CW00952416

THE IRISH TIMES

THE IRISH TIMES

150 Years of Influence

Terence Brown

BLOOMSBURY

LONDON · NEW DELHI · NEW YORK · SYDNEY

Bloomsbury Continuum
An imprint of Bloomsbury Publishing Plc

50 Bedford Square   1385 Broadway
London   New York
WC1B 3DP   NY 10018
UK   USA

www.bloomsbury.com

Bloomsbury, Continuum and the Diana logo are trademarks of Bloomsbury Publishing Plc

First published 2015

© Terence Brown, 2015

Terence Brown has asserted his right under the Copyright, Designs and
Patents Act, 1988, to be identified as Author of this work.

All rights reserved. No part of this publication may be reproduced or
transmitted in any form or by any means, electronic or mechanical, including
photocopying, recording, or any information storage or retrieval system,
without prior permission in writing from the publishers.

No responsibility for loss caused to any individual or organization acting on
or refraining from action as a result of the material in this publication
can be accepted by Bloomsbury or the author.

British Library Cataloguing-in-Publication Data
A catalogue record for this book is available from the British Library.

Library of Congress Cataloguing-in-Publication data has been applied for.

ISBN HB: 9781472919069
ISBN ePDF: 9781472919083
ISBN ePub: 9781472919076

2 4 6 8 10 9 7 5 3 1

Typeset by seagulls.net
Printed and bound in Great Britain by CPI Group (UK) Ltd, Croydon CR0 4YY

To find out more about our authors and books visit www.bloomsbury.com.
Here you will find extracts, author interviews, details of forthcoming events
and the option to sign up for our newsletters.

In memory of my father
Henry Montgomery Brown
Journalist, Missionary, Preacher

CONTENTS

List of Illustrations

The Berghof, Nazi Chancellor Adolf Hitler's home in the Bavarian Alps, 1936 (Getty Images)

Adolf Hitler at The Berghof, 1938 (Getty Images)

SECOND PLATE SECTION

Bomb damage in Belfast after German bombing (Getty Images)

Damage caused by German bombing of the North Strand, Dublin, 1941 (© Dublin City Council, image courtesy of Dublin City Library and Archive)

President John F. Kennedy arrives at Dublin Airport, 1963 (Irish Photo Archive)

The Second Vatican Council, Saint Peter's Basilica, Rome, 1962 (Getty Images)

The Beatles arrive at Dublin Airport, 7 November 1963 (Irish Photo Archive)

Pope John Paul II in Phoenix Park, Dublin during his visit to Ireland, September 1979 (Getty Images)

Police battle with rioters in the Bogside area of Derry, 1969 (Press Association)

A funeral mass for eleven of the thirteen Bloody Sunday victims taking place in St Mary's Roman Catholic Church, Creggan, Derry, 1972 (Victor Patterson)

A British soldier patrols the Falls Road, Belfast, May 1981 (Getty Images)

Prime Minister Margaret Thatcher and the Irish Taoiseach Garret FitzGerald signing the Anglo-Irish Agreement, Hillsborough Castle, November 1985 (*Irish Times*)

The Archbishop of Armagh, Dr Cahal Daly, greets President Robinson in St Patrick's Cathedral, Armagh, December 1990 (*Irish Times*)

Sinn Féin President Gerry Adams addresses the crowd gathered at Connolly House following the IRA Ceasefire Announcement, watched by Martin McGuinness (Press Association)

The *Irish Times* 'X case' cartoon, by Martyn Turner, 1992 (*Irish Times*/Martyn Turner)

PREFACE AND ACKNOWLEDGEMENTS

In April 2007 I was approached by the then Chairman of the Irish Times Trust, Professor David McConnell, asking for advice. He explained that the newspaper would celebrate its 150th birthday in 2009 and that the Trust was keen that a history of the *Irish Times* might be written to mark the role it had played in Irish life since 1859. He wondered if I could suggest the name of anyone who might be invited to undertake such a task. When we met again a week or so later, he surprised me greatly by asking, on behalf of the Trust, whether I myself might be willing to accept such an invitation. I informed David (whom I have known since our student days in Trinity College Dublin in the 1960s, when I first began to read the newspaper on a daily basis) that I would give the matter serious thought. Having discussed McConnell's proposal in detail with my literary agent, Jonathan Williams, by the autumn of 2007 I had reached an agreement with the *Irish Times* that I would write a book on the history of the newspaper. In striking this agreement, I made it clear that it would take until much later than 2009 to complete such a work and that the book I envisaged writing would not be a conventional institutional history with a primary focus on such things as its finances, business affairs and administration. Rather, it would have as the paper's main concern the analysis of how the newspaper had reported and reflected on Ireland and the world over the course of the 150 turbulent years since 1859 when the *Irish Times* was founded.

In agreeing with pleasure to undertake this task, I was emboldened by two things. First, I was aware that in September 2009 I could take early retirement from my Chair in Trinity College, so before long I would have time to write a book of the length necessary. Secondly, in 2004 I had published a revised version of my book of 1981, *Ireland: A Social and Cultural History 1922–1979*. This had involved doing research on the country's recent past, 1979–2002, which I believed would prove useful when I came to write about the *Irish Times* of the 1980s and 1990s. I was aware, too, that David McConnell had been prompted by my *Ireland* to consider extending to me the invitation he had done, since it covered an important period in the newspaper's history and this fitted me for the kind of work he thought I might agree to attempt.

Accordingly, this book is the product of the first years of my retirement and I hope it justifies the hopes Professor McConnell and the Trust placed in me. While I was working on and writing the book, The Irish Times Ltd afforded me some financial support, though it is important to state that this book is independent of the newspaper and is in no sense an 'official' publication.

In writing this book I was aided by other authors who have broached the topic. I am thinking especially of Mark O'Brien's conscientious *The Irish Times: A History*, to which I am significantly indebted (as citations in this book indicate). John Martin's contentious *The Irish Times: Past and Present,* kept me alert to the role of ideology in the paper's attitudes, while the theme of Dermot James's *From the Margins to the Centre: A History of the Irish Times* helped me to shape the narrative I wished to present in my book. For James's book presents the history of the paper as one which inscribes how an organ of a peripheral caste, the Protestant Anglo-Irish, became adapted to the emergent Irish nation and eventually central to its life. By contrast, as I read the nineteenth-century newspaper I became increasingly aware how, as the voice of imperial Unionism in the period, the newspaper felt itself as basically secure in its Tory patriotism in a Victorian world, and so at the centre of things. Its experience in the twentieth century, examined in detail in the main body of this book, was that of a challenging modernity, in which the Victorian frame of mind experienced repeated assaults in a time of science, new technologies and social forces, world wars, the claims of nation states, of economic crises, political extremisms and political violence. The adaptation of the newspaper this book traces is to modernity itself, in the context of an island nation within the European Union trading in the globalized economy of the late twentieth and early twenty-first centuries.

In writing this book I accrued various debts. I am grateful to Liam Kavanagh of the *Irish Times*, who arranged access for me to the newspaper's digital archive. Searchable electronic resources of this kind have made newspapers available to researchers in exciting new ways and this book is I hope evidence of that. I am also grateful to Professor David McConnell for introducing me to the late Major Thomas McDowell. Over dinner in the latter's home I had the valuable opportunity to gain an impression of his character and personality. Geraldine Kennedy kindly allowed me to listen to a recording of an excellent interview she had conducted with Major McDowell. John Horgan supplied me with a very interesting written account of the early phase of his career with the *Irish Times*. Conversations with him were helpful, indeed, as they were with James Downey, with Ambassador to Finland, Dónal Denham (whose father was an employee of the newspaper) and with Gerry Smyth.

I am grateful, too, for Jonathan Williams's constant encouragement, for his faith in the book, and for the loyal support of my wife Suzanne, who patiently endured my obsession with an engrossing, time-consuming project.

Terence Brown
Dublin, 18 September 2014

1

THE *IRISH TIMES* AND VICTORIAN IRELAND

In 1869 Anthony Trollope, that eminent Victorian, published what many consider to be his masterwork, *He Knew He Was Right*. A grim tale of marital discord and insane jealousy that imagines an obsession of Othello-like intensity in a world of telegraphs and anger, the novel, in many of its details, reflects the fact that it was the product of an information and communications age. In a world of almost instantaneous postal delivery and journeys by train, the author, in frequent topical references, assumes that he is writing for an informed audience, one that will have been reading newspaper discussions of the implications of the Reform Act of 1867. That journalism is a fact of the modern life the novelist evokes throughout his book is made clear inasmuch as a main character in one of its subsidiary plot-lines is a young man attempting to carve out a position for himself as a member of the Victorian fourth estate. Trollope, as always in his fiction, is alert to the social and economic aspects of his characters' aspirations.

Hugh Stanbury, in *He Knew He Was Right*, son of a deceased Devonshire clergyman, has a Harrow and Oxford education behind him, courtesy of a rich aunt who has settled £100 per annum on her nephew (at a time when it was possible to marry and raise a family in modest but decent circumstances on about £150 a year) provided he make his way in the world as a barrister. Trollope informs us: 'The very hour in which Miss Stanbury learnt that her nephew was writing for a penny newspaper she sent off a dispatch that he must give her up or the penny paper.' Journalism for her is social disgrace. Hugh's friend Louis Trevelyan (the villain of the book) shares Miss Stanbury's low view of journalists and journalism, telling Hugh 'that he did not think much of the trade of a journalist ... that he was sinking from the highest to almost the lowest business by which an educated man and a gentleman could earn his bread'. At the time the novel begins, Stanbury is just about managing to replace his aunt's subvention by his writings, but he prefers the prompt payments involved and the bohemian life his profession permits to the exiguous conditions of the Western Circuit. By the end of the novel, Stanbury is so well established in his 'trade' that he is able to propose and be accepted, assuring his bride-to-be of an income of £500 per annum, a life insurance policy of £1,000 and the opportunity to live if not in Whitehall Gardens or Belgrave Square, then in one of the burgeoning middle-class suburbs of the nation's capital. When they marry, their nuptials are noted in 'various metropolitan newspapers'; and the fact that a journalist could marry well is greeted by his peers as proof of 'what a Bohemian could do. And that men of the press in England might gradually hope to force their way almost anywhere.' Trollope leaves his happy couple with the assurance, 'It is our opinion that Mr and Mrs Stanbury will never want for a beef-steak in the cupboard.'

Trollope's novel captures some of the ambiguity of the journalist's role in mid-Victorian British society. Scarcely a profession in the eyes of many, journalism, nonetheless, afforded significant career prospects for the intelligent, educated young man without means, and the social success of such a man as young Stanbury might be read as indicative of a social trend in which the views of a Trevelyan would become increasingly anachronistic. In her study *Victorian News and Newspapers* (1985), Lucy Brown notes that when London clubs, those precise arbiters of social standing in the second half of the nineteenth century, were 'at the height of their prestige and prosperity' (p. 127), 'there is substantial evidence to suggest that journalists were elected into equal membership with other candidates in a wide range' of them. She paints a picture of a minority of well-placed journalists moving easily in a world of 'actors, literary people, military experts, travellers and the aristocracy in the general social vortex' (Brown 1985, p. 129) and notes that that measure of respectable success, the *Dictionary of National Biography*, planned from 1882, by no means excluded gentlemen of the press. It was clear, therefore, that mid- and late-Victorian Britain was seeing a cohort of men and some women emerging who in national and provincial newspapers, in an age of increasingly immediate news distribution, was augmenting that body of commentators and opinion-makers who contributed to the monthly and weekly reviews and magazines, and who made Victoria's reign an age of printed, political, social and cultural reflection. As the second half of the nineteenth century progressed, newspaper editors and the most respected journalists began to share in their power. In 1881 the British Museum opened a special newspaper reading room to mark what the *Edinburgh Review* had noted as early as 1855: 'Journalism is now truly an estate of the realm' ('The newspaper press', p. 447).

Concurrently, society was affected, as Victoria's long reign wore on, by a process of professionalization, which began to undermine the commentator who could contribute as a generalist to the great reviews, as he, and occasionally she, began to be replaced by the professional expert. In this context, the journalist as a professional in the field of information began to seek and gain enhanced credibility. The founding of the Press Association as a professional body in 1868 can be seen as a sign of this process at work.

The career of a journalist who spent his working life in Victorian Ireland suggests that similar forces and processes were in train in that country as well as in Britain. Andrew Dunlop, who left a valuable account of his life in the profession in *Fifty Years of Irish Journalism* (1911), was a Scottish lad o' parts from near Glasgow who took up residence in Ireland as a sub-editor and cub-reporter in 1856. Remembering his youth in Scotland, when the bug for journalism entered his veins, he associated his ambitions not only with newspapers but with the kind of high cultural periodicals, such as the *Edinburgh Review* and the *Quarterly Review*, that were the house journals, as it were, of the United Kingdom's ruling elites.

The country Dunlop came to in 1856 lacked, with one possible exception, a publication to rival the great British Victorian quarterlies or monthlies, but possessed a vibrant national, provincial and local newspaper culture associated with its contentious politics in the decade following the Famine. As his career progressed, Dunlop was happy to note that the exercise of journalism in Ireland attracted no noticeable social opprobrium or bar to advancement in other fields. Indeed, he was pleased to record that when he worked for the Dublin *Daily Express*, among those willing to contribute leaders were 'the Right Hon. Lord Rathmore, the then Hon. David Plunkett, one who is now a Judge of the High Court of Justice in Ireland, one who became a County Court judge, three who became Queen's Counsel, one a bishop of the Church of Ireland' (Dunlop 1911, p. 45). He reported, too, that Sir William Thompson, a distinguished surgeon and twice president of the Royal College of Surgeons, had been a student member of the reporting staff and was 'always proud of having been so connected with the press'. That senior politicians maintained contact with the press bespoke the power they held over public opinion. Dunlop observed that Parnell was 'always civil and courteous to journalists' (Dunlop 1911, p. 30) and that 'he frequently travelled in the same compartment with the reporters when going to or from a meeting in the country' (Dunlop 1911, p. 30). Parnell's awareness as leader of the National Party of the significance of journalism also meant that it could be a route to career advancement. As historians George Boyce and Alan O'Day remark: 'The linkage of politics and the press received reinforcement with the induction of many journalists, editors and newspaper proprietors into the National Party as MPs, while others were prominent in the local organisation of its infrastructure' (Boyce and O'Day 2004, p. 4). By 1890 a writer in the London *Observer* could comment rather caustically of the English capital, 'Journalism is well-nigh swamped with Irishmen, most of whom do exceedingly well in it' (cited *Irish Times*, 5 April 1890). And there was a considerable pool of such men in Ireland, too, as newspapers proliferated in the provinces in the 1870s. By 1886 there were 55 nationalist newspapers in the country (Boyce and O'Day 2004, p. 4).

What further emerges from Dunlop's recollections is that, as his career developed, it was incumbent on him to develop specialist credentials and expertise in particular fields. Between 1879 and 1886, for example, he effectively became a crime correspondent. During this stint of reporting on all too frequent Irish murders, he also spent a hectic four days just before one Christmas covering 350 miles by train and 120 miles by road to investigate social distress in north-west Donegal. Later, when he had found a secure berth for himself with the *Irish Times*, he functioned less as a jobbing reporter than as a correspondent for special subjects. One such involved a series of lengthy articles on 'Ulster and compulsory purchase', to obtain the material for which he 'travelled for over a week, visiting every county and all the principal towns of the province' (Dunlop 1911, p. 248). Dunlop's standing in his profession allowed him to be a contributor in 1897 to the *Proceedings of the Institute of Journalists*.

The one organ in Ireland extant when Dunlop made his move to the country, which might have competed with the august periodicals he read as a youth in Glasgow, was the *Dublin University Magazine*. Founded in 1833 by a group of young Trinity College-educated radical Tories, in its heyday the *DUM* had propagated a heady mix of robust support for the 1801 Union of Ireland with Britain with a fully formed cultural nationalism. It did not shy away from espousing Protestant supremacism. Among its editors had been Isaac Butt, before his conversion to Home Rule, and the novelist Charles Lever (who could on his day give Dickens a run for his money in the Victorian fiction popularity stakes). In 1859 the editor of a minor rival, the *Harp*, subtitled the *Irish Catholic Monthly*, admitted, 'The first magazine in Ireland is the *Dublin University [Magazine]*. With a large highly educated reading public, peculiarly liberal in supporting a congenial literature, and fully alive to its importance, aided by a large proportion of the upper-class Catholics, the *University Magazine* is, of course, all that might be expected, in the style in which it is placed before the public' (McBride 1987, p. 353). This serene estimate was probably possible since by 1859 the *DUM* had lost its crusading political zeal and had, as one study of the magazine puts it, largely 'retreated to an emasculated literary sphere' (McBride 1987, p. 337). It does, however, in its identification of an educated readership in the country and of a caste of upper-class Catholics sufficiently eirenic in temperament to enjoy a periodical clearly identified with the Protestant unionist interest, suggest that a space certainly existed for a newspaper that could appeal to the same constituency, representing Protestant unionist Ireland but in a spirit of moderation and fair-mindedness.

In the year in which the editor of the *Harp* so generously saluted the *DUM*, the first edition of the *Irish Times and Intelligencer* rolled from the presses. Dunlop again (by 1911 an old *Irish Times* hand and perhaps *parti pris*): 'It soon became a formidable rival to the previously existing dailies *The Freeman's Journal*, *The Daily Express*, and *Saunders Newsletter*. The *Irish Times* is now, and has been for years, well in front of all its contemporaries' (Dunlop 1911, p. 288).

It would have been interesting to have heard Trollope's views as a chroni-cler of clerical life on the early history of the *Irish Times* which seemed to conjoin Barchester with Fleet Street in what might on the face of it seem a very curious marriage.

The paper was founded by a young member of Ireland's Protestant Ascendancy caste, Lawrence A. Knox, 'eldest son of Arthur Knox from Co. Mayo and Lady Jane Parsons, daughter of the Earl of Rosse' (Mark O'Brien 2008, p. 16). Knox had seen service in the British Army in the Crimea with the rank of captain. Still very much the dashing young soldier, he was only 22 when he returned to civvy street and embarked on his career as a newspaper proprietor, in which role he would prove himself as effective as he had as a military man. However, it was from the ranks of Ireland's Christian soldiers that he sought his editor. The paper in the initial weeks of its existence was editorially in the hands of a member of the staff of the Protestant university, Trinity College Dublin, one Dr George Frederick Shaw. The post then demanded the oversight of six editions of the paper a week (two editions appeared each Tuesday, Thursday and Saturday), and Shaw's university duties and other activities, for he was a busy man-about-town, probably precluded him from continuing in the editorship. By July the paper had began to publish daily (excluding Sundays) and the editorship formally passed to a relative of the senior academic Shaw, one George Bomford Wheeler (he had been involved as a leader writer from the newspaper's earliest days). Wheeler was in holy orders when he took on his editorial duties in Dublin, where he had served as a curate and a chaplain (he also had a career as a freelance contributor to Irish and British periodicals behind him). His journalistic avocation was not seen by the Church of Ireland hierarchy as an impediment to his spiritual vocation, for in 1865 he was appointed to a Rectorship in Ballysax, Co. Kildare, from where he continued to edit the paper until his death in a coaching accident in 1877. Weekdays in this latter period of his life saw him in Dublin, while at weekends he attended to his parochial duties. There was no sense that the occupancy of a newspaper editor's chair in any way compromised the general esteem in which this classical scholar, writer and parson was held. His career is further evidence that journalism in Victorian Ireland, as in England, was in fact gathering a certain prestige about it. Wheeler's own paper noted on his death that 'By virtue of his position in connection with Trinity College, the church, this paper and his own abilities and social virtues, he might have commanded the welcome *entrée* into any society ...' (James 2008, p. 26).

Wheeler's joint role as parson and print man, which would surely have intrigued Trollope, might have been a matter of dilettantism and amateur dabbling, but in fact was nothing of the kind. For during his tenure the newspaper consolidated its existence as the primary journalistic expression and defender of Protestant conservative interests in the country. That a clergyman should have been at the tiller of the journalistic ship was to a certain degree apt, for the interests of the Church of Ireland in the second half of the nineteenth century were often to be bound up with those of Protestant Ireland more generally. And as one historian of the Church of Ireland has bluntly put it: the Church in the 1850s and 1860s 'was increasingly an entity in a world unsympathetic to its very existence' (Akenson 1971, p. 224). As a clergyman of a church that stood at the heart of Protestant Ascendancy until the disestablishment of 1869 and the subsequent efforts to shore up its somewhat depleted powers, Wheeler was perhaps well placed to comment on public affairs at a time when, as the historian F. S. L. Lyons states in *Ireland since the Famine* (1971), religion 'for most Irishmen ... remained not only at the centre of their personal lives but stood out as one of the most formidable of the barriers separating them from each other'. For 'religious rivalries – unhappily complicated by the fact that they coincided closely (though not completely) with division between native and settler, conquered and conquerors – had been part of the very fabric of Irish history since the Reformation' (Lyons 1971, p. 17).

The newspaper's first editorial of 29 March 1859 was confident that ancient animosities were abating, even though only a decade had passed since the terrible depredations of the Famine of the late 1840s. It advised:

> Every year sees a larger and larger proportion of our population indifferent to the manoeuvres of faction, disgusted at the arts of the demagogue and sincerely desirous of laying aside their natural prejudices and labouring together for the good of their common country. Men of this stamp dislike to be classed and ticketed off even under such mild denominations as Liberal or Conservative.

It was to this progressive readership, as factionalism waned, that Knox hoped his paper would speak. But one principle must remain inviolate: that of association with Britain within the Empire:

> As Irishmen we shall think and speak; but it shall be as Irishmen loyal to the British connection, and proud to share in the destiny of the only first-rate Power in Europe that has known how to combine social order with individual freedom.

In 1868 Lawrence Knox himself was elected as MP for Sligo in the 'Conservative interest', but not before affirming as early as 1860 that the *Irish Times* was 'the Protestant and Conservative daily newspaper' (Mark O'Brien 2008, p. 18).

The political, social and cultural pillars of that Protestant and conservative interest in 1859 were clear to all whom the editor held to be right-thinking: the Union (though its conditions could be redefined), the established position of the Church of Ireland as effectively a state Church (the Act of Union had united the Irish Church with the Church of England), rights of property and land ownership, the primacy of the English language as the instrument of governance, law, education and social exchange. Over the next half-century all these pillars would suffer shocks and several of them would be toppled. A kind of teleology that might read the disestablishment of the Church of Ireland in 1869 as prelude to the Land War, Home Rule crises, the rise of militant republicanism and eventual separatism might suggest that a newspaper with such an ideology and purpose would have a simple task to perform: it should be to mount a rearguard defence against the inevitable drift of history. That the tides were flowing with force in a particular direction at any given time was, however, not easily evident even to the most perspicacious conservatives, caught up as they were in the currents and cross-currents of political life. When to defend and when to attack could not always be clear; no editor was gifted with hindsight before the event. And, more crucially, it could not be assumed that the term 'Protestant' covered a homogeneous interest.

When the *Irish Times* began publishing in 1859, what has come to be termed 'Anglo-Ireland' held much of the country's acreage and exercised considerable political power. Numerically small, this group of resident Irish gentry, Protestant in religion and in their own minds English by extraction, of about 3,000 families in all, constituted the main bulwark of conservative feeling in the country. Their view of the world combined often intense rural and local loyalties with imperial commitments. In a land robbed of its parliament by the vote of many of their forefathers in 1800, such people often looked to London as their capital (where Irish peers, some of them absentees, had seats in the House of Lords at Westminster). Even if they kept townhouses for the Vice-Regal season in Dublin, they sought to marry within the ambit of their own rural social world which included similarly placed people in Britain. Although they certainly did not deserve the poet Louis MacNeice's indictment of them when he dismissed their Big House tradition as having 'maintained no culture worth speaking of – nothing but an obsolete bravado, an insidious bonhomie and a way with horses' (MacNeice 1941, pp. 104–5), their kind of conservatism and the social attitudes that underpinned them were to become increasingly moribund.

Had the new newspaper sought to depend for its readership on this threatened elite, it would surely have foundered in defending what was becoming a minority increasingly marked by anachronism. In social terms Anglo-Ireland did occupy the apex of a Protestant Ireland that, according to the Census of 1861, stood at just less than one-quarter of the island's population of 5,800,000 persons. However, Protestantism was unevenly spread throughout the country, contributing to its difficulties in meeting political and social challenges when they came. The main Protestant denominations were Anglicanism and Presbyterianism, the former being represented throughout the country, a majority of its adherents in the northern province of Ulster, and the latter concentrated in the same northern province and only marginally present elsewhere. Leinster, with Dublin and its environs to the fore, was the principal centre of Anglicanism outside Ulster.

The Dublin, which in 1859 saw a newspaper appear (that soon would become a daily) to speak for the Protestant and conservative interest, was still a city where Protestantism, nonetheless, stood for quite a deal. The waning of factional tensions that the *Irish Times* optimistically welcomed in its first editorial probably reflected the fact that for 'a brief period in the 1850s, the newly reformed Dublin corporation contained a healthy combination of liberals and conservatives, elite catholics and protestants' (Cosgrove, 1988, p. 113). It was to such a constituency that the *Irish Times* undoubtedly hoped to speak with its moderate, if imperial, unionist voice. Protestants furthermore occupied a disproportionate number of positions in the public administration of the city and of the country, centred in Dublin, as they did in such professions as medicine, the law and in the upper levels of service provision in an economy where industrialization had taken hold only modestly.

The latter half of the nineteenth century in Dublin saw a flight to the suburbs as a condition of urban gentility when the former townhouses of the rural gentry were increasingly abandoned to become the tenements of an immiserated labouring class; and the demographic changes this involved bore an unmistakably confessional aspect. Some southern suburbs of Dublin became markedly Protestant, while the developing suburbs north of the city (apart from Clontarf) were inhabited predominantly by Catholics (the term 'suburb' was firmly in the property advertising lexicon of the *Irish Times* from its early years). Dublin south-side suburbs, such as Rathmines, Pembroke and Blackrock, became identified as Protestant enclaves in a Catholic city, with Clontarf a northern outpost, as it were. As Mary Daly has put it:

> The flight to the suburbs made it possible for the middle classes, and particularly for wives and families, to escape the more distasteful aspects of Victorian city life ... Dublin suburbs offered a further attraction in that the predominantly protestant and unionist Dublin middle class could evade the unpleasant reality that they were a minority which was increasingly losing control both in Ireland and the city of Dublin. (Daly 1984, p. 122)

It was undoubtedly among this Dublin Protestant middle class that the *Irish Times* could expect a loyal readership anxious for a newspaper that spoke to its concerns and met its informational requirements.

The early subscription success of the paper indicated that a market certainly existed for what it had to offer. Between February 1860 and June 1862 the newspaper reported daily on its sales. In that period it could claim a rise in sold copies per day from 8,720 to 16,988. By the late 1860s it claimed that it had 20,000 daily purchasers.

The conditions for such an auspicious start, even in the economic depression of the early 1860s, had been created in 1855 when legislation had been passed in the United Kingdom parliament abolishing stamp duty on newspapers (though Dublin was slower than London in adapting to the opportunities so created). The era of cheap news distribution had begun, for in the same year the *Daily Telegraph* was relaunched as a penny-print, challenging *The Times* as the leading British newspaper. The railway system allowed for distribution beyond the English capital (in Ireland the postal system and the railways meant that *The Times* had become and remained the paper-of-choice among many of the rural Anglo-Irish gentry). But as L. M. Cullen has advised of the 1860s in Ireland: 'Beyond the metropolis there was only a small market for daily newspapers at any price' (Cullen 1989 p. 44). In Dublin paperboys at stations on the Dublin–Kingstown line played a key role in selling the new cheap prints to the capital's middle class. In 1859 these were, along with the *Irish Times*, the *Morning News*, the *Freeman's Journal* and the *Dublin Daily Express* (the last two existing prints that had reduced their price). The *Freeman's Journal* was a liberal nationalist organ, while the *Dublin Daily Express* was conservative in its politics. Cullen reports that in the 1860s the *Daily Express* lost ground commercially in Dublin, leaving the field there to the *Freeman's Journal* and the *Irish Times*. However, he judges that in the Victorian period an Irish 'mass market for daily newspapers did not exist' (Cullen 1989 p. 78). By the 1870s he notes that 'an interesting dichotomy' had clearly emerged of 'dominance by a unionist paper in Dublin, and by a nationalist paper outside the capital' (Cullen 1989 p. 79). By the 1880s, Cullen further notes that 'the one daily which had a wide circulation outside the city of publication was *The Freeman's Journal*' (Cullen 1989 p. 78*)*.

If then we must consider the *Irish Times* in its Victorian manifestation as essentially a Dublin newspaper (and the extensive advertisements it carried do reflect a largely Dublin-based, middle- and upper-middle-class readership) then, as an organ concerned to reflect a conservative and imperial view of the world, it was less likely to focus with ready sympathy on the concerns of the rural Anglo-Irish gentry (it was not loath to inveigh against absentee landlordism). Nor was the industrializing Protestant north of the country a natural constituency for the paper. The second half of the nineteenth century would see Belfast surpass Dublin as the country's most populous city as ship-building and engineering made it a powerhouse of north-British capitalism. There, distinctive forms of Protestantism and conservatism would emerge in an increasingly sectarian climate, remote from the more managed confessional divisions and encounters that characterized social life in Dublin.

A symptom of the North's difference presented in the first year of the *Irish Times*'s existence and the reports in its columns on this perhaps suggests a certain bemused incomprehension of events there, as if to anticipate how the Dublin paper would often have to engage with northern particularity and difference throughout its history.

The year 1859 in Antrim and Down was the 'Year of Grace', when religious life was affected by an extraordinary outburst of revivalist enthusiasm, akin to the 'Great Awakening' that had struck New England in the eighteenth century. The Church of Ireland in the nineteenth century had, it is true, become 'predominately evangelical' (Akenson 1971, p. 132) in theological outlook, but that scarcely allowed for the outpourings of emotion, ecstatic fervour and speakings-in-tongues which were occurring at mass meetings in the north, often outside the control of either Anglican or Presbyterian Church authorities. On 2 July 1859 the *Irish Times* reported on 'a most extraordinary and apparently uncontrollable religious movement' underway in Ulster and struck a note of conservative concern: 'As yet, providentially, there has been little of that violation of decorum which history tells us has occurred in the case of prior revivals.' On 7 July the paper published one of its earliest letters from a reader, R. Allen of Ahoghill near Ballymena, Co. Antrim, who sought to set the 'extraordinary' events of that summer in historical perspective. By 9 August the *Irish Times* was copying a report from the *Belfast Newsletter* which indicated that decorum was certainly at risk as the summer of revival turned towards a harvest of 'saved' souls:

> The number of those who fall into a sort of trance is on the increase. In each instance there are professed converts, and after being restored to consciousness, their joy is unbounded. Several – strangers in Belfast and others – have visited those individuals, and to all the cases are the subject of much astonishment.

The rest of the *Newsletter*'s account indicates that the northern clergy were anxious to gain control of a force that could escape their oversight in disturbing ways.

Twentieth-century analysis of 1859's 'Great Awakening' (which, although it affected other parts of the country, had its epicentre in Ulster) has tended to read the phenomenon in Marxist and sociological terms, analysing the violent emotionalism of the revival as a product of social and economic anxieties in a region undergoing rapid industrialization. In 1859, one senses that for the *Irish Times*'s respectable, middle-class, essentially Dublin readership, it was an insight into how the north, compared with their capital city, was a place apart, though as they read, they might have reflected that the very newsprint they held in their hands was the product of technological developments in the industrialized Victorian world. These, indeed, had made the communication of daily news from around the globe a feature of what one cultural historian has termed the era of the 'reading nation' (St Clair 2004, p. 13) in the United Kingdom.

Steamships and the rise of the railways (which expanded in Ireland between 1850 and 1866 from 537 to 1,909 miles of track) had brought the peoples of the British Isles closer together than they had ever been. In the eighteenth century, when London to Holyhead was 'one of great post-roads of England' (Munter 1967, p. 72), post could take three to five days to make that journey; thereafter it took 18 to 20 hours to make the sea voyage to Dublin in good weather. Rail services in Britain and the faster steamships, together with the expansion of the rail service in Ireland from the 1850s, had opened up the country to news from the Irish and English capitals. Then, in an event that would signal a leap forward in communications technology, the first telegraphy link between Britain and Ireland was laid in 1852 (it stretched from Holyhead in Wales to Howth, just north of Dublin). By 1866 Europe could be in touch with North America when Valentia Island in County Kerry became connected to Newfoundland. Australia would be linked to the world's burgeoning telegraphic system in 1871, together with Japan and China. South America went 'on line', as it were, in 1874, with Africa slowly getting connected between 1879 and 1884. As Christopher Morash has observed, 'the telegraphy effectively created a global informational field' (Morash 2010, p. 86) in the Victorian era as news became a commodity that could be acquired, packaged and sold on. From this period come the great news-gathering agencies: Reuters, founded by Julius Reuter in 1851, and the Press Association, founded in 1868 – alert as they were in responding to this opportunity. The nationalization of the telegraph services in Britain and Ireland in 1870, with the Post Office as the overseeing authority, indicated that the state recognized that the distribution of news was a public good. Lucy Brown comments that this development was 'an important landmark in Victorian administrative history' (Brown 1985, p. 121); but it also suggested that a shift in consciousness had taken place, since the state accepted that the transmission of information was so important in a modern society that it could not be left to private enterprise alone.

The effects of this technological, and the concomitant institutional, innovation are not far to seek. News increasingly became a matter of near instantaneous communication and there was a great deal more of it available on a daily basis. In the early 1860s, when the *Irish Times* sought to report on transatlantic affairs, for example, and most crucially on the America Civil War of 1861–5 (one of its first great international news stories; the other being the unification of Italy), there was a time-lag of more than a week before news became available. It was 1 January 1863 before the newspaper reported and commented at length on the defeat of Union forces at the Battle of Fredericksburg, which had taken place on 13 December ('The commotion in New York, on receipt of this intelligence, resembles that at Athens when it was announced that the army at Syracuse was lost'). When Atlanta fell to Sherman's army on 2 September 1864, the *Irish Times* picked up a London *Times* report from New York of 7 September on that momentous event: 'The capture of Atlanta is officially confirmed'. By the end of the decade, events in Britain, Europe and North America could be learnt about by the same or the next day. What this meant for an editor was that decisions about what constituted 'news', with the balance between international and local events at issue, became more complex, since matters of import had to vie on the wire services with floods of trivia.

Technological developments allowed *Irish Times* editors greater space to cope with this new instantaneity and informational embarrassment of riches. For the nineteenth century saw advances in the means of print production. The shift towards machine-made paper as the basic material of the news business was almost complete in the United Kingdom by 1859; and the mechanization of printing, a key element of the Industrial Revolution, had contributed to the most profound change in the spread of information since the invention of moveable type. At its inception, the *Irish Times* employed a printing press that allowed each issue to comprise only four pages. In the early years the expansion of 'news' was accommodated by increasing the size of the individual pages and printing more columns per page, but this was markedly unsatisfactory. In 1869 the paper bought a new rotary printing press (the first Dublin newspaper to do so), which allowed it to expand to become 12 pages per issue by 1873. Its engagement with the agencies that the age of print generated had been signalled in 1862 when the *Irish Times* struck a deal with the British book and newspaper distribution firm W.H. Smith, whereby that company (which under the name of Eason and Son would occupy for many decades the commanding heights of such activity in Ireland) would distribute 'the entire stamped distribution of the *Irish Times* to its regular subscribers' (Cullen 1989, p. 56).

That news was becoming big business was made clear in 1873 when the first owner of the *Irish Times*, Captain Knox, died of scarlatina at the comparatively youthful age of 36. His widow almost immediately put the business up for sale and it was purchased by a major Victorian businessman, Sir John Arnott. A Scotsman who had settled in Ireland, Arnott would over time accumulate a portfolio that ranged from department stores to horse-racing, and extended to shipping and brewing. He anticipated, indeed, how in the twentieth century in the United Kingdom a business magnate could choose to include among his interests a national newspaper or group of newspapers that reflected his own political views (Sir John's were conservative). Ireland had acquired its own version of the kind of newspaper proprietor who combined business with opinion-forming, public service and philanthropy, a Hibernian Beaverbrook on a mini-scale. In Arnott's hands the paper prospered, moving in 1882 from Lower Abbey Street, where it had first been edited and printed, to larger premises in D'Olier Street, where it would remain until 2006. The newspaper had adopted the more market-friendly name 'the *Irish Times*' in 1874 and from July 1875 had been issuing a Saturday magazine-like edition.

Under Geoge Bomford Wheeler's editorial guidance, the *Irish Times* basically stood for the settled order of things (and when ownership passed from Knox to Arnott there was no appreciable change in its fundamentally conservative outlook, even if the new owner hoped for greater attention to 'commercial and industrial matters' than had pertained in its first 14 years, including developments in the industrialized north of the country, which he hoped could be a model for general progress). A telling instance, early in the paper's life, of such deep-rooted and instinctive conservatism of mind was its editorial of 14 January 1863 which criticised Abraham Lincoln's final Emancipation Proclamation freeing slaves in territories held by the Confederates (an event of world historical significance, as time would tell). 'Mr Lincoln,' judges the *Irish Times*, 'has risked all, upon a throw.' For the writer, Lincoln had stirred a hornet's nest:

> If a proclamation could make slaves free, there were on the first of January no slaves in the South. Mr Lincoln, however, is aware that he must obtain the negroes before he can manumit [free from bondage] them. Therefore he directs 'that the military and naval authorities of the States will recognise their freedom'. This means that the Union troops and the Union gunboats are to favour a servile revolt. The hot blood and cruel temper of the negroes are to be aroused against the families of the planters, and horrors which the pen refuses to describe are to be perpetrated by the Federal authority.

This will be, it seems, an inevitable consequence of Lincoln's rashness, the editorial continued, and the blame will lie with him, since:

> Throughout the whole war nothing is so remarkable as the unexpected loyalty of the negroes to their masters. They have adhered to their owners with affectionate fidelity, they have followed them to the armies, joined with them in the encounters, nursed them in sickness, cultivated the fields and guarded the families of the planters. Mr Lincoln's proclamation will have no effect on the great body of these men.

This idyllic version of the old South contrasts strikingly with the newspaper's jaundiced assessment of the condition of the Confederates' foe. On 5 January 1863, the *Irish Times* had opined:

> As yet neither Northerners or Westerners had been called upon to pay the cost of the war. They have been enjoying a Fool's Paradise and are about to be crudely awakened to their real condition. When war had to be maintained by the expenditure of 'cash' and when the Irish and Germans refuse to be led out as sheep to the slaughter, then the war must end.

The Irish men in the Union armies (along with the Germans), who, for the *Irish Times*, by contrast with the noble negroes who had fought for the

Confederacy out of loyalty to their masters, and had displayed an ignoble tendency to sheep-like acquiescence to their fate, were, of course, emigrants from a country where famine had driven them to an Irish version of the Black Atlantic. Survivors of the coffin ships of the Famine years and after, through their involvement in the affairs of their abandoned country, whose shores they had recently departed, they would over the course of the Victorian era prove themselves anything but supine about what they considered to be the enslaved condition of their native land.

The *Irish Times* in 1863 could not perhaps have been expected to be prescient about the role Irish-America would play in Irish separatist politics of the period. It did, however, have evidence as early as 1861 that a new force was at work in Irish politics, with a powerful North American axis; for in that year the remains of Terence Bellew McManus were brought to Ireland from California, by way of New York, for reinterment.

The Fermanagh-born McManus had been transported to Van Diemen's Land as a result of his participation in the Young Ireland rebellion of 1848. He had escaped in 1851 and settled in California, where he died in poverty in 1861. On 11 November 1861 the *Irish Times* published a lengthy report on the funeral (McManus's remains had been repatriated) that had taken place the day before (a Sunday) in Dublin. It had been a vast affair in which the cortège passed through the city streets from Lower Abbey Street to Glasnevin cemetery, observed by large crowds. 'The procession,' noted the newspaper's reporter, with admirable objectivity, 'included about 20,000 people, principally of the lower orders, mixed with some respectably-dressed persons.' An American 'Deputation' was present and it was from its ranks that a Californian, N. C. Smith, was drawn to give the oration over the grave (from which the paper published extracts). Smith made it clear in his eulogy that the nascent Fenianism of North America regarded the funeral as a test case for the Irish: 'in our minds out there the spirit of Irish liberty went hand in hand with the spirit of the dead. We believed that the funeral of M'Manus would test the truth. If the Irish people, we reasoned, fail to know this man, we shall look on them as a doomed race.'

The huge popular response in Dublin to the dead McManus surely gave him and North America the answer they had hoped for. It was one, however, guaranteed to discomfit the conservative *Irish Times*. Considerable tetchiness was evinced, therefore, in its editorial of 2 December, less than a month later, when it noted how a New York newspaper had defended actions of the United States government by citing the seizure of McManus by the British authorities from an American ship in Cork harbour in 1848 as a kind of precedent: 'The stress laid ... on this pretended precedent would seem to indicate that the exportation of the remains of M'Manus to this country was really a political movement undertaken by the friends of the Federal Government, with a view to future contingencies.' In truth it was far more than that.

The spirit of the dead was stirring in Ireland as in North America. Indeed, the historian J. J. Lee has observed of the McManus obsequies: 'in some respects the funeral signalled a turning point in the history of Irish public opinion' (Lee 1973 p. 55). The *Irish Times* was alert enough to the dangers of this subterranean tide of militant Irish nationalist feeling and to the role played by what Fintan O'Toole has termed 'funerary propaganda' (O'Toole, *Irish Times* 2 October 2001) in fomenting it, to reprint in September 1865 from the *St Louis Republican* the report of an episcopal interdiction on priestly attendance at a similar 'deferred interment and ... pageant which is to accompany the burial' of an American Fenian who had died in Minnesota. The *Irish Times* seemed to hope, despite the evidence that Dublin had presented, that Fenianism was a foreign import and not really native to Ireland. The spirit of the dead would, however, if only briefly, walk again in Ireland in the Fenian revolts of 1867.

The military endeavours of the Fenian Rising took place in February and early March 1867. The February events were local, while those in March, intended to herald a national rising, were centred on Dublin and counties Tipperary, Limerick and Cork. On 16 February the paper was pleased to report that the Fenian 'army' had been routed in Kerry, its soldiers driven ignominiously into the hills. The 'peasantry to a man' had 'refused to have any participation in the movement'; the Fenian forces had been unimpressive. Indeed, some of them, the report noted with scarcely concealed contempt, 'bore strong resemblance to the dilapidated specimens of humanity which were landed on our quays from the purlieus of the manufacturing towns in England'. Outsiders were obviously to blame and the *Irish Times* suspected that 'the leaders of this most insane and wicked raid in Kerry are Americans'.

By mid-March, following the wider attempt at insurrection, the newspaper was gratified to inform its readers '"All is tranquil". "No Fenians appear upon the hills". These are now the stereotyped headings of the reports which reach us from the country.' At the end of the month, the paper could refer to recent events in Ireland as 'a burlesque of rebellion' (*Irish Times*, 29 March 1867). This was in an editorial that still had its eye on North America as the source of the Fenian infection. Outrages in Manchester and in London put England in the paper's editorial sights later in the year and in very curious terms. In an editorial on 24 September, following the violent springing of Fenian prisoners in Manchester, the writer was in full-throated, rhetorical mode:

> Fenianism, which has completely died out in Ireland, exists in England, but this is not the old Fenianism, with which in this country we were acquainted. A few deluded youths played at drilling – it was fun to them in the way it was conducted – or marched down a country road on moonlit nights. For few moments a few waifs and strays followed American leaders – men of large promises – to Tallaght or Kilmallock, but

they slipped away the moment they found what they were expected to do.
But Fenianism in England is desperate and murderous; it arms its instruments to the teeth; it wars in the open streets against the public force, it
wounds and slays. (*Irish Times*, 24 September 1867)

But in England, the editorial was at pains to insist, it was not simply an Irish
phenomenon, and the writer objects, indeed, to the fact that, because of the
recent outrage, the entire Irish population of Manchester had automatically
become suspect in the eyes of English public opinion. To blame are also, he
believes, as well as Fenian desperadoes, 'The debauched English artisans – the
roughs who stab and wound in midnight brawls – the wife beaters of English
manufacturing society.' They 'are amongst the men who have been engaged
in this desperate but successful affray'. The writer is convinced, indeed, that
'among the lowest members of English trades' union there are to be found
members ready to commit any act of violence'.

An editorial on 11 September 1867 puts such reactionary, offensive
fulmination in the context of what might be termed the conservative patriotism
of the newspaper's early decades. In September former prime minister 1st Earl
Russell passed through Dublin en route for a holiday in Killarney, Co. Kerry
(the Whig grandee had retired from active politics when he left office as prime
minister in 1866). Though the *Irish Times* regarded the reformer Russell as a
political opponent, it offered him good wishes for his vacation (in 'the most
beautiful scenery in the world'), spiced with advice. The earl should get to
know the Irish peasantry: 'He may see the peasantry in their homes, at their
work, or at fair, market, and patron festival. He will find them civil even to
a polished degree of courtesy. He will soon learn that they are intelligent,
quick-witted, ready of reply, and not averse to state what would benefit them
and their class' (*Irish Times*, 11 September 1867). Yet the newspaper does
not let representatives of the peasantry speak for themselves, since it suggests
that Russell will not find among them support for the kind of reform English
Whigs and Liberals would thrust upon them (disestablishment of the Church
of Ireland among these).

The Irish peasantry, it seems, are a model peasantry (loyal to their masters,
like the slaves of the old South during the American Civil War). They do not
seek political reform but economic opportunity. Fenianism was an aberration
that should not blind the English statesman Russell to what could truly
improve their lot and stem emigration: the means to 'obtain a better home ...
decent clothing ... proper food and lodging such as a man should have'. The
editorial combines, therefore, a genuine, if somewhat sentimental, regard for
the Irish countryman (which notably contrasts with the paper's distaste for
the English artisan), with an unrealistic assessment that he lacks a political
consciousness. It was this benign view of the Irish masses that would essentially

underpin a patriotism in the newspaper until the Land War, the Phoenix Park murders and the Plan of Campaign made even the most sanguine of conservatives in the country think again.

Conservative Irish patriotism, in the first two decades of its existence, governed the attitude of the *Irish Times* to the growing phenomenon of Home Rule nationalism. Theorists of nineteenth-century European nationalism tend to see it as progressing through three distinct phases. In the first stage, members of a country's intellectual elite begin to cultivate an interest in a territory's ancient past, its antiquities, language and artefacts. In the second phase, as this group enlarges, some of its number, as Alan O'Day has put it, 'seek to develop a political programme and seek to incorporate the masses into their conception of the nation (Boyce and O'Day 2004, p. 20). A third stage involves mass mobilization to pursue the goal of national liberation. Although this pattern does not hold precisely in all the circumstances in which European nationalism came to life in the nineteenth century, it does illumine the course of Irish nationalism in significant ways. The late eighteenth century had seen the growth of a version of colonial patriotism among members of the Protestant Ascendancy which was given expression in the founding of the Royal Irish Academy in 1785 and in the publication of such works as Charlotte Brooke's *Reliques of Irish Poetry* (1789). In the 1820s Daniel O'Connell had forged from the Irish masses a constituency that could be appealed to in the name of his Liberal constitutionalism, which bore fruit in Catholic Emancipation in 1829; but this did not translate into a full-blooded nationalist movement. O'Connell had, however, prepared the ground for the second phase of nationalist endeavour, that in which an elite seeks to instil national consciousness into the populace at large. The key figure in this during the 1860s and 1870s was Isaac Butt.

Butt had begun his public career as a radical Tory, one of those who had founded the *Dublin University Magazine* (he acted as editor from 1834 to 1838). His conservatism had been a matter of devotion to the Union while his radicalism had involved outrage at the English maladministration of Ireland and love of his nation's culture and traditions. He served as Tory MP for Youghal, Co. Cork, from 1852 to 1865 as his views became more and more liberal. That experience, together with his work as a barrister on behalf of Fenian prisoners after the rising of 1867, bred in him the belief that Ireland's future was to be best secured within the Empire by a native parliament. He formed the Home Government Association in 1870 and served and led a Home Rule party in Westminster (representing Limerick) until his death in 1879.

The *Irish Times* under Wheeler's editorship seemed to recognize that Butt's patriotism was not so very different from its own (and from that of its first owner Captain Knox's sympathy for Butt's vision of Home Rule). After all, the paper stood for reconciliation among the various strands of Irish life, and the kind of federalism in the British Isles Butt envisaged would, so he claimed, help bring that about: 'It is from the joint deliberations of all classes of Irishmen that we may most confidently hope to present a plan of a national legislature, in which the just influence of property and education, and rank may be harmoniously combined with popular privileges and power, so as to make the legislature the real representation of the nation' (Boyce and O'Day 2004, p. 23). So when in November 1873 Butt summoned a kind of parliament in waiting to found the Home Rule League, the paper reported its deliberations fully and afterwards editorialized in calm, respectful tones. 'The Home Rule Conference,' it judged, was 'an event in the history of Ireland.' It continued in like high-flown vein:

> It is unnecessary to say to anyone who has perused our reporting columns that the Home Rule Conference has been marked by the display of dialectic talent, of self-control, of mutual concession, and of patriotism, which would have done credit to many a National Assembly more strictly representative in character. (*Irish Times*, 22 November 1873)

The editorial, indeed, strikes, in a mood Butt sometimes echoed, a distinctly anti-English note, expressing impatience at how the conference proceedings had been misrepresented in the English press ('Well considered gabble,' said the London *Daily News*). By contrast, the *Irish Times* could with calm authority aver:

> A large number of Irishmen have met in decorous assembly; they have given expression to a programme, which if it be sincerely carried out, does not seem to threaten the stability of the Empire; and that by the terms of their resolutions they have anticipated all demands that could be made for a substantial guarantee of their intentions.

In 1877 James Scott was appointed editor by the paper's second owner, Sir John Arnott. Scott set the paper on a course of unambiguous support for the Union. In 1882 it declared itself 'Moderate-Conservative'; in 1887 'Independent', meaning 'Liberal-Conservative'; by 1895 it made no bones about being 'Unionist' (Mark O'Brien 2008, pp. 26 and 30), having no truck with dangerous ideas like Home Rule. Nonetheless, when Isaac Butt died in May 1879, the newspaper greeted the occasion with a weighty editorial that saluted a great man, as if to acknowledge a patriotism that transcended party. 'His personality,' the paper observed, 'filled so much space in the recent history of Ireland that one feels as if a great spring in the political machinery of the nation had just snapped.' As with the career of Daniel O'Connell, Butt's life work had ended in disappointment:

> Like O'Connell, he had promised much and done much. Like him, the irresistible force of circumstances barred his progress to the goal on which he had fixed the straining eyes of a nation ... Both will be remembered

as men who toiled devotedly for the country of their love; and the name of each will survive when the mannikins who stung them have sunk into deserved oblivion. (*Irish Times*, 6 May 1879)

The truth was that Butt's death marked a watershed in the course of Irish nationalism in the nineteenth century and confirmed a shift in power that had been in the making for some years, as younger, more militant members of the Irish Parliamentary Party at Westminster sought to put muscle into the Home Rule project by the use of obstructionist tactics (by adopting what in the United States had come to be known as the filibuster). Charles Stewart Parnell, no mannikin, would emerge in the 1880s as the focus of this more robust engagement with *realpolitik*. And Parnell's rise to power in nationalist Ireland would be accompanied by a mass movement for fair rents, fixity of tenure and right of sale, among the country's tenant farmers, led by Michael Davitt's Land League, which, while the Land War raged, gave an economic edge to constitutional ambition. At the same time, eruptions of politically inspired violence roused the spectre of the radical separatism that had, apparently, been defeated with the suppression of the Fenian uprising in 1867. When to this inflammatory set of circumstances was added William Gladstone's decision in 1886 to legislate for Home Rule, then unionism was confronted in the 1880s by threats to its position of a graver, more immediate kind than had ever been represented by Buttite nationalism, with which the *Irish Times* had been able to feel moderately at ease.

In respect of Gladstone, the unionist *Irish Times* had good reason to feel deeply suspicious in the 1880s. He unquestionably had a history of disregarding the views of loyal Protestant folk, for it had been he who had brought about the disestablishment of the Church of Ireland in 1869. From the earliest editions of the *Irish Times*, the affairs of that ecclesiastical body had been close to its heart (understandably so since its second editor was in holy orders) and disestablishment had presented it with a notable challenge. It had learnt then that when Gladstone had made up his mind, he pursued his objectives with resolute determination. When in February 1869 the *Irish Times* commented on Queen Victoria's speech outlining the British government's legislative programme, it observed, vis-à-vis disestablishment, that those 'who were loudest in their demands for the destruction of the Irish Established Church' (*Irish Times*, 17 February 1869) never disguised the fact that they had other concerns as well, which they could use to foment dangerous agitation: land ownership and the issue of denominational education. Presented with a *fait accompli* on 18 June 1869, when the House of Lords passed the second reading of the Established Church (Ireland) Bill, the *Irish Times* had made the best of what most Irish Anglicans thought was a distinctly bad job. In key with its patriotic conservatism, the newspaper used the occasion to highlight again that a measured solution to the land question was the real issue confronting the country, if that were not to be used as a dangerous bone of contention by disloyal elements. Accordingly, the *Irish Times*'s editorial of 19 June 1869 made clear that, with the religious question now, one way or another, en route to settlement (the paper held hopes of necessary amendments tabled in the Upper House), the matter of landlord and tenant should now take centre stage. 'Every day,' said the editorial, 'is furnishing illustrations of the evils attendant upon the existing nature of the relations between landlord and tenant in Ireland. This all-important subject can now be discussed without being embittered by religious feuds fought over with polemical acerbity.' The subtext of the piece is that English statesmen, with Gladstone a case in point, tend to adopt grand strategies for an Ireland weakened by disunity, and they disregard the complex social realities of Irish life. National unity can be the only bulwark against English meddling, of which the enacted Bill was a signal example.

A ghastly event in Dublin in 1882 served notice that English politicians in Ireland in the 1880s and those Irish men and women who supported the Union faced extra-parliamentary political forces not only of a redoubtable kind, as evidenced by the Land League, but of a cruel and savage nature. On 6 May the Chief Secretary for Ireland, Lord Frederick Cavendish, and his undersecretary, Thomas Burke, were bloodily assassinated in Dublin's Phoenix Park. Unusually, the *Irish Times* published the day after, a Sunday, to register its horror. The paper stated that it was publishing that morning 'under circumstances of the most unexampled and startling character' and solemnly reported that 'public feeling [had] received a shock such as never has been experienced in the country before'. The paper described in graphic detail how Cavendish and Burke had been dispatched with knives or daggers, lingering on the horror of their wounds as evidence that 'The history of Ireland – at least of the period in which we live – may be searched in vain for a record of a crime more terrible, or one carried out with more deliberation or determination.' Something, it seemed, had surfaced from the lower depths to call itself 'The Invincibles'.

Even in the febrile atmosphere that marked Irish public life in the years following this grisly assault on the body politic, the *Irish Times* sought to sustain the kind of liberal balance that had marked its response to Irish nationalism in the era of Isaac Butt. Not even the Phoenix Park murders could quite persuade it that it was operating in very changed times. Accordingly, in 1884, as Gladstone's Franchise Act to expand the British and Irish electorate was working its tortuous way through the Commons and Lords (the Conservative *Irish Times* took a fairly jaundiced view of the proposal, strongly supporting the ideas about distribution of members in constituencies that reactionary elements in parliament had foisted on Gladstone as the price for enacting his Bill), it kept true to its long-term vision of an Irish society at one with itself, untroubled by political malcontents, with the Irish countryman as the base upon which all could contentedly rest. On 8 January 1884 the *Irish Times* reiterated what had been its attitude to land reform since the 1860s – it should proceed, provided it was managed in an orderly fashion (this did not inhibit supporters of Davitt denouncing the paper as 'The Liarish Times'): 'What is desired is that everything should be done in a lawful and just manner.' Then the Irish peasantry would be 'the mainstay of order and of religion also, and the best supporters of its spiritual authorities. The growth of such a class of agriculturalists would be a rejoicing for every true patriot of every persuasion.'

Admiration for the Irish peasantry had long been a feature of the *Irish Times*'s social vision. A review of one of the most successful Irish plays of the Victorian age is a telling example of what was a settled attitude that found expression in its columns. In April 1861 Dion Boucicault's *The Colleen Bawn* (1860) had begun a run at the Theatre Royal, Dublin (which the *Irish Times*'s theatre reviewer invoked as 'the temple of Irish drama', *Irish Times* 1 April 1861). The paper's review of this quintessential Victorian melodrama, already an international hit, was at pains to make clear that this work, 'one of the finest Irish dramas ever put upon the stage', based on a novel of rural crime, *The Collegians* (1829), by Gerald Griffin, was no piece of gratuitous stage Irishry, but a celebration of the Irish peasantry. The reviewer commented: 'In further notices we shall refer to this admirable drama, which is no burlesque of Irish character, but a truthful and thrilling picture of real life, interpreted by those who understand the peculiarities of the Irish peasant, and admire his virtues and many estimable qualities, of which honour and integrity are not the least conspicuous' (*Irish Times*, 1 April 1861).

On 21 May 1884 the paper reported on a speech on the Franchise Bill by the conservatively minded, though independent, Lord Randolph Churchill. It noted that Churchill believed in 'the enfranchisement of the agricultural labourer'. In so doing, the *Irish Times* affirmed that at least one English politician showed 'a large and intelligent acquaintance with Ireland', for the Irish labourer was certainly well equipped for enfranchisement in any just extension of the electorate (with a 'fair and equitable adjustment of seats according to population'); for 'the Irish labourer is superior to the English labourer. He is not ignorant of politics or his own interests. He is a lively reader of newspapers and forms his judgement sharply and quickly – too sharply and quickly very often for those who would trade on his prejudices.' When at the end of 1884 the Bill became law, the *Irish Times* noted of the promised redistribution of MPs in the United Kingdom on the basis of population (of which it approved) that it would 'extinguish boroughs and throw the representation into counties'. This was to the paper's satisfaction for it might result in 'an enlargement of the ideas upon which members will be elected'. No doubt these could include the thoughts of some of the country's newspaper-reading, well-informed countrymen, able now to cast votes free of those who would exploit their grievances for nefarious purposes. Generally, the paper had seemed hopeful about the parliamentary future: 'The future Irish representation will be made as truly representative as is possible for the whole people, and not of mere clamourers and revolutionaries' (*Irish Times*, 20 November 1884).

Within a year the newspaper and unionist Ireland was to be confronted with the unpalatable fact that Gladstone would lay a Home Rule Bill in parliament that would shatter any hopes that the 'whole people' of Ireland (by which it meant unionists as well as nationalists, Protestants as well as Catholics) could share an agreed constitutional future (in passing, one must note that, although the issue of women's suffrage arose during the debates and controversies about the Franchise Act, the right to vote in Britain after 1884 remained restricted to adult males). For many Irish unionists it seemed that a revolutionary had pitched his tent in the very grounds of the mother of parliaments.

That revolutionary was Charles Stewart Parnell and his betraying abettor in casting Irish Protestant and unionist sheep to Catholic nationalist wolves was William Ewart Gladstone. On 19 December 1885 the *Irish Times* made its position crystal clear. It advised unionist Ireland, as the substance of Gladstone's intention became known, 'that their interests are already betrayed as far as Mr Gladstone can betray them, and that there is not a day to lose in declaring their obstinate resistance to the betrayal'. Gladstone, it seemed, wanted to rid England of an Irish burden without regard for the deepest feelings of loyal citizens of the United Kingdom residing in Ireland: 'England casts us off, gets rid of us – that is the great temptation offered to her by Mr Gladstone' (*Irish Times*, 9 April 1886). The next day the paper was pleased to reprint the view of *The Times* that Gladstone's Bill amounted to a 'cruel and cowardly betrayal of our loyal fellow-subjects'.

In the event, the Bill foundered, but its defeat perhaps masked the fact that its very proposal had been a reaction to the changed condition of Ireland where mass mobilization on the land question, parliamentary obstructionism and the threat of anarchist violence had inaugurated a new phase of Irish nationalism. Furthermore, the charged atmosphere in which the debates about Home Rule had been conducted affected the country in a marked way, as politics took on a keener sectarian inflection. This was pronounced in Ulster, a province long scarred by outbreaks of inter-communal violence in the streets of Belfast and in some towns in the province. The proposal and defeat of Gladstone's Bill in the House of Commons in June 1886 was a prelude to outbreaks of serious rioting in Belfast throughout the early summer which surpassed in intensity anything that had occurred before. Lord Randolph Churchill, the Tory MP and vicious opponent of Gladstone, had been determined to play the Orange Card in 1886 to defeat Home Rule and so bring down the government (both things in fact transpired but not solely because of Churchill's intervention). Events in June and July in Belfast showed how bloody a hand Churchill had held, when he had stirred the flames of Orange Order resistance to Home Rule. Gladstone, he declared in Belfast's Ulster Hall on 22 February, was an assassin like Macbeth, who was ready to plunge 'the knife into the heart of the British Empire' (*Weekly Irish Times*, 27 February 1886). He suggested 'that the struggle is not likely to remain within the lines of what we are accustomed to look upon as constitutional action' and posited provocatively: 'But now may be the time to show whether all those ceremonies and forms which are practised in your Orange lodges are really living symbols or idle and meaningless shibboleths.' An article published in the *Irish Times* on 10 April 1886 proved that there were influential figures in the north of Ireland prepared to meet Churchill's challenge. Under the headline 'Will the Orangemen Fight?' the paper reported on an interview given to a representative of the *Pall Mall Gazette* by the well-known Orange firebrand and MP for South Belfast, William Johnston. Johnston had made it clear that 'Orangemen would not accept any scheme of Home Rule on any terms.' What was striking about Johnston's replies to his journalist interlocutor was that, although the Orange Order was an all-Ireland institution, with its headquarters in Dublin, he saw possible armed Orange resistance to any Irish parliament in the capital as having its epicentre in Belfast. Reckoning that if Home Rule were granted, the 'Orange Party' would consider itself as being 'placed under a foreign domination', Johnston continued menacingly and revealingly: 'Yes we would have nothing to do with it, but the form of resistance would depend on the overt act of the Parliament. We could not, of course, initiate an invasion directed against them, but where they sought to reach us we would drive them out.' So *Irish Times* readers were introduced to the idea of fortress North and the birth of a modern siege mentality that would thereafter affect Irish politics for more than a century. Johnston also set before their minds the prospect of civil war:

> I said twelve years ago on Mr Butt's motion in March 1874, that any attempt to promote a separate Parliament would produce civil war. The other day when I was in Ballykilbeg 100 men assembled to confer as to the best kind of arms they could secure, and I was to consult with some military gentlemen in England on the best means of defence.

A letter, published on 20 May under the byline 'The Feeling of Ulster', gave voice in more measured terms to the growing sense of Ulster exceptionalism which was one effect of the 1886 Home Rule crisis. 'Suppose it is passed,' suggested 'An Ulsterman' of Gladstone's Bill, 'in the face of all this determined opposition on the part of those who have made Ulster prosperous, and have preserved Ireland from utter ruin, what would be the result? Loyal Ulster will not submit calmly. Its people inherit much of the courage and determination of their Scotch forefathers. I, for one, venture to think that they will not be abandoned in the present crisis.' On 18 May 1886 the *Irish Times* itself seemed to indicate sympathy with the province's mood when it noted approvingly a pamphlet by a Methodist minister who had, it was claimed, shown 'what Ulster has to expect from a Parnellite Government' and had 'borne witness to the deep-seated and growing sentiment of antagonism to that fate which no denunciation of civil war can get rid of'.

On 8 June, when the bill was defeated, although the newspaper was at pains to direct its readers to 'the constitutional confusions which would be the result of the Premier's plan', the *Irish Times* struck a conciliatory note. It observed: 'Vast changes of sentiment, as well as of party relations, are sure to spring from this morning's work [news of the division in the House of Commons had reached the paper at 1.20 a.m. by its own private line to Westminster]. Let us hope that in Ireland the public will bear what has happened with equanimity.'

Violent sectarian rioting in Belfast and in Lurgan, Co. Armagh, involving loss of life, and sectarian commotions in Sligo town in the immediate aftermath of the Westminster vote did not augur well for public equanimity in places where the Home Rule crisis had inflamed confessional tensions. In its responses to these lamentable events, the *Irish Times* on 15 June chose, oddly enough, largely to disregard how religion and politics mixed in a noxious brew in parts of Ireland, and took a high Tory attitude as it opined:

> The serious part of these tumults, however, in the Northern town as well as in the Western, lies in the proof which they give that the socialist contempt for prosperity or personal superiority is extending ... It is necessary to bear this ever in mind. We are not contending any longer with a form of rancour between potential factions only – we have something worse and more dangerous, and going deeper, to concern ourselves with. The vicious spirit which takes possession of a class of the population when their minds have become perverted, and an insatiable unrest afflicts them, is a danger that those responsible for the public peace have need always to be on their guard against in dense communities.

This rodomontade, combining as it does a distinctively Burkean note with the *Irish Times*'s characteristic Victorian distaste for concentrations of urban working-class people, is an Irish version of Victorian middle-class panic in face of potential social disorder. However, the *Irish Times*'s apparent unwillingness to confront how sectarianism was grievously deforming the Irish body politic may have derived from something more commendable. Arguably that was its own innate sense of religious decency, which meant that it found the idea of purely sectarian violence difficult to fathom.

As a newspaper that spoke to and for the Protestant interest in the country, the *Irish Times*'s reportage of Church of Ireland affairs had always played a significant part in its pages during the period. Frequent Church Notes were those relating to the Church of many of its readers, and the newspaper took good care to deal with issues that affected Irish Protestantism as they arose. It did so, however, in a way that simultaneously sought in a liberal and good-mannered fashion to pay due respect to Catholic feelings and the demands of the majority of Christian believers in the country. An interesting case in point was the *Irish Times*'s response of 5 April 1873 to Fawcett's Act of that year. This was the parliamentary statute proposed by a radical Englishman, Henry Fawcett, which provided for the abolition of religious tests in Trinity College Dublin. Some of these had been removed in 1793 when Catholics and dissenters were permitted to matriculate and to take degrees, but the Act of 1873, as the *Irish Times* put it, enabled the college (the single constituent college of the University of Dublin, founded by Queen Elizabeth I to promote the Protestant religion in Ireland), 'to fill her chairs and her Fellowships with the ablest men among the candidates for them, instead of, at present, filling them with the ablest men of one particular denomination'. 'Mr Fawcett's Bill', therefore, was 'an excellent thing for Trinity College'.

In reacting in this way to Fawcett's parliamentary intervention in Irish educational affairs, the *Irish Times* was in broader terms, it could be argued, merely bowing to demographic and social reality which in the post-Famine period involved Irish Catholicism consolidating itself in a major church-building programme and in the flexing of political muscle as the first Irish cardinal, the redoubtable Paul Cullen, centralized ecclesiastical authority in obedience to Rome's spiritual jurisdiction. But in key *Irish Times* editorials and reports in the period, the paper evinced in tone and manner more than a fatalistic bowing to the inevitable rise of Catholic power in Ireland, set on its way by the Emancipation Act of 1829, but a true regard for the faith of the majority of the island's inhabitants. A symbolic moment in the life of the Victorian Irish Catholic Church was the dedication of St Patrick's Cathedral in Armagh in 1873. On 7 July of that year the *Irish Times* carried a report from a correspondent that the building, a 'noble edifice, one of the finest if not the finest in the kingdom', was near completion. The correspondent was of a mind that 'Men of all shades of political opinions must regard it as an ornament to the city.' On 25 August the paper drew lengthily and admiringly from its own reporters at the scene of the dedication, which had taken place the day before (a Sunday) in a full-scale evocation of a momentous event in the history of Irish Catholicism. The Church, which a century earlier had been under interdiction (the renowned Dominican preacher Father Thomas Burke in his homily on the day adverted to 'the growth, persecutions and revival of the Catholic Church in Ireland', while honouring the Christian efficacy of forgiveness), now would have a cathedral in Armagh which would surpass in splendour the Anglican cathedral in that city. And the *Irish Times* did not hesitate to mark the occasion with full journalistic coverage of what was judged to be a 'highly important occurrence'. The paper's reporting team was glad to note what would now be thought of as the ecumenical nature of the day's proceedings: 'A most remarkable and gratifying element of the vast assemblage was the number of Protestants of rank and station' who had been present. And they could express satisfaction that among the list of those who had contributed to the cost of the building could be 'found Protestants, Presbyterians and Catholics happily blended in the common object to a cathedral for Catholic worship'.

Also in 1873, the *Irish Times* had a building achievement closer to its Protestant heart to celebrate. In 1865 the paper, in an editorial, had greeted the completed restoration of St Patrick's Cathedral in Dublin as the 'noblest work of our age'; and this at a time when the 'pence and shillings of the Roman Catholic, like rain drops forming the river, have accumulated and sufficed to rear ecclesiastical structures which are an honour to any age or country' (*Irish Times,* 25 February 1865). In 1873 the paper again celebrated the completed restoration of Christ Church Cathedral in Dublin by publishing an account 'of the foundation and history of one of the most deeply interesting of our great cathedrals' (*Irish Times,* 11 September 1873). The introductory remarks to this contribution are fascinating, for they make explicit how the newspaper saw Irish Anglicanism as by no means an alien confession of a planter stock in the land but as a part of Ireland's rich Celtic deposit of Christian faith. The introductory note affirmed that the Church of Ireland's acts of church restoration were a revival of the 'primitive spirit' of the 'ancient Ages of Faith' in the country (an Irish echo of the Victorian Gothic craze), but were also a part of the estimably religious character of the present-day country. Together with the restoration of Church of Ireland cathedrals and churches and the 'the erection of the handsome Presbyterian Church in Rutland [now Parnell] Square, by the late Mr Alexander Findlater' (an exquisite example in Dublin of Gothic revival architecture), the article reminded its readers how 'the numerous catholic cathedrals, churches, colleges, convents, schools, parochial houses and charitable institutions that cover the kingdom, upon the erection of which several millions have been expended, within a period of less than 50 years, testify, in a still stronger manner, the depth and strength of the same religious feeling, on the part of the poorer members of the mass of the people of Ireland'. With such a vision of the Christian faith as a shared inheritance in Ireland, the *Irish Times* was able in a leading article to eulogize Cardinal Paul Cullen on his death in 1878 as one 'in the true sense a priest', whose demise had 'been received with unmixed regret by all sections of our fellow citizens' (25 October 1878). It is not to be wondered at that the *Irish Times*, thinking as it did, found the sectarian excesses of the 1886 Home Rule crisis an affront difficult to deal with. For the newspaper liked to think of Ireland as a Christian country with its confessional differences transcended by a profound, instinctively national respect for apolitical religious feeling. Its conservative patriotism meant that it could view the marked ecclesiastical quality of Irish life as an inherited strength and not as a political problem that could, especially in the north of the country, express itself in overtly sectarian terms.

The 1890s were to be an object lesson, which nobody could ignore, of how in Ireland religion and politics were inextricably bound up with one another. The fall of Charles Stewart Parnell, leader of the Nationalist Party in Westminster, on account of the divorce action taken by Captain William O'Shea against his wife (and Parnell's mistress), Katharine, would not only split the party, but bring the Catholic hierarchy to the fore in commenting decisively on a matter of great political moment. On 4 December 1890 the *Irish Times* published a statement that the hierarchy had released which judged Parnell to be unfit for office. The prelates sought to defend their intervention as driven only by their moral recoil from what the divorce action in London had revealed and not by politics, but it was evident that they had politics very much on their minds since they concluded: 'we see nothing but inevitable defeat at the approaching elections and as a result Home Rule indefinitely postponed, coercion perpetuated, the hands of the evictor strengthened, and the tenants already evicted left without the shadow of a hope of being ever restored to their homes.' The *Irish Times* commented on this statement, identifying it as an 'extremely important document', reflecting that 'the conclusions which it pronounces will be well received universally with the respect which is due to the position and authority of those eminent prelates'. It was sure 'This weighty decision thus announced will, no doubt, exercise the largest effect.' And it was sure, too, that that effect would be immediate, bearing on the progress of a Land Purchase Bill (which the paper approved) then before the House of Lords; for it followed the above editorial with a further one on parliamentary developments that could ensue as a consequence of the ecclesiastics' statement.

The extensive editorial the *Irish Times* published on 8 October 1891, two days after Parnell's sudden death, suggested that it was not what it called his 'moral lapse' which troubled it (though when the divorce case had concluded in November 1890 the paper had deprecated Parnell's 'duplicity'), but his politics. In this way it sought to keep religion and politics separate in its evaluation of Parnell, where the hierarchy had conjoined them, while denying that they had done so. By contrast with the hierarchy, the *Irish Times* had little doubt that Parnell was fit to be a leader, for 'his worst personal antagonist never imputed to him any treachery or sacrifice of his associates'. It was his policy of Home Rule for Ireland it opposed, even if it granted, true to its traditions, that Parnell had worked to improve the condition of the Irish poor. It was his own caste he had put at risk:

As to the estimate of Mr Parnell which those not of that political connexion [the Irish Party] will be justified in entertaining, it is enough to add that his errors were great and the injustice which he did to his own social class flagrant, and excused in its extravagance in no measure by faults of theirs.

In sum, the *Irish Times* regretted 'the waste' of Parnell's energies 'in a labour that has proved a momentous failure'. It judged that 'his death closes a chapter in Irish affairs'.

The tone of this editorial (almost rancidly bitter about Parnell's betraying associates and about a cynically manipulative Gladstone), when compared with the eulogy the *Irish Times* had published 12 years earlier to mark the death of Isaac Butt, may perhaps be explained by the fact that Butt had never seemed a class enemy. The polemical edge (the occasion of Parnell's death being employed to challenge Gladstone to come clean about his intentions vis-à-vis the fractured Irish Parliamentary Party, which had split apart over their leader's 'moral lapse') of the *Irish Times*'s leading article on Parnell's demise indicates that he had been feared by unionists in a way Butt had never been and that, although his 'failure' to bring about Home Rule could be deemed 'momentous', Parnell's near success in 1886 had been peculiarly unnerving. What Butt had talked about, Parnell had almost made happen in a climate of threatened and actual violence, land agitation, religious division in the north of the country and portended civil war. The attitudes expressed in the editorial betray an existential anxiety that had not really been felt in Butt's time.

The fact was, did the newspaper but know it, that the rise of Parnell, the Home Rule crisis and the fall and death of Parnell were placing enormous strains on the edifice that the *Irish Times* constituted, striking at the ideological foundations of its outlook. This involved viewing the world through imperial eyes. The Union of Britain and Ireland, a good in itself, had allowed the Irish people, the paper assumed, to be partners in the great outreach of civilizing power constituted by the British Empire. This key reality of the age was reflected in the first four decades of the paper's life (in the period when that empire grew exponentially) in the constant, detailed attention the *Irish Times* paid to events in the United Kingdom's far-flung territories. This had reached an emotional apotheosis in 1884 when the paper had followed the vicissitudes and eventual fate of General Gordon (that Victorian icon of imperial imagining) in the Sudan with obsessive zeal, on 1 April damning a statement by Gladstone in parliament as 'amongst the most disingenuous and sophisticated that have ever proceeded from the PRIME MINISTER', while it lamented 'GORDON has been *abandoned*, the Soudan has been abandoned and Egypt proper has been abandoned.'

This view of the world involved a bifocal perspective that did not really constitute a unified field of vision. From one point of view, the *Irish Times* spoke as if it were expressing the settled, shared imperial attitudes of the governing caste of the United Kingdom, from the centre as it were. In Ireland, however, the paper increasingly represented the interests and spoke only for a national minority who did not share the Irish nationalism of the majority of the country's population. It was the voice of a powerful constituency, to be sure, with secure footholds in the administrative and business worlds in Dublin, but, outside the province of Ulster, becoming marginal in Irish life. The degree to which the paper was increasingly aware of this was evidenced in 1892 when Gladstone in old age began his second failed attempt to enact Home Rule for Ireland. As in 1886, the most potent forces arrayed against him were mustered in Ulster, when the Ulster Unionist Convention was held on 17 June with 12,000 delegates present. The *Irish Times* noted in one leader that Ulster had spoken and that its voice would 'ring through the constituencies of the United Kingdom'. But whereas in 1886 the *Irish Times* had seemed almost embarrassed by the robust, sectarian forms that political expression took in Belfast and its environs, by 1892 it was now earnest to emphasize that northern unionist strength was an asset all-Ireland unionism might be forced to draw on. The paper editorialized in glowing terms on the strength of purpose northern unionism had exhibited. The Convention held out-of-doors in Belfast had been a show of unity, which had commanded the support not only of Protestants and Presbyterians but of Catholics too (the paper thought it a display of 'praiseworthy Christianity'). Most significantly, it was an endorsement of the Union of 1801, which could not be gainsaid, for

> The Act of Union, submitted again to the judgement of the best and most responsible men of every class amongst us, could not find a jury more entitled to declare that it shall ever continue, than those who, on the memorable 17th June, met in the Northern capital to register their decree, and send it on in anticipation of the Gladstone manifesto, to every English or Scottish constituency. The work, which was serious in its obligation and difficult in its management, has been brought to a splendid culmination, and the first grand national effort of Belfast as a city remains recorded to its imperishable glory.

The Second Boer War of 1899 to 1902 was a moment in the newspaper's history when its imperial and local perspectives came into sharp conflict; and they did so in a way that tended to highlight the complexities involved in the paper's position as defender of British imperial interests and of Protestant unionist Ireland. Like most British newspapers, the *Irish Times* followed the course of that dismal war in a distant land with obsessive concern. The fact that some of of its decisive encounters were sieges that achieved the status of imperial legends (Kimberley, Ladysmith and Mafeking) gave the events there a kind of local significance in the Ireland where unionism itself felt increasingly besieged (what were deemed British attempts to kill Home Rule by kindness in the last years of the century had scarcely moderated the intentions of militant Irish nationalism).

On 19 May 1900 the *Irish Times* greeted the relief of Mafeking with unbounded enthusiasm in a country that had in fact been divided in its support for the belligerents in South Africa. The 'long suspense ... is over. A Reuters dispatch in London last night from Pretoria announced that the Boers had raised the siege after having their forts and laargers severely bombarded.' The paper exuberantly shared in the joy that had erupted in the British capital. An empire had triumphed:

> As the news was flashed over the wires, every part of the Kingdom joined
> in the demonstration and soon, wherever a telegraph cable could spread
> the glad tidings and a man of British blood was there to hear it, a prayer
> of thankfulness and of praise went up to heaven.

In reporting this denouement, the *Irish Times* revealed a distinctly colonialist mindset when it complacently concluded 'Boer cunning' has been 'defeated by superior intelligence'. By 28 May the paper's satisfaction with events in the southern hemisphere had taken on a triumphalist tone, as it noted: '"A correspondent with Lord Roberts's army" states that the splendid handling of the forces has completely out-manoeuvred the Boers. The advance is quite irresistible, and now even the most irreconcilable Transvaaler realises the hopelessness of the struggle.'

Closer to home, from early October 1899 the *Irish Times* had increasingly been made aware that there were those in Dublin who hoped for different kinds of news from South Africa. On 30 September an Irish Transvaal Committee (ITC) had signalled its existence, and at a rally of some 20,000 people in Dublin the next day it was announced that an Irish Brigade to fight alongside the Boers would be formed when war began. Notable Irish nationalists spoke to the throng. On 11 October battle was joined between the British and the Boers. Irish regiments in the British Army were to be mobilized for action in South Africa and enlistments were sought. By 16 October the *Irish Times* was stating that it had refused to publish material submitted to it by the Irish Transvaal Committee. It reported that a placard had been 'extensively posted up throughout Dublin', by order of that committee, which under the heading 'Enlisting in the English Army Treason to Ireland' had advised: 'In preventing recruiting for the English Army you are working for Ireland's honour and you are doing something to help the Boers in their struggle for freedom.' Initially the paper responded with disdain to these developments, suggesting on 25 October that the committee was 'not worth an instant's notice' as the product of 'some obscure tenement'. And they were likely to be a bunch of ineffective cowards who would inspire nobody: 'The recruiting sergeants for the Boers have not found a single man, as far as we know, to enlist from any of our four provinces.'

The newspaper, in provocative mood, wanted to know who exactly comprised this committee. In December it got its answer and it was not to its liking.

Under the headline 'Dublin and the South African War', on 18 December 1899 the paper reported how the previous week a meeting had been summoned by the ITC to object to the awarding of an honorary degree to the British Colonial Secretary, Joseph Chamberlain, identifying him as the 'author' of 'the robber war being waged to-day by England'. The chair was to be taken by John O'Leary, an old Fenian leader. It had also been indicated that Michael Davitt and William Redmond (brother of John Redmond, leader of the National Party at Westminster), would attend and speak. This suggested that the various strands within Irish nationalism (separatist militancy, social agitation and constitutionalism) were finding common cause in opposition to Britain's imperialist adventures. The authorities were sufficiently alarmed to proscribe the meeting. Nonetheless, the organizers proceeded, with resultant disorder in the capital as the police sought to disperse the crowds that had formed in Sackville (now O'Connell) Street. Among the fomenters of the street protest were Maud Gonne and James Connolly.

At the meeting itself, under O'Leary's chairmanship, Davitt, Redmond and Gonne spoke and were joined in doing so by Patrick O'Brien, MP. A motion was passed 'condemning the Transvaal war'. John Dillon, a prominent member of Redmond's party, had written to give his support.

The *Irish Times* chose not to remain on the journalistic sidelines on the question of the Boer War. It established an Irish Regiments' Widows' and Orphans' Fund, and in the weeks after the proscribed meeting of the ITC it printed frequent reminders of where donations were being received. It was gratified to report on 2 February 1900 that between 24 October and 30 December 1899 these donations had amounted to £11,567. By January £13,040 had been received. The paper also arranged for substantial quantities of clothing to be sent to the Irish soldiers who were at war with the Boers.

The Boer War was a turning point for Irish nationalism which had been in disarray since the Parnell split, Parnell's death and the defeat of the second Home Rule Bill in 1893 (though the Local Government Act of 1898 had given it substantial powers at local level). As P. J. Mathews has argued, the war 'provided the Irish Parliamentary Party, shell-shocked from almost a decade of in-fighting, with an opportunity to unite around an issue that had no direct bearing on Irish affairs and was, therefore, less likely to cause dissension. In many respects it provided Irish nationalist MPs with a common cause and held the various factions together long enough for a degree of mutual trust to be formed' (Mathews 2003, pp. 99–100). The party was also being challenged by the United Irish League, founded in 1898 to represent the interests of small farmers. Unity was necessary for survival. Accordingly, when the *Irish Times* became directly involved in support for the British Army in South Africa it was taking sides in a very pronounced way at a time when, as Roy Foster has put it, 'The Boer War had aligned Irish nationalism across a broad front' (Foster 1998, p. 229). And as Mathews has further argued, the Boer War protests, against which the *Irish Times* resolutely, even truculently, set its face, were also changing the nature of Irish nationalism since they allowed what in the past had usually been clandestine forces of militant separatism to achieve crucial public visibility and increasing political credibility. Among those who enlisted in the Irish Brigade to fight for the Boers was John MacBride, who would subsequently marry Maud Gonne, the revolutionary firebrand and W. B. Yeats's unattainable muse, while a key figure in the ITC was Arthur Griffith, who in 1905 would found Sinn Féin.

In its direct support of an imperial war, the *Irish Times* at the turn of the century may have seen itself as speaking from the high ground of establishment British opinion-making. Locally, it was making significant enemies, who in the future would be in the ascendant. And they were enemies who would increasingly view Protestant unionist Ireland not as a national minority but as an alien presence in the land. It was in 1900 that the pugnacious journalist D. P. Moran founded his journal *The Leader* where he would launch a sustained polemical crusade against Protestant control of much of Irish business life. And in a series of essays published in 1899 (collected in 1905 under the title *The Philosophy of Irish Ireland*) Moran would help make the term Anglo-Irish one of opprobrium.

It was assuredly from the high ground of imperial certitudes that the *Irish Times* spoke when Queen Victoria passed away on 22 January 1901. The paper editorialised two days later in elevated terms:

> The QUEEN was so much a part of the established order of things that it is difficult to realise that anything can go on without her. Men have been born, have had children born to them and seen their children's children without ever knowing another Monarch besides VICTORIA. There are officers in the army to-day whose grandfathers received their first commissions with her sign-manual upon them. There are flourishing Colonies called by her name, containing great cities, supplied by all the latest products of civilisation, that were trackless deserts when first she ascended the Throne. The letters 'V.R.' seem to most of us an integral portion of the British constitution.

For the *Irish Times* it was self-evident that the Victorian age in which Ireland had played its part was an age of grandeur, with the British constitution a bulwark of greatness, questioned only by a minority. In the general grief occasioned by the death of the Queen, the newspaper could ignore the fact that many in Ireland had no liking for the British Empire. In the *Irish Times*'s celebration of the civilizing effects of empire that involved the foundation of 'great cities', the paper could bury any troubling consciousness that Dublin itself had declined as a city during Victoria's lengthy imperial reign.

Mary Daly, in her book *Dublin: The Deposed Capital: A Social and Economic History, 1860–1914* (1984), has painted a dispiriting picture of a city that endured a protracted economic decline in the nineteenth century when the imperial parliament at Westminster did little to arrest social problems of poverty, unemployment, congested housing, ill-health. Where efforts at amelioration were made, they tended to illustrate, as Daly has it, 'the inappropriateness of transferring administrative practices unchanged to Ireland' (Daly 1984, p. 320). She argues that when Westminster at last began to confront Irish social conditions in 1870 in response to the Land War, it did so by concentrating on rural affairs, to the disadvantage of Irish cities (with the exception of Belfast where manufacturing was making a north-British industrial city of what at the end of the eighteenth century had been an Irish town). In 1875 the *Irish Times* itself had passed a damning judgement on the city where misery accumulated. 'A Study of Dublin Streets: Specially Written for the *Irish Times*' pondered the city's inveterate social lethargy in puzzled terms:

> We have wandered much through the liberties on the south side and their counter part about Church Street on the north side of the river. And never knew which most to marvel at – the contentment of the thousands who herd together in these wretched abodes, or the stupid inactivity of our philanthropists who, while they continually are promulgating patent schemes for the reform of our masses, forget that the character of people depends in great degree on their dwellings, and till decent lodgings can be obtained at a moderate price it is vain to hope for any real amelioration of the bulk of our bread winners. Indeed, as it is, the unfortunate tenants of these broken down courts and alleys deserve considerable respect for preserving so many domestic virtues, and such a sunshiny nature in the centre of dark haunts of dirty misery. (*Irish Times*, 6 December 1875)

The truth was that as Britain became an industrial powerhouse, post-Famine Ireland outside Ulster remained largely an agricultural country. When in 1895 and 1896 a committee organized by Sir Horace Plunkett considered the economic future of Ireland (including in its membership, which brought unionists and nationalists together, the *Irish Times*'s proprietor Sir John Arnott), it concluded in a report of 418 pages, which covered most aspects of Irish production, and highlighted the role agriculture played in the Irish economy, that an Irish Department of Agriculture and Industries should be established. The *Irish Times* gave the report (which had been presented unanimously to the Lord Lieutenant) extensive coverage when it was published in August 1896, but, despite the presence of Arnott on the committee, the newspaper was lukewarm in its support. The report had been dismissive of the

Royal Dublin Society, to which no doubt many influential *Irish Times* readers belonged, and its implicit criticism of Westminster's governance of Ireland was scarcely to be welcomed by Dublin unionists, who depended on the imperial parliament for political protection (in a more self-confident Belfast the report was given an enthusiastic welcome by both the Belfast *Newsletter* and the *Northern Whig* (West 1986, p. 47). Perhaps the report's dismissal of cities as centres of industry offended the civic pride of a newspaper that saw itself as an important journalistic voice in the second city of a great empire.

Although municipal Dublin had failed to enhance the nation's capital with notable public building in the period, the cultural resources of the city had in fact been markedly increased in the late nineteenth century by the construction of the National Library of Ireland and the Science and Art Museum, both of which were made possible by monies granted from the British exchequer. Thereby Dublin was included in the Victorian enthusiasm for the collection and tabulation of knowledge and for government taking a role in the improvement of civil society, which was a marked feature of cultural life in Victorian Britain. For unionists, the complex of buildings that began to be assembled adjacent to Trinity College were proof positive in stone of the value of the British connection and could be celebrated unreservedly by the *Irish Times* as one of the glories of the age. The paper was loud in its praise of these additions to the city's fabric. On 14 June 1890 the *Irish Times* welcomed the near completion of the National Library buildings in Kildare Street as a 'vast and splendid structure', in their 'magnificence' to be compared with the British Museum in London. Local pride extended even to the provision of water-closets, about which the *Irish Times* waxed lyrical: 'the lavatories ... in the basement, are perhaps the completest and finest to be found in any part of the *United Kingdom* or elsewhere'. The fruits of the Union were, indeed, wondrous to behold. On 29 July in the same year the *Irish Times* editorialized in portentous terms on the planned joint opening ceremony for the Science and Art Museum (on the other side of the Leinster House lawn) and the National Library. It observed that the work had been completed 'in somewhat troubled times' but was pleased that 'amid all our contentions they have arisen as a permanent demonstration in favour of the pursuits of learning and mental improvement among the masses in preference to political warfare'. On this occasion local pride was subsumed in national gratification: 'There is not in any capital in England a group of buildings all in all more beautiful.' The paper looked forward to the opening ceremony with a characteristically Victorian blend of high-mindedness and condescension:

> It may be anticipated that every circumstance of public dignity and evidence of public satisfaction will supplement the proceedings, and that the working classes, we may say more than any, will give proof that

they appreciate the large consideration for them and their interest, and recreation, which is stamped upon every principle and feature of this magnificent provision for public education and national progress.

In writing thus in 1890, the *Irish Times* was echoing its response to the Great International Exhibition held in Dublin twenty-five years earlier (which had bequeathed to the city one of the few other nineteenth-century public buildings to vie with the Museum and Library complex for architectural recognition; it is now the National Concert Hall). Then the paper had regretted that the working classes had not attended the exhibition in expected numbers, but was gratified that the display of Irish art and manufactures in an international context had seemed to transcend politics. It had observed on 10 November 1865 that: 'Exaggerated rumours of disloyalty and intended rebellion were spread abroad, yet our foreign visitors did not even see a ripple on the surface of society.' By contrast, the exhibition had, 'undoubtedly, given a great impetus to trade, and a stimulus to the inventive power of our countrymen'.

What was being expressed on both these occasions separated by two-and-a-half decades was the spirit of conservative patriotism, for which the *Irish Times* was a major voice, as we have seen, which modulated as time went on into what came to be termed, by the century's end, 'Constructive Unionism'. This approach to Irish governance in the period 1895–1905 was based on an assumption that the resolution of specific Irish grievances could dissipate support for Home Rule (though it is moot how coherent as a political philosophy and programme this was). It was given impetus by those who believed that social, economic and cultural provision could blur political conflict and reconcile the majority of the Irish to the constitutional status quo. The *Irish Times*, in the kinds of support it gave to projects such as the International Exhibition in 1865 and the opening of the Library and Museum buildings in 1890, helped to create the ideological space in which ideas about improvement as a substitute for party politics could be developed by unionists and government officials. The last years of the Victorian era in Ireland accordingly saw much public support for small local industries and craft associations in a period when Sir Horace Plunkett sought to encourage co-operation among Irish farmers, in a rural world where land agitation had sunk deep roots. Wives of the Lords Lieutenant were to the fore in this encouragement of native ingenuity since it gave them the chance 'to do active charitable work without getting involved in anything politically contentious' (Sheehy 1980, p. 147). In November 1895 the *Irish Times* allocated ample space to reporting on the opening of an Arts and Crafts exhibition in Dublin by the Lord Lieutenant, accompanied by his wife, Lady Cadogan. Lord Mayo presented an address, after a performance of an Arthur Sullivan setting of a fervently nationalistic poem by T. W. Rolleston. The address was written by Professor Edward Dowden, Professor of English Literature at Trinity College

Dublin and a staunch, imperially minded unionist. Dowden, in a burst of wishful thinking, had insisted of those who had organized the event (the Arts and Craft Society of Ireland had been founded in 1894), 'Our work such as it is, is the work of a united people.'

The complex of buildings in Kildare Street which was so impressively added to in 1890 included a Natural History Museum, which had been opened to exhibit artefacts presented to it by the Ascendancy-based Royal Dublin Society. It was transferred to state ownership in 1877 and granted funding from the exchequer. Ascendancy origins and British government support were reflected in an imperial age by its collection which represented the wonders of the animal world in the United Kingdom's expanding empire. At the heart of Dublin, it was a symbol of the global reach of the empire that the *Irish Times* so sedulously supported in its columns. It was also a testament to the purchase science was cumulatively gaining on the Victorian frame of mind. Opened two years before Charles Darwin published *On the Origin of Species*, with its variegated collection of fossils, specimens, skeletons and geological objects, it offered the Irish public a window on a new naturalistic vision of the world that was gaining power in Victorian society and recruiting committed authoritative advocates.

The *Irish Times* had first appeared in the year in which Darwin published his masterwork. An advertisement in the paper on 23 July 1860 is evidence that the Kingstown Circulating Library numbered Darwin's opus among 'New and Popular Works' and on 8 May 1862 the *Irish Times* noted that a paper on the book had been read at Trinity College Dublin's Philosophical Society, but until the 1870s allusions to Darwin are rare in the *Irish Times* and tend occasionally to the waggish rather than to the considered. As late as 28 October 1872, the paper expressed surprise at the reported observations of a Professor Corcoran: 'we are astounded at the Professor's apparent adoption of Darwin's theory that we all come originally from apes and have lost our tails'.

The general Victorian response in 1874 to John Tyndall's British Association for the Advancement of Science address, given on 19 August in Belfast, was anything but jocose. Tyndall, a renowned Victorian scientist and eminent Irishman, was the incoming president of the association and he chose to mark the occasion by delivering a powerful lecture, rooted in an evolutionist's convictions, on the materialist basis of science. The *Irish Times*'s report of 20 August managed to be bland about an event that was to provoke much controversy, noting how the learned professor had spoken with 'grace and fluency', although some of the audience, about the middle of his long address, 'showed signs of weariness'. The *Irish Times*'s reporter, himself perhaps lacking full concentration throughout, celebrated the point towards the end of Tyndall's speech, where he genuflected before the ultimate mystery of things. In so doing, he missed the highly contentious crux of the lecturer's argument, which in its published form asserted that matter contained 'the promise and potency of every form and quality of life'. Others did not, concluding that Tyndall's address was a definite attack on the Judaeo-Christian world-view and on revealed religion. In Ireland the controversy stirred up by the address was imbricated with confessional matters. On 1 November the *Irish Times* reported that a pastoral letter had been read in every Catholic church in the diocese of Dublin, stating: 'Their lordships declare that the theory which recognises in matter the promise of every form of life is of Pagan origin and was that which was first taught by the Pagan philosophers who flourished 600 years before Christ and whose condemnation was pronounced by Plato and Aristotle.' Two bishops in County Galway were less measured. They damned Tyndall, as the *Irish Times* reported on 10 November, as a 'degenerate Irishman' who had dared to ventilate at 'our doors his startling theories of evolution and materialism'. The *Freeman's Journal* spoke for Catholic nationalism in general when it editorialized on the controversy: 'These phantoms will disappear like last visions of the night, and the Darwinian theory and the doctrine of evolution will be placed in the well-filled museum, where are deposited the Dreams of Errors of the over wise' (cited Bew 2007, p. 292).

Such an immoderate reaction suggests a more than philosophic animus. That Tyndall was an avowed unionist in politics probably added insult to the injury many Catholics felt (though, as John Wilson Foster (1997) has shown, Tyndall's address also caused much fluttering in Presbyterian dovecotes in Belfast as well, though they were predominantly of the unionist persuasion). For the role of science in Victorian Irish cultural life was a vexed issue, intricately and sometimes damagingly linked with the question of university-level educational provision and confessional politics.

Associated in the public mind with such Ascendancy institutions as the Royal Dublin Society and the Royal Irish Academy, the Royal College of Surgeons and Trinity College Dublin, science in Ireland could easily be identified by those alarmed by its overweening epistemological claims and gathering authority in the intellectual domain with the English conquest and unwelcome colonial governance. Accordingly, science became entangled with politics and a struggle for intellectual control in the period. How fraught all this was had been revealed in 1873, when, as the *Irish Times* reported from London on 1 December, a major protest was presented to Cardinal Cullen and the Catholic hierarchy on 'the defective educational system and general management of the Irish Catholic University' (the Catholic University was the offspring of the college founded in Dublin partly by John Henry Newman in 1854). The nub of the case against the university, according to the signatories to the protest, was its neglect of science, which gave to the enemies of the Church grounds to argue that it 'was on principle opposed to modern sciences'.

The protesters, who included students past and present, lamented that 'No one can deny that the Irish Catholics are miserably deficient in scientific education.' They threatened, in deliberate provocation, that if things did not improve, Irish Catholics would seek scientific enlightenment at 'Trinity or the Queen's colleges' where they would 'study for themselves the works of Herschel, Darwin, Huxley, Tyndall and Lyall'. So, as is clear from this report, Tyndall's name had already been entered in the lists of Irish polemics and their sometimes bitter exchanges about conflicting centres of ideological power by the time he gave his British Association address. However even the *Irish Freeman* had to admit, in the midst of the controversy that followed Tyndall's speech, that the 'literary side of the national character has always been stronger than the scientific, and the triumphs of our countrymen in invention and contrivance have been quite poor' (cited Bew 2007, p. 293).

In August 1874 the *Irish Times* swiftly followed up its initially bland account of the Belfast meeting by publications that indicated that it understood how Tyndall's address was a matter of real moment in the United Kingdom. On 21 August it redacted material from the London journals on the subject in a lengthy article, while on the same day printing a quietly appreciative account of Tyndall the man and gifted scientific lecturer. On 15 October it published a report of the Protestant Bishop of Meath's annual visitation with his clergy to Dublin's Metropolitan Hall. His address to his clergy on that occasion suggested that ecclesiastical reaction to Darwinism did not have to be as negatively blunt as that of some members of the Irish Catholic hierarchy. In measured terms the bishop took issue with the materialism of Tyndall's version of evolutionary theory, arguing for an accommodation between the Christian world-view and a less severe theory of the origin of species. In his address, the bishop struck a note that was to characterize the way in which the *Irish Times*, as a Victorian organ, in subsequent decades treated one of the central intellectual conflicts of the age: that between science and revealed religion. It gave proper attention to lectures and addresses that promoted the evolutionary idea, while giving space to religious thinkers who sought to soften its vision of nature 'red in tooth and claw', which its proponents were sometimes overzealous in propagating. What could not be denied, however, was the centrality of Darwinism to Victorian debate. The substantial report of a lecture given by George John Romanes (biologist, psychologist and young friend of Darwin) in Dublin in August 1878 gave ample evidence of this fact. His subject was 'Animal Intelligence'. He stated in the course of his detailed reflections:

> We are living in a generation which has witnessed a revolution in thought
> unparalleled in the history of our race. I do not merely allude to the fact
> that this is a generation in which all the sciences, without exception,
> have made a leap of progress such as widely to surpass all previous eras of

intellectual activity; but I allude to the fact that in the special science of biology it has been reserved for us to see the first rational enunciation, the first practical demonstration, and first universal acceptance of the doctrine of evolution.

Towards the end of his address the lecturer declared that 'in all the history of science there is no single name worthy of aveneration more profound than the now immortal name of Charles Darwin' (*Irish Times*, 17 August 1878). In publishing this speaker's views as a very lengthy article, the *Irish Times* was proving itself attentive to the zeitgeist, prepared as it was to give scientific thought its position in the marketplace of ideas in Ireland.

If the conflict between science and religion was something that gave Victorian intellectual life a distinctive edge, social relations between men and women in the period were affected more intimately by an intensifying demand for female suffrage and emancipation. The year 1884 was, as we have noted, one when franchise reform dominated political life in Ireland and Britain. That enterprise introduced to the public in a forthright way a topic that was to generate considerable debate in the last years of the century and which would become a matter of inflamed agitation in the first two decades of the next. The possibility of votes for women was raised, contested and defeated in 1884, but thereafter what came to be known as the 'woman question' would increasingly demand an answer.

Readers of the *Irish Times* would have been made fully aware of the demand for women's parliamentary and municipal suffrage (municipal female suffrage had been granted in England and Wales in 1869) when on 21 January 1876 the paper published a substantial report of a meeting of the National Society for Women's Suffrage, held in Dublin the evening before. It had been 'largely and respectably attended' and the Lord Mayor sent a letter regretting his absence. The speeches of a number of English delegates were reported at length, granting the speakers the kind of space usually afforded only to male orators in the *Irish Times*'s columns. The women exhibited rhetorical skills at least as elevated and dialectically assured as many of the speeches from the United Kingdom's parliament which the paper so conscientiously made it its business to print when the Houses were sitting. However, the *Irish Times*'s reporter could not resist pointing out that it was 'evident that a portion of the audience attended the meeting more with a view to hear lady orators and be amused by their arguments than to indicate by their presence that they considered the women of these countries laboured under an extraordinary grievance in not having the right to the Parliamentary franchise. They were certainly in sportive humour ...'

That the issue of women's rights and the 'woman question' was associated here with the 'sportive humour' of part of an audience's reaction tells us something about the discursive space in which such matters were addressed in late Victorian British and Irish society. Newspapers with pretensions to the full authority of the fourth estate, such as *The Times* of London and the *Irish Times* of Dublin, in their house style presented themselves as models of high-toned, judiciously argued prose. As Lucy Brown has wittily observed, such nineteenth-century newspapers were often written 'as if their natural habitat was the chancelleries of Europe', eschewing advertising displays since the goods they sold 'did not belong in such society: cough cures and underwear were for the servants' hall and the terraced suburb' (Brown 1985, p. 22). However, the 1880s saw the emergence of what the English poet, critic and social analyst Matthew Arnold dubbed the 'New Journalism', aimed at both servants' hall and the terraced suburb. The Irish journalist T. P. O'Connor, a noted practitioner of the new form in London, noted in 1889 in an article in the intellectually respectable *New Review*, that it involved 'a more personal tone' (O'Connor 1889, p. 423). He observed: 'Beyond doubt we are on the eve of a new departure in English journalism. All the new journals adopt the new methods, and even the oldest and most staid, cautiously and tentatively, and with a certain air of self-reproach, admit some of the features of the New Journalism' (O'Connor 1889, p. 423). O'Connor's essay was responding to Arnold's intervention of 1887 in the even more respectable *Nineteenth Century* where he had deprecated the way journalism was going. He had opined in that periodical: 'the New Journalism ... is full of ability, novelty, variety, sensation, sympathy, generous instincts. Its one great fault is that it is *feather-brained*' (Arnold 1887, p. 638). And as Martin Conboy has argued, Arnold's use of the word 'feather-brained' here is strikingly revelatory: 'In his accusation that the New Journalism was 'feather brained' Arnold's ... criticism was not only based on cultural elitism, it was also implicitly critical of its engagement with ... hitherto feminized characteristics' (Conboy 2004, p. 143). To a considerable degree, therefore, the New Journalism was admitting women's concerns to the journalistic field, but in ways that challenged the tone, style and presentation of papers that would have preferred to operate uniformly at what they considered to be a higher level. It does not surprise in this context that 'serious' papers like the *Irish Times* in the 1880s and 1890s, when they addressed the role of women in society and dealt with the issue of female emancipation and suffrage were inclined to do so in the 'sportive' manner that the New Journalism had popularized. High style was maintained for matters of state and politics; the woman question could allow for racier writing, a lighter touch, the house style of the *Weekly Irish Times*.

For the *Irish Times*, the American press (in which the New Journalism had sprung to life with Joseph Pulitzer's *New York World*) supplied appropriately frothy copy on women's issues for it to reprint. For example, on 17 November 1888 (in the paper's Saturday magazine section, itself a concession to a lowering of the paper's general tone), it was reported from the *Boston Gazette*, under the byline 'Independent Young Women': 'there is nothing that shows the growing independence of women' more than the fact that young women in that city 'were setting up establishments of their own' where they live 'without a chaperone'. A young woman could hire a summer house, where, provided she was not 'too "larky"', as the report coyly has it, 'she is as happy as the day is long, for she has her own little nest in which she can follow all the innocent inclinations of her own sweet will'. In that nest of her own, the occupant's inclination may have been less than innocent, as the paper suggested in a reprint on 10 September 1887 from the *Globe* on 'Girl Smokers', when a writer offered a droll commentary on a social trend: 'One of the earliest ambitions of girlhood when emancipated from the thralldom of the school room and the French grammar, is to learn to smoke.' For the girl who wants to make a statement, it seems, 'there is only one thing she can do which has the satisfactory savor of wickedness and wildness, and that is to smoke'. Unfortunately, the 'manipulation of a cigarette, which the expert male can combine with other light occupations such as beer and conversations with barmaids, is a task of no small magnitude'.

The matter of gender difference, however, was not always treated as the stuff of persiflage. On 8 September 1891 the *Irish Times*'s readers could have heard the voice of male reaction to the advance of women when an extensive speech by a Mr Frederick Harrison, president of the English Positivist Society on 'Women's True Function' was printed. That eminence's view was that a woman was the angel in the house, for 'The natural and normal work of women was by personal influence in the home.' He decried what he saw as the implications of the demand 'in the present day for the *emancipation of women*, for complete freedom for every adult individual, male or female'. In striking contrast, the *Weekly Irish Times* on 26 December regaled its post-Christmas readers with an article by Lady Cook, née Tennessee Claflin (a renowned American advocate of female emancipation), on 'Women and Progress'. The redoubtable Claflin, with her sister Victoria Woodhull reputedly the first female stockbrokers on Wall Street and magazine printers of the *Communist Manifesto*, was uncompromising in her view that 'No people and no scheme of progress ever succeeded and became lasting which did not include the advancement of women equally with men.' An editorial that the *Irish Times* published on 20 May 1901, which unfavourably compared contemporary educated womanhood, the twentieth-century 'College girl', with the 'Early Victorian "Miss"' would undoubtedly have pleased Ms Claflin for it welcomed 'a revolt among the best and noblest part of feminine humanity against remaining in passive idleness, contributing nothing, mentally or physically, to the fund of labour which sustains the State'.

One facet of Victorian life in which women were vying with men for success was that of literature. Yet the *Irish Times*'s reportage on literary life and its reviewing policies did not in the main reflect this in an appreciable way. Indeed, its literary sense of things was markedly conservative, with books and publishing being treated with a kind of *belletrist* amateurism in an age which Matthew Arnold had characterized as an age of criticism. Reports on forthcoming publications were joined by occasional reviews or reprints of reviews from British organs without any sense developing of criticism as a social function a newspaper should seek to provide in a systematic way. The main focus was on London-published material, although articles on forthcoming books of Irish interest were also featured. Until the 1880s and 1890s there was little sense that Ireland possessed a literature of its own in the English language and one could read many editions of the paper without being made aware that Irish was spoken in various parts of the country and that in Gaelic the nation was inheritor of one of the oldest of the vernacular literatures of Europe.

This began to change, however, as what became known as the Irish Literary Revival began to make its impact on cultural life. In 1886 when the poet and antiquarian Sir Samuel Ferguson died, the *Irish Times* reprinted an appreciation by the Trinity College Dublin classicist (and tutor of Oscar Wilde) John Pentland Mahaffy, published in the *Athenaeum*, which took account of the deceased's national ambitions as a poet for, in the writer's view, 'In his anxiety to revive a distinctively Irish literature he perhaps sacrificed some of the popularity of his books' (16 August 1886). Mahaffy when he penned this tribute to Ferguson, who had served as president of the Royal Irish Academy, could not have known that within three years a young Irish poet, inspired by Ferguson, whom he called 'the most central because the most Celtic' of his Irish precursors who composed poetry in English, would publish a volume of verse as the first assured step in a literary career that would take him to the award of the Nobel Prize for Literature in 1923. W. B. Yeats's *The Wanderings of Oisin and Other Poems* (1889) in the title poem followed Ferguson in its foray into the world of the pagan Celtic past. The *Irish Times*, exhibiting literary prescience, despite its rather limited critical horizons, published a full review, in which it was judged that 'Mr Yeats is more brilliantly imaginative, original and self-reliant than ever' (4 March 1889). In 1890 it found itself publishing an article from the London *Observer* on 'Ireland and Her Literature' which took to task the Irish journalist Justin M'Carthy for suggesting that the country could boast no contemporary literature of her own. The *Observer* a little sourly observed that, *pace* M'Carthy, 'if we quit the political arena we are confronted on all sides with manifold evidences of the activity and influence of Ireland', including those in the literary sphere. For 'in every department of literature Ireland is strongly represented'. And in 1892 the *Irish Times* reported not only on the founding of a National Literary Society but printed a letter of 15 October that year from W. B. Yeats, himself as honorary secretary of the society's library committee, announcing the formation of lending libraries where reading rooms already existed in the country to distribute among the population 'a fairly representative collection of books of both Irish and general literature'.

In the 1890s, therefore, Yeats provided copy for the paper's contributors and journalists as his doings in poetry, in the theatre and in literary polemics were deemed, in the context of a revival of Irish literature, inherently newsworthy. For he was unquestionably becoming a celebrity in a decade in which his fellow countryman Oscar Wilde (the paper reported on his triumphs and his disgrace and on 22 December 1900 published a letter claiming that at the end he was received into the Roman Catholic Church) was spectacularly proving the power and the danger of that propensity. In 1892 his Irish friend the poet Katharine Tynan observed of the young man who spent much of his time in the London Wilde was taking by storm:

> Mr Yeats is now living in London, and is as striking a figure as was the young Shelley or the young Keats. A long delicate oval face of pure olive colour, eyes of great beauty, dark hair which falls away heavily from a broad brow; these make a head an antique sculptor might have modelled ... But in London Mr Yeats has had the wisdom to let no English voice claim his poetry. What colour it has taken on is the pure colour of the old Gaelic poems – the secret of which hitherto has only been discovered by two men, and they little understood by the English – Edward Walsh and Samuel Ferguson (*Irish Times*, 11 June 1892).

A measure of the new nationalistic context literary revivalism was creating in the 1890s is supplied by a leading article in the *Irish Times* of 7 December 1897. This directed readers' attention to a new book, *The Life and Writings of James Clarence Mangan* by D. J. O'Donoghue, which the leader judged 'a book which all Irishmen will welcome'. The article had no doubt that Mangan, an early nineteenth-century, Dublin-born, English-language poet who would soon benefit from the admiring critical support of the young James Joyce, was a figure worthy of rescue from undeserved obscurity. For O'Donoghue's work had redeemed 'the reputation of the poet'. 'Few more intense Irishmen,' the Irish Times reckoned, 'than CLARENCE MANGAN have ever contributed to our national literature and few amongst all our writers have ever more generously nourished their intellect.' The unionist *Irish Times* was willing to indulge the idea of an Irish national literature despite the imperial fulminations of Trinity College's famous Professor of English Literature, Professor Edward Dowden, who in the 1890s, in polemic jousts with W. B. Yeats, deprecated such thought as literary provincialism. When the National Library of Ireland was about to be opened in 1890, the paper had hoped, indeed, that the Science and Art Museum as well as the Library would serve 'as a permanent demonstration in favour of pursuits of learning and mental improvement among the masses in preference to political warfare' (29 July 1890). It hoped that the shelves of the Library would 'bear all that is best of Irish as well as general literature'.

W. B. Yeats in the 1890s was in the vanguard of a movement that sought to invest Irish culture with what he believed was the spirituality of the ancient Celts, for he was determined that the Irish Literary Theatre (founded in 1899) would encourage the production of plays to challenge the way the Dublin theatres – the Gaiety, the Queen's Royal Theatre and the Theatre Royal – presented programmes (advertised and reviewed in the *Irish Times*) often mounted by English touring companies, which reflected London theatrical fashions and tastes and gave cultural life in the Irish capital, with a steady diet of melodramas, plays of sensation and music hall variety shows, a distinctly English Victorian flavour. How very much at ease the newspaper felt itself in the cultural life of mid-Victorian Dublin is evidenced by its report of an evening 'Conversazione' held in the Round Room of the Rotunda on 31 March 1871 in aid of 'the poor of Dublin of all denominations'. The Superintendent of the Telegraph Department of the General Post Office had charge of the arrangements. The first part of the programme consisted of a display of various telegraph instruments. There was present a 'troupe of negro melodists who were to charm the audience ... with their beautiful songs and laughter-provoking eccentricities' (*Irish Times*, 1 April 1871). During the evening the band of the *Irish Times* played a selection of music; much admired was the lately published 'Little Nell Waltz'. A new gallop, 'Blue Eyes', 'was heartily encored'. There were a Strauss waltz and some operatic favourites in the band's repertoire. Perhaps it was the middle-brow bourgeois complacency of the *Irish Times*'s cultural outlook, openly displayed on such an occasion, which made Yeats in his collection of Irish folk tales, *The Celtic Twilight* (1893), include a tale told him by a Mayo woman of how the Devil had once appeared to her in the guise of a flapping newspaper she knew by its size was the *Irish Times*.

It was in the field of music that the *Irish Times* in the last decade of the century was most willing to acknowledge that a distinctive Irish tradition existed. For inasmuch as it sponsored any particular critic of cultural production in this period, it was Dr Annie Patterson, composer, musicologist, minor poet and teacher at the Royal Academy of Music in Dublin, who could have laid claim to the status of *Irish Times* critic. She wrote extensively on music matters in the *Weekly Irish Times* magazine from 1899 onwards and was evangelical on behalf of the Irish musical tradition. In 1896 she had been to the fore in establishing the Dublin *Feis Ceoil* (first held in 1897), with its emphasis on traditional music and song. An article on 'The Native Music of Ireland', written on the occasion of Queen Victoria's 1900 visit to Ireland, had her enthuse about 'the confessedly matchless Native Music of Ireland'.

What is clear from such *Irish Times* cultural commentary in the 1890s and at the turn of the century was that, as a unionist organ, it sensed that the idea of national culture, in a period of literary and linguistic revivalism, could not be the sole preserve of nationalists and especially separatists. So the Annie Patterson who welcomed the Queen's visit to Dublin could also hope for the emergence of an Irish Grieg or Smetana. On 21 April 1900, in an article on 'Famous Irish Composers', she wrote:

> It ... yet remains for a foremost Irish musician to produce a work of art, based upon the foundation of native minstrelsy and legendary lore; and let us hope that the present brilliant era may not pass without some such worthy specimen of Gaelic home-grown genius being added to its records.

Perhaps the paper intuitively grasped as the Victorian age drew towards its end what was to prove to be the case: that the Irish debates and conflicts that awaited its journalistic attention in the twentieth century would often involve fraught matters where culture (not just religion) and politics intertwined.

2

THE *IRISH TIMES* AND TWENTIETH-CENTURY MODERNITY

The 'Aeolus' episode of James Joyce's epic of Dublin life, *Ulysses* (1922), is set in the office of the *Freeman's Journal* (and *Evening Telegraph*). It is, of course, appropriate that this novel, the action of which takes place over the course of 16 and early 17 June 1904, should pay an ambiguous compliment to the trade of journalism, which is so occupied by the quotidian. Joyce, in this seventh episode of his masterpiece, satirizes in brilliant parodies the high-flown rhetoric and dusty fustian of Victorian and Edwardian journalese, plays with the headline-writers' propensity to encapsulate complex affairs in pithy phrase-making, and suggests how editorial high-mindedness depends on the less exalted business of advertising revenue. Yet he also salutes journalism as the epitome of modernity, along with the much-vaunted Dublin tram system, bound up as it is with the machinery of production, circulation and distri-bution which comprises a twentieth-century metropolis. In the episode we hear the clang of the electrified tram echo with the 'sllt ... sllt ... sllt' of the newspaper press in a kind of hymn to technological progress.

The *Irish Times*, the *Freeman's Journal*'s Dublin rival, had in fact composed its own anthem to progress in an editorial on the third day of the twentieth century in which the city's tram system was included in a roll-call of Dublin's historic achievements. In an article entitled 'Dublin at the Close of Century', the paper expressed its gratification that 'The Dublin of today presents the appearance of a handsome and prosperous city with broad streets, fine shops and stately edifices.' For the *Irish Times*, 'locomotion' was a key indicator of undeniable progress and a source of urban pride: 'It is admitted that in the system of electric tram service we have advanced far ahead, and made London and even Paris seem old-fashioned in this respect.' Although 'the bitter cry of the poor' was 'ever sounding' in the *Irish Times*'s ears, the paper celebrated a city in vibrant motion: 'The opening up of new districts and the communication established between them, as well as the means of easily reaching all the suburbs within a certain radius, are incalenlable [*sic*] benefits.' Like Joyce's 'Aeolus' episode in *Ulysses*, the *Irish Times* placed Dublin not on the periphery of Europe but at the heart of the modern world, as a city in which 'steam and electricity have found their uses here as elsewhere'.

Indeed, so ardent was the paper at the birth of a new century that on 1 January 1901 it had indulged in some optimistic future-gazing:

> Let us look forward to a time when increased knowledge of one another has taught the nations that war is a fool's game; when surgical science, aided by some new development of Röntgen rays, has made mental disease as easily curable as many physical ailments are now; when by the discovery of a light-weight accumulator electricity may be stored as readily as water and be the willing servant of the poorest household; when the working classes as a whole are as sober as the gentry today; when National Education has brought real culture into the humblest home; when the Government of the State will in the truest sense be an aristocracy – the rule of the Best.

That modernity was, nonetheless, an ambiguous condition was poignantly evidenced at the turn-of-century when, as its possibilities were hopefully raised in its columns, the *Irish Times* reported the sad news that 'an old woman named Catherine Lindley ... was knocked down by a tramcar in College Green on Christmas ... who died in the hospital on Sunday'. In coming decades the paper would have ample opportunity to ponder the mixed blessings of the modern age, but in the first decade of the century it reported zestfully on the quickening pace of technological development. No more so than when in 1903 it gave generous coverage, as did all the Dublin papers, to the Gordon-Bennett Cup motor race which was held that year in Ireland, starting and finishing in the capital.

That Ireland was chosen to host this salute to motorized speed and the internal combustion engine was no small fillip to national reputation. The first four races had taken place in France, Germany and Austria, and in 1903 England had been ruled out as unable to supply a suitable location and for legal reasons. Certainly patriotic blood was roused when the Irish midlands were chosen for the course by the race's organizers. The *Irish Times* climaxed its extensive reportage of the preparation for and the running of the race with its reporter's claim of 3 July 1903: 'There is no parallel in Irish history for the scenes which were witnessed yesterday along the course traversed by the competitors for the Gordon-Bennett Cup.' The reporter was struck by the speed of the racing cars (in fact, no more than 40 miles per hour, or thereabouts, on average). He was familiar with 'the magnificently-built, comfortable-looking mechanical contrivances which are to be seen any day careering along the streets of our cities' which had penetrated even 'the most belated districts'; but the racing cars were objects of wonderment: 'Built primarily for speed, with the wind resistance reduced to the lowest point, the racers were utterly unlike the ordinary type of car, while their tremendous powers of endurance and potent possibilities appeared to exercise a sort of fascination on the thousands who watched them flying past at different points of the course.' The leader of the day on the event was couched less like this anticipation of Italian Futurism, with its worship of speed and power, than as a somewhat headmasterly tribute to the crowds (in reality smaller than had been expected outside the city) who had behaved themselves well, without troubling the Royal Irish Constabulary, on what was undoubtedly a day that could be interpreted variously. The *Irish Times*'s reporter wrote excitedly: 'The event was unique so far as this country is concerned, and engendered an amount of public excitement which it would be impossible to pourtray [*sic*].' The young, cynical James Joyce (who from Paris in April of that year had himself contributed to the *Irish Times* an unimpressive interview with a French driver who would take part in the race) wrote bitterly of the race in his story 'After the Race'. In Glasgow on the same day, the *Irish Times* reported, under the headline 'Alarming Motor Accident', that a car had been driven into the Clyde when a brake failed. Happily no lives were lost in the Irish motor race (though an English driver and his mechanic were hurt when their car overturned on a corner). Nor were they in September 1904 when the Irish Automobile Club (founded in Dublin in January 1901) held a series of motor races on Portmarnock Strand in north County Dublin. The *Irish Times*'s reporter observed of the choice of venue that none 'more suitable' could have been found in 'the whole of the United Kingdom' (7 September 1904).

That the horseless carriage had come to stay was made abundantly clear in January 1907 when the Irish Automobile Club held its first Dublin Motor Show in Ballsbridge. The *Irish Times* marked the occasion not only by stating in its Saturday magazine that it promised 'to be one of the most interesting and successful motor shows ever held in the United Kingdom' but by publishing a technical article by a Mr P. McCredy (one of the founders of the Irish Automobile Club) entitled 'Lessons of the Motor Show'. He not only judged that there was 'no reason' why Ireland should not eventually become as famous for its motors as its shipbuilding, but informed the paper's readership of the competing claims of the chain and propeller drive shaft, the several gear systems available to manufacturers and the need or otherwise for a clutch. A new trade was coming into being with its mysteries and terms of art. The *Irish Times* had begun publishing 'Motor Notes' in 1902, which later in the decade sometimes became 'Motor and Cycling Notes', and the feature had also familiarized readers with a new argot. McCredy's passion for motorized transport extended to the motor cycle and in this article he also reported on the various producers of this machine (on 13 August 1907 the *Weekly Irish Times* noted that Ireland had 1,224 registered motor cycle owners). In 1908 the second Dublin Motor Show, which was opened by the Lord Lieutenant, was welcomed by the *Weekly Irish Times* as providing 'many signs of the awakening of our people to a full sense of the possibilities of this form of locomotion, both for commercial and pleasure-giving purposes' (*Weekly Irish Times*, 4 January 1908).

In 1905 George Bernard Shaw had put a motor car on the stage of the Royal Court Theatre in London, in Act II of his play *Man and Superman*, associating it with the new phase of human evolution that the life force was bringing into being. Not everyone greeted the coming of the car with the same élan. In the *Weekly Irish Times* of 15 August 1903 (the year in which Shaw wrote *Man and Superman*) it was noted how a 'strong anti-motor spirit' pervaded the House of Commons at Westminster, as members agreed to enforce a speed limit of 20 miles per hour. The question of speed remained contentious and on 21 September 1908 the *Irish Times* wrote about a Local Government Board circular that had been sent around 'in consequence of the numerous representations which have been made, both in Parliament and elsewhere, respecting the danger and annoyance not infrequently caused by the driving of motor cars'. The article appeared under the headline 'Speed and the Dust Nuisance'. It was clear that the coming of the car was affecting the environment and the experience of city life. The board recommended the trimming of hedgerows in the countryside to improve sight-lines at crossroads, while the concept of motorized urban traffic and its attendant problems was entering popular consciousness. In October 1904 the newspaper had published a series of letters about the varying rights of cyclists and motor drivers on the capital's roads in relation to 'the rules of the road' (a vexed issue to the present day). On 26 May 1908 the *Irish Times* expressed concern that the Parnell monument to be erected at one end of Sackville Street would be 'a serious obstacle to traffic'. It reported that the businessman A. S. Findlater had shown that 'Cyclists and drivers of motor cars descending the hill will have their vision obscured by the monument, and, in any case, traffic inwards and outwards of the city must often suffer prolonged and annoying delay.' The frustrations of the traffic jam were at hand.

That the car was inserting itself as a permanent fixture of modern life was perhaps evidenced when, as the *Irish Times* reported on 14 August 1908, King Edward VII persuaded Emperor Franz Joseph 'to take his first ride in a motor car'. Neither, of course, could have known then that a motor journey undertaken in Sarajevo by the Emperor's nephew Archduke Franz Ferdinand, heir to the Hapsburg throne, would in July 1914 result in the unleashing of mechanized slaughter on an unparalleled scale in Europe, which would do much to define the nature of twentieth-century modernity. Nevertheless, that royal jaunt in 1908 works its powerful symbolism of the way that technology had inaugurated the era of the internal combustion engine.

The *Irish Times* was equally alert in the first decade of the century to how mechanized flight was promising to fulfil humankind's age-old longing to conquer the air. From 1908 to 1910 it was caught up in the general modern excitement at the daring exploits of the Wright brothers and of Louis Blériot. For example, on 12 August 1908 its readers could read how the Paris correspondent of the *Globe* waxed lyrical when Wilbur Wright made a 1 minutes, 45 seconds' flight at Le Mans in France at a speed of 65 kilometres per hour, saluting how 'Mr Wilbur Wright's perfect command of his machine as it glided in the air at a height of thirty-five or forty feet, rising and falling at his will, threw even the scoffers into a fever of excitement.'

Flight was registering as something magically new in the history of humankind, an apotheosis of technology. Indeed, on 13 November 1909 the *Weekly Irish Times* republished an article on 'The Sensation of Flight in the Air: A Lady's Adventure', in which a 'well-known lady aeronaut' recalled her first flight as something so new, so transmogrifying, that it almost defied description. After take-off, she thrilled, 'The engine still roared, the wind still rushed past but all of a sudden there had come into the motion a *something* new, unimaginable, indescribable ... Oh, the rapture of that swift moonlight flight through the gloaming.' On a less gushing level the *Irish Times* reported on 23 October 1909 a communication from a Mr Reginald F. O'Donnell of Lower Mount Street, Dublin, that he was at work constructing his own version of an aeroplane. On 15 January 1910 the *Irish Times*, under the headline 'Mr Ferguson's Aeroplane: First flight in Ireland' could record that one H. G. Ferguson in Belfast had managed a flight of over 1,000 yards at about 15 feet above the ground.

While the effects of the motor car on the environment and on the cyclists of Dublin took some of the edge off the excitement that the coming of the motor car fomented in the columns of the *Irish Times*, the conquest of the air also stirred more deep-rooted anxieties. The invasion panic that spread through Edwardian society in Britain had an impact on the newspaper's content. It published nervous reports on the development of the German Zeppelin. In 1907 the paper reported fully on a lecture given in Birmingham on 'The Navigation of the Air' by a Major B. Baden-Powell. He was satisfied that 'little remained to be done ... until aeroplanes were absolutely perfect' (*Irish Times*, 18 November 1907) and he hoped that 'the era of flying machines', soon to be 'travelling in thousands and in all directions through the air', would 'hasten the coming of universal peace'. However, Baden-Powell had also counselled gravely: 'If foreign nations were able to command airships, and England had none, we must suffer very heavily in the event of war.' On 11 December the paper reported on the ominous conclusions of Sir Hiram Maxim, the inventor of the Maxim machine-gun, under the headline 'Is a German Aerial Invasion Possible? An English View'. Maxim, described in the report as 'an authority of aeroplanes', envisaged planes soon being constructed solely for military purposes, capable of carrying a ton weight across the English Channel. He imagined such machines serving as troop carriers, but the concept of aerial bombardment as a possibility was taking hold (Maxim, later, would himself attempt to design a bomber-plane).

In the field of communications, technology was rapidly advancing too. The doings of Guglielmo Marconi (with his Irish commercial interests and, after 1905, Irish wife) in the development of wireless telegraphy were assiduously reported on. The *Weekly Irish Times*, on 17 January 1903, indeed commented that his experiments amounted to 'One of the greatest exploits of modern times, like the transatlantic cables, which have taken fifty years to gain their present efficiency, still in its infancy.' In 1909, the year in which Marconi shared the Nobel Prize for Physics, the *Irish Times* recorded that the White Star Shipping Line had equipped itself with the Marconi telegraph system. Moving pictures as entertainment were also becoming popular in Irish cities, as the cinema became a marked feature of popular culture. The opening of new cinemas was duly noted by the newspaper. The paper was attending the birth of a new medium. On 20 January it had reported that the *Money Market Review* had concluded that cinema in England was no passing fad, like 'the skating rink craze', but something that had 'come to stay'.

Readers of the *Irish Times*, as the new century progressed, were being given, therefore, a sense that they were living in a time of exciting technological possibility. The newspaper itself at the turn of the century had, indeed, adopted a new printing technology when it made the transition from 'hand-set type to mechanized production by Linotype machines' (Mark O'Brien 2008, pp. 67–8). Such hot metal typesetting would remain the basis of production until the late 1980s when digital electronics would represent a further revolution in communications methods. Ironically, the actual paper that readers held in their hands in the first decades of the twentieth century, as artefact, did little to reflect this quickening pace of technological innovation that the *Irish Times* both reported on and, on the level of print production, participated in. The Victorian period had in fact seen a remarkable flourishing of illustrated books and visually attractive magazines and journals. Photography had begun to accompany text as a partner in communication and not just as illustrations. Throughout all this, like *The Times* of London, the *Irish Times* had with studied disdain eschewed pictorial matter, even rejecting cartoons almost entirely, in offering their purchasers only closely packed columns of often dense printed matter. This stylistic resolution had begun to weaken somewhat in the field of advertising, where drawings could be indulged, and in the first decade of the twentieth century the *Weekly Irish Times* more and more began to accompany text with illustrations and sometimes with photographs. One gets no sense, however, in the daily paper that the editor and owner were aware in a responsive way of the new technologies that were expanding the possibilities of travel, communication and visually based reportage. The paper retained its deeply conservative appearance (no doubt costs were involved) as an era of mass communications dawned.

In 1912 an event of such significance occurred that it would test newspapers' capacity to deal with disaster on the kind of overwhelming scale modernity would repeatedly unleash upon humanity.

On 3 April 1912 the *Irish Times* reported that 'The White Star liner *Titanic* ... the largest in the world' had been launched in Belfast. It noted that the 'stately proportions of the mammoth were greatly admired by the large crowds' who had gathered to watch the event. On 11 April the *Irish Times* could record that the *Titanic* had left Southampton the day before, on her maiden voyage. For the newspaper, the ship was a testament to 'progress in modern shipbuilding': 'she made an impressive picture as she quietly slipped in brilliant sunshine down Southampton water, quite dwarfing all adjacent shipping'. Then on 16 April the paper announced gravely: 'Almost as we go to press the awful news reaches us of the loss of the *Titanic* with nearly seventeen hundred out of the two thousand three hundred and fifty passengers and crew who formed her immense burden of human life.' The sinking of the ship, which had taken place on the night of 14 April and before dawn, was to preoccupy the journalistic world for weeks to come. For as one historian has argued, 'the entire English-speaking world was shaken' (Wyn Craig Wade, cited John Wilson Foster 1997, p. 22) by an occurrence that marked 'a watershed between the nineteenth and twentieth centuries' (Foster 1997, p. 23).

From the outset the *Irish Times* was conscious that an event of shattering proportions had taken place which offered individual human stories bound up in a narrative of mythic proportions. The names and professions of Dubliners who had been on board were published in the *Weekly Irish Times* on 20 April. The *Irish Times*'s first account of what had transpired struck a note of awe appropriate to the scarcely comprehensible fact of the liner's loss: 'the imagination halts at the suggestion that the latest and most marvellous mechanisms of ocean travel are exposed to dangers every whit as awful as those which lie before any tramp steamer of a few tons burden'. If, the paper determined, the loss of 675 women and children were to be confirmed, then the disaster would be 'one of the supreme tragedies of the sea'. In pondering what had occurred, this leader painted an impressive picture of the ship as a floating hotel of surpassing grandeur and luxury, 'appointed throughout in a way in which no hotel on solid earth could hope to rival', brought miserably to ruin. By 22 April, in a leader, the *Irish Times* felt able to draw a lesson from the terrible event. For it saw in the *Titanic*'s sinking (in what was a representational commonplace in much contemporary and subsequent commentary) an example of modernity's hubris: 'The loss of the *Titanic* came as a rude and awful reminder to humanity of the fact that the marvellous inventions by means of which we men presume to scorn the forces of nature are nothing but the playthings of the elements.'

The toll of the *Titanic*'s dead was a warning that 'our vaunted conquest of the air is a thing of sufferance, and even on these terms, dearly bought'. It was, in this reading of things, as if nature were indicting modernity for its presumption. On the Saturday before, the *Weekly Irish Times* had played a full part in establishing how the disaster would be interpreted. What the novelist Henry James had termed in 1896 'the imagination of disaster' had been confronted with something almost beyond imagining which demanded 'graphic stories of survivors' (duly supplied), but also a prose account that drew on Victorian and Edwardian melodrama's fascination with disaster (represented on stage by technological *coups de théâtre*) and anticipating the sensationalism of the disaster movie. Under a photograph of the doomed vessel, the 'story of the *Titanic*' was unfolded to its heart-rending conclusion (the experienced seaman and author Joseph Conrad was soon to object to the false, written-up, Drury Lane aspects of an event he judged simply the result of 'arrogant folly').

Much subsequent reportage in the paper involved the inquiries that were quickly established in the United States and in the United Kingdom and involved considerable, scrupulously detailed, technical matters. A mounting impression was created of an attempt to set what had occurred within some rational framework, but the almost religious significance of the tragedy could not easily be denied. A report from Belfast on 27 April spoke of how the event had 'cast a deep and sad shadow over Belfast, whose citizens feel a personal loss in the catastrophe'. Commentators were at pains, as the Belfast writer had it, to emphasize how humanity had excelled itself in face of the horrors with which it had been confronted at sea: 'acts of heroism and altruism persuaded that our highest common humanity [was] vindicated'.

So the *Irish Times* can be seen at work from the moment the news broke in helping to set in place the key elements of a widely credited, if in parts dubious, *Titanic* narrative (involving the hubris the ship represented, luxury and opulence overwhelmed by the forces of nature, the spectacular demise of a behemoth of modernity, the unassailable humanity of the species in extremity, the proneness of technology to unanticipated design flaws, the affecting poignancy of individual sufferings), against some of which George Bernard Shaw, for one, set his face. What strikes the reader now about the *Irish Times*'s treatment of the event was that it had been confronted as a print medium, at the dawn of the age of the electronic image and sound recording, that took it to the edge of its capabilities. For the event as described and commented upon by newspapers, including the *Irish Times*, seemed to yearn for the visual representation which the conservative production values expressed in regular columns of print were unable to match in representational power. For modernity was beginning a challenge to print's hegemony in the informational, communicative and mass entertainment fields which would continue late into the twentieth century.

John Wilson Foster, in *The Titanic Complex* (1997), has convincingly argued that '*Titanic* ... sailed and sank at the very centre of contemporary cultural preoccupations' (Foster, pp. 54–5). These included not only the obsession with technological progress which achieved a kind of apotheosis and *Götterdämmerung* in the *Titanic*'s voyage and loss, but ideas about collective agency and social forces that were vigorously at work in the twentieth century in ways that they had not been before. Much was made in contemporary commentary of how male chivalry was reasserted as a vital component of civilization as the catastrophe struck, as if to give the lie to the uncomfortable implications of suffragist activism in the recent past. The *Irish Times*'s Belfast reporter joined in this reactionary setting of things in their proper place: 'In that darkest hour of destiny the order "women and children first" was sedulously obeyed' (*Weekly Irish Times*, 27 April 1912). And when the great ship had set sail, the *Irish Times* had noted, as if it were the natural order of things, that the passengers were divided by class, the White Line offering First- to Third-class facilities for its customers. The numerical relativities of these, some commentators would soon observe, reflected the class composition of British society. So the *Titanic* sank as a simulacrum of a society that at its apex knew apparently unbounded wealth, while lower orders endured the straitened conditions of the poor. In the actual world, the strict demarcations of shipboard life did not, however, obtain, because class conflict and the political movements that fomented and sustained it grew in potency in what became a period of revolutionary fervour and action.

In the period before the outbreak of the Great War, the conservative *Irish Times* was often affronted by the activities of a newly militant suffragism. Conservative folk in Ireland had had to endure the agitational role women had played in the Land War of the early 1880s, when the Ladies Land League, led by Parnell's sister Anna, had for the first time in the country made the female voice a distinctive one in a political cause. But that had been short-lived. The 'extremism' of modern English suffragism, especially in the years 1908–12 , was for the *Irish Times*, in its outrageous refusal to bow to legitimate state power, truly shocking to behold. As militancy increased in those years, including interruptions of parliament, the breaking of windows, the confrontation of politicians about their business, and hunger strikes (with forced-feeding), the paper reported on events in the tones of outrage. Though on 7 November 1907 the newspaper did print a letter from Anna Parnell defending the Suffragists and their tactics ('they seem to me to be at least trying to do something ... And the suffragettes have certainly managed to make the House of Commons a little more ridiculous than it already was').

A headline of 29 October 1909 catches the tenor of much of the paper's reporting of suffragist activity: 'Disgraceful Outrage. Acid Thrown at Ballot Boxes. Returning Officer Seriously Injured', while an attack on Winston Churchill (then President of the Board of Trade) in November in which he had been 'horse-whipped by a suffragette on alighting from the train in Bristol station' (*Irish Times*, 15 November 1909) warranted an article in the *Weekly Irish Times*, that made the redoubtable Churchill (who in fact favoured a limited female enfranchisement) a hero of reaction and a victim of evident hysteria. The *sang-froid* of the British male had won the day: 'The reception given to Mr Churchill at Colston Hall, Bristol [where he fulfilled his speaking engagement] was of such a demonstrative nature as to suggest recognition of his successful resistance of the suffragette attack.'

The *Irish Times* had made its position clear on such disturbances of the peace of the realm and the threat to government ministers posed by militant suffragism. In a leading article on 31 January 1908 it had expressed its exasperation in a forthright manner: 'The militant female Suffragists are becoming a serious nuisance to the Government. It is ridiculous, and it is also scandalous, that the King's Ministers should have to go about their business under police protection.' A deputation from the National Union of Women's Suffrage in Britain had just been told by the prime minister that there was no probability of a Female Suffrage Bill being placed before parliament in the then current session, and the *Irish Times* feared 'further outbursts of "Suffragette" disorder on a very considerable scale'. Ominously, one of the Union's leaders had suggested that this parliamentary impasse might in fact provoke violence which, although deplorable, '"they would regard as not altogether unreasonable or inexcusable"'. The *Irish Times* responded with a shudder of revulsion, but could not deny itself a certain *Schadenfreude* at the prospect of English prime-ministerial discomfiture in the face of violent agitation:

> This is the language of the Irish political agitator, and it will fall upon minds not less ignorant and excitable than those which were so profoundly influenced by ... cattle-driving orations. We can only hope that, if the Suffragettes are going to put Mr Asquith and his colleagues to really serious inconvenience, these gentlemen may be able to find solid comfort in the platitudes with which they are so fond of defending agrarian lawlessness in Ireland.

In comparing implied suffragist threats with the tactics of Irish nationalists and land reformers, the *Irish Times* at the end of 1908 would have known that suffragism was not confined to Britain. For in that year an Irish Women's Franchise League had been formed, with some of its key supporters notorious nationalist propagandists, well versed in the methods of the putative threat of violence. At its second meeting in Dublin in March 1909, one Irish speaker, responding to the main address by an English suffragist, stated, to cries of 'hear, hear' and laughter: 'As to the methods employed in England, she thought that women undergoing imprisonment were encouraging the brutality of men. She would rather be inclined to have a revolver in her hand' (*Irish Times*, 4 March 1909).

In March 1912 Emmeline Pankhurst came to Dublin to address the League, speaking for the first time at a meeting in Ireland. The *Weekly Irish Times* fully reported the event, at which the speaker assured her audience that she hoped to 'hand on to the Irish women her flaming torch' (*Irish Times*, 12 March 1912).

The fact was that suffragism was beginning to have an impact on the body politic which even the *Irish Times* could not ignore. On 3 February 1910 it had reported that the nationalist leader John Redmond, under pressure from the Women's Freedom League, although 'said to be an avowed opponent of the movement', had stated his readiness 'to act in accordance with the views of the majority of the party', where feeling was 'divided on the question'. And while the unionist *Irish Times* could view such a development objectively, it could not be expected to be completely neutral when its owner's wife, Lady Arnott, with Lady Balfour in attendance, on 30 November chaired a *Conversazione* in Dublin of the recently founded Conservative and Unionist Women's Franchise Association in the Café Cairo on Grafton Street. The paper reported respectfully on this genteel if not insignificant occasion. By 1911 when it suspected that members of the Irish Women's Suffrage League were planning to subvert the Census of that year by evading it, it divulged the plot as if it were a grave act of subversion and domestic rebellion: 'It is not too much to say that many members spent last night long distances from their homes' (*Irish Times*, 3 April 1911).

Nor was the *Weekly Irish Times* averse at the height of the suffragist agitation to giving space to those who found the women's movement both an affront to nature and a matter of comedy. On 6 November 1909 it chose to reprint from the *London Magazine* some of the best-selling novelist Marie Corelli's extraordinary views on the woman question. She is 'a mistake' declared Corelli imperiously of the suffragette:

> And it is a curious and deplorable sight to see even a few women of the great majority descending from their heights of security and peace, shrieking to be allowed to dabble their garments in the blood of the fray, clamouring for weapons ... but it has its comic side. A woman with clenched fists is always funny – much funnier than a man in the same condition. Everything rough, violent, ungraceful, and unseemly has the immediate effect of making a woman look ridiculous.

In her book *The Irish Women's Movement: From Revolution to Devolution* (2003), Linda Connolly has argued that while the early years of the twentieth century saw the expansion in Ireland of 'a more broad-based and concerted women's social movement' (Connolly 2003, p. 61) than had existed in the second half of the nineteenth century, and the emergence of a 'militant suffrage strand' (Connolly 2003, p. 62), the movement was 'divided (not unified) by the national question'. This meant that while women could press their demands respectively on unionists and on the Irish Party, their aspirations might get lost when the issue between these two became not matters of social policy and franchise reform but the legislative status of Ireland itself. The cause of women could be judged to be a minority concern when the Union was actually at stake or when national freedom immediately beckoned. The fact, too, that suffragism as a political commitment in Ireland was largely the concern of upper-middle-class and middle-class, well-educated people further militated in the period against its becoming a fully effective force with mass appeal. By contrast, class politics in the decade before the Great War threatened to overturn the settled order through mass mobilizations (women's demands became linked to those of labour in the early twentieth century when they also tended to be occluded as a subordinate matter at times of industrial dispute).

Belfast was the site of the century's first great struggle in Ireland between the power of capital and the urban force of organized labour. It was a prelude of things to come in Dublin. A labour-relations dispute began with what seemed a limited if ill-tempered fracas when the *Irish Times* reported on 10 May 1907 that about 50 labourers, members of the Dockers Union in the service of the Belfast Steamship Company, were on strike about their employer's use of non-union workers. The company responded, amid some nasty violence, by locking out the union members, and the conflict quickly intensified into a confrontation between workers and bosses which by the early autumn had led to riots in the streets, a police mutiny, two civilian deaths and the deployment of the soldiery in support of the civil power. The dispute rapidly became almost as an augury of a later bitter duel in Dublin, a test of strength between two men: Thomas Gallaher, who not only was chairman of the shipping company party but proprietor of a major cigarette factory in the city, and James Larkin, a coming man in the burgeoning Irish labour movement of the early twentieth century. An Irish immigrant from Liverpool, Larkin had been at work organizing the National Union of Dock Workers in Belfast since the beginning of the year and the dispute in the docks offered him a chance to flex his muscles. His rhetorical powers were considerable and by July, as supportive strikes spread to other workforces, he found himself addressing mass meetings in an atmosphere that to some commentators seemed to verge on the revolutionary. By the end of August, as the employer starved out the increasingly desperate workers (strike funds were inadequate), a settlement was arrived at, with the Dockers' Union a victim of its own and especially of Larkin's tactical folly. Larkin would shortly thereafter abandon the trade union to form in Dublin the Transport and General Workers' Union.

Throughout the turbulent months of this northern imbroglio, the *Irish Times* published regular reports from its own correspondent which expressed the mood of alarm that Larkin's adventurism had provoked in many Belfast citizens. The term 'Labour' became normalized in frequent headlines in a way it had not been before in its columns. Sometimes graphic accounts of street commotions were mixed with sombre reportage that did not disguise class interest. When in early July the leadership called on every member of the Dockers' Union to cease work in order to 'stop every ship in the harbour', the *Irish Times* reported: 'The threat to completely dislocate the traffic of the port has aroused much indignation among local merchants, and the cross-Channel companies who gave way to the Union whether they should not now, in view of the threatened violation of their agreement, abrogate the agreement altogether' (*Irish Times*, 8 July 1907). Trade might seize up in Belfast port with unknown consequences. As the lockout drew to its climax, the paper, in an article by its Belfast correspondent which chronicled the history of the dispute and Larkin's role in it, gave space to Gallaher to claim, 'There is now a spirit of extreme lawlessness rampant in the city, and that is entirely caused by the laxity of the authorities in dealing firmly with the strikers and their sympathisers. The origin of the whole business, I think, is due to the uprising of the forces of Socialism, which has become so powerful a factor in the party politics of the day' (*Irish Times*, 19 July). In the interest of balance, the organizing secretary of the Dockers' Union was also given space to put the case for the strikers in this report, but the *Irish Times*'s correspondent's sympathies were clearly with Gallaher, whom he describes as controlling 'an immense business' and as one who 'can claim to speak with the greatest authority on the trade matter'. The union's spokesman was afforded no balancing accolade. Interestingly, in some of the reportage women are seen in supportive roles in the midst of the workers' struggle.

It was another urban plutocrat with whom Larkin unsuccessfully fought in 1913 when Dublin, as Belfast had before it, became an Irish cockpit of the kind of large-scale urban labour disputes with revolutionary potential that erupted in the United Kingdom and rocked Europe in the first three decades of the century (in 1907 the *Northern Whig* newspaper had portentously told its readers, 'We are on the eve of an experience something akin to that which paralysed Russian cities during the last couple of years' (cited Bardon 1992, pp. 427–8).

Dublin in 1913 was a repetition on a metropolitan scale of what had occurred in Belfast in 1907. Once again the issue was that of union recognition which developed into an epic power struggle between capital and labour, played out as if it were a fight to the death between two strong-willed men. Since 1907 Larkin had been establishing the Irish Transport and General Workers' Union as a force to be reckoned with in the city until William Martin Murphy (owner of the *Irish Times*'s principal journalistic rival, Independent Newspapers, and of the Dublin United Tramway Company), an entrepreneur of imperial ambition and hubris, resolved to bring it to its knees. Having gained the support of many of the capital's main employers, Murphy declared war on the union, on unions and the socialism and syndicalism that increasingly inspired them (the Marxist and syndicalist James Connolly was another major figure who took to the stage as the drama of 1913 unfolded in Dublin) when in August he simply sacked all those of his employees who refused to renounce union membership. Other employers followed Murphy's lead in what quickly became a near general lockout that threatened industrial anarchy and the continuance of normal social life in the nation's capital. Where the events of 1907 in Belfast had been a matter of provincial reportage by a 'correspondent', the unfolding of the Dublin lockout involved the *Irish Times* in what seemed to it an existential threat to its conservative ideology and to the way of life that ideology sustained. From the start, it was unabashed, and rebarbatively so, in its support of the employer's interest even as the immiseration of Dublin's army of low-paid workers and of their families intensified. It sensed that what was taking place in its city was not only of local consequence but a manifestation of a more general crisis of civilization. On 13 September it delivered itself of an implacable jeremiad. Assuring it readers that it had no quarrel with the collective bargaining procedures of normal trade unionism, it set its face against the evil of syndicalism it associated with the Transport and General Workers' Union. It was necessary, it judged, 'to dislodge from the body of Dublin an octopus which [was] draining its very life-blood'. So it thundered editorially:

> There is no possibility of negotiation with James Larkin's Union. It must either crush or be crushed. The Great Anarch has been crushed in other cities where he has been tackled boldly and strongly. He will be crushed in Dublin also. However protracted this battle may be, it can have only one end. The whole industry and intelligence of the city are behind the employees. We deplore the suffering which this struggle is going to inflict on the workers and on their innocent families, but that suffering will bear fruit in the disenchantment of experience. With one or two conspicuous exceptions, the employers are resolute and united. This fight will see the end of syndicalism in Dublin.

In the same leading article on 'The Labour Crisis', the *Irish Times* warned flesh-crawlingly: 'The very existence of Dublin is at stake.'

The month of September, in the midst of the lockout, had in fact served notice that limited sections of the city were in truth under a threat of actual disintegration. Two tenement houses in Church Street (in a part of the city notorious for grotesquely overcrowded slum conditions) collapsed, with the loss of seven lives. Even the *Irish Times* in its fervent conservatism in face of union agitation could not but comment on this tragic occurrence. Tellingly, it did so in the paternalistic tones it had often adopted about the Irish peasantry in the nineteenth century. If living conditions could be improved, extremist politics would wither on the vine. Of the denizens of tenement Dublin, the paper condescendingly wrote: 'The members of the Irish Transport Workers' Union live, for the most part, in slums like Church Street. Their domestic conditions make them an easy prey to plausible agitators. We believe that if every unskilled labourer in Dublin were the tenant of a decent cottage of three, or even two, rooms, the city would not be divided into two hostile camps' (*Irish Times*, 4 September 1913). In the spirit of this lofty commentary (the paper's almost-pastoral vision of urban unity was not likely to be realized without fundamental political change), the *Irish Times* established a charitable fund in aid of the children made homeless in the disaster, but without moderating its support for the employers in the conflict (some of whom were themselves tenement landlords). When, however, in the early autumn the employers rejected a report on the lockout delivered by the Board of Trade, the *Irish Times* published a remarkable letter that put an entirely different complexion on the whole affair.

George Russell, or AE as he had become among the mystics and occultists with whom he often consorted, was a northern Protestant, settled in Dublin, a poet and painter who had rejected orthodox Christianity for the esotericism and orientalism favoured by the poets of the Celtic School and the Irish Literary Revival. Surprisingly, given his otherworldly preoccupations, Russell had been recruited by Horace Plunkett as an organizer for the co-operative agency, the Irish Agricultural Organisation Society. In this role he had in fact proved remarkably effective and in 1905 he had become editor of the society's periodical, the *Irish Homestead*, where he honed a considerable journalistic talent. In September 1913 he was one of a number of people unattached to the unions who formed a committee for industrial peace. His letter to the *Irish Times*, published on 7 October 1913 under the heading 'To the Masters of Dublin', was anything but eirenic, since it was a no-holds-barred attack on the employers. Russell denounced a boss class as people who by their 'devilish policy of starvation' have sullied their very souls: 'The souls you have got cast upon the screen of publicity appear like the horrid and writhing creatures enlarged from the insect world, and revealed to us by the cinematograph.' In employing a metaphor from current communications technology to damn the employers, Russell was heightening the sense that he wished to create in his letter, that the Masters of Dublin were dangerous anachronisms the city could ill afford. As he bluntly stated it: 'Your insolence and ignorance of the rights conceded to workers universally in the modern world were incredible, and as great as your inhumanity.' The letter was damning in its judgement: 'your collective and conscious action as a class in the present labour dispute has revealed you to the world in so malign an aspect that the mirror must be held up to you, so that you may see yourselves as every humane person sees you'.

The question arises as to why the *Irish Times* chose to print this carefully aimed broadside (the first major prose statement about Irish affairs by a writer associated with the Irish Literary Revival to appear in its columns), particularly since it so unambiguously represented the labour dispute in class terms. Perhaps the editor was moved to give Russell such ample space to express views that ran so counter to his own editorial line because the letter was in fact essentially an indictment of nationalist Ireland. For Russell had begun his polemic by casting the employers of Dublin as 'the aristocracy of industry in this city' and continued, 'Some of you have helped Irish farmers to upset a landed aristocracy in this island, an aristocracy richer and more powerful in its sphere than you are in yours, with its roots deep in history.' Russell's rhetorical strategy was well managed. Some of those who were leading the lockout were the very people, he was saying, who had helped to unseat the Protestant Ascendancy in the countryside. They were now behaving, in the city, Russell argued, in the manner that the aristocracy had done in the countryside. Since they were weaker in many ways than the old Ascendancy, Russell was inviting them to mend their ways lest they share the fate of Anglo-Ireland in becoming cast as enemies of the people. So while the *Irish Times* supported the employers as employers and was not very concerned about them changing their policies (though choosing to publish Russell's broadside just when they had rejected the Board of Trade's report was indicative of reservations about their battle tactics), it was certainly not averse to seeing key nationalist leaders among them rebuked as a new 'aristocracy' whose powers must be held in check. One senses that the *Irish Times*, at a level deeper than the dispute in question, was operating on the principle that 'my enemy's enemy is my friend'. For since early in the century the *Irish Times* had been in almost constant open warfare with the burgeoning forces of twentieth-century democratic Irish nationalism.

On 7 May 1912, the *Irish Times* had published a letter to the editor reporting how passing through St Stephen's Green in Dublin a few days before, the correspondent had heard 'an itinerant orator, holding forth to a select audience, say: "The *Titanic* could not have luck; every rivet put in her was driven home to the accompaniment of 'To Hell with the Pope'"'. An event that had been mythologized since April of that year as a crisis of modernity on a grand scale, in Ireland was, it seems, capable of being absorbed into local mythologies that bespoke the fundamental divide in the country between nationalists and unionists, Protestants and Catholics; just as Russell's commentary on the lockout, conscious as it was of the international context of the labour issue, was rooted in a reading of Irish history. How events of international import and more local political concerns were played out in the reportage of the paper was starkly evidenced when on 18 May 1912, amid extensive coverage of the *Titanic* disaster, the paper advised: 'The text of a Government of Ireland Bill was issued yesterday. The measure provides for the establishment in Ireland of an Irish Parliament, consisting of the King, Irish Senate, and Irish House of Commons. The supreme power and authority of the Parliament of the United Kingdom is to remain unaffected.'

That the *Irish Times* over the following two years would vigorously oppose this decision of the governing Liberal Party in Westminster was scarcely surprising. The newspaper had for over a decade staked its colours so firmly to the mast of unionism that any shift in its position on Home Rule would have been read as a flag of surrender, had it been inclined to make any such adjustment. It was not so disposed.

On the death of Sir John Arnott in 1898, a legal process had ensued by which by 1900 the Irish Times Limited came into existence to publish the *Irish Times*, the *Weekly Irish Times* and the *Evening Irish Times*. The board included four members of the Arnott family, and its first chairman and managing director was Sir John Alexander Arnott, who remained in these posts until 1940 (Mark

O'Brien 2008, pp. 30–1). Arnott family tradition was markedly conservative and unionist. When James A. Scott died in 1899, William Algernon Locker was appointed editor of the daily paper. A Londoner who had cut his journalistic teeth on British newspapers, his focus seems to have been on the English metropolis, where from 1915 to 1929 he was assistant editor of *Punch* (a magazine notorious for its insulting cartoon versions of the Irish in the nineteenth century and no friend of Ireland in much of the twentieth). Locker gave up his *Irish Times* post in 1907 and was succeeded immediately by John Edward Healy, who would occupy the editorial chair until 1934 (the longest tenure of any editor in the paper's history to date). His politics, like those of his immediate predecessor and those of his proprietor Sir John Alexander Arnott, were unshakably unionist. From 1911 to 1918 Healy had the help of an assistant editor leader writer, the Dublin-born Warre Bradley Wells, who had worked for the *Liverpool Daily Post and Echo* in England (Ian d'Alton 2014, p. 103). In the 1920s Wells would help edit George Russell's *Irish Statesman*, which gave important support to the Irish Free State as a force for stability.

Healy, indeed, was the quintessential product of the Protestant professional middle class, among whose members in Dublin the paper found its principal readership in the early decades of the twentieth century, as it had in the nineteenth. He had been born on St Patrick's Day 1872 in Drogheda, Co. Louth. The entry on Healy in the Royal Irish Academy's *Dictionary of Irish Biography* (contributed by the historian Diarmaid Ferriter) portrays a man in whose person key Protestant and unionist institutions found their living expression. His father was a provincial solicitor and his mother was a daughter of a Church of Ireland clergyman. A scholarship took him to Trinity College Dublin, where having initially seemed set fair to follow in his maternal grandfather's footsteps into the Anglican priesthood, he read classics and modern literature (among his tutors was John Pentland Mahaffy, renowned classicist, tutor of Oscar Wilde, controversialist, wit and staunch unionist royalist). Healy's academic reputation was such that as a student and young graduate he was already teaching at a Rathmines school and was soon lecturing on a part-time basis at Alexandra College (among its pedagogic activities was the preparation of young women for the examinations of the Royal University). On graduation, journalism and the law beckoned as career possibilities, with journalism remaining Healy's true avocation as he read for the bar (at college he had edited a student magazine). Experience as Dublin correspondent for *The Times*, a brief stint as editor of the Dublin *Daily Express*, a longer sojourn as editor with the *Church of Ireland Gazette*, occasional leader writing for the *Irish Times*, culminated in his abandoning the law (having been called to the bar in 1906) for the editorial chair he took at the *Irish Times* in 1907. He brought with him, therefore, despite being a reserved and private man, contacts in the law, Church, education and academe (the last of these of an intimate kind, for in 1899 he had married the daughter of a Trinity classics don, Dr Ernest Henry Alton, who would rise to the Provostship of his college). When to this was added his friendship with Sir John Alexander Arnott (with his business associates and wide knowledge of Irish commercial life), then it seemed that Healy was just the man to adapt the paper's nineteenth-century traditional Tory patriotism for the new era.

Fintan O'Toole has written well of the kind of unionism that Healy, along with his proprietor, would have wished to sponsor in their paper: 'the unionism of both Arnott and Healy was not that of the Protestant landlords, nostalgic for the good old days of Ascendancy rule. It was modernizing, industrial and urban, anxious to see the rest of Ireland follow the lead of industrial Belfast into the twentieth century. Healy, in particular, was also sympathetic to the notion of a federalist unionism that would keep Ireland within the United Kingdom but give it more control over local affairs' (Fintan O'Toole, *The Irish Times: The Book of the Century*, 1999, p. 18). With the emphasis adjusted to the industrial future, where in the nineteenth century the paper had more frequently focused on the achievement of stability in the countryside, such an outlook was largely of a piece with that which had governed the paper's attitude to Ireland in the previous century. The problem was that the modern world was in the throes of fundamental changes and Ireland was caught up in these in its own ways. Unionism of whatever kind would be challenged as it had never been before and Healy's gentlemanly patriotism (expressed in prose of studied punctiliousness) would prove itself ineffective in sustaining itself as a workable ideology for his threatened caste.

The process of democratization that marked the early twentieth century in many countries as governments attempted to subdue revolutionary energies (including the kind of syndicalism that was defeated in Dublin in 1913) by judicious reforms, had been anticipated in Ireland by the British government's Local Government Act of 1898 (though no immediate pressure was on the Irish Chief Secretary, Gerald Balfour, to bring forward such a Bill when he did) and the Wyndham Act of 1903. The first of these reformed local government in a way that allowed for the emergence of powerful local authorities. F. S. L. Lyons has judged the 1898 Act as 'one of the most important measures of conciliation passed during the whole period of the Union' (Lyons 1971, p. 212). Of the local authorities he writes:

> Once they began to operate, they were, of course, dominated by the Catholic and nationalist majority who found in them an invaluable training ground for self-government. In social terms, also, the effect of the Local Government Act was not far short of revolutionary, for it marked a decisive shift of power and influence over the country at large away from the landlord ascendancy class and towards 'the democracy' of farmers, shopkeepers and publicans. (Lyons 1971, p. 212)

The *Irish Times* greeted a Bill that was to prove so socially and politically significant with a surprising aplomb which seemed to be bred of wishful thinking. On 21 June the paper, in supporting a three-year tenure for councillors, spoke in comfortable Burkean categories of such a term-of-office producing people who would be 'independent ... of those who voted them into office, acting not as delegates, but truly as representatives'. When the Bill left the House of Commons for the Lords, the *Irish Times* between late July and early August (the Bill received the royal assent on 12 August) published it in full over several editions, suggesting that it should be widely discussed. The paper gave its own measured, if unrealistic, view on 22 July: 'It is not to be expected that so complex a system will work with perfect ease at first. But we see no reason to fear serious difficulty.' The paper argued that it should conciliate nationalists for 'It is meant for the good of the people. It endows them with full powers over their own affairs. It gives them command in local administration which is home rule in the very essence.' The leader writer did acknowledge that there were risks. He observed: 'We may expect party men, of course, to be in evidence, especially at the start. They have pledged themselves to a view of the Act as a stepping-stone towards a revolution, not in local administration, but in the constitutional system.' However, the paper felt there was a safeguard against such an outcome, for it considered that Ireland was so firmly cemented in an empire that had increased in importance since the failure of the last Home Rule Bill, experience of governance at the local level in Ireland would educate young men not for membership of a native parliament but for imperial service: 'the quickening of the local genius to be expected from the operations of the Local Government Bill will help to prepare Irishmen for larger undertakings beyond the bounds of their native land'.

When, by November, divisive Parnellite politics seemed indeed to be rearing its head in anticipation of a local election to be held in Galway in January of the next year, the paper confessed itself at ease with the possibility of nationalist majorities in all the authorities throughout the country's 32 counties, for that 'would do absolutely nothing to further a Home Rule Bill' (*Irish Times*, 15 November 1898). Its head firmly stuck in the sand, the paper assured its readers: 'The more successful the scheme to establish political control in the Councils should be, the less likely would it become that it could promote "Ireland a nation". For if such an appalling vista were to emerge, the British Parliament would surely kill Home Rule not with kindness but with customary firmness.'

The Purchase of Land (Ireland) Act of 1903 (popularly known as the Wyndham Act, after its sponsor, the Irish Chief Secretary George Wyndham) was a further attempt by government to secure the country within the Union by removing the main causes of social and economic discontent in the countryside. It sought to resolve the issue of land ownership. Whereas the Local Government Act had not been passed in response to current destabilizing agitation, the

Wyndham Act was a direct reaction to developments that threatened to reignite the Land War of the early 1880s as agitation brought the condition endured by tenant farmers in Ireland once more centre stage in Irish politics. The outcome of this was, as Lyons has it, that 'the Land Act triumphantly passed through parliament in the session of 1903' (Lyons 1971, p. 218).

Given its long-term commitment to land reform as the basis of political stability within the Union, the *Irish Times* was scarcely likely to do other than give a welcome, albeit a cautious one, to Wyndham's Act. It had been instigated following a Land Conference chaired by Lord Dunraven, one of Anglo-Ireland's most distinguished sons, and it had even managed to bring William O'Brien, the founder and leader of the United Irish League, to the point of moderation as the Bill worked its way through parliament. The tone of the paper's leader on the Act, published on 3 November, the day the act became operative, was oddly low key, given how momentous the occasion was (and proved to be such almost immediately as the paper's columns began filling up with reports of meetings between tenants and landlords or landlords' agents to fix the terms by which, under the provisions of the Act, land would be transferred from landlord to tenant). The *Irish Times* on 3 November was concerned that insufficient monies had been set aside to allow for 'the transference of all the agricultural land in the country from its present owners to the occupying tenants – in a comparatively short time'. Accordingly, it expected 'friction' in the short term but its eyes were really directed to posterity and it was not assured by what could unfold as a consequence of the Act:

> What the ultimate result may be no man can foretell. If the landlords as a rule remain in the country, and if there is such a diminution in class feeling as to enable them to resume their natural place in the administration of local affairs, the results of the Act will be almost wholly beneficial. If on the other hand they should as a rule betake themselves and their purchase-money from Ireland, through lack of inducement to remain, then the last state of the country will be worse than the first, and a hundred years hence our descendants will witness the growth of a new race of landlords less regardful of the principle of *noblesse oblige* and far more greedy after getting the full commercial rent from their tenants than those who now own the land of Ireland.

By 1 December the *Irish Times* was happy, nonetheless, to report that the Act was 'progressing steadily'. Tenants were meeting their landlords or their landlords' representatives and the paper judged that 'Nothing but good should result from this intercourse.'

Emboldened by the smooth resolution of the land question, Lord Dunraven pressed on in the spirit of conciliatory unionism. He formed the Irish Reform Association and in August and September 1904 it published proposals for a limited form of legislative devolution by representative council in the country. The newspaper was less than impressed, in terms that contrasted with its support of the Wyndham Act. It was ready enough to open its pages to discussion of the proposals, though it advised on 26 September, 'while congratulating the reformers on the ingenuity of their proposals, we are not prepared at present to do more than take note of them'. Such caution quickly became superseded by acrimonious controversy when Chief Secretary Wyndham himself, in a letter to *The Times* of London, rejected the proposals. Amid unionist and nationalist anger at the Irish Reform Association, the part played by Wyndham's under-secretary in the formulation of the proposals came under serious question, as did Wyndham's own role in the matter. Wyndham was forced to resign in 1905 when his private involvement in what he had publicly repudiated became undeniable. He had been caught in fact (his fate compounded by incompetence) between two opposing forces, unionism and nationalism, which no amount of conciliation could really render quiescent in their fundamental opposition to one another. Lord Dunraven, in a lengthy letter to the *Irish Times*, pithily expressed how he felt caught in the pincers of that career-wrecking machine: 'Our message of peace seems, alas! to serve only as an invitation to paint their war drums a brighter orange; it only excites extreme Nationalists to wave more frantically a greener flag' (*Irish Times*, 8 October 1904). The reference here to orange war drums was to prove prescient, for in 1905 northern unionism, with its vibrant Orange associations, was to form, in direct consequence of the devolution crisis, an Ulster Unionist Council, institutionalizing a reality that had obtained since the first Home Rule crisis, in which unionist muscle-power was demographically centred on Belfast.

The contrast between the *Irish Times*'s positive response to the Wyndham Act and its lukewarm-at-best reaction to the Irish Reform Association's proposals (in both of which Lord Dunraven was a key figure) can in part be explained by an altering political and cultural climate. Modernity, with its technological innovations, its broadening horizons implicit in greater ease of travel and communications, its new forms of mass entertainment, also involved in the early twentieth century various kinds of reaction in many parts of Europe to the shock of the new. In Ireland these included not only enthusiasms for cultural nationalism and linguistic revival, with their emphasis in a homogenizing age on Irish distinctiveness, but a kind of hardening of attitudes in the political and cultural spheres. In the midst of the devolution crisis, the *Weekly Irish Times* chose to republish from the *National Review* an article by Professor Edward Dowden of Trinity College on 'Irish Unionists and the Present Administration', which reflected this chilling in the cultural climate. It was a bleak intervention from the cultivated Professor of English Literature, who in the 1890s had jousted in print with the young W. B. Yeats over the poet's nativist tendencies. By 1904 Dowden was giving a good deal of his time to the defence of a union he felt was increasingly endangered. His article was a word to the wise about a situation he thought could not be other than polarized: 'The logic of the situation will not be altered,' he insisted; 'two ideas essentially antagonistic will confront each other – now as in 1886 – until one or the other has obtained the mastery'. Dowden thought the early years of the new century had been marked by an intensification of that dialectic, which no acts of conciliation could impede:

> A great contention is not yet closed between two irreconcilable political ideas – there is no half-way house. The era of conciliation in Ireland of the new century had been marked by the rise and progress of the Gaelic League. The era of conciliation has also been distinguished by an outbreak of religious intolerance of quite exceptional virulence. The Irish Unionist party during the next session of Parliament will be thoroughly justified in making its protest against the substitution of partiality for justice in methods of administration in Ireland. (*Weekly Irish Times*, 1 October 1904)

In responding as cautiously as it did to the Reform Association's proposals, one senses that the *Irish Times* was beginning to understand that it was living in new and interesting Irish times. Issues would present with greater severity than they had done during Victoria's reign, when an imperial foundation had usually seemed a secure basis for a conservative equanimity in the second city of the empire, however challenging the local circumstances. In this context it is possible to understand why the *Irish Times* was somewhat ambivalent about the Irish Literary Revival, which, with the founding of the Abbey Theatre by W. B. Yeats and others in 1904, was catching the attention of the world. It was as if it was understood instinctively that cultural revival, like Gaelic revival, could underpin unwelcome demands for political separatism.

Writing about the Home Rule crisis of 1886 and the intensity of opposition it provoked in Belfast and the counties of north-east Ireland, Thomas Bartlett has argued that Home Rule was never just about home rule, and that this was understood almost viscerally by those who came to be known as Ulster Unionists. They appreciated that what was couched as a demand for legislative change was in fact about 'undoing the conquest and, so far as Ulster Unionists were concerned, it was about undoing the plantation' of the seventeenth century (Bartlett 2010, p. 338). Home Rule politics were the expression of a *mentalité* in part constituted by 'the intoxication of grievance' and by 'hatred of England pure and simple'. So while the first decade of the twentieth century in Ireland saw many commentators and writers pondering what the century held in store for the country, such animus, if we accept Bartlett's almost Manichean view, was the deep structure of Irish reality, which governed social and cultural relations and which no amount of discussion or conciliation could substantially alter. In the decade following Queen Victoria's death, the *Irish Times* had ample opportunity to reflect on how the forces of Irish nationalism were regrouping and how intensely they might focus their energies on undoing Protestant and unionist power in the land. The sense that Ulster Unionists had long lived with an Irish nationalism that challenged their right to the very land and properties they occupied, settled as they had been at the point of a sword, was to surface in the anxieties that affected their southern compatriots in the Edwardian period.

When in 1904 Dowden argued that the era of conciliation had been characterized by 'an outbreak of religious intolerance of quite exceptional virulence', he may have been referring to the increasing determination by Catholic organizations in Dublin (among which was the Catholic Association) to advance Catholic participation in the professions and in the civil service, but he was also likely to have had in mind reprehensible events in Limerick of that year. For in January 1904 a demagogic Redemptorist priest, one Father John Creagh, had fomented antagonism to the small population of Jews resident in Limerick. His message was the usual noxious anti-Semitic mixture, in which claims of Jewish exploitation were blended with theological obloquy. He called for a boycott of Jewish interests in the city and was unfortunately soon heeded. For much of the year Jewish traders were shunned by their Catholic neighbours and individual members of their community suffered assaults. Most of the Jews in the city left, some of them having lost their businesses. As historian Dermot Keogh has concluded of this unhappy episode, 'the Jewish community in Limerick had been dealt a severe blow' (Keogh 1998, p. 51).

The *Irish Times* played a part in the contention these events precipitated. On 1 April 1904 it published a letter from the director of 'The Irish Mission to the Jews', I. Julian Grande (he gave a Dublin address). Grande bluntly claimed: 'No Jew or Jewess can walk along the streets of Limerick without being insulted or assaulted. The police give them, so far as I was able to see, passive protection.' Grande appealed to 'all who pity the down-trodden and persecuted Jew, to come to the assistance of the perishing and boycotted Israelites in Limerick'. This intervention and that of the Protestant Bishop of Limerick, Thomas Bunbury (whose defence of Jews in his diocese was carried in a report in the *Irish Times*), caused grave offence in the city itself, where the mayor was on record as stating 'there was no persecution' (*Irish Times*, 21 April 1904) of Jews because of their religion (and that the 'the only objection to them was due to their usurious method of dealing'). A motion was passed at the City Council: 'That we condemn and repudiate in the most emphatic manner the attack made by Dr Bunbury on the good name of the city, and also by the English Press, as we consider such attacks most unjustifiable and uncalled for.' The *Irish Times* clearly thought there was a case to answer because it had published a second letter from I. Julian Grande on 13 April, calling for funds to help the Jews of 'lawless Limerick'.

Prominent Irish nationalists denounced Creagh and the boycott. Among them was Michael Davitt (whose Land League in the 1880s had honed the boycott to a sharp-edged weapon). This fact makes it initially surprising that when the issue came up at the Church of Ireland Synod in Dublin in April, there were those ready to link what was happening to Jews in Limerick to what could happen to Protestants in Ireland more generally. One asked, as the *Irish Times* reported, 'what was to be done in Ireland if persecutions, such as the Limerick Jews were experiencing, were to go on. In the case of the Jews they had a glimpse of what was likely to be done with regard to small communities' (*Irish Times*, 16 April 1904). Another made explicit that he suspected the hand of the Catholic Association (whose main aim was displacing Protestants in key employment sectors) behind the Limerick boycott. After a good deal of discussion, in which Davitt's boycott tactics were recalled, the Synod unanimously passed a resolution deploring 'the persecution of Protestants and Jews in Ireland'.

That such a note of paranoia was struck at the Church of Ireland Synod (duly reported by the *Irish Times*) in 1904, when a Conservative government was in power at Westminster, is very telling. It suggests that, although the political conflict between nationalist and unionist Ireland was often played out as a kind of well-managed shadow boxing at the beginning of the century and the constitutional position seemed reasonably secure, Protestant and unionist Ireland was aware of underground currents of a fundamental hostility to it gathering strength beneath an apparently calm surface, which could lead to its shipwreck. The return to power of a Liberal administration in 1905 did nothing to calm such nerves and in the following years the *Irish Times* reported on and expressed the anxieties of a caste increasingly aware of its possible minority status outside the nine counties of Ulster.

Among things likely to unsettle the island's Protestants in this period was the papal *Ne Temere* decree of 1907, made applicable in 1908. This change in canon law effectively made it possible for Catholic parish priests to require non-Catholic partners of a church marriage to agree to raise children of the union as Catholics before they would solemnize the nuptials. Ireland was not the only country where this caused consternation and controversy, but in a society where religion and politics had for so long been intertwined, it was the source of predictable contention and even outrage.

Objections to this ecclesiastical policy were raised in various Protestant Church bodies. At the Church of Ireland Synod, for example, held shortly after Archbishop William Walsh had informed the Catholic faithful of the city about the decree and its implications (the *Irish Times* fully reported his missive), very considerable disquiet was expressed. George Chadwick, the Bishop of Derry, raised the issue (his remarks were included in the usual extensive *Irish Times* report of such meetings) and he expressed a fear that canon law could be treated as superior to the law of the land (*Irish Times*, 29 April 1908) in terms that belittled Catholic Ireland's Irish respect for law. The topic kept recurring at Church level until on 30 January 1911 a public meeting was held in the Metropolitan Hall in Dublin, under the chairmanship of the Protestant Archbishop of Dublin, Joseph Peacocke, to protest against the decree 'In Connection with Mixed Marriages'. It was an expression of Protestant solidarity in the city, attended by Anglicans, Presbyterians and other dissenters. A counter meeting was consequently held (in a way that echoed the sectarian Bible wars that had marked Dublin life in the 1820s, when theological disputation had almost become a blood sport) at the Hibernian Club in Rutland (now Parnell) Square where a Father Ambrose Coleman stated: 'All who read the newspapers lately could not have failed to have seen that a great deal was written about the *Ne Temere* decree as an act of papal aggression upon this unfortunate country.' He would show, he claimed, that 'this was only a bogey, a bogey concocted of imagination and ignorance' (*Irish Times*, 15 February 1911). Father Coleman's main argument, as the *Irish Times* reported it, was that Protestants had shamelessly proselytized in Ireland in the past and that it was hypocrisy and Orange bigotry to object to the Catholic Church's clarity on the matter. The flavour of Father Coleman's discourse can be caught when he is recorded as observing: 'For hundreds of years every effort has been made by the English Government and their representatives in Ireland to bring the Irish people out of the Church of Rome, as they call it, into the Church of confusion.'

More significant than such outbreaks of religious bad manners, in allowing us to take the temperature of inter-confessional exchanges in the period from the columns of the *Irish Times*, was an editorial in the paper itself on 15 December 1910, which linked renewed fears about Home Rule (once more in the Liberal government's sights) and the *Ne Temere* decree. The editorial concerned the matter of Protestant premonitions that Home Rule could be Rome rule. The writer expressed confidence that no Irish parliament would establish the Roman Catholic Church ('It is one of things that Governments in the twentieth century do not do') and would not lay any claim to 'the funds of the Church of Ireland'. 'The minority,' the paper asserted, 'do not fear a crude and barbarous assault which would disgrace the Government in the eyes of Europe.' What it did fear was laid out in a compelling passage of signal candour, which indicates how deeply anxiety had entered twentieth-century Protestant and unionist souls: 'The minority are open to aggression from three sources. They may be attacked as Protestants, as Unionists, or as owners of property.' In respect of the first of these, the paper expatiated with evident, exacerbated feeling:

> We desire to say that from the great majority of their fellow-countrymen they fear no unfair assault. But they do fear it from small and organized bands of undisciplined and intolerant men ... As Protestants our fear is largely based on two grounds. A very considerable part of Nationalist political life is openly and avowedly controlled by a secret society from which Protestants are rigidly excluded. The existence of these political

secret societies is an anachronism in a modern State ... We could trust our fellow-countrymen if they were let alone. But we cannot trust these secret and irresponsible committees who are capturing the machine of government, and crushing beneath a rigid tyranny even those of the same party ... There is another matter in this connection which is even more delicate, but must be mentioned. The Papal Decree on Mixed Marriages has caused the greatest resentment and regrets among Protestants of the whole country. We have nothing to do with questions that affect the internal discipline and control of the Roman Catholic Church ... we must be resolved upon one matter. It must not be open to the temporal power to enforce the spiritual penalties in this respect. The first safeguard that we demand is that the law of civil marriage and legitimation shall be placed beyond the control of any Irish parliament. (*Irish Times*, 15 December 1910)

A distinctively ethnic form of nationalism was in fact making itself felt in Ireland's new century which increasingly would establish Catholicism as a marker of Irish identity, setting in question the nationality of the country's Protestants. Furthermore, the cultural nationalism of the Gaelic revival movement (which had been inaugurated in the 1890s with the founding of the Gaelic League in 1893), was establishing Irish (so named to invest 'Gaelic' with national status) as an essential component of Irishness. The idea of an Irish Ireland, Catholic and Gaelic, was taking hold and by the middle of the second decade of the twentieth century the new political party Sinn Féin, formed in 1905 to challenge the hegemony of the Irish Party in nationalist Ireland, had to all intents and purposes, despite an avowed republican understanding of citizenship, absorbed Irish Irelandism as a controlling ethnic ideology.

The Gaelic revival movement in its early stages had not been overtly political in complexion. Many Protestants and unionists had initially been affected by the sociable aspects of the league's activities and were minded to join with their compatriots in promoting knowledge of the language. However, quite quickly, issues of linguistic usage took on a distinctly political hue (individuals, for example, who chose to use Irish versions of their names resisted the Post Office's insistence that English was the official language of communication), opening a fissure among those who regarded the league as a force for cultural enrichment and those who saw it as inevitably expressive of separatist impulses.

The *Irish Times* to a degree aligned itself with those who approved of or indulged the Irish language movement as effecting cultural enrichment (this was of a piece with its benign attitude to the revival of Irish music and literature, noted in Chapter 1). The *Weekly Irish Times* published a regular section on 'Irish Language Notes' (which among other things introduced the occasional usage of Gaelic script to its columns) contributed by one who gave his name as 'Murnán'. A piece from his pen on 10 January 1903 nicely caught the blend of cultural enthusiasm with less attractive exclusionary instincts that tended to vie for supremacy in the movement. He wrote:

> One frequently hears the question asked – What has this movement so far, accomplished. I answer that there is scarcely a phase of Irish life in which its influence is not apparent. Is it nothing to have stimulated the people to mental effort, to have taught them for the first time to think for themselves, to have helped them to turn their minds on the industrial problems of the country, to have sweetened their imaginations by substituting the clean songs and beautiful music of their own land for the tawdry and often vicious songs imported from abroad?

In March 1903 the Gaelic League inaugurated an annual march in Dublin in support of the language revival. The second of these in 1904 stimulated the *Irish Times* to editorialize on the event and the cause it promulgated. The leader writer noted in curiously patronizing tones that the march had drawn 'a noticeable preponderance of young men and women obviously belonging to the respectable and comfortable estates'. Assured by this, the editorial observed of the successful march: 'The Gaelic League deserves immense credit for this achievement.' Hoping that the league would eschew sectarianism, the *Irish Times* concluded of that body on 14 March:

> If it can keep out of politics and confine itself entirely to industrial and educational developments and to the encouragement of national pastimes, we see no reason why it should not play a tremendous part in the moulding of the youth of Ireland, the shaping of the national character and the advancement of our native industries. In a movement conducted for these objects, without any political aims sandwiched between them, every patriotic Unionist can, and we feel sure would, join.

This editorial provoked a bitter response from a Dublin reader, one Ella MacMahon, who strenuously doubted the good faith of the Gaelic League. She asserted with force: 'It is a pity, but it is a fact, that wherever you go you find the Irish language movement prominently put forward there you find undisguised and unbridled hatred of England. Wherever the League is there are seditionists gathered together' (*Irish Times*, 15 March 1904). By September 1905 the *Irish Times* had begun to incline more to the position of its distrustful letter-writer than to its former condescending approval of the league's activities. On 8 September it published a lengthy editorial on the language movement that reflected a far from sanguine attitude to its possible effects on the country.

Perhaps the editor's attention had been caught by a legal case taken against a carter in County Donegal who had insisted on painting his name in Irish on the back of his cart (the case had been reported on at length in the *Irish Times*'s own columns) where the accused had been defended by a 'Mr Pearse', no less. Whatever the reason, and the editorial does make passing reference to this case, as well to more recent examples of what it considered excessive linguistic zeal (it damned these as 'the most provincial form of patriotism run stark mad'), the paper's mood had darkened by September 1905. For it had come to think that the Gaelic League had been too successful. It had 'seized the imagination of a very vigorous and very pugnacious body of Irishmen and they have raised it to the position of a national problem' (*Irish Times*, 8 September 1905). The problem for the *Irish Times* comprised two things: 'the ulterior purpose of the Irish language movement and the present and possible effects of this movement on the material welfare of the country' which might isolate it behind, as it were, a Gaelic curtain. The paper considered that the nation was being 'bullied' into accepting the Irish language and that this would have deleterious consequences for the economy. It seemed acutely aware of how the matter of ethnicity was being foregrounded in cultural and political discourse, that such alleged bullying particularly involved 'Nationalist public bodies': 'They have been told,' the paper gloomily warned, 'until some of them perhaps believe it, that to reject the Irish language is to be "anti-national".' The *Irish Times* averred that it had no 'feeling of hostility to the Irish language' but it objected strongly to what it sensed was an 'ill-directed zeal which would make Irish take the place of far more important instruments of intellectual culture'.

What these other instruments of culture might have been, in the *Irish Times*'s frame-of-reference, is suggested by the historian Paul Bew in his book *Ireland: The Politics of Enmity 1789–2006* (2007), where he argues that in the first decade of a modernising century

> ... the language movement provided ... a new world of meanings and a potential basis for the constitution of new hierarchies: it was all the more necessary because Irish unionism had the support of so many eminent and internationally renowned Irish-born scientists who could not be dismissed as privileged layabouts of the Ascendancy. The emotional intensity of Irish-language activists was, in part, designed to block out the prestige of men like the scientist and Unionist John Tyndall ... (Bew 2007, p. 367)

Substance is given to Bew's analysis, which might otherwise seem too simple, when we note how Irish became a matter of heated public interventions as the National University of Ireland was coming into being in 1908 and 1909.

The National University of Ireland was the answer to the Irish university question which had been a political conundrum, like a miniature version of the Irish question itself, for much of the nineteenth century. One of the Queen's colleges founded in 1845, that in Belfast, became the stand-alone Queen's University of Belfast. The other two Queen's colleges, those in Galway and Cork, were incorporated in a federal university system of the National University, along with University College Dublin, offspring of the university college John Henry Newman helped to found in 1854. Trinity College Dublin was issued with new letters patent, assuring its future as another stand-alone university in the country. So much to many people's satisfaction. However, what exercised other Irish minds at this crucial point in the country's intellectual history (the federal system survived as such for a century) was not what role the science and technology that were so rapidly affecting daily life could play in the National University, but whether Irish should be made compulsory for matriculation at its colleges (the concept of 'compulsory Irish' was born in reportage, including that in the *Irish Times*). In 1908, 1909 and 1910 the *Irish Times* repeatedly published reports on how local authorities had passed motions demanding that knowledge of Irish be a condition of university entry and criticised the activities of the Gaelic League as leaders of the crusade such motions represented.

In June 1910 the Senate of the National University (the university had come into existence on 1 October 1908) announced that Irish would be compulsory for matriculation in 1913. The *Irish Times* on 24 June published an unhappy editorial which acknowledged how concepts of ethnicity had been at work in the debate which had culminated in that decision.

So demoralized was the *Irish Times* by this outcome that it did not see fit to challenge such a starkly adversarial characterization of Irish cultural life as a matter of the anglicized and the native. It acknowledged how the Senate had been forced into a decision that the *Irish Times* judged was 'bad' and for which 'the Irish people [would] have to pay a heavy price', comforting itself by reckoning that a strict application of the new requirement could help to 'swell the constantly increasing numbers of the students at Trinity College and Belfast' where no such impediment to entry would obtain. With some prescience, however, the editorialist advised: 'The devotion which makes a man master of a subject does not depend upon compulsion and is not even stimulated by it.' The *Irish Times*'s conclusive disillusionment with the Gaelic League came in 1915, when, amid the anxieties of the Great War, it judged that the end had come to 'all the hopes and enthusiasm which begot the League and maintained it for some years as an honest and youthful organisation. It has been captured by a small body of political extremists and cannot pretend in future to be anything but a political organisation' (*Irish Times*, 30 July 1915).

That the times were indeed marked by intense feelings about ethnic purity and by nationalist rigours about identity had been made dramatically evident at the Abbey Theatre in Dublin in January 1907. John Millington Synge's comic masterpiece *The Playboy of the Western World* had been greeted then by a riotous response from nationalists and damned as a calumny upon western Irish rural society. Its tale of a patricide feted in a Mayo village aroused violent opposition from elements in Sinn Féin and from among its followers, who considered figures such as Lady Augusta Gregory and W. B. Yeats (who had founded the theatre as a national institution in 1904) as Ascendancy types, who, despite their culturally nationalist aspirations, had, they thought, encouraged Synge to impugn Irish womanhood. The *Irish Times* had not been, as we have noted, especially supportive of Yeats and his enterprises before this event. The plays mounted by the Abbey Theatre had been reviewed by the paper as they were produced but without much sense that it was making theatrical history. The books associated with the Irish Literary Revival, among them works by Yeats and Lady Gregory (the latter's fine versions of Irish saga material were admired), were courteously noted by reviewers, but only as part of the paper's essentially *belletrist* treatment of English language literature in general. In 1907, however, it was more than happy to come to Yeats's support and to that of his theatre, reckoning, one suspects, that if Yeats and the Abbey Theatre could be so targeted, then who was safe in the new unabashedly aggressively nationalist Ireland that was coming into being?

The *Irish Times*, of course, like the other Dublin newspapers, recognized a good story when it saw it; so some of its reportage on the riotous and disputatious events provoked by Synge's play was treated as good knock-about copy. The editorial of Wednesday, 30 January 1907 (the play had opened the previous Saturday), struck an altogether more portentous note. Regretting that Synge's play, which it considered flawed, was not the best plank to stand on in making a plea for freedom of expression, the *Irish Times*, nonetheless, insisted: 'The claim – not now advocated for the first time – that people should be allowed to howl down a play or a book merely because it offends their crude notion of patriotism cannot be tolerated for a moment.' With no holds barred, the newspaper declared: 'We sympathise with the plucky stand which the National Theatre Company is making against the organised tyranny of the clap-trap patriots.' No doubt the *Irish Times*'s appreciation of Yeats's stance on Synge's play was also enhanced by the fact that the poet shared the paper's other concerns. At the meeting called to debate Synge's play, to which the paper's editorial of 30 January was a commentary, Yeats had in fact unfavourably compared the Ireland of his boyhood with that of 1907. He had argued that in the past the country had been led by genuine leaders; in the present it was at the mercy of 'coteries' and only understood conversion by terror, threats and abuse'. The *Irish Times* was happy to say, despite the hyperbole of Yeatsian rhetoric: 'We heartily endorse everything Mr Yeats said yesterday.'

Thereafter the *Irish Times* gave more coverage to Yeatsian interventions in public debate (it reported fully, for example, on a speech in which Yeats attacked the Irish 'bourgeoisie' in 1907 and published responsive letters to it). It was as if, for all Yeats's past as a republican who had helped to organize the United Irish commemoration in 1898, who had publicly opposed the visit of Queen Victoria to Dublin in 1900, the *Irish Times* sensed that they shared an almost caste interest with the poet in opposing those it had so contemptuously dubbed, with an almost Yeatsian venom, 'clap-trap patriots'.

If the *Irish Times* felt the values of Protestant and unionist Ireland, which it continued to articulate, were at risk from what Yeats called 'coteries' in a period of deficient leadership, the paper itself had in the first decade of the century to contend not only with new aggressive forces in the nationalist movement but with a new competitor in the battle for readership. In 1905 William Martin Murphy launched the *Irish Independent* in tabloid style at a halfpenny per issue, undercutting both the *Irish Times* and the declining *Freeman's Journal* (which merged with the *Irish Independent* in 1924). Basically an Irish version of the Harmsworth (Northcliffe) model in England, the *Irish Independent* quickly prospered, gaining a readership both in Dublin and provincial Ireland (where the *Irish Times*, as in the previous century, scarcely circulated). Murphy was indisputably a leader in nationalist Ireland at this time, but not the elitist, romantically daring sort of whom Yeats increasingly approved, for the sphere in which he excelled was commercial. The newspaper he founded reflected his entrepreneurial and commercial concerns while expressing Catholic nationalist sentiments of a broadly conservative kind in a way that meant it appealed to a wide constituency. So the *Irish Times*'s minority status in the country was being redefined in not-so-subtle ways both by the emergence of militant forces ready to do religious/cultural battle against anglicized and Protestant Ireland, and by a confident national majority prepared to flex its economic muscle, led by entrepreneurs of Murphy's stamp.

All this helps us to understand, why, in the middle of the lockout of 1913, the *Irish Times*, although it supported William Martin Murphy in that dispute, chose to publish Yeats's bitterly dismissive ballad 'Romance in Ireland' (afterwards renamed 'September 1913'). Composed, as Yeats had it, 'On Reading Much of the Correspondence against the Art Gallery', the poem was an attack on those in Dublin Corporation who had spurned a benefactor's generosity by refusing to vote for sufficient funds to build a gallery in Dublin to house the French works of art involved. Yeats's poem made much of how there were those in contemporary Ireland who fumbled 'in the greasy till' in miserable contrast with the true heroes of the romantic past: 'all that delirium of the brave' (Yeats 1992, p. 160). There was a shudder of caste revulsion in this poem of elitist, minority disdain. The *Irish Times*'s editorial suggested that it, too, had recoiled in distaste from Murphy's reported remark on the art gallery issue that public money should not be spent, at a time when conditions in tenement dwellings were so desperate, 'in building a picture palace over the Liffey'. An editorial in the issue in which Yeats's poem was published prissily signalled its agreement with the Yeatsian hauteur in face of creeping philistinism and vulgarity: 'Mr Yeats sees behind the opposition to the Art Gallery Project a tendency of mind which he fears may grow on us in Ireland ... He feels that there is a danger of our people becoming hardened to the worship of materialism and commercialism' (*Irish Times*, 8 September 1913).

Ireland in fact did possess leaders at this time, if not of the cavalier, romantic, self-sacrificing variety favoured by Yeats. The Irish Party at Westminster was led by the gentlemanly, generally competent figure of John Redmond, while the Irish Unionist Parliamentary Party there was led by the formidable Edward Carson. The issue was, for a third time, Home Rule. If the matter had been decided by force of personality, then it would have been no contest, for Carson, who came to the leadership of unionism as one of the most powerful politicians in the United Kingdom, was a forceful orator, a charismatic presence and a combative court advocate; above all, he was ruthless. By contrast, Redmond was reserved, a capable if scarcely electrifying speaker and instinctively tolerant, where Carson was strategically focused. With the Liberals in power at the behest of the Irish Party at Westminster, and the House of Lords veto on legislation passed in the Commons removed in 1911 (Bills could not be dismissed more than twice in the upper house), Redmond held a winning hand that, with the support of his more robust second-in-command, John Dillon, could scarcely fail. That Redmond saw a Home Rule Act finally on the statute book only after a crisis that brought the country to the point of civil war and challenged the existence of the United Kingdom itself is evidence of the skill and daring with which Carson played his hand at this time and the powerful forces he could call on in opposition to the settled will of a majority of Irish men and women who supported Home Rule. As a principal organ of southern bourgeois unionism (from which background Carson in fact hailed), the *Irish Times* was not unsurprisingly preoccupied by Home Rule as the foundations of the constitution trembled in the years before the outbreak of war in August 1914.

The *Irish Times* in the twentieth century, under the editorship of John Edward Healy, was, as stated earlier, as staunchly opposed to Home Rule as it had been in the nineteenth century. However, when events in the north of the country made clear that partition was a likely outcome of the eventual enactment of the Home Rule Bill, first read in 1912, then the *Irish Times* faced the appalling vista that unionism in the rest of the country could be left as a vulnerable minority in nationalist and Catholic Ireland. Were such circumstances to arise, it came to reflect, Home Rule for the whole island might be the lesser of two evils.

In 1911 the newspaper drew comfort from Ulster Unionist expressions of solidarity with their southern brethren as they declared that there would be no split between them in opposition to Home Rule. The alacrity, however, with which the *Irish Times* fell on these assurances suggests that the paper was not entirely convinced that such promises would hold good in the fires of *realpolitik*. Ulster, it sought to convince itself, 'would never make a mockery of her Unionism by an inglorious and base attempt to shelter herself within a separate parliament' (*Irish Times*, 11 October 1911). It was this editorial whistling in the dark about a province with which it had never really felt in sympathy which accounts for what amounted to the support the paper gave to the essentially rebellious and revolutionary steps that Ulster Unionism took in 1912 and 1913 at the urging of Carson and his northern lieutenant, James Craig. Ulster Unionist muscle was so well developed that it could not be opposed by the British government, which must in consequence abandon Home Rule for the entire island – or so was the *Irish Times*'s fond hope in 1912, the year in which a new Home Rule Bill was first laid in the Westminster parliament. For when in September 1912 nearly a quarter of a million Ulstermen signed a covenant declaring that 'all means necessary' could be employed to oppose Home Rule in their province, the *Irish Times* reckoned their temerity was decisive when it editorialized that 'they had convinced every open mind in the United Kingdom that the men who sign the Covenant today will keep their word. This is the only fact that counts. They may be right or wrong, loyal or disloyal, patriots or rebels; but they have taken a course, and nothing will turn them from it' (*Irish Times*, 28 September 1912). Only a civil war could halt them in their purposes and that, the editorial implied, was unthinkable, so Home Rule must fall.

On 1 January 1913 the *Irish Times* realized that it could not depend on Carson and the northern unionists, when Carson moved an amendment at the report stage of the Home Rule Bill that would permit 'the exclusion of Ulster from the operation' of the Bill. Although the amendment was rejected, the *Irish Times* was clearly shaken (the shock that such an amendment was the work of one of its own, so to speak, must have compounded the discomfiture; Carson represented the University of Dublin in the Commons). Initially the *Irish Times* had thought that Carson was acting in a merely strategic manner, knowing, as he did, that his proposal would be rejected. However, the paper's editorial expressing gratification that the amendment had been rejected had an extra edge since it had come to suspect that Carson had in fact been serious in tabling the amendment that would mean that 'Southern Unionists should be left to shift for themselves'. The editorialist was unimpressed by Carson's argument that their interests would be protected by Ulster Unionist MPs in Westminster. Carson was, it seemed, prepared to contemplate their 'political banishment' which 'did not offer a single gleam of hope'. The paper thundered:

> Ulster rejects a Home Rule Parliament. If it is not to be forced into such
> a Parliament – a coercion which we believe to be impossible – it must
> find some better plan than Sir Edward Carson's for rewarding the trust
> and loyalty of its brethren in the South. Ulster must stand or fall with the
> whole of Unionist Ireland.

And if such a fall involved the granting of Home Rule and a parliament in Dublin, it would be better for southern Unionists if there were Ulster Unionists sitting there alongside their southern compatriots.

There were ironies and complications for the *Irish Times* in all this. Despite the paper's expressed anxiety, in January 1913 Carson *was* probably acting strategically when he tabled his amendment. He was, after all, as imperially minded a unionist as the editor of the *Irish Times* and it was not until towards the end of the year that he became fully convinced that southern unionism was not to be saved in the existing circumstances. For Carson, the exclusion of Ulster (meaning all nine counties of the province) would so complicate the Home Rule project that a federal arrangement would have to be devised in time which could accommodate the imperial reality to which Carson gave his allegiance. So in 1913 and 1914 as Ulster unionism threatened open rebellion, supported in the spring of 1914 by the newly imported and illegal guns of the recently formed Ulster Volunteer Force (UVF), Carson was to the fore in representing the Ulster cause, rather than the all-Ireland one. In September 1913 he had stated that were Home Rule to come into effect, a provisional government would be established in Ulster and the UVF could have supplied it with some basic military support (though how effectively is a moot point). For him the northern province was where the power lay to complicate Home Rule in a creative if dangerous way. It was where the *Irish Times* hoped it would founder. This, of course, meant that both Carson and the *Irish Times* were playing with fire, for the forces of Ulster loyalism might have lit a general conflagration.

Understandably, editorial tone in these unnerving times took on a hectic, febrile note. When, for example, the Bill was presented in parliament for the third time in April 1914, an editorial inveighed against it as 'calamitous and anti-national'. It 'would set up a sham and bankrupt parliament' (*Irish Times*, 2 April 1914). In July of the same year the *Irish Times* declared that, were the Bill to become law without a general election to test its public support in the United Kingdom, then 'Ulster will be absolutely justified in resisting it by every means in her power. She'll be in fact the champion of British liberties against an unexampled tyranny' (*Irish Times*, 16 July 1914).

It seemed that the titanic struggle between unionism and Home Rule nationalism that Edward Dowden had identified in 1904 as being resolvable only in the victory of one or the other was inevitably coming to a head. As it did so, Dowden himself died. The passing of such a man in the midst of political turmoil was not without poignancy; for Dowden was the closest thing to a fully developed resident intellectual that Irish imperial Tory unionism could boast. His quitting the scene when he did could be read as the end of an era when men like him could hope to affect the body politic. A Shakespearean scholar of world renown, Dowden had founded the Unionist Alliance to protect the union he thought essential to Ireland's place in the world (his work on Shakespeare can be analysed as substantiating his politics). He was a seasoned and effective polemicist. So the *Irish Times*'s obituary reflected the range of his achievements but did so in a manner that suggested that it knew Dowden's day was done in more than the obvious literal sense. It commented:

> Culture carries its own atmosphere about with it. Its influence is the greatest of all educators. In Professor Dowden it meant learning, wisdom, humour, charity, an imperturbable sweetness of mind. He was a strong and serious politician. In the hottest days of the Home Rule conflict he made fighting speeches for the Unionist cause. Yet he never wounded a human soul. The secret of his political effectiveness was a benignant and crushing suavity. (*Irish Times*, 5 April 1913)

The paper thought contemporary Ireland needed the 'gift of culture' only a Dowden could bestow as it lamented on how the country had been affected of late by 'gloomy enthusiasms'. His commendable universalism of outlook, even in an Ireland renascent with cultural energy ('We have', the obituarist admitted, 'a new and fertile school of Irish drama', as well as other signs of cultural life), was being superseded by 'a certain narrowness of vision'. For the writer, 'Our national imagination and national ambitions seem to be shutting themselves up within the four walls of Ireland.' The note of a threnody for a vanishing unionist hegemony in the cultural as well as the political sphere lingers in the obituary therefore, as if to acknowledge that the time was fast fading when 'a benignant and crushing suavity' would cut any ice in modern Ireland. 'We record,' the paper grieved (and its editor had sat at Dowden's feet in Trinity College), 'Dr Dowden's death with something of that sinking of heart which Wordsworth felt at the passing of brother after brother, "from sunshine to the sunless land". He was, it seems, to us, one of the last of an old school – a school that has kept us in touch for so many years with the intellectual movements of the world.'

The year 1914 gave mounting evidence that 'suavity', whether benign, crushing or both, held little currency in Ireland or in a Europe careering towards disastrous warfare that would involve much of the world.

For the *Irish Times* the outbreak of war in Europe on 1 August 1914 removed it from the horns of a very uncomfortable dilemma (the paper, unusually, published on a Sunday to report on the declaration by Germany of war on Russia). For the *Irish Times*'s dependence on Ulster to defeat Home Rule meant thinking of loyalist threats of violence as a bargaining chip in the game of statecraft. However, that spring and summer it had seemed that the phony war in Ireland might become a real one. As noted above, the Ulster Volunteer Force imported significant weaponry, and British army units stationed at the Curragh, Co. Kildare (near where the paper's second editor had ministered), ordered to move against them, refused to do so. A paramilitary force, the Irish Volunteers, had mustered in the south of Ireland to oppose the Ulstermen. When that body also imported arms, the British army met them with the force they had declined to use against the UVF. Having supported the Ulster Unionist cause, the *Irish Times* could hardly resile from its position when Ulster unionism sought to acquire the means to give it muscle. That, however, meant providing succour to rebellion against the imperial parliament and the throne, things anathema to the Tory unionist mindset. Editorials in this dangerous time, when the country seemed doomed to civil war, amounted to an anxious wringing of the hands as the paper was pinned to the collar of its own ambivalence about the situation. Ulster had right on its side, and must be the engine that would destroy Home Rule, so the contemplated use of force against it was 'tragic and terrible'. But the Curragh mutiny was 'even more important and more sinister' since that threatened order at a fundamental level in the United Kingdom. Yet the Irish Volunteers' arms-smuggling could be understood as a reaction to events in the north. The *Irish Times*'s impotent angst reached a crescendo in an editorial of 27 July 1914, the day following the attack by the British army on the Irish Volunteers in Dublin. The paper uttered an anguished jeremiad, entitled 'Danger and Duty':

> The state of our country is desperately critical. The Administration is helpless and discredited. Everywhere men are taking the law into their own hands. The nation is divided into two rival armies. Passions run stern and high. British statesmanship is distracted between the menace of the Irish problem and the imminent fear of European complications. None of us knows what the morrow may bring forth. Anything may happen in Ulster, and yesterday's incidents prove that even the safety and welfare of the capital city of Ireland are trembling in the balance ...
>
> Ireland demands at this critical moment that all her sons shall unite in a great effort of self-restraint and good-will.

The outbreak of war meant that the operation of the Home Rule Act was postponed for the duration. Redmond encouraged nationalist Ireland to support the British war effort and the Irish Volunteers to enlist in the imperial army. He hoped that such Irish 'loyalty' would be rewarded and much was made of German atrocities in Catholic Belgium to stir up Irish feeling against the depredations of the Hun. For the *Irish Times*, the outbreak of war meant that Ireland's sons could unite not in 'self-restraint and good-will' but in martial opposition to a common foe.

Paul Fussell, in *The Great War and Modern Memory* (1975), recounts how in many parts of Europe the war that began on that fateful day in August 1914 was greeted with enthusiasm and a spirit of chivalric self-sacrifice. The English poet Rupert Brooke caught a general mood, which early in the war welcomed conflict (experience of actual warfare would soon dissipate such naivety) as some kind of cleansing process for a civilization that had seemed sullied by age, when he wrote in 'Peace' of a generation meeting the call to arms 'as swimmers into cleansing leaping' (Brooke 1987, p. 1). The *Irish Times*, more realistically, initially reacted to the outbreak of war with a genuine trepidation. It seemed to grasp that modern warfare represented a new and terrifying chapter in the bloody history of humankind: 'We are face to face with the certainty of war on such a scale and of a character so terrible as civilisation (if we can use the word without irony) has never yet known ...' (*Irish Times*, 2 August 1914) However, the paper quickly became affected by widespread exultation at the thought of sacrifices to come and blood shed in a noble cause. When Redmond suggested that the Irish Volunteers should constitute divisions of the British army, the paper approved, certain that 'the eager manhood of Nationalist Ireland' (*Irish Times*, 17 September 1914) would troop to the colours. It enthusiastically welcomed the fact that unionists and nationalists were 'going to fight shoulder to shoulder ... to share the same baptism of blood, the same suffering and glory in the same holy cause ...'

The *Irish Times*'s elevated zeal at the prospect of war was not simply a local version of the jingoism that overtook so many that fateful autumn. With its chauvinist fervour was mingled a paradoxical relief that the Irish crisis of that summer had been superseded by an altogether greater one. By 5 August the paper had managed to convince itself that 'the people of these kingdoms are more cheerful than they have been at any time since the war clouds began to gather over Europe' because uncertainty had ended. In Ireland there was cause for 'thankfulness – even exultation', for the nation was finding itself again, uniting in an 'hour of trial'. And it hoped, too, that in the experience of shared glory and sacrifice on what it termed 'the familiar plains of Northern Europe' (*Irish Times*, 17 September 1914), where Irishmen had won battle honours in the past, the Irish question would find happy resolution. For the paper imagined that

> ... the end of the war will find a new situation in Ireland. Many things will have changed: much will have been learned and much forgotten. By that time, it may well happen, the great political problem which all our statesmen have failed to resolve will have found its own solution.

The *Irish Times*'s reportage of the Great War was a complex matter. The newspaper was unassailably convinced of the justice of the imperial cause and was not above scaremongering about what could happen to Ireland if Germany triumphed and occupied the country (that would, the newspaper warned, be 'worse than any other calamity that [had] ever overtaken it in all its mournful history' (*Irish Times*, 25 September 1914). From this point of certitude that the war was a 'fight for civilisation and liberty' (*Irish Times*, 2 August 1915), the paper made sure in editorials and reports that its readers were kept as informed as possible of the course of the war. Special Sunday editions, for example, provided maps of the various theatres of conflict, and editorials were frequently devoted to close, often extensive, analyses of military strategies and their outcomes. So while the columns of names of Irish dead and missing grew longer and the roll of honour the paper published in respect for the Irish fallen grew poignantly, there was a dominant tone effected by the newspaper that war as politics by other means could somehow be retained within rational comprehension (as earlier it had sought to make the loss of the *Titanic* seem amenable to reason). The great battles were afforded appropriately generous space for analysis, while day by day brief reports from far-flung sites of conflict (derived, as the war became a prolonged affair, from Association Press messages) gave a sense of a great empire in a vital struggle for survival against an unprincipled foe. However, this almost Olympian perspective on the titanic events of the war could reach a height where rationality seemed to betray itself in the *reductio ad absurdum* of the analytic method. On 26 August 1915, for example, the *Irish Times* pondered 'The Factor of Numbers', computing the appalling losses on both sides to that date and in cold calculation concluding: 'We may fairly reckon ... that the total losses of the Kaiser's Armies up to June 30 must have been not less than two and a half million or about 225,000 for every one of the eleven months that the war had lasted.' The paper was confident that 'A war of attrition would bring Germany to its knees', and without too long a delay.

Often, however much the newspaper sought to make the war seem open to rational understanding, it was clear that its editorialists appreciated that they were dealing with a matter of undeniable emotional import. The terrible experiences of Irish soldiers in Flanders and at Gallipoli in 1915 demanded some properly heartfelt response. The paper attempted to sound a patriotic bugle, as it affirmed in an editorial entitled 'The Irish in Gallipoli': 'The fighting in the Dardanelles will be a landmark in the history of the Irish people' (*Irish Times*, 4 September 1915). It admitted high sentiment when it recalled 'the laughing lads who marched along the Dublin quays' bound for battle. The paper judged, however, that the slaughter had been worth it, for many of those young lads had died for their country as well as for the Empire. The writer fell back on the argument the newspaper had promulgated at the war's outbreak. In an emotional peroration he celebrated the unifying power of military sacrifice, now made good by much shedding of Irish blood:

> A little more than a year ago they were planning to kill one another. To-day many of them have died for one another. When this war is ended we shall resume our political controversies in a new Ireland. The Unionists and Nationalists who fought at Ypres and stormed the hill at Suvla have sealed a new bond of patriotism. The spirit of our dead Irish soldiers will cry trumpet-tongued against the deep damnation of inter-necine strife in Ireland.

Just over a year later, even after the horrendous losses at the Somme in July 1916, which the paper admitted had demanded 'a heavy price of British manhood'

(*Irish Times*, 9 August 1916), it thought a similar emotional equation could be written in defence of mass carnage. On 19 September 1916, in an editorial entitled 'Loss and Gain', the writer weighed the war in the balance of conflicting feelings and found that what he termed 'the cleansing fires of war' were purgative fires for the British Empire as a whole, including its Irish corner:

> Spiritually and morally, the British Empire is infinitely the better for the war. Knowledge by suffering entereth, and already the war has done two great things for us. It has established a bond of brotherhood between all classes. They have had the same hardships and bereavements in the same cause. The peers and trade unionists who, during many profitless years, are now binding one another's wounds in the trenches, and facing death together in front of the same machine guns. Captains of industry have got to know the British working man better in France than they ever knew him in factories at home. For Ulster Unionists and Southern Nationalists in the Irish regiments the Somme is undoing the dismal work of the Boyne.

The writer of this almost Panglossian effusion accompanied it with a maudlin description of how 'Thousands of lads, still almost school boys have gone to their deaths ... as proud and happy as when they were leading their teams to victory at cricket or football.' The opposite extreme of the paper's moments of cold-blooded calculation, was, it seems, a mawkishness about doomed youth. The newspaper was determined, however, that there should be no shortage of youthful Irish recruits for the charnel house that it thought was so spiritually renewing for empire and country. Shirkers must play their part.

So when the *Irish Times* reflected on Irish losses in Flanders and on the 'terrible wastage of war', this did not affect its hopes for greater enlistment. It bemoaned the fact that 'the farmers' sons cannot be persuaded to enlist on any terms' (*Irish Times*, 3 August 1915). On 26 August of the same year the paper published an article on the Royal Dublin Fusiliers and the 'pluck and determination' of its men in the Dardanelles, but noted how 'there were at least 500 young men of military age on the promenade in Bray yesterday, who regarded the war as "no concern of ours".' Shop assistants who had declined to follow the colours attracted the writer's particular contempt, for 'The men in the campers at Bray, Kingstown, and Sutton are not of the class who loaf around public houses of an afternoon.' Following the mass blood-letting on the Somme, the *Irish Times* editorialized on 'Recruiting in Ireland', returning to the theme of dereliction of duty, though this time it was the Irish countryman who was the object of disapproval: 'The upper and professional classes and the working classes in the towns have done their part. They formed the three Irish Divisions. There are now yawning gaps in those Divisions and there are tens of thousands of young countrymen in Ireland who can fill them if they choose' (*Irish Times*, 30 August 1916). When conscription in Ireland became a live issue in 1918, the *Irish Times* supported its imposition against the widespread antagonism that defeated the proposal.

Any of the shopkeepers and countrymen the *Irish Times* had identified as shirkers in the war effort, if they had been minded to read the newspaper that had berated them in this way, would, despite the many articles and editorials that wrote about the war in the elevated terms of patriotism, sacrifice, honour and military glory, have had ample opportunity to consider the likely personal cost of taking 'the King's shilling'. For as well as the lengthy analyses of military advances and strategy that the *Irish Times* published throughout the conflict, there were many reports from the war fronts that made all too graphically clear what mechanized, modern war involved. Of the Second Battle of Ypres, for example, readers of the *Weekly Irish Times* could have learnt how, according to a dispatch from the front, from Sir John French,

> ... the fighting [had] been characterised on the enemy's side by a cynical and barbarous disregard of the well-known usages of civilised war and a flagrant defiance of the Hague Convention [of 1899 for the pacific settlement of international disputes]. All the scientific resources of Germany have apparently been brought into play to produce a gas of so virulent and poisonous a nature that any human being brought into contact with it is first paralysed and then meets with a lingering and agonising death. (*Weekly Irish Times*, 17 July 1915)

It was all too obvious that trench warfare was a monstrous experience. By mid-August, as Associated Press reports of German atrocities came in (with stories of human shields, the shooting of prisoners and of the wounded, the use of flat-nosed bullets to chill the blood), the *Irish Times* felt itself obliged to remind its readers, in a less than convincing fashion (in an editorial entitled 'Germany Besieged'), of the permanence of the human spirit amid the horrendous novelties of industrialized warfare:

> Sometimes when we read of the havoc created by the new engines of destruction – the monstrous guns, the torpedoes, the gas and flame projectors, and all the other horrid paraphernalia with which our enemies have made us familiar – we are apt to forget that success in war is, after all, an affair of the spirit. (*Irish Times*, 19 August 1915)

Reports in the *Irish Times* were in fact giving its readers to understand that modern technology was affecting both the conduct and the nature of war. It noted how wireless telegraphy had 'found itself' in this war. 'There is no danger that it will ever suffer again from indifference or neglect of British governments. It is today an essential part of the equipment of Empire' (*Irish Times*, 27 July 1915). In August of the same year, under the headline 'Science and War', a Sir Oliver Lodge was reported celebrating long-range telegraphy as a 'true contribution to science ... which will outlast all the engines of destruction' (*Irish Times*, 14 August 1915).

Among such 'engines of destruction' was the submarine; and Ireland was caught up in the aftermath of a grim lesson on how this craft, with its deadly cargo of torpedoes, was a new element in warfare which placed civilians directly in the line of fire. The sinking by a German submarine of the *Lusitania* passenger liner off the Old Head of Kinsale on 7 May 1915, with the then reported loss of 1,502 persons aboard, provoked extensive journalistic coverage. This was in some ways a rerun of the reportage of the *Titanic* disaster, but this time laced with fury that human agency was involved. There were the same graphic accounts from those who had been rescued, along with affecting descriptions of the survivors limping into railway stations in Cork and Dublin. The *Irish Times* had no doubt that this was a villainous act of a villainous enemy: 'These men, women and children have been murdered deliberately and with forethought' (*Irish Times*, 9 May 1915). Among those who had perished was Sir Hugh Lane. In an 'Appreciation' of the life of this philanthropic art dealer and connoisseur, Thomas Bodkin (subsequently director of the National Gallery of Ireland) wrote of a 'most foul and wanton murder' (*Irish Times*, 10 May 1915). What had been termed 'German frightfulness' against Belgian civilians in British polemics in the early months of the war, was showing its lethal hand close to home. The *Irish Times* would have further cause to employ the term when Germany targeted British citizens from the air.

From early in the war, the concept of aerial combat became a staple of commentary, but it was 1915, the year of the Zeppelin raids on England that brought home how all-out industrial war, with technology adding new instruments of destruction to national armouries, threatened civilian populations, as well as those in military uniform. These attacks, fulfilling anxious pre-war prophecies, had begun on 19 January and continued sporadically throughout that year and the next. At first, the *Irish Times* treated these as pinpricks that, even after a raid in May which left 7 dead and 35 injured, would serve only to increase British recruitment (in fact the Zeppelin raids had been causing high levels of local panic in Britain). It noted, too, how the Zeppelins attracted fascinated spectators. By 4 September, supplying details of a Zeppelin raid on London, the paper referred, however, to 'the murder that flies by night'. Following the most deadly raid on London of 8 September, the tone darkened markedly as the paper commented in its editorial 'Air Raids': 'It [aerial bombardment of a city] is a form of military activity that is developing in parallel degree with the increasing importance of the submarine in naval warfare. In the next war operations on terra firma will hardly count' (*Irish Times*, 11 September 1915). On 15 September the paper welcomed a Sir Percy Scott to the central gunnery defence of London to counteract 'the most remorseless weapon in the whole history of warfare'. The *Irish Times* felt sure, however, that Britain was learning to combat 'the novel menace of the submarine and will deal with the Zeppelin'. The paper, indeed, felt sufficiently confident about this to publish on 24 September a graphic cockpit-eye account by a Zeppelin commander, the ace-pilot Heinrich Mathy, on the most recent raid on London, that of 8 September. It came by way of the New York correspondent of the *Daily Mail* who had telegraphed about the account given to the correspondent of the *New York World* in Germany. In this piece, which arrived so circuitously in Dublin by way of the international network of news distribution technology had developed, *Irish Times* readers were supplied with one of the earliest descriptions of what was to become a tragic commonplace of twentieth-century conflicts: an aerial assault by night on an inadequately defended city. The commander described how:

> As the sun sank in the west we were a considerable distance out over the North Sea. In the distance we could see the Thames, which points the way to London. The English can darken London as much as they want, but they can never eradicate or cover the Thames.

Guided by the river to the heart of London, the commander tries to bomb the Bank of England and Tower Bridge. Over Liverpool Street Station, he drops his final load of bombs:

> I shouted 'Rapid Fire!' through the tube and the bombs rained down. There was a succession of detonations and bursts of fire, and I could see that they had hit well, and caused apparently great damage, which has been confirmed by reliable reports we have since received. Flames burst forth in several places in that vicinity. Having dropped all my bombs I turned my airship towards home.

Mathy left 22 Londoners dead, 87 injured and considerable destruction behind him as he flew east. In October 1916 he himself would die just north of London when his craft went down in flames.

The *Irish Times* accompanied Mathy's eyewitness account of his military and aeronautical prowess with the following official caveat, in square brackets:

> [The Home Office have passed the above telegram for publication, with the comment that it contains numerous statements which are quite untrue, and one (to the effect that an anti-aircraft gun has been placed under cover of St Paul's), which can only be characterised as a falsehood, apparently invented to excuse what German aircraft are attempting to do.]

The British authorities had been exercising censorship and control of reports from the actual war fronts and from the home front since the outbreak of war. The publication of Mathy's 'Narrative' (as the headline writer termed it) with the Home Office's explicit warning made abundantly clear that in time of war newspapers had their own battle for truth in the news on their hands. The

Irish Times's editor, John Edward Healy, from early in the conflict indicated that he was alert to this. We know that he was 'a member of almost the first group of journalists to visit the Western Front' (Mark O'Brien 2008, p. 47, citing *Irish Times* obituary), no doubt keen to see for himself what conditions were like there. He clearly felt it important to inform his readers that news in wartime was no innocent thing, and that truth could be war's first victim. On 17 August 1915, in an editorial entitled 'Eye-Witness', the paper reflected on how restricted access to hard information about the progress of the war had in fact been to that date. It complained that 'until very recently war correspondents had to content themselves with rumours and anecdotes picked up from stragglers at the ports of Northern France or patients in the hospitals'. Fortunately, things had begun to improve, in the paper's estimate. 'Eye-Witness' accounts had begun to be released by the army's Press Bureau, with descriptions of the actual fighting. Even more recently, it was noted, newspaper and agency correspondents had 'cautiously' begun to base their own reports on these releases, dating their copy from 'British Headquarters' so that there was as 'close a return to the accepted idea of war correspondence' as was likely in the circumstances. The need for the army's 'Eye-Witness' was declining as messages were sent by accredited press representatives at headquarters. On 6 July 1916, in the middle of reports from the Somme, the newspaper took the trouble to consider the kind of access to information correspondents were getting to front line action. In an article entitled 'The Press Camp', the paper told how a few discreet press correspondents, 'admitted to the Army headquarters', had become sufficiently trusted to be afforded the opportunity to write 'battle pictures'. These reporters, the *Irish Times* told its readers, 'were allowed to be on the spot when the attack was launched between the Somme and the Ancre ... and were told beforehand when it would begin'. The presence of such 'embedded' war correspondents, as we would now call them, meant that their accounts could be 'battle pictures' delivered 'at the moment when such pictures are worth the drawing'. On 15 July the paper published a vivid description, recording how the soldiers of the Ulster Division sacrificed themselves for the Empire, and the Ulster Volunteer Force had 'won a name which equals any in history':

> When I saw the men emerge through the smoke and form up as if on parade, I could hardly believe my eyes. Then I saw them attack, beginning at a slow walk over no man's land, and suddenly let loose as they charged over the two front lines of enemy trenches, shouting 'No surrender, boys'. The enemy's gunfire raked them from the left, and machine guns in a village enfiladed them on the right, but battalion after battalion came out of the awful wood as steadily as I have seen them at Ballykinlar, Clandeboye or Shane's Castle.

Such a 'battle picture', by a correspondent who could 'hardly believe' his eyes, suggests that, as with the mass disasters of the modern age epitomized by the sinking of the *Titanic*, reportage was being confronted in the Great War with things that beggared credulity and required more than verbal representation. The British government grasped this fact and appointed its own official war artists from 1916 onwards; initially expected to produce propaganda material, such painters as Percy Wyndham Lewis, Paul Nash and the Irishman William Orpen were soon encouraged to supply the public with art that might offer an imaginative interpretation of the war experience, as well as provide visual reportage. As if conscious of the need for the artist's contribution at such a terrible time, on 25 July 1915 the *Irish Times* had republished an essay by the sculptor Henri Gaudier-Brzeska, first published in the London Vorticist periodical *Blast*. An avant-garde artist (and friend of T. S. Eliot), Brzeska had been killed serving as a soldier in French uniform. His essay 'Intensity of Life', 'a curiously human and pathetic document ... probably the last he wrote' (*Irish Times*, 25 July 1915), bore witness to the indestructible power of the impulse even amid 'the bursting shells, the volleys, wire entanglements, projectors, aesthetic motors, the chaos of war'.

In less than a year, in April 1916, the *Irish Times* would find itself caught up in a pitched-battle for the control of central Dublin, which would test its powers of reportage to the limit, a battle with its own artist victims and 'human and pathetic' documents.

When insurrectionists occupied key buildings in central Dublin on 24 April 1916, the *Irish Times* was at the epicentre of a battle zone. For the rebels had occupied, among other buildings, the General Post Office in the city's principal thoroughfare, and it was near that building that their leader, the poet, barrister and schoolmaster Patrick Pearse, proclaimed an Irish republic. The *Irish Times*'s editorial office was just several hundred yards from where this momentous event took place and close to Trinity College, where British forces took up positions to put down a dangerous rebellion. So their building was in the line of fire of the belligerents. From reporting and commenting on a war at a distance, the newspaper was suddenly confronted by the challenge of dealing close-up, as it were, with the phenomenon of armed conflict in the central streets of a modern city in the United Kingdom.

The paper sought to sustain publication in conditions where reporting and editorial staff were restricted to their offices because of the heavy firing in the immediate vicinity. Military censorship was imposed and the edition of the Tuesday morning was issued in reduced form at the request of the authorities. It contained a 'Proclamation' from them which stated they had 'taken active and energetic measures to cope with the situation. These measures are proceeding favourably.' As if to support such official *sang-froid*, the paper calmly observed: 'We are glad to learn that in spite of the current troubles in Dublin, the Royal Dublin Society's Spring Show will be opened today.' Further attenuated editions followed as the week unfolded, the contents of which could have been seen as undermining the show of confidence Tuesday's paper affected. On 26 April the paper included the Proclamation of Martial Law and, surely a sign of things getting serious in Dublin, the closing of all licensed premises. The next day an editorial gave full support to martial law. It recorded how 'We have all noticed the cool and almost indifferent behaviour of the well-disposed crowds in our streets during the last few days' but advised that 'the present military operations are not public entertainments, but a grim and dangerous business'. As if by its silence to give force to this assertion, the paper did not appear again until Monday, 1 May.

Newsgathering and publication were prodigiously difficult in Dublin in the final week of April 1916. There was not only censorship, martial law (imposed by the newly appointed Commander-in-Chief of the British army in Ireland, Sir John Maxwell) and immediate dangers to persons and property, but the city was cut off from contact with the outside world (the authorities had commandeered the telephone exchange and the telegraph). Other newspaper offices were immediately affected by the chaos of Easter Week (as the days of insurrection and suppression came to be known). The offices of Independent Newspapers were occupied by the rebels and the offices of the *Freeman's Journal* suffered damage from shell fire (Mark O'Brien 2008, p. 48). The *Irish Times* saw its own store in Abbey Street raided by the insurgents, and in a moment of powerful symbolism of the uneasy relationship between print media and politics, 'big reels of paper ... rolled out on the street' (*Irish Times*, 1 May 1916) to make barricades.

The renewal of publication on 1 May, with the dateline 28, 29 April, 1 May, gave the *Irish Times* the opportunity to publish a considered editorial on all that had transpired during the previous week, culminating with the surrender of the rebels on the Saturday. It was a minatory study in denunciation. The paper was grimly satisfied that a 'criminal adventure' had largely been snuffed out by a superior force. 'The Dublin Insurrection of 1916', it confidently predicted, would 'pass into history with the equally unsuccessful insurrections of the past. It will have only the distinction – that it was more daringly and systematically planned and more recklessly invoked, than any of its predecessors.' The paper did admit that there may have been a 'certain desperate courage' in the 'wretched men' who had so revolted, but it reserved honour in the matter to all those who had helped put down an insurrection that would 'leave behind it a long trail of sorrow, poverty and shame'. The editorial reached a severe conclusion in a trope that drew on colonialist rhetoric as old as the conquest itself:

> The State has struck, but its work has not finished. The surgeon's knife has been put to the corruption in the body of Ireland, and its course must not be stayed until the whole malignant growth is removed.

Arguably, this unflinching statement (which was matched in its intensity of feeling by the antagonism expressed against the rebels in the nationalist *Irish*

Independent) was not a direct call for the series of executions by firing squad following military tribunals that began on 4 May, but the *Irish Times* did not resile from its stern position, nor from its medical metaphor, even as the executions took their ghastly toll. By 6 May, when eight men had died, the *Irish Times* defended itself from the *Freeman's Journal*'s accusation that it was instigating an Alvar campaign in Ireland. It insisted: 'We said, and we repeat, that the surgeon's knife of the State must not be stayed "until the whole malignant growth has been removed".' On 11 May the *Irish Times* censured the *Freeman's Journal*: 'Confronted amid the ruins of Princes Street [where its offices had been], with the fruits of its timidity and nervelessness, it is timid and nerveless still'; but by 11 May its own stance had moderated somewhat, because in its editorial, 'Rebellion and Settlement', it stated solemnly: 'We hope sincerely that no further executions may be found necessary, though we hope also that no convicted murderer will escape the penalty of his crime.'

Punishment for crime, the rooting out of sedition, the insanity of the action undertaken by the insurrectionists was the tenor of the reaction of the *Irish Times* to the fateful events of Easter Week. By late May and June its focus became the political consequences of what had occurred. But throughout those extraordinary events the newspaper had been more than a mouthpiece for the unionist and loyalist interest in the city and the country. The *Irish Times* was a newspaper that knew it had an extraordinary story to cover. Indeed, the editorial of the edition of 25 April, which had appeared in reduced form, began: 'This newspaper has never been published in stranger circumstances than those which obtain today. An attempt has been made to overthrow the constitutional government of Ireland.' The editor and staff could scarcely have considered themselves newspapermen if the *Irish Times* had restricted itself to fulminations against all and sundry. They bravely tried to grasp the journalistic opportunity that had befallen them.

By 13 May the company had gathered sufficient information and reportage, photographs and comment to issue a bumper edition of the *Weekly Irish Times*. This attempted a full narrative of the event, with reports from the different theatres of engagement between the rebels and the British (some of these drew on reports that had already been published in the daily paper). Photographs of the 13 leaders put human faces on the insurrectionists, some of whom had already paid the ultimate price for their actions. The story of how Joseph Plunkett, poet and rebel, had married Grace Gifford in his prison cell before his execution added pathos to the extensive coverage, which helped lay the basis for a volume on the rebellion which the company would publish a year later.

Some of the most colourful reportage was of the looting of department stores in central Dublin, as the urban poor took advantage of a breakdown in everyday law and order, but the predominant sense in this edition was that a functioning modern city in the United Kingdom and a seat of government had been brought to the point of near-collapse in a military putsch led by a small body of armed and determined men and women. A new kind of warfare, now known as urban guerrilla warfare, though the wearing of uniforms by the insurgents was a romantic anachronism, was being enacted for the first time in a European city (the *Irish Times* had published a report about the suppression of the Paris commune in 1871, an event that to a degree anticipated what in the twentieth century would be one pattern of warfare, an urban uprising put down by superior force).

It was in fact a day-to-day account of the Rising published as 'A Citizen's Diary' on 2 May that gave the most tangible sense of the almost surreal conditions that the Rising had fomented in the city. Random images in this diary, that of a Mr J. R. Clegg, function as metonyms of the widespread subversion of customary order that had taken place: 'a woman in an old dressing gown sits in the open, on a chair, placidly reading a book, taking no interest in the looting that is progressing around'; 'From across the street, towards the G.P.O., come several volunteers with wooden trays of jam rolls, buns etc. evidently for the garrison'; on the north side of St Stephen's Green a 'deserted tramcar on this route has its glass riddled by bullets. A severed electric wire lies in coils on the ground'; 'On a street corner lies a man's felt hat. The owner, it is stated, "was shot there this morning".'

A powerful impression develops of a city under a new kind of siege, with all participants caught up in a deadly game for which the rules have not yet been written (the attempt in St Stephen's Green to dig trenches as if in emulation of the more formalized warfare then raging in Europe, seems oddly out-of-key in the general mayhem). The diarist summed up in a way that bespoke how unsettling the whole week had been, how hard to comprehend as something that had happened in real time:

> The severance for such a length of time of all communications with places outside the city; the complete collapse of communications inside; the absence of the daily papers; the disappearance of the police; the cessation of the tramcar and other wheeled traffic; the problem of getting house supplies; the total stoppage of business; the vague and often alarming reports of casualties; the paucity of authentic information; the unfamiliar and menacing detonations, night and day, of rifles, Maxims, and the heavy guns – and many other associated features of the time gave a unprecedentedly strange colour to the daily life of Dublin.

Yeats was famously to characterize the Easter Rising as the birth of a 'terrible beauty'. If it was that, it was a birth whose coming to term involved a new kind of modern warfare that blurred the distinction between the battle front and the home front, between civil society and military action.

The Great War itself, both more conventional in its methods and vastly more terrible in its human cost than the insurrection in Dublin, because of the immense destructive power of modern armaments and technology, dragged on until 11 November 1918. The *Irish Times*, unambiguously supportive of the Allies to the last, despite those recurrent sacrifices, which were proudly if poignantly registered in its columns, on 11 November greeted the collapse of the German Empire with a mordant summary (in an editorial entitled 'A Headless Empire': 'The whole tradition of blood-and-iron has perished in confusion and anarchy.') The paper was concerned that any disorder in a defeated Germany should be contained, for if it were not, it 'would be a calamity not only for herself but for the world'. Nonetheless, 11 November was 'a red-letter day in the progress of mankind'. An awareness of the world historical significance of imperial disintegration in central and eastern Europe helped to define the zeitgeist as hostilities ended, and the *Irish Times* caught the general mood when it expressed the hope that 'the danger of Bolshevism in Germany' was being averted. For events in Russia were beginning to threaten a new kind of tyranny that could rise out of the ashes of the old in Europe.

It was aware, too, that other forces were at work in the world which would define the future. On 27 December 1917 the paper had celebrated the recent taking of Jerusalem by British forces, following the Balfour Declaration in November of that year, which had promised British government support for the establishment of a Jewish homeland in Palestine. The paper had observed then that 'The deep-seated pride of Jews all over the world is daily becoming more manifest.' But it was conscious that the international scope and cosmopolitanism of Jewry was not the whole story, for Zionism was indisputably a manifestation of the recrudescent nationalisms that also were helping to define the zeitgeist as the war reached its conclusion. The *Irish Times* had reminded its readers of the Jew's 'passionate fidelity to the ancient shrine and ancient traditions of his race' and observed, 'Today he is linking himself anew to the old Jewish Kingdom.' Such rhetoric of race and soil was certainly not foreign to the Irish nationalism that had helped to foment the Easter Rising, and the sentiments it expressed were settled features of Irish national feeling. In the immediate post-war years the paper's unionist and conservative ideology would be confronted by a militant Irish nationalism that was intent that the country's right to self-determination would be heard and accepted. For twentieth-century modernity, as well as opening up the world through mass communications and technological innovations of one kind and another, which had allowed a 'world war' to be fought, would also be the era when the nation state proved its enduring tenacity in the face of universalizing tendencies.

3

The *Irish Times* and the Nation State

In April 1921 W. B. Yeats began work on a sequence poem that would eventually carry the title 'Nineteen Hundred and Nineteen'. On its first publication, however, it was entitled 'Thoughts upon the Present State of the World'. Its central preoccupation was how the long period of Victorian peace was giving way to a time of violent transition. Readers of newspapers in Britain and Ireland and the many families in the United Kingdom who had lost loved ones in the Great War, had they read Yeats's poem in 1921 might have been surprised by the way his work, so determined to be a commentary on the current state of things world-wide, seemed to elide history by shifting from the broad vistas of the Victorian *Pax Britannica* to the local skirmishes of the Anglo-Irish War of 1919–21 and its atrocities and counter-atrocities. The Great War seems absent from the poem's apocalyptic historiography. Yet the poem, it can be argued, as it contemplates, in a kind of aggravated horror, the condition of the world in the immediate aftermath of the Great War, speaks, in its profound awareness of how one age can give way to another in the long history of humankind, of what it is to live in a period of fundamental transition, one greater than that between peace and war. And the poem identifies that transition as involving in 1919 a shift from universalizing tendencies at work in society to the shaping forces of native atavisms. The economist John Maynard Keynes expressed the same sense of things less hectically but no less powerfully when he wrote of this stage of human history: 'We have been moved almost beyond endurance, and need rest. Never in the lifetime of men now living has the universal element in the soul of man burnt so dimly' (cited Bardon 1992, p. 466).

Yet as if to give the lie to Yeats's vision of the universal in the affairs of man giving way in 1919 to the inflamed passions of autochthonous memory and feeling, the columns of the *Irish Times* (as did those of newspapers in various parts of the globe) in the winter after the Great War contained many reports of how disease in a modern mass society was no respecter of national borders. The influenza pandemic of the winter of 1918/19 was a reminder that internationalism could not be sacrificed to too narrow a commitment to the self-determination of nations. Public notices about the affliction had appeared in the paper as early as July 1918 but, as autumn turned to winter, reports of its effects and death notices made all too clear that the world was now at war with an enemy as deadly as any of the forces that had been unleashed by the Great War. February and October in 1918 and February and March in 1919 were when Ireland was most affected by the pandemic. By 8 March 1919 the *Weekly Irish Times* noted the global impact of the disease: 'The ravages of influenza this winter have had a world-wide effect that is still apparent.' And on 8 April 1919 the *Irish Times* editorialized on 'International Health'. It noted how 'The problems associated with the establishment of peace have engrossed men's mind to such an extent that the International Health Conference which is sitting in Cannes has almost escaped notice.'

The Versailles Peace Conference, which was concerned with the political consequences of the recently ended war, had begun in January and its controlling principle (promulgated vigorously by the US President, Woodrow Wilson) was the right of nations to self-determination. By contrast, the Cannes conference, to the *Irish Times*'s approval, was international in outlook. It had discussed the immediate establishment of a Central Health Bureau. The paper commented: 'If such a Bureau had existed last year, the medical profession throughout the world would have been in a better position to cope with the influenza epidemic.' (*Irish Times*, 8 April 1919) The *Irish Times* hoped that each national Red Cross Society would 'launch a great health crusade in its own country'.

By April 1919 a crusade of a different kind had entered on a new and terrible phase in Ireland, which made such international perspectives seem strangely quixotic and remote, however much they could be defended on rational grounds. For January 1919, as the Peace Conference began its deliberations, saw the first shots of what would become the Anglo-Irish War, fought by an Irish guerrilla army against British forces with the intent of establishing the Irish Republic Patrick Pearse had idealistically declared on 24 April 1916. The *Irish Times*, as we saw, had deployed a medical metaphor then, to excoriate armed separatist action by a revolutionary minority. From its point of view in 1919 to 1921, the cancer that had presented in 1916, metastasized virulently, putting the body politic at possibly terminal risk.

The insurrection of 1916 had had profound consequences for the government of Ireland. As early as May 1916 the *Irish Times* had recognized that the Rising had affected the terms of Anglo-Irish relations in very dangerous ways. The resignation of the Chief Secretary, Augustine Birrell, and other members of the Irish administration had set in motion Lloyd George's negotiations about the future governance of the country, in which, as the *Irish Times* had it on 4 June: 'The rebellion has been defeated, but the spirit of protest survives, fiercer we think, and even more bitter than before.' Southern unionism was in grave danger in such a climate and the newspaper was at pains to emphasize its claims to a sympathetic hearing. For unionists 'in proportion to their numbers ... [had] given more fighting men and better brains to the great war than any other class in Ireland, or, perhaps, in the empire'.

Even in 1916 there was an air of poignant insecurity in such utterances, as there was when on 6 June the paper declared: 'A scheme that ignored the claims of the Unionists of the three southern provinces would invite disaster, and we shall resist any such scheme by every means in our power.' On 27 June an editorial damned Home Rule without Ulster (which Lloyd George envisaged) as 'national suicide', for

> If an Irish Parliament is to escape disaster, the extreme conservatism of the South must be balanced by the progressive spirit of the North. In a word, the permanent partition of Ireland is inconceivable, and if it were conceivable, it would open a prospect hardly less terrible than the subjection of our whole country to the Prussian armies.

In the event, Lloyd George's negotiations failed and the country entered on a period of great uncertainty, with the country's constitutional future once again cast into the melting pot of conflicting aspirations. From 25 July 1917 to 4/5 April 1918 an Irish Home Rule Convention was held in Dublin (meeting in Trinity College), seeking to square the circle of the Irish political conundrum.

The convention was probably doomed from the start since Sinn Féin, which was taking on the mantle of the kind of Irish separatist republicanism that had made its presence so spectacularly felt in 1916, chose not to attend. Eamon de Valera had won a by-election victory in East Clare in the summer of 1917 as the Irish Parliamentary Party's star waned, so what was evidently an increasingly significant voice in Irish politics was not heard at the convention's many meetings. A moving spirit in establishing the convention, who would in fact chair its deliberations, was the progressive Unionist Horace Plunkett, which, as Nicholas Allen has surmised (Allen, 2003, p. 78), probably explains why the *Irish Times*, before the convention assembled, gave ample space to George Russell to set out his vision of Irish Home Rule. The paper stated on 26 May: 'We take no responsibility for Mr Russell's opinions, many of which we are unable to accept ... It is important that, on the eve of this National Convention, Irish Unionists should have understanding of the various currents of Nationalist opinion which this Memorandum affords.' In three contributions Russell mapped out for a unionist readership key aspects of contemporary opinion on the national question (agreeing, it can be noted, with the *Irish Times*'s own analysis that progressive industrial energy was a preserve of the northern counties). Significantly, Russell's intervention in the debate about Ireland's future seemed to take for granted that the forces of unionism were now arrayed against not the Irish Parliamentary Party (whose time, it is implied, was well and truly over), but against the vital energy of Sinn Féin. Perceptive unionist readers of Russell's idealistic tract perhaps would have been inclined to view this polarity as one that could not easily be managed in the dominion status Russell envisaged for the country as an optimal outcome of constitutional negotiations between Irish and British interests.

Be that as it may, Russell laboured earnestly, but to no avail, as a committee-man among the abundant papers, memoranda, agendas and reports that the convention generated. By December 1917, wearied by what he saw as the intransigence of northern unionism, and all too aware of the crippling absence of Sinn Féin in the discussion, Russell wrote a telling letter to the *Irish Times*. Entitled 'The New Nation', this lamented how the convention had revealed the deep fissures in understanding that divided Irishmen. Unionist and nationalist did not appreciate the force of opponents' arguments, the depth of feeling that supported them, nor did they respect each other as fellow countrymen. In a telling sentence, Russell stated that he was convinced that Irish enmities were 'perpetuated because we live by memory rather than hope'. Russell followed up this missive, published on 19 December, with a letter composed on Christmas Day and printed in the *Irish Times* on 27 December, which raised his plea for Irish mutual understanding to a spiritual plane, where forgiveness might enter the moral equation of Irish conflict, to allow unity to prevail in a nation riven by 'an eternity of opposites'. The letter had a distinct air of an indulgence in wish fulfilment.

As if to dispel that mood in advance, the letter of 19 December was marked by gloomy prescience. For Russell had grasped that the blood sacrifice of the Easter Rising had set in question for many the vastly bloodier sacrifice of Irishmen in the King's uniform and how survivors of the Great War would be treated in Ireland when they returned from action. 'I ask', he wrote, 'our national extremists in what mood do they propose to meet those who return, men of temper as strong as their own? Will these endure being termed traitors to Ireland?' Anticipating that the welcome to be given to the demobbed soldiery would be hostile, Russell concluded his letter with a challenging poem entitled 'To the Memory of Some I Knew Who Are Dead and Who Loved Ireland'. In this he set in apposition the names of dead Irish volunteers to the British army with those of key figures who had been executed in Dublin after the Easter Rising. Yet each group is afforded equal respect in the poem as the poet longed for a '... confluence of dreams/That clashed together in our night,/ One river born of many streams ...'. He apostrophized the Irish dead in the Great War in poignant terms:

> You who have fought on fields afar
> That other Ireland did you wrong
> Who said you shadowed Ireland's star,
> Nor gave you laurel wreath nor song.

Russell's moral balancing act in this poem must have been troubling for many of the *Irish Times*'s unionist readers. They would certainly have been gratified to have a well-known nationalist writer and poet pay due tribute to the Irish fallen; but that this involved the names of Patrick Pearse, Thomas MacDonagh and James Connolly (whom Russell dubbed 'my man') being afforded equal veneration must have seemed a step too far for many of them in Russell's call for a 'confluence of dreams' few of them desired. On 28 December 1917 a Dublin correspondent made clear that he wanted none of Russell's moral algebra. He reminded readers that Easter 1916 had involved 'foul murder' and grieving relatives. To forgive on their behalf would involve, he stated bluntly, 'the cheapest kind of vicarious Christianity'.

Russell's articles and letters in late 1917 were the first extended contributions by a notable Irish writer in the columns of the newspaper. As such, they can be seen to anticipate how in later decades the newspaper would offer a platform to writers and critics who would provide a dissenting voice in the monolithic cultural consensus that underpinned an independent Irish state after 1922. Indeed, Russell's letter of 19 December anticipated in its detail some of what would be a recurrent theme of significant dissentient opinion when the new state, which was established in 1922, tended to define itself in markedly ethnic terms as Gaelic and Catholic. For Russell made it axiomatic, in his plea for parity of esteem for the various strands that constituted Irish national life, that none could claim to exercise political and cultural hegemony by reason of its indigenous status. For Ireland, in Russell's view, was a composite nation formed by its history of invasion and settlement: 'It would be difficult to find even in the Western Coast a family which has not lost ... its Celtic purity of race. The character of all is fed from many streams which have mingled in them and given them a new distinctiveness.'

Russell's idealistic hopes for an Ireland in which all strands of national life would harmoniously co-operate were scarcely realized and the five years following the publication of his idealistic articles, letters and poem in the *Irish Times* would see Irish division underlined by mass agitation, violence, partition and civil war. That the use of direct action as epitomized in the Easter Rising had taken firm hold in twentieth-century Ireland was quickly made evident once again in April 1918, when a general strike against the possibility of military conscription being extended to Ireland closed all newspaper offices in the capital (Mark O'Brien 2008, p. 51); there was no edition of the *Irish Times* on 23 April. On the political front Sinn Féin would rout the Irish Party in the general election in December 1918, setting in motion a process that through political manoeuvring and revolutionary violence would see the *Irish Times*'s worst nightmares come to pass. For by 1922 it found itself representing the southern Irish unionist interest in what was, in effect, a small nation state carved out of the United Kingdom, which left six northern counties of the island still under British jurisdiction.

The Anglo-Irish War, which began with shots fired in January 1919 by a small group of republican mavericks acting on their own behalf, initially involved sporadic acts of violence conducted without much sense of central planning or overall strategy. By mid-1920, however, the number of such attacks and their wide dispersal in countryside and town meant that what was occurring was to all intents and purposes a revolutionary war. Accordingly, on 14 July 1920 the *Irish Times* recognized that a watershed in Irish affairs was fast approaching. In an editorial entitled 'The State of Ireland', the paper advised that all efforts to apply Home Rule for Ireland should be abandoned to allow for British authority to be reinstated as 'a prelude to negotiating an all-Ireland settlement'. The leader writer, in grimly Manichean mood, judged: 'Then, and then only, can [Ireland] escape the choice between a republic and re-conquest. Nature abhors a vacuum. If British law ceases to exist in Ireland – and the rattle is in its throat now – the laws of an Irish republic will take its place.'

In November 1920 that vacuum was to be filled not by Nature but by an act of guerrilla ruthlessness that made it fully clear to the British authorities and to those like the majority of readers of the *Irish Times* that they in truth faced a deadly enemy in what had come to be known as the Irish Republican Army (IRA).

On Sunday 21 November the IRA, under the direction of Michael Collins, killed 13 men and injured six others in Dublin in an attack aimed at breaking the British intelligence services in the city. Three Irishmen in British custody on the same day were shot, while, it was alleged, trying to escape. That afternoon Croke Park, Dublin headquarters of the Gaelic Athletic Association (GAA), where a football match was in progress, was the scene of a British Army atrocity when soldiers fired on the crowd, killing 12 people (one a player on the Tipperary team). The day went into popular memory as 'Bloody Sunday'.

The *Irish Times* was appalled by the day's events (supplying, indeed, a vivid report of the Croke Park outrage), but was most exercised by the immediate danger to British rule posed by Collins's coup. It warned in an editorial on 22 November: 'A country whose capital can be the scene of fourteen [*sic*] callous and cowardly murders on one Sunday morning, has reached a nadir of moral and political degradation.' On 25 November the paper, under the headline 'Law and Murder', declared: 'For the time being, the suppression of murder and the restoration of law are the beginning and end of the Irish problem.' The next day the *Irish Times* gave ample space to report how Dublin had shut its shops as crowds lined the streets in respect for Collins's English victims as their coffins were taken to the boat for England. It was as if the newspaper was trying to convince itself that what it termed in a headline a 'Conspiracy to Smash the British Empire' was a *conspiracy* and not a movement that was increasingly attracting mass support in the country. There was ample evidence in the contents of its own columns in November and December 1920 that something more fundamental was in train. For day by day there were accounts of IRA actions and of reprisals taken by British troops. On 30 November the paper reported on the ambush and killing of 15 auxiliary policemen (the auxiliary wing of the Royal Irish Constabulary had been established to help meet the IRA threat) near Macroom Castle in County Cork. Vicious reprisals followed which the paper judged 'utterly wrong', but even though the *Irish Times* believed the ambush had involved between 80 and 100 men (in fact it was perpetrated by about 40), it still invoked the concept of a clandestine enemy: 'Blood and fire continue to mark the course of the insane conspiracy that is speeding Ireland to her ruin.' By 6 December the paper was driven to include the term 'truce' in its lexicon, indicating that it knew that the British authorities were confronted by much more than a 'conspiracy' in Ireland, but was as yet uncertain about with whom such a truce could be negotiated. In the absence of such, in early 1921 the paper continued to insist, as it had done through much of 1920, that the rule of law was of paramount importance in a country where martial law had had to be declared in counties Cork, Tipperary, Kerry and Limerick in December 1920.

Frequent reports in the paper in 1920 and 1921 gave its readers a painful sense of how law and order were being overwhelmed. Grim accounts of attacks on police stations and military convoys vied for space with reports of reprisals by the military and the auxiliary police, particularly in the latter half of 1920 when the specially recruited police force dubbed the Black and Tans was savagely operational (the sacking of Cork city by auxiliaries and Black and Tans in December 1920 being a particularly egregious example of official lawlessness). That the 'war' was often being fought on the basis of opportunist attacks, in which local knowledge and local animosities fed into a more general threat to established order, was evinced in distressing stories of random kidnappings, abductions and killings by armed groups whose motives went unexplained. A report on 6 December is typical. It ominously stated how Cork's chief constable had been kidnapped while home on leave, when a 'party of armed men took him into custody, and had him conveyed to a destination unknown'. The same issue, under a headline 'Labourer Shot Near Skerries' (*Irish Times*, 6 December 1920), reported on the hunting down by armed men of a young quarry labourer and trade union official in his mother's home. He had been 'an arbitrator in the Republican courts', a participant in the 1916 Rising, and an ardent student of Irish; he had chosen to stay with his mother after being on the run for two weeks, away from his wife and family who lived in the town. He was shot dead trying to escape from a back window 'in the presence of his terror-stricken mother, brother, and sisters'. It was clear that cold-blooded murder was a weapon employed by Crown forces as well as the IRA, in a bitter and embittering struggle.

Some of these stories, while giving the *Irish Times*'s readers grounds for anxious fears that parts of the country were close to anarchy, were also windows on a republican culture that was increasingly consolidating itself, with its own rules of engagement, moral universe, sense of legitimacy, shibboleths and symbols. Drawing on traditions that went back to the Catholic Defenders of the late eighteenth century, to the United Irishmen, to the various land agitators of the nineteenth century, to the Fenians and the Irish Republican Brotherhood, modern Irish republicanism was forging a moral community and political identity that would consecrate the violence of 1916 and of the Anglo-Irish War as foundational achievements of a generation that was challenging the power of the British Empire and clearing the way for Irish independence. For all its reportage of the violent daily events in its columns during this period, there is little sense that the *Irish Times*, still reflecting the cultural values of the increasingly anxious southern Protestant community, had any true understanding of what inspired those it simply reckoned to be murderers and criminals. In that editorial of 6 December 1920 (an issue which, as we noted, contained its typical complement of reported violent incident), while it mooted the possibility of a truce, it still clung to an ideal of law and order which bore little relationship to a conflict involving a guerrilla war of attrition and state-sponsored reprisals: 'there cannot be truce with crime,' it admonished. 'With or without the help of the Irish people, the fight against moral and political anarchy must be fought to the end.'

In the event, the battle between the British state and its armed forces against revolutionary Irish republicanism was not fought to an end. A truce of the summer of 1921 led to protracted negotiations so that a treaty was agreed between the government of the United Kingdom and representatives of those who had fought and supported the guerrilla struggle. The Anglo-Irish Treaty granted dominion status within the British Commonwealth to the 26 counties of southern Ireland. Northern Ireland was to remain under British rule, exercised through a devolved parliament that had been made possible by the Government of Ireland Act, passed in December 1920. The *Irish Times* had vigorously opposed the Government of Ireland Bill, since it would place southern unionists in the invidious position of being a small minority in whatever polity might emerge in the country. The tenor of its opposition to Irish partition suggests that it was driven by more than simply self-interest. Rather, it sensed that partition would deliver many absurdities and create the conditions for recurrent national crises. It presciently and bitterly observed when the Ulster Unionist Council signalled its support for partition:

> In passing this Bill, it will pass a measure for the permanent division of
> Ireland, for the maintenance of sectarian strife, for the perpetuation of
> all the grotesque machinery of tri-sected railways and double judiciaries.
> It will doom the Irish people to secular unsettlement, and will convert
> thousands of law-abiding men to the cause of revolution. (*Irish Times*,
> 11 March 1920)

Less than two years later, in January 1922, in the south of Ireland the newly constituted parliament (Dáil Eireann, whose members had been elected the previous summer) voted by a small majority to accept the terms of the treaty ('a stepping stone to freedom'). Given its apocalyptic sense of what partition involved both for what was now the southern minority and for the country at large, the *Irish Times* could have merely raised its hands in horror as its worst nightmares were realized. In fact, it welcomed the Anglo-Irish Treaty with surprising grace, reckoning that it gave to the new state 'a place of profit and honour in the community of the Empire' (*Irish Times*, 9 December 1921). It avowed: 'The loyalist minority are ready to put their faith in the good-will of which Mr Arthur Griffith [one of the republican leaders who, along with Michael Collins, had negotiated the treaty] has assured them' and made clear its view that 'the Downing Street agreement offers to Ireland the greatest measure of freedom, the richest prospects of peace and progress, that ever were, or can be, within her grasp'.

Such graciousness (in what was essentially defeat for the all-Ireland unionism the *Irish Times* had almost unfailingly promulgated since its foundation in 1859) was, one assumes, sincerely motivated (though John Edward Healy, as editor, had many times over the years inveighed against the kind of outcome to the Irish imbroglio which had now come to pass). The paper's support of the Anglo-Irish Treaty was also a matter of strategy. For it feared the split of the Sinn Féin party over acceptance of the Treaty (with its leader Eamon de Valera questioning what the negotiators had achieved in London) could lead to a civil war as damaging to the country as anything that had gone before. Accordingly, when in early January the Dáil had ratified the Treaty by a mere seven votes, the *Irish Times* was unambiguous in its support of the majority. It said it could 'sympathise with Mr de Valera's honest and, no doubt, unselfish sorrow in defeat' (de Valera had led the opposition to acceptance of the treaty's provisions), but it was certain 'no man or party of men has any right to sacrifice a nation's welfare to the pursuit of an ideal' (*Irish Times*, 9 January 1922). It understood that 'any conflict in Ireland must now be civil conflict between Irishmen and Irishmen' and it earnestly hoped that de Valera would not precipitate such a catastrophe. In such circumstances the *Irish Times* took it upon itself to 'speak for the vast majority of Southern loyalists' in putting its faith in the fair-mindedness of the administration that was about to be formed. However, it could but not reflect on how great a shock to the system of the southern unionist family the new dispensation would be:

> All their old landmarks have disappeared. They have reached a point where they must break with traditions that were very dear to them. They are forced to adjust their minds to an entirely new set of ideals and ideas. They are invited to launch the ship of their hopes and fortunes upon an

uncharted sea. For the moment at any rate a wide gap seems to divide them from all the Imperial institutions which they still honour and helped to build.

Nonetheless, the newspaper – true, it might be argued, to its best traditions of a conservative patriotism – signalled its commitment to helping the new order to function. Of southern loyalists, it declared:

> To one article of faith, however, they continue to fix an unshaken mind. Ireland is their country and her future must be their future. The talk of a Babylonian exodus ... has irritated them. If they must make a new start, they prefer to make it in their own land ... The Southern loyalists will do their best to make the new settlement a success. They demand only equality of opportunity and they ask for no confidence which they are not prepared to earn.

Resigned pragmatism, of course, was also involved. This stood in striking contrast to the apocalyptic tone the paper had affected since the events of 1912 and 1916 had put the possibility of an independent Irish state firmly on the agenda. In acceding to the unfolding of events, the *Irish Times* was effectively engaging in a volte-face that was not just an expression of conservative patriotism; sound business sense was playing its part.

It was not that southern Protestantism was not at considerable risk as the new dispensation took hold. An exodus, if not of Babylonian proportions, which saw a whole people in exile, did in fact take place between 1922 and 1923. At independence, many Protestants who had served in the armed forces, or who were currently members of the police, left the country or crossed the new border for life in Northern Ireland. In Dublin, where before independence there had been about 10,000 working-class men with their dependants, the exodus was particularly marked, as the social composition of the capital's suburbs became predominantly middle class and Catholic. In other parts of the country the scattered Protestant community was directly threatened by the national revolution and subsequent Civil War. The residences of the Ascendancy were especially vulnerable, directly associated as they were with landlordism and the *ancien régime*. Between 6 December 1921 and 22 March 1923, as reported in the *Morning Post*, 192 country houses fell victim to incendiaries. Humbler Protestant folk also found themselves threatened or attacked, with County Cork accounting for a distressing number of enforced departures and fatalities. On 14 June 1923 the *Irish Times* reported that the Church of Ireland Bishop of Cork, at the Cork annual synod, had stated in some anguish: 'During the past two-and-a-half years our Church population has declined by 8 per cent ... Their houses have been burned. Destruction has moved through the land. The ruins of Ireland may well make all who really love her weep.'

In May 1922, while this lamentable process was at work, the British government raised the issue of southern Irish refugees with what then was still the Provisional Government of Ireland (this was succeeded by the Government of Ireland which came into being on 5 December 1922). The Provisional Government replied, admitting liability for compensation, owing to a 'number of persons who have arrived in Great Britain, having been driven from their homes in Ireland by intimidation, or by actual violence at the hands of disaffected persons' (*Irish Times*, 1 June 1922), but pointed out that there were those keen to discredit the new power in the land. It informed the British that they had assured a delegation from the Church of Ireland Synod as recently as 12 June that 'the Government would protect its citizens, would ensure civil and religious liberty in Ireland, and that spoliation and confiscation would be discountenanced in Ireland'. It reminded the British that what was occurring on a limited scale was significantly exceeded north of the Irish border, where 'For many months an organised campaign of violence and intimidation had been pursued against the Catholic inhabitants of Belfast and the surrounding counties of North-East Ulster. With the result that many thousands of persons have been driven from their employment, their property destroyed and looted, and in many cases the bread winners of families murdered.'

The publication the next day in the paper's columns of a statement on the position of southern loyalists, issued by the Irish Registration Bureau (Compensation Claim Committee), expressed scepticism about the new state's assertion that it would protect its citizens (though the article had as its subheading 'Protection of *British* Citizens', my italics). It listed six categories of persons who had been made refugees in the upheaval of Irish independence and civil war. The list ranged from large landowners to small traders, ex-government employees and English people who had simply made their homes in Ireland. It was noted that the 'expulsion' was not confined to Protestants, since 'The armed bands have made a special set against all those who either sent their sons to fight in the British Army, or who assisted recruiting in Ireland during the European war. In most cases these people have arrived with nothing but the clothes in which they stand up.' Though Catholic Redmondites also bore the opprobrium of republicans, it was observed that in 'some villages – notably in West Cork – nearly every Protestant trader and small farmer has been expelled at the point of a revolver, and many of their relatives have been shot'. The committee regarded the situation of 'loyalists' in southern Ireland to be so threatened that, in a fevered passage, the committee summoned the spectre of international Bolshevism to account for what it termed 'the Irish terror'.

Nonetheless, an editorial on the same day, headlined 'Southern Refugees', was strangely muted, even sanguine, about the situation. It took the Provisional Government at its word, admitting 'no doubt, there has been some political exaggeration of the exodus'. It even envisaged that within a couple of months the refugees would be able to return safely to their homes in an Ireland in which it would be an immediate duty of the administration 'to restore houses and property to all who have lost them through violence or intimidation'. How exactly the editorialist thought the many scores of country houses with their furnishings, pictures, libraries – many of which had been razed to the ground – could be restored is not clear. A note of wan wishful thinking sounded in an almost disassociated reflection on a turbulent scene.

The summer of 1922 cleared the editorial mind. On 2 October the paper published a lengthy leader on 'The Southern Minority'. This accepted that the number of Irish refugees in England was rousing British antagonism to the Free State and that the exiles were deserving of compensation. For the *Irish Times*, however, that was only 'the fringe of the problem'. The real issue was the fate of the 'very large majority of the ex-Unionists of Southern and Western Ireland' who had 'refused to go into exile'. The editorialist accepted that there was no well-organized system 'in this campaign of destruction' which had affected 'farmers and shopkeepers' as well as 'the owners of great estates and lordly mansions'. And he judged that loyalists were likely victims because they were vulnerable as wealthier members of society in a period of 'lawlessness and greed'. What could not be gainsaid was that a section of the population was being subjected to almost impossible pressures:

> Many of them have suffered grievous harm and loss. Many of them are exposed to daily and nightly danger of attack. They cling to their homes and businesses, partly, no doubt, because they dare not surrender their only means of livelihood, but partly, as we rejoice to believe, in a spirit of truest patriotism. They have not lost faith in their country's destiny.

The newspaper now demanded of the Irish government that it make good its promise to defend its citizens by bringing 'the current disorders to an end'.

The paper's editor, John Edward Healy, had good reason to demand that order be restored, for the 'Troubles' had seen him, along with a fellow employee of the paper, mistakenly arrested and threatened with immediate execution by a group of drunken auxiliary soldiers, and a bullet was shot through one of the windows of his Dublin home, presumably by republicans who disapproved of what the newspaper stood for.

As it became clear that the Provisional Government was the only bulwark in the state against what it perceived as threatened anarchy and when the new constitution created a parliamentary upper house in which the southern minority was granted significant representation, the *Irish Times*, in the first decade of independence, became a staunch if sometimes critical supporter of the ruling party, Cumann na nGaedheal. The fact that the government's economic policies in the 1920s were strikingly conservative in complexion undoubtedly helped the paper to be reconciled with, if less than fully supportive of, the new order.

Although the southern Irish minority had been depleted in the south and west and the Dublin Protestant working class was almost lost to history in this period of political and constitutional upheaval, much of the capital's Protestant middle and upper-middle class remained intact, their standing in manufacture, business and commerce, law, higher education largely undisturbed. However, there were new figures in the Dublin business world who were willing to co-operate with rising Catholic businessmen and entrepreneurs in such bodies as the Dublin Chamber of Commerce. To the Protestant Jamesons (proprietors of the principal whiskey distillery in the city) and the Guinnesses (with their famous brewery) were added in the chamber members of the Eason and Jacob families (the latter renowned for their biscuits). The Easons were Presbyterians and the Jacobs Quakers. The Catholic William Martin Murphy's son Lombard was co-opted on to the council in 1919, on the death of his father, and became president in 1924. It was to this cohort of business-orientated pragmatists (from which a number of parliamentary representatives would emerge) and others like them that the conservative *Irish Times* of the 1920s was undoubtedly pleased to direct its appeal, as well as to the middle-class Protestant lawyers, academics, clergy, teachers and to the Protestant civil servants and administrators who had chosen to remain in posts in the new dispensation. It also hoped to attract a readership among similarly placed people in the city's Catholic nationalist middle class who predominantly welcomed the country's new status. Accordingly, what might be termed conservatism with something of a green tinge characterized the paper in the first decade of the Irish nation state. And since all these groups had a stake in stability, the *Irish Times* gave its qualified support to the political party and government most able to supply it. In the 1920s the paper had a circulation that rose from 32,500 in 1920 to 36,500 by 1926 (Mark O'Brien 2008, p. 58), indicating that a dependable readership for its offerings continued to exist at a time of transition.

A measure of the depth of the paper's basic support for the new Irish administration is the *Irish Times*'s attitude to the government's largest industrial and economic investment in the 1920s: the construction of a massive hydro-electrical plant on the River Shannon at Ardnacrusha, Co. Clare. When what was termed 'The Shannon Scheme' was mooted in 1925, it met with considerable opposition, some of it coming from former unionists, who argued that the Liffey was a more appropriate river for electricity generation in the south of Ireland. In this context the *Irish Times* trod carefully.

The paper's innate economic prudence and its instinctive concern for the views of those who had represented the unionist interest in the recent past did not preclude it from giving due respect to a government it felt it had no option but to support as the dam holding back the frightening waters of chaos.

A fear of chaos was a major element in the paper's *Weltanschauung* in the 1920s. And in May 1926 chaos did, indeed, seem truly at hand in the neighbouring island of Britain when the Trades Union Congress called a general strike in defence of workers in the coal-mining industry. The *Irish Times*'s deep-dyed conservatism on economic matters, which had allowed it to see the dread hand of Bolshevism at work at home and abroad since 1917, became a reactionary jeremiad as it contemplated a ruination in Britain that could have a disastrous impact on Ireland and, even more alarmingly, on world trade. On 3 May, the day before the strike began, the paper warned that 'a general strike of a month's duration would deal a staggering blow to the very life of Great Britain' (*Irish Times*, 3 May 1926). However, the editorialist did not shrink from the prospect of class war to defeat Britain's 3,600,000 trade unionists. Though the skies might fall, the paper thundered in the notorious manner of its London namesake,

> If the alternative to a general strike is submission to the irrational demands
> of organised labour, the British Government must reject those demands
> and must win its battle with the help of a people who have not crushed
> a foreign tyranny merely to become the slaves of class tyranny at home.

When the strike ended on 12 May, the paper rejoiced in 'England's Victory', with 'the authority of the State ... vindicated' (*Irish Times*, 13 May 1926). The following day the editorialist, in a leader entitled 'The Reckoning', could not resist a turning of the victor's knife. To the charges that strikers were being victimized by employers, the editorial line was unbendingly severe: 'If this be "victimisation", those who are responsible for it are the strikers themselves. Somebody must pay the penalty of a general strike.' So spoke the voice of an unabashed class interest.

That the *Irish Times* in the 1920s was as conservative on local economic matters as it was on the broader stage of British national life was made clear as the new administration settled to the task of government. In the exiguous circumstances in which the new Irish state was seeking to balance its budgets, the paper gave its firm approval to one of the most niggardly decisions of the Free State government, a decision that would come to haunt it and which probably contributed to the defeat of the Cumann na nGaelheal party in the general election of 1932. In one of his budgets the Minister for Finance, Ernest Blythe, cut the old-age pension by a shilling per week (a 10 per cent reduction). When he proposed this draconian step, an *Irish Times* editorial offered sympathy to the minister, who 'became automatically one of the most unpopular men in the country' (*Irish Times*, 22 February 1922), while commending his economic volte-face (for 'last year's budget' had been 'ridiculous'). To its credit, the paper did advise a campaign to ensure that those improperly in receipt of the state pension (of whom the editorialist was certain there were many) should have payments cut off, to allow 'wise discrimination' for those who 'depended altogether on their weekly pensions' . However, the tone of the editorial reflected a settled conservatism of mind on economic matters that allowed it to assert: 'Mr Blythe must persist in his project.'

In the early years of independence, the *Irish Times*'s support for the Free State government as a force for political and economic stability was accompanied by a certain broadening of its sympathies in respect of Irish cultural achievement at a time when it wished to extend its readership among the Catholic nationalist middle class. The greening of the paper was never more than a pastel affair at this time but noticeable nonetheless. Sport, for example, in the Victorian, Edwardian and pre-revolutionary decades had, as well as horse-racing, meant that rugby and cricket reported on with a fine sense of Corinthian values as activities worthy of imperial subjects and gentlemen. In the 1920s the paper began to take some account of Gaelic games (hurling and football) with their mass appeal and advanced nationalist ethos. Hitherto, the paper had given notice to results of only select Gaelic fixtures (in 1915, for example, it cursorily recorded that the All Ireland football final had taken place at Croke Park in Dublin and it deigned to provide the final score). That Gaelic games could be incorporated in the *Irish Times*'s value system, although their participants might not be gentlemen of quite the kind to be found on cricket and rugby pitches, was evidenced in the paper's report on the 1922 All Ireland football final, again at Croke Park between Dublin and Tipperary. After welcoming 'a new era in Irish sport' (*Irish Times*, 17 June 1922), bred of increased co-operation between the various codes, the writer, under the curious headline 'Gaelic Athletic Pastimes', swiftly fell into the kind of military analogies that had been the staple of the *Irish Times*'s rugby reportage, to represent the game as a battle between the Pale and the Gael: in the event 'dash and vigour triumphed over art and skill'. Subsequent occasional reports in the 1920s appeared as 'Gaelic Pastimes' in the same slightly elevated rhetorical vein.

A reference to 'a new era in Irish sport' in the editorial cited above also noted how preparations for the Tailteann Games were bringing sporting bodies together in the planning.

The Tailteann Games, under the auspices of the arguably chauvinist Gaelic Athletic Association (founded in 1884), were an expression of the cultural nationalism of the period. In ancient Ireland, mythology had it, the Celtic King Lug had inaugurated an athletic festival in honour of his foster mother, Tailte. Newly independent Ireland would call together the international Irish diaspora to celebrate the country's status in a festival of athletics and other sports (but not including the 'foreign games' of rugby, soccer, field hockey and cricket). The first such event took place in Dublin in 1924.

The games were accompanied by a good deal of the Celtic flummery (druidic costumes, ceremonial arches, elaborate processions) which was the legacy of the cultural revival movement that had preceded independence. The *Irish Times* was happy to indulge this soft-focus version of Irish identity (and more nationalist pageant propaganda) and gave the proceedings full

and sympathetic coverage. It published the entire programme in advance and
noted the international dignitaries who had accepted invitations to attend,
who included eminences from as far away as Persia, as well as the American
poet Ezra Pound. On 4 August, after the weekend opening, the paper waxed
lyrical at the success of the inaugural ceremonies. It particularly welcomed how
the Games had brought our little State into the stream of world affairs and
continued: 'The elevated tenor of this effusion was not affected by the fact that
Eamon de Valera, on behalf of Sinn Féin, had boycotted the Tailteann Games.

While the games were in progress, the Dublin Horse Show took place at the
grounds of the Royal Dublin Society at Ballsbridge, in Dublin. The *Irish Times*
was pleased to link this event, with its Ascendancy associations and traditions,
with the Tailteann Games, reckoning the two had 'joined hands' (*Irish Times*,
5 August 1924) in a city where 'the gloom of revolution' was 'passing away';
and on 16 August, in an editorial entitled 'Sport in Ireland', as the paper
judged that 'The Tailteann Games have given a tremendous impetus to Irish
sport', it also welcomed the MCC cricket team to Dublin to play against the
Gentlemen of Ireland. The paper saw in all this an earnest of an eirenic future
(blithely failing to consider how the issue of 'foreign games' must rumble on for
decades): 'In every aspect of athletics we seem to be entering a period of revival,
which political differences are powerless to prevent. It is a happy omen for the
future; for where sport is honoured there can be no room for despair.'

The Tailteann Games also sponsored a variety of cultural events. There
were musical concerts and art displays. Prizes for literature were awarded for
work by Irish writers, including for those who published in English. By so
doing, the organizing committee was acknowledging that, against the strident
voices of some ideologues who denied national standing to literature other
than that composed in the Irish language, what was then termed Anglo-Irish
literature was a legitimate aspect of the native culture. The *Irish Times*, which
in the pre-independence period had tended to treat the literature produced in
English by Irish men and women as simply a branch of English literature (a
view Professor Edward Dowden of Trinity College had zealously propagated),
in the 1920s began to change its tune, aligning it with the position taken by
the Tailteann committee and with others who saw in the provenance of Irish
literature in English a kind of litmus test of the cultural values of the new
state. In treating Anglo-Irish literature as a distinctly native phenomenon in
the 1920s, the *Irish Times* was, therefore, not only seeking to attract a liberal
nationalist readership, but making (whether it fully realized this or not) an
ideological point about cultural identity in the new Ireland.

A series of 28 articles published in 1923 under the heading 'Some Irish
Artists' suggests that the paper had deliberately chosen to give prominence
to Irish cultural production, broadly conceived, at the new state's inception.
Among the painters, sculptors, composers, workers in glass entered in this

mini-pantheon assembled pseudonymously by 'Bruyere', were distinguished figures like the painter Sir William Orpen, the composer Herbert Hamilton Harty, and such literary ex-patriots as George Bernard Shaw and the critic Robert Lynd, who, like Shaw, plied his trade in London. All these individuals in various ways were products of Protestant Ireland, as were some of the more local figures included in the series, such as the dramatist Lennox Robinson, the painter Paul Henry and the poet Seumas O'Sullivan. However, the Catholic nationalist majority was also at work in the Irish cultural sphere, as evidenced by the inclusion of Austin Clarke, whom Bruyere evoked as 'one of the more distinguished of the younger Irish poets' (*Irish Times*, 15 September 1923), and whose verse was permeated, the writer sensed, with the 'Gaelic spirit'; for 'his writing breathes the tradition and spirit of native Ireland'.

Bruyere clearly envisioned Irish cultural achievement in broad church terms (though it was a male church). His purview even extended to James Joyce, whose *Ulysses*, published in 1922, had been admired by very few; it was deemed by many to be obscene, drawing the attention of censors in the United Kingdom and in the United States. Bruyere's assessment of Joyce as an 'Irish Artist' was cautious enough, but brave in its recognition of true literary power: 'Whether one likes or dislikes his work, one cannot fail to be impressed by its force ...' (*Irish Times*, 5 May 1923). W. B. Yeats, though, could be celebrated unambiguously as 'the greatest living poet writing in the English language'. When Yeats was awarded the Nobel Prize for Literature in November 1923, the newspaper wrote of the former republican agitator, nationalist and recently appointed senator in the Irish parliament's upper house, with unabashed enthusiasm. 'This prize', an editorial entitled 'The Poet's Crown' gave its readers to know, 'is the highest honour that can be won by a man of letters, and Irishmen throughout the world will rejoice that the genius of one of their countrymen has been crowned by its gift' (*Irish Times*, 15 November 1923). The writer of the editorial was at pains to make a political and a cultural point at this historic moment in the poet's and the nation's life:

> His success is a national, as well as personal, triumph, and it constitutes a fitting sequel to the recent admission of the Free State to membership of the League of Nations; for although Mr Yeats writes in the English language, he is purely an Irish poet. The folk-lore of Ireland was his sole inspiration; the spirit of the Gael is the warp and woof of his thought.

So in Yeats the paper had a role model for political internationalism in foreign relations (it had unreservedly welcomed the Free State's entry to the League of Nations in September 1923) and cultural fusion in the national context. The poet's Church of Ireland ancestry and his unionist Sligo-merchant relatives, his use of the English language, did not exclude him from the Irish pantheon. He was 'purely an *Irish* poet'.

It is likely that this editorial on Yeats's success was by the author who, as Bruyere, had contributed the series on Some Irish Artists. And it may be, too, that Bruyere was a young journalist named Robert Maire Smyllie, whom the newspaper had recruited in 1920. For not only did the editorial reflect that journalist's internationalist outlook in his aligning of Yeats's Nobel Prize with the Free State's accession to the League of Nations, but the Bruyere series gave much evidence that its author knew many of the subjects personally. Later, when he was the legendary editor of the *Irish Times*, Smyllie would spend much of his leisure time in the company of Irish writers in the sociable purlieus of public houses adjacent to the newspaper's premises. The Bruyere series, if indeed it was Smyllie who wrote it, suggests that he cultivated literary and artistic associations from early in his career in a way that it is impossible to imagine the reclusive, invincibly respectable, John Edward Healy doing.

Robert M. Smyllie was born in Glasgow in 1894, the eldest son of a Scottish Presbyterian also named Robert. His mother hailed from Cork. Smyllie's father, who was a printer by profession, was working in Sligo town when his first son was born. Smyllie senior eventually became owner/editor of the local pro-unionist paper, the *Sligo Times*, so printer's and journalistic ink ran in the family veins. Education at Sligo Grammar School took Smyllie to Trinity College Dublin in 1912, but he soon abandoned academia and struck out on his own, taking up a tutoring job in Germany, where he found himself incarcerated as an alien enemy for the duration of the Great War. The prison camp near Berlin may have supplied the kind of general education that prepared him for a life in journalism which a small Irish university may not have done. At the very least, he became fluent in German and was introduced to a wide variety of political opinion that gave him a broader perspective on international affairs than many of his Irish Protestant contemporaries, whose views on the world did not often include European vistas. After the armistice, Smyllie returned to Ireland where in 1919 the editor identified him as a suitable person to cover the Versailles Peace Conference. The apprentice newspaperman had the satisfaction of seeing a lengthy series of articles on the conference and on world politics appear under the byline 'From Our Special Correspondent', dateline Paris.

Irish readers of these would no doubt have been concerned to learn how a Sinn Féin delegation led by de Valera had fared in seeking to have the cause of Ireland placed before a conference that sought to give expression to the concept of national self-determination in the interests of peace. Smyllie duly obliged by informing them that the conference did not 'take the Irish question very seriously'. He was keenly alert to the fact that in the era of the nation state, when it was 'in the interest of all of Europe to see a strong and prosperous Poland, able to prevent German encroachment into Russia or to stem the march of Bolshevism into Europe' (*Irish Times*, 29 March 1919), border and ethnic disputes were erupting in central Europe which threatened renewed instability. Smyllie understood these were like the one developing in Ireland writ large: 'Central Europe is strewn with Irelands,' he observed. He was conscious, too, that the matter of German reparations was fraught with danger ('It would be useless and foolish to ask Germany for a sum we know she could not pay') and with remarkable prescience Smyllie envisaged how if the Polish question were to be badly answered by a conference unwilling to give sufficient time to its resolution, then a recovered Russia might be 'prepared to support Germany in annexing this territory'. He pondered 'would the other Powers care to risk another European war to prevent it?' 'It is infinitely better,' he advised, 'to spend a few days longer in arriving at a settlement which can leave no danger of a new upheaval.'

The appalling effects of and the upheaval caused by the Great War were to the fore in Smyllie's mind as he supplied these detailed and carefully argued reports from victorious France and from defeated Germany, which he revisited. In February, for example, he sent a graphic dispatch about the area around Verdun, which evoked the 'terrible and merciless suffering' that had been 'inflicted upon those unfortunate subjects of our greatest ally' (*Irish Times*, 28 February 1919).

In a report published in March 1919 Smyllie celebrated how 'modern means of transit and communication' (*Irish Times*, 6 March 1919) were bringing the world together ('Every part of the world is inseparably linked to every other part').

In the 1920s, the *Irish Times* was determined to keep the memory of the war fresh in its readers' minds. For the paper, Irish participation in the Great War had been an imperial duty and the deaths of Irish soldiers had shown to the world that Ireland was part of the United Kingdom's Commonwealth of Nations. In the early years of Irish independence, the *Irish Times* considered that commemoration ceremonies were not simply occasions to honour the Irish dead in the titanic struggle that had recently ended, but were opportunities to sustain Ireland's continuing membership of that Commonwealth and its sense of international responsibility. They were also times to argue that the new state could ill afford to reject a crucial part of its national inheritance in which Protestant Ireland, north and south, had played a signal part. In November 1923, under the headline 'Remembered Valour', an editorial struck an internationalist note: 'Ireland's recent tragedies of revolution and bloodshed will not be allowed to dim the value and glory of her contribution to freedom's victory in the battlefields of three Continents' (*Irish Times*, 12 November 1923).

The following year, a decade after the outbreak of European hostilities, the *Irish Times* could take comfort that the war was being properly commemorated when a Celtic cross was temporarily erected in College Green in Dublin to the memory of the dead of the 16th (Irish) Division of the British army (which had in fact included many Irish Volunteers who had answered John Redmond's call that they should enlist). The writer reported that a huge gathering of up to 100,000 had assembled in the capital ('all Dublin people', *Irish Times*, 12 November 1924). The Free State government was represented at the wreath-laying ceremony. Mrs Despard, a well-known suffragist firebrand and sister of Field Marshal Lord French, was also present; Mrs Tom Kettle, widow of a distinguished Irish intellectual (and friend of James Joyce) who had perished in France, laid a wreath; 'virtually everyone had a Flanders poppy'. Again, the *Irish Times* editorialized in wistfully hopeful terms: 'Loyalty to the Empire is seen to be consistent with perfect loyalty to the Free State ... To-day the cross in College Green – the very fact of its presence – is proof that within the Free State itself men of all parties are coming together in a new and broader creed of patriotism.'

In the 1920s, therefore, the *Irish Times*, in matters ranging from sport to war commemoration, raised a well-educated voice (Healy's relish for the untranslated Latin tag and Smyllie's always punctilious if uninspiring prose assumed a certain kind of literacy) and defended an internationalist outlook and political and cultural tolerance on national matters, 'a new and broader creed of patriotism'. There was, however, substantial evidence that the tide of Irish cultural affairs was not flowing in the generally pluralist direction desired by the newspaper. The most obvious sign of this was the Irish Free State's policy of gaelicization.

The drive for Irish separatism in the twentieth century had always involved cultural aspirations. The reversal of the conquest would allow its cultural consequences to be extirpated and the new nation state would prove its authenticity by stamping the new social order with the outlines of an ancient, indigenous civilization, with the grandeur of the Gael. To the fore in this project was an attempt to revive the Irish language so that it would become the first language of the people. Before independence, an examination qualification in Irish had been made a prerequisite for matriculation in the National University of Ireland. With the foundation of the Free State, the Department of Education, under the direction of Professor Eoin MacNeill (formerly leader of the Irish Volunteers), made Irish a compulsory subject in all secondary schools, as it was in the country's primary schools, and initiated a process that could mean that all education in the country would eventually be conducted in that language. A kind of *Kulturkampf* was in motion.

The *Irish Times* felt ambiguously about the revival movement. In the first blush of its soft-focus 'greening' in the early phase of independence, it recognized that Irish would gain in national respect in the new dispensation. In April 1922 it even published a droll article by a P. Donnelly entitled 'Learning Irish: How It Is Done', which amusingly outlined the linguistic obstacle course that awaited civil servants who wished to acquire, on fear of demotion or exclusion, 'the ability within a prescribed period to fill up in Irish the longer or shorter space that comes between "a chara" and "le meas *more*" in the official correspondence' (*Irish Times*, 17 April 1922). In 1923 the *Weekly Irish Times* published a series of Irish language lessons. In the same year the paper greeted the issuance of the new Free State halfpenny stamp, with its 'Sword of Light' symbol (in Irish that concept had been used as the title of the Gaelic League's magazine). The stamp, with its Celtic image, design and Irish language (all of which were to be repeated in the penny, fivepenny and sixpenny stamps), was judged 'altogether very artistic and interesting' (*Irish Times*, 21 April 1923). Plays in Irish at the Abbey Theatre in March 1924 warranted praise under the subheading 'Some Excellent Acting' ('Nothing better could be desired than the first play given last night', *Irish Times*, 11 March 1923). Other manifestations of gaelicization, however, met with the paper's concern. It set its face against a proposal that the wig and gown should be abandoned in the Free State's courts ('Wig and Gown', *Irish Times*, 12 October 1923) and it was unimpressed by the 'post-colonial' impulse to change anglicized versions of place names (it repeatedly preferred Kingstown to Dún Laoghaire, which had adopted the Irish name in 1921) back to their Irish originals or, in the case of Dublin itself, to a former Irish name. When it was proposed in 1923 to change the name of Bray, Co. Wicklow (a tourist resort to the south of Dublin), to Brí Chuallan, the paper, in tones that suggested irritation as well as economic realism, advised against it. About 'compulsory Irish' in the schools, the paper entertained no ambiguity.

As early as November 1923, in an editorial entitled 'Culture and Politics', the *Irish Times* indicated that a cultural war was being waged in the new state that had just managed to end an actual civil war. And if the issue of the national authenticity of Anglo-Irish literature was a skirmish in the struggle this involved, a major front was the matter of Ireland's Gaelic identity and the place Irish played in underpinning it. For the Irish Ireland ideologue, Ireland was nothing without its Gaelic identity, and the English language and culture an alien imposition that must be absorbed by the living, restored nation. In 'Culture and Politics', the writer expatiated on what a speaker at the Trinity College Dublin Gaelic Society had termed 'Pseudo-Gaelicism'. The editorialist approved the speaker's iconoclasm which had identified a good deal of what was thought to be ancient Gaelic cultural practice as modern invention, with 'no root in the history of Gaelic Ireland' (*Irish Times*, 14 November 1923). The newspaper observed: 'The Gaelic movement was one of the weapons in the Anglo-Irish conflict and, as such, was soiled by much ignoble use.' It was to be hoped that the weapon had been put aside, but it was feared that it might still be wielded to divisive effect. The editorial warned:

> If ... the Irish language is made a touchstone of patriotism or, on any large scale, a condition of employment – if it is to be forced upon the rising generation under positive or negative penalties – those who love it with the most knowledge will have every cause for regret. Such a policy will foster 'pseudo-Gaelicism' in its most mischievous and most degrading form.

In July 1924 a report suggested that W. B. Yeats agreed with this assessment, for he was reported as telling Seanad Eireann how he had tried to learn Irish, but had failed. He chastised his fellow senators 'for pretending that they know a language they did not' and observed that 'the language has caused irritation and that irritation was growing in the country' (*Weekly Irish Times*, 12 July 1924). By November of the same year, when it had become fully clear that the Department of Education was set – if possible and despite all objections – on gaelicizing all Irish schools, the paper was mounting a mini-crusade against 'Compulsory Irish'. In an editorial so entitled, the *Irish Times* recognized that a strong body of opinion in the country was of the mind 'that the Irish language not only must be revived, but must be made universal in Ireland as a mark of distinct nationality' (*Irish Times*, 24 November 1924). It stated: 'Unhappily the school which values the Irish language merely as a political weapon exerts too large an influence in the counsels of the Free State Government.' The paper contended that this policy, rather than fostering 'the cherishing of the common heritage of a people', would in a context where it was 'farcical to attempt more in the schools than the teaching of the language and literature on its own merits' mean 'our children's minds may be cramped within a new-fangled and barbarous jargon'. This leader brought a swift riposte from Eoin MacNeill himself, who denied that his plans were as draconian as the *Irish Times* had represented them as being. On 22 November, responding to the correspondence and articles that this editorial and MacNeill's intervention had provoked, the paper reiterated that it was not an enemy of the Irish language but insisted that 'the greatest condemnation of compulsory Irish lies ... in the fact that it is a sin against nationhood' (*Irish Times*, 22 November 1924). It was, indeed, that in the editorialist's mind since it offended against 'the principle of full and equal freedom for all citizens of the Free State'. By this, the *Irish Times* meant that many Irish citizens would be compelled to learn a language they did not wish to learn simply to gain access to state employment.

That the climate was unpropitious for the kind of case the paper was making about the principal weapon (and it is telling how often this martial metaphor was employed in exchanges on this topic) the proponents of gaelicization possessed, was made clear when in 1925 the Gaelic Athletic Association 'affirmed afresh' (*Irish Times*, 13 April 1925) its ban on 'foreign games', even disallowing attendance at such sports by its members. 'By its policy of exclusion,' the paper judged, 'the Association has degraded sport, making it a mere tool for political or racial discrimination.' It saw, too, using a classical allusion, the decision as symptomatic of a wider malaise: 'There is too much negative patriotism in our country: men are making a desert and calling it Gaelic Ireland.'

It was perhaps inevitable that the controversy over 'compulsory Irish' was also inflected with religio/political concerns. The paper itself had identified the policy as bearing with special force on Protestant schools. In June 1924 it had inveighed against the minister's proposals as an attack on the Protestant community: it was 'interfering with their liberty of thought and action and wounding them through their children' (*Irish Times*, 25 June 1924). And although subsequent editorials of that year shifted the emphasis to cultural considerations, the fact that attitudes to Irish could follow the religious divide in Ireland, north and south, was never too far from the surface. When in 1926 the paper published a letter from an eminent Trinity College philosopher, who bluntly stated that the government's Irish language policy was 'an instrument of religious and political tyranny', the gloves came off. MacNeill's successor as Minister for Education, J. M. O'Sullivan, to the *Irish Times*'s outrage, accused the paper of 'an attempt "to stir up sectarian strife" and of "hostility to the native language"' (Mark O'Brien 2008, p. 62). The *Catholic Bulletin* – republican, nationalistic and resolutely Catholic – had no compunction about entering the fray in starkly adversarial terms. It damned the *Irish Times* as one more pernicious outpost of England's Protestant garrison in Ireland. The *Catholic Bulletin*, dogmatic in its conviction that Ireland was a Gaelic and a Catholic nation, saw the *Irish Times*'s attitude to Irish as an attack on the very essence of Irish identity. To question the policy of 'compulsory Irish' (a chief advocate of that policy was a Catholic priest and Professor of Education at University College Dublin, Father Timothy Corcoran, who contributed vigorously to the *Catholic Bulletin*) was to be an enemy of Catholic as well as Gaelic Ireland. No mercy should be shown in a cultural war.

It may be that the intensity with which some advocates of 'compulsory Irish' and the project of Gaelic revival fought their battles in the 1920s was a reflection of the parlous condition of the language in that decade. For, apart from small tracts of the west and north of the 26 county state, the populace was English-speaking. To change that state of affairs would require not only enormous effort but a secure conviction rooted in an unwavering ideology. No 'Ascendancy' organ like the *Irish Times* could be allowed to stand in the way of a national crusade.

There was no possible reason to doubt Ireland's Catholic identity, for, unlike the country's Gaelic identity, it was a demographic and sociological given. The Census of 1926 confirmed this, with the Catholic population being recorded at 92.6 per cent. Of these, the vast majority were regularly in attendance at Mass and at least conventionally devout. Independent Ireland was one of the Catholic nations of the new post-war Europe. Nonetheless, the 1920s and early 1930s saw efforts to consolidate the role of Catholicism in Irish life and to emphasize how religion and national feeling coalesced.

The Church hierarchy had its own reasons for supporting this development. It had opposed the physical force aspects of Irish republicanism and nationalism in both the nineteenth and twentieth centuries and now it had to find an accommodation with a government that contained a complement of former gunmen and their supporters. As it happened, many of these were only too anxious to make their peace with the Church, so the first decade of independence was a propitious one for those who desired to flex the muscles of Catholic cultural and political power. The celebration of the centenary of Catholic Emancipation in 1929 and the Eucharistic Congress, held in Dublin in 1932, were occasions when Irish Catholic nationalism could demonstrate how convincingly it gave a powerful popular identity to the new state.

The celebrations of 1929, for which the state issued a commemorative stamp, culminated with a Mass in the Phoenix Park on Sunday, 23 June, attended by 300,000 people (and broadcast to the nation). The day before that, the *Irish Times*, in an editorial, reckoned the Act of Emancipation to be 'one of the greatest events – perhaps the cardinal event – of Irish history' (*Irish Times*, 22 June 1929) and expressed gratification that the liberator Daniel O'Connell had been supported by 'enlightened Protestants'. All had not been sweetness and light, however, at meetings held in Dublin during the week, for the paper observed:

> Most of the addresses at the Dublin Mansion House this week have ended
> on a note of social tolerance and good-will. We welcome it most heartily,
> but we regret the too frequent disparagement of the Protestant churches
> in Ireland, the too frequent suggestion that they represent not only an
> alien creed but an alien culture and alien aspirations.

The editorial felt it necessary to remind its readers that the Catholics of Ireland had no monopoly on patriotism; though by referring to them as 'Roman Catholics' in the Protestant habit of the period, the writer perhaps betrayed his own confessional partiality.

The impressive gathering in the park on the Sunday warranted an extensive colour piece the next day, contributed by a 'Special Representative' who grasped the symbolic significance of what had occurred. A nation that had suffered much under a foreign yoke had achieved its freedom: 'The silver hair of an age that remembered the famine was blent with the golden curls of adolescence and a dozen phases of Irish history co-mingled in a throng that must have been without precedent in the life of our island' (*Irish Times*, 24 June 1929). The editorial of the same day, 'Church and People', was awestruck before the spectacle of organized Catholic piety: 'No observer ever again can question – if he ever questioned – the loyalty which the mass of the Irish people give to their Church, the simple and profound devotion which they bring to the mysteries of their faith.' The Eucharistic Congress of 1932 would give the paper further ample evidence of how Church and people could unite as a nation at prayer when about a million people congregated for Mass in the same Phoenix Park.

Given the centrality of Catholicism to Irish social life, it was scarcely surprising that the Free State government took steps to ensure that Catholic social and moral teaching was protected by Irish legislation. The Irish people were certainly Catholic, Ireland was a Catholic country if not yet an Irish-speaking one, but no harm would be done by ensuring that they remained so in morals as well as in public expressions of faith. In 1922 and 1923 the introduction of Bills for divorce in the Dáil were met with horror and in 1925, by changing standing orders, the legislature made it impossible for any resident of the Free State to be divorced in the jurisdiction. This action provoked an impassioned speech in the Senate by W. B. Yeats which the *Irish Times* printed in full while berating its tenor and tone. Yeats damned the ban on divorce as an assault on the Protestants of Ireland ('No petty people,' he thundered). The *Irish Times* itself had been more circumspect, less partisan, since the step had been mooted in February 1925, but genuinely discomfited. On 12 June 1925 it admitted how difficult it would be to reconcile 'the minority's constitutional freedom with the dictates of the majority's conscience' but advised that prohibition of divorce could become a 'canker' in the body politic, making a united Ireland more difficult of achievement. By 26 June, when divorce had effectively been made impossible in the Free State, an editorial affirmed: 'It is because this issue involves not merely the rights of a few victims of wretched marriages, but the liberties of every citizen of every creed, that we view the *Dail*'s decision with extreme concern.'

Rigorous censorship was also recruited in the 1920s to protect the virtue of the people. To a degree this merely reflected international concerns that the Great War had loosened the moral fabric of life and that modern media – cheap prints, radio and film – were coarsening popular culture. In Ireland, however, the censorship mentality took a particularly firm hold. This was made dramatically evident when Sean O'Casey's play *The Plough and the Stars* was brought to a halt by republican protesters in February 1926. The play, mounted at the Abbey Theatre (which since 1925 had been in receipt of a state subsidy), gave offence on many levels. It allowed the flags of the 1916 Easter Rising to be carried into a public house where a cheerful prostitute was complaining about how politics were interfering with business. At a deeper level the play was a challenge to the ideology and developing cult of the Easter Rising and of Patrick Pearse, in the name of the playwright's socialist solidarity with the capital's urban poor.

The *Irish Times* played a direct role in the commotion and controversy stirred up by O'Casey's epic drama of the Easter Rising. Yeats, a director of the theatre, in anticipation of trouble, had prepared a speech, placing it in the hands of the paper's editor. When rioting erupted in the theatre, he informed the rioters that they had 'disgraced themselves again', in reference to the tumult that had interrupted almost two decades earlier the first performance of *The Playboy of the Western World*. The next day the paper carried Yeats's speech in full (allowing those who had failed to hear it in the din in the theatre the opportunity to take further offence at its tone of imperious disdain for a philistine mob). In its editorial, 'Cant and Facts', the *Irish Times* bemoaned the fact that, despite the vast sums expended on education in the country, there were 'numbers of Irishmen and women [among the protesters had been widows of republican martyrs] whose only answers to arguments are the raucous shout and the closed fist' (*Irish Times*, 13 February 1926). It advised that intolerance sprang from a 'refusal to see what one does not want to see' and represented O'Casey as the Hogarth of the Dublin tenements, and of a vice-ridden city. Tellingly, the editorial linked the response to the play with the 'smug voice of cant' which was beginning to agitate for a press and literary censorship 'to prohibit the importation of indecent books and newspapers – especially Sunday newspapers – from England'.

The next three years saw agitation for literary and press censorship intensify until in 1929 the government passed the Censorship of Publications Act. In the climate of the times, this was no less than could be expected. Other states were concerned about the proliferation of pornography, and Ireland followed them in drafting legislation to control its dissemination. Furthermore, the yellow press in Britain was associated with salacious reportage. Nationalistic *amour propre* could accordingly be appealed to by those who attributed all things ill in Ireland to the old enemy, and they called for a *cordon sanitaire* around the state. Gaelic revivalists, too, could welcome the restriction on imports of English-language material that consolidated the anglicization of the populace. And the majority of faithful Catholics could rest satisfied that immorality would not receive implicit sanction by its treatment in literary art, and the concept of artificial contraception would not find any place in the public domain.

In 1928 and 1929 the *Irish Times* gave extensive coverage to debate about the Censorship Bill in a society that was largely supportive where it was not indifferent to the issue at hand. It also reported on the outrages that were accompanying the demands for censorship. On 20 May 1928, for example, the Dublin to Wexford train was held up by seven young men, and thousands of copies of English Sunday newspapers were destroyed. The *Irish Times* invoked the name of Savonarola as it expressed its distaste and alarm. It was not that the high-mindedly respectable newspaper was opposed to the suppression of obscene material. Rather, it feared that the Bill before parliament would prove a dangerously blunt instrument, a threat to the literate class and to the Protestant minority. So when the Bill first reached the Seanad, an editorial regretted that it was proposed 'to smash a dung-beetle with a sledge-hammer' (*Irish Times*, 13 April 1929) and warned that the Act would authorize 'a single minister, advised by a board of censors, to act as a warden over the whole field of ancient and modern literature – to tell educated citizens that they must not read certain books. The claim is outrageous and ought to be intolerable.' Running through the paper's response to the Bill was a fear that it would impinge on the rights of the individual, deform Irish cultural life and allow the morality of the majority Church to restrict access to the 'movement of modern thought' (*Irish Times*, 17 May 1928). Even Darwin's *On the Origin of Species* could be indicted. ('Will the Bill', an editorial entitled 'Immoral Literature', provocatively queried, 'seek to impose upon the whole State the principles and views of any institution or class of the state? The proposed Bill will be an unjust censorship if it challenges in the slightest degree the intellectual freedom of any educated Irishman.') By the second reading of the Bill in the Dáil in October, the *Irish Times* was forthright, if instinctively, in its condemnation, and prescient, too, when it stated:

> The suppression of deliberately lewd newspapers is an acknowledged need, but the proposed censorship of books is a most sinister invasion of public and private liberty. It will make the Free State ridiculous in the eyes of the world; it will discourage learning and letters, and it will advertise immorality; no ingenuity can save it from the worst excesses.

The version of national identity the Censorship Bill seemed designed to protect was not one the country's Protestant minority could comfortably embrace. Protestant Ireland could 'gladly concede a Gaelic-Catholic culture to all who desire it', but resisted its imposition 'upon citizens who have no desire for it' (Mark O'Brien 2008, p. 69).

The force of the *Irish Times*'s critique of the Censorship of Publications Act was vitiated, it must be said, by its elitist assumption that popular culture was inherently unhealthy and that it was reasonable that certain subjects should not be discussed in 'newspapers which have large circulations among the uneducated classes' (*Irish Times*, 23 November 1928). One suspects, too, that the *Irish Times*'s editorialists did not really see their own reading and intellectual lives being affected by the Act's strictures. They probably agreed with Mrs Sheehy-Skeffington, renowned feminist and widow of a victim of the Easter Rising, when she declared apropos of the proposed Bill: 'we shall probably read in the end exactly what we want' (*Irish Times*, 23 November 1928). Such high-minded individualism, when combined as it was in the *Irish Times*'s case with patrician condescension, was reflected in the paper's attitude to the censorship of films. The advent of the 'talkies' presented particular problems. 'Hitherto,' the newspaper opined, 'only one sense has been exposed to danger through vulgar or licentious films; but a nasty talking film can corrupt a youthful mind simultaneously through the sense of sight and hearing' (*Irish Times*, 16 September 1929). It righteously approved strict censorship of film to protect the nation's youth.

The 1930s was in Ireland, as elsewhere in the English-speaking world, the decade when film, about which the *Irish Times* in 1929 seemed so exercised, would become a form of mass entertainment, which knew few boundaries of nation or state. It was also a decade of mass unemployment and of an international depression that would have seismic effects on many of Europe's nation states. Ireland would not remain unaffected by these. As the 1920s drew to a close, in November 1929 the newspaper published reports on the Wall Street Crash, the stock exchange collapse that helped to set in motion the economic miseries of the decade to come. On 19 November the paper copied a chilling report from a special correspondent of the *Daily Express*, which could have been read as a universal warning:

> Not since the dark days of the 'South Sea Bubble' in the early years of the eighteenth century ... have the rank and file of a nation's people been driven by a single staggering thrust of the hand of fate to such irrecoverable depths of distress ...' (*Irish Times*, 19 November 1929).

4

THE *IRISH TIMES* AND DE VALERA'S IRELAND

In 1939 the Irish-born poet Louis MacNeice published in London his long poem *Autumn Journal*. A quintessential work of the British 1930s, viewed from a liberal/left perspective, this marvellously readable work makes the Spanish Civil War a litmus test of political integrity as it responds anxiously to the Munich crisis of the previous autumn, when armed conflict with Germany had seemed an immediate and terrible possibility. The poem is heavily inflected with social guilt about the economic depression of the 1930s. For in what MacNeice's friend the English poet W. H. Auden would later dub a 'low dishonest decade', the depression had immiserated millions, while the governing class had failed the population of England's industrial cities. As the sense of international crisis deepened, the poet, whose west of Ireland father ministered as Church of Ireland Bishop of Down and Connor in unionist Belfast, rounded on his native land with impatient disdain. Northern Ireland, the poet judged, was mired in invincible sectarianism ('the minority always guilty'), while the southern state had become a byword for isolationist self-regard and cultural myopia:

> Ourselves alone! Let the round tower stand aloof
>> In a world of bursting mortar!
> Let the school-children fumble their sums
>> In a half-dead language;
> Let the censor be busy on the books; pull down the Georgian slums
>> Let the games be played in Gaelic.
>> (MacNeice 1939, pp. 139–40)

The era of nation states was being challenged by greater forces than they could individually muster to protect their citizens from social catastrophe ('Put up what flag you like, It is too late/To save your soul with bunting'); and in such a context, where

> 'Castles are out of date', it is absurd for Ireland to think 'everyone cares/
> Who is the king of your castle'
>> (MacNeice 1939, p. 140).

In fact, in the Irish Free State in the 1930s the question of who in fact ruled and on whose terms (who *was* king of the castle?) was central in the public life of the nation, affecting the country's internal politics and its international relations in definitive ways. It was a decade, indeed, in which the *Irish Times*, still the voice of the southern Protestant minority, predominantly resident in Dublin, would find most of what it stood for politically and socially under-mined by the determined, focused efforts of Eamon de Valera, who rose to commanding prominence in Irish political life.

In April 1926 de Valera founded Fianna Fáil, carrying with him, in a new political party that clearly intended to enter the Dáil, members of Sinn Féin who had taken the republican side in the Civil War and IRA volunteers who had fought it, who thought they could combine a continued commitment to opportunistic militarism with membership of a party named in English translation 'Soldiers of Ireland'. It immediately became clear that the governing party of William T. Cosgrave (to which the *Irish Times* gave its support, despite many caveats) viewed the new party as a threat to constitutional order in a way the existing parliamentary opposition of the Labour Party had never been. From early in the life of Fianna Fáil (which would come to dominate Irish politics until the second decade of the twenty-first century) de Valera made no bones about the fact that he intended to revisit the terms of the Anglo-Irish Treaty. At the founding of a Blackrock branch of the party in Dublin in June 1926, he stated that the Constitution of the Free State 'was a denial of liberty ... By it they had taken out indentures of slavery' (*Irish Times*, 18 June 1926). In the general election of June 1927, the *Irish Times* uninhibitedly made it clear that it took a jaundiced view of de Valera and his attitude to the oath of allegiance to the Crown. In an editorial on 3 June the paper advised, 'The parties which openly declare their intention to wreck the State will poll to their maximum strength ... Every man and woman who believes in ordered government must combine to defeat them.' Next day an editorial opened up an appalling vista as it imagined what would occur 'if the electorate should be mad enough to give [de Valera] a majority'. It would effect the 'shipwreck of the state' (*Irish Times*, 4 June 1927).

The June election, which gave Cosgrove's Cumann na nGaedheal 27.4 per cent of the vote to Fianna Fáil's 26.1 per cent, with Labour taking 12.6 (Bew 2007, p. 449), suggested that, although the waters were choppy, the ship of state could still take to sea. The assassination of Kevin O'Higgins by a small group of anti-Treaty republicans as he was on his way to Mass on Sunday, 10 July, gave deadly evidence that it was not only de Valera who threatened the state and that the question as to who would rule in Ireland was still moot.

The *Irish Times* responded to this event with unmitigated horror. O'Higgins had proved himself a stalwart enemy of those who had taken up arms against the Treaty settlement (it was he who had sanctioned the death warrants of republican prisoners executed in response to republican atrocities, thereby, as it proved, effectively signing his own death warrant) and while he was no monarchist, he was not a republican purist; he had been to the fore at the Commonwealth Conference in 1926 which had helped to solidify the concept of the dominion status the Free State shared with other 'British' jurisdictions. The *Irish Times* respected that achievement. So, for the newspaper, his assassination was simply murder most foul: 'No more hideous or more cowardly crime has disgraced the records of modern Ireland' pronounced an editorial the next day, which amounted to a eulogy to O'Higgins, who had not only played a statesman's part at the Commonwealth Conference but had been crucial, in his unstinting defence of the rule of law, in bringing the national minority to trust the new state. 'May our special tribute to his memory be the statement that his influence was, perhaps, the most compelling factor in the reconciliation of Southern Unionists to the new *régime*' (*Irish Times*, 11 July 1927). On 12 July an editorial saluted the young minister (he was only 35 when he died) as one who had overseen the transition of the Free State 'from anarchy to peace'. And most tellingly, perhaps, the day after O'Higgins's death under the headline 'Kevin O'Higgins: A Personal Memory' signed by 'Nichevo', the pen-name occasionally used by R. M. Smyllie, the paper allowed its readers to sense what the nation had lost in the untimely passing of a paragon among men. Smyllie recalled a recent meeting with O'Higgins in London where he felt he had glimpsed the soul of the man and had 'learnt more about the inner history of *Sinn Fein* than [he] ever had before' (*Irish Times*, 11 July 1927). That Smyllie felt able to pen what amounted to a threnody for a fallen warrior to one who had been to the fore in the struggle for independence the paper had so vigorously opposed (O'Higgins was a Collins man to his core) suggests both the impact of O'Higgins as a man on those with whom he came in contact and how the *Irish Times* had adjusted to the circumstances of what was in effect dominion status: 'Staunch friend; stout foe; man of genius and humble-hearted gentleman, peace to your ashes. We shall not see your like again.'

O'Higgins's death removed from the stage of Irish politics the one figure who might have proved a capable antagonist for Eamon de Valera, who was set on usurping the role of protagonist in the national drama. By the ironies of history it was the assassination that in fact propelled de Valera, in August 1927, into the Dáil he would come to dominate in the 1930s. For, in the aftermath of the tragedy, the government passed draconian acts of legislation, among which was a requirement that would force de Valera and his party quickly to resolve the issue of the oath of allegiance (following the June election, Fianna Fáil had been prevented from entering the Dáil when its members declined to take the oath). And de Valera rose to the challenge, by devising a form of words and mode of action that went beyond casuistry to allow his party to take their seats. The *Irish Times*, still in shock at the demise of the Minister for Justice and

External Affairs, exhibited near panic when the parliamentary arithmetic of the newly constituted house with Fianna Fáil deputies in their seats threatened to hand effective power to de Valera. When it seemed that a minority government might be formed with Fianna Fáil support, the *Irish Times* was fierce in condemnation. In the event, the vote to bring about this state of affairs was tied in the house and was decided by the negative vote of the chair. The day before, by dint of some expert journalistic sleuthing by no other than Smyllie himself (Mark O'Brien 2008, p. 65), the paper had been able to publish the names of prospective Labour Party ministers in the putative new government. This scoop, which involved a degree of skulduggery, probably helped to create a climate of suspicion about the vote in the Dáil, which had been deadlocked because one deputy, who was expected to vote in favour, had absented himself before the division. It was widely believed at the time and for years thereafter that one John Jinks had been leant on by an independent Unionist, Bryan Cooper, and by Smyllie (Smyllie was already an ample presence, as in later life he would become notably corpulent!) or rendered unfit after an excessive lunch or even dispatched by train to Sligo (from where all three men hailed). Jinks denied any such machinations had been involved, but the stories were too colourful to be set aside by sober facts; and the paper's evident sense of triumph when the motion was defeated only fanned the flames of suspicion that something untoward had occurred with the *Irish Times* involved.

Eternal vigilance, even in triumph, remained the paper's byword where de Valera was concerned. Two by-elections were to take place on 24 August 1927. Once more the future of the nation was on a knife-edge. On that day an editorial warned that 'the capture of one seat' could bring about a dreadful reversal for the body politic. It reckoned Fianna Fáil's declared aims of abolishing the oath and revisiting the financial settlement with the United Kingdom would amount to a declaration of war with Britain (and also with Northern Ireland, it provocatively, if somewhat disingenuously, pointed out). The paper damned de Valera as a man of 'vain and insensate violence' and characterized his political goals as a 'crazy and malignant policy' likely to bankrupt the nation. In September 1927, happily for the *Irish Times*, that 'calamitous' outcome did not arise, for Cosgrove called a general election at which he won a majority sufficient to govern for a further four-and-a half years. Alarmingly, however, the election, with a declining vote for Labour and near extinction for smaller parties, cast Irish politics in an essentially bipolar mould, which in time would settle structurally as Fianna Fáil versus the rest. In the 1930s there was no doubt that the *Irish Times* raised its voice repeatedly among those of the rest. This was not a comfortable position, however, for de Valera would prove himself a cunning and resolutely effective antagonist and the ranks of his opponents were often to be filled by individuals at the head of movements and forces with whom the paper could scarcely feel comfortable.

Moreover, the paper's adjustment to the new state, which had been effected to a carefully measured degree in the first decade of independence, would be set in question as that state was radically redefined.

Given its editorial excoriation of de Valera when he seemed to be on the brink of power in 1927, the *Irish Times* greeted its *bête noire*'s actual accession to government office on 9 March 1932 with surprising equanimity. De Valera took power as President of the Executive Office of the Irish Free State which he had opposed less than a decade earlier, and also reserved to himself the portfolio of External Affairs. He did so with the support of the Labour Party and some independents, since his own party did not command an overall majority. An editorial the next day, hoping that the government's minority status would hold its radical enthusiasm in check ('The Labour Party will not permit the new Pharaoh to rush blindly into any Red Sea of political controversy', *Irish Times*, 10 March 1932), was prepared to give de Valera a large benefit of the doubt:

> Sensible Irishmen, whatever their present fears may be, will not cry before they are hurt ... Mr de Valera's intentions are admirable. He breathes goodwill towards all classes and creeds of his countrymen. He desires, as we all desire, the unity of Ireland. He approaches social problems in the high temper of a Christian reformer, and has visions of a self-contained and self-supporting State ... He dreams of utter independence for the Irish Free State ... We shall soon see how *Fianna Fáil*'s Sir Philip Sidney will fare in his fight with facts, and how he reacts to the handicaps of his new position ... It seems, therefore, that Mr de Valera's Government may be good with ease, but may not be bad without much difficulty. A judgment so moderately hopeful cannot be passed on all the Governments of Europe.

Such editorial *sang-froid* was short-lived, for the new leader was quickly to prove himself more the Machiavelli of Irish politics than the Renaissance gentleman. And it soon became clear that he had kept External Affairs in his own hands since he had precise intentions in respect of the state's most vital 'external' relation, that with the United Kingdom.

By 23 March the paper was informing its readers in apocalyptic tones that de Valera intended unilaterally to abrogate a key element of the Anglo-Irish Treaty and related financial commitments. He would remove the oath of allegiance from the constitution and would withhold payments of the land annuities (generated by the Land Acts that had transferred ownership to 'native' proprietors) that the state owed British bondholders. On 23 March the *Irish Times* deemed the situation a 'national emergency' and de Valera's plans 'cataclysmic'. Sir Philip Sidney was proving 'the sheer autocrat' with the country's democratic liberties at stake. On 24 March, when Britain had given its reply to de Valera's announcement (it would hold the Free State to the

Anglo-Irish Treaty and to the financial settlement), the *Irish Times* envisioned a fraught future for the country, which might mean 'even the sternest doom of all. Britain may leave the Free State to her mournful destinies as an isolated republic' (*Irish Times*, 24 March 1932). The irony was, apparently, lost on the writer, that de Valera in fact intended to make the Free State a republic in all but name and would welcome the diminution and eventual disappearance of the state's constitutional entanglement with the United Kingdom. That would be no cause for national mourning.

From its inception to its conclusion in 1938, the *Irish Times* regarded the economic war with Britain as an unmitigated disaster for the country. Certainly the paper was entirely sincere in its urging that it would lead to financial ruin. In late 1932 it contemplated 'national destitution' (*Irish Times*, 3 November 1932) and queried whether an obdurate de Valera would remain unaffected by the spectacle of increasing immiseration: 'Hungry men are becoming a grimly common sight in the Free State.'

As a conservative organ, the newspaper was, as well as being sympathetic to those in misery, anxious about the toll such need would place on the rates. As such, it was also genuinely alarmed that de Valera was a dangerous social leveller. It warned, for example in July 1933, that the policy of his government was 'a crude, merciless and progressive proletarianism. Its deliberate aim is to submerge capital; to annihilate the right to property and to establish a common standard of low living in an isolated land' (*Irish Times*, 4 July 1933). A week or so later it vociferated: 'It is not too much to say that if Lenin or Stalin had sought to prepare Ireland – a Christian and conservative country – for Communism, his plans would have coincided largely with the Free State's Government's present policy' (*Irish Times*, 13 July 1933). In less heated terms, the paper was happy to have the support of none other than John Maynard Keynes, in questioning the direction in which de Valera was leading the country. The *Irish Times* was pleased to report in an editorial how at a lecture at University College Dublin, Keynes had pondered whether the Free State was 'a large enough unit geographically, with sufficiently diversified natural resources, for more than a very modest measure of self-sufficiency to be feasible, without a disastrous reduction in a standard of life which is already none to high' (*Irish Times*, 20 April 1933).

So we may not doubt the *Irish Times*'s genuine fear for the economic well-being of the Free State and its populace in the 1930s as the economic war rumbled on. However, one senses, too, that its opposition to the depredations inflicted on the cattle trade by de Valera's policy and on the more substantial farmers in the country was part of its assault on his constitutional ambitions, about which it felt even more keenly. Tellingly, in an editorial entitled 'Mr de Valera's Challenge' in May 1933, the paper observed how if de Valera were to be successful in his constitutional efforts and so effectively carve the Free State out of the 'Empire', the then current economic war would have given the Free State 'merely a slight foretaste' of the incalculable 'losses and miseries' that would ensue: 'She will lose the British market for ever, and her sons in Great Britain and throughout the Commonwealth will become aliens. Her people will be thrown back upon the slender and isolated resources of a twenty-six county republic ...' (*Irish Times*, 6 May 1933). Therefore, in highlighting the deleterious effects of the economic war on Irish life in the 1930s, the paper was fighting its own war against constitutional change. It was saying that if you think things are bad now, imagine what they will be like if de Valera, the Irish Lenin, gets his way.

De Valera's determination to impose his will on the body politic had quickly become evident when he had, in his first period in office, hollowed out the institutions that gave public expression to what was effectively dominion status, just as the *Irish Times* in 'Mr de Valera's Challenge' had feared he would do, leaving behind only the 'surviving fragments of the Treaty' to be 'removed in a wheelbarrow' (*Irish Times*, 6 May 1933). He ostentatiously downgraded the standing of the Governor General (the notable political figure who occupied the role was summarily dismissed and replaced by a compliant nonentity), but it was his attitude to Irish access to the Privy Council in London that stuck most uncomfortably in the craw of the *Irish Times* (as it did in those of many others and not all of them former unionists). For this, more than whether or not the Governor General occupied the Vice-Regal Lodge in Dublin's Phoenix Park (the new incumbent had been dispatched to the suburbs), even more than continued membership of the British Commonwealth, held very dear as it was, seemed symbolically to strike straight at the heart of the minority's interests and the British identity its members had not been obliged to abandon at independence.

The *Irish Times*'s hopes that the Labour Party might prove a brake on de Valera's outrageous plans, ill-founded as it thought they were, received a body blow when in January 1933 de Valera called a snap election and was returned to power with an augmented party representation, while Labour was reduced to eight deputies, who were prepared to sustain him in government. This gave de Valera his opportunity to press on with what must have seemed 'to orthodox imperialists ... a veritable rake's progress' (Lyons 1971, p. 519) of constitutional change. When in August 1933 de Valera presented three Bills to the Dáil, the single object of which was, as the *Irish Times* had it, 'to abolish the power of the King in the Irish Free State', an editorial waxed indignant at what at that moment seemed mere play-acting on his part to appease republican opinion; access to the Privy Council had already been made almost impossible, and the third of de Valera's new Bills would merely 'give legal sanction to an already accomplished fact' (*Irish Times*, 10 August 1933). By October the same year, however, when the three bills had passed a second reading in the Senate, an editorial returned to the Privy Council issue, indicating that it remained a worrisome sore point, and that, as a powerful symbol, it played on minority fears for the future. The paper reported how in the Seanad Sir John Keane (a renowned former unionist) claimed that there had been a 'gentlemen's agreement' between the Irish negotiators of the Treaty and the unionist minority that 'the right of appeal' would be respected. The *Irish Times*'s editorial of 19 October 1933 made clear that what had happened and was happening to the right of appeal to the Privy Council was an injury inflicted on the minority which boded ill for the values to which it adhered:

> The minority did not fear then, and does not fear now, any such perils as a corrupt judicature or religious persecution; but it regards the right of appeal as a precious – indeed the only surviving – link with the Crown. Of course, it is as a link with the Crown that Mr de Valera's Government has doomed the right of appeal. These three bills are part of the deliberate process by which finally the Free State, like Alice's Cheshire cat, will fade altogether out of the empire, leaving behind her the last traces of a cynical smile. (*Irish Times*, 19 October 1933)

De Valera's rise in the early 1930s to near-hegemonic power was not politically unopposed. His winning of government office had alarmed more than the *Irish Times* and its constituency. It was feared that he would be less than even-handed between the forces of the state and the IRA which still opposed its very existence. The fact that one of de Valera's earliest actions in power was to release IRA prisoners from prison did little to dampen such anxieties; nor did his apparent willingness to turn a blind eye to the increasingly bellicose activities of some IRA members. Furthermore, many in public office feared that the new government would institute a spoils system and were afraid that they might lose their posts as a new dispensation took hold. Just before the 1933 election was held, an Army Comrades Association (ACA) was formed, ostensibly a veterans' society but in reality a body that would quickly mutate into a group of men prepared to use strong-arm tactics against the IRA, Communism and a government that might prove itself indulgent towards these malign phenomena. When de Valera, only briefly in office once again, in February 1933 peremptorily sacked the colourful and popular chief of police, General Eoin O'Duffy, the ACA was galvanized in a way that by the end of the summer saw O'Duffy as head of what had become a National Guard and as leader of a new party, the United Ireland Party or Fine Gael, which emerged when Cosgrave's Cumann na nGaedheal sought association with this new power in the land (the *Irish Times* in September immediately pledged its support for this party).

For the *Irish Times* all this represented an acute difficulty. It had responded to O'Duffy's dismissal with outrage: 'this distinguished and serving officer has been dismissed without cause stated and without notice, as no householder would dare to dismiss a domestic servant' (*Irish Times*, 24 February 1933), but as O'Duffy's influence on the body politic waxed, unambiguous support for what he espoused became highly problematic. On the one hand, O'Duffy and his strong-arm comrades in the National Guard – dubbed 'the Blueshirts' on account of their quasi-military uniform – seemed to represent a force capable of interrupting de Valera's rise to unalloyed ascendancy. On the other hand, the 'Blueshirt' movement was willing to present itself as an Irish cousin of Italian fascism with its anti-democratic ideology. For the *Irish Times*, which had for a decade been vocal in support (qualified as it often had been) of the democratically elected Cumann na nGaedheal party, to see the dangerous de Valera and Fianna Fáil challenged by a putatively anti-democratic force (O'Duffy favoured the version of state power then in operation in fascist Italy, coloured with ideals of Catholic corporatism) that might in fact bring down de Valera was, indeed, compelling, if disorientating, to behold. That Cosgrave's party in 1933 seemed to be absorbed by O'Duffy's movement thickened a recipe for editorial confusion and possible equivocation. Adding to the ingredients of this *Irish Times* stew was the fact that the newspaper's stance on Mussolini and Italian fascism had at times been moderately supportive. In 1926, for example, the paper had assessed, in an anti-communist mood, the Italy of fascist dictatorship: 'Under her new autocrat Italy is a well-managed, peaceful and economically progressive land' (*Irish Times*, 29 March 1926). The paper admitted such governance involved 'losses' for the people which might be felt in an economic downturn, but Mussolini's 'bold experiment' had brought undoubted prosperity to a grateful populace. De Valera's adventurism and instinct for autocracy was not likely to prove so successful either in prosperity or in popular gratitude.

By August 1933, as O'Duffy seemed on the point of mounting a *coup d'état* by summoning his supporters to march en masse on Dublin, the paper's dilemma became almost embarrassingly obvious. On 9 August it may have published a poem entitled 'Old Ireland' by a Hilda F. North-Bomford which plaintively enquired

> *What does it matter what shirt you wear,*
> *If its [sic] blue – or green – or white.*
> *'Tis the heart beneath*
> *We want to beat*
> *For old Ireland's right ...*

but the paper's editorials of that month clearly demonstrated the truth of another stanza in the poem which lamented that 'Beneath each shirt of different hue ... /There's great unrest.' Ten days later, in an editorial entitled 'Danger and Duty', the *Irish Times* reflected on that unrest in terms that indicated how conditions in the country had certainly unsettled its editorial equipoise. The government had threatened that if O'Duffy were to proceed with his plan to parade in Dublin, the National Guard would be proclaimed under the Public Safety Act. The paper hoped O'Duffy would 'cancel his arrangements', but it could not prevent itself, in its distaste for de Valera, from offering its readers a benign perspective on O'Duffy, while admitting his National Guard ('distinctly fascist' in its organization, if 'democratic' in 'its professions') was a force for national disunity that could only benefit Fianna Fáil: 'General O'Duffy has brought into public affairs a spirit of energy and discipline which, when it has found a proper place, will be a national asset of first importance.' The paper advised O'Duffy that he should make common cause with the parliamentary opposition to bring down de Valera's government, and then his 'proposals of parliamentary change' could 'be discussed quietly on their merits'. When on 22 August the government did in fact proclaim the National Guard, the *Irish Times* remained cautiously inclined to see O'Duffy as a force for good in Irish politics. In its editorial 'Proclaimed' of 23 August, it accepted that the state was entitled to, indeed ought to, suppress the semi-military body O'Duffy's more bellicose supporters had become, while questioning querulously why the fully military IRA 'flourishes without check'. Where earlier in the month O'Duffy had been granted the benefit of political doubt as someone who could help to dislodge de Valera, by 23 August the same partial licence was extended to the Guard itself: 'The best qualities of the National Guard were the new hopefulness, vigour and discipline which it has injected into Irish affairs. That spirit can save the country if it is applied now solely to the tasks of political organisation and unity.'

On 26 August the *Irish Times* made clear how it hoped the country could both ride the tiger of O'Duffy's and the National Guards' spirit while taming it so that it could be credibly recruited to bring down de Valera's government. It advised that the government could not 'be dethroned by shirts of any tinge' and warned, despite the indulgence the paper had afforded him, that 'As a semi-military *dux* and the head of a banned organisation General O'Duffy can create nothing except trouble'; but as 'an organiser of much ability with a large following in the country' he could 'make himself really formidable to the Government, and can smile in vain at the terrors of the Public Safety Act'. At the year's end, as de Valera asserted his authority once again when he proscribed the Young Ireland Association (offspring of the banned National Guard and inheritor of the 'Blueshirt' sobriquet), the paper found in disarray its tactic of both commending O'Duffy as a possible force for good, while deprecating the undemocratic nature of his ideology and activities. For de Valera had proved himself a more formidable, possibly sinister, foe than even the *Irish Times* had expected. It asked 'What does the Government mean?' in proscribing the Young Ireland Association and it continued in a damning denunciation that spoke of political impotence:

It professes to be democratic, relying entirely on the people's will; yet it does not hesitate to act as ruthlessly as the Nazi Government in Germany when it thinks that it is being threatened by a powerful opponent. No British Government ever took more drastic action in this country than President de Valera's ministry has taken. (*Irish Times*, 9 December 1933)

Sir Philip Sidney was now Adolf Hitler in an unlikely transmutation that had included Lenin and Stalin.

In early 1934 that note of near-hysteria recurred in the paper's editorials as John Edward Healy's long incumbency drew towards its end. Their combination of outrage and settled despair make for uncomfortable reading when one considers how Healy had carried the paper through the Anglo-Irish War and the Civil War and had sought to come to terms with the Free State's existence. De Valera is represented as a dictator, responsible for the ruination of the country: 'Mr de Valera and his colleagues are making themselves absolute rulers of the Free State, the only disposers of the people's lives and fortunes' (*Irish Times*, 1 March 1934). The paper was not sure that the Irish were 'fit for self-government', so great had been the 'moral degradation' effected by de Valera's disregard for the rule of law: 'the tragedy of a nation's soul is reaching its climax amid wanton accompaniments of economic distress'. On 3 March the paper shuddered as it contemplated 'a day when Communism may flourish like a rank weed in a devastated Ireland'. When later in the same month de Valera announced that he would abolish the Senate for rejecting his Restriction of Uniforms Bill, the paper bewailed his 'resort to sheer despotism' and lamented: 'Today the unabashed dictator stands revealed. Mr de Valera has no use for a constitution that is not his slave' (*Irish Times*, 24 March 1934). Another Civil War was at hand if he persisted in his folly. A new comparison came to the editorial mind: 'If he takes that course, he will become a tragic figure in history – the Samson of Irish politics.'

O'Duffy's short-lived thrust for power, it is now generally accepted by historians, was less a full-blooded Irish version of European fascism than a fevered response to local conditions in which IRA intimidation and violence, unimpeded by the government, seemed to threaten the democratic future of the state. When, following an egregious act of pointless terror (the murder of the elderly Henry Somerville on the grounds that he had supplied references for Irish recruits to the Royal Navy), de Valera moved decisively to suppress his erstwhile allies in the legion of the rearguard, the *raison d'être* for the Blueshirts rapidly declined, together with their capacity to affect the body politic. However, for a time they had seemed able to provide a muscular counterforce to de Valera's Fianna Fáil. When it is understood that O'Duffy's probably opportunist interest in a corporatist restructuring of the state allied him with the Catholic Church, the other great institution that was concerned with power in the Free State, then it can be seen why the *Irish Times* in the early

1930s was inclined to place a cautious bet on O'Duffy (quickly withdrawn as it was when his true colours became clear). For in the 1930s the Catholic Church in Ireland, powerfully influenced by the corporatist ideas contained in the papal encyclical *Quadragesimo Anno* (1931), was making sure its role in Irish life, especially as an arbiter of social policy, would be respected and given legislative teeth. O'Duffy, with his corporatist ideas, at the head of the new party, Fine Gael, plus the Church should surely have been enough to inhibit the dangerous adventurism of a de Valera.

How powerful the Catholic Church was in Ireland as almost a state religion had been amply demonstrated in the Catholic Emancipation centenary celebrations of 1929. The Eucharistic Congress in Dublin in June 1932 again reminded politicians and people alike that the Church held not only the keys of a spiritual kingdom but could and probably would also continue to exercise its considerable authority in the temporal sphere, too. To seek to be king of the Irish castle in independent Ireland meant reckoning with the fact that the Church could bar the door if its interests were threatened.

The Eucharistic Congress surpassed the Catholic Emancipation celebrations in scale and in the international attention it drew to the Irish capital. True, once again, to its traditions of respect for the faith of the majority of Irish men and women and to its own churchy origins, the *Irish Times* gave extensive coverage to activities that lasted for an entire week. On Saturday, 25 June, the day before a great gathering for Mass in the Phoenix Park, an editorial welcomed the week as perhaps the 'most notable' in the city's history – 'a week of rich and wonderful experience'. For all Irish Christians, indeed, the congress was an impressive demonstration of the power of faith in an increasingly secular world:

> During the week Roman Catholic Ireland testified to her faith with unanimous and whole-hearted fervour, to which Protestant Ireland must render the highest tribute ... The grandeur of this national devotion has made the deepest impact on all foreign visitors. Ecclesiastics from other lands know how decadent is the state of the modern world ...

During the week of the Eucharistic Congress, as the *Irish Times* reported on 22 June, an exhibition mounted in the National Museum in Kildare Street, reminded those who visited there of an earlier momentous week in Dublin. An exhibition of the relics of Easter Week 1916 evoked another of the Irish forces that vied for power in the country in the 1930s, that of militant republican separatism. There were displayed a 'revolver used by the same man in 1867 and 1916, the day-to-day diary of Commandant Joseph Plunkett, written in the General Post Office, and a uniform used by the Citizen Army'. The editorial in which the *Irish Times* honoured Ireland as an isle of faith in a wicked world, as if reminded by this exhibition that 'Religion and Politics' (the headline chosen for the leader article) could never be really separated in the country, having honoured the piety of the multitude, could not but turn to more mundane matters: the threat posed by de Valera, newly in office and breathing republican fire. For, as the paper prophesied, 'When the Free State turns next week from heaven to earth she will face a cloudy and menacing prospect.' The possibility loomed of an imminent breach between Ireland and the United Kingdom which would place the whole future in the melting pot. It was the editorialist's fervent hope that the spirit of the congress would 'irradiate the political clouds, as during the week the word *Adoremus* [had] lit the skies over Dublin'. De Valera's divisive policies, with their 'unappeased hatreds and unforgotten wrongs', could accordingly be dissolved in beneficent streams of spiritually inspired goodwill. The paper apparently hoped that de Valera's radicalism could be swamped by the flood of harmonious feeling released by the congress and that de Valera, among those who in 1922 had been condemned by the Church for splitting the nation, would be bound to moderate his policies. The problem was, however, that de Valera was all too ready to strike his own entente cordiale with Church power as it related to social life, while pressing on with his republican project. In terms of *realpolitik*, this would prove an accommodation satisfactory to both parties.

De Valera was in fact a social conservative of a profoundly Catholic complexion, despite his revolutionary past and constitutional ambitions. During the Eucharistic Congress, De Valera's government had hosted a state reception for visiting dignitaries at which there were 4,000 guests. Although Fianna Fáil struck an egalitarian gesture about dress codes during the week, one can interpret that state function as a moment when the Church and Fianna Fáil made their peace. And as historian John Whyte outlines it, in following years de Valera and his ministers were assiduous in signalling their devotion to Mother Church (Whyte 1971, pp 40–61). Any hopes the *Irish Times* had entertained that a conservative Church might curtail de Valera's wilder ideas were proved fond indeed. Since de Valera granted the Church control, where it wanted control, he could be left to his own devices in the constitutional sphere.

In June 1934 a Criminal Law Amendment Bill was passed. Among many provisions that sought to prevent various forms of vice in the state was a clause which made illegal the sale and importation of contraceptive devices (discussion or advocacy of their use had been banned in the Censorship of Publications Act, 1929). The *Irish Times*, under its recently installed new editor R. M. Smyllie, John Edward Healy's crown-prince successor, opined, in a broadly supportive editorial on the Bill, that clause 17 was 'likely to arouse much controversy' (*Irish Times*, 25 June 1934). Perhaps aware that this was an exaggerated claim in a socially conservative country, the paper let controversy flourish for some weeks in its own letters column. One such letter, signed 'Husband and Father', succinctly stated a firm Protestant position. He observed of the state's Catholic majority: 'whether they form 90 per cent of the population, or even more, they have no right to enforce their standards, by legislation, upon those of us who have equally strong moral convictions on the other side of the question' (*Irish Times*, 27 June 1934). Another letter warned of the kind of Ireland that was being created where the drabness of life in the countryside was proving a stimulus to vice, while considering that 'the growth of vice among our young people is largely due to the cruelty and lack of charity among their elders towards any departure from the strict law of charity' (*Irish Times*, 6 July 1934). The drabness of rural existence was not to be alleviated by government intervention when in the next year it passed the Public Dance Halls Act.

The Irish hierarchy, as uncharitable elders, had for decades been inveighing against rustic 'company-keeping' in unpatrolled locations. A 1935 Act sought to ease episcopal moral panic by making it a requirement that dance halls be licensed accordingly to strict criteria, overseen by the judiciary. A letter to the paper on 14 June 1935 from one who termed himself 'Non Grex Sed Lex' reflected the inter-generational tension that had resulted in the passing of the two Acts, when he warned: 'The primitive herd instincts of undisciplined youth must be firmly controlled and yield to the law.' On the same day another letter-writer objected to how 'persons of both sexes undressed together for swimming, on riverbanks as well as at the sea-shore', while lamenting the 'disgraceful conduct of hyper-amorous couples' who 'were to be seen along the sides of ... public roads'. On 6 September a Dublin Jesuit offered his severe analysis of the current moral malaise: the country was engaged in an economic war, and rural dances were subverting that crusade. They were 'a grave menace to the nation' since young farm workers were lying too long abed after night-time revelries. A district judge in Donegal, hearing an application for a dance hall licence in September, reckoned: 'The craze for dancing was not so much a cause' of moral desuetude 'as a symptom. The country was full of restless, ill-disciplined, often idle, young people, in whom [the] schools had failed, in the main, to develop a taste for reading or intellectual pleasure' (*Irish Times*, 5 September 1935). On 18 September the paper recorded the first prosecution and fine for holding an unlicensed dance (a tame enough affair conducted to the strains of a melodeon). In this fairly widespread climate of intrusive, legalistic puritanism, it must have come as a relief to many a lad and lassie when a district judge determined, as reported in the *Weekly Irish Times* on 21 December 1935, in time for the mistletoe, that kissing in public 'was not an indecent offence' under the Criminal Law Amendment Act. A young fellow had been hauled before a court 'for embracing and kissing a girl outside a dance hall' just before midnight.

The *Irish Times* gave its own considered view on this efflorescence of Mrs Grundyism, inflected through Church pastorals and statute law, in an editorial entitled 'Dance Halls'. It admitted that there was a credible case against unregulated dance halls, but its tone was mildly ironic about the moral outrage they occasioned: 'If all the statements made at District Courts are correct, dancing is one of the greatest causes of evil in modern Ireland' (*Irish*

Times, 25 October 1935). The editorialist seemed amused enough by some of this, quoting one Catholic bishop who had wonderfully commented: 'Of all the amusements, there seems to be a curse on dancing since the days of John the Baptist. Seldom can a person attend a dance without catching something of the immoral state.' The *Irish Times*, in demurral, was unconcerned that folk could lose their heads at dances, at least in the capital, for 'the atmosphere of almost painful respectability at most dances in Dublin contrasts strongly with the assertion that modern dancing is indecent and suggestive, and that even the tunes to which it is performed are capable of great moral harm.' It well understood that the real bugbear was jazz, which in 1930s' Ireland had become a metonym for evil, along with the foreign yellow press and 'immoral literature'.

The editorial tone in this leader, with its mild good humour before arriving at the unexceptionable if banal conclusion that dancing should not be 'forbidden altogether', probably reflected the lighter hand of Smyllie at the helm. Healy as editor, especially when roused by the doings of de Valera, had repeatedly struck a note of high-flown alarm in the paper's leader columns as constitutional crisis followed constitutional crisis. The literary effect was often to suggest frozen outrage, fixed in statuesque irrelevancy to the vulgar and colourful energies of Irish political life as it was actually practised. The rigorous template Healy favoured for leading articles (the first leader always had to consist of three paragraphs of 22 lines each; the second leader had to be a single paragraph of 35 lines; Gray 1991, 1994 pp. 30–1; Fleming 1965, p. 161) heightened this impression of a near-formulaic, deeply conservative antipathy to the republican ethos that was the ideological underpinning of the Free State. Lionel Fleming, in his recollection of this period, recalled Healy as 'a man of remarkable inflexibility of mind' (Fleming 1965, p. 160). For all that the newspaper had given its qualified support to the new dispensation in the 26 counties as the one most likely to impose and sustain law and order, Healy's style seemed a relic of the imperial days for which he certainly hankered. By contrast, although he remained essentially a unionist by social formation and conservative by inclination on most political and social matters, Smyllie, albeit no stylist of marked ability, was capable of an unbuttoned discursiveness (when he contributed 'An Irishman's Diary' as 'Nichevo', for example) and an editorial unbending that bespoke a far from reclusive personality.

In fact, Smyllie was very much the social animal, whereas Healy had sedulously protected his privacy. The latter preferred the private dinner party when he sought a social contact; the former was a pub-man of the traditional journalistic type, who soon acquired a reputation as a Dublin character, which made him a recognized landmark of city life in general, in a way that his predecessors had mostly not been. His larger-than-life persona – Chestertonian in girth and spirit, cheerfully bawdy in male company, punctilious in personal address, mired in procrastination and managerial disorder, a keen if ineffective golfer – attracted from Smyllie's fellow journalists and employees on the paper the kind of loyalty and affection, mingled with frequent frustration, that only the truly remarkable can command. The forceful peculiarities of his personality were registered, indeed, in four vivid volumes of memoir by his colleagues, more than a few articles, and were widely referenced in accounts of the period, where the previous incumbents had stimulated only respectful obituary prose.

Patrick Campbell (son and heir to Baron Glenavy), wit and future TV panellist, who worked on the paper from 1935 to 1938 and again between 1944 and 1947, famously set Smyllie in comic aspic, when he recalled in a *Spectator* article how he counted himself fortunate, in an era of grey anonymity on Fleet Street, to have served under an editor 'who wore a green sombrero, weighed twenty-two stone, sang parts of his leading articles in operatic recitative, and grew the nail on his little finger into the shape of a pen nib, like Keats' (cited in Inglis 1962 p. 47). That the paper appeared on time every day under Smyllie's unconventional editorship was a testament to the persistent energy and acumen of the long-serving general manager, John Simington; that the *Irish Times* was worth buying and became more so under Smyllie's editorship was testament to the fact that creativity often flourishes in the purlieus of eccentricity, bohemianism and an affected, studied indolence. Smyllie, in determined flight from the demands of his manager and much neglected correspondence (he was a procrastinator of genius), spent a great deal of his time in what was effectively a branch office, the Palace Bar, across the street from the office building on D'Olier Street. There most evenings, he enjoyed the company of an eclectic selection of Dublin's writers, poets, dramatists, actors, painters and their conversational hangers-on until duty called and he returned to headquarters to write an editorial or other pressing piece and to see the paper printed in the early hours of the morning, having shared music and further drink with congenial members of the staff.

Irish literary life was in transition in the 1930s. The Irish Literary Revival of the 1890s and early decades of the century, which had put the country on the international cultural map, had been led by the poet Yeats and had found its spiritual home in Lady Augusta Gregory's residence at Coole Park in County Galway. It was redolent of the Ascendancy Protestant world from which it mainly derived. In Dublin, 'evenings' in middle-class homes in such respectable suburbs as Rathmines and Rathgar had been the 'salons' at which culture, politics and literary reputation were discussed over tea, sherry and biscuits in an atmosphere that did not preclude the presence of women. By the mid-1930s, with Yeats mostly abroad and AE (George Russell) dead (both of whose 'evenings' in the 1920s had been the focus of such intellectual exchange), the capital's cultural life was finding its centre of gravity in the public house rather than in the genteel drawing-room. The company was almost exclusively male and the social mix more representative of the country at large than

Yeats's evenings at his grand residence in Merrion Square, for example, had ever been. That the demotic attractions of the lounge and public bar were replacing the refinement of the salon bespoke how the country's literary and artistic practitioners were themselves becoming more interested in the daily life of the nation's citizenry than in the romantic idealism that had inspired the Irish Literary Revival at its inception. That editor Smyllie sat among them on a near-nightly basis, holding court, as it were, suggests that he, too, was part of that transition, combining as he did membership of the almost exclusively Protestant Masonic Order, playing the 'island golf course' in Malahide to the north of Dublin (itself opening its fairways to the better sort of Catholic business and professional men, though Smyllie himself never became a paid-up member) with an advanced taste for pub life in the city centre.

If Smyllie was king of the castle in the Palace Bar and endured a kind of joint monarchy with his general manager in D'Olier Street, in the years immediately following the editor's appointment, de Valera was tightening his hold on actual republican power. When he flexed his political muscles threateningly, the *Irish Times*, under Smyllie's editorship, was perfectly prepared to let the paper oppose him as vehemently as Healy had done. In October 1934, for example, an editorial indulged itself in an expansive comparison of the Free State governed by de Valera with European despotism, as if to assure its readers that the spirit of Healy had not left the building:

> To all intents and purposes President de Valera, although he relies on a democratic vote – possibly the most democratic in the world – is a dictator. Herr Hitler abolishes the entire Constitution of Weimar with a stroke of a pen; President de Valera tears up the Free State's Constitution piecemeal. The one is a dictator and boasts of the fact; the other preserves the *façade* of democracy, behind which he works his own unfettered will. When the Reichstag was in Hitler's way, he promptly got rid of it, just as Signor Mussolini got rid of the Italian parliament. When the Free State tried to thwart President de Valera's dictatorial plans, he did precisely the same thing in a different way. (*Irish Times*, 18 October 1934)

However, as Smyllie settled into his editorial chair, the tenor of editorials about de Valera's Ireland became more circumspect, even pragmatic. This was most evident in the paper's response to the adoption in 1937 of the constitution promulgated by de Valera to bring his constitutional crusade as far as he could in the prevailing circumstances (in which partition of the island had become an undeniable roadblock to the realization of the republic envisaged in 1916).

In February 1936, in an editorial, the paper made clear that whatever de Valera attempted in the constitutional sphere (and the writer admitted: 'On many points of policy we agree, more or less cordially, with Mr de Valera', *Irish Times*, 17 February 1936), the issue of Commonwealth membership should be non-negotiable. When in April 1937 de Valera published the draft of a new constitution for the state, where Healy might immediately have turned the big guns of his apocalyptic rhetoric on it, the *Irish Times* set out in measured and sometimes cleverly ironic terms to expose the document as flawed and in broad terms perhaps little more than a paper tiger for all its apparent claws. On 1 May an editorial entitled 'Eire' (with an epigraph from an eighteenth-century Munster poet), judged de Valera's work as 'a long and rather dreary document' that had achieved the dubious feat of ignoring Britain and her Commonwealth almost completely:

> There is an oblique reference to it – a kind of shamefaced attempt to keep a last-minute grip on the painter, as it were – but for the rest Great Britain might be just as far away as Aldebarran [*sic*] [a star in the Taurus constellation], although everybody knows perfectly well that the thing that matters most is its relationship with the neighbouring island.

The rest of this editorial identified the draft constitution's main provisions, welcoming the restoration of a Senate in a new form and commending the establishment of a Council of State as a kind of Privy Council. It reckoned, however, that '*Eire* is neither fish, flesh, fowl nor good red herring. It does not tell us whether we are in the Commonwealth or out of it. Can it be that Mr de Valera does not know?' (*Irish Times*, 1 May 1937). Subsequent editorials speculated about what manner of creature the new state would be, especially with regard to the British Commonwealth, coming to the conclusion that de Valera's document was a very strange animal, a paper tiger with the potential to become the real thing.

On 8 May an editorial provocatively quoted W. B. Yeats's poem of national disillusionment from 1913, which as we noted, first appeared in the *Irish Times* as 'Romance in Ireland'. Concluding that the provisions of the new constitution had not 'set the Liffey on fire' (*Irish Times*, 8 May 1937) and that '*plus ça change, plus c'est la même chose* so far as essentials are concerned *Eire* will not be one whit more or less independent than *Saorstát Eireann*.' 'Was it for this', the writer queried, 'that the civil war was fought in 1922, that so many young lives were sacrificed, that all those fine old Irish mansions were burned down and their owners driven from their country?' As for de Valera himself, the tone adopted was snide, reckoning his constitution a masterpiece of sham, 'an elaborate pretence' for he would be

> ... able to tell the groundlings at the next general election that he has given the final twist to the lion's tale ... [He] will be able to convince the more credulous among their followers that the British connection has been severed; and in all likelihood, they will come back to power for another five years as a reward for their sea-green incorruptibility.

By the end of the month, as the dangerous subtlety of de Valera's proposal became more fully understood, the newspaper's attitude became more searching, as expressed in a leader entitled 'The Republican Charter'. It had become clear that the wily politician had drafted a document that could allow for continued membership of the Commonwealth or for secession from it. In this, the new position of elected President was highly significant, for he could serve as a kind of Governor General until such time as a fully functioning Irish republic came into being. Then he would be 'ready and equipped to assume the duties of President of the Republic' (*Irish Times*, 27 May 1937). Since the *Irish Times* did not think that would occur until partition was ended, and that was not likely to happen in the foreseeable future, the editorial continued to view the draft constitution as toothless: 'while we admire its ingenuity, we deplore its futility'. However, on 4 June the paper expressed its alarm that the proposed Article 40 of the constitution, which set limits to free speech (it envisaged that the right of free speech should not be 'used to undermine public order or morality, or the authority of the state'), might curtail the freedom of the press. Invoking Mussolini and Hitler's similar view of press freedom, the editorial 'Farewell Freedom' warned: 'The Constitution proposes to cripple the public's judgment; it opens the way for a condition of affairs in which no view but the Government's will be available to the people at large.' The paper worried about the issue again on 9 June, this time referring to the high-ranking Nazi Hermann Goering, as it dismissed the draft document imperiously as 'in its essentials ... so much eyewash' (*Irish Times*, 9 June 1937). So while the constitution was toothless, the man who drafted it was a dangerous beast indeed, who as king of the Irish jungle might use it for his own nefarious ends; he was a 'supreme egoist', an editorial entitled 'L'État c'est moi' advised, one who some years earlier had 'announced blandly that when he wished to know what the Irish people wanted, he merely looked into his own heart, where it seems, he was able to discover the clue to every riddle' (*Irish Times*, 5 June 1937).

Since the newspaper was anxiously exercised about the threat to press freedom, opposed to the article prohibiting divorce, supportive of the idea of a presidency, for which post it recommended the Church of Ireland Gaelic scholar, folklorist and language revivalist Douglas Hyde, it is striking that the issue of women's role in society did not become a matter of controversy in the *Irish Times* coverage of the constitution debate. That Articles 40, 41 and 45 were points of contention, however, was made clear by an advertisement placed in the paper on 30 June 1937 by the National University Women Graduates Association, advising women voters to reject the constitution, since 'your equality of status guaranteed in the 1916 Proclamation and the old Constitution can be taken away; the State can interfere in the private concerns of the Home; the State can interfere in a woman's choice of occupation' (*Irish Times*, 30 June 1937).

When the constitution became effective on 29 December 1937, the *Irish Times* published a considered editorial that summed up the main points that had been made in its columns during the referendum debate: the new constitution, where it was not simply 'eyewash', was an exercise in ingenious double-think (de Valera's mind was assessed as 'entirely logical, and almost entirely impractical' (*Irish Times*, 29 December 1937); it would not 'make the slightest difference to the lives of the people', who would continue to enjoy their dominion status while abroad and a kind of republican citizenship at home. More seriously, acknowledging that the constitution was now the law of the land and must consequently be respected, the editorial doubted whether or not what it accepted were de Valera's sincere principal intentions in promulgating the constitution could be realized by the document. These were, as the writer judged: 'to put an end to civil strife in the twenty-six counties by providing for the extreme Republicans all the essentials of an independent Republic; and the other was to advance the cause of Irish unity'. The paper noted how Sinn Féin at midnight on 29 December had hoisted a black flag over its headquarters in Dublin 'to symbolise the party's mourning at the birth of the new dispensation'. It would be, the editorialist grimly warned, as disloyal to the new as to the old state and would settle for 'nothing less than an isolated Republic'.

A force that the *Irish Times* was happy to see constraining isolationist tendencies in independent Ireland was the quickening pace of technological development underpinned by modern science. On 7 July 1937, a week after de Valera's constitution received its popular mandate, the paper was pleased to report and editorialize on a double trip that sent a flying-boat, the *Caledonia*, from Ireland to Newfoundland and welcomed another such craft that had made the flight from Canada to land at Foynes on the Shannon estuary. The editorial expressed gratification that the transatlantic passenger services that were sure to follow would strengthen relations between the British and North American people, 'and the Irish people ought to be proud of the important part that is being played by their country in this wonderful achievement' (*Irish Times*, 7 July 1937). The occasion could not pass, however, without the *Irish Times* making a political point, playing on de Valera's terminology in relation to Ireland's relationship with the United Kingdom and the British Commonwealth:

> The future of Foynes and Rynanna [there was a flying boat base at Foynes and an airport at Rynanna, both on the Shannon] depends in large part on the continued association with the Commonwealth. Whether that association proves to be 'internal' or 'external' does not amount in the last analysis to a row of beans. What does matter is that Ireland shall not be a separate Republic; and those Irishmen who think at all ought to realise that yesterday's double flight to and from the United States [*sic*] is one of

the most cogent arguments against separation that have [sic] ever been adduced. (*Irish Times*, 7 July 1937)

The shrinking globe, the *Irish Times* hoped, was making separatism anachronistic.

Earlier in the decade, indeed, under Healy's editorship, the paper had continued to be, as it had been in the period before independence, an enthusiastic advocate for the 'science' and technology that were changing the world and humankind's understanding of the universe (the term 'science' itself was by the 1930s fully registered in its lexicon, along with the honorific 'men of science'), though not usually in such obviously tendentious terms. As might be expected, technology was respected, especially where it bore on imperial defence (the memories of the Great War were still all too fresh; a new searchlight, for example, was welcomed on 4 December 1931 as 'further proof of Britain's supremacy in the art and science of aviation'). 'Science' was treated more disinterestedly, if, nonetheless, as an aspect of a more secular, liberal and humanistic discourse than was generally current in the Free State in the early 1930s. In so doing, it set the paper in implicit opposition to a prevailing Irish assumption that national goals were limited to the political, economic and linguistic spheres.

With obvious deliberation, Healy's newspaper drew attention to scientific landmarks and centenaries. The hundred years since Michael Faraday had produced electricity from magnetism was noted in an editorial on 22 September 1931. The death of Thomas Edison on 18 October 1931 warranted a further editorial devoted to scientific and technological achievement. The leader, simply headed 'Edison', observed: 'His contribution to the world's material progress and welfare has been, at least, as large as the contribution of any other single man; for virtually the whole of modern electrical development must be ascribed to his account' (*Irish Times*, 19 October 1931).

The meeting in London on 23 September 1931, to mark the centenary of the founding of the British Association for the Advancement of Science, had a few weeks earlier given the *Irish Times* a similar opportunity to reflect further on the role of science in society. The paper gave ample coverage to General Jan Smuts's presidential address to 5,000 delegates, in which he claimed that 'Science is at last coming into its own as one of the supreme goods of the human race' (24 September 1931). An editorial of the same day, entitled 'Science and Life', was a resounding panegyric to the scientific spirit:

When we view the nineteenth century in retrospect it stands out – perhaps more than any other period in the history of the universe – as a century glorified by the ever soaring and ever conquering spirit of man ... We, in the opening of a new century, have seen the old philosophical conception of the physical universe melt away before the adventurous speculations of pure reason, founded on research and discovery ... Not only does science touch the business of the workaday world at every point, but ... science today makes an increasing aesthetic appeal to people, with its vision of order and beauty and the selfless pursuit of truth.

When the *Irish Times* published a report on 2 May 1932 under the headline 'The Atom Split: Young Dublin Doctor's Discovery', it was accompanied by a leader hailing the work of John Cockroft and Ernest Walton (both future Nobel Laureates) at Lord Rutherford's Cambridge laboratory. The editorial agreed with Lord Rutherford that 'a page not only new, but momentous, is being turned in the story of scientific progress', while stating: 'It must be a cause of pride to all Irishmen that one of the two victors of the atom – Dr. E. T. S. Walton – is a young graduate of Dublin University.'

Under Smyllie's editorship, the paper's attitude to science became more nuanced. It was no longer simply treated as a triumph of reason to be set against the unreason of a narrow nationalism with its Gaelic pretensions and rural orientation (de Valera, along with numbers of his compatriots, was a sentimentalist about the benefits of rustic life). A more literary atmosphere in the paper, with an enhanced book page and a greater awareness of Irish cultural achievement, allowed for a sense that science and technology were no longer unmixed blessings; and they could be viewed, too, through the lens of cultivated whimsy. When, for example, in August 1936 television images were broadcast from the BBC's new Alexandra Palace transmitter, the *Irish Times* indulged itself with a droll leader, 'The Age of Miracles', which reflected on the way the public accepted 'so complacently the bewildering gifts of science'. The public would quickly begin to complain about the quality of the broadcasts on offer and become blasé about the science underpinning their transmission: 'We accept the sun, the moon, and the stars without question, impotent before such wonders; and now we have learned to accept each new invention of science, however incredible, in the same unruffled manner' (*Irish Times*, 25 August 1936).

By contrast, the following month the paper published a sombre editorial that responded to a presidential address to that year's meeting of the British Association for the Advancement of Science (reported on in an article in *The Times* of London) that had considered the impact of science on society. For the writer of the editorial on 'Science and Man', the Great War had been a terrible proof that 'the gifts of science, although they have brought happiness and prosperity to thousands of people, are double-edged' (*Irish Times*, 10 September 1936). One cannot imagine so gloomy a view of science being taken in Healy's paper as was expressed in this editorial's conclusion: 'Yet control of some kind seems to be essential if mankind is to preserve itself; for the tyranny of science has proved itself already to be worse than any other tyranny' (10 September 1936).

The paper in 1938 did indicate, however, that Healy's more consistently rational, and humanistic spirit still inhabited D'Olier Street when the paper marked the 50 years since Louis Pasteur had assumed the directorship of the

Pasteur Institute, with an editorial entitled 'Benefactor of Mankind'. Pasteur's 'abiding contribution,' the paper judged, was 'to be found in a safer and cleaner world ... He was born into a world sunk in disease; it is to his glory that he cleansed that world' (*Irish Times*, 15 November 1938).

Perhaps Smyllie's greatest gift as an editor was his eye for youthful talent. He himself had been recruited somewhat unconventionally and he was inclined to return the compliment in kind. On his own appointment he was happy to see a 29-year-old junior promoted to be his deputy. Alec Newman, who in fact became Smyllie's successor in 1954, was a Waterford-born man who had been educated at the Royal Belfast Academical Institution and at Trinity College Dublin, where he read Classics while cutting his journalistic teeth on the college's student magazine *T.C.D. Weekly*. An Irish nationalist, where Smyllie remained essentially a unionist in sensibility, Newman was deeply interested in literary culture. In 1934 and 1935 the paper published, probably on his prompting, a fortnightly series of poems by Irish poets, for the first time highlighting the work of younger Irish poets. Patrick Kavanagh, for example, was published twice in the series. In the second half of the 1930s under Newman's influence, the weekly book page began to be a thing of serious critical account, where hitherto on literary matters the *Irish Times* had been at best *belletrist* in outlook, when it was not simply provincial. Indeed, it may well have been Newman who helped shift the paper's attitude to science, identifying as it increasingly did the conflict between science and culture in general (in anticipation of C. P. Snow, one might claim) and between science and religion as more salient under modern conditions than any opposition between an introverted national culture and international, science-driven progress. Significantly perhaps, in February 1936 the paper published a damning review of A. J. Ayer's *Language, Truth and Logic*, curtly dismissing its scientific positivism.

In the 1940s Irish letters would seek to organize itself as a force that could effectively oppose the monolithic Irish Ireland ideology that helped to sustain de Valera in power. In 1932 the *Irish Times* had given its support to W. B. Yeats's establishment of an Irish Academy of Letters, which could stand for freedom of expression against the draconian actions of the Censorship Board and the cultural conformity of the period, with de Valera at its apex. It never, however, gained much purchase on Irish life (its onlie begetter, Yeats, spent much of his life abroad because of ill-health before his death on 28 January 1939). In the 1930s, when the Irish Ireland ideology was in the ascendant in the literary Ice Age that the censorship seemed intent on imposing on the country, what and how a paper chose to review literature in its columns was a measure of how seriously it took its commitment to artistic liberty and cultural inclusiveness. The case of James Joyce offers a ready litmus test.

The paper, as we indicated, had published a brief interview-article by James Joyce on a French racing driver in 1903; in 1904 it noted that a Mr

Joyce had been highly commended at that year's Feis Ceoil in Dublin for his tenor singing. The works that established the author's name, *Dubliners* and *A Portrait of the Artist as a Young Man*, did not attract the notice of the paper. Bruyere did, however, as we saw, include Joyce in the 'Some Irish Artists' series published in 1923, when a cautious estimate reckoned of *Ulysses* (1922) that 'in writing it Mr Joyce had made an entry into European literature' (*Irish Times*, 5 May 1923). In November the same year, in a report on a lecture given in Dublin, readers could have learnt of W. B. Yeats's admiration for the book; but on the same occasion a future member of the Censorship Board had denounced *Ulysses* for its moral filth. Yeats's defence of *Ulysses* at the prize-giving ceremony of the first Tailteann Games had not really been helpful to Joyce's Irish reputation when he described the novel as 'obscene as Rabelais' but 'more indubitably a work of genius than any prose written by an Irishman since the death of Synge' (*Irish Times*, 11 August 1924).

By the 1930s Joyce was an internationally renowned figure and the *Irish Times*, in recognition of his indisputable status, noted items on his doings and health as they were picked up on the wire services. In 1931 it reported on his marriage to Norah Barnacle in a register office in London 'for testamentary reasons' (*Irish Times*, 4 July 1931). In December 1933 the *Irish Times* reported the famous judgement of a New York court that *Ulysses* was not obscene. More locally, the novelist Brinsley MacNamara, who contributed an article on Irish literature to the lengthy supplement the *Irish Times* issued to mark the first decade of the Free State, observed that the book went largely unread in Ireland. It may have caught the attention of the world, but, although 'no Dubliner' could 'escape its authentic Dublin quality', in Ireland it was 'quietly referred to as "an open sewer," and left at that' (*Irish Times*, 21 December 1932). A year later a review of a study of Joyce acknowledged more thoughtfully that, far from being an impenetrable book, as many of those who had attempted to read it claimed (Brinsley MacNamara had found it artistically 'amorphous'), *Ulysses* would 'give up its meaning to anybody with sufficient time to read it more than once' (*Irish Times*, 23 December 1933). That reviewer felt less secure with the *Work in Progress* that would become *Finnegans Wake*, but a contributor in 1934 was more open to avant-garde modernism when he observed of 'James Joyce's Experiment with Language' that he was 'trying to mould language to his own ends' in 'portmanteau words' (*Irish Times*, 27 October 1934), as Lewis Carroll had done.

The publication of *Finnegans Wake* in 1939 was greeted by an editorial in the *Irish Times* of 6 May 1939, entitled 'Ancient and Modern'. The young man who had contributed the desultory interview-article with a racing driver in 1903 had travelled a long road. The leader writer acknowledged that the author's new book was not easy reading since 'It is written in English that is not English, and it makes sense that is not sense.' He grasped, nonetheless, that 'The thousands of Irish people who have read "Ulysses" in defiance of an

English ban will recognise the genesis of its style in the last, admirable "hour" of greatest of modern novels.' This key critical insight, that *Finnegans Wake* is a book of the night, of the kind of reverie-filled darkness in which Molly Bloom had concluded *Ulysses*, that seeks to 'express those half-rational conceptions which lie in the borderland between conscious thought and semi-conscious or unconscious perception', was joined by further insightful critical observations in the review the paper published the following month.

This review headlined 'Sixteen Years Work by James Joyce: New Novel is "Endlessly Exciting in Its Impenetrability"', gave readers a vivid sense of the book's linguistic bravura ('One feels its power, the kind of gleaming genius behind it') and supplied suggestions as to how it might be thought of as 'The convolutions of a dream, as a game in which only the author knows the rules and in which the sounds of words in infinite variety fascinate him'. The writer commented: 'One thinks of an arrangement of sound, of music' and suggested that the work could be usefully read aloud. He sensed, too, that it was a text overwhelmed by the demotic speech of Dublin. More profoundly, the reviewer stated: 'Time and space and identity as we have known them are here no more.' Such literary acumen about *Finnegans Wake* can be said to be the moment when the *Irish Times* came critically of age, as it were. It was manifestly determined to give full intellectual attention to a highly controversial work by one of Catholic Ireland's most remarkable sons, and to what came to be termed the 'revolution of the word'. The review itself considered that 'a new language may have been born'.

Joyce's death in Zurich in 1941 warranted an editorial, simply entitled 'James Joyce', on his life and achievements. It was a full-throated encomium that identified *Ulysses* as the work that would place him among the immortals (as a greater writer in his field than Yeats in his):

> Joyce's contribution to the world's literature will be judged by 'Ulysses', one of the most remarkable books ever written. It has been hailed as a work of consummate genius, fit to be included in the first rank of the masterpieces of human thought. It has been condemned as a crude essay in pornography, unworthy of an Irish writer, the product of a diseased mind, and fit to be read – if indeed it could be read at all – only by persons as depraved as the author himself. The fact is that 'Ulysses' has had a bigger influence on contemporary literature than any other single work of modern times. (*Irish Times*, 14 January 1941)

This compelling editorial about one of Ireland's 'most highly gifted sons', one who had not been honoured as a prophet in his own country, was at pains to insist on Joyce's national patrimony: 'James Joyce was an Irishman of the Irish'. In so emphatically identifying Joyce as quintessentially Irish, the *Irish Times* was doing more than expressing Irish patriotism about an international figure who had spent most of his adult life abroad. It was nailing its colours definitively to the mast of a cultural pluralism and hybridity that stood opposed to the dominant Irish Ireland consensus of the day, a consensus that would be more effectively challenged by Irish writers themselves from the 1940s onwards. That exclusivist ideology had found its most persuasive advocate in the 1930s (as D. P. Moran had been at the turn-of-century) in a book published in 1931 by the Professor of English at University College Cork, Daniel Corkery. In *Synge and Anglo-Irish Literature*, Corkery had damned most Irish writing in English as essentially non-national and provincial (the *Irish Times*'s review had responded: 'To our mind it would seem the real "provincial" in this matter is Mr Corkery himself', *Irish Times*, 12 June 1931). And the paper had signalled clearly in 1934 that a culture war was afoot in de Valera's Ireland; it knew, too, on which side it found itself. The occasion was the first presentation of prizes awarded to Irish writers by the recently formed Irish Academy of Letters. An editorial entitled 'An Irish Culture' was gratified that the members of the academy were 'drawn from all parts of our island', continuing: 'There are men of pure Gaelic stock among them, as well as Normans, Ulster-Scots, and even Cromwellians; but they are all writing in the English language, and the culture which they represent is, as it ought to be, an amalgam of all the elements of which our race to-day is composed' (*Irish Times*, 8 December 1934). The editorial forcefully drew the political lesson that was inscribed in the controversy about national culture:

> At a time when small-minded persons would wish to imprison literature in this country in parochial fetters – just as the politicians are seeking to create the narrowest form of economic nationalism – it is encouraging to find that so many of our writers are breaking through their artificial bonds and compelling the world to take notice of them. These men are intensely national in outlook, but they realise that the Irish nation is the monopoly of no party or of no class.

The editorial marked the occasion not only by this salvo in the culture war but by berating the government's attitude to 'the artist's liberty of expression'. So in asserting in 1941 that James Joyce – Catholic, writer in English, whose major work was ignored in his native city, when it was not dismissed as obscene – was Irish of the Irish, the *Irish Times* was sticking steadfastly to its pluralist guns.

That the *Irish Times*'s endorsement of cultural pluralism (including literature and science in its purview) was no mere strategy to protect the interests of Normans, Ulster-Scots and even Cromwellians (and Joyce as known apostate could have been seen as a useful recruit to the ranks of dissent) was evidenced by its willingness to give space to the creative endeavours of younger Irish writers in a way it had not done before. It also allowed them to criticize their elders and indulged their attacks on sacred cows. On 26 February 1935, for example, when the Nobel Laureate W. B. Yeats announced that he was setting up an Abbey

Theatre advisory board, the paper published a highly critical letter from Frank O'Connor and Seán O'Faolain. Both had been nurtured as writers by Daniel Corkery, though by 1935 they had broken with his austere form of nationalism. However, they felt Yeats was betraying the national ideals of his own theatre when he indicated that he hoped to expand its repertoire with English and continental plays. And they bemoaned the fact that younger playwrights were being ignored: 'To fall back on the revival of old plays is merely a confession of incapacity to encourage.' On 2 March O'Faolain was given the opportunity to expand on the case, when he concluded in an article that, at the Abbey, the young writer 'meets no atmosphere of ideals'. On the same day the paper even published a generally supportive editorial on O'Faolain's piece, an intervention that was to all intents and purposes a criticism of the grand old man of Irish letters, the Anglo-Irish Yeats. 'We welcome,' the editorial confessed, 'the controversy which Mr. Yeats's plan has brought; for it means that people have become suddenly aware that the Abbey represents something which Ireland cannot afford to lose.' At the end of the decade, in a further turn of the screw, O'Faolain and O'Connor, who had themselves become part of a new literary establishment, would find themselves assailed in the letters column of the paper by a writer who, under the pseudonym Flann O'Brien, was mischievously prepared to puncture their intellectual pretensions. In closing a spirited and comical correspondence, Smyllie gave his readership to understand that the identity of that rancorously irreverent spirit was known to him.

The *Irish Times* in the 1930s under Smyllie's editorship remained a markedly conservative organ. Its fundamental social outlook continued to be that of educated, prosperous folk (Latin tags were not abandoned in leading articles when Healy died) who occupied comfortable positions in business, the legal and medical professions, and in the public service. Increased use of photography, which had been occasional in the 1920s, had, however, freshened with visual immediacy the severe columns of text that in earlier decades had given its pages a distinctly forbidding aspect (and one page was dedicated to photographs). Advertisements were livelier, deploying the wit and playfulness of the adman as well as attractive drawings. The front page was largely devoted to such advertisements, and others were distributed elsewhere in the paper. The 'Court and Personal' section still recorded the comings-and-goings of the titled and high-ranking in the archipelago, as if to give the impression that the Irish *ancien régime*, with its links to the British well born, somehow was still intact and had been joined by a new, respectable Irish elite. 'Church Notes' might, as well as the Church of Ireland, encompass matters affecting Presbyterians and Methodists, but not readers of the majority confession. Where the *Weekly Irish Times* in late Victorian times had realized that women were an important constituency in its readership, in the daily paper in the 1930s they were catered for by the patronizing column 'Of Interest to Women'. Matters motoring commanded

RMS Titanic, the White Star Line's Olympic-class ship in Harland and Wolff's shipyard, Belfast, shortly before her launch in April 1912; she sunk on her maiden voyage to New York, on the night of 14th April 1912, with the loss of more than 1,500 lives

Irish Guardsmen stand at their post five minutes before the Armistice, near Maubeuge on 11th November 1918

Two women walking past jewellers, Grafton Street, Dublin, c.1900

John William Stocks behind the wheel of the Napier motorcar he
drove in the Gordon Bennett race of 1903

Soldiers survey the interior of the wrecked Post Office in Sackville Street, Dublin, during the Easter Rising of 1916

View of the junction of Lower Abbey Street and Sackville Street, 1916. On the left are the remains of the Hibernian Bank Branch Office, and on the right the skeleton of the Dublin Bakery Company Restaurant

Two men in Irish costume with wolfhounds at the opening
parade of the Tailteann Games, 1924

The huge turbines under construction at the Shannon
hydroelectric scheme at Ardnacrusha

Irish Free State politician and Minister for Justice and External Affairs,
Kevin O'Higgins (1892–1927) addressing a gathering

Crowds at the 31st International Eucharistic Congress,
Dublin, June 1932

General Eoin O'Duffy, leader of the Blueshirts

An Imperial Airways seaplane, *Maia* docked at Foynes, July 1938

Dr Ernest Walton with Cockroft-Walton apparatus, 1932.
Physicists Walton and Cockroft developed the accelerator
in the Cavendish Laboratory at Cambridge University to
artificially accelerate atomic particles to high energies

View of the Berghof, Nazi Chancellor Adolf Hitler's home
in the Bavarian Alps, 1936

Adolf Hitler looks out at the Obersalzburg Mountains
from a balcony near the Berghof, 1938

more respect as the middle-class family car began to become the norm, with the paterfamilias at the wheel. The newspaper's circulation stayed at about 25,500 (Mark O'Brien 2008, p. 82), which did not perturb the editor (whatever about the general manager and the proprietor, though the accounts stayed in the black), content as he was to oversee a paper of quality, disdaining populism.

Nonetheless, in the early years of Smyllie's reign, as suggested by the genuine interest the paper took for the first time in current, local literary production, there was a convincing impression given that the *Irish Times* was seeking to become a willing participant in the new Ireland's life and not a somewhat aloof and occasionally seriously jaundiced observer of it. The *Irish Times* was open for conversation, as it were, with the emergent nation of which it accepted it was a part. It is that which probably accounts for the fact that even those who might have been expected to be immune to its appeal, in retrospect recognized the sea-change that had begun to take place on Smyllie's appointment. One such figure was Todd Andrews, a republican who had fought in the War of Independence and taken the anti-Treaty side in the Civil War. He was very much a mover-and-shaker in de Valera's Ireland and no friend of Protestant privilege. In 1982 Andrews recalled of Smyllie's impact as editor on the paper:

> Smyllie accepted that he was an Irishman owing an unequivocal allegiance to Ireland ... his influence derived from the fact that he wrote from the standpoint of a free independent Ireland rather from that of a province, regrettably and possibly temporarily separated from the motherland ... Smyllie, in fact, integrated the *Irish Times* and what it stood for and he was more than welcomed by the ruling group and the civil servants in particular ... Favourable comment from the *Irish Times* made a minister's day. Favourable comment from the other two Dublin dailies was of no importance to them. (Andrews, cited Mark O'Brien 2008, p. 82)

This tells us that the editor's studied bohemianism had been the effective disguise of a person of substantial, practical achievement.

Irish political and administrative culture was not, of course, coterminous with the nation, and Andrews's retrospective endorsement of Smyllie's 'revolution' was probably the exaggeration of one for whom the political class constituted a defining element of the community. There remained, however, swathes of Irish society in which the clerically minded *Irish Independent* and the *Irish Press* (founded in 1931 by de Valera to give broad republican support to Fianna Fáil) had the unswerving loyalty of the partisan. For many of these it would have been unthinkable to take the *Irish Times*, still regarded, as it was, as alien and as an occasion of possible sin. The newspaper's attitude to the international crises of the 1930s and to World War II would not, one senses, have given such people much reason to change journalistic allegiances and habits had they been minded in those times to sample its daily offerings.

5

THE *IRISH TIMES* AND THE WORLD CRISIS

I n 1942 the poet Patrick Kavanagh, two of whose early pastoral poems had
been published by the *Irish Times* in 1935, wrote but did not publish a long
work entitled *Lough Derg*. It was a successor poem to what is recognized as
Kavanagh's masterwork, *The Great Hunger*, which appeared in 1942. In that
latter poem of 14 sections, the poet had presented an excoriatingly realistic
report from the heart of rural Ireland that gave the lie to Eamon de Valera's
vision of a bucolic, countryside supporting a free, self-sufficient nation. In
Lough Derg (1978) Kavanagh turned his attention to the religious life of the
common people, following them on a pilgrimage to the penitential island of
Lough Derg in County Donegal. There he found the devotion to things of the
spirit reduced to a petty materialism and the country mired in a self-defeating
isolation in time of war. 'All Ireland,' he observed, '... froze for want of Europe.'

It was apt that *Lough Derg*, with its striking plea for European perspectives
to mitigate Irish provincialism, was not published during World War II (it in
fact was published posthumously many years later), for the period 1939–45
was one in which news from Europe was to a large degree suppressed by a
government determined that the populace should not have its support for Irish
military and political neutrality affected by partisan reportage of any kind, or
even by much information. This posed considerable problems for newspapers
in Ireland, and it can be argued, especially for the *Irish Times*, which had
earnestly made it its business in the 1930s to cover extensively international
affairs both in the Anglo-Saxon world and in Europe as aspects of an ongoing
world crisis that came to a head in the declaration of war in September 1939
and in the terrible events that then ensued.

The *Irish Times* had in the 1930s given thoughtful attention from its
conservative viewpoint to the economic blizzard that had blown through so
many countries (though little actual reportage was done, it must be said, of what
day-to-day poverty involved on a human level) that was so much a fomenter of
the crisis. In October 1936, for example, the protest march of 200 men from
Jarrow in the north-east of England to the Westminster parliament to draw
attention to the impoverishment of their town, drew from the conservative
paper the cautious opinion that, although 'from one point of view, these

marches are useless' (*Irish Times*, 16 October 1936), they could influence public opinion to demand that the government take action. Twelve days later, as the *Irish Times* contemplated forthcoming election tests for the British government, the paper noted how the insular, self-regarding concerns of a British electorate were set against an alarming international panorama (it adduced in this regard the Spanish rebellion, the Abyssinian War and the rearmament programme, as realities alongside 'the large-scale attempts to relieve unemployment at home' [*Irish Times*, 28 October 1936]). It counselled: 'there have been reminders – such as the march of the Jarrow workers to London – that unemployment still is acute in many parts of England and more than one industrial town in the north has been complaining that the State has forgotten its plight' (*Irish Times*, 28 October 1936). The following month an editorial drew a more internationalist conclusion when it warned: 'No country, indeed, can feel safe if it allows whole areas to remain poverty-stricken, and from every point of view it is well that the situation should be changed' (*Irish Times*, 19 November 1936). Closer to home, the *Irish Times* had had the opportunity to consider the dangerous effects of economic depression on industrial society in the lamentable outbreaks of sectarian rioting and violence which occurred in Belfast in 1935.

A weapon in the *Irish Times*'s case against de Valera's economic war in the 1930s was that it would help to copper-fasten partition. The newspaper hoped Northern unionists would in time become willing to contemplate Irish unity within the Commonwealth, with the entire island enjoying the dominion status that had been granted to the Free State in 1922. An impoverished state south of the border, especially a state that had loosened its constitutional ties with Britain, would certainly not attract unionist attention as one worth joining. In this context, Northern prosperity within the United Kingdom could be cited as a counter to de Valera's linked economic and constitutional policies. Economic crisis and sectarian violence in Belfast undermined that argument, while it made locally visible the kinds of stresses the Great Depression was inflicting on the body politic in other parts of Europe.

In 1928 the *Irish Times* had been pleased to editorialize on 'Northern Ireland's Progress'. Its economy was improving after a downturn in the shipbuilding and linen industries ('the clang of the hammer on the Queen's island [the shipyard in Belfast] is being heard again ...' *Irish Times*, 18 December 1928). And while 'the whole idea of two fiscal units in such a small island is absurd to the point of fantasy', the people of Northern Ireland were 'working out their own salvation'. 'None but the most prejudiced observer,' the paper commented, 'will deny that they are doing it well.' By 1933, with the worst effects of the economic crash of 1929 apparently overcome in the United Kingdom, the paper declared that it 'was no longer possible to decry the signs of Britain's returning prosperity' (*Irish Times*, 18 December 1933). Suggesting improbably that de Valera, by 'crafts and assaults', had 'hoped actually to check a return of prosperity to Britain', the writer reckoned the Free State was 'on the verge of bankruptcy'. The editorial concluded: 'Even now, if Mr de Valera could swallow his petty emotions, the twenty-six counties might yet share the fortunes of their great neighbour.' Readers might have discerned as a subtext here a recognition that the six counties were fortunate to be part of a union in which 'new markets open before the British manufacturer' because 'the Free State farmer is deprived of the great market which ought to have been his permanent possession'.

The reality was that the 1930s brought deep economic depression to Belfast which exacerbated political tensions there between nationalists and unionists which in turn found expression in sectarian conflict. In his history of Ulster, Jonathan Bardon records that 'Not a single ship was launched at Queen's Island between 10 December 1931 and 1 May 1934, and the number of employees in the Belfast shipyard was reduced from 10,428 in 1930 to 1,554 in 1932' (Bardon 1992, p. 526). At the same time the linen export trade collapsed to a degree that 'around one third of the workers in the industry became unemployed' (Bardon 1992, p. 526). Briefly in 1932, it had seemed that near-starving Catholic and Protestant workers might unite in the simple demand for bread ('throughout the disturbances there was a full-throated chorus from men and women shouting "we must have bread"', *Irish Times*, 12 October 1932) and increases in outdoor relief. In the event such solidarity was expressed not only in marches but by the rioting and looting that brought an armed police response. Three were left dead and many were injured. The *Irish Times* on 17 October of that year expressed relief that a moment when 'signs of incipient Communism' had appeared in Belfast had been successfully dealt with by the authorities. It considered with conservative rigour that accession to strikers' and rioters' full demands would have 'involved an acknowledgment of socialistic doctrine hitherto unknown in these islands' (*Irish Times*, 17 October 1932). As the city settled down, the paper blandly welcomed the Northern government's 'sympathy' for its 'distressed citizens' and reckoned that it had emerged 'with credit' from a dangerous situation.

Things reverted to a more traditional form in the summer of 1935 when economic deprivation and inflamed political feeling fomented vicious sectarian attacks, rioting and widespread damage to and destruction of domestic property in Catholic districts of Belfast, where many fled their homes. On this occasion the *Irish Times* could not afford the rather distant if strict ideological stance it had taken in 1932, for the violence north of the border threatened to affect the Protestant community in the Free State in direct ways. For, along with graphic reports of the Belfast troubles, the paper was also recording how, in the Free State, Protestant churches were being attacked in reprisal for Orange crimes in the North. Running through editorial commentary at this time is an anxious wish to disassociate southern Protestants from their unlovely brethren in Northern Ireland.

On 22 July the paper declared with outrage: 'Whoever is to blame for the orgy of shooting and stone-throwing in Belfast – and neither side can be absolved, although the majority deserves the greater censure – it is obvious that the Protestants of the South have had nothing to do with it. They have given no sympathy to the state of mind which made those riots possible' (*Irish Times*, 22 July 1935). The next day an editorial used the occasion of George Russell/ AE's Church of Ireland interment in Dublin, which had been attended by Catholics and Protestants, roundly to denounce Orangeism, as if it were solely a Northern phenomenon:

> We hold no brief at all for the Orangemen, whose ignorant bigotry would be a disgrace to any community that calls itself civilised, and whose leaders, many of whom occupy high places in the State, have been guilty of conduct on many occasions that is beneath contempt. The Orange attitude to the Roman Catholic religion is disgusting, and no honest man, whatever his religious views may be, could attempt for a moment to defend it, or even to make excuses for it. (*Irish Times*, 23 July 1935)

This frank condemnation was accompanied, however, by an uneasy sense that it might not be universally believed, for the paper went on to consider how, since the Protestant community in the south was so small and so spread out, even, an admittedly rare, 'outbreak of fanaticism ... gives rise to the gravest anxiety'. An editorial on 27 July was accordingly pleased to report, as if it proved its bona fides in the Free State, that 'This newspaper has been stigmatised in Belfast as an "anti-Orange" journal' (*Irish Times*, 27 July 1935). The editorial was entitled 'Aftermath', since 'the first fury of the sectarian riots in Belfast' had 'spent itself'. It was time for reflection on what had happened. The paper's instinctive class interest, its essential distaste for the workers of an industrial city, was evident. The Belfast ratepayers would have to bear the burden of the disturbances, 'while the real culprits, who belong to the lowest class of Belfast society, will escape scot-free'. However, even more telling was its frisson of horror at the spectacle of religious bigotry it saw in the Northern capital. The impulse to analyse, comprehend and sympathize was overcome in a curse on both their houses: 'The fact is that in the city of Belfast there are two mobs, almost equally depraved in their outlook, who try to cloak their brutalities under the guise of religious zeal.' God forfend, the unnerved editorial implies, that the foul spirit of Belfast should spread to the Free State, where 'disquieting evidence of anti-Protestant feeling in several parts of the country' was giving cause for serious concern. Such feeling, the *Irish Times* sought to assure its readers, 'is foreign to the kindly character of the people of the South'.

What is striking in all this is how, under pressure of Northern events, symptomatic at a local level of the general world economic crisis, the *Irish Times* fell back on unthinking conservative rhetoric and attitudes that belied its oft-repeated anti-partitionism, as it recoiled in respectable horror from what it thought set Belfast apart from the rest of Ireland. Elsewhere in Europe, as Belfast's industrial society fell apart when economic deprivation bit deep in a divided community, equally disturbing events were challenging the social order with violent upheaval. It was clear that the Versailles settlement of 1919 was at risk as the Great Depression exacerbated the political fault-lines it had sought to set in stone (Vinem 2002, pp. 211–14). The *Irish Times* in the 1930s, viewing these events at some distance, was able to achieve a less strident, more analytic, tone than that adopted in response to Northern Irish commotions. In its treatment of the rise of Hitler, of the Spanish Civil War, the Munich crisis of the autumn of 1938, while its liberal instincts were more to the fore, its innate social conservatism was challenged by a profound sense that the world was on the edge of barbarism and a new cataclysm.

On 22 February 1933 the *Irish Times*, contemplating the German general election that was to take place on 5 March, was sanguine enough about the fact that 'Probably Herr Hitler will get his majority' (*Irish Times*, 22 February 1933). It supposed complacently that 'the German race has a deeply-rooted love of order' and 'has been accustomed for centuries to submit to authority'. The editorial identified Hitlerism as '... a symptom rather than a condition in itself' and opined 'A few years of Hitlerism may work a change ...'

When the Reichstag burned in Berlin on 27 February 1933, raising the political mood to a fever pitch, the *Irish Times*'s conservative fear of Bolshevism emerged in full-bloom. It took at face value Nazi claims that communists had been responsible for the arson attack. On 4 March, in an editorial 'Herr Hitler's Way', it stated that 'Communist extremists were almost certainly to blame'. And the paper, indeed, seemed willing to grant some political leeway to the Nazi leader as hammer of the Reds ('Omelettes cannot be prepared without the smashing of eggs'), (*Irish Times*, 4 March 1933), while deprecating his anti-Semitism ('His insensate hatred of Jewry is the weakest plank in Herr Hitler's programme'). The danger posed by Soviet Communism allowed the paper to indulge Hitler with his 'praiseworthy scheme of national regeneration' (with its 'blot of unreasoning anti-Semitism'). The editorial thought Hitler had earned his chance at power and gave him its muted blessing: 'At the moment he is Europe's standard bearer against Muscovite terrorism, and, although some of his methods certainly are open to question, nobody doubts his entire sincerity.'

When Hitler gained his majority on 5 March, the *Irish Times*'s tune began to change. It accounted for Hitler's rise to near-untrammelled power by focusing on the disappointments the German people had suffered since the Great War. Now, the paper concluded, 'they have yielded to the glamour of Hitlerism, with its Swastika banners, its gaudy uniforms, its catch words and its fantastic promises' (*Irish Times*, 7 March 1933). But it remained confident that 'behind all the trumpery and false glitter of the Hitler movement, the German genius remains sound'. The fear was that Hitler might reopen the Polish question. By 11 March, the paper was clearly unsettled by the revolutionary excesses unleashed by Hitler's accession to power: 'It is all very tragic. Herr Hitler's young men, with their brown shirts and their heated heads, are exceeding the bounds of political decency' (*Irish Times*, 11 March 1933) read an editorial entitled 'German Fascism'. It noted with dismay, 'Throughout the Reich the Jews are folding up their tents and stealing quietly away.' Fearing that the German nation was a victim of 'political quackery' the editorial fell back on a Germanophile bout of wishful thinking:

> Everybody who knows and appreciates Germany's real *Kultur* must grieve
> at this great nation's abandonment to an unworthy hysteria. We have no
> doubt that the people who gave birth to the men of the stamp of Goethe,
> Beethoven, Hegel, Mozart, Schiller and Bach will not tolerate for long the
> arrogant pretensions of a Hitler.

No such optimism was possible on 24 March when the *Irish Times* acknowledged that the Austrian house painter had unquestionably become Germany's dictator.

Two editorials published in March and April 1933, both entitled 'Germany and the Jews', indicate how, at the inception of Nazi rule, the *Irish Times's* liberalism made the newspaper, despite its opposition to the Communism Hitler was excising from the body politic, an outspoken critic of that party's anti-Semitism. On 27 March an editorial stated bluntly, 'Chancellor Hitler has allowed the anti-Semitic proclivities of his followers to reach wicked lengths' (*Irish Times*, 27 March 1933). It could not yet bring itself to admit that 'the ignorant passions of the Nazi rank and file' were shared by the leadership, but it was certain German Jews did not merit 'the atrocious treatment which is being allotted to them', despite the fact that many German Jews were communists, 'just as Russian Jews were the brains of the 1917 revolution in Russia'. The second editorial on the subject in April was more forthright, attributing anti-Semitism to the Führer himself. 'The persecution of the Jews,' the paper judged, 'is Herr Hitler's deepest and most flagrant blunder' (*Irish Times*, 20 April 1933). It was a blunder because it endangered German culture; it had provoked the ill-will of Jewry throughout the world, but most injuriously for the German nation itself, it had 'revived civilisation's distrust of the German temper and of German ambitions'.

In 1935 the newspaper was disgusted by Joseph Goebbels, when he gave as his opinion that 'The Jews might be human beings ... just as fleas were animals, and would be tolerated in the new Germany so long as they did not abuse the laws of hospitality or did not try to behave as if they were the equals of Aryan Germans' (*Irish Times*, 1 July 1935). It deprecated, too, Nazi attacks on the Christian Churches, as it plaintively asked, 'How can any Christian people ... deal on terms of real friendship with a Government that openly proclaims its bitter animosity against a small Jewish minority and continues to persecute the Churches with all the evidences of relentless hatred?'

One can take it that much of the *Irish Times*'s commentary on German affairs in 1933 came from or was influenced by Robert Smyllie. Fluent in German, his interest in and admiration for German culture were of long standing. A holiday in Germany in 1929 had supplied him with material for a series of articles on 'The New Germany'. In the autumn of 1936 he repeated the exercise, producing 14 articles on 'Germany under Adolf Hitler' (using his pen-name Nichevo). Once again the reader is struck by how an essentially conservative frame-of-mind, admiring of order and fearful of social anarchy, is in conflict with generous liberal feeling outraged by flagrant infractions of human decencies.

Much of the content of Smyllie's series is jarringly positive, given the increasingly antagonistic tone of the paper's 1933 opinions and subsequent editorials. A visit to Hitler's mountain retreat at Berchtesgaden draws from Smyllie admiration for how well kept everything is, as it demonstrated 'the German's amazing love of order'. On 4 November 1936 Smyllie surprisingly observed: 'My respect for Herr Hitler has increased a hundred-fold since I visited Obersalzburg. One may not be enamoured of his politics, but there must be something at least unusual about a man who chooses to live and do his work in such heavenly surroundings' (Smyllie was referring to Hitler's idyllic mountain retreat in Bavaria). A further article on attractive features of the new regime even went so far as to state: 'There is no doubt whatsoever that Adolf Hitler has done great things for the German people. One may as well be frank about that' (*Irish Times*, 6 November 1936). 'Now,' Smyllie declared, with what seemed like respect, 'she is one of the strongest powers in the world ...' And he liked 'the clean-limbed' young German soldiers he observed in a militarized society. However, he cannot but acknowledge in another article that, for the country's Jews, 'The Nuremberg laws ... represent the most reactionary legislation in any country since the middle ages' (*Irish Times*, 10 November 1936) and he does not disguise his revulsion at their cruel application. He grasps that Germany is a society kept in order by fear, though 'many Germans like this sort of life'. Jews, however, are promised, and the word is telling, 'extermination'. He discounts what one German Jew tells him about conditions at Dachau, since he had not himself been incarcerated there, but does report how people do disappear 'into one or other of the concentration camps, to which no polite person ever refers. Domestic espionage has been brought to a high art, and no one ever knows to whom one is speaking' (*Irish Times*, 10 November 1936). Perhaps most alarmingly for his readers, Smyllie found that, while Germans over 30 years of age did not want another war for the German people, 'in the long run war will be inevitable ... because there is no other conceivable way out of their current difficulties'. The *Irish Times*'s editor asserted of Germany, with mingled awe and alarm, that 'there is one thing she can do consummately well, and that is to make war'. On 17 November Smyllie supplied a cogent analysis of the European political and strategic state of affairs that could foment a new outbreak of universal hostilities.

In a famously controversial essay on the fascist leanings of the poet W. B. Yeats, Conor Cruise O'Brien asserted that 'such feelings were quite usual in the Irish Protestant middle class to which Yeats belonged' (Conor Cruise O'Brien 1998, p. 41). He observed that 'The *Irish Times*, spokesman of that class, aroused no protest from its readers when it hailed Hitler in March 1933 as Europe's standard bearer against Muscovite terrorism.' O'Brien recalled what he termed 'the pro-Fascist tendencies of the *Irish Times*'; tendencies all-too-evident, one must record, in a respectful obituary for Edward Carson which the paper published on 23 October 1935. His career for the *Irish Times* had been a failure, an Irish tragedy of unfulfilment: 'If he had been forty years younger, Lord Carson of Duncairn might have been a British Hitler or Mussolini' (cited John Martin 2008, p. 143).

Smyllie's series on contemporary Germany under Adolf Hitler drew a powerful letter to the editor from one of Dublin's leading Jewish inhabitants, who fully understood what Nazism and Fascism represented: Henry M. Sinclair, proprietor of an antique shop in the city (the founder of the firm, Sinclair's grandfather, had been vice-president and treasurer of the Jewish congregation in Dublin (Knowlson 1996, p. 277). Sinclair's brother and his family had lived in Germany for a time, until the legislation against Jews there had brought them back to Ireland. In 1937 Henry Sinclair would take a famous action for libel on account of an allegedly anti-Semitic passage in a lively memoir by Oliver St John Gogarty. At the heart of the case had been the right to his good name of a Jew and an Irish citizen. In seeking to defend that right, which was in fact vindicated, the young Samuel Beckett appeared for the plaintiff and had found his own good name wilfully traduced. His fate had been oddly Jewish, with vilification and victimization driving him abroad to Paris where he would serve in the wartime Resistance.

Sinclair's lengthy letter in November 1936 had directly addressed the psychological sources of anti-Semitism and the political expediency of scapegoating. It fully warranted its heading 'Mehr Licht' (echoing Goethe's famous reputed last words – more light – though that heading had first been used by the paper to cover news of the Electricity Supply Board, before it came to be used for letters on Jewish issues) in its thoughtful analysis of what Sinclair termed 'one of the most baffling phenomena of modern statecraft' (*Irish Times*, 12 November 1936). His letter is a powerful statement on how sustained propaganda can induce mob hysteria that suppresses awareness of past wrongs done to the Jews in a new consensus – 'that, no matter what you do you can't do wrong to the Jews, because they are Jews'. Sinclair, indeed, was exploring the psychic condition that could license 'extermination' and genocide, and which would bring the German people to ruin:

That the vast mass of the people have need of something to hate is a well-known fact to students of sociology; and, furthermore, if you successfully orient the latent capacity for hatred to the mob, you can exploit the opposite quality of this hatred for your own objects and nucleate to yourself and your group that mysterious power that comes forth from the collective adoration of the mob. And this is what actually happened in Germany, and why, strangely faithful as he is ... Hitler adopted the Hakenkreuz [the swastika] as the badge of his party – deeply significant of the ultimate nemesis this very symbol will be. Without the Jews Herr Hitler might still be dreaming of another Putsch!

That the noxious germs of anti-Semitism had found a few hosts in Dublin in the 1930s became clear when in February 1939 the *Irish Times* reported that an undated circular letter had been sent by post to a number of prominent Dublin citizens. The paper published its contents. Sent by an A. J. Browne from a Dublin address on behalf of the self-styled Irish-Ireland Research Society, the document proposed an inaugural meeting. Professing no ill will to 'the Jews as a whole', it offered the usual farrago of accusation and insinuation (including by implication the blood libel: 'even in this century a famous ritual murder trial took place at Tisa-Eslar in Austria', *Irish Times*, 23 February 1939) before disingenuously asking: 'But since the same people are blamed in so many different places at so many different times, can everyone else be wrong and the Jews alone right?' The *Irish Times* no doubt published this nasty document to alert its readership to the dangerous, if very limited, pool of the anti-Semitic infection in the capital (police investigation in fact suggested that the Irish-Ireland Research Society did not exist but was merely one journalist, possibly in the pay of the Italian or German legations, seeking, with two assistants, to foment anti-Semitic feeling (Keogh 1998, p. 148).

Wars and rumours of wars around the world in the 1930s added to a sense of an unfolding international crisis that might end in disaster. Some of these had little direct impact on public opinion in Ireland, whereas the Spanish Civil War of 1936–9 became a source of considerable inflamed feeling. When Italy invaded the state of Abyssinia in 1935, the immediate significance for Ireland was somewhat nebulous. De Valera understood, however, that in such an unsettled era small nations could depend for their survival only on robust international institutions. So the Irish government led by de Valera was strong in its support of the League of Nations, which sought (to little effect) to indict Mussolini before the international community. The *Irish Times* broadly supported this stance (though it kept a sympathetic eye also on how the British government responded to the Italian dictator's adventurism). On 19 February it firmly stated that 'he has defied the whole world' (*Irish Times*, 19 February 1936) and that 'no sort of excuse can be found for Italy's conduct'. Of Mussolini, it observed in sombre tones and in terms that had an ominous quality indeed: 'If he refuses now to cut his losses and make a reasonable peace with the Abyssinians, he will be guilty not only of crimes against humanity, but also of a blunder of the first magnitude.' When by March Mussolini was consolidating his African 'triumph', the *Irish Times* regretted the delay in imposing sanctions on Italy, since that would 'destroy much of the small nations' faith in the League of Nations' (*Irish Times*, 3 March 1936). Later in the month the paper reasserted its support for the league in face of Italy's 'unprovoked assault' (*Irish Times*, 31 March 1936) on such a small nation.

The Italo-Abyssinian War, though fought in Africa, involved a western European power, which meant that, although the Irish public did not become particularly agitated about the war's conduct and outcome, the Irish government could see itself as a voice able to speak for peaceful resolution (and the *Irish Times* was happy to add its own editorial voice in the same cause). The Japanese invasion and occupation of much of China in the late summer and autumn of 1937 was an altogether different matter. The paper admitted as much in December of that year when an editorial reflected: 'China is so far away from Western Europe that the people of these islands have not awakened yet to the gravity of the situation that has been precipitated in the Far East, by the piratical activities of Japan' (*Irish Times*, 7 December 1937). The paper, nonetheless, understood that the invasion was an event of world historical significance as it continued: 'The establishment of the puppet-State of Manchukuo [the Japanese had seized Manchuria and a part of inner Mongolia in 1931 and in 1932 had installed a government there] has passed into history, and will rank with Italy's seizure of Abyssinia as one of the major crimes of all time.' On 17 December, the paper tried to alert its readers, in an editorial entitled 'The Waste Land', to the international impact the event would have (the full horror of the rape of Nanking was not yet known) and to how Japan's actions had even struck close to home: 'Already the Chinese war has had a devastating effect upon the linen industry of Northern Ireland, and the quiet closing of the ports will be deadly to the cotton mills of Lancashire and a host of American industries' (*Irish Times*, 17 December 1937).

In May 1938 in an editorial entitled 'Death from the Air', the *Irish Times* linked, in a burst of similar global analysis, an incident in the Sino-Japanese War with an equivalent event on the other side of the world and recalled Mussolini's campaign in East Africa. The paper was clearly alarmed that a general crisis was in motion which involved a transformation of values that could result in total war being waged on civilians as well as on armed combatants. 'Two great cities have spent a week-end of horror,' the editorial informed its readers. 'Barcelona had endured twelve hours of aerial bombing at the hands of Franco's forces in Spain, while Canton in China was raided from the air by the Japanese with grievous loss of civilian life.' The writer continued in a kind of awed apprehension at a generalized spectacle of air-borne disaster:

In one hemisphere Madrid has been shaken many times by General
Franco's bombers; the town of Guernica has been wiped out of existence;
only last week 200 people were killed in a murderous assault on the port
of Alicante. In the other hemisphere nearly all the great towns along the
line of the Japanese advance have been assailed without mercy from the
air ... Thus East and West improve upon the lesson which they learnt from
Signor Mussolini's warplanes in Abyssinia, and thus they establish the
technique for future wars. (*Irish Times*, 30 May 1938)

What so alarmingly was being demonstrated was that civilians would be
targeted in any new world war.

The *Irish Times* had in fact been conscientiously and extensively reporting
on the Spanish Civil War, to which the destruction of Guernica in 1937 was
one terrible climax, since it began in July 1936. This reflected not only how that
epic struggle commanded the attention of all Europe, but also how it had had
a considerable impact on Ireland itself.

In Ireland, the Spanish Civil War, which in most European countries was
seen as a conflict between Left and Right, was widely perceived as an assault
upon a Catholic nation by the malign forces of godless Communism. The press,
in the powerful guise of the ostentatiously clerical *Irish Independent*, led the
pack in its sustained propaganda on behalf of Franco's junta. It devoted more
attention to the war than any other Irish daily and in terms that deliberately hid
from view or attempted to explain away atrocities committed by the rebel forces.
As Fearghal McGarry observes, 'a steady stream of atrocity stories outlining
actual and invented accounts of horrific violence against the Spanish clergy was
printed on an almost daily basis throughout the opening months of the conflict'
(McGarry 2003, p. 70). For the *Irish Independent* was determined to win Irish
hearts and minds for Franco's cause, since it saw the world in so Manichean a
fashion that victory for evil in Spain would mean victory for evil in Ireland, too.
There could be no neutrality in what that newspaper viewed as a holy war. And
it knew where its journalistic enemy was to be found as, in August 1936, a brief
newspaper war on the coverage of events in Spain broke out.

The *Irish Times* from the first had sought to report the conflict objectively.
It sent its own correspondent, Lionel Fleming, to counter the *Independent*'s
man by, as well as reporting on Anarchist and Communist excesses, 'put[ting]
on record the fact that this was a legitimate struggle, both against the evils
of Nazism and Fascism ... and the claim of the Catholic Church, that it
should be allowed to control almost every aspect of Spanish life' (Fleming
1965, pp. 169–70). In several editorials in August 1936 the paper sought to
defend the integrity of the press in wartime, noting that it was the duty of a
newspaper to 'avoid hysterical overstatements which are calculated to create
an atmosphere of hatred and ill-feeling' (*Irish Times*, 26 August 1936). The

Irish Independent was well aware that the *Irish Times* had it in its sights when it so editorialized and it responded with a well-aimed counterblast: 'Certain journals ... erstwhile if not at present pillars of robust Conservatism at home, are now so pro-Anarchist and pro-Communist that these eulogies of these new-found allies must surely startle their regular readers' (*Irish Independent*, 22 August 1936, cited McGarry 2003, p. 74).

This was, of course, an absurd characterization of the *Irish Times's* position, which, although it offered two cheers for Spanish democracy, it was only two cheers at the very most. For, as opposed to the *Irish Independent*, it saw the conflict in Spain as essentially political and rooted in the complex history and social conditions of Spanish life. It was not a religious struggle per se. The paper's editorial of 5 August 1936, entitled 'The Spanish Problem', stated the case forcefully, while warning from an international point of view that 'a false move in Spain by one or other of the European Powers might lead to a general upheaval' and deprecating much 'unscrupulous propaganda in the world's Press'. It argued that a democratic and legitimate government had recently been elected in Spain with which 'The Spanish people were evidently fairly well satisfied', until 'certain highly placed army officers began to get busy' (*Irish Times*, 5 August 1936). In the event, 'the stage was set for a bitter struggle between the Popular Front and the allied forces of conservatism' (*Irish Times*, 5 August 1936). No uncritical defender of the Popular Front, the paper well understood that if the front should succeed, it would 'establish a military dictatorship in Madrid'.

The *Irish Independent*, with its mass readership, undoubtedly influenced the Irish public to see events in Spain through a religious lens, where the *Irish Times's* liberal values shone amid its customary conservatism to present an altogether more convincing picture of a highly complex situation (the *Irish Press* followed the line held by its founder, the Taoiseach Eamon de Valera, in supporting Spain's Catholics, while recognizing the Republican government as legitimate). The fact that the Catholic hierarchy largely shared the *Irish Independent's* belief that the conflict involved the forces of light and the forces of darkness, made the *Irish Times's* stand a markedly unpopular one. There were those ready to assume that its views were determined by an eye on British interests in the southern Mediterranean. Others attributed its insistence that the war in Spain was not essentially a religious war to a habitually covert anti-Catholicism unmasked in the heat of controversy (McGarry 2003, p. 72).

The Catholic hierarchy, in taking a close interest in how the war was being reported, sharing as it did the *Irish Independent's* view that spiritual things were at stake in the peninsula, was signalling how fully, as a body of senior churchmen, they understood that a climate of opinion antithetical to their interests could be fomented by a free press. Nor were they averse to Catholic agencies working to limit that freedom by boycotts, blacklists and threats. The *Irish Times* was affected in a direct way by actions of this kind, when, as a consequence of its position on the war, a significant number of Catholic schools ceased advertising in its pages. As an expensive paper selling at threepence a copy (the *Irish Independent* sold at a mere one penny a copy) with a circulation no higher than 30,000, at best, the paper could ill afford to lose this revenue stream. Smyllie, nonetheless, stood firm, adamantly refusing to bow to such censorious pressure.

The *Irish Times*'s response to the destruction of Guernica by German bombers on 26 April 1937 was unequivocal (it printed the Press Association's man Eamon Holmes's account of the 'ghastly slaughter' there and the 'Terrible Scenes in Smouldering Town'). An editorial on 3 May entitled 'The Agony of Spain' treated with disdain the idea some entertained that republicans had bombed the town to discredit Franco and was less than impressed by his claims and by those of the German government that they were innocent in the matter. It was blunt enough about what it dubbed 'a sickening business' and 'the most ruthless air raid in the history of warfare ... there is no doubt the raiders were German'.

On 7 May the paper evoked the event as atrocity and as terrifying portent: the town had been 'razed to the ground within a few hours; men, women and children alike were massacred, and civilisation was given an awful foretaste of what will be likely to happen if ever another world war should occur' (*Irish Times*, 7 May 1937).

The possibility of a new and even more terrible world war than that which had raged in the second decade of the century was a reiterated theme of *Irish Times* editorials in the second half of the 1930s (at the time when *The Times* of London, in the persons of its editor, Geoffrey Dawson, and his deputy editor, Robert Barrington-Ward, were advocates for the appeasement of Hitler). The implication of its stance was that Hitler would have to be stopped in his tracks if a full-scale catastrophe were to be avoided. In March 1936, as German troops re-entered the demilitarized Rhineland, the paper judged that 'Herr Hitler has told the world in so many words that it must either concede [to] her demands or be prepared to fight her' (*Irish Times*, 13 March 1936). The following year, in an editorial entitled 'War-Mongering', the paper asked, 'Are the dictators of Europe determined to bring about another war?' (*Irish Times*, 24 June 1937), concluding: 'Sooner or later a stop must be put to all this sabre-rattling. The continent of Europe is in a condition of chronic hysteria ... When a dog goes mad nobody is safe; and there are many mad dogs on the continent today.' In 1938 it became all too clear that sabre-rattling could quickly give way to the unsheathed sword and that the mad dogs of Europe would once again be at one another's throats.

The *Irish Times* responded to Hitler's annexation of Austria on 12 March 1938 with horror and foreboding, as it recorded how a special law had been passed 'to legalise the *Anschluss*'; in a few hours 'the historic nation of Austria [had] been wiped off the map' (*Irish Times*, 14 March 1938). 'History,' the writer insisted, 'holds no parallel to Herr Hitler's shameless bludgeoning of a defenceless State' in what amounted to 'international brigandage'. Events in Austria, the paper sadly recognized, proved 'that nothing matters but force. The only argument that the Nazis ever will understand is greater force. Europe today is under jungle law.'

News from the Soviet Union that spring gave warning that another great power was in the grip of its own kind of hysteria. There seemed little hope that Stalin's Russia would be anything but a force for continental instability. In May 1937 the paper had admitted: 'Stalin is incontestably the most powerful man in Europe; he is also the least safe and the least enviable' (*Irish Times,* 13 May 1937). In February and March 1938 the *Irish Times* published full reports of the Moscow show trials (product of the dictator's paranoia and insecurity; the paper had in November 1937 claimed that the Stalinist dictatorship was 'as stringent and tyrannous as ever was known upon the earth', *Irish Times,* 23 November 1937). An editorial on 24 March 1938, which acknowledged Stalin's uncanny power to carry the Russian masses with him, nonetheless reckoned his future as uncertain as it was 'unenviable', despite the terrible efficiency of his purges: 'Stalin's chief hope of survival, perhaps, will be the outbreak of another world war; for the pressure from outside may serve to weld together the elements of a people which must otherwise burst its bonds' (*Irish Times,* 24 March 1938).

The autumn of 1938 brought Europe to the brink of general war, when Hitler threatened Czechoslovakia with armed conflict if it did not cede the Sudetenland to him. The British prime minister, Neville Chamberlain, who was intensely anxious to settle this crisis peacefully, met the German Chancellor at the Berchtesgaden the *Irish Times*'s editor had so much enjoyed in 1936. Its idyllic atmosphere did little to pacify Hitler, who restated his bellicose claims, to which Chamberlain acceded. A second meeting at the Bavarian resort allowed Hitler to increase his demands. At the end of September four powers met at Munich in a last-ditch effort to maintain the peace. For Smyllie, the events of the autumn of 1938 represented not only a grave threat to international order, but something of a personal crisis. For less than a year earlier he had travelled widely in a country now in grave danger. His resulting series of articles, published as 'Carpathian Contrasts', had showed him to be a friend of Czechoslovak democracy. But he knew, as was stated in his newspaper on 24 May 1936, that conflict between Germany and Czechoslovakia could 'precipitate a general war'; and that could not be countenanced for, as the writer on that day had it: 'we cannot believe that any man who was blinded in the last war could condemn the people of Europe to such an appalling fate'.

On 29 September the Munich Agreement was signed by four powers (Britain, France, Italy and Germany) essentially giving *carte blanche* to German designs on the Sudetenland, thereby making it well-nigh impossible for the Czechs to oppose Hitler. Even the deputy editor of the London *Times*, Robert

Barrington-Ward, who had followed his editor in preaching appeasement of Germany, baulked at this. The *Irish Times* published editorials around this date that amounted to elaborate hand-wringing exercises as it nurtured fond hopes that peace could be prolonged. Yet it recognized a brutal truth: 'Unhappily for the Czechs, their destiny is now in the hands of others. If they wish to rebel against the decision, whatever it may be, of the four Great Powers, they will be abandoned to their doom ...' (*Irish Times*, 30 September 1938). By the spring of 1939 the paper knew the die was cast, when Hitler, unsatisfied by occupation of the Sudetenland, annexed Bohemia and Moravia under threat of immediate and terrible war. It understood, as it expressed it in an editorial entitled 'Germania Contra Mundum', that had the Czechoslovakian president resisted Germany's demands, 'Goering's bombing aeroplanes would have been over Prague in a few hours, and one of the loveliest cities in the world would have shared the fate of Guernica.' It now accepted that 'So far as the outsider can judge at present, the Fuehrer and his lieutenants are utterly contemptuous of world opinion. They have become drunk with power, and seem prepared to go to any lengths in pursuit of their mad desire for world domination' (*Irish Times*, 21 March 1939). The newspaper wondered where Germany might strike next. In 1937 it had opined 'that there is a closer affinity between modern Russia and Germany than between Great Britain or the United States and Russia' (*Irish Times*, 23 November 1937). Nonetheless, the German-Soviet non-aggression pact of August 1939 was a shock that provoked a stunned awareness of a threatened apocalypse: 'People talk glibly of war ... but let there be no mistake, if war comes, the light of civilisation will be quenched. Once it goes out it never will be relit in our generation ...' (*Irish Times*, 24 August 1939). On 1 September German forces invaded Poland, and the United Kingdom, along with France, almost immediately declared war on Germany.

On 3 September, the Sunday on which Neville Chamberlain told the world that Britain and its empire were now at war with Germany, the *Irish Times* published a special edition (it had not published on the Sabbath since the Sunday following the Easter Rising of 1916). It pondered wistfully on that momentous day the possibility that the major European democracies might give Hitler a last chance to prove his bona fides as it realized 'We can merely wait and pray.' Monday brought a leading article entitled 'Dies Irae', reporting that 'Britain side by side with France is going to the aid of Poland, that gallant folk whose mournful history has earned for it the sympathy of all honest men' (*Irish Times*, 4 September 1939). Poland's recent ignominious participation in the dismemberment of Czechoslovakia (it had used the time following Munich to seize territory from its neighbour) was no longer an issue as the country itself fell victim to Nazi ambition. The paper had to set aside its own oft-proclaimed aversion to and scepticism about the idea of Irish neutrality in any European war (it considered that in the event of war with Germany, such neutrality would be as impractical as Scottish neutrality: Mark O'Brien 2008, p. 99). De Valera had made absolutely clear, as events that summer rushed to what seemed an inevitable conclusion, that Ireland would be neutral in what was to be described as 'the Emergency'. 'Dies Irae' for Ireland would involve, despite the country's many social and personal links with Britain, an insecure isolation:

> Ireland faces the uncertain future with a heavy heart. She is a tiny nation, whose sole interest is in peace; but her geographic position, her economic system and, to a large extent, her history, place her at the mercy of a warring world. Mr de Valera has proclaimed a policy of strict *neutrality. In all circumstances*, it is the only policy that the Irish Government could pursue.

The second half of the all-Ireland hurling final the day before between Cork and Kilkenny had taken place in Dublin amid violent thunder, lightning and a deluge. It seemed Mars was in the ascendant. As a second leader, 'Storm Prelude', had it: 'For the superstitious, yesterday's strange weather was full of signs and portents' (*Irish Times*, 4 September 1939).

Weather was also on the poet Patrick Kavanagh's mind, in an article he contributed to the paper that October. Under the headline 'Europe Is at War' with subheadings 'A Rural Irish Contrast' and 'Remembering Its Pastoral Peace', the poet began his exercise in bucolic nostalgia with an evocative description:

> Midnight in Dublin. A wild, but not cold October wind is driving rain against my window. The last buses are swishing by on the glassy-bright streets. The radio in the flat above me has stopped forwarding to this address the mixture of blather and jazz which is called propaganda and which is supposed to influence the masses. (*Irish Times*, 25 October 1939)

As journalist and wordsmith, Kavanagh knew the war would involve competing narratives and biased reportage in the interests of propaganda, but he perhaps could not have realized as he composed this piece that future contributions to the newspapers could not include references to current meteorological conditions. For the extraordinary censorship regime that the Free State imposed as a principal instrument of its policy of strict neutrality in the unfolding world war, extended to suppressing weather reports that might aid any of the belligerents. On one notorious occasion this would involve the banning of a photograph the *Irish Times* wished to print of a government minister skating on a frozen pond in a Dublin park, lest awareness of an unusual cold-snap in the city could aid a belligerent.

The *Irish Times* in 1945 was to characterize wartime censorship in Ireland in damning terms. It was, an editorial fulminated, 'as Draconian and irrational as anything that ever was devised in the fertile brain of the late Joseph Goebbels' (*Irish Times*, 12 May 1945). That intemperate outburst was the undoubted product of over five years of sapping frustration in which Robert Smyllie and

Alec Newman had fought their own long, dispiriting battle (relieved only by a few minor if amusing victories) with an obsessively vigilant censor. Smyllie's opponents in this hand-to-hand fight were civil servants who were directly answerable to the Minister for the Co-ordination of Defence Measures, Frank Aiken (appointed on 8 September 1939). A strong-willed Ulsterman who had fought to great effect in both the War of Independence and the Civil War, Aiken had the unwavering trust of de Valera and was left by him to impose censorship as he saw fit. The minister's attitude to freedom of expression in a time of 'emergency' can be readily discerned in a passage in a memorandum for government on the subject 'Neutrality, Censorship and Democracy' he prepared in January 1940. There he stated without embarrassment:

> There are some self-styled democrats who would hold on to the peace time liberalistic trimmings of democracy while the fundamental basis of democracy was being swept from under their feet by the foreign or domestic enemies of their democratic State. Wise men, however, discard these trimmings when necessary in order successfully to maintain the fundamental right of the citizens freely to choose by whom they shall be governed. Wise Constitutions provide for such emergencies. (Ó Drisceoil 1996, p. 310)

That Aiken considered an uncensored press a 'liberalistic' trimming of a democratic society in peacetime meant that he was not likely to brook any opposition to the regime in wartime. That the *Irish Times*, with its Ascendancy origins and its presumed pro-British stance in that war, was a stout proponent of such 'trimmings' meant that the battle-lines between Aiken and Smyllie were sharply drawn. For in a letter to one of Aiken's civil servants about what seemed an egregiously petty act of suppression, Smyllie indicated how passionately he believed in the freedom of the press. At risk of imprisonment under the emergency powers passed at the outset of the war, Smyllie stated of his refusal to bow to a threat that the newspaper might be closed:

> I am not a bit ashamed of it. I should be ashamed if I felt otherwise; and I am glad to think sometimes that when all this filthy business is over, I at least will be able to walk through the streets with my head up, even if you do put me into gaol, fine me whatever you can extract from a harassed bank manager and/or put me or my colleagues of the *Irish Times* on the bread line. (cited Mark O'Brien 2008, p. 116)

Irish neutrality was a policy bred of military weakness. Although the land defence forces (national and local) were significantly strengthened in the first year of the war, the government knew that without naval and air power it would be unable to withstand a military invasion by either Germany or the old enemy Britain (a Britain that yearned to deploy in the Battle of the Atlantic the resources of Irish ports it had recently assigned to Irish control at the end of the economic war). In the absence of military capacity, the government, with Aiken as its powerful agent, was determined that no public hint of partisanship could be seized on by any of the belligerents as an excuse to invade the country. And the Irish people, who were almost entirely supportive of this policy, were to be sustained in their faith in the government line by a view of neutrality that made a national strategy seem like an ethical imperative.

The censorship was certainly pursued with the intensity of a moral crusade. It had in its sights as those to be affected by its interdictions not just the broad mass of citizens, but republicans who had never accepted the legitimacy of the Free State and those who still felt some allegiance to Britain and her Commonwealth. The former included the IRA, which had launched a lethal bombing campaign against the United Kingdom in 1939 and which sought to make common cause with Nazi Germany during the war in the hope that a defeat for Britain could lead to the ending of partition. The latter constituted many of the *Irish Times*'s readers, who were pro-British in general outlook and who may well have had relatives and friends serving in the British forces (despite its avowed neutrality, Ireland did not seek to prevent its citizens enlisting in the service of the United Kingdom during World War II). The policy sought to suppress whatever could be deemed in the least degree supportive of either of these contrasting positions, making neutrality seem both inevitable and morally worthy (during the War of the Atlantic and the Battle of Britain, British public opinion was roused by an antagonistic press in London to view Irish neutrality as cowardly and ignobly self-serving; after the United States entered the war, similar attacks on Ireland's stance were mounted from that quarter). The government felt that not only was neutrality, supported by a rigorous censorship, its only real defence against invasion but was necessary to the stability of the state itself. Aiken, in the memorandum cited above, expressed this belief in striking terms. Having explained how neutrality and censorship were linked ('it behoves neutrals who want to remain at peace to walk warily in the zone of the propaganda war', Ó Drisceoil 1996, p. 309), he continued:

> As a nation we have a definite grievance against the nearest belligerent, but the Government have declared with general consent that we would be unwise, in the interest of the nation, to engage in a war against this bellig- erent. Not all of our people approve of this policy, and if a certain section were allowed to talk offensively about the morals of Germany in relation to its aggression in Poland and elsewhere, we can be quite sure that others would try to express in even more offensive terms their detestation of British morality ... And if a competition of this sort were allowed to start between gentlemen who would confine themselves to words, they would

quickly get supporters who would wish to use stronger arguments, and it
might very well be that we would have a civil war to decide the question as
to which of the European belligerents we should declare war upon.

Leaving aside the obvious fact that the victor in such a putative civil war as
Aiken envisaged would scarcely be able to wage effective war on anybody, one
apprehends here a mixture of deep-dyed nationalist principle with pronounced
insecurity that resulted in a censorship that sought to disallow any comment
whatsoever in Irish newspapers, partisan or otherwise, on the course of the
war. Reportage could not extend beyond the record of events as they unfolded,
because commentary and opinion were, as far as was possible, repressed. The
kind of vivid reporting from front lines that had appeared in the paper from
embedded correspondents during the Great War was forbidden (and no Irish
paper had a reporter in theatre). The result was that Irish press coverage of one
of the world's greatest ever catastrophes was often marked by a weird objectivity. It was as if a titanic struggle were taking place on another planet, to
be observed, to be sure, but without noticeable affect, in a kind of emotional
neutrality that actualized the state's attempt to control all printed information
about the war. Editors frequently fell back on the use of maps to display the
comings and goings of armies and navies, as if on planet Mars, adding to the
sense of a military spectacle in train, with the blood and suffering expunged.

For the *Irish Times* and its redoubtable editor and his staff, these conditions
were well-nigh intolerable. The fact that the censorship policy was conducted
with a nit-picking attention to detail must have particularly irked Smyllie,
for he had always been a man with his eye on the big picture. He had clearly
relished writing and publishing editorials in the 1920s and 1930s which
had uninhibitedly surveyed mankind from China to Peru. The censorship
policy meant that he could not comment on the progress of the war with
the same unfettered amplitude (though he resolutely tried to do so) while he
had to attend at the micro-level to the censor's insistent, and from Smyllie's
point of view, picayune demands. These included the insistence in 1941 that
henceforth the paper could list only the names of Irish fallen in the war in the
normal 'In Memoriam' list, occluding the particular circumstances of their
deaths. Smyllie had some fun at his tormentor's expense (deaths in action
were attributed to 'lead poisoning'; famously on one occasion he allowed a
reference to a war-death at sea to be described as a 'boating accident'), but the
result of his minor triumphs in a war of attrition with the censor was that after
29 December 1942 the newspaper had to submit 'each issue in full for
censorship before publication' (Ó Drisceoil 1996, p. 164).

Adding to Smyllie's fury at these augmenting impediments to his trade
were the facts that English newspapers with their pro-British reportage and
propaganda were on sale in the country and that the BBC was easily picked up

THE WORLD CRISIS 169

by those who had receiving sets and the batteries to use them (as the war went on, acquiring such batteries became very difficult). The *Irish Times* itself drew attention in May 1940 to the role it thought the BBC played in Irish life, when the standard of broadcasts from Radio Eireann was at issue: 'No matter how bad Irish programmes may become,' it opined, '170,000 will continue to take out licences every year in order that they may listen to the BBC' (cited Wills 2007, p. 192), if not to local offerings. On that station, in late 1941, Irish listeners could have heard *Irish Half Hour*, which as Claire Wills has it, while 'Ostensibly designed for Irish people serving in the [British] forces,' had as its 'real target ... the Irish audience at home' (cited Wills 2007, p. 192). Printed journalism was beginning to have a serious rival in radio in the field of day-to-day reportage. Furthermore, Irish men and women serving in the British forces were allowed to spend periods of leave in the Free State, bringing with them direct information about the war itself and about conditions in Britain. They undoubtedly talked with relations and friends about their experiences, but none of these conversations could be reported frankly. For Smyllie to find himself considerably restricted in this context must have felt like an attack on his very *raison d'être*.

The Luftwaffe's bombing attacks on Belfast in April and May 1941 gave ample evidence of the bizarre conditions in which Irish newspapers were operating during 'the Emergency'. On the night of 15 and 16 April, German planes dropped 203 metric tons of bombs and 800 firebomb canisters (Bardon 1992, p. 566) on the almost undefended city, to devastating effect. At least 900 people lost their lives, a larger number in a single night than in any other city in the United Kingdom apart from London, where the Blitz took thousands of lives in 1941. A second raid on 4 and 5 May completed the destruction of much of the city (more than half of the housing stock was either flattened or badly damaged as a consequence of the two raids). A firestorm of awesome power in the shipyard district anticipated the future fate of Dresden.

These dreadful events created a major problem for the Irish government and its censorship policy. The policy had been to affect a studied neutrality as between the moral claims of right of the British and their allies and the Germans (although the government was in fact giving much surreptitious help to the British). The sanitized reporting of the war in the Irish press was supposed to underpin that moral neutrality and even to create the sense that neutrality itself was not only justified as a means of self-preservation but was a moral response to the conflict. Reports on the terrible effects of raids on British cities from October 1940 onwards, and their impact on panic-stricken civilian populations, had been strictly kept out of the columns of Irish newspapers (as, indeed, they were to a considerable extent in British newspapers, at the direction of the Ministry of Information in London). The Belfast bombings, which brought the war in all its gruesome horror very close to home, challenged that ideological construct in stark ways. For it was men and women whom the

Constitution considered full Irish citizens in waiting, as it were, who were dying under the Luftwaffe's assault. And many of them would have had relatives or friends living south of the border. The refugees who poured over that border seeking sanctuary added to the sense of a policy facing a real challenge. For how could people remain morally neutral when their nearest neighbours and putative fellow citizens were perishing under the undefended skies of Belfast?

On the night of the April bombings, de Valera had given permission for 13 fire-engines to be sent to Belfast in response to a request for help (to little effect, unfortunately, since water pressure had collapsed in the city). This was all the more reason to ensure that the newspapers did not use the bombings to imperil censorship itself. De Valera sanctioned mention of how he had allowed fire-engines to go northwards provided 'no stress was laid on the part they played' (Ó Drisceoil 1996, p. 119), limited as it in fact was. His decision was to be represented as simply an act of good-neighbourliness, and in no way an infringement of neutrality itself. The newspapers were not to think that any licence would be extended to them in their desire to tell the full story of what had happened in Belfast.

The coverage of the April bombings began in Irish newspapers on the evening of the 16th. The *Irish Times*'s edition on the morning of 17 April carried reports of the man-made catastrophe in the kind of objective terms it was advised to adopt in all its war-reporting. Its editorial of that morning was an altogether different kind of thing. Entitled 'A Terrible Beauty', to echo Yeats's incantatory evocation of Dublin's Easter Rising in 1916 (Easter Day had fallen on 13 April 1941), it must have stretched the censor's indulgence to the limit; it expressed heartfelt opinion in moving prose. The air of strategic reflection on the course of the conflict, which was a prevailing tone of *Irish Times* commentary in 'the Emergency', was abandoned for emotional identification with war's civilian victims.

The paper probably got away with this editorial stance since, in evoking the suffering of ordinary people in Belfast, it made much of Belfast as an Irish city, the home ground in the eighteenth century of some of the founding fathers of Irish republicanism; and it treated de Valera's decision to send fire-engines to the city's aid as 'the hand of good fellowship reached across the border'. Nonetheless, since it judged that the populace of the Free State had been made fully aware of what aerial bombardment meant, it could assert openly:

> The sight of trainloads of destitute refugees arriving at Amiens Street Station brought home to the people of Dublin as no story of Coventry or Glasgow ever could have brought home, the appalling tragedy of the present war ... For the first time since the outbreak of war the people of Ireland have been made to realise what it means; for previous bombings had been trivial affairs, with little or no loss of life.

The following day brought a photograph of some of those refugees on their arrival in Dublin, but the prose reportage of the death-toll in Belfast was of a near-concussed disassociation that leant an air of objective unreality to the ghastly topic in hand. The paper's reporter in Belfast communicated how:

> The death toll in Belfast as the result of the air-raid on Wednesday morning is growing hourly as the debris from the wrecked houses is being removed. Up to noon it was officially announced that two hundred persons were known to be dead, but a large number of people are untraced, and it is feared that some at least of the missing are also dead.
>
> The task of clearing up the debris and extricating bodies still buried is proceeding.
>
> Close on sixty rest centres have been set up in different halls and religious buildings in the city, where homeless and foodless people are able to procure cheap and hot meals.

One observes how the report delivers its grim messages in anodyne phrasing ('rest centres' seems a grim enough euphemism).

An editorial of 19 April was as disinclined to euphemism as the 'Terrible Beauty' editorial of midweek. It presented an argument, based on the Belfast blitz, under the headline 'The Barbarous Bomb', which at one point cast in obvious doubt the moral equivalency of the belligerents, a linchpin of Irish neutrality as a political doctrine. It contrasted eerily with the almost detached reportage of the actual effects of the Belfast bombing that the paper had been carrying all week. The editorial's theme was how aerial bombardment of civilian populations, which it had reported on with horror in the 1930s, when Spain and China had suffered grievously from such attacks, had now become an accepted norm of 'total war'. And the almost daily torpedoing of 'unarmed merchantmen' was 'taken as a matter of course' (*Irish Times*, 19 April 1941). The writer continued, highlighting how Ireland, which up to then had had 'ringside seats' at this immense spectacle, was now aware of what terror from the air and ruined cities actually involved:

> Modern war, in all its stark reality, was brought within less than half-an-hour's flight from Dublin ... in Belfast as almost everywhere else, the real victims were harmless – men, women and little children – whose homes were wrecked over their innocent heads, and who if they survived, lived through hours of deadly terror, the memory of which they will carry to their graves.

'Since the raid on Belfast,' the paper judged, 'the people of Dublin have begun to realise as they never could have realised otherwise, something of the sufferings that have fallen to the lot of less fortunate cities.' The *Irish Times* was gratified that a generous response to its own appeal for funds for the relief of distress among refugees proved that Ireland was still 'a civilised country'.

It is probable that the censor allowed reportage of the Belfast blitz to pass his eagle-eye since the general tenor of the *Irish Times*'s editorials at the time was supportive, whether consciously or not, like the first editorial on the matter, of how de Valera hoped southern responses to the Belfast bombings could be orchestrated in the Free State. Claire Wills, in her study of Irish neutrality, describes how at what could have proved a crisis point for de Valera's policy, he himself deployed a 'rhetoric of humanitarianism and popular national unity' (Wills 2007, p. 217) that 'did resonate widely in the population'. In its emphasis on how North and South could be seen as essentially one in shared compassion at this moment of suffering ('The arrival at Amiens Street Station of some thousands of homeless refugees from the North has pierced the hearts of the most thoughtless'), the paper was in fact in effective sympathy with an emotional means of reaction to the carnage and destruction north of the border that did not demand any of the rethinking of neutrality which otherwise might have been necessary. So the unsettling dissonance in the paper in the aftermath of the bombing, which we have explored above, between emotionally charged editorials that must have given the censor pause and the cold reportage he encouraged, was really a superficial thing, however disconcerting to the readership, affording us a clear sense that a newspaper was being bent to the will of a powerful hegemony, despite its own impulse to test the limits of censorship in various ways.

The *Irish Times*'s reporting of a German bomb attack on the North Strand district of Dublin (perhaps misdirected by British interference with German radio waves) on the night of 30/31 May 1941, for all its efforts since September 1939 to report the war fully and by inference to reflect the pro-British feeling of much of its readership, is further evidence of a newspaper operating under effective restraint. Given that 28 people were killed, 90 injured and 300 houses were in ruins, the paper could be more graphic in its reportage, since the censor, in a city where news passed quickly by word-of-mouth, could not without attracting ridicule have disallowed some such material in the papers. So the *Irish Times* printed pictures of the devastation, and its reports quoted a doctor describing maimed children on 'relays of stretchers' passing 'to and fro with the moaning children crying for their mothers' (*Irish Times*, 31 May 1941). However, at a moment when the paper might have been minded at least to raise issues about Germany's conduct of warfare, an editorial on 2 June returned to a familiar theme: the vulnerability of civilian populations to aerial attack, when 'No neutral country is safe ... from the ruthlessness of war.' On 9 June the *Irish Times* informed its readers that it was directing some of the money raised for refugees from Belfast to those affected by the Dublin bombings. An actual German assault on Irish sovereign territory, with significant loss of civilian life, was being treated as a humanitarian matter. In reacting in this manner, the paper was again giving comfort to its tormentor in the person of the censor; for such an editorial stance was clearly not at odds with de Valera's handling of affairs at this delicate period for his policy of strict neutrality. That most of the population, genuinely frightened by what had happened to Belfast and shaken by the bombing in Dublin, were more than anxious not to provoke any further German attacks on a country the *Irish Times* itself had described as possessing 'grossly inadequate defences' only made the paper's situation more invidious.

A sense of how the *Irish Times* was forced to view the war as if from a panopticon, all-seeing but with itself paradoxically as prisoner, unable to express itself freely, can be caught in its response to the Japanese attack on Pearl Harbor in December 1941. Headlines on 8 December, the day after the raid, reported the event along with reports of military developments in North Africa. An editorial that morning, entitled 'Japan at War', did take note of a White House release that referred to 'Severe damage' and of how 'the loss of life' was 'expected to be heavy' (*Irish Times,* 8 December 1941), but the greater part of the editorial was given over to the large-scale implications for the course of the general war. Instead of writing about how this bloody and nefarious turn of events, which brought the United States to a state of war (to which Irish-America had been resolutely opposed), could be a watershed, the editorial drifted into an almost 'academic' series of ruminations, concluding:

> Now the thing that everybody knew must happen sooner or later has occurred; the greatest of the oceans has become the scene of war, and the last two of the Great Powers are at each other's throats. From now onwards the student of events will follow them not on a map of Russia, or of Libya, or all of Europe, but on his map of the world.

A column from the paper's 'Military Correspondent' (who offered occasional analyses of the war's progression) the next day appeared on the sports page, alongside accounts of recent team engagements (Trinity's rugby fifteen had defeated Queen's Belfast in a closely fought contest). It was a compacted exercise in the elevated abstractions of an imaginary High Command.

The next day, in a further editorial, entitled 'War in the East', the writer pondered at length on how things had come to the pass as they had. It judged Japanese perfidy in Hawaii as a sad example of how in modern warfare a nation had got its blow in first. The chivalry of Crécy and Agincourt was dead.

All this seems bland, even detached (though that was surely not the intent) in its enforced judiciousness as between the embattled armies, navies and air forces. The human cost of the war, its courage and malignity, were being covered in fustian and elaborate theorizing about strategy.

There were times, however, even under the conditions of the strict censorship, when the leader writer rose to the occasion. D-Day in June 1944 brought a powerful editorial, 'Days of Doom', that struck a genuinely tragic note. It made even-handedness (the views of both the British and the German governments on the vital significance of 6 June were given) less a legal requirement than an opportunity for an anthem for dead youth, for an affecting reflection on 'the pity of war. The pity war distilled' (Blunden 1965, p. 116).

> The world is watching these prodigious events with bated breath. It is far too soon yet even to guess at their outcome. One thing, however, is certain. Many thousands of gay young lives already have been lost, and no man can tell how many others are committed to their doom. This hour is one of the most solemn and tragic hours in human history. Mankind's destiny has been flung upon a cruel fate. (*Irish Times*, 7 June 1944)

When in 1945, with censorship lifted, Robert Smyllie inveighed against those who had imposed de Valera's policy as no better than 'the late Josef [*sic*] Goebbels', his ire was aroused by the fact of censorship in general but also because he believed his own newspaper had been 'singled out for particular attention' (*Irish Times*, 12 May 1945). Not only had the paper been unable 'to express, or even hint at its convictions' that an Allied victory was devoutly to be wished for since that involved the defeat of 'tyranny and injustice', but it had 'alone among the Dublin dailies ... been compelled to submit to the autocrats of Dublin Castle every line that we proposed to print, from the leading article down to the humblest prepaid advertisement'. So exacting and tiresome had been this experience that Smyllie claimed, in a heated exaggeration, that 'it was seldom ... that our leading articles were not hacked and mutilated in such a way as to make them almost meaningless'. He believed the *Irish Times*'s unionist past and its Protestant, anglicized culture had made it a target for an Anglophobia that was intent on suppressing its view of the world, as well as its view of the belligerents. The *Irish Times*'s preference for English-language place names (for example, Kingstown for Dún Laoghaire, had irked the censor).

There was an irony involved if, indeed, the *Irish Times* was the victim during the war years of a prejudiced Irish-Ireland mindset among some of the censorship officials (one of them who had served as an airman in the Great War, a career civil servant of undoubted ability and intelligence, could scarcely be accused of that). For in the war years the paper in certain respects became more closely involved with mainstream Irish life than it had been hitherto. On a popular level, this was evidenced by the now regular reporting of Gaelic games, which gave colour to life each summer and autumn throughout the country at a time of drab deprivation. Where once the All Ireland football final at Croke Park in Dublin had been given the most cursory of references, in September 1941 it warranted an editorial entitled 'The Big Match'. The writer was grudging enough about the GAA in his leader, bemoaning how the rule on foreign games meant that the county teams could not draw on all the talent available. However, the leader conceded that 'a well-fought game under the Gaelic code can be as exciting as any other, and the fact that its rules can be so quickly appreciated is a point in its favour. Furthermore, the inter-county aspect, which never has been of importance under the other codes, is a source of great enthusiasm' (*Irish Times*, 8 September 1941). The paper's suspicion of the GAA's Irish-Ireland nationalism could not easily be set aside. Rugby, cricket and to a lesser degree soccer were the sports of preference of its assumed readership, along with horse-racing, which in Ireland drew support from all classes and creeds.

It was not likely that the *Irish Times*'s attitude to Gaelic games was not going to affect the robust nationalism of an organization that thought of the culture of the Gael as republican, Catholic (a bishop threw in the ball at the start of All Ireland finals) and most true to itself when expressed in the Irish language. Where the paper could have an influence, though in a much narrower sphere, was in the field of literary culture. For there it could convincingly challenge the doctrine, promulgated vigorously by Irish Ireland ideologues, that the only literature that could worthily be described as 'Irish' was Gaelic, in the Irish language. We have seen how in the early 1920s the *Irish Times* had begun to treat Irish writing in English as something more than English literature with an Irish accent. By the 1940s, Smyllie's Palace Bar contacts with a range of Irish writers, together with the acumen of his deputy, Alec Newman, had made the Saturday book page (which Smyllie had inaugurated) a place where a post-Yeatsian generation of poets could see their work in print, proving that Irish writing in English was no mere Ascendancy appendix, to be excised when Irish was restored as the national language, but a vital organ of cultural expression.

The paper that had honoured both Yeats and Joyce in its columns now gave space for poems by such as Patrick Kavanagh, Donagh MacDonagh (son of the executed 1916 leader Thomas MacDonagh) and Valentin Iremonger. Young Irish writers were recruited as reviewers and among these were the poet, playwright and novelist Austin Clarke. He had cut his teeth as a literary journalist in London in the 1920s and 1930s. During the war years he served as the paper's main poetry critic, bringing to his reviews a determination that new work in English by Irish poets would be judged alongside that of their contemporaries abroad. For example, he reviewed the Ulster poet W. R. Rodgers's first book, *Awake! And Other Poems* (1941), together with T. S. Eliot's *The Dry Salvages* (1941) (the third of that poet's *Four Quartets*). In this review Clarke claimed that there was 'a very definite imaginative stir in this country at present' (*Irish Times*, 4 October 1941). Elsewhere, however, he had bemoaned the conditions under which Irish poets and other writers were forced to labour. In the period of the Irish Literary Revival it had been possible to publish in Ireland. Now, he complained, 'while our politicians squabble and boast in their horrible way, the novels, poems and plays of Irish writers to-day are scattered among the catalogues of London publishing firms' (*Irish Times*, 9 November 1940). And there was no recent tradition of informed literary criticism in Ireland against which the poet could refine his art (in the past, Clarke stated, that had existed in robust oral form). In reviewing Donagh MacDonagh's first book of verse very critically, Clarke by implication attributed its weaknesses to this national deficiency, which he was evidently trying to make good. His reviews could be acerbic (Louis MacNeice's collection *Plant and Phantom* (1941) did not impress, except where it eschewed 'journalism and politics': *Irish Times*, 24 May 1941), for Clarke had his doubts about the artistry of some of his poetic peers. He thought 'the tradition of fine craftsmanship' was 'passing over' to short-story writers, who worked 'with the same conscientious care which our poets formerly gave to lyrics' (*Irish Times*, 19 April 1941). What was not in doubt, however, is that Clarke took for granted that the work in English by Irish writers was Irish literature. And he was bold enough as a critic with claws to have his own work published in the newspaper where he took others to task. One of his finest poems, 'The Blackbird of Derrycairn', was published on the book page on 18 October 1941.

Austin Clarke was a graduate of University College Dublin. So was Donagh MacDonagh. Indeed, MacDonagh, on 15 March 1941, had contributed an article on a young poet, Charles Donnelly, who had died in Spain while fighting on the republican side, which movingly evoked their time together at University College; in the 1930s University College Dublin produced a crop of graduates who could compare with anyone who had emerged recently from the altogether more ancient Trinity College. From its inception, the *Irish Times* had been edited by Trinity men (even Smyllie had spent a short time there) and its contributors and writers, if not many of its rather more plebeian reporting and printing staff, were often recruited by means of an Irish version of the old school tie. The book page in the 1930s and 1940s began to break up that semi-closed shop, since it allowed well-educated Irish nationalists to have their say on literature and drama. Smyllie, moreover, saw to it that the paper served as a showcase for contemporary, especially younger Irish poets. The paper gave space on its literary page to an original poem on a weekly basis. In 1944, under it own imprint, it issued an anthology entitled *Poems from Ireland*. Edited by Donagh MacDonagh, this volume gathered 93 poems (by 41 poets, of whom six were women and seven were Northerners), most of which had 'appeared since the outbreak of the war'. In his introduction the editor argued that 'The best poetry written in this country, though in language it may be English, has yet a native quality which is difficult to define; and this may be due to the fact though English has been the vernacular here for over two centuries, the Irish voice has never quite forgotten the native language' (MacDonagh 1944, p. 1). He continued, noting how in the schools 'the majority of teaching is completed through Irish': in 'these circumstances it seems reasonable to suppose that either a new native poetry will begin to develop, or, at the very least, a poetry written in English will show ever more signs of the Gaelic influence' (MacDonagh 1944, p. 2). In the preface that R. M. Smyllie contributed (he signed it as 'Editor, *Irish Times*', dated December 1944) he made another significant cultural observation of what was a wartime publication, printed in Dublin, the capital of a neutral state: 'it will be seen that those poets who have been writing in Ireland have been almost wholly unaffected by the impact of the world struggle. To what extent this fact has affected the quality of their work I will leave the critics to determine.' Critics in 1944 could have noted how many of the selected poems in the book were traditionally formal and topographical in content and how a melancholic mood prevailed. Some of the finest poems in the book were love poems (among them Patrick Kavanagh's 'Renewal' – subsequently renamed 'Advent'). It was at the level of imagery if not at that of content that the reality of warfare was artistically being registered. For example, Valentin Iremonger's 'Spring Stops Me Suddenly' notes in Audenesque manner: 'Summer is there, screwed and fused, compressed,/Neat as a bomb, its casing a dull brown' (MacDonagh 1944, p. 38). Heart mysteries and imagery of conflict combine with memorable power in Patrick MacDonogh's 'Over the Water' (one of the finest poems by an Irish poet in the period). The poem concludes:

> Here skies have scarcely room
> To house their clouds of bombers, yet had I but my darling,
> We'd mix our hate with pity for stripling airmen doomed
> To their own strange damnation, and in a night of horror
> Softly we'd lie together under a bomber's moon.
>
> (MacDonogh, 1944, p.53)

The biographical notes on the poets, compiled by the volume's editor, almost inadvertently indicate, in defiance of the censor, as it were, that some Irish people were participants in the European struggle entering its final months. A number of poets are identified as currently living in England, where Frank O'Connor was 'working in films'. The reader is informed that Louis MacNeice is 'at present working for the British Broadcasting Corporation' and that C. Day Lewis 'is at present working for the British Ministry of Information'. Of the novelist and poet Francis Stuart, it was recorded that 'He has been in Germany since before the present war', reminding readers who may have heard his propaganda broadcasts to Ireland from Berlin that Irish citizens varied in their attitudes to the country's neutrality. Some of the poems in *Poems from Ireland* could be read, too, as serving poignant notice that a world in crisis was enduring a humanitarian calamity. The 25-year-old Peter Wells's 'Lament for Victory' provided what could have been a poetic dispatch from the Russian front:

Since there are no more beaches to conquer, and slow
Poverty has struck down those whom no leaves cover:
Since the quiet shell, the impenetrable factory have uttered
Their final proclamation, and no gun
Echoes again the weeping, the defeated;
Like iron manacles, grinding all hope, the inconsolable losers:
Since all is fallen, now not even the flowers shall perish,
>But the tired women shall come out on to the snow with crosses.
>(MacDonagh, 1944, p. 88)

Among the writers whose work was represented in *Poems from Ireland* was Myles na gCopaleen, one of the several pseudonyms of Brian O'Nolan, a graduate of University College Dublin, who had already established a role in the paper as its most remarkable columnist. The paper had recruited him as a columnist in 1940.

O'Nolan was the Ulster-born son of a peripatetic Irish civil servant who had insisted that the language of the home, even in Dublin, be almost exclusively Irish. O'Nolan was educated at Blackrock College and he graduated from University College Dublin in 1933. After two years when he worked on a Masters degree, he soon followed his father into the Irish civil service by entering the Department of Local Government, where by 1937 he was private secretary to the minister. In that role he was never to be the conventional office-bearer, for he nurtured the literary ambitions of his coterie at University College Dublin, who felt the achievement of their predecessor there, James Joyce, as a challenge to their own capacities.

O'Nolan as an undergraduate had contributed enthusiastically to a college literary magazine and in 1935 had even attempted with one of his brothers and a friend to found a magazine. An admired uncle was a sports journalist. So newspaper ink, if not running in his veins, was not something, as an aspiring literary man, he was inclined to scorn. He took the chance Smyllie offered with no sign that he thought such an endeavour beneath him. Indeed, his recruitment to the *Irish Times* was the result of his gleeful participation in elaborate fake controversies fought out in the letters column of the newspaper. O'Nolan signed some of his contributions to this *blague* Flann O'Brien, though the affair was conducted through 'a multiplicity of pseudonyms' (Cronin 1989, p. 108). Then in 1940 he was joined by another of his University College Dublin friends, Niall Montgomery, in a similar fake correspondence about a dramatic production at Dublin's Gate Theatre. Obvious pseudonyms ('Oscar Love', 'Luna O'Connor') brought an air of rather wearisome undergraduate whimsy to the exchanges.

A further epistolary controversy was sharper and cut a little closer to the bone. The poet Patrick Kavanagh had published a review of a book by a popular Irish novelist (in passing, he criticized the Irish Boy Scout movement, bringing its own angry ripostes from disgruntled readers) in which he reflected on the relationship between popular success and artistic achievement. When the following week Kavanagh's poem of rural recollection entitled 'Spraying the Potatoes', with its vision of a 'poet lost to potato fields', appeared on the *Irish Times*'s book page, the literary conspirators had a field day. As townies and university men, they could patronize the peasant poet in their literary japes. And while these controversies were going on in the summer of 1940, the same cabal of humorists were bombarding the paper with pseudonymous missives on such arcane matters as 'Ibsen's problems with dandruff, the use of sewers by Ireland's artistic elite, and the dearth of hair on the legs of the Hitler Jugend' (Wyse Jackson 1999, p. 8). Smyllie himself joined in the fun as 'The O'Maden' but he knew the nonsense had to stop, or at least be controlled. So when Niall Montgomery introduced the editor to O'Nolan, he quickly took to him, and offered the improbable civil servant a second job.

Initially O'Nolan was to write a thrice-weekly column in the Irish language. O'Nolan chose to call it '*Cruiskeen Lawn*' ('A Full Jug') and to write under a further pseudonym, Myles na gCopaleen. He took this name from that of a horse-dealer in Dion Boucicault's hugely successful play *The Colleen Bawn* (1860). In that Victorian Irish melodrama, Myles in fact sings about the '*Cruiskeen Lawn*'. In the *Irish Times*'s column, na gCopaleen would swell over the years in a stream of about four million words (which throughout its run appeared on the leader page of the paper) into one of the most extraordinary figures in twentieth-century literature, prolifically self-inventing as he is, to become a gargantua of self-esteem and a fount of grotesque trivia, deploying a gallery of 'surrogates to speak for him' (Wyse Jackson 1999, p. 12).

Smyllie probably asked O'Nolan to write his column in Irish as a deliberate attempt to appeal to those younger nationalists among the paper's readership, many of them, like O'Nolan, civil servants of the new state, who, having acquired the language at school or college, could not be expected to share the instinctive antipathy for linguistic revivalism its more traditional readership readily felt. The latter would surely have been more in sympathy with the views expressed by no less an eminence than George Bernard Shaw, when, in a special interview for the paper in December 1941, that luminary iconoclastically stated that he disapproved of teaching Irish in the schools. He considered that the Irish were already too Irish and should be more European. 'I have,' he said,

> no patience with this atavistic folly of planting a dead language on Irish schools as Latin verse is planted in English ones. Our greatest achievement in this field has been our conquest and annexation of the English language which we handle more easily than the English do. It gives us power over the minds and imaginations of the human race in all continents. It is

read and spoken everywhere, and this school Gaelic is read and spoken nowhere. (*Irish Times*, 6 December 1941)

The former, those who had experienced and benefited from the school system (knowledge of Irish was required for civil service employment) might have been expected to be more in tune with O'Nolan's sense of the value of the language to Irish people and to the culture in general, even if compulsion had made many of them cynical about the revival enterprise. In a '*Cruiskeen Lawn*' column in 1943, which responded to a leader that had questioned the worth of the revival policy, Myles commented:

> There is probably no basis at all for the theory that a people cannot preserve a separate national identity without a distinct language but it is beyond dispute that Irish enshrines the national ethos and in a subtle way Irish persists very vigorously in English. In advocating the preser-vation of Irish culture, it is not to be inferred *that this* culture is superior to the English or any other but simply that certain Irish modes are *more comfortable and suitable* for Irish people; otherwise these modes would not exist. It is therefore dangerous to discourage the use of Irish because the revival movement, even if completely ineffective, is a valuable preser-vation of certain native values. (*Irish Times*, 18 October 1943, cited in Taaffe 2008, p. 117)

Such moderation, of course, was not likely to appease those zealots who insisted that national identity could not be realized in a language other than Irish. Nor was the unlikely phenomenon of a column in the old Gaelic script appearing on a regular basis on the leader page of the *Irish Times* a matter for their gratification. For Myles was quickly damned in a rival paper's squib as 'a native anti-Irish chick' who had found a perch for himself in a Protestant broadsheet, where it squeaked 'neo-Gaelic through/the back of its head' (cited in Taaffe 2008, p. 97). And the column itself (it appeared mostly in Irish until September 1941 when it began to alternate between Irish and English on a daily basis, before in 1944 settling for English almost completely) was nothing the respectable language enthusiast with his or her school Irish would have been inclined to favour. For, in John Wyse Jackson's words, it was 'scurrilous, highly inventive and almost untranslatable. Nothing like it had ever been perpetrated in the language' (Wyse Jackson 1999, p. 9). And one of the principal targets of its humour and burgeoning satire was just the kind of puritanical, chauvinist über-Gael who would have viewed O'Nolan's column in the *Irish Times* with suspicion and distaste. Indeed, in a series of parodies of Gaelic folk tales, entitled 'Tales from Corkadorky', Myles prepared the way for the novel he published in Irish in 1941, *An Beal Bocht* (*The Poor Mouth*), which comprehensively rendered the Irish-speaking west-of-Ireland Gael, as represented to critical acclaim in literature and memoir, bleakly and terminally absurd. The *Irish Times*'s own review of the book grasped its explosive character as it noted how 'Enemy after enemy goes down in as funny a piece of debunking as has been done in any language' (*Irish Times*, 13 September 1941).

Caricature had not been a feature of the rather staid pages of Smyllie's earnestly responsible newspaper. In 1939 and 1940 it had, however, published a series of cartoons of Dublin figures by the New Zealand artist Alan Reeves (who in the city's humorous magazine *Dublin Opinion* had contributed a famous cartoon of the *Irish Times*'s editor among his literary cronies in the Palace Bar; that was perhaps an advance on a earlier *Dublin Opinion* cartoon which had wickedly represented the editorial office as an old-dufferish Senior Common Room with mortarboards de rigueur). None of these cartoons, which ran a gamut from the city's lord mayor to the poet Austin Clarke, had anything of the acidulous contempt with which Myles na gCopaleen caricatured in this period the obnoxiousness of those he found 'the most nauseating phenomenon in Europe ... the baby-brained dawnburst brigade, who are ignorant of everything, including the Irish language itself' (cited in Clissmann 1975, p. 238). And in the 1940s he had good reason to wage satiric war in verbal cartoons against at least some of the more rebarbative of language enthusiasts who were then trying to rouse the populace out of its linguistic lethargy.

The early 1940s are now seen as a moment in independent Ireland when a genuine revival of Irish-language literature, with O'Nolan himself (author of *At Swim-Two-Birds*, 1939) a key figure in this, began to stir. However, it was also a moment when small political ginger-groups with distinctly fascist overtones were flexing their muscles in the public domain. They combined (as Hugo Hamilton's compelling memoir *The Speckled People* [2003] reveals of one of them) a dedication to the Irish language along with racist xenophobia. In attacking such folk in his column, O'Nolan was in fact reminding the *Irish Times*'s readership of what was at stake in the European war. And, in so doing, he was subverting the censorship policy in a more telling way than his editor ever managed to do. As their activities intensified, Myles drew heavily ironic attention to how such groups had their very nasty equivalents on the Continent:

I was recently held up at a Dublin street corner by a small crowd who were listening to a young man with a strong North of Ireland accent who was aloft on a little Irish scaffold.

'Glún na Buaidhe' he roared 'has its own ideas about the banks, has its own ideas about amusements, has its own ideas about dancing. There is one sort of dancing that Glún na Buaidhe will not permit and that is jazz dancing. Because jazz dancing is the product of the dirty nigger culture of America ...'

Substitute jew for nigger here and you have something beautiful and modern. (cited in Taaffe 2008, p. 115)

It would be wrong, however, to characterize 'Cruiskeen Lawn' as simply a vehicle for satire. It was not simply anything, but an extraordinary, inspired literary potpourri that defies easy description. Its controlling energy is humour which must have lightened the mood of many a reader, who in a period of straitened circumstances found the daily grind a challenge. In its paragraphs the reader would have learned of the doings of Keats and Chapman (he of Keats's famous poem about Chapman's *Homer*) as the prose wound its way to a piece of groan-making wordplay (Myles delighted in multi-lingual punning). The observations of 'the Brother' and of 'the Plain People of Ireland' brought hilarious demotic Dublinese to a page often dominated by high-flown opinionation. The pretentious affectations of the city's *soi disant* intelligentsia were an easy target of 'Cruiskeen Lawn''s feline derision (O'Nolan dubbed them 'Corduroys'). The doings of the da, Sir Myles na gCopaleen, afforded international vistas that exceeded even Smyllie's near-universal gaze. A bare-faced assumption of academic superiority on any subject in heaven or on earth made the collegiate decorousness of the paper's ideolect seem oddly timorous. A familiar phrase could provoke elaborate narratives that worked a *reductio ad absurdum*. And there was the 'Catechism of Clichés' (which must have arrested the flow of many a contributor, as it can, to employ a cliché, the present writer). 'What,' Myles would ask, 'is the nature of clockwork? It is regular'; 'And what is the nature of daylight? It is broad.'

If the energy of 'Cruiskeen Lawn' was essentially humorous, despite occasional rancorous rants when the bile rose, its obsession was language itself. The bravura displays of literary ventriloquism in its various exercises in pastiche were a constant reminder, therefore, that language was not a simple mirror on the world but distortion of it. The effect was highly subversive in a newspaper that took itself, despite its editor's eccentricities, very seriously indeed. A leading article might wish to strike an authoritative note on a topic of great moment but there on the same page was Myles's column exhibiting how all forms of discourse are tricks of style and rhetoric. And in a period of close censorship, the sheer linguistic inventiveness of Myles na gCopaleen was a kind of health warning to readers that the rest of the paper, with its constrained attempts to report and comment on the course of the war, was an etiolated thing, the lifeblood of actuality edited away. One critic has suggested that in his column O'Nolan was publishing a kind of 'bizarre newspaper *inside* the newspaper'. (Stephen Young cited in Taaffe p. 137) More accurately, one might say that 'Cruiskeen Lawn' was an anti-newspaper inside the *Irish Times*, drawing attention as it did, in self-referential literary and textual antics, to the artificial construct a newspaper is, for all its implied claims to be 'the truth in the news'.

Myles as subversive had the temerity not only to mock editorial attitudes in his column, but at the same time to parody Smyllie's style:

> Keep this under your hat but the editor of the *Irish Times* is ... Irish!
> Owing to physical propinquity of two islands, destinies inextricably
> intertwined, commonwealth of nations, futility of dwelling on history,
> promotion of amity and goodwill, tongue that Shakespeare spoke, our
> indefeasible claim to a seat at the peace conference. Ha-ho. (*Irish Times*,
> 13 April 1944)

And his instinct for wordplay even infected the rather ponderous humour of
his editor when he, too, employed a pseudonym.When 'Nichevo' published
a list of British naval and military officers commended for their part in the
war by Winston Churchill, as if they hailed from the north and south islands
of Japan (to the censor's humourless annoyance), Myles concluded, 'As that
venerable member of the samurai, San Tiok Eli, might or might not have put it:
"Quae regio in terra plena laboris?" Gimmemewhip' (*Irish Times*, 11 February
1941). We may surmise that the then Tánaiste (deputy prime minister), Seán
T. O'Kelly, was not so very amused by this cheeky play on his name or by the
condescending tone of its delivery, but we can hope Myles approved.

Smyllie's newspaper in the war years was, we can credibly say, making
distinct efforts, especially in its book page, to appeal to a new generation of
readers, to the kind of educated nationally minded people who were impatient
with the simple nostrums of the political class about such things as language
and identity, but who unfussily saw themselves as Irish without qualification.
That Brian O'Nolan, writing as Myles na gCopaleen, was a key factor in making
the *Irish Times* the paper of choice in this constituency is evidenced by the
recollection of Anthony Cronin, Wexford-born poet, critic, cultural adviser to
Taoiseach Charles Haughey, and O'Nolan's biographer. He recalls how, as an
undergraduate in digs in Dublin (in itself a Mylesean situation), as the D-Day
invasion of Europe was unfolding, he was lent a copy of Flann O'Brien's *At
Swim-Two-Birds* (1939). He continues, before telling us how pleased he had
been to be informed that the said Flann O'Brien was also Myles na gCopaleen:

> As a first-year student in UCD I was in search of sophistication, in art
> and, to some timorous extent, in life. I bought the *Irish Times* whenever
> I could afford it because the *Irish Times* was a symbol of liberation from
> the values of one's *Irish Independent*-reading forebears and of graduation
> to intellectual Dublin; and in it I read Myles na gCopaleen whose column
> was by far the most sophisticated production one could find or hope to
> find in any native publication; indeed, like others, I bought the paper
> largely in order to read it. (Cronin 1989, p. 145)

One of roles O'Nolan played in the *Irish Times* in the years of World War II
was, by his choice of subject, to highlight how 'the Emergency' in Ireland was
affecting day-to-day life. His inventive offer in November 1942 of tobacco

smoke collected in bags and offered for sale second-hand, tells us that, although Ireland did not suffer the very severe rationing the war brought to Britain, some privations were hitting hard. Myles's 'Research Bureau' in its madcap inventions further suggested humorously how citizens were being cast back on their own resources to solve the minor difficulties of life in a society where fuel to run cars, trains and machines was increasingly unobtainable.

The 'Research Bureau' was, it also has to be said, a satirical shot at the Institute for Advanced Studies that Eamon de Valera had established in 1940. With its three sections devoted to Celtic Studies, Cosmic Physics and Theoretical Physics, it was a rare attempt by the Free State government to acknowledge both the international scholarly importance of the country's linguistic inheritance and the significance of fundamental scientific research. The renowned physicist Erwin Schrödinger, at de Valera's invitation, was a founding member of the institute. Myles's disdain for intellectual pretension of any kind meant that this ambitious venture provoked him to humorous flights of fancy.

In so reacting, of course, O'Nolan was flaying if not exactly slaying what had been earlier in the century one of the *Irish Times*'s sacred cows: science as an international avocation which made Irish nationalism's 'obsession' with the revival of a native tongue seem preposterously provincial. In O'Nolan's way of looking at the world, that attitude was itself provincial. For despite his attitude to de Valera's institute, he was himself attentive to the extraordinary advances in twentieth-century physics. That did not necessarily involve seeing the Irish language and scientific modernity as necessarily antithetical. In a further crucial way O'Nolan's characteristic outlook was essentially at odds with the ethos the *Irish Times* liked to think represented its best instincts. For by the 1940s, particularly as it struggled with the wartime censorship, it saw itself as a bulwark of liberal values in a hostile world. By contrast, O'Nolan had no time for liberals, especially those of the Irish variety like Frank O'Connor and Seán O'Faolain (the later of whom founded the liberal nationalist monthly, *The Bell*, in 1940). In Myles's column they were frequently the target of his precisely directly impatience, since, in his view, they self-interestedly exaggerated the malign effects of the literary censorship on their careers. He thought little of them as writers.

It was in fact the matter of literary censorship that provoked the *Irish Times* in 1942 to make explicit what it felt were its core values. On 9 October the paper published a letter from Frank O'Connor protesting about the recent banning by the Censorship Board of a book by Eric Cross based on the rural reminiscences of a County Cork tailor and his wife, *The Tailor and Ansty*. Seán O'Faolain, whose *Bell* had been waging war on the literary censorship since its earliest numbers, quickly joined his name to O'Connor's opening salvo in a controversy about the board's activities which ran until in mid-November when a Protestant senator, Sir John Keane, tabled a motion in the upper house of the parliament. It stated: '... the Censorship of Publications Act, 1929, has ceased to retain public confidence and that steps should be taken by the Minister to reconstitute the Board' (cited Adams 1968, p. 84). This stimulated a lengthy debate in the house before it was defeated.

The *Irish Times* gave its verdict on the Censorship Board and on the debate on 3 December 1942 in an editorial that expressed a liberal belief in the primacy of individual judgement and free thought where state power sought unwarrantedly to intrude. It bluntly damned the board as an 'immoral body' (*Irish Times*, 3 December 1942). With clumsy irony an editorial entitled 'Censorship' suggested that the five members should be remunerated, since, as educated and civilized men, they were making themselves ridiculous. Were they to be paid, the people would more readily object to what, as a liberal organ, it thought an 'obnoxious, insulting doctrine that no adult citizen of this country is capable of reading a book without the acquisition of dirty thoughts, and that a board of five people is capable of directing the morals of a country of three millions'. Such literary censorship in a word was 'stupid'.

One contibutor to the Senate debate had accused Sir John Keane of taking some of his ideas about censorship from letters in the *Irish Times*, as if that were enough to condemn them in the minds of all right-thinking people. And he had support for that dismaying view in the pages of the influential Jesuit periodical *Studies*, where some of University College Dublin's foremost intellectuals liked to publish on social policy topics and on ideological themes (corporatism on the Italianate model had been a 1930s' preoccupation for a few of them). There, a Father Patrick Gannon inveighed against the *Irish Times* in a way that indicated that the paper's willingness to accept the reality of the new Irish state cut little ice in some quarters:

> Everyone remembers ... what a storm of protest the very notion of [censorship] aroused. You would fancy that all the liberties of the land were in danger. Characteristically enough, the campaign was led by a newspaper which, throughout its history, fought with all its influence against political liberty and had no word of protest against the suppression of such organs of opinion as voiced the aspirations of the Irish nation for political emancipation. (Adams 1968, p. 94)

It was being implied that the dangerous leopard, for all its literary vapourings, had not changed its non-national spots.

The other national dailies in the capital also gave the *Irish Times* to know that it was on its own in respect of an almost quixotic assault on the Censorship Board (it was a structure that could depend on firm support in important places). As Michael Adams reports: 'The *Irish Independent* in its only comment on the debate "preferred to err on the side of stringency rather than of laxity"' (Adams 1968, pp. 92–3). The *Irish Press* was content that, although some works of literary worth had been banned, 'in no case' had the Board 'taken action arbitrarily or through caprice'.

In the war years, it must be said, it was the *Irish Times* itself that was the more insecure edifice in the Irish landscape. The very issue in which the board's literary censorship was dismissed as stupid was a mere four pages; wartime newsprint shortages were hitting hard. The proprietor, Sir John Arnott, died in July 1940, to be succeeded by his brother Loftus Arnott. Sir John's son, Sir Laureston Arnott, became managing director (Mark O'Brien 2008, p. 122). The *Irish Times*'s new board was keen to see greater business acumen at work in the paper and looked to a co-opted businessman, Frank A. Lowe, to help it wield a new broom. There was a good deal that needed his reforming zeal. Smyllie clearly thought mere accountancy beneath him and his own eccentricity had allowed the paper's D'Olier Street offices to become a kind of indoor relief site for indigent newspapermen and other hangers-on who had no actual role in the *Irish Times* itself. Among these parasitic elements, Smyllie came and went like a minor potentate, oblivious of the fact that their presence indicated that his kingdom was truly a temporal one that could easily fall. Niall Sheridan has left an evocative verbal sketch of Smyllie arriving for work which tells us how business efficiency was the last thing on the editor's mind in an office long lost to sound administrative procedures (that the paper appeared with the regularity it did during Smyllie's disorganized reign is surely a testament to the skills of the reporting team and to the sturdy artisans of the printing press):

> In anticipation of [Smyllie's] coming, the front office was frequently occupied by a straggle of suppliants – impoverished old acquaintances to whom he gave small sums of money, crackpots seeking publicity for their crazy schemes, a well-known briefless barrister needing money for a cocaine 'fix'. An elderly lady from some respectable suburb, banging her umbrella on the counter and demanding an interview with the Editor. (Sheridan, cited in Cronin 1989, p. 111)

In the editor's inner sanctum, unopened correspondence piled up, 'an Everest of mail that towered over him' (Gray 1994, p. 134). It achieved this impressive height since Smyllie operated a technique of 'Masterful Inactivity'. Explaining this to a neophyte journalist, he patiently advised:

> In principle it is very simple. It consists, in the main, of doing absolutely nothing about anything. Apply it to letters to the editor, and you come up with a very simple solution: if you don't answer their letters, they will go away, or emigrate to England, or die perhaps, and that'll be the end of that. No bother, no trouble, no fuss. (Gray 1994, p. 136)

One letter, however, of which the editor was required to take note in 1942 was from a solicitor acting on behalf of the Institute for Advanced Studies. Erwin

Schrödinger had given a lecture questioning the need for a cosmological first cause. An institute Celticist in another lecture had pondered whether the St Patrick of faith and fable was a composite of two figures. Myles na gCopaleen gleefully announced, 'in a witticism much admired in Dublin' (Cronin, p. 177), that all de Valera's Institute had achieved was to 'show that there were two Patricks and no God'. The ensuing libel case was settled out of court for the sum of £100, of which only £50 was ever paid. Smyllie's other principle of 'Eternal Vigilance' (Gray 1994, p. 138) had failed him.

The fact that the *Irish Times* was ever vigilant to the newsworthy received emphasis when on 21 April 1941, perhaps as a sign that Lowe was about his Augean task of reform, the paper abandoned its traditional format, in which the front page had been given over to advertisements. Thereafter the wartime reader of the first daily edition was greeted each morning by the screaming headlines that announced news of a world enduring cataclysmic events. Distressed by such an upfront assertion of the paper's national and international attentiveness, the same reader could easily turn to news of less disturbing alarms and excursions: the sports news, with the racing results and race cards, was promoted to a position immediately after the front page.

6

The *Irish Times* and the Post-war World

I t is one of the major ironies of European cultural history that the author who in the 1950s most fully seemed to express the anomie and existential despair that overcame many in the post-war world was a citizen of a country that had remained neutral throughout a war that had ravaged the Continent between 1939 and 1945. It was Samuel Beckett's play *En attendant Godot* (first performed in Paris in 1953 and then in English as *Waiting for Godot* in London in 1955) that in its tragi-comic angst caught a mood of near-desolation that helped to define the zeitgeist for a generation. So much had been destroyed, swept away in the cataclysm, so many people had been uprooted and made homeless or stateless, so many innocents slaughtered, that a play that offered an image of human suffering in the persons of two loquacious derelicts in a kind of waste land, futilely awaiting some redefinition of their existence, struck a chord of pained recognition in the many audiences who made it an almost instant classic of twentieth-century literature. Its representation, too, of the cruel, arbitrary power that comprises the master–slave relationship was exactingly germane in a period in which a continent had only begun to come to terms with the fact that the attempt of a 'master race' to impose its will on its neighbours had involved an unimaginably abominable attempt at genocide.

The *Irish Times* marked the ending of the war in Europe, in which so many had perished, with its editorial 'Laus Deo' on 8 May 1945. World War II had, the editorialist averred, been 'an ordeal which [had] no parallel in the world's history' (*Irish Times*, 8 May 1945). The surrender by German forces, the death of Hitler and the disintegration of the Third Reich meant that Germany's collapse had been 'complete and overwhelming'. For the *Irish Times*, it was 'the end of an era, but the beginning of a new and completely unpredictable chapter in the history of the world'. At a less global level, the ending of European hostilities incited controversies that suggested that age-old animosities between Britain and Ireland had outlasted the deluge, had, perhaps, been exacerbated by Irish neutrality. On 1 May, in an act that the victorious allies found incredible and the survivors of Nazi terror unconscionable, Eamon de Valera called on the German representative in Dublin to offer the condolences of the Irish people on the death of the German Chancellor, Adolf Hitler. The exact niceties of diplomatic protocol were to be observed, it seemed, though the heavens fall. Minor, though ugly, demonstrations in Dublin and in a few places elsewhere also indicated that there were a few in Ireland who regretted that an enemy of the old enemy had been defeated. Strident voices were raised in Britain which berated Ireland for her craven neutrality during the war. Winston Churchill, who at various stages of the conflict had sought to entice Ireland to grant the Allies the use of her country's ports and airfields (the reward would be the ending of partition), crystallized such opinion when in a broadcast of 13 May, he inveighed against what he considered a shameful period in Ireland's history. Even though, in what he invoked as 'a deadly moment in our life', the British had left 'the de Valera government to frolic with the German and later with Japanese representatives to their heart's content' (Wills 2007, p. 391), Churchill argued that, but for the loyalty and friendship of Northern Ireland (Derry had been a key port, giving as it does on the North Atlantic), Britain might have been forced to 'come to close quarters with Mr de Valera'. De Valera responded to this choleric example of imperial rodomontade (Churchill had been quite prepared to sacrifice his friends in Northern Ireland when it had seemed necessary) with a resolute dignity that salvaged a reputation compromised by his visit to the German representative earlier in the month. In a broadcast reply, de Valera challenged Churchillian rhetoric with effective rhetoric of his own, reminding the British prime minister that Ireland was a 'small nation that stood alone, not for a year or two, but for several hundred years against aggression ... a small nation that could never be got to accept defeat and has never surrendered her soul'.

This chain of events placed the *Irish Times* in a delicate position. De Valera's reply to Churchill was widely admired and steadied support for his policy of neutrality which had been shaken somewhat by the peculiar punctiliousness of his consolatory visit to the German legation. The newspaper sought both to keep its integrity with respect to its view of neutrality and its awareness that the British war-leader had insulted Ireland. On 15 May, in an editorial that admitted 'This newspaper has never been neutral', although it had 'acquiesced in it' since it was the policy of the nation it sought to serve, the writer entered a mild rebuke to the British prime minister. While accepting that Churchill had been speaking in the flush of victory, it did acknowledge, nonetheless, 'an uneasy feeling that possibly he went just a little too far' (*Irish Times*, 15 May 1945). This mealy-mouthed demurral at Churchill's intemperance was joined by a bland opinion: 'his suggestion that Mr de Valera's Government spent its time during the war in "frolics" with the Germans and the Japanese was, to say the least of it, a slight overstatement'. Three days later the paper's editorial 'Turning Away Wrath' gave a firmer, more considered response to Churchill, which expressed gratification that the always courteous de Valera had offered the biblical 'soft answer' to assuage the Englishman's anger. This afforded the paper an opportunity to describe and defend the actual role many Irish people and the state itself had actually played in the war. In the de facto ambiguities of Anglo-Irish relations (the twenty-six county state was neither a full republic nor a dominion) 'Ireland's neutrality from the very start operated in favour of the United Nations and particularly of Great Britain' (*Irish Times*, 18 May 1945). In face of understandable anti-Irish feeling in Britain and the United States, the editorialist was at pains to point out that 'at least 100,000 – and probably more – of her sons had joined the British forces'. The country had sent 'many scores of thousands of workers' to Britain who aided the war effort. Food exports in 'vast quantities' helped to 'relieve the economic strain, and in some measure to alleviate the rigours of rationing'. So, while de Valera's abstract, almost metaphysical, mind saw Anglo-Irish relations in stark if always politely expressed terms, Irish links with Britain, the *Irish Times* implied, had stood the test of a terrible war and had not been broken. The paper even went so far as to argue, despite the peril imposed on Britain by Ireland's denial of its ports to the Allies, that 'for most practical purposes, the mere existence of this little country on Britain's western flank constituted a military safeguard'. And the airport at Foynes on the Shannon had been of 'incalculable value both to the British and to the Americans'. Ireland's neutrality had by no means been ignoble either. The country had played its part in the defeat of fascism. As these editorials were appearing, it was becoming gruesomely clear what fascism and Nazism had truly involved.

On 14 May 1945 the *Irish Times* published a letter from a Senta Woods (who gave a Drogheda address) to express dismay at the way 'the general public doubt the truth of the articles and photographs which have been published in all the leading British newspapers about the atrocities committed by the Germans in the concentration camps in Germany' (*Irish Times*, 14 May 1945). She suggested that a mission be sent to ascertain the truth. On 15 May the newspaper, under the headline 'Irish Officers View German Prison Camps', gave readers to know that beatings, hangings, shootings and scientific starvation had taken place in the camps. Private letters by two Irish officers to their families were quoted. One reported how an RAF chaplain had said, 'You will be reading in the newspapers about the atrocities perpetrated in those camps. Well if you multiply what you read by 100% you will arrive at something like the truth. The absolute horror is indescribable' (*Irish Times*, 15 May 1945). An army captain was also quoted as saying, 'All these facts that I have given to you are absolutely true. Folks in Ireland have been slow to believe such things. They need to be shaken badly. They don't understand the horror of this war because it had not been brought home to them. They have spun their own little cocoon, and have been indifferent, to a great extent, to the sufferings of humanity.' The paper that day was invading that cocoon with its horrific reports of mass murder of Jews, of how 'pyres had burnt for fully six months'. One survivor of Auschwitz, a Harry Spitz, former conductor of the Berlin and

Vienna State Opera Orchestras, was reported as telling how 40,000 Jews were gassed every week, with 'the ultra-modern gas chambers able to take 6,000 at a time'. He himself, in an encapsulation of the unfathomable barbarity that had overtaken German culture, told of how 'he was beaten with a steel baton and then forced to conduct Beethoven's Fifth Symphony'.

The following day a W. P. le Clerk wrote to the paper, questioning the need for any truth mission to Germany (he wished to concentrate on 'building the peace'). 'The reason' for any such tour of inspection, he contended, 'is obscure, but if we are to celebrate the removal of censorship by washing other countries' dirty linen in our public press, why not send the party of ghouls to India, China, Palestine or Russia' (*Irish Times*, 16 May 1945). It seems that some readers were unwilling to, or could not take in, the depth of depravity that Nazism represented. How it had affected 'thirty-two citizens of Eire' (*Irish Times*, 17 May 1945) was revealed the next day when the paper reported on their experience at a camp outside Bremen. Five of their number had died of typhus fever and they had witnessed random acts of murderous violence. A month before, the camp commandant had 'shot sixteen prisoners after announcing that he knew he would be shot or hanged by the Allied armies, and he would "take as many as he could with him"'. The headline for this report on information provided by one of the Irish survivors to an 'Irish Times reporter' was, as Claire Wills has pointed out (Wills 2007, p. 401), oddly cautious as to the veracity of what was being alleged about Nazi atrocities. 'Irishman's Story of "Horror" Camps' left room, with its inverted commas, for doubters to continue in their doubts. Indeed, Robert Smyllie himself confessed, writing as Nichevo on 26 May, that he had been 'bothered' in his mind 'regarding the behaviour of the Nazis to their victims in the concentration camps'. We recall his scepticism when in 1938 he had doubted a report on conditions in a camp and, as a Germanophile and a journalist, he now stated: 'Newspaper men are not easily impressed by propaganda; and I must confess candidly that I took a lot of the talk about the German camps with a grain of salt.' A conversation with the Irish dramatist and intrepid war reporter Denis Johnston had dispelled any scepticism about what had happened. Johnston, another confirmed Irish Germanophile, had been taken to the camp at Buchenwald, where what he saw registered in the moment as simply beyond description. Nichevo's column of 26 May sought to express a horrified acknowledgement of the truth of the reports his newspaper had carried, but the tone was strangely costive, as if the mind was absorbing the ghastly fact of organized mass murder Johnston had communicated to him, but the emotions were not able to respond to something so unimaginable (Johnston in his autobiography, *Nine Rivers from Jordan*, 1953, would later manage to evoke in memory, with heart-rending, poignant immediacy, his experience of entering Buchenwald in 1945 to discover its all-too-actual horrors). (cited Adams 2002, p 278)

Perhaps a sign that the enormity of what had happened to European Jewry in World War II had not really sunk in in the immediate aftermath of hostilities was the fact that editorials published in the paper in the summer and autumn of 1945 on the future of the Jewish people failed to take account of the fact that the Holocaust had altered everything. In an even-handed editorial, for example, in September 1945, which criticized the British government's intention to resile from the Balfour Declaration of 1917, the writer judged that 'A final solution may be expected only when the United Nations, to which the British Government has referred the matter, has had time to deliberate' (*Irish Times*, 25 September 1945). The phrase 'final solution' in respect of the Palestine question recurred in the paper's lexicon without apparent awareness of the shocking import of that lapidary phrase in Europe's very recent history. One notes, too, that when almost a year later the *Irish Times* commented on the impending verdicts to be delivered on the Nazi leadership following the Nuremberg trials, as it considered that regime's crimes, it was not the Shoah that concerned it, but the fact that Hitler and his henchmen had 'brought a great nation of more than 60,000,000 people crashing to its doom' (*Irish Times*, 3 August 1946). The editorial, entitled 'Hangman's House' (which posited as its conclusion that 'Humanity is sick of executions'), referred to what had overtaken the German people as 'a dreadful holocaust'. The term 'holocaust' in 1945 had only begun to be applied to the Nazi attempted genocide, but its use here in an editorial, which makes no reference to the fate of the Jews while bewailing the 'doom' of the German nation, is rather telling in a paper that had excoriated Nazi anti-Semitism in the 1930s. Perhaps the awful scale of Nazi criminality had not yet fully sunk in.

A book review published in the *Irish Times* in September 1945 had in fact presented its readers with the stark facts of attempted genocide. Under the heading 'The Future of the Jews', Samuel Beckett's friend A. J. Leventhal, who had replaced Beckett as lecturer in French at Trinity College Dublin in 1932, reviewed a pamphlet by the British publisher Victor Gollancz, *Nowhere to Lay their Heads*, and a book, *Jewish Labour Economy in Palestine* by a G. Muenzner. Writing of Gollancz's pamphlet, Leventhal noted how the author 'writes of misery and agony in undertones' (*Irish Times*, 8 September 1945). Leventhal understood this as a rhetorical strategy by which 'eloquence' is left to 'statistics', but he was not loath to reinforce the impact of what he identified as 'the cold reasoning of revelatory numbers':

> Four million Jews, he [Gollancz] declares, have been put to death in Europe since the beginning of the Second World War. This is an understatement. At the Zionist conference which has just been held in London the number of murdered Jews has been estimated as nearly five million. In any case, it's a number larger than the ultimate casualties of any of the fighting peoples with the exception of Russia and possibly Poland. He dismisses with an

ominous calm the manner of their death; slow torture in some cases, starvation, gas chambers, gangster beatings in others. Quietly practical, Mr Gollancz forgets the dead, and asks what is to happen to the survivors.

The full horror of the Shoah took time, it can truthfully be said, to register in Ireland. That the *Irish Times* was at first uncertain about what British reportage was revealing is in that context significant, for respect for British sources of information was in its DNA. Other organs, lacking such genetic imprinting, were openly sceptical about atrocity stories emerging from Britain. The *Irish Press*, greatly exaggerating what had appeared in the *Irish Times*, even went so far as to claim in an editorial attacking the paper on 17 May 1945 that 'Now in 1945 that little Ascendancy group which is still un-reconciled to the loss of its powers and privileges has begun to fawn around the knees of the victors, or perhaps "grovel" might be a better term, in view of its atrocity stories and atrocity photographs' (Wills 2007, pp. 399–400).

August 1945 had brought an event that in its immediate shattering effects trumped the protracted if appalling narrative of the attempted Jewish genocide that awaited its full recounting in Ireland as elsewhere. The explosion of an atom bomb over the Japanese city of Hiroshima by the United States Air Force on 6 August was reported as an event of monumental significance by all the Irish dailies. The immediately subsequent atomic bombing of Nagasaki added to the alarm and anxiety. The *Irish Times* entrusted its editorial on the attack on Hiroshima to a young staffer, Jack White (Gray 1994, p. 138), a recently recruited Trinity College Dublin graduate, later to become a distinguished Irish television executive and author. He rose to the challenge, delivering a resonant statement on how the century's fear of aerial bombardment in war had been awfully fulfilled in the explosion of 'The Mighty Atom':

> No single disclosure of the war – not even that of the rocket bomb – has had so profoundly disturbing an influence on the mind of the ordinary man. He sees he has entered an era in which the means of destruction have become so powerful that any further war must be almost an Armageddon.
> (*Irish Times*, 8 August 1945)

White wrote that the bomb, which had fulfilled the worst imaginings of science fiction, had altered the nature of world politics for ever. With considerable prescience, White imagined how what later became known as the doctrine of mutually assured destruction might check the hand over the nuclear button. He hoped that the new agency of the United Nations might be a surer guarantor of peace.

The *Irish Times* could hardly have avoided publishing an editorial on so signal an event as the atomic bomb attack on Hiroshima. Smyllie must have been aware, however, that what the United States had done would tend to confirm in many Irish minds their belief in the virtue of Ireland's neutrality. Indeed, the paper in May had acknowledged that de Valera had 'elevated the idea of neutrality into a principle ... he contrived to convince the people ... that Irish neutrality had a high spiritual basis' (*Irish Times*, 15 May 1945). And while the *Irish Times* had then pointed out that Ireland had been effectively neutral in favour of the Allies throughout the war, he probably realized that the atomic bombing of Japanese cities, with tens of thousands of civilian casualties, could be grist to the mill of those who were concerned to exonerate Ireland from the charge that it had not understood the full evil of Nazism and had immorally cocooned itself from humanity's sufferings. For was the deliberate slaughter of Japanese civilians not as abhorrent as anything the Nazis has inflicted on subject peoples and on the Jews, the argument might run, and Irish neutrality a properly pacifist stance?

On 11 August 1945, as the paper's front-page headline announced 'Japan Offers Conditional Surrender', a less circumspect editorial than that which White had initially supplied accordingly weighed in on the question of the morality of the bombing. Agreeing that weapons of mass destruction represented an existential challenge to humankind ('man now possesses such terrible weapons that the future must offer either peace or the destruction of civilisation': *Irish Times*, 11 August 1945), the editorial, nonetheless, posited of the concluding hostilities: 'The final blows ... were decisive; and it may be that the immolation of the people of Hiroshima has prevented, in the end, a greater slaughter.' And as if further to set what had occurred in Japan in a moral equation, the leader reminded how 'twelve million Germans evicted from the area occupied by the Poles and Czechs are on the move. Twenty or thirty thousand arrive in Berlin every day.'

Claire Wills has considered in some detail why, as she puts it, 'the Irish response to Hiroshima and Nagasaki' was 'so much more forthright than the reaction to the death camps' (Wills 2007, p. 420). She admits that among the explanations may, indeed, have been the fact 'that Hiroshima was experienced as helping to relieve the pressure on neutrality at the end of the war. Ireland had been tragically vindicated in refusing to see the conflict in terms of black and white.' So Smyllie, with his pro-Allied attitudes, must have been considerably discomfited by Myles na gCopaleen's contributions on the matter in Smyllie's own newspaper. Myles treated the bombing as a peculiarly barbaric crime, as a product of racism. On 20 August, in his '*Cruiskeen Lawn*' column, he asked: 'Why should this outsize barbarity be visited on Japanese?' (*Irish Times*, 20 August 1945). The American decision to use atomic weapons in Japan, Myles was letting it be known, was a crassly racist one and the manifestation of an inveterate fallen human nature. For: 'There is only one war and to think that it will cease within the bourne of humanity's tenure of the soil is to think as one thought in the nursery ... When the world is at peace, horror camps are not photographed' (cited in Cronin 1989, p. 158).

On 25 August in an editorial celebrating Australia's contribution to the war effort (they had fought 'like tigers' in North Africa), what one may take to be Smyllie's voice rang loud and clear. 'Now it is over,' he declaimed, 'Germany and Japan have been crushed, together with their miserable following of satellites. Once more the British Commonwealth has emerged in triumph from a world of conflict' (*Irish Times*, 25 August 1945). Myles was incensed by this and on 10 September declared his own war on his editor. In a column of contorted ironies, he disdainfully quoted Smyllie's bombastic editorial and demanded 'the question which I must crave entitlement to put to that great pro-consular figure, the reverend editor of the *Irish Times*, is simply this. *Are you, Sir, really satisfied that Irish culture, that great achievement of T.C.D.* is such that you are justified in referring to the civilisation of Imperial Japan as a miserable satellite thereof.' For the rest of the week Myles wrote of the superior achievements of the Orient as compared with the hubristic West. Part of the humour of the '*Cruiskeen Lawn*' column had been that O'Nolan had been allowed to take issue with editorial matter (a comic arrow sometimes directed the reader to the adjacent column). This was different. There was a certain venom involved as the Irish Catholic and University College Dublin man put Trinity College Dublin and its pro-British Protestant scion in their place. Friday brought a patronizing tone and a withering disdain for the ideals of social progress, things the paper liked to think it espoused, which may have overstepped the mark: '*Cruiskeen Lawn*' did not appear again until later in the month. The hiatus probably signalled editorial displeasure.

Writing of the immediate aftermath of World War II as experienced in Ireland, historian Thomas Bartlett has observed that the successful maintenance of neutrality had a deleterious effect on the body politic. This was inasmuch as its apparent success gave a kind of endorsement to the isolationist economic policies the state had imposed in the 1930s:

> Politicians in the Irish Free State were secure, complacent and even arrogant in their vision of what they wanted Ireland to be and confident that with perseverance a Gaelic-speaking self-sufficient, agriculturally based, Catholic moral community could finally be realised. The 'Emergency' had seemingly vindicated the policies pursued by Fianna Fáil in the 1930s towards achieving these goals. (Bartlett 2010, p. 474)

Events would quickly demonstrate that the post-war period at home and abroad would be marked by major changes. The bombing of Hiroshima and Nagasaki did, indeed, as the *Irish Times*'s editorials had surmised, herald a new era of change from which Ireland could not be immune. As that new age dawned, a fortuitous anniversary gave the paper an opportunity to reflect on its own values that it undoubtedly hoped could sustain it in the challenging days ahead.

The occasion was the centenary of the untimely death in 1845 of the Young Ireland leader, the journalist, poet and patriot Thomas Davis. The newspaper chose to publish a special issue to honour his memory. On the face of it, this must have seemed an unlikely editorial decision, for as one contributor, the young University College Dublin historian Robin Dudley-Edwards, argued, it had been Davis who in three brief years of political work had, in the tradition of the United Irishmen of 1798, brought the concept of Irish separatism to the fore once again in the Irish/English imbroglio. However, it was Davis's anti-sectarian patriotism that made him for the *Irish Times* a man to honour almost above all other Irishmen. It fell to a Trinity College Dublin historian, T. W. Moody, to pen a panegyric to the long-dead patriot. Davis was a paragon among Irishmen, Moody enthused, for no one had 'ever dedicated himself to the service of Ireland more single-mindedly than did Davis, and no man [had] ever laboured in that service more intensely, more honourably and more memorably'. It helped no doubt in both this writer's and the editor's mind that Davis, and most of the Young Ireland leaders, whether Protestant or Catholic, were Trinity men. It was, however, the idealistic values Moody discerned as inspiring Davis that made the Young Irelander a fit subject for extensive commemoration in the *Irish Times*:

> Though Davis sang of 'a nation once again' he was in truth seeking to build a nation such as had never existed before – a nation in which all sections of Ireland's population, whatever their origin, class or religion, would be joined in mutual respect and the will to share a distinctive destiny as Irishmen; a nation rooted in the will and affections of its people and not any exclusive principle of blood or creed or culture. (*Irish Times*, 7 September 1945)

The special issue, to which Donagh MacDonagh contributed an appropriate poem, also included a lengthy editorial on 'Davis and his Work', which expanded on Moody's encomium, drawing lessons for the conduct of current Irish affairs. Quoting Thackeray, who had in 1843 reflected that 'in Ireland there are two truths – the Catholic truth and the Protestant truth', the editorial sadly admitted, 'Thackeray was correct: he would be only a little less correct if he were writing in 1945 instead of 1843.' For the writer, however, Davis held out the ideals of an Irish nationality in which Protestant and Catholic could share and all classes could feel at home. It saw that Davis's 'chief aim' had been 'to restore Ireland's sense of pride and tradition and dignity, and to unite the jarring creeds and classes for a common objective ...' The *Irish Times* was signalling, therefore, that it held to Davis's ideals; in a sense was taking them for its own as it bemoaned the fact that Davis's Ireland remained unborn. The editorial concluded:

> His dream of a Protestant and Catholic *concordat* has been very imper-
> fectly realised, and to this fact may be traced the tragic division of our
> island into what amounts to a Catholic and a Protestant State. If Davis's

teaching had been taken fully to heart, would our country to-day be victim of the great sin of partition?

Events, as we shall see, would soon test in dramatic fashion the *Irish Times*'s proposition that the Irish Free State was essentially a Catholic state. Ironically enough, the circumstances that provoked a highly revelatory Church–state crisis developed from an attempt by a government minister minimally to follow Britain's example in the war's aftermath by giving a slightly greater role to the state in the matter of social welfare. The irony consists in the fact that the *Irish Times* in its economic conservatism had been dubious about that kind of state intervention both in Britain and Ireland. Indeed, in commending Davis in 1945, it made much of the Young Islander's doctrine of self-reliance and regretted a contemporary 'increasing tendency to rely upon the kindly offices of "Government," rather than the virtues of hard work and discipline'.

In the United Kingdom the Beveridge Report of 1942 had laid the groundwork for the welfare state that the Labour government of 1945 began to put in place. With many Irish people living in Britain and with Northern Ireland set to be affected by the major involvement by the state in the social welfare of its citizens, it was inevitable that the Irish government would have to consider making similar provisions in the 26 counties. It was obvious, however, that change would have to come, given that in 1947/8 the state was paying a mere £830,000 towards the provision of health services (with local authorities still 'supplying over eighty per cent of the cost of their services', Lyons 1971, p. 662).

The extension of the new British welfare state to Northern Ireland inevitably created difficulties for those who hoped for the ending of partition (they included in his own distinctive fashion the editor of the *Irish Times*). Unionists were unlikely to be willing to join a state that could afford them fewer social benefits than the United Kingdom. When during a campaign for an election that would oust de Valera's government and replace it with a coalition in which a new radical party, Clann na Poblachta, would play a part with the Labour Party, the issue of the North and the welfare state would be given prominence. Seán MacBride, leader of Clann na Poblachta (son of Maud Gonne and the 1916 martyr John MacBride and former commanding officer of the IRA in the 1930s), wrote a long letter to the *Irish Times*, addressing the problem of partition. In this he admitted that 'unless and until we establish economic conditions and social services here that will be at least as attractive as those that prevail in the Six Counties, we cannot hope to arouse real enthusiasm for the ending of partition, even among the Nationalist population of the Six Counties' (*Irish Times*, 28 January 1948). The paper editorialized on the matter. It agreed that MacBride was correct about the significance of economic and social disparities between North and South on the likelihood of Irish reunification, but it doubted that such things were as important as MacBride supposed. The editorial listed other impediments to Irish unity, blaming de Valera especially for seeking to achieve 'a thirty-two County Republic which shall be Gaelic-speaking'. The effect was to suggest that the editorialist was less focused on the Free State's lack of developed social services (the provision of which might, it allowed, lessen unionist opposition to the idea of unity) than on broader constitutional and cultural issues. Events over the following 18 months were to challenge the newspaper's instinctively conservative outlook on social issues.

In the February 1948 election, de Valera's Fianna Fáil party lost its parliamentary majority, indicating that post-war political complacency had been unwarranted. The Irish Free State was not immune to the pressures for change that had been building up in many parts of the world. Indeed, the recent founding of Clann na Poblachta and the reinvigoration of a party, Clann na Talmhan, which spoke for small farmers in the west of the country, indicated a hearty appetite for change in Ireland itself. And among the changes it got were those that markedly affected public health.

The new coalition, which took power in February 1948 with the socially conservative Fine Gael as the major partner (that party supplied the Taoiseach, John A. Costello), appointed as Minister for Health Noel Browne, a young Trinity College educated Catholic medical doctor and member of MacBride's party. Clann na Poblachta had stood not only on a republican ticket, but was committed to the state provision of social welfare. Browne quickly moved to make good his party's promise to the electorate. His own family had been tragically affected by tuberculosis and he himself had survived the disease. His ambition was to eradicate TB in Ireland as new medication made that an achievable goal (when he came to office tuberculosis was 'killing between 3,000 and 4,000 people every year' in Ireland, Lyons 1971, p. 572). A mass radiography programme had helped to reduce such fatalities but the country lacked sanatoria and hospital beds set aside for the treatment of the afflicted. Browne made it his business to supply these. Departmental funds (together with the direction of monies from the Irish Sweepstake lottery funds) were earmarked for the supply and staffing of sanatoria throughout the country.

The *Irish Times*, despite its prudent attitude to state intervention in social provision, could not but be impressed by the minister's ardour. As early as April 1948, an editorial was welcoming 'Dr Browne's zeal in his campaign against tuberculosis' and saluting the fact that 'appreciable progress [had] been made in regard to the provision of beds for tubercular patients' (*Irish Times*, 10 April 1948). 'The young minister [had] been able to infect many of his assistants with some of his own enthusiasm.' Just over a year later, in an editorial entitled 'The Nation's Health', reflecting on the state of health in the population of Britain, gave its clear support for the way 'The present Government [was] pledged to introduce a national health service, which, even if it cannot hope to vie with its costly British counterpart, will ensure that no citizen, however poor, will be permitted to die for lack of medical or surgical attention' (*Irish Times*, 9 May 1949). In June, writing as Nichevo in 'An Irishman's Diary', Smyllie praised Noel Browne, who 'had worked wonders' (*Irish Times*, 11 June 1949) since coming to office.

On 23 September 1949 the paper reported that a contract had been signed for a regional tuberculosis sanatorium near Galway which would cost one million pounds; 'the contract is said to be one of the largest building contracts ever placed in Ireland' (*Irish Times*, 23 September 1949). Such a report indicates how in the later 1940s and early 1950s medical science and medical matters were becoming a specific focus of journalistic attention. Reports about new drugs (among them streptomycin, which was a weapon in Browne's battle against TB), about vaccination and the control of infection became a feature of reportage, along with announcements about the opening of new sanatoria. While the paper published the weekly number of those made ill by infectious diseases in Dublin, much of the coverage of medical matters was couched in optimistic terms, reminding one of the excitement technological advances had generated in the newspaper in the first decade of the century. From 1947 onwards it retained its own medical correspondent, who in the 1950s was afforded a frequently published column. On 24 October 1952 the *Irish Times* reported that a Nobel Prize had been awarded to Professor Dr Selman Waksman, the discoverer of streptomycin.

By 1950 the welfare state was a given in Britain, and Irish commentators could not but take note of it. An *Irish Times* editorial in March 1950 bemoaned the 'gross-overspending' (*Irish Times*, 9 March 1950) the health service in Britain had given rise to. Aneurin Bevan, Minister of Health there, was a 'stormy petrel', allowed to perch in office by an indulgent prime minister. In an *Irish Times* review of Louis MacNeice's *Collected Poems*, however, the poet Austin Clarke took for granted that the era of revolutionary politics, in which MacNeice had found his poetic voice, was over in Britain, and the new permanent order was that put in place by the British Labour government: 'The revolution has come and gone and England has now a welfare state' (*Irish Times*, 16 September 1950), he stated with finality. The same month an editorial in the paper on 'Man and Medicine' attempted a measured audit of the British National Health Service which it judged 'one of the most revolutionary developments of the Socialist *régime*' (*Irish Times*, 14 September 1950). It had, the paper observed again, 'proved appallingly expensive ... Abuses abounded, and safeguards against them proved inadequate or impotent.' Nonetheless, it could not be denied that 'the comprehensive new State services yielded benefits to multitudes of deserving folk'. The editorial now gave greater weight to the effect the United Kingdom's welfare state was having in cementing partition. The writer posed the question: 'Will the Irish system of private medicine, seconded by State services only in regard to extraordinary needs, be found sufficient not only to maintain and improve public health, but also to satisfy people who see their cousins enjoying what may be termed medical luxury just over the border?' The writer, still marching to a conservative drum, remained cautious, however, about radical change in the Free State, for 'Complete socialisation of medicine goes even farther than socialisation of industry, and invades privacy in the very home. It inevitably entails a threat to personal freedom.' Despite such views, by 1951 the paper was frankly acknowledging that the existence of the welfare state in the United Kingdom had not had the deleterious effects on individual effort that it had earlier feared would be the case. In an editorial explicitly entitled 'The Welfare State', the writer took account of published evidence on how the quality of life had improved in one English city and concluded: 'the changes there show what the Welfare State can do to confound its critics. There is no evidence that it has pauperised the community, or made for indolence or apathy. On the contrary, it appears the British are healthier and harder-working than ever' (*Irish Times*, 20 October 1951). Notwithstanding the financial difficulties for the Irish state that an empowered trades union movement might create, the editorial writer was now convinced that 'the problem will not be solved by abandoning the road to the Welfare State before our journey is well begun'. One might identify the first decisive steps of that journey in the announcement made by the Minister for Health on 7 February 1950 (although he had clearly signalled his intentions earlier) at a sod-turning ceremony for the sanatorium near Galway city. As the paper reported it, Noel Browne had

> ... declared that he would soon extend the scope of the medical services and hospital facilities to give protection to mothers during motherhood and to children in their early life and during stages of adolescence. The Government had decided that every man and woman and their children should have the best health service that money could provide. (*Irish Times*, 7 February 1950)

The minister had made his Christian socialist convictions more than clear as he stated: 'I intend ... to make available to all our people as a fundamental right of his membership of our Society, all that the science of medicine holds for man in his time of ill-health and sickness.' In doing so, he was challenging not only the conservative consensus in the country about social provision, of which the *Irish Times* (along with most of the medical profession) was a part, but throwing down the gauntlet to the Catholic hierarchy, who believed such provision was essentially a matter for families whose consciences in the matter of human reproduction had been guided by Church authority. The stage was being set for a dramatic clash between Church and state, in which the *Irish Times* would play a role. It would be a drama that would test in stark fashion the newspaper's claim that Thomas Davis's pluralist ideals for the Irish nation had scarcely been realized in the 26-county Irish Free State.

In 1950 the *Irish Times* had had grounds to fear that the Irish state was not neutral as between the rights of its Catholic and Protestant citizens when Catholic Church interests entered the frame. For in that year the legal implications of the *Ne Temere* decree (which had caused Protestant alarm when it was promulgated) were tested all the way to the Supreme Court in what became known as the Tilson Case. The judge in the High Court, by reason of the clause in the 1937 Constitution that recognized the special position of the Catholic Church, ruled that promises made by non-Catholic partners in 'mixed' marriages to educate their children as Catholics must be binding. The Supreme Court, on narrower and on less than convincing grounds, upheld the judgement, with the only Protestant member of the five-man bench dissenting. The paper published a series of furious letters protesting about the decision. Its editorial on the issue was more circumspect, even sanguine, in contrast to the *Irish Times*'s fears earlier in the century, in opposition to its most splenetic correspondents. It summarized the facts of the 'sordid case', analysed the judgement and concurred with both the majority and minority on the Supreme Court that the Common Law that gave authority to the father in such cases was archaic. It concluded with admirable, if slightly disassociated, aplomb:

> ... it is difficult to avoid the impression that the philosophy underlying Irish jurisprudence is tending slowly but surely to be informed by the principles of the Roman Catholic Church. *A priori* there can be no great objection to that so long as the issue is faced squarely by everybody concerned. (*Irish Times*, 7 August 1950)

Such equanimity could not be maintained in the crisis between Church and state which erupted in October 1950 and continued until April 1951.

In 1947 de Valera's government had introduced a Health Act. Among its provisions was legislation that would allow for the state to make medical services freely available to mothers and their offspring. It was Browne's intention, as a minister in the new coalition government, to put in place by an Act of the Oireachtas the arrangements necessary to realize this intention. His efforts were met with opposition from the Irish Medical Council, which insisted that such provision should be means-tested, giving the cost of the scheme to justify a position that derived in part from self-interest (that Browne was himself a medical doctor did not commend the scheme to its most conservative members, nor to some members of the cabinet who were professional men). More significantly, it reinvigorated the profound opposition of the Catholic Church, which had in fact raised its concerns about the mother and child aspects of the Act with de Valera in 1947. Dublin's Catholic Archbishop, John Charles McQuaid, led the charge against Browne's Bill. The Church's concerted opposition to

Browne's proposed scheme was based on the belief that his proposals infringed Catholic social teachings about the rights of parents, about the limited role the state should play in social welfare, and that it risked Catholic mothers being given advice on reproductive matters that could include advice on artificial contraception and abortion (Whyte 1971, p. 215). More fundamentally, it involved an assertion of ecclesiastical power in a manner that raised questions about the substance of Irish democracy.

Browne published the full details of his scheme on 6 March 1951. On 5 April Archbishop McQuaid delivered a death-blow to his plans. On behalf of the hierarchy, McQuaid told the government that the Minister for Health's scheme was 'opposed to Catholic social thinking' (Whyte 1971, p. 223). At cabinet the next day Browne found that none of his colleagues would support him in pressing on with the enactment of his Bill. The scheme was abandoned with unseemly haste and Browne was required to resign from office by MacBride, the leader of his party (they had long been at loggerheads, MacBride suspecting Browne of wishing to unseat him as party leader). He did not go quietly. Before tendering his required resignation, he had asked Robert Smyllie to publish in their entirety the contents of letters that had 'passed between himself, the Taoiseach and the hierarchy' on the issue (Whyte 1971, p. 239). Smyllie promised to do so, thereby putting it up to the other Dublin morning dailies to follow suit (Browne later recalled in his autobiography how 'Smyllie, an editor with genuine liberal beliefs, had promised me that should ... an embargo be attempted, then, at risk of going to prison, he would "publish and be damned"', Browne 1986, p. 186). On 12 April the *Irish Times*, the *Irish Independent* and the *Irish Press* carried these documents. It was an extraordinary moment in Irish journalism, in which Smyllie played a brave role (for the Official Secrets Act might have been invoked). For the first time the Irish public had an extensive insight into how the government conducted its business in private, and to how deferential government ministers, including Browne himself it must be said, were to Church authority. The release of this material, which came from Browne by way of a sympathetic civil servant, must have confirmed to many of his parliamentary colleagues that he was a loose cannon, who by reason of his hyper-sensitive personality and obdurate stances at negotiating tables, had brought his troubles down on his own head. For Smyllie, such considerations did not weigh at all. His editorial of 12 April was a no-holds-barred assault on the integrity of the Irish state. It was as if the frustration of the war years and a deep-seated ambivalence about the state itself, for all his efforts to adapt to Irish independence, found expression in a bitter conclusion. The Free State was effectively a theocracy.

For Smyllie, Browne was a pure victim of a 'gallant fight'. Forces too great to confront alone had been 'both openly and covertly arrayed against him' (*Irish Times*, 12 April 1951). Though the paper had been critical of Browne's plan (and its medical correspondent as recently as 19 March 1951 had supplied a fair-minded account of the medical profession's attitude to the scheme), the editor was outraged at the means by which it had been terminally obstructed. The editorial was contemptuous in the broad sarcasm of its tone:

> This is a sad day for Ireland. It is not so important that the Mother and Child Scheme has been withdrawn, to be replaced by an alternative project embodying a means test. What matters is that an honest, far-sighted and energetic man has been driven out of active politics. The most serious revelation, however, is that the Roman Catholic Church would seem to be the effective Government of this country. In the circumstances may we appeal to Mr Costello and his colleagues to admit the futility of their pitiful efforts to 'abolish the border' – their Mansion House Committees, their anti-partition speeches at international assemblies, their pathetic appeals to the majority in the Six Counties to recognise that its advantage lies in a United Ireland? To that majority, the domination of the State by the Church – any Church – is anathema, and from now onwards it can plead some justification for all its fears. It seems that the merits of a theocratic Twenty-six Counties outweigh those of a normally democratic Thirty-two. Has the Government made its choice?

Grist to the *Irish Times*'s polemical mill was provided in the parliamentary debate on Browne's resignation, as deputies sought to outdo each other in affirming fealty to their Church, eagerly ready as the majority of them were to obey its teachings on social policy.

In entitling its bitter editorial on the Mother and Child controversy 'Contra Mundum', the *Irish Times* was paying tribute to what it saw as Noel Browne's heroic, solitary stand against the serried ranks of the bishops. The newspaper may not have quite realized that in coming to Browne's defence in the fashion it did, it was joining him as the target of widespread obloquy. The Taoiseach and his Minister for Defence, Tom O'Higgins, set the tone in the debate on the matter, when they declared that the opinion of the *Irish Times* was of no moment as compared to their primary religious allegiance (Mark O'Brien 2008, p. 139). Others took the opportunity to inveigh against Smyllie and his newspaper, which published a 'flood of correspondence on the subject, in which the balance of opinion was critical of the hierarchy and government' (Whyte 1971, p. 240). One parliamentarian dared to agree with Smyllie's main point: that the Church had usurped the power of the state. For their pains, as John Whyte puts it, 'the newspaper and the deputy were subjected to an avalanche of polemic' (Whyte 1971, p. 242). The most colourful, hard-hitting and damaging criticism came from the widely read *Catholic Standard*, where the president of University College Cork, Professor Alfred O'Rahilly, published two articles on the *Irish Times*'s coverage of the debacle, which mingled spirited abuse with cogent argument. For the professor was a vociferous controversialist, gifted with a profound belief in his own omniscience. He declared it 'utterly nonsensical' that 'the *Irish Times* claims the right to subject the Government to a daily barrage of school masterish scolding, while denying to the Catholic Episcopate the right of an occasional restrained intervention purely on matters of principle' (cited Mark O'Brien 2008, p. 142). O'Rahilly's argument was expressed with the peculiar force of a conviction equal to anything Smyllie might muster. He was exercised by what had happened to civil society under fascism and concerned about the current position of the Catholic and other Churches in the USSR and the Soviet bloc. His argument against totalitarianism was telling. Smyllie must have been chagrined when the Protestant *Church of Ireland Gazette* also came out against his editorial, on roughly the same grounds as O'Rahilly.

It was left to Brian O'Nolan to put the Cork professor in his place. In a '*Cruiskeen Lawn*' column he characterized the *Catholic Standard* as 'a small pious weekly taken by the innocent to be the voice of the Catholic Church and as such profitably sold at church doors' (the controversy in fact boosted circulation to 83,000, its highest ever to that date: Whyte 1971, p. 240) and dismissed O'Rahilly's contribution to it: 'I have read his stuff. It is a tirade saturated with arrogance and ignorance' (*Irish Times*, 2 May 1951). O'Nolan mocked the professor's polymathic interests (almost equal to Sir Myles na gCopaleen's own), nevertheless taking his points in order, to rebut them in mock jocular fashion (it was absurd, he thought, that a 'Tory Protestant' paper should be accused of consorting with a Leftist clique). He concluded in balanced enough mode:

> My own real view? The Editor, in writing the leading article in question, lacked prudence. The bishops, making a perfectly legitimate intervention on a vital matter, should have done so overtly, if only for the benefit of the faithful. Lenten Pastorals are obvious occasions for the enunciation of their views. In failing therein, they lacked prudence. (*Irish Times*, 2 May 1951)

Smyllie's response to Browne's fate was imprudent and arguably excessive. The *Irish Times*, in relation to the Tilson Case, had accepted in 1950 that in a country in which the majority of the population were Catholic, the law would reflect that fact. Was it not equally likely that on social policy the views of the hierarchy would be sought by government and taken into account? What had happened may have been more revelatory about the miscalculations of a headstrong if idealistic minister than an exposure of rule from the Vatican by way of the conference of bishops. Serious imprudence lay in the fact that, by making such an overheated accusation, the *Irish Times* could be suspected of revealing its true bigoted colours and its opinion even more impatiently set aside by the nationally minded as the irrelevant maunderings of an *ancien régime* voice. This was unfortunate not only for the paper itself but for society in general. For the 1950s, with Dr John Charles McQuaid as the face of a church militant, was to see (as shall be shown in the next chapter) more overt exercises of Church power and Catholic action than had been the case hitherto. A fully credible liberal counterweight would have been helpful in ensuring healthy democratic debate. In time it would become clear that any attempt to organize effective liberal opinion in the country would be met not only by focused hierarchical opposition but by muscle-flexing from a vigorous Catholic right. That one of the chief organs of liberal thought in Ireland (another was the more nationalist *The Bell*, now edited by the socialist and republican Peadar O'Donnell) could be dismissed, on account of an ill-judged editorial, as a colonial throwback, could not but do disservice to that cause.

The *Irish Times,* in the months leading up to the Mother and Child crisis, had in fact been immersed in an attempt to define what was meant by liberalism in Ireland, as if it was preparing for battles to come. This had resulted when the paper responded to an unpleasant lecture by a professor of Philosophy at University College Galway, which revealed the outlook of certain conservative ideologues among the Catholic majority. The Very Reverend Professor Felim Ó Briain's field was medieval Irish Christianity, but that did not inhibit him from commenting in robust terms on the current challenges to the Catholic faith in the country. As the *Irish Times* reported, the professor had, in a public lecture on 23 January 1950, claimed 'that the only freedom that would triumph in the absence of the full Christian code was the freedom of the armed man to suppress the liberty of all who differed from his views' (*Irish Times*, 24 January 1951). Among those likely to speed the imposition of such tyranny, Ó Briain fixed his gaze on socialists and liberals who were at one, he suspected, in their support of sexual licence: 'One of the fields of freedom in which Socialists agreed with Liberals was a free morality – the ethic of free love.' And such 'sexual freedom', where it could be achieved, 'would entail, as a necessary consequence, artificial prevention of births. As this was not infallible there must also be freedom of abortion, divorce and the state education of the children, who in the new free society, were an obstacle to the pleasures and fun of the parent.' Against this dystopian nightmare, the professor judged: 'The Liberal ethic met everywhere and in all points of its programme one obstinate opponent – the Catholic Church.' In Ireland, however, the threat had its feeble, essentially ludicrous side, where 'At its most innocent and futile [the liberal ethic] appeared as an occasional letter in the *Irish Times* about "priest-ridden Irish" or "the domination of the clergy".'

As if to prove to the very reverend professor that the liberal ethic as understood by the *Irish Times* was in fact neither foolishly innocent nor futile, the paper over the next few months opened its letters column to a full-scale debate on the topic. The first contributor to this was Owen Sheehy-Skeffington, a well-known socialist, lecturer in French at Trinity College, Dublin and by reason of the fact that in 1916 his father had been murdered by an out-of-control British officer during the Easter Rising, one vested with a certain republican/nationalist kudos. He made it his business quickly to repudiate the idea that socialists and liberals were in effect disguised libertines united in their enthusiasm for 'free love'. And he suggested that 'In Ireland there are some who would have us be considerably more Papal than the Pope' (*Irish Times*, 26 January 1950), seeking to characterize Ó Briain as an extremist. That extremism was pernicious, Sheehy-Skeffington observed, 'in this land where a religion based on transcending love finds all too commonly its expression in uncharitable and misinformed attacks on any who dare to hold differing views, be they Socialist or Liberal'.

This was a clever riposte (and Sheehy-Skeffington was a skilled polemicist, as his later career as a senator would amply demonstrate) for it turned the issue away from that of sexual morality to that of freedom of opinion and of expression. Ó Briain would have none of it. Employing what his opponent called 'the science of formal logic' (*Irish Times*, 16 February 1950) to forbidding effect, he reiterated his claim that Liberalism must involve what he now called 'the full free love programme' (*Irish Times*, 31 January 1950). Almost comically, he provided a long list of the living and dead, liberals to a man, whom he claimed had preached the free love doctrine. He argued: 'No genuine Liberal or Socialist will ever accept the concept of sin and so their claims to man's right to free love, contraception, abortion, divorce, homosexuality, etc. are merely the inescapable consequence of their basic teaching.' Brian Inglis, a former journalist on the *Irish Times*, wrote in to suggest that the professor's identification of people, which a correspondent humorously described the next day as a 'long list of moral disintegrators', raised a question: 'Can it be – dare it be said – that there may be something in an ethic which includes so distinguished a gathering' (*Irish Times*, 2 March 1950). The very reverend professor was immune to such persiflage, certain as he was that 'Only where free men agree to accept a clear, definite, dogmatic code of duties, based on the natural law and divine law, can human rights be protected and freedom upheld' (*Irish Times*, 11 February 1950).

Sheehy-Skeffington a few days later boiled down Ó Briain's argument to two key propositions: 'It has become clear that basically Father Ó Briain believes that (a) all who are not Catholics are in danger of becoming Liberals and Socialists, who if they are "logical" will necessarily be sexual maniacs and monsters of depravity; and that consequently (b) no Catholic can be a Socialist and a Liberal' (*Irish Times*, 16 February 1950). The Trinity man here was being less than fair to his antagonist, for Ó Briain also dismissed liberalism and socialism as proven to be weak defences against twentieth-century totalitarianisms. He was not quite as obsessed by the issue of the sexual profligacy that liberalism and socialism could unleash in Ireland as Sheehy-Skeffington had implied. Other correspondents took up broader themes, too, since the debate covered matters constitutional (a rump of councillors in County Westmeath had just voted to raise the matter of Article 44 of the Irish Constitution, hoping to strengthen the position of the Catholic Church), the workings of the Censorship Board, the impact of the controversy on partition. Extreme views found expression. A Protestant canon, responding to letters on Article 44, dubbed the papacy 'the father and mother of totalitarianism' (*Irish Times*, 2 March 1950) which had supplied Hitler with a model for his own form of tyranny. Not to be outdone, the secretary of Maria Duce, one of the more formidable of a number of right-wing ginger groups that were intent on maintaining and augmenting Catholic power in Ireland, wrote to describe 'The ideal for Catholic States such as Spain and Ireland' (*Irish Times*, 7 March 1950). It would be 'while extending full liberty and official recognition to the Catholic Church alone' that the state 'should not only not connive at the proselytism of non-Catholic sects, but should suppress them as inimical to the public good'.

Despite the range of subjects covered by the 'liberal ethic' debate in the newspaper (the *Irish Times* published it as a booklet in June 1950), the controversy, one may posit, had a consequence Smyllie could not have intended. By responding so vigorously to an agenda set by the Very Reverend Professor Ó Briain, the ensuing debate never quite managed to escape from giving the impression that the 'liberal ethic' was a form of special pleading for sexual laxity of one kind or another. Instead of countering the voice of Catholic absolutism with a robust defence of the Davisite pluralism the paper had honoured in 1945, the attempt, by even so astute a political operator as Sheehy-Skeffington, to meet Ó Briain on his own ground, made it seem that the idea of ethics was something that was applicable only to sexual mores and practices and not related to the matter of virtue or otherwise in private, public and commercial life. In later decades liberalism, indeed, would come to be associated almost exclusively with such issues as contraception, divorce and homosexuality (the 'liberal agenda', which encompassed these subjects, as we shall see, became the focus of debate and social activism). By the law of unintended consequences, the 'liberal ethics' controversy in the *Irish Times* in 1950 may, in a small way, have contributed to a narrowing of the meaning of the term 'ethics' to simply meaning 'sexual ethics'.

One satirical correspondent, an Eamon O'Murphy, seemed to suggest that, one way or another, for all the high-toned argumentation, the controversy involved (as with the editor himself, Latin tags came easily to many of the contributors) an Irish dedication to an impossible sexual purity. He wrote: 'Regarding the censorship, it is too tolerant – it is too narrow in its scope. Only the other day I heard the authorities had declined to ban the import of typewriters with the disgusting words "shift lock" on the keys. Imagine these indecently combined words staring at Ireland's pure womanhood day after day. Shame, sir' (*Irish Times*, 3 March 1950). O'Murphy was having fun with the fact that the Abbey audience had rioted at the insult to Irish womanhood at the mention of 'shifts' in Synge's *The Playboy of the Western World*. He supplied his own artistic commentary on the current controversy:

> Allow me to conclude in the words of a well-known poet, whose name escapes me at the moment:
>
> *O bliss of the purified! bliss of the free!*
> *I plunge in the cleansing tide opened for me;*
> *O'er sin and uncleanness exulting I stand*
> *And give thanks I was born in pure Ireland.*

Myles na gCopaleen gave his splenetic view of the 'liberal ethic' controversy in mid-February: 'my problem is concerned with how to spend two columns saying the simple word "Bah!"' (*Irish Times*, 13 February 1950).

The imprudence that marked Smyllie's reaction to Noel Browne's resignation in 1951 may in part have been stimulated by a belief that what was at stake were the liberal values that had been so extensively analysed in the columns of his newspaper in the early 1950s. The emphasis in his notorious editorial on that event, with its highlighting of how unionist opinion in Northern Ireland would be affected by a display of what certainly appeared to be governmental subservience to Church authority, suggests that he had a more fundamental bone of contention to pick with Costello's administration. That probably disinclined him to be anything other than very frankly outraged by the Mother and Child fiasco.

Since 1922 the *Irish Times* had envisaged partition being ended only on the basis of whole-hearted membership of the Commonwealth. Costello's government, to Smyllie's horror, later in 1948 had in fact taken the monumental step of declaring that Ireland would become a republic outside that very Commonwealth. This decision of September 1948, which took effect on Easter Monday, 18 April 1949, traduced all that Smyllie and Healy had sought to protect as editors of a national newspaper with a unionist patrimony. Costello's decision not only made the ending of partition more unlikely, but threatened the near dual citizenship enjoyed by the populace of the 26-county state. Unionists, like Smyllie himself, had managed to adapt to their post-independence context, comforted by the fact that the state was a member of a commonwealth of nations with the Crown at its head. From 1949 onwards that would no longer pertain, though Irish citizens would be permitted to live and work in the United Kingdom as if they were, to all intents and purposes, British subjects.

How seismic a disturbance this represented for the paper may be judged by two observations published on New Year's Day 1948 and on New Year's Day a year later. An editorial on the first of these occasions noted how 'Passing from the transitional upheavals of another post-war year', the future could be welcomed since the state was 'entering into new economic bonds between this nation and nations of the British Commonwealth' (*Irish Times*, 1 January 1948). A year later 'An Irishman's Diary' commented: 'The greatest events of the last twelve months in Ireland of course have been the political eclipse of Mr de Valera and the secession of Eire from the Commonwealth' (*Irish Times*, 1 January 1949).

In the early months of 1949 the paper sought to analyse in a series of troubled editorials what the passing of the Republic Bill, signed into law on 21 December 1948, would mean for Ireland north and south and for relations with Britain. As the date approached when the new Republic would actually come into existence, an editorial entitled 'A Great Sum' began by quoting Yeats's poem 'September 1913' ('Was it for this the wild geese spread/The grey wing upon every tide ... ?') to affirm 'There will not be many rejoicings on Easter Monday; for if the truth be told, there is not much enthusiasm among the people for the new Republic' (*Irish Times*, 2 April 1949). Following the coming into existence of the Republic, the paper published a fatalistic editorial entitled 'Looking Ahead'. It was relieved that although 'the last remaining link with the British Crown and the Commonwealth has been severed' (*Irish Times*, 20 April 1949), a relationship with Britain had been established so that 'Irishmen [would] not be regarded as aliens in Great Britain'. However, its acceptance of the new order of things was scarcely gracious: 'We always have been opposed to the idea of an Irish Republic. In particular we have been, and still are, opposed to secession from the Commonwealth; but the milk has been spilled now, and we must accept things not as we might like them to be, but rather as they are.' That the spilt milk was no unfortunate accident exercised the writer. He knew where responsibility lay and clearly would not forget it:

> We ... are convinced that the standard of political honesty in Ireland has been lowered grievously by the action of Mr Costello and his Fine Gael colleagues; they will be judged not by us, but by history ...
>
> Nevertheless, the die has been cast, and it is the duty of every citizen, whatever his or her personal views may be, to give unconditional loyalty to the new State.

A day earlier, the *Irish Times* had published a set of answers to questions posed to George Bernard Shaw by the paper's London editor. The first of these asked: 'Do you regard the Republic of Ireland Act as marking a step forward or a step backward in Ireland's development?' The canny, if optimistic, sage of Ayot St Lawrence (then in his nineties) was more circumspect than the paper's editor, while affecting iconoclasm. He replied: 'Ask me in 5 years hence. If our terrible vital statistics improve to a civilised level, then our steps will have been steps forward. If not, there will be nothing for us but the ancient purification of the submergence of the island for ten minutes in the Irish Sea' (*Irish Times*, 19 April 1949).

Ireland's change of status in 1949 was, we can now more fully understand, part of a pattern that was affecting the world in general in the immediate aftermath of World War II. The *Irish Times* was, nonetheless, conscious as it occurred that a sea-change was taking place in world affairs. It had its editorial eye on the Orient. As Dennis Kennedy, then writing editorials for the paper about European integration, has recorded it, Bruce Williamson, a voracious reader, 'was the nearest thing' the paper had 'to a regular leader writer, almost always on foreign topics' (Kennedy 2009, p. 87). In March 1947, commenting on the meeting of the Asian Relations Conference (held in New Delhi to draw together Asian countries seeking independence), the *Irish Times* published a reflective editorial entitled 'Aspirant Asia', which pondered how tectonic plates were shifting:

> Asia for the last two centuries has been disunited and distraught ...
> Generations may pass before Asia can organise herself to advantage. The fact remains that her bemused consciousness has been awakened, that self-determination is the dynamo which drives her various peoples, and that, for better or worse, she has become the warden of her own destiny. (*Irish Times*, 27 March 1947)

One notes here the writer's instinctive orientalist categories ('her bemused consciousness') but is struck by the editorial's firm commitment to change: 'So far as the East is concerned, Europe's day is over, and a historical episode, which, in general, has not been notably to the white man's credit, has come to an end.' India's achievement of independence in the same year was accordingly greeted, despite the partitioning of the subcontinent, with no expression of regret that the British Empire was being diminished: 'Britain has stepped from her seat of power with a good grace, and the Indian people themselves now must undertake the obligations of a destiny, that can be noble and spacious' (*Irish Times*, 27 August 1947).

Any residual imperialism entertained by the *Irish Times* editorial team could have focused on the hope that both the new India and Pakistan would remain members of the British Commonwealth (the editorial that marked the ceding of British power in August 1947 was entitled 'The New Dominions'). The newspaper's vision for that organization in a post-colonial world was expressed in an editorial of 12 April 1948. There, it, indeed, envisaged that, even as the new United Nations appeared 'on the scene' (*Irish Times*, 12 April 1948), the Commonwealth could be adjusted to encompass nations that still owed allegiance to the British Crown and those, like India, that, as republics, did not. 'To people who may be disposed to dismiss the whole idea as illogical and unworkable,' the paper argued, 'we can only say that many things that seemed impossible have been accomplished by the British genius for compromise and readiness to deal with problems as they arise. Within the span of thirty years the conception of a Commonwealth of self-governing nations has made such headway that nobody now dares fix the limits of its influence.' When on 11 April 1949 the *Irish Times* reported that the Indian prime minister, Pandit Nehru, hoped that India as a republic would retain its membership of the Commonwealth, Smyllie must have felt both vindicated and rueful. For Ireland was on the point of leaving the Commonwealth in the very month in which Nehru hoped it could be restructured to allow a republic to enjoy full membership. Nehru paid Ireland a seven-hour visit after the Asian Relations Conference. The next day the *Irish Times* saluted both the 'inspired leadership of Pandit Nehru' and 'the traditional genius of the British people for compromise' (*Irish Times*, 29 April 1949) which had made it possible for the circle of republicanism and Commonwealth membership to be squared. 'Is it possible,' the editorial enquired plaintively, 'that Pandit Nehru has set a headline for Mr Costello? If one republic can be a member of the Commonwealth, why should the same privilege not be open to another?'

By the early winter of 1949, an event of truly seismic proportions in Asia drew from the paper an editorial in which a broad historical perspective allowed for a surprising if slightly naive optimism. In Peking on 1 October 1949, Mao Tse-tung, as victor of a civil war which had raged since the 1930s, declared the formation of the People's Republic of China. On 3 October an editorial acknowledged that Mao was 'entitled to a place beside the great revolutionary leaders of this century of fundamental change' (*Irish Times*, 3 October 1949). It further granted that 'The Chinese leader [had] become the central political figure of the Far East, and the focus of the attention of extremists and revolutionaries in every corner of South-east Asia.' Yet the writer seemed to prefer Mao to his nationalist enemy Chiang Kai-shek, acknowledging that he was 'an abler and more far-seeing politician'. It judged: 'There is no doubt that both men are fanatics; but equally it is undeniable that Mao's fanaticism is in tune with his time, while Chiang continuously has been at variance with it.'

No such calm in the columns of the *Irish Times* attended the establishment of 'a Jewish State in Palestine, to be called "Israel"' (*Irish Times*, 17 May 1948). The violence that accompanied that event ensured a much less complacent response. An editorial on 17 May feared that the bloody birth of the new state presaged 'far more blood ... before it is set upon its feet' for 'the war will continue until either Arab or Jew is compelled to admit defeat'. The editorialist, however, expressed astonishment that, even as the new state was at war for its very survival, the United States had recognized it. This raised a larger issue that held great cause for concern. As the *Irish Times* put it: 'The cause of this embarrassingly hasty action on the American part throws a lurid light on the delicate condition of world politics. The diplomatic correspondents of two continents agree, without exception, that the White House acted in order to forestall the Soviet Union.'

The newspaper was, of course, referring here to the 'Cold War' which had ominously developed between the Soviet Union and the Western democracies since the ending of armed hostilities in 1945. In this, the *Irish Times* was consistently firm in its defence of democracy, but that advocacy was sometimes accompanied, as in this editorial, by a certain irritation at United States' foreign policy. One can detect in its editorial observations on the new world order that the *Irish Times*, still emotionally attached in so many ways to the United Kingdom (the 'London Letter' was a journalistic hardy perennial), was conscious that a shift of power across the Atlantic was in process, and was discomfited as a new super-power began to flex its muscles.

Winston Churchill had delivered his famous peroration on the post-war freezing of relations with Stalin's empire in March 1946. The *Irish Times* managed to report and editorialize on this wide-ranging analysis of global politics, which caught the attention of the world, without mentioning its most resonant phrase. Nonetheless, it recognized the cogency and salience of what a man whom it judged 'with the possible exception of Marshal Stalin, the greatest world figure of to-day' (*Irish Times*, 7 March 1946) was saying. His gloomy prognostications about the Soviet threat could not, the paper implied, be easily set aside. And his term 'the iron curtain' quickly became in the *Irish Times*, as it did throughout the English-speaking world, a staple of political commentary.

The broadly dispersed related term 'Cold War' entered the paper's lexicon in 1947 (the year in which Walter Lippmann published his famous book of that name), and would remain lodged in numerous accounts of strategic and global affairs for decades to come. It was ubiquitous in the 1950s when the Cold War dangerously threatened to turn white hot – in Korea, Hungary and around the Suez Canal. In this dangerous polarized world, with the Soviet Union and the United States in frozen confrontation, the *Irish Times* was perfectly clear about its fundamental loyalty to the West. Indeed, it viewed with some scorn the Republic's refusal to join the emergent North Atlantic Treaty Organization (NATO), not taking seriously the state's assertion that it could not participate since it was in dispute with Britain over the issue of partition: for 'Ireland's strategic position is of the utmost importance. If there should be another war our island would be exposed to appalling risks' (*Irish Times*, 24 March 1949). In 1950, noting that 'within the last twelve months the cold war [had] been intensified to freezing point' (*Irish Times*, 9 May 1950), an editorial laid the blame for the deterioration in international relations firmly on Soviet shoulders. Yet the *Irish Times*'s support for the United States, the main bulwark against the expansionist threat of Soviet Communism, was sometimes grudging. For example, even in 1949 as it was criticizing the Republic for its myopic attitude to NATO, it was at best lukewarm about the power that would underwrite it militarily. In view of the Soviet threat, an editorial entitled 'War and Peace' advised: 'common prudence demands that no unnecessary risks shall be taken by the democracies.'

One may not be particularly fond of the methods of American capitalism; at any rate, they are preferable to those of the egregious Cominform [the Communist Information Bureau, formed in 1947 among Europe communist states to help to spread that ideology]' (*Irish Times*, 24 March 1949). And in 1950, even as he called for the strengthening of the Western alliance, the writer of the editorial ('Defence in Depth') on the matter reflected that, while 'There must be no gaps in the anti-Communist front' (*Irish Times*, 9 May 1950), the spectacle of a 'divided world' was 'most unwholesome'. Any melting of the Soviet diplomatic heart should be seized upon by the Western powers. The editorialist deprecated the emergence of the anti-communist witch hunt led Senator Joseph McCarthy in the United States. It denounced the Senator's 'deplorable attitude of mind', while regretting that it was 'not confined to him, although he affords it the most dramatic medium of expression'.

An overt expression of a tendency towards anti-Americanism in at least one of its leader writers during the early phase of the Cold War, even if the need for secure defences was accepted, was in fact supplied in February 1951. The decision of the US president Harry S. Truman to sanction the manufacture of a hydrogen bomb was greeted in the paper by an unusually passionate editorial. Entitled 'Mid-winter Madness', the leader wondered how the president, 'this average product of a comparatively small American city' (*Irish Times*, 4 February 1951), could have taken a decision 'which may be capable of the complete destruction of the civilised world, as we know it'. The writer, in mingled condescension and resentful distaste, blamed a new imperialism that would inevitably foment an alarming arms race:

> The Americans, on the whole, are a peace-loving people. They may be naïve in many ways; but there is a streak of genuine idealism in them which cannot be gainsaid. Their trouble at present is that they seem to be suffering from a power-complex, springing from their unprecedented material prosperity.
>
> As a monetary unit, the dollar is all powerful in the world to-day. The Americans have control of all the dollars; therefore they feel they ought to have control of everything else, including weapons of destruction in every form.

By 1955, when the Korean War and the violent suppression by the Soviet Union of an insurrection in East Germany had not unleashed a general conflagration, the Irish Times had learned to live, if uneasily, in the nuclear age. An editorial, 'Dragon's Teeth', though warning of the dangers of political miscalculation and suggesting how a war begun with conventional weapons could lead to a nuclear catastrophe, neverthless conceded that what became known as mutually assured destruction mitigated those risks. However, the writer still feared that improved defences and protection in one country might induce it to attempt an overwhelming first strike. It feared 'the dangers of world suicide may be greater than ever before' (*Irish Times*, 29 January 1955). Events in 1956 would test such anxious forebodings. They were events, in the period of major international change that followed World War II, which had effects in Ireland, reminding Irish people immediately that their island nation was not immune to the impact of world events.

The insurrection in Hungary, which began in late October 1956, was extensively reported on in Irish newspapers. Eyewitness reports were printed in the *Irish Times* on 26 October of Soviet tanks opening fire on unarmed demonstrators in central Budapest as the paper acknowledged 'A popular rebellion is in progress' (*Irish Times*, 26 October 1956). In an editorial on 29 October the writer feared that a tragedy was unfolding in Hungary since the attempted revolution there made what it termed 'a reversion to old-fashioned Stalinism' all too likely. By 4 November its fears were realized. As the Soviet forces invaded the country, the last messages of the beleaguered government and people were broadcast and printed in the Irish media. Affectingly, the *Irish Times* reported how at 8.10 a.m. Budapest Radio went silent and was not on the air again until 10 p.m. when a woman's voice was heard before the station closed down. Speaking in German she said, 'Help Hungary, Help ... Help.' There was no help to be had, since the only force that could have threatened the Soviet Union with punishment for its action, the United States, was in no way inclined to risk a head-on confrontation with the Soviet Union over one of its satellites.

The *Irish Times* joined the other Irish dailies and the Western press in general in condemning the invasion of Hungary. On 5 November, its editorial, 'Russia's Treachery', stated: 'All the civilised world has been shocked by yesterday's event in Hungary. The Soviet Union has acted with a brutality unsurpassed even by the cynical indifference with which it left the partisans of Warsaw to their fate in 1944 ... What will follow can only be imagined, for a dark curtain has been drawn across Hungary; but it is certain that no considerations of humanity will move the Russian soldier' (*Irish Times*, 5 November 1956). On 10 November, as the Soviet occupation was consolidated amid much bloodshed, a leading article in the paper honoured the 'gallantry of the Hungarian insurgents in the face of seemingly insuperable odds' and observed in pain: 'What the Soviet Union hopes to gain by this insane massacre is beyond normal comprehension' (*Irish Times*, 10 November 1956).

Desmond Fennell, a young Irish journalist at that time stationed in central Europe, sent articles on the Hungarian tragedy to the paper from Vienna. One of these reported on conditions in a transit camp for refugees near that city. He recorded that 6,000 Hungarians fleeing their country had passed through the camp since it had opened. Fennell expressed concern for 'Uprooted lives' and 'personal tragedies' but sensed 'an atmosphere of hope, of escape from a nightmare' (*Irish Times*, 13 November 1956). Hope was engendered, it is clear from the article, because transit from the camp was swift and the occupants were bound for the various countries that had agreed to help resettle them. Among such countries was Ireland. So for the rest of the year the *Irish Times* would publish reports on Hungarian refugees who had been received in an army camp in County Clare. By 30 November, the camp was home to 235 Hungarian men, women and children. In all, the Irish state gave entry to 541 Hungarians (200,000 persons had fled the Soviet invasion). Itself a country long affected by emigration, Ireland now had a small contingent of displaced persons to accommodate. Regrettably, problems quickly arose (they were specified in a few letters to the *Irish Times*). The men wanted jobs in a depressed economy. The camp in Clare was unsuitable for families. In fact, by the end of 1957 most of the refugees had chosen to depart for Canada. Yet Ireland, in stark contrast with its wartime and immediate post-war record on the admittance of Jewish refugees, was taking an internationalist view and acting in concert with the recently established United Nations High Commission for Refugees (Ireland had achieved United Nations membership in 1955). Fennell's articles in the *Irish Times* encouraged readers to understand that this was the right thing to do, even as some of them were forced by unemployment to emigrate themselves. He gave human faces to the bare statistics of diaspora.

If the insurrection in Hungary and its brutal suppression, which brought refugees to Ireland, demonstrated in recognizable human terms how the Cold War was more than a gigantic shadow-boxing match between the super-powers, concurrent events in the Middle East were a further lesson in the fragile interconnectedness of the post-war international order. The Israeli, British and French military response to Egypt's nationalization of the Suez Canal quickly resulted in acute petrol shortages in Britain and in France. On 27 November 1956 the *Irish Times*'s front-page headline alarmingly read 'British Petrol Supply Running Dry'. On 1 December the paper reported that the Irish government would impose petrol rationing from the New Year onwards. On 11 December a report from Northern Ireland told readers that transport problems there had become acute.

The destabilizing shock to the international political order that the Anglo-French attack on Egypt represented was marked by two surprisingly forthright editorials in the *Irish Times*. On 31 October 1956, under the heading 'Partners in Folly', the editorialist warned that the ultimatum Britain and France had given Nasser on 30 October (to observe a ceasefire or face Anglo-French intervention, ostensibly to separate Israeli and Egyptian forces) had put the Western alliance in peril; for they had 'delivered their ultimatum without even the courtesy of asking American opinion' (*Irish Times*, 31 October 1956). The writer accused the putative belligerents of acting with 'hysterical haste' and continued: 'Doubtless they have given a striking testimony to Anglo-French "solidarity", but that solidarity will be a poor, hollow thing if it implies the final rupture of the weakening bond with America.' Moreover, the editorialist regretted the reputational damage that an attack on Egypt would involve for Britain and France. It would 'damn their prestige for ever among the Arabs of Asia and Africa'.

The following day the paper carried a report on a White House statement that the United States 'stood by its intention to go to the aid of any victim of aggression in the Middle East'. The report also indicated that an American official had declined to answer when asked if that pledge could involve offering aid to Egypt in the event of an Anglo-French attack on its territory. The term 'aggression' would be picked up on in an editorial that appeared on 1 November 1956, when the imminent invasion was presaged by bombing attacks on the Suez Canal. 'So begins,' an editorial entitled 'Invasion', told its readers, '... one of the most deplorable acts of aggression in post-war history. Britain and France have behaved with flagrant dishonesty. It is true that the Egyptians have given Israel every provocation; but the gross offender on this particular occasion was Israel ...' (*Irish Times*, 1 November 1956). So incensed was the writer that he envisaged a spectacular break-up of the Western strategic community. Of the Anglo-French partners in folly, he advised: 'Already they have shaken the Atlantic alliance to its foundations.'

It did not come to that, nor was it ever likely to as it quickly became obvious where true political and military power now lay in the western hemisphere. And the Britain that had lost India in 1947 was now revealed as a toothless lion, its imperial reach, for all that it possessed nuclear weapons, a thing of the past in a world divided between the super-powers and an awakening giant in China.

Desmond Fennell, in an article published in the *Irish Times* on 8 November 1956, identified the damage done by this military and political adventurism to Western claims of moral superiority to the Soviet regime which was in the process of cruelly crushing the Hungarian uprising. 'With relief the embarrassed Communist press of Eastern Europe turned from Hungary to the old familiar hunting ground of "imperial aggression", he observed; 'the moral advantage was lost' (*Irish Times*, 8 November 1956).

This was a consequence of the Suez crisis that did not go unremarked in the United Kingdom as well, where the action of the government in Egypt met with forthright opposition and unleashed a torrent of national self-doubt about Britain's changed role in the world. In such a context it perhaps should not surprise that the *Irish Times*, which had sustained respect for and sympathy with British interests since the foundation of the Irish state, was so outspoken about the Suez fiasco. Its traditional stance of special regard vis-à-vis Ireland's nearest neighbour should not necessarily, it is true, have precluded the expression of frank opinion where that neighbour was making serious errors of judgement. And when that neighbour itself was engaging in self-examination, it would have been curious, indeed, if a paper such as the *Irish Times* had chosen to exclude itself from the debate. However, there was an astringency in the two *Irish Times* editorials I have cited, and a severity that suggests less sympathy with British discomfiture than censure by an independent mind.

That mind was that of the paper's editor, Alec Newman, who had succeded Robert Smyllie in that post on the latter's death-in-harness in September 1954. We know Newman was responsible for the leading article on 1 November since he subsequently wrote of how the board of the paper had discussed its contents (Mark O'Brien 2008, p. 150). John Edward Healy had recruited Newman for the *Irish Times* staff in 1930 and over the years he had established a close working relationship with Smyllie which made them almost a comic duo of Dublin's journalistic world. For alongside the larger-than life Smyllie, Newman's 'lean and schoolmasterly aspect' (Long 2008, p. 901) and scholarly, polite, reserve acted as a foil to the former's ebullience. When Healy died in 1934 and Smyllie was appointed editor, Newman, as we saw, became his assistant. Never actually friends, the two men enjoyed acting out a mini-drama of elaborate formality in their professional dealings.

They differed in their politics. Newman, as we noted earlier, although born in Waterford, had spent much of his boyhood in Belfast, to which city his family had moved in 1912. His experience of sectarian division there, at what was a period of great turbulence, laid the foundation for a self-conscious adoption of an Irish nationalist outlook, when, after graduating from Trinity College Dublin, he chose to make his career south of the border. During 'the Emergency' he served as a reserve signals officer in the Irish defence forces and on occasion wore the uniform to work in the *Irish Times* office, as if to make a point. Like many converts to a creed, Newman's adoption of a considered form of nationalism (we may take it that the celebration of Thomas Davis in 1945 reflected his commitment to a pluralist republic yet to be realized), involved moments when the principles of the adopted faith must be emphasized. Newman's editorial of 1 November 1956 was, one senses, one such moment. Nor was he to be shaken in his outspokenness. Despite the editorial being subject to some criticism at board level, when the British prime minister, Anthony Eden, was forced from office early in the following year on account of his disastrous Suez policy, Newman commented unequivocally that Eden had 'clouded the end of his long political career by a blunder of the first magnitude [and] weakened his country's authority to speak even as a diminished Great Power' (Mark O'Brien 2008, p. 150).

Newman's nationalism was sufficiently developed by 1961, when he was dismissed by the *Irish Times* (largely because he did not seem likely to be able to improve the newspaper's insecure financial position), for him to transfer as a leader writer, without apparent difficulty, to the robustly republican *Irish Press*, with its support for the Fianna Fáil party and commitment to uniting Ireland. No doubt the fact that in 1951 the *Irish Times* – outraged by the coalition government's policy on the Commonwealth and by the Mother and Child capitulation – had recommended electoral support for de Valera's party, aided his passage to the paper de Valera had founded. In the 1950s, it is important to stress, however, the *Irish Times*'s analysis of what was termed 'the national question' was distinctive in its understanding of Northern Protestant opinion and of its significance in respect of attempts to end partition.

When de Valera lost office in 1948, although he had paid little close attention to the matter while in power, he set off on a world tour to raise international attention to the wrong done to Ireland by partition. Not to be outdone, the coalition government, with Seán MacBride, Minister for External Affairs, as the moving force, set in place an all-party committee to publicize Ireland's right to unity. At a time when borders were being redrawn in Europe and the international order was creating new institutions, it did not seem fanciful that the Irish question should be put on the table once again. Exactly what that question was, however, was a matter of considerable import. Since 1922 the political class in the Free State had believed that partition was something that, since it was imposed by Britain, would have to be solved by negotiations between the Irish and the British governments. The Northern Irish government in Belfast, with its devolved powers, was viewed as an illegitimate junta that served the interests of a ruling class of landowners and industrialists. The unionist populace there had been duped or bribed into thinking themselves British. If Britain could be persuaded to remove itself from the equation, the unionist population would quickly come to its senses and accept the authority of an all-Ireland state. In the meantime they could be wooed in a desultory fashion and, more often than not, berated for their (admittedly all too actual) sectarian prejudices. Some in the Free State and the Republic believed that political pressure might induce Britain to withdraw its claim of sovereignty over Northern Ireland. A small minority had always believed violence directed against the United Kingdom might act as a catalyst of constitutional change.

During de Valera's several periods in office, while he shared with the IRA the view that partition was ultimately a responsibility of the British, his government had rigorously suppressed any of its volunteers who had tried to make war on the United Kingdom. As a consequence, the ending of partition had begun to take on the aspect of an unrealizable national ideal, like draining the Shannon, or reviving the Irish language, referred to at elections but deferred when Fianna Fáil was actually in power. In the aftermath of World War II, however, as the Irish Free State was declared a republic, discussion about the unification of the country became less perfunctory. The *Irish Times* responded to this by stating its own position in unambiguous terms. It differed from the mainstream ideological position inasmuch as it took seriously the determination of the Northern Unionist population to resist being incorporated against their will in an all-Ireland polity. A meeting of an anti-partition league in the Mansion House in Dublin in March 1949 drew from the paper a long editorial on 'Partition'. At the meeting some speakers had attacked the *Irish Times* for conducting 'a "foul campaign" against the cause of Irish unity' (*Irish Times*, 12 March 1949). Against that charge, the paper defended itself forcefully, asserting that it devoutly wished for the end of partition and stated:

> We have been criticised sharply because, it is alleged, we have failed to make any constructive proposals to persuade the people of the Six Counties to throw in their lot with the rest of us. That charge is blatantly untrue. We have pleaded with them time and again; but our efforts have always been thwarted by the ineptitude of Southern politicians ... During the past twenty-five years they have been doing everything possible to estrange the majority in the North.

Among things such politicians had done to dissuade Northern unionists from even considering unity were, the *Irish Times* averred: secession from the Commonwealth, the intention to create a Gaelic-speaking republic (dubbed 'a crazy plan') and the habit of 'pouring abuse on the heads of those whom they profess to have been wooing'. Crucially, however, the editorial focused on the unionists of Northern Ireland as the real impediment to Irish unity, and not the British: 'To blame the British is to ignore the outstanding fact – namely, that the majority in the North does not want to join the Republic and that, if the British should try to compel it, matters would become infinitely worse even than they are to-day.' In April the paper reinforced this point when it asked 'does Mr MacBride, or any other Minister, believe that the majority of the Six Counties would submit quietly to coercion by the South, or even by Britain?' (*Irish Times*, 20 April 1949). By the summer of 1949 the paper was convinced that the 'cold war' the Irish government had declared against the British 'and a slightly warmer propaganda war against the "puppet junta" in the North' (*Irish Times*, 7 July 1949) had failed miserably: 'The unhappy truth about the whole business is that, as a result of almost incredible bungling, a solution of the border problem is farther away than ever it was.'

These editorials of 1949 probably reflected the mind of Robert Smyllie on the matter of partition. Alec Newman's accession to Smyllie's chair in 1954 did not alter the paper's fundamental view that partition could not be ended without the agreement of Northern unionists, and in this way its ideological position on a key issue of Irish policy remained a minority one in the 1950s. When in 1956 a conciliatory speech by Seán Lemass (who in the 1960s would seek to break the ideological logjam between north and south) at Queen's University Belfast was immediately followed by IRA attacks in five of the six Northern counties (among the first shots over two nights of a long-planned border campaign against partition to be waged by that body between 1956 and

1962), the paper declared it an act of national sabotage. It predicted that these actions could have only one outcome: 'the net effect ... is only to harden the Unionist heart – and there are 900,000 Unionists to be persuaded – in favour of the present constitutional position and against Irish reunification' (*Irish Times*, 13 December 1956). The editorial concluded that the worst and most damaging result of such futile militarism 'is the long-term one of alienating more and more the solid and steady mass of Six County Unionists whose loyal adherence will be the *sine qua non* of our nation's eventual reunion'. For, like Smyllie's before him, Newman's newspaper took seriously the 'outstanding fact' of unionist opposition to any change, in a post-war world undergoing rapid change, that would rob them of their political patrimony as subjects of the Crown and citizens of the United Kingdom.

7

THE *IRISH TIMES* AND A CHANGING IRELAND

In 1966, the year when the Irish state held the commemoration of the Easter Rising, which had changed the course of Irish history 50 years earlier, John Montague published a sequence poem entitled 'Patriotic Suite'. Poem nine of the sequence evoked the atmosphere at a festival of Irish traditional music and song held in the west of Ireland, in terms that suggested the country was no longer the sexually repressed, deeply conservative society that the revolution earlier in the century had done little to alter. Indeed, the energy released at the festival indicated that the demand for change which had existed then, in the 1960s was surfacing at last:

> At the Fleadh Cheoil in Mullingar
> There were two sounds, the breaking
> Of glass, and the background pulse
> Of music. Young girls roamed
> The streets with eager faces,
> Shoving for men. Bottles in
> Hand, they rowed out a song:
> *Puritan Ireland's dead and gone,*
> *A myth of O'Connor and Ó Faoláin.*
>
> In the early morning the lovers
> Lay on both sides of the canal
> Listening on Sony transistors
> To the agony of Pope John.
> Yet it didn't seem strange or blasphemous,
> This ground bass of death and
> Resurrection, as we strolled along:
> *Puritan Ireland's dead and gone*
> *A myth of O'Connor and Ó'Faoláin.*

(Montague 2012, p. 79)

These two stanzas, with their ironic echoing of Yeats's famous poem of disdain for the Ireland of his day ('September 1913'), registered a poet's pleasure at the changes that were afoot in the country as it turned in memory to the hallowed past. The new Ireland was hedonistic, sexually uninhibited, with women asserting their powers, in sympathy with the good Pope John XXIII whose Second Vatican Council had breathed renewal into the Church, and was open to the world and its technological wonders. A kind of national resurrection was in process, a throwing-off of an inhibiting self-image.

The Irish Times in the 1960s was to report on, reflect on, and, in its own metamorphosis, to be a part of this Irish *Risorgimento* to a degree that made the early and middle years of the decade among the most exciting and creative in the country's modern history. By the end of the decade, in a changed Ireland, the newspaper would have transformed itself into a publication that both represented and expressed the life of the nation in a distinctive and widely admired way.

The auspices for such transformation in the reputation of a newspaper that marked its centenary in 1959, as the 1950s ended, were not good. In the first instance, the public response in 1957 to an incident in the IRA's border campaign had made the paper's expressed position on the national question seem simply a characteristic reversion to type. On 1 January an IRA attack on a police station in Brookeborough, Co. Fermanagh, left two of the raiding party mortally wounded. Other raiders managed to escape southward, leaving dead and injured behind them. The Northern police found one of them, Seán South, dead in a byre, his dying companion, Fergal O'Hanlon, beside him. Their deaths and funerals unleashed a huge wave of public sorrow and widespread admiration in the Republic for their desperate courage in giving their lives for the cause of Irish unity. As J. Bowyer Bell in his history of the IRA has it: 'There began a week of near national mourning' (Bell 1997, p. 353). Large crowds attended their obsequies in Monaghan and in Limerick. As the *Irish Times* itself reported, when O'Hanlon's remains were brought to church in Monaghan: 'For nearly a mile outside the town people lined the road' (*Irish Times*, 4 January 1957). In Limerick when the highly respected South (devout Catholic, devotee of the Irish language, and talented in the arts) was laid to rest, the leaders of the city's corporation presided over a major civic occasion. Even the *Irish Times*'s rather muted report could not but give some sense of the import of what was an event in a national tradition of political funerals that stretched back to the interment of Terence Bellew McManus in 1861. 'People,' it reported, 'streamed into the church in large numbers from early morning to file past the coffin which was covered with hundreds of Mass cards, and surrounded by about fifty wreaths from different organisations' (*Irish Times*, 7 January 1957).

The Taoiseach, John A. Costello, who had returned to power in a coalition government in 1954, broadcast to the nation on the evening of 6 January to assert the authority of the state in opposition to the militants, who by their actions had declared war on the United Kingdom on behalf of the Irish people. Costello had been willing enough to challenge Britain about partition by international diplomacy during his first term in office. For a minority to take it upon themselves militarily to attack United Kingdom forces in Northern Ireland was quite a different matter. He indicated that the full force of the state would be directed against the IRA. The *Irish Times*, in its editorial of 7 January, gave Costello unflinching support. The problem was, however, that while Costello was speaking for many Irish nationalists who did not want to see the Republic's authority usurped by the hotheads of the republican movement, the severity of the *Irish Times*'s response to what had transpired, with O'Hanlon and South barely cold in their graves, could not but have aroused ill-feeling even among those who held no regard for the IRA. The *Irish Times*'s editorial mingled ideological purity of its own special kind with revulsion from activities that many in the country found understandable, if regrettable. It stated with cold logic: 'Deeply as we in this part of the country may deplore the establishment and continued existence of the entity known as Northern Ireland, it nevertheless survives by the will of a substantial majority of its Irish population, and any attempt to alter its constitution in defiance of that will is undemocratic and vicious' (*Irish Times*, 7 January 1957). And where Costello had sought to make emotion his friend when he lamented how 'Within the past week, three young Irishmen have been killed in the course of attacks on police stations in the Six-county area', the *Irish Times* leader would have none of such appeals to better feeling:

> It is one of our Irish weaknesses that we are apt to let emotion – too often, misplaced emotion – prevail over cooler, more realistic judgment. Public men, in particular, must be careful lest they should seem, even indirectly, to condone the irresponsible and, in the long run, tragically unpatriotic conduct of illegal organisations.

This did not sit well on a day when on another page of the newspaper the report of South's funeral in Limerick included a lengthy list of the dignitaries who had been present. Fergal O'Hanlon and Seán South were in the process of being elevated to the status of patriotic martyrs. An editorial that damned them as enemies of the people risked reminding readers of what the *Irish Times* had said about the martyrs of 1916. It certainly reminded its readers, in its chilly, even condescending, integrity that the paper had always spoken primarily for a self-conscious minority and that its purview was less than fully national.

Also in 1957, what became known as the 'Fethard-on-sea Boycott' of Protestant shopkeepers in a small County Wexford town, drew the paper into a controversy that further meant the adoption of its Protestant tone of voice and attitudes, which many found distinctly alien.

This regrettable manifestation of overt organized sectarianism, almost unique in independent Ireland's history, was instigated when a Protestant mother married to a Catholic man refused to honour her promise (made under the terms of the *Ne Temere* decree) to have her two children raised in the Catholic faith. She fled with them to Belfast, with the result that the Protestants of the Wexford town were ostracized by the Catholic community there. The boycott began on 13 March and petered out only in the autumn (Whyte 1971, p. 324). It received significant episcopal support, as well as causing acute embarrassment to the significant number of Catholics in the country who deplored such tactics. Among those was the writer Ulick O'Connor, who wrote to the *Irish Times* to remind its readers that Pope Leo XIII had condemned boycotting in 1888 as 'altogether foreign to natural justice and Christian charity' (*Irish Times*, 3 July 1957). Another correspondent, signing as 'Catholic Citizen', had in June compared what was happening to the recent past in Germany: 'It smacks a bit too much of the pagan Nazi doctrine justifying widespread reprisals against the innocent, the uncharged and unconvicted, a punishment for a crime committed' (*Irish Times*, 11 June 1957). The paper itself raised the spectre of totalitarianism on the same day in an editorial that fumed: 'it is the sort of conduct, which while official practice in the nations under Communist yoke, has no place in a 20th-century democracy'. On 5 July the *Irish Times* expanded on this theme when it stated in an editorial entitled 'The Boycott': 'This unlovely principle, in one form or another, has characterised every tyranny in history' (*Irish Times*, 5 July 1957). On 15 July it stated bluntly that the boycott was 'undemocratic, unchristian and in every way detestable' (*Irish Times*, 15 July 1957).

The *Irish Times* took particular offence at the statement of the Catholic Bishop of Galway on the action of the townsfolk, when he pronounced that the boycott was 'a peaceful and moderate protest' (*Irish Times*, 5 July 1957). The editorialist found Bishop Michael Browne's intervention 'hurtful, unhelpful and mischievous' and concluded by reverting to a term it had recently used to condemn the IRA: 'Whether they know it or not, the Fethard boycotters are acting as enemies of the people – the whole people. The course which they have been following is bad in itself and bad in all its conceivable consequences.' If the Catholic citizens of a small Wexford town were 'enemies of the people', what exactly did that make the Bishop of Galway and other clerics who supported them in their stand?

Further militating against the *Irish Times* becoming widely accepted as a genuinely national publication was the fact that in the late 1950s aggressively Catholic lay organizations, with the implicit blessing of leading figures in the hierarchy, were vigorously intent on opposing the liberal values about personal conduct and freedom of expression that the paper espoused. This highlighted for many that the *Irish Times* was a newspaper with what to many seemed a particular and even perverse agenda, rooted in its Protestant past and present. One critic of the newspaper accused it of being afflicted by the disease of 'Chronic Episcopophagy'. Such criticism helped to confirm the wide suspicions that were held about the *Irish Times*. For as Mark O'Brien comments: 'Such malevolence towards the paper was not unusual. As one reporter remembered, the paper was seen as the devil incarnate by a lot of Catholics; we were the people who read banned books. To be in the *Irish Times* was almost an occasion of sin' (Mark O'Brien 2008, p. 153).

Arguably, the fashion in which the *Irish Times* as late as the final years of the 1950s was still regarded by many in the country as at best the voice of a recalcitrant minority wilfully clinging to a dream of empire, where it wasn't to be regarded as a colonial cuckoo in a Catholic nationalist nest, was demonstrably unfair. Under the editorships of Healy, Smyllie and their successor, Newman, the paper had in a determined and fairly consistent way adjusted to the reality of Irish independence, bringing to the experience of state formation its own distinctive Irish voice: sceptical, questioning, concerned with social stability and fiscal prudence in its conservative manner, respectful of the democratic process, even when the will of the people seemed to take the country in directions the paper thought ill-advised, perhaps perverse, valuing and giving due credit to the nation's scientific and artistic achievements, open to the expression in its columns of a spectrum of viewpoints.

Indicative of its quality as a newspaper was the high professional competence of some of the journalists it had discovered and fostered, the critical content of its literary pages and the intellectual rigour of contributions it welcomed to its pages. And, of course, it had 'discovered' Myles na gCopaleen.

Among journalists who cut their professional teeth on the *Irish Times* in the post-independence period were Patrick Campbell, Brian Inglis and Jack White. Its literary page by the end of the 1950s had become as attentive to Irish creativity as it was to international developments and, in giving space to such an independent thinker as Hubert Butler, the paper signalled its own independence of mind.

Campbell, the final Lord Glenavy, was taken on by Smyllie in 1935, when, to his father's despair, the heir to the title had seemed incapable of earning a living. Campbell quickly adapted to the newspaperman's life in a profession which, he later argued, happily involved 'no degrees, no diplomas, no training, and no specialised knowledge of any kind' (Campbell 1967, p. 117). In fact a social gadfly, Campbell got sound on-the-job training from Smyllie, especially in matters of style and correct usage, as he wrote humorous sub-leaders, did film reviews and served for a time as literary editor. He found his métier, however, in the writing of a drolly acerbic Dáil sketch in what he himself would characterize as the 'spirit of probing derision' (Campbell 1967, p. 128) that had never been far absent from Dublin's devotion to engaging talk. Bored by the process of producing this column but exhilarated by the powers it seemed to allow him, the young Campbell took off for London and Beaverbrook's *Daily Express* (the family name initially impressed that proprietor) and the London

Evening Standard, where he did not prosper. The war saw him back in Ireland serving in a Dublin-based role in the Irish navy. In 1944 Smyllie welcomed back the prodigal, who for three years crafted the 'Quidnunc' column into a good-humoured, vivid window on the social life of the city's only partly imaginary beau monde. Campbell's column served the salutary purpose at a drab time of suggesting that life had not become universally dreary. Patrick Campbell's legacy to the paper was that 'Quidnunc' became a permanent feature, surviving his second defection in 1947 (to Smyllie's forcibly expressed irritation), which took him to prominent journalistic success in England on such titles as *Spectator*, *Punch* and the *Sunday Times* (Maume 2008, p. 299), as a writer of engaging persiflage and of sketches and to a lucrative career as a 'personality' of the burgeoning television age in the 1960s and '70s.

By contrast, Brian Inglis's journalistic apprenticeship in Smyllie's *Irish Times* was the nursery of a career of some moment at the more consequential levels of British journalism and publishing. Where Campbell became a contributor to the *Spectator*, Inglis was appointed that weekly's editor in 1959. Like Campbell, Inglis had been recruited by Smyllie in the 1930s, but, in further contrast to his colleague, he served in the British forces during the war. He rejoined the paper in 1946, when, despite his Ascendancy background in the snobbish north County Dublin town of Malahide, he associated on the best of terms with highly gifted young intellectuals of nationalist outlook such as Conor Cruise O'Brien, the economist Patrick Lynch and the journalist and University College Dublin academic historian Desmond Williams. He easily held his own in such challenging company. A colleague on the newspaper at that time remembers Inglis as 'the most effortlessly capable journalist that my generation in the *Irish Times* can ever have known' (Dudley Edwards 2009, p. 900). A combination of strength of intellect, the journalist's curiosity and a ready pen in later life would make him a successful popularizing author on serious subjects. His two engaging memoirs, *West Briton* (1962) and *Downstart* (1990), contain vital portraits of his first editor, Robert Smyllie.

If the *Irish Times* helped propel Campbell and Inglis into the metropolitan excitements of London journalism and television, Jack White was inducted by the paper into a career that would make him an *éminence grise* in the new medium of Irish television. A Protestant (he was raised as a Congregationalist in County Cork), White was recruited by the *Irish Times* immediately after he completed a postgraduate degree in law (he had graduated with a first in classics) at Trinity College Dublin. At Trinity he had won prizes for English prose and verse and edited a literary magazine. He served as London editor from 1946 to 1952 (introducing an admired 'London Letter' to the paper). From 1952 he was features and literary editor (though deliberately impeded in the features department of the paper by his rival Alec Newman), until in 1961 he accepted the post of head of public affairs in RTE, just as the national broadcaster was

A CHANGING IRELAND 227

about to launch its television service. In RTE he rose to be controller of television programmes and subsequently head of resources. The literary promise of White's college days was fulfilled by the writing of three novels and a successful Abbey play. Other journalists whom Smyllie recruited who also gave sterling service to the paper were Bruce Williamson, a future literary editor and film critic on the paper, and Cathal O'Shannon, who would become one of RTE's most gifted makers of documentary programmes. Seamus Kelly settled into the post of 'Quidnunc', supplying the 'Dubliner's Diary' for many years.

In the 1950s, under White's direction, the weekly literary page consolidated the reputation it had begun to establish in the late 1930s, when it had turned its attention in a serious way to the work of current Irish writers and poets, as well as giving due prominence to international letters. By the end of the decade it had become, as it remains, the place to be reviewed in Ireland, and where it was possible to establish a reputation as a newspaper critic. And the weekly poets' corner was a much-coveted space. Among those who joined Austin Clarke (who retained his role as the principal reviewer of new volumes of poetry, as well as enlarging his purview to include general literature) as regular or occasional reviewers were such figures as Terence de Vere White, who would succeed Jack White as literary editor in 1961, the novelists Kate O'Brien and John Broderick, the poets Monk Gibbon and John Montague, and Joseph Hone (W. B. Yeats's first biographer). The universities supplied their complement of experts in various fields, sometimes giving the literary page a distinctively donnish tone. From the English Department at University College Dublin came reveiws by Denis Donoghue, at the beginning of a career that would bring him international renown as a critic. From the English Department in Trinity College Dublin came poems (on Dublin and Ireland) and reviews from Donald Davie, who would also achieve an international reputation in subsequent years as one of England's most scrupulous twentieth-century poet/critics. F. S. L. Lyons, a future Provost of Trinity and in his day the doyen of Irish historians, supplied elegantly lucid reviews of historical texts. So on a typical Saturday such as one in the summer of 1958, a reader could find a review by a Florence O'Donoghue of A. L. Rowse's *The Later Churchills* rubbing shoulders with a new poem by Patrick Kavanagh ('Dear Folks') and a scholarly assessment by the Professor of French at Trinity College Dublin, E. J. F. Arnould, of a volume on the illuminated book. Alongside these appeared on that day a review by one of Ireland's most remarkable twentieth-century writers of prose, the essayist Hubert Butler. His subject that Saturday was a book by T. G. E. Powell on the Celts. It appeared under the headline 'The Elusive Celts'.

Butler was an appropriate choice to review such a work, for among his many interests as a man of passionately intent curiosity was the world of early Christian sainthood in what was popularly thought of as Celtic Ireland. Powell's book dealt with the complex and obscure European provenance of the idea of the Celt, allowing Butler to conclude: 'It is difficult to isolate purely Celtic elements anywhere' (*Irish Times*, 12 July 1958). In the world of scholarship, this was not an especially surprising thing to say; in 1950s' Ireland, however, it was to court iconoclasm. For the Irish Ireland movement that had made the revival of Gaelic its defining project, was much given to thinking of the Irish people as an ethnic homogeneity, with the Irish language as a marker of an ancient Celtic identity that had been suppressed by the colonial power with its English language. Butler's airily expressed statement in the tongue of the conqueror was capable of giving offence to those primed to take it (though elsewhere in his writing he himself deployed the term 'Celt' without such scholarly reservation).

Butler was no stranger to being suspected as an impertinent, alien iconoclast. As the scion of minor gentry with a distinguished Norman name, this Oxford-educated son of a former High Sheriff of County Kilkenny, where he resided at the rural family seat, was not advantageously placed to take on the role, in his effortlessly adroit, superbly judged prose, of public intellectual in the Republic of Ireland. People of his background could be tolerated, even indulged, as writers of poetry, fiction or drama. Essays, articles and lectures on issues of moral and political moment, which fearlessly took on established authorities in the name of individual liberty and radical beliefs about community well-being, were altogether less welcome in many quarters.

Nothing daunted, in the 1950s Butler made his country house the centre of his life, from where in letters to the press and in essays, serial articles and reviews he steadily began to accumulate what would prove to be his life work: the production of a body of prose writings that has won international admiration in recent years.

Butler wrote for publications at home and abroad, among which was the *Irish Times* in the 1950s, when its columns afforded him the space to develop his ideas and hone his subtly acerbic, pellucid style (in modern times only George Orwell wrote English with the same transparency of manner). Among the subjects he addressed with unabashed aplomb was the role of the Protestant community in independent Ireland. In May 1955 the *Irish Times* published a series of articles by Hubert Butler on that subject under the headline 'No Petty People?' The series sought to establish whether W. B. Yeats's statement in his 'divorce' speech in the Senate in 1925, when he had claimed that the Protestants of Ireland were 'no petty people', really obtained. Butler's damningly caustic judgement was uttered forthwith: 'In the last few years Southern Irish Protestants, once renowned for their eloquence and intellectual daring, have become one of the most inarticulate minorities in the world' (*Irish Times*, 13 May 1955). Much of the rest of the series of five articles seemed bent on single-handedly making good that failure of nerve, as Butler unapologetically asserts that the right of private judgement, for the Protestant, is non-negotiable. And he showed himself indignantly direct when needs be: 'Twenty years ago an Irishman who still believed that an Irish-speaking Ireland was possible was an idealist. Ten years ago he was an amiable self-deceiver; to-day he is a crook or a dangerous paranoiac whose judgment on no single subject could be trusted' (*Irish Times*, 17 May 1955), though he later admitted that had such a transition been achieved in an earlier century, the effects might have been beneficial. What gives this series its touch of genius, raising it above a merely rhetorical performance, refreshing as that is in its bold clarity of tone, is that Butler invents a typical Anglo-Irish Protestant, pusillanimous and time-serving, to bear the brunt of his patrician scorn for co-religionists who settle for keeping their heads down in the new order, ready to take flight for Sussex or the Antipodes if things get too tricky at home. 'The avoidance of unpleasantness,' avers Butler of this imaginary trimmer, 'has become the fortieth article of his religion' (*Irish Times*, 14 May 1955).

Other articles by Butler in the *Irish Times* in the 1950s displayed his idiosyncratic, even quixotic, spirit. Few readers could have expected to find, for example, a series on Spanish Protestants, in an Irish newspaper in that or in any period. In May 1958 Butler duly obliged. Yet such arcane knowledge about a faraway country was a measure of the internationalist reach of Butler's concerns as a writer and thinker. In 1956 he was a member of a cultural delegation to China, and an insightful series of articles on that new polity in an ancient land followed. The condition of Europe was his abiding concern and particularly the toxic blends of ethnicity, nationalism and religion which had disfigured the borderland territories of its central and eastern regions and had poisoned relationships with Jewry. A series of articles in 1951, on 'Europe's Debatable Lands', surveyed the contested landscape. And in 1956 a short review of a major study of the Holocaust drew from him the observation, as if warning his fellow countrymen of their own capacity for air-brushing atrocity from the collective memory, that in Germany tens of thousands of civilians must have seen the deportees en route to their terrible fate: 'Ignorance cannot possibly be pleaded' (*Irish Times*, 4 April 1956). The measured irony with which Butler relates how tyranny creates the conditions for complicity with evil is exemplary of his feline skills as a writer:

> The nation-wide miracle of not-noticing and later not-recollecting could not have been carried through if the Nazi Government had not made things as easy as possible for tender consciences and unreliable nerves. At Nuremberg, Captain Schubert, of the composer's family, explained some of the devices for allaying '*seelische Belastung*', of which 'spiritual strain' is a better translation than 'guilty conscience'. One might instance also Treblinka railway station, which was so gay with posters that it was just possible to be ignorant that it was a terminus from which no traveller returned.

Butler drew a profound lesson for his readers, in a sentence characteristic of this writer's unclouded, exacting moral vision: 'These volumes are not so damning to any particular nation as to the vast international army of the respectable, who smother their private consciences under the cloak of public duty.'

Hubert Butler's effectiveness as a writer of a strenuously ethical turn-of-mind is dependent on the sustained empiricism of his engagement with the world. His essays were consistently illuminated by telling points of fact and by a grasp of how history permeates the texture of life at the most local levels. His internationalist perspectives were grounded in a deep, realistic affection for the home ground. Accordingly, his essays and articles on Irish life and society published in the *Irish Times* and elsewhere in the 1950s made convincingly actual the kind of patriotic feeling about the country that the paper had so often expressed at the level of the leading article, with its elevated formalities. An article of July 1956 on the effects of emigration evokes a provincial landscape with a poetic lyricism and a novelist's sense of the living fabric of Irish reality:

> The river Erne shambles undecidedly through this ambiguous land, to the thousand islands of Upper Lough Erne. It hesitates at every bog and makes a lake, it winds round every small hill and makes an island. Because of all these hills and lakes, communities are isolated, there are letter-boxes on trees, lonely petrol pumps, and small shops in boreens where you can buy bootlaces, doses for bullocks and long-bladed Cavan spades. You used to get fine rush hats for haymaking very cheap, and potato baskets and clogs made from the local willows and alders, but I have not seen them there lately; more exotic commodities, like chocolate creams, grow soft and blotchy with long waiting. (*Irish Times*, 27 July 1956)

It was this combination of a literary sensibility with the social historian's grasp of cultural implication that made Butler a fine reviewer of contemporary writing. His review of Pasternak's *Doctor Zhivago* (one of the publishing highlights of the decade because it breached the 'Iron Curtain') appeared in the paper in 1958; his review concluded as if with a salute to a fellow spirit: 'As in the old Russia, the writer still has power to undermine pomposity with humour and irony, and to tame vast distances with detailed and intimate sketches of the things near-by' (*Irish Times*, 27 September 1958).

The article by Butler on County Cavan in 1956 began by noting that emigration figures demonstrated that there was 'no county in Ireland which its natives leave so precipitately'. Given that precipitate departure from Ireland was a marked feature of this border county, what the essayist termed a lemming-like 'stampede to the sea' was also in train in many parts of the Republic at this time. Indeed, a year earlier Butler had noted with asperity of the charge that the anglicized Irish were West Britons, that because of the economic state of the country and emigration, in fact 'they [were] becoming plain, unhyphenated Britons' (*Irish*

Times, 18 May 1955). He was no doubt thinking of the many Irish people who had left for British towns and cities with their long-settled Irish communities.

In the late 1950s the parlous state of the country's economy and the debilitating effects of mass emigration on national morale, were recurrent matters for concern in the *Irish Times* as they were for the other national dailies. The stark statistical facts about emigration had first been made widely available by the report of a Commission on Emigration in 1954 (it had been established in 1948).

The preliminary report of the 1956 census, which was made public in June of that year, sounded a shrill alarm bell in the editorial office of the *Irish Times*. An editorial asserted that the figures proved that the 'country's most important capital asset – her people – is being allowed to drain away' (*Irish Times*, 12 June 1956). It reckoned that 'a national emergency' was unfolding, as it warned: 'It is quite certain that depopulation at the present rate need not continue for many years in order to kill the country.' The writer concluded: 'No problem which the Government is facing is as serious as emigration, which is simply another word for national suicide.' A year later an editorial concurred with the claim by Seán MacBride, at Clann na Poblachta's annual congress, that the economic situation of the country threatened the state itself, for as it bluntly declared, 'Nothing less ... is at stake than the survival of the twenty-six Counties as a separated and independent entity' (*Irish Times*, 10 June 1957). In such a context, it was, the paper argued, unsurprising that 'so many of our young people take the first opportunity of shaking the dust of Ireland from their feet'.

With Alec Newman in the editorial chair (though Smyllie was often referred to in the office as if he was still in post), it was unlikely that the economic problems of the state and the alarming pace at which emigration was increasing, would be adduced to question the wisdom of Ireland's strike for independence earlier in the century. In April 1956, nonetheless, the issue hovered as it were in the background when in an editorial entitled 'Vanishing Irish?' (the title of a recently published book on the country's depressing demographic prospects), the writer observed: 'it is frightening to reflect that to-day, more than 30 years after achieving independence, this state may conceivably be in the throes of the worst emigration crisis in its history' (*Irish Times*, 5 April 1956). Two months later, in an editorial on 12 June, however, the paper came even closer to drawing that existential inference, as it implied that independence had been squandered by government:

> How many people really understand that the Census revealed nothing less than a national emergency.
>
> It is quite certain that depopulation at the present rate need not continue for many years in order to kill the country ... emigration is simply another word for national suicide. (*Irish Times*, 12 June 1956)

One can almost imagine Robert Smyllie's ghost at the writer's elbow urging him to draw a negative conclusion about independence itself.

What in fact the editor did do in response to national crisis was to give ample space in his paper for various experts to provide thorough analyses of the effects of emigration and of the economic and social state of the country. One significant consequence of this was that attention became focused on the experience of the Irish diaspora. Where in the past the 'emigrant wake' had thrust individuals into a kind of terra incognita from which only private letters to families tried to cross the space between separate worlds, in the second half of the 1950s the fate of the emigrant Irish became a public subject of study and reportage. For example, in December 1958 F. S. L. Lyons supplied an extensive review-article on a book on the nineteenth-century Irish emigration to the United States, which took account of the individual pain it had involved. Lyons ended on a note with stark contemporary resonance: 'And while the hard necessity for emigration could be, and often was, argued by economists, yet in terms of human suffering, it was a devastating experience, the full effects of which we are even yet discovering. Ill fares the land which can only live by such drastic surgery, and which now, after a hundred years, still cannot staunch the wound' (*Irish Times*, 5 December 1958). In February 1959 the social historian E. R. R. Green was given space for two long articles on 'The Irish in America' (with the subheading 'Why and How They Went') and 'The Difficulties of Assimilation', which offered modern social substance to the idea of Irish America. At a practical human level, an article by the Irish international badminton player F. W. Peard (entitled 'How to Get There: An Emigrant's Guide to New York') provided valuable information on the transatlantic journey and what would confront Irishmen and women at US Immigration.

An article published in 1956 dealt with the issue of Irish migration to the United Kingdom. By dint of careful statistical analysis, it reached the conclusion that the emigration of the 1950s had 'created new centres of Irish population, which subsequently serve as a focus of attention for each year's new and ever-larger crop of arrivals from Ireland' (*Irish Times*, 28 January 1956). It was clear that the Irish as a demographic entity had bypassed the traditional settlements in coastal cities and had 'penetrated inland to areas of full-employment'. These findings appeared under the byline 'Analyst', the pseudonym employed by Garret FitzGerald, future politician and Taoiseach. In the 1950s FitzGerald's employment in public bodies necessitated journalistic anonymity. The article in which these findings appeared, with its blend of analytic detachment and a fascination for statistics, was entirely characteristic of the many articles he contributed to the paper during the decade, on topics as diverse as the declining numbers studying Irish in the country's universities to patterns of car sales. His writings bore the marks of an invincible curiosity and a zest for his subjects that never quite managed to convince the reader that he or she should fully share it. By the end of the decade, under his own name, he was contributing a regular column of economic comment. It can truthfully be said that FitzGerald, by such writings, almost single-handedly brought to life the 'concept' of 'the economy' as a category of thought salient to Irish self-understanding.

The demographic crisis of the late 1950s bore particularly on Irish minorities since their low numbers made them peculiarly vulnerable to the effects of emigration. At the end of 1957, for example, Seán Ó Maoilbhride asked in an article 'Can the Gaeltacht Be Preserved?' (*Irish Times*, 9 December 1957). In a telling image, he warned his readers how over three centuries the geographic areas in which Irish was the mother-tongue of the inhabitants had inexorably been shrinking: 'With the passage of time the perimeter [of the Gaeltacht] has gradually receded like the hair-line of a balding man.' Emigration was taking such a toll that the 'actual number of people living in the Gaeltacht districts' was 'dwindling all the time'. As confidence waned in such areas that they could survive economically, English was gaining 'more and more currency' and 'the proportion of people within the Gaeltacht itself' that remained '*exclusively or even mainly Irish-speaking* [was] also decreasing at a pretty fast rate'.

The Protestant community too felt the impact of a quickening pace of emigration which made their presence as a distinctive element in the nation similarly fragile. In an editorial in June 1959, entitled 'The Protestant Exodus', the writer pondered the choices facing Irish Protestants. Generally more affluent than many of the majority, who in hard times had no choice but to seek employment beyond the seas, Irish Protestants were, nonetheless, attracted by superior conditions and salaries abroad. So 'the fact' remained 'that a great many Protestants [had] shaken the earth of their native country from their heels over the last few decades, and their departure has been a loss not merely to their various Churches, but to the nation at large' (*Irish Times*, 1 June 1959).

A secure future for the paper itself was not unrelated to the decline in the Protestant population which had taken place since independence, for its core readership was to be found in that community in Dublin, for all that liberal-minded Catholics, the civil service and the political elite were also to be found among its readership (not all of whom thought it an 'occasion of sin'). The company had, as we have seen, sought to set the paper on a sounder administrative basis during the war years, but this had met with significant in-house resistance. In 1947 the *Irish Times*, along with its fellow national titles, had been forced to meet trade union demands for minimum wages and more social hours in the newspaper industry. In this newly regulated context, proprietors had to deal in 1952 with a seven-week strike in a dispute with the print unions. The *Irish Times* faced this interruption, when no copies were published, only eight months into the aftermath of a fire that had caused significant damage to its printing presses and linotype machines in its central Dublin premises.

Alec Newman, like his immediate predecessor, was not inclined to view sales figures with much concern so long as they remained stable at about 35,000. The new management which took over in the 1950s, conscious that the paper's core readership could not be depended upon indefinitely, adopted a much less relaxed position. After Smyllie's death in 1954, the Arnott family had, at Frank Lowe's instigation, sold the majority of the shares they held in the company to a number of highly respectable Dublin businessmen (maintaining continuity, one member of the Arnott family was appointed to the new board) who were keen to oversee diversification of company activities if the risks involved would mean rising profits. The company already owned the *Irish Field*, and in 1941 the *Weekly Irish Times* had mutated into the *Times Pictorial*, with its largely photographic content. In November 1957 the board enlarged its portfolio when it launched a new title, the *Sunday Review*, a lively, populist tabloid that never fulfilled its commercial promise as a focus for advertisers, despite healthy circulation figures. Not apparently deterred, in 1960 the company, in an ever riskier venture, purchased the long-standing *Dublin Evening Mail*, which could not even under the new management compete with the popular Dublin evening papers, the *Evening Herald* and the *Evening Press*. It was wound up in 1962, but not before its costs had almost ruined the company. In the late 1950s the board had commissioned a consultancy company, McDowell Management Directors Ltd, to examine its business and management structures. Major Thomas McDowell of that agency was to play a role in the closing down of the *Evening Mail* and a highly significant part in the future of the *Irish Times* itself. In 1961, as we noted earlier, the board, unnerved by the company's shaky financial position, summarily removed Alec Newman from his post as editor, replacing him with Alan Montgomery, who had served as news editor under both Smyllie and Newman. Effective in that post as a skilled reporter, Montgomery did not excel as an editor and he left journalism for commerce in 1963.

So the late 1950s and the early 1960s were a time of uncertainty and problematic change for the *Irish Times* titles. By contrast, the country, confronted by the threat of mass emigration, a balance of payments crisis in 1956 and economic stagnation, was decisively taking the steps necessary to shore up and strengthen the economic basis of the hard-won political independence the state had achieved. For the sense of failure that emigration and lack of economic expansion had bred in the official mind made the time propitious for those who wanted radical change. This meant that when a young civil servant, T. K. Whitaker, newly appointed secretary in the Department of Finance, wrote a document on 'Economic Development', which essentially proposed the abandonment of protectionism in favour of free trade and the encouragement of direct foreign investment, his message did not fall on deaf ears. In 1959 Seán Lemass succeeded de Valera as Taoiseach, and he, despite long fearing that such a policy would increase Irish dependency on Britain, gave his support to Whitaker's proposal for what amounted to a national volte-face.

A series of two articles in the *Irish Times* in May 1959 by Patrick Lynch (chairman of Aer Lingus and lecturer in Economics at University College Dublin) on 'The Economics of Independence' made very clear that the state had, indeed, changed course. Commending Whitaker's 'masterly survey and the discussion it has provoked' (*Irish Times*, 25 May 1959), Lynch continued:

> The Sinn Fein myth, which has been a decisive influence on public thinking and policy for more than two generations, has assumed that Irish political independence implied economic independence. The shadow of this unfounded dogma which identified political independence with economic self-sufficiency still remains. Experience should have taught that in Ireland, political, geographic and economic boundaries do not coincide, but the lesson has been slowly learnt ... It is because so many emigrate that those who remain at home are able to afford a standard of living that could not be maintained if Irish political independence implied the obligation to cater on their own terms for all the people born in Ireland since the State was established.

This was heretical enough, but Lynch went on to describe how acceptance of Whitaker's ideas would inevitably mean a closer relationship with Britain, as a prerequisite for future involvement in the developing European Economic Community (EEC). He stated bluntly that 'There is such a mobility of labour, capital and ideas between Britain and Ireland that for all these purposes at least the two countries have become, to a considerable extent, a common market.' In the third article, heresy bloomed fully, as Lynch stated: 'Closer economic association with Britain is entirely compatible with an intelligent concept of Irish nationhood, if only because so many Irish people are domiciled in Britain and the movement of people between the two countries is regional migration, not international emigration' (*Irish Times*, 27 May 1959).

Lynch's understanding of what might constitute 'an intelligent concept of Irish nationhood' was not one likely to appeal to the new Taoiseach, who was anxious to present the state's about-face in economic policy as compatible with his party's perennial aspiration for the achievement of full Irish sovereignty. Yet Lynch's message, while not exactly music to the *Irish Times*'s ears, was something many of its readers would have been pleased to hear, confirming their view that the 'Sinn Féin myth' had been deleterious to the country's interests. So when Lynch had delivered the lecture on which his articles would be based, the paper had hailed its 'Straight Talking' (the title of an editorial) and its 'revolutionary ... calm acceptance of the interdependence of the Irish economy and that of Britain' (*Irish Times*, 13 April 1959). The writer of this second leader even went so far as to suggest that the 'embracing of this economic truth should be logically followed by a similar political adjustment'. A year later the paper was welcoming the fact that the state was adopting Whitaker's proposal with a five-year plan for economic expansion in a context where men like Lynch provided advice on 'matters of realistic principle' (*Irish Times*, 8 April 1960). In July of that year, under the headline 'Economists Unanimous', the paper reflected in broad terms on the historic shift in economic policy that was now well advanced:

> It is, perhaps, paradoxical that the so-called 'Economic War' of the 1930s was well over when this country began to think seriously about economics. The flowering of the Sinn Féin myth of industrial self-suffi-ciency was probably a necessary aftermath of the birth-pangs of a new state but it did a great deal of damage, not only through its expression in Government policy from the late 1920s up to the early 1950s, but also in the attitude of mind it created among economists and the people as a whole ... the fact is that the last four or five years have witnessed the birth of a positive economic mould of thought which has not been equalled since the days of Griffith and Horace Plunkett. (*Irish Times*, 8 July 1960)

The *Irish Times* was, therefore, giving its full support to these ideological devel-opments, which included not only a novel commitment to free trade, but to strategic economic planning of the kind Patrick Lynch (judged 'an outstanding interpreter and guide in Irish economic affairs') advised. How far-seeing Patrick Lynch, indeed, was, is revealed in a further two articles he published in the *Irish Times* at this time (the topic was 'Economic Planning in Ireland'). In March 1960, touching on a subject near to the paper's heart during an earlier dispensation, he wrote: 'Science occupies too modest a place in the educational system, and the research departments of the universities are too penurious to keep step with the needs of industry, much less point the way towards revolu-tionary forms of innovation' (*Irish Times*, 30 March 1960). It would be four decades before the state began to heed this perspicacious piece of advice.

It took only six years for the impact of Whitaker's report and of the new economic thinking to produce a major change in Anglo-Irish relations. For at the end of 1965, after intensive negotiations, Ireland signed a Free Trade Agreement with the United Kingdom. The *Irish Times* adopted an air of refined pragmatism to mark this outcome, which seemed to represent a resetting of the Irish question itself. 'Let us hope,' it suggested,

> that it is a settling down in the form of a final answer. Certainly by most Irishmen and by all Englishmen it is conceded that there is nothing left to fight about. Forty years of toddling have taught us to walk. The only question (with a small q) left is in which direction. (*Irish Times*, 15 December 1965)

One cannot imagine the *Irish Times* of the earlier decades of Irish independence responding to an agreement that confirmed the close ties that existed between the two countries in quite the same way. For the editorial in fact insisted, in terms that would probably have offended Robert Smyllie, had he been alive to read it, that the 'acid test' of Irish 'political independence was September, 1939'. The new agreement could not disturb that reality, for as the writer insisted: 'There is no reason to believe that in the unlikely event that a similar choice offered itself tomorrow', Ireland 'would choose differently'. This marked change in tone and outlook can be attributed to the fact that, after several years of ineffective experiment with new titles and the editorship, the board had found a man who could make the *Irish Times* a paper brilliantly able to reflect and comment on a rapidly changing country. His impact and influence was to exceed that of even the legendary Smyllie, whose essentially pro-British spirit had hovered in the office of the paper long after his bodily departure.

Douglas Gageby had been co-opted to the board of the *Irish Times* as joint managing director in 1959, to serve alongside Frank Lowe's nephew, George Hetherington (Lowe himself died shortly after Gageby's co-option, never having achieved the profitable reordering of the company's affairs he had been appointed to effect). When Hetherington gave up his management role, Gageby was in place as 'sole managing director' (Mark O'Brien 2008, p. 157). When, therefore, Gageby was appointed editor following Alan Montgomery's departure in 1963, he obtained the kind of power in the paper no one had possessed hitherto and which he certainly had not enjoyed in any of his earlier journalistic positions. Happily he proved more than worthy of the power thus vested in him.

The new editor was the only son of a Belfast Protestant father and a mother who hailed from County Meath. His father, with a paternal background in the Protestant working-class heartland of Belfast's Shankill Road, had moved with his wife to Dublin where Douglas was born in 1918. In 1922 the family moved back to Belfast where Gageby Senior entered the new Northern Ireland civil service. Thereafter the journalist-to-be was afforded the education that only a small minority of Belfast's citizens experienced at that time: attendance at a good grammar school (Belfast Royal Academy) and matriculation at university. Gageby graduated with a degree in modern languages (French and German) from Trinity College Dublin in 1941. The trajectory of his childhood, youth and young manhood was of a kind that might have been expected to make of him what could be termed a typical '*Irish Times* liberal' of the period (Protestant grammar school boy, from a solid middle-class family in Belfast, going south to Trinity with its liberal Protestant ethos). In fact, it helped to make him a Protestant nationalist with strong republican leanings.

Perhaps Gageby's republican nationalism was a product not just of his emotional attachment to his native city but to the Belfast in which his grandfather as a trade union official and left-wing local politician had in his day stood up to the forces of unionist conservatism. In his later life he recalled in fact that, though born in Dublin and having lived there by choice for most of his life, Belfast was in his bones. 'I love Belfast, I have family graves there ...' (*Irish Times*, 28 May 1991) he confessed, in an article on the city that breathes anger at how British politicians had played the Orange card there and made respectable the Orange lodges which his grandfather in the 1880s had thought were facing oblivion, 'fit only for louts and layabouts, for boozers and brawlers'. Gageby's republican, almost Anglophobic, contempt in this article for what he termed 'Gallopers' (F. E. Smith, who, as Lord Birkenhead, helped draft the Anglo-Irish Treaty of 1921, was often referred to as 'Galloper Smith') is palpable. For, he fumes:

> There were gallopers before F. E. Smith or Lord Birkenhead, among them Lord Randolph Churchill. These gentlemen came to the North, stirred us up and then went back to their broad acres and their London clubs and their Oxford and Cambridge colleges, leaving us to get on with the usual business of hating and murdering each other, only with more intensity.

Gageby, true to his convictions, enlisted in the Irish armed forces during World War II, where his knowledge of German made him a useful intelligence officer. After the war he began his journalistic career on de Valera's paper, the *Irish Press*, and in 1949 he became deputy editor of the sister publication, the *Sunday Press*. That he was a strong republican nationalist is evidenced not only by the fact that he prospered in the largely Fianna Fáil-supporting Irish Press group, but by his appointment in 1951 as editor-in-chief of Seán MacBride's Irish News Agency, which was a less than successful feature of the international anti-partitionist efforts of the coalition administration in power at that date. In 1954 he returned to the Irish Press group as the first editor of the *Evening Press* which for decades competed successfully with the *Evening Herald* for a Dublin readership. Gageby's evening paper was both entertaining and driven by its editor's nose for a good story. Its parent paper the *Irish Press* has been characterized with a measure of accuracy as 'both radical and rumbustious' (Michael O'Toole 1992, p. 66). It had been the first Irish daily to put news on the front page, and it published the hugely popular 'Roddy the Rover' column by Aodh de Blacam' whose genial tales of the byways of Irish rural life and his Irish Ireland outlook on culture and tradition meant that the paper found a readership far beyond the Pale. De Blacam had in fact reviewed books and written leaders for the *Irish Press* in the 1920s (Maume 2009, p. 125).

Gageby, therefore, brought to the fundamentally staid *Irish Times* the Press group's instinct for economic survival (the *Irish Press* had been sustained by the firm commitment of its politically partisan readership) and commercialism, together with an astute eye for the newsworthy and colourful in a society on the cusp of rapid change. He was determined that the paper should reflect the new Ireland, where much that had been taken for granted in the recent past was being vigorously debated. Nonetheless, in the Press group he had seen how uncertain lines of authority between proprietor and paper might compromise editorial independence. There would be no such confusion in his case at the *Irish Times*. And behind the air of an agreeably encouraging senior executive (who welcomed diversity of opinion as a wind that would blow away the stuffy atmosphere in the paper he had inherited) were the values and expectations of the officer corps. Tim Pat Coogan, who began his own distinguished career in journalism as a tyro sub-editor on the *Evening Press*, when Gageby was editor, recalled in a memoir how the 'weapons' of Gageby's displeasure 'developed in officers' training courses, were the vitriol bottle and the rapier' (Coogan 2008, p. 92). At editorial meetings he could reduce grown men to tears by the severity of his censure. At the same time he commanded considerable loyalty and respect, even from some of those who suffered the sharpness of his tongue which is the measure of really effective leadership. From those who have written about Gageby the man, it is possible to distinguish a particular gift: he seemed able to inspire in juniors an earnest desire for his approbation and approval. He was certainly no plaster saint. James Downey, who joined the paper in the 1960s and served as deputy editor from 1978 to 1986, while aware of Gageby's virtues has left a severe summary of his complex character and personality: 'It would be an understatement to say he was sparing of praise. He was ungrateful, liverish, erratic, often unjust and dictatorial, sometimes deceitful' (Whittaker 2006, p. 28).

Gageby, as editor of the *Irish Times* in the early 1960s, with his rare mix of well-judged journalistic enthusiasm and business acumen, was unquestionably a man who could revitalize the title, functioning as he was at a time of Irish renewal. For the early years of the decade in Ireland were marked by an upsurge of national confidence that made change possible. People began to speak of a watershed in Irish affairs as the pessimism of the late 1950s gave way to a more optimistic spirit, in which novelty could be embraced, not as a desperate last measure in face of crisis, but as an exciting challenge. Remembering the 1950s, Gageby himself damned them as a 'dull and inconsequent' (Lee 1979, p. 131) decade that had followed the 1940s, when Ireland was recovering from 'a lame neutrality' (Lee 1979, p. 131). In retrospect, he clearly saw himself and his newspaper as integral to the new, more stimulating Ireland in the making in the 1960s. Downey writes appositely of Gageby's first, successful, period as editor which meant that between 1963 and 1986 (during three years of that span he was in what would prove a temporary retirement) the circulation more than trebled:

> He had many advantages and plenty of luck. The proportion of educated people in the population rose. Spectacular political events stimulated interest in current affairs and created a demand for more analytical and independent coverage and commentary. Ireland became more open, both internally and in our relations with the outside world, and readers wanted

a newspaper which could reflect that. But the achievement was still awesome. (Whittaker 2006, p. 23)

Certainly Gageby's dismissal of the 1950s as an 'inconsequent' decade was exaggerated. In that decade the *Irish Times* had had to respond to such issues as the Mother and Child crisis, to the renewal of IRA violence at home, and the Suez and Hungarian crises abroad, with the Cold War as a permanent backdrop to the news. In many respects the decade had been neither dull nor inconsequential. Nonetheless, in Ireland, as elsewhere, people were quick to think of the 1960s as somehow inaugurating a less constricted, more glamorous time, with wartime austerity receding and exciting opportunities opening up for the young.

A great boost to Ireland's renewed self-confidence was supplied by the visit to the country in late June 1963 of the president of the United States of America. That the young Harvard-educated scion of the Boston Irish, who had played to win in a dangerous nuclear poker game with the Soviet Nikita Khrushchev when the Cuban missile crisis had brought the world to the brink of doom the previous autumn, was visiting the land of his forefathers was an enormous fillip to national morale. It was gratifying, indeed, for a country that had recently feared for its very survival, to hear John Fitzgerald Kennedy in Wexford say (as reported on the front page of the *Irish Times* on the second day of the visit): 'Ireland's experience had a special significance for the world because, after hundreds of years of foreign domination and religious persecution, she had maintained her identity and loyalty to the Faith and the Fatherland' (*Irish Times*, 28 June 1963). It was gratifying too, to hear, as Seamus O'Kelly pointed out in the paper on 29 June, that an American president was proud of the nation's literary heritage (even if, one must reflect, not all the Irish had taken the authors he named – Joyce, Yeats and Shaw – to their bosoms). The same day the *Irish Times* editorialized on the president's arrival in the capital as a 'triumphant progress'. Of Ireland's reaction to Kennedy and a visit which was both historic and informal, the paper affirmed: 'It was a reception which had no equal in the 40 years of our independence' (*Irish Times*, 29 June 1963). The banner headline on the front page that day read simply 'Ireland Honours Kennedy'.

By November the nation was in mourning for the assassinated president. The *Irish Times* on the day following his death compared him to Abraham Lincoln, as it remembered his visit, which had 'left a deep and lasting impression on the land of his forebears', continuing: 'Every Irishman will feel a personal sorrow.'

In the improved economic conditions of the 1960s, paradoxically, the *Irish Times*, especially under Gageby's direction, turned its attention to what might be termed 'the condition of Ireland'. Where in the second half of the 1950s, 'the economy' had become a clearly defined focus of attention, in the new decade it was 'society' that now demanded analysis. Among new recruits to the paper were Michael Viney and the University College Dublin-educated John Horgan, who under their own bylines, itself an innovation, as 'correspondents' for specific societal areas of concern (industry, agriculture, politics), would supply well-researched articles and series of articles that helped readers to gain an understanding of the kind of society in which they were living.

As a young Englishman (born in Brighton in 1933 and appointed to the paper in 1961 from Fleet Street, after he had spent a year living in a west of Ireland cottage) of liberal/left disposition, Michael Viney brought to the analysis of Irish reality a dedicated objectivity and a lack of innate respect for inherited sacred cows. Viney took on such subjects as the experience of unwed mothers; growing old in Ireland; mental health; the numerical decline of the Protestant minority (reduced by the early 1960s by emigration and a low birth rate, as compared to the Catholic majority, to five per cent); and the state of the Irish language. To such topics Viney brought a bracing instinct for sympathetic truth-telling. Concluding, for example, his series on the state of the Irish language, published in 1963, he recognized, in a way the *Irish Times* had never really done, that compulsory instruction in schools was a necessity if any hopes for revival were to be realized. However, when a language commission reported in 1964, he responded with a tonic realism about the most sacred of Irish cows. He observed coolly that the report was 'a unique challenge to national and personal honesty of opinion in Ireland ... It comes at a time when a mistake in national objectives would not only be wasteful of time, energy and money, but also damaging to the national fund of optimism and self-confidence. The real patriot at this moment, whether he is for or against a renewed effort to revive the Irish language, is the man who tells the truth' (*Irish Times*, 15 January 1964). Vincy's own form of truth-telling was evident in his firm conclusion: 'a decision to proceed with revival which is not backed by individual resolution to learn and use the language would be a tragic piece of national self-deception'. As it was, too, when he broke a social taboo by examining the prevalence and effects of alcohol abuse in the country.

Perhaps the most devastating of the social reports (some of which the *Irish Times* published as stand-alone pamphlets) Viney contributed to the *Irish Times* in the first phase of his career in Ireland was a 1966 series on young offenders. In this he responded to a highly critical study which had been published in London on the way such young people were treated in Ireland. Viney made it his business to travel around the country visiting reformatories and industrial schools to see for himself. What he found was bleak indeed. He noted that the state had largely ignored the recommendations of a commission of enquiry established thirty years earlier. The state had presided over a system of religious-run institutions that struggled with inadequate funding and made do with personnel who had little or no training, to cope with young offenders, many of whom were really the rejects of society and not the villains in the making of popular prejudice. Viney's report from St Conleth's reformatory in Daingean, Co. Offaly (where the inmates had in fact been convicted of criminal offences) was particularly appalling. There, one of the Oblate fathers (whose order managed and ran the school in an eighteenth-century cavalry barracks leased to it by the Board of Works) candidly told Viney that the only solution for Daingean was 'obliteration' (*Irish Times*, 4 May 1966). He noted the Fathers' and Brothers' intense resentment at the niggardly state support for their work. Viney painted a stark picture of life in St Conleth's, based on the 'State's parsimony'. Of the boys, he wrote: 'Theirs is a world of overriding shabbiness and decrepitude. Their everyday clothes are greasy and unkempt or even straightforwardly tattered. One of the boys made perfectly clear that a brutal regime of corporal punishment held sway at St Conleth's.'

On the fates that awaited the victims of Ireland's reformatories and industrial schools, Viney was very blunt. He advised:

> Some, *whatever* the original reasons for committal to industrial schools, will drift quickly into crime. Others, seeking to survive in the more squalid corners of our cities, will be seduced into homosexual prostitution while still in their teens. Very many, institutionalised out of all initiative and independence, will take refuge in the Army, in hospital or hotel kitchens, or in the domestic staff of wealthy families ('They jump to the whistle,' a priest said in Cork. 'It's in their blood').

It took a full 33 years for the full truth about St Conleth's, Daingean, to emerge. A lengthy section of the Ryan Report on Child Abuse in religious institutions in Ireland, issued in 2009, revealed the horrors that had been perpetrated there, which not only included ritualistic floggings but acts of sexual depredation. In an interview given in 2010, Viney spoke of his feelings then about his 1966 articles. He remembered how little public response there had been to his findings at that time and expressed remorse that he had not confronted the possibility of sexual abuse in his reports. He commented: 'When everything came out later, I felt a terrible guilt for not having gone into the child-abuse side of things ... At least the physical. That was clear. I may have had my suspicions about the sexual abuse, but nobody at the time would have credited it' (Rosita Boland, 1910). And, indeed, Viney was surely right about how such revelations would have been greeted in the 1960s and is accordingly unduly harsh about himself in feeling guilt of the kind he describes. For the government and the religious orders had no wish to see their dirty linen washed in public in 1966, particularly in the month after the state had solemnly commemorated the Easter Rising as the foundational myth of the state. That Viney's articles appeared at all indicates not only the journalist's clear-eyed moral vision, but editorial courage too.

If the climate of the time made it well-nigh impossible for a newspaper to accuse members of religious orders of sexual impropriety, this was not because religion itself was off-limits in the press. On the contrary, the calling in 1962 by Pope John XXIII of a Second Vatican Council to consider relations between the Church and the modern world had put religious affairs on the front pages of Irish newspapers. Gageby, guided by a recently appointed news editor, astutely saw that this colloquy should be given extensive coverage by his newspaper. So the young John Horgan (appointed by Alan Montgomery just before his resignation) was moved from his post as education correspondent to that of religious affairs correspondent. Horgan brought a Catholic social formation, a brief period working on the *Catholic Standard* and a left-wing social conscience to bear on this epochal moment in the Church's long history. From Rome he cabled substantial reports and analyses that made Church debates seem matters of immediate moment for modern man, with direct implications for Irish society. Such prominence being afforded to Catholic thought and action in the columns of the *Irish Times* was quite new. As we have seen, the newspaper had often expressed a Tory-like sympathy and regard for the Catholic Church, but always as an outsider, as the voice of non-Catholic Ireland. Its columns had, however, systematically carried reports on the mainstream Protestant Churches, as if they had the right to be so acknowledged, while the weekly Church notices advised of the times of Sunday services from the highest Church of Ireland cathedral to the lowest evangelical meeting house. Now the Roman Church was taking centre stage, as it were, and paper and populace had their eyes properly turned on Rome.

So Horgan reported on the impressive opening of the final, fourth session of the Vatican Council, now under the authority of the new pope, Paul VI, as a moment that blended tradition with modernity: 'The nave of the basilica, bathed in arc-lights for the benefit of the television cameras, was flanked by wide swathes of episcopal purple with a splash of scarlet at the top where the cardinals sat on the right-hand side of the altar' (*Irish Times*, 16 September 1965). The next day the paper's front page headline read 'Objections to Decision on Religious Liberty: Position in Ireland Used as Example'. In an editorial on 18 September, entitled 'Onward', the *Irish Times* welcomed the reforming impetus at work in the Church, remarking that, despite fear that bureaucracy would impede change, 'expectations raised so high cannot be stopped ...' (*Irish Times*, 18 September 1965). The effect of such reports and editorial priorities was to suggest that it was natural for an Irish newspaper to report and comment on Catholic developments, not as a generally polite bystander, but as a voice for the people to be immediately affected by such things as Mass in the vernacular and the proposed participation of the laity in church governance. The newspaper's highlighting of the Vatican Council was crucial in making it seem a truly national organ.

Religion and even theology in the first half of the 1960s, in the wake of the Second Vatican Council, became a 'story' for the *Irish Times*. Horgan was dispatched to Spain and Holland to take the temperature of *aggiornamento* in two contrasting Church polities (the paper's internationalism was given prominence at this time by a monthly column, 'Eye on Russia'). Terms such as 'collegiality', 'ecumenism', 'church unity' became the counters of debate, in letters to the paper and in ecclesiastic pronouncement. Tellingly, when the question of Rome's attitude to artificial contraception was raised in the *Irish Times*, it was no longer simply as an infringement of Protestant rights, but as a matter that bore on the personal lives of all. As the debate raged in the Holy City and through Catholic Christendom, the paper commented:

> One aspect of the matter strikes us forcibly. Here is a topic of overwhelming interest, particularly for Roman Catholics. It affects therefore, acutely, the people of this country. And this is a topic, of all topics, that is of interest to the laity. Its practical effect does not have any bearing on the clergy. (*Irish Times*, 15 March 1965)

The editorial noted that publishing an article on artificial contraception, other than by means of the 'rhythm method', would involve prosecution under the Censorship of Publications Act. The paper judged that the existence of that law, which, among its provisions, forbade the advocacy of 'any form of birth control other than that which is currently approved of by the Church ... deprives Irish Catholics of a fundamental right. And the State, not the Church, is responsible.'

From such statements one can date the emergence of a liberal Catholic commentary in the newspaper, which would enrich its traditional liberal ethos for the rest of the century. Horgan's five-part series of articles on 'Christians and New Left' in November 1966, which discussed publications by the Slant Group in England (among them the later internationally renowned literary critic Terry Eagleton), even allowed radical perspectives on Catholic theology to be entered in *Irish Times* dialogue about Christianity's future, that the Vatican Council had stimulated in Ireland as elsewhere.

The manner in which Gageby gave Viney and Horgan freedom to explore the 'condition of Ireland' and the religious context, in the first years of his editorship, was one of the ways in which he was transforming the *Irish Times* so that it could no longer be regarded as the mouthpiece of the *ancien régime*. Smyllie and Newman in their different ways had, as we have seen, significantly adjusted the paper to the new state of affairs, but core attitudes had remained to remind readers of its patrimony. Gageby simply allowed the new Ireland, with its variety of opinion, space in the paper, permitting individuals to express how they felt and thought about the country. And he himself did not seem unduly concerned to give any special attention to members of the Protestant minority (who still had their Church Notes and Social and Personal columns as a reminder of what many still thought of as the proper order of things). Among journalists whom Gageby had on his team who helped give the paper its new, unselfconsciously, unambiguously Irish complexion, were John Healy and Donal Foley.

John Healy was a Mayo man, who had worked alongside Gageby in the *Irish Press*. Like Gageby, he had been an employee of the Irish News Agency in the early 1950s. He had been an active force, together with Ted Nealon (who would later gain renown as a television journalist, as a compiler of the standard guide to the Dáil and Seanad, and as a Fine Gael politician), on the *Sunday Review* (the two of them were largely responsible for such success as it had). He had also served a stint as editor of the doomed *Evening Mail*. Tim Pat Coogan has left a vivid pen-portrait and estimate of an extrovert who lived and wrote with an infectious ebullience.

> He ... had the physical appearance of a Guinness barrel wrapped in a cardigan and topped by a large bald head. His mannerisms, such as buttonholing someone and (literally) bouncing them off balance with a thump of his belly while commencing a monologue (he did not hold conversations) with the words 'Say, fella', made him a number of enemies ... As a journalist, he had one of the finest instincts for impending changes in society that I ever encountered. (Coogan 2008, p. 88)

In comparison with the assertive Healy (whose public persona actually masked a quieter man, interested in the creative arts), Donal Foley was a more engagingly sociable individual who had made many contacts among English socialists when he worked in the London office of the *Irish Times* in the 1950s. Born the son of a rural headmaster in 1922 in the Ring Gaeltacht in County Waterford, Foley was bilingual in Irish and English. When Gageby in 1963 called him to Dublin to serve as his news editor, he brought to the paper a wide, deeply appreciative knowledge of Gaelic culture and games and an instinctive understanding of how the Irish language could play a liberating role in a healthy nationalism. Unlike some Gaelgeori, he possessed a droll sense of humour and an eye for the absurd in Irish political life (both evident in his humorously satiric column 'Man Bites Dog', which ran weekly in the paper for the years 1971–81); like Smyllie before him, he was a good pub-man (Gageby, with whom he made up a working duo of Douglas and Donal at the beating heart of the paper, was moderation personified) and a convivial companion. Where John Edward Healy, as editor, had insisted that leading articles should be constructed according to a strict pattern of paragraphs, Foley as news editor became a stickler for brevity as the mark of good reportage and commentary. Where Healy was keenly aware of an Ireland forsaking old ways for a more entrepreneurial and aggressive future in an era of free trade, Foley, who was remembered by a future editor of the paper as one possessed of 'an enormous sense of the country in all its moods and flavours' (Brady 2005, p. 27), was sensitive to how innovation did not imply abandoning the duty of respectful preservation where it was warranted. Deaglán de Bréadún has written how Donal Foley was 'the moving spirit' (de Bréadún 2009, p. 78) behind the way in which from that period onwards 'The *Irish Times* became the prime outlet for good journalism in Irish.' Among the writers who would give substance to de Bréadún's claim over the years ahead would be such notable contributors as Breandán Ó hEithir, Seán Mac Réamoinn, Eileen O'Brien and de Bréadún himself (appointed Irish language editor in 1987). Foley's influence in broadening the paper's cultural sympathies meant that de Bréadún could write in 2009, as he celebrated the *Irish Times*'s continued commitment to Irish language journalism under a successor Irish language editor, Pól Ó Muirí: 'Few would have forecast back in the 1920s that what was then seen as the unionist, asccendancy paper would be virtually the last bastion of Irish in the mainstream print media more than 80 years later' (de Bréadún 2009, p. 78).

John Healy's early contributions to the *Irish Times* came while he was still writing an 'Inside Politics' column for the *Sunday Review*. Until that paper closed in November 1963, Gageby simply reprinted Healy's Sunday column in the *Irish Times* the following Saturday. So readers who had missed Healy's welcome to President Kennedy in June 1963 got to read it in the *Irish Times*. He struck a note of self-confident omniscience about Irish political life which he would sustain for years to come: 'You are welcome to the old scene. Allow me to introduce myself. I am Ireland's best-known political commentator' (*Irish Times*, 25 June 1963) and as such he took it upon himself to introduce the leader of the Western world to the political movers and shakers he would encounter during his visit. Among them was Charles Haughey, who would figure repeatedly over the years in both Healy's 'Backbencher' column 'Inside Politics' and in the Dáil notes he also contributed to the paper. He informed the president:

> Of course, there's Bonnie Prince Charles. I am not referring to the brandy-gulping heir apparent to the British Throne, but rather to the apparent heir to the Taoiseach's seat in Dáil Eireann, MR CHARLES HAUGHEY. He is the son-in-law of Mr Lemass. He has been scuttling about the country to personally ensure our cops are on the ball for your visit. He is as powerful as J. Edgar Hoover.

Those who took the tabloid-style *Sunday Review* (about 19,000 of them in its last days) may have become accustomed to such jocular iconoclasm about the Irish polity. To many *Irish Times* readers and to the figures who were the subjects of Backbencher's robust, highly personalized reports and analyses, it must have come as quite a shock. In the past, readers could accept the kind of patronizingly humorous Dáil reports of a Patrick Campbell as just what you would expect from the *Irish Times*; but here was what seemed to be a highly informed insider writing about political shenanigans as if they were an intimate drama staged for the public's entertainment. Yet there was an under-lying seriousness of purpose in what the man was writing. He unapologetically took for granted that the citizen of a democracy deserved frank reports from the political front line and that deference was the tribute pusillanimity paid to power. When the *Irish Times* announced in November 1963 that Backbencher was joining its journalistic team, the paper informed its reader: 'He is a senior politician whose identity has been the best-kept secret in Irish journalism, and so it will remain' (*Irish Times*, 29 November 1963).

So detailed was Backbencher's information about developments in political parties and in the Dáil and Seanad that some suspected that he was no single individual, but a group of disaffected politicians who were feeding material to the paper's news reporters. In fact, Healy had the ear of some of the young Turks in the Fianna Fáil party, who were enthusiastically relishing the opportunities Lemass's conversion to free trade had opened up (those admiringly, if satirically, dubbed 'mohair-suited politicians'). Healy himself, at an imaginary dinner with Lemass, had counselled the ageing leader that Ireland was doing better than it ever had and that now was time for 'Young blood. Fresh blood. Blood to match the mood and spirit of the country' (*Irish Times*, 30 July 1963). He gave his support to the pragmatic nationalism this volte-face had unleashed. Among those he was close to were Brian Lenihan and, in particular, Donagh O'Malley (though, as Mark O'Brien has shown, this did not inhibit criticism of O'Malley, when Healy thought he deserved it: Mark O'Brien 2008, p. 174). Healy was an early, and as the years would prove, a consistent admirer of Charles J. Haughey, whom he frequently referred to as 'the golden boy' of Irish politics, in a way that was only minimally humorous.

What is clear about Healy's writings in the early and mid-1960s was not only that he possessed a keen understanding of the day-to-day rough-and-tumble of political life, but that he grasped how Irish political culture was in flux, as the power of the image took hold in the formation of public opinion. A witty article he published in 1964, 'The Lean and Hungry Look of Success', carried, therefore, a weighty political message about the importance of a political profile. Healy liked to preface his observations with a Shakespearean allusion. So he argued that Cassius, the lean and hungry man of *Julius Caesar*, was still dangerous to those in power:

> In American politics just now there is a sharp division as to whether the fat man has a place on the political scene. Since Kennedy the American public had been conditioned into accepting the lean man. Historically, it is on the shoulders of the gaunt and lean that the cloak of power had been flung.

Alone among so many, Daniel O'Connell of the dripping haunches merely proves the consistency of a rule to which he was the great exception. (*Irish Times*, 27 March 1964)

All this sent a message to the Golden Boy, who was beginning to understand how much appearance mattered: 'Mr Haughey is as aware as I am of the need for a trim figure: he is given to riding to hounds in an effort to forestall the small man's nightmare: a paunch.'

Healy's analysis of how de Valera defeated Kevin O'Higgins's son Thomas in the race for the presidency of Ireland in 1966 displays even more fully and seriously how he had understood that what he termed 'subliminal propaganda' (*Irish Times*, 28 May1966) had immense force in modern politics. He himself deploys compelling imagery to make an incisive point about the workings of illusion in vote-gathering, observing of the Fianna Fáil campaign:

> It turned back the clock. The mohair suits were put back in mothballs and the old pair of National Aims were taken out and dusted down, taken in a bit at the shoulders, the folds of the trousers turned up and narrowed a bit by Mr Sean Lemass, 'tailor and cutter, second-hand suits turned a speciality.' To be sure it was a bit moth-eaten but the navy serge (or is it herringbone?) pattern of The Language always wore well and suited him, especially with his height. (*Irish Times*, 28 May 1966)

Healy saw how such massaging of the electorate with the gentle strokes of unrealizable dreams clothed the naked lust for power which helped to define the Fianna Fáil party. He also identified Haughey as a politician who possessed such ambition to a high degree. For all Healy's friendship with O'Malley, it was Haughey whom in one article he evoked as 'the Golden Outsider' who, almost because he was resented inside the party for 'his arrogance, his ambition, his cold-blooded calculating' (*Irish Times*, 27 August 1966), could be a future party leader. As the complete pragmatist, he was the man to take the baton from his father-in-law Lemass. The 'challenge of the future' was not to Haughey but to the party, as to whether it would allow him to seize the day. When in November 1966 the paper published a poem in memory of John F. Kennedy by the Northern poet Roy McFadden entitled 'The Golden Boy', there may have been those who initially mistook the subject of a poem that spoke of 'the necessary man' (*Irish Times*, 22 November 1966).

Donal Foley's role as news editor meant that his impact on the paper was more pervasive than Healy's, for all the latter's close association with Gageby, with whom the Mayo man shared a passion for angling. Foley's mark on the paper was evident in the commissioning of articles in the Irish language by such people as Seán Mac Réamoinn and Breandán Ó hEithir (in time this commitment to the language bore fruit in 'Tuarascáil' which afforded half a page weekly writing in Irish about current affairs, life in the west and in the Gaeltacht. This brought highly gifted Irish-speaking journalists within the ambit of the paper, who before the coming of Donal Foley would have been inclined to view the *Irish Times* as uncomfortably monoglot). Coverage of Gaelic games was extended, with Foley himself providing colourful reportage. One senses that the influence of his personality softened the harder edges of Gageby's distinctive character in a way Healy's could not and that the remarkably broad range of contributors the paper began to publish reflected his intuitive, innately hospitable nature which was open to good writing from whatever source. So readers of an increasingly capacious paper (it expanded in the 1960s to 16 and sometimes more pages on weekdays, with Saturday a bumper edition of at least 18 pages) could find themselves reading a thoughtful account of 'Irish and Modern Life' by a national school teacher, that reported on how the modern Irish words for such things as '*toffee, diaper, fuse, decanter, syphon, sprayer, change-over-switch, enamel, plaster-of-Paris*' (*Irish Times*, 3 October 1963) were probably incomprehensible to native speakers in the Gaeltacht (this article appeared just before Foley took up his post in Dublin, but it reflects his interests and the kind of realistic coverage of things Gaelic he encouraged; he may well have suggested the author).

They could also enjoy Oxford-educated Alec Reid (who as 'Michael George' wrote drama criticism and anonymously provided 'pups' or humorous final leaders), on the seventieth birthday of Lord Iveagh (in March 1964 for example). What this variety implied was not conflict between contrasting Irish worlds but a genuine enthusiasm for the complex weave of the country's life. If Gageby's deepest attachment in Ireland was to the Belfast of his youth, Foley's was to the Ring district and to its Irish-speaking people, whom he memorably evoked in an article in September 1966. There on 'a poor, scattered haphazard rocky peninsula, almost cut off by the sea,' he recalled, where 'spuds and mackerel were the staple ... the Ring fisherman, the small farmers and their children won fame from Celtic scholars for their fluency and the idiomatic musical-sounding Irish which they spoke' (*Irish Times*, 19 September 1966). Such unembarrassed rootedness and local pride gave both men the confidence to report on the new Ireland in the making with a generously democratic spirit. It also made Douglas and Donal, the townie and the countryman, a fruitful partnership.

The paper they oversaw in the 1960s quickly adapted to a decade in which readers expected their daily paper not only to be the source of news, serious opinion and basic information on sports results and birth and death notices, but a magazine as well. The layout was more carefully conceived and copy more attractively presented, with much greater use of photographs. The concept of lifestyle was being born as a consumer society took hold in a country that had once made frugality almost a political virtue. Columns on *haute couture* by Terry Keane and on cooking as a bourgeois accomplishment by Mary Frances Keating gave a sense that life in independent Ireland could be stylish and cultivated. The paper carried gardening columns, and garden centres placed advertisements. Where, in the recent past, advertisements in the paper had tended to come, as Michael O'Toole pointed out (citing Joe Walsh, editor of the *Irish Press* from 1962 to 1968), from major Protestant firms and, with, oddly enough, large detergent advertisements vying for space with those for department stores, insurance companies and building societies (Michael O'Toole 1992, p. 70), ads more and more became focused on products that added to the pleasure of daily existence. Travel agents and companies were now offering package holidays to continental resorts (the paper carried a travel column), even to the ski slopes in winter, as well as for agreeably inexpensive weekend stays in the country. Television sets, cameras, the new mass-produced mini cars, even motorized lawnmowers, were the advertised appurtenances of what was bruited as 'modern living'. The property pages burgeoned to three pages on a Friday, with an ample use of photographs. Many of the properties on display in these ads were the extensive homes set in their own grounds on the south-side of Dublin or in such north-side suburbs as Sutton, Howth and Malahide, which could not easily be run without domestic help (and personal ads seeking domestics, or announcing the availability of such, remained a secure source of income for the *Irish Times* throughout the decade). Increasingly there were ads, too, for smaller housing units in new estates that catered for lower middle-class folk keen to get on to the property ladder (job advertisements on the back pages indicated the diversifying workforce that inward investment was creating). Companies advertised the novel idea of central heating. The idea of 'a property market' and the concept of 'development' took a firm hold in the business pages. In September 1966 the paper carried an ad for the First International Furniture Fair, to be held over four days in the Intercontinental Hotel in Dublin. Even drink ads suggested the broadening of middle-class taste in a changing Ireland, with wider horizons opening up for many. As the wine and drink writer T. P. Whelehan noted in February 1964, a noticeable shift had taken place to such lighter spirits as vodka. In December 1966, Findlaters, a Dublin grocery store, thought it worth contributing a 'Guide to Wine' to advise those new to the pleasures of the grape.

On 10 April 1964 an editorial took rather crotchety note of the country's ready conversion to consumerism. Pondering how the queue was a part of life, the writer expressed concern at the way the release of new housing stock generated queues among those anxious to make deposits on property. Our editorialist felt sufficiently alarmed by this phenomenon to question 'the affluent society' which had been 'fomented by the great consumption conspiracy, which claims that as long as everyone increases both the quantity and the quality of what he consumes or acquires, the world must automatically become a better and a happier place'. The leader expressed the view that Ireland had escaped 'the worst excesses of this particular madness', but feared 'there are many signs that our happy immunity is drawing to a close'. However, the *Irish Times* rather undermined this plea for community and a sustainable economy, by following it with a leader on 'The Business of Pleasure', which explored the intimate relationship between a man and his wine merchant. It advised, in the plummy voice of the wine snob: 'consumption has risen without, necessarily, an accompanying growth in knowledge and judgement'.

The idea of the leisure society was also gaining ground as disposable incomes allowed for more and more people not only to purchase television sets to receive programmes from British channels and the national service which began broadcasting in 1962, but the funds to buy long-playing records and to attend concerts and musical entertainments. The roles of film, television and music critics in the journalistic world were becoming markedly more significant in a period of new electronic media. The young people with their transistor radios in Montague's poem 'Patriotic Suite', with which we began this chapter, were certainly tuning in to such stations as Radio Luxembourg and the pirate station Radio Caroline with their diet of pop music. Among their parents there was an increasing audience for classical music which the vinyl disc and the gramophone made available in high quality sound. Among the *Irish Times* critics of this period who were responding to how culture in the 1960s was increasingly being consumed electronically were Ken Gray on television, Fergus Linehan on film and Bill Meek on folk and traditional Irish music. Charles Acton, the paper's classical music critic, who began work on a freelance basis in the 1950s, was perhaps the *Irish Times* critic who most effectively made his position in the paper in the 1960s a platform for influencing public taste and arts policy (the lack of a dedicated concert hall in Dublin was an obsessive concern). Acton's reviews of the many concerts he attended in Dublin and around the country were informative, opinionated, sometimes wounding to artistic egos (though he was enthusiastically supportive of the young Irish musical talent that was emerging in the 1960s (Pine 2010, pp. 301–2 *passim*). His regular record column brought to the reviewing of recorded music the kind of professionalism and knowledge of a wide field that readers had come to depend upon in the literary pages.

Fortunately, Acton's own taste was catholic; for it would have been difficult for a purist with an Anglo-Irish background such as his to have become the paper's 'official' apostle for classsical music. A regard for classical music had until the 1940s been almost completely associated in Ireland with the alien Ascendancy caste (though it had in fact made only a scant contri- bution to the European canon). Traditional music, enjoying a revival in the 1960s, was considered by many to be the expression of national authenticity. Acton was capable of celebrating both and other kinds of music too. Yet his caustic, colourful turns of phrase and frank judgements made his columns frequently controversial (they drew angry letters to the editor). Even when in broad approval of an artistic institution, he could not resist pawky humour which inevitably disconcerted its subjects. So he could report in April 1965, in the first of three articles on the Dublin Feis Ceoil, that the annual festival which the paper's earlier music critic, Annie Patterson, had helped to found, was, as it stood, 'extremely valuable' as a 'focus of interest for all sorts of diverse musicians who might not otherwise come together' (*Irish Times*, 20 April 1965); nonetheless, he feared that the Feis risked becoming moribund, in terms that surely gave offence:

> This is a time when the whole festival impetus is under fire and when there is an urgent need for its leadership in our musical life. At this time the Feis Ceoil appears to many people like an old lady wintering in a sea-side boarding house, trying to live as much as possible as she did in the past and regretting that the value of her income is steadily declining.

Acton's musical catholicity even extended to the pop music that was an expression of the youth culture that was helping to define the 1960s as a decade in the English-speaking world. For in an article in 1964, on where a concert hall might be sited in Dublin, Acton accepted 'music is not only symphonies and quartets; it is also brass bands and Clancys and fesieanna and light music shows and jazz and Hootenanny and even Beatles' (*Irish Times*, 12 May 1964). Not all contributors to the paper shared Acton's tolerance. The spectacle of Beatlemania, following a concert by the 'fab four' in Dublin in November 1963, drew from the paper a dyspeptic leader entitled 'The Death Watch'. The writer alluded to Juvenal's satires to reassure readers that explanations for 'youthful depravity' were as ancient as Rome itself, but laid the blame for such excesses on the 'older generation ... who feed children with the wretched mental food on which their minds live' (*Irish Times*, 9 November 1963). For 'the money makers' had 'discovered an enormous market. As travellers long ago bartered beads for jewels with savages, so do these enterprising people put out films, records and television programmes which youth pays for.'

Subsequent reportage on the effects of pop music on the young tended to emphasize 'hysteria' and mass emotion. A distinct snobbishness could be detected in some reactions to 60s' youth culture. Fergus Linehan, for example, reviewing the Beatles' film *A Hard Day's Night* in 1964, commented on how the Liverpudlians gave out 'with that deflating, mocking sham humour of the sort that can be heard, for instance, on the cheap side of Dalymount Park' (*Irish Times*, 27 July 1964), home of Bohemians, a Dublin soccer team. When The Rolling Stones appeared in Dublin in January 1965, a report reckoned their act amounted to 'gymnastics and noise' (*Irish Times*, 7 January 1965). Quidnunc in 'An Irishman's Diary' added a sexist note in May 1964, to reportage on indigenous popular music, when he described 'an outfit called the Royal Showband', in performance in Dublin in 1964, as seven figures who 'leap about the stage, jerking convulsively and yelling at the top of their lungs, while antiphonally, little girls in the auditorium screech in unison a couple of octaves above high C' (*Irish Times*, 9 May 1964). It was the paper's freelance jazz critic George D. Hodnett, who had the insight to sense that the times were a-changing in more fundamental ways. 'Bob Dylan is a phenomenon,' he began a review of a concert in Dublin by the American singer/musician. Neither Dylan's voice nor his musicianship impressed Hodnett (whose markedly bohemian dishevelment disguised a sharp intelligence), but he grasped that 'Mr Dylan is a poet, and that though he might be but a minor one were he to publish in slim volumes without the assistance of guitar, harmonica and publicity machine, it is something to sell poetry to a mass audience at all' (*Irish Times*, 6 May 1966). Hodnett concluded: 'this isn't music, but something else; something sociologically interesting even after allowing for the admen, and anyway, a man who can write such a line as "like a fire in the sun" whatever it means, has something'.

If the *Irish Times* in the 1960s was scarcely tuned to rock and roll, 'The Death Watch' leader spoke censoriously of how the young had been 'given opportunities for self-indulgence that their fathers never knew. In thousands of homes Radio Luxembourg is blaring out the "Top Twenty" tunes and children are sitting with their ears glued to transistors or their eyes glued to the "telly".' In many ways, however, the paper had adjusted to an Ireland that was undergoing genuine change. Certainly the newspaper's improved economic performance (once the incubus of the *Evening Mail* was exorcized and Major Thomas McDowell, with his sound business acumen, was in place as joint managing director from November 1962 onwards) evidenced its attractiveness to a wider readership. Circulation figures rose 'between 1962 and 1966 to over 44,000 copies a day' (Mark O'Brien 2008, p. 177), where they had at best been averaging about about 30,000 when Gageby took over. Indeed, the company was sufficiently well funded to survive even the fraught labour relations of the period which had a direct effect on the newspaper industry when a printers' strike closed down the national press for 13 weeks in 1965. James Downey, who joined the staff of the *Irish Times* in 1960, has provided a warm and astute assessment of the newspaper's standing in the 1960s under Gageby's innovative editorship:

> In many ways, the *Irish Times* epitomised the spirit of the age. It sat on a tripod composed of these elements: the perception that it had retained the standards of the past while shaking off the less desirable parts of its unionist and 'West British' background; Gageby's overwhelming person-ality, combined with his integrity and his eccentric but attractive political views, and its enthusiastic campaign for a new and more liberal Ireland.

All these came together in a way that gave it a unique status in Irish journalism and something of an international reputation. Along with the exceptional talents of the journalists, they made it almost, but not quite, a great newspaper. (Downey 2009, p. 103)

Perhaps the most surprising claim here is that the *Irish Times* was gaining an international reputation. At the beginning of the decade its very survival had been in doubt (no dividend was paid to shareholders from 1960 to 1964). By 1968 an American, Harvard-educated writer who had worked as a foreign correspondent for *Time* and *Life* magazines, in his book on the new Ireland that had emerged in the 1960s, could claim with a real chance of being believed: 'it is possible to assert that, in terms of constructive impact on its particular community of readers, the *Irish Times* is the most influential newspaper in the British Isles' (Connery 1968, p. 248). He continued: 'for an outside observer seeking knowledge of contemporary Ireland, it is absolutely indispensable'. The newspaper had become national inasmuch as it was hard to think of the country without it.

8

THE *IRISH TIMES*, THE NORTH AND A EUROPEAN IRELAND

I
n the spring of 1966 Faber and Faber published in London a first collection by a young County Derry poet, then resident in Belfast. Entitled *Death of a Naturalist*, it contained 'Docker', a poem, which, in cartoonish, stereotypical images, it must be said, lampooned the Protestant industrial proletariat of the city:

> There, in the corner, staring at his drink.
> The cap juts like a gantry's crossbeam,
> Cowling plated forehead and sledgehead jaw.
> Speech is clamped in the lips' vice.
>
> (Heaney, 1966, p. 41)

The second stanza began ominously: 'That fist would drop a hammer on a Catholic –/Oh yes, that kind of thing could start again' (Heaney 1966, p. 41). The poem in fact dates from 1963 (Parker 1994, p. 71) the year after the IRA called off the failed border campaign it had begun in 1956. Sectarian tensions in Belfast had been heightened during those years of threatened and actual violence; by 1966, however, when Seamus Heaney published 'Docker' in *Death of a Naturalist*, hopes were being widely entertained that sectarianism, violence and the gun were being removed from Irish politics. The free trade agreement with the United Kingdom had reset the relationship between the Irish Republic and its immediate neighbour which had involved so much friction in the recent past. It was generally accepted that the future for both countries lay in simultaneous accession to the European Economic Community, when the French president, Charles de Gaulle could no longer exercise his veto on British membership (on 8 April 1966 an *Irish Times* editorial stated bluntly, 'Nobody can seriously question the need for Britain ultimately to join the Common Market; or the need for Ireland, Denmark and Norway to follow suit'). In that context a dispute about a border on the island of Ireland would, it could be expected, fade into insignificance. However, in the review of Heaney's volume the *Irish Times* carried in May 1966 , by his fellow Northerner and poet Michael Longley, it was suggested that 'Many of these poems seem like attempts at exorcism' (*Irish Times*, 24 May 1966). Events would prove that the spirit of communal strife, detected by Heaney in his satiric poem, had not been banished in Northern Ireland. but remained at hand for the right voice to summon it.

Eighteen months earlier the auspices in Ireland, north and south, had looked more propitious. For in January 1965 Taoiseach Seán Lemass had broken through the walls of republican nationalist ideology by paying a visit to the Northern parliament building at Stormont in Belfast, there to meet the recently installed prime minister, Captain Terence O'Neill. The purpose was improved relations and co-operation between the two parts of the island, expressed in the hyper-cautious language of diplomacy as 'matters in which there may be the possibility of a degree of common interest'. The *Irish Times*'s response to what it designated a 'coup', in face of anticipated opposition from unionists and from republicans, was to state that the 'unqualified good wishes of everyone in Ireland should go out' to both men. A hint of euphoria coloured the editorial prose: 'No doubt, both men, in the next few days, will realise that they have underestimated their countrymen and that such criticism as arises will be drowned in the chorus of approval. The meeting has caught the imagination of people far beyond our shores ...' (*Irish Times*, 15 January 1965).

If the young Seamus Heaney in 1966 feared the possibility of violence in Belfast, there were those in the southern capital who had been prepared to remind citizens there that advocates of physical force still had the means to challenge Lemass's pragmatism about Northern Ireland, about relations with the United Kingdom and about new European alignments. Early on the Tuesday morning of 8 March a powerful bomb damaged the Nelson Pillar in O'Connell Street, Dublin. This monument had stood almost opposite the General Post Office, where the Republic of Ireland had been declared 50 years before. This act of violence and vandalism (the pillar was a focal point at the heart of city) was clearly designed to send a message. The government did not own the revolutionary tradition of 1916 which was to be honoured on the fiftieth anniversary of the Easter Rising the following month. Nor could it assume that the abandonment in 1962 of the IRA campaign was the end of armed action by paramilitaries. There were those who had their own hopes for an alternative Irish future than that which Lemass envisaged. The pure 32-county republic declared in 1916 still remained to be delivered.

The next day the *Irish Times* published an editorial on the event entitled 'Splinter Group' (assuming in its word-play that it was a small republican gang who had planted the explosives). The writer drolly regretted the loss of the monument as another example of the city's indifference to its architectural heritage: 'there is a tradition to ignore aesthetic considerations when something is to be blown up in Dublin. No people have more gaily blown away their heritage in stone' (*Irish Times*, 9 March 1966). More sombrely, the writer reflected: 'If the spirit of 1916 is represented ... by the blowing up of the Pillar, it is, indeed, a spirit that suggests the sowing of dragon's teeth.' And a blow had been struck against the authority of the government by 'this coup in the heart of the capital city'. Two days later, the *Irish Times* reminded its readers that what had happened was no laughing matter, even though there had been no casualties other than the admiral himself. It angrily denounced 'this tactic, which the most primitive emergent nation could hardly equal' (*Irish Times*, 11 March 1966) as it advised, given the challenge posed by what it termed 'groups of dissidents', that the paper did not hold 'any brief for the view that the 1916 celebrations should in any way be curtailed or amended'.

Curiously enough, the Dublin bomb, which the *Irish Times* strenuously deprecated, afforded the paper an opportunity not only to display its nationalist credentials (it took umbrage on behalf of the nation at how dissidents had infringed on its sovereignty), but to signal its support for the elected Irish government and for its programme of events to be staged in commemoration and celebration of the Easter Rising. For an editorial staff who must have been perfectly aware of how their paper had responded to the insurrection in 1916, the March explosion allowed the paper to position itself in the public domain as a loyal inheritor and defender of a republican tradition it had formerly excoriated, which now held legitimate power in the land.

With this adroitly managed in these two editorials, the *Irish Times* chose to publish a special 16-page section of the paper on the Easter Rising on 7 April, two days before the two weeks of planned state ceremonials began. Perhaps this is indicative of the editor's concern that his paper's mature appreciation of the Irish past should receive thoughtful consideration before the commemoration itself became the focus of journalistic attention. Be that as it may, Gageby's editorial on the same day, 'Call of the Past', was a personal statement of his own creed of United Irish republicanism and a summons to statesmanship on the issue of partition.

For Gageby, the fiftieth anniversary was a chance to assess how much the 50 years since the Rising had given true expression to Wolfe Tone's United Ireland desire in the 1790s to 'abolish the differences of Catholic, Dissenter and Protestant, and to substitute the common name of Irishman' (*Irish Times*, 7 April 1966). Apart from the Irish government's 'feeling for the religious susceptibilities of those of Tone's persuasion' (Tone was a Protestant by social formation), Gageby judged the achievement in that regard had been 'lamentable'. What exercised him was that neither government nor people had really taken seriously the settled will of the Northern Protestant community to resist incorporation into an all-Ireland polity.

In adopting this stance Gageby was in fact echoing what the *Irish Times* had, as we saw, stated cogently enough in the 1950s, even if he was less outspoken about how some Irish laws were not conducive to liberalism. However, where he differed from Robert Smyllie and even Alec Newman was that he was fervently committed to the unity of the country and ready to do his part in peacefully bringing it about. He believed the two parts of the island needed each other and that 'the tide' was 'with those' who favoured 'the unity of the country'.

A good deal has been written by those who worked with him about Gageby's almost visceral Anglophobia (evident to a degree in his encomium for Belfast, quoted in the last chapter) and his instinctive lack of sympathy for Northern Unionist politicians. In this editorial, however, he showed himself, while scornful of their past manoeuvres, at least capable of discerning how unionists' current position (with Harold Wilson's Labour government in London not enamoured of the Ulster Unionist Party and unenthusiastic about the union itself) was a difficult one. He commented: 'The Northern Government, with the present Administration in Britain likely to be well entrenched for a long time to come, is in many ways in an invidious position. It is a corner from which it is hoped it will be helped out, rather than blasted out.' The note of republican disdain, it is true, accompanied this appreciation of unionist difficulty ('Not again can the Unionists do a Carson manoeuvre. No German kaiser or princelings are available'), yet the editorial concluded with a wise awareness that the immediate days of commemoration ahead held both hope and peril for the country.

The special supplement on the Easter Rising was a substantial document (subsequently published in book form in 1968), which drew on a cohort of well-informed commentators and respected academics. The impression created collectively was of a balanced, considered assessment, together with underlying respect for the polity that had emerged in the early twentieth century, with 1916 as a foundational event. This in itself was an achievement, since it brought an event that could still inflame old and some not-so-old wounds within a field of professional reflection. Trinity College political scientist Basil Chubb's sober conclusion in his article, for example, that the momentous occurrences of revolution and state formation had produced an 'Ireland ... well provided with an adequate range of tried forms of administrative organisation' was unlikely to stir the blood as the nation remembered a blood sacrifice, but it could give welcome perspective to debates about a past that in many respects was still a matter for heated contention.

Two articles, in particular, broke the measured, senior common room judiciousness of the supplement as a whole. Desmond FitzGerald, former Free State government minister, who had been among the rebels in the Post Office in 1916, contributed a vivid account of how Patrick Pearse and other leaders had behaved as the event unfolded. He reported how Pearse 'talked of the Rising as a glorious thing in itself, without reference to what it might or might not achieve in the light of the position at the moment' (*Irish Times*, 7 April 1966). He and Joseph Mary Plunkett, as defeat awaited them, had talked of installing a German prince as an Irish figurehead 'after the English were beaten'. For the man they had in mind, Prince Joachim, could be depended upon to endorse a policy of de-Anglicization through support for the revival of Gaelic, since 'the non-nationalist element' in Irish society 'had shown themselves to be so bitterly anti-German'. Conor Cruise O'Brien, in his own piece of historical fantasizing, pondered on what might have happened had the rebels waited until 1918 to launch their assault on the British Empire. Had they postponed their premature rebellion until that year, in the conditions then pertaining, he reckoned, 'it was reasonable to assume that ... the revolutionary leaders could have brought about an insurrection' which might have altered world history. Not content with indicting the heroes of 1916 with a mistiming of epic proportions, O'Brien, in withering terms, went on to imagine how the 1916 martyrs might judge the Ireland of 1966. He observed, 'What would come as a painful surprise would be the ease with which this position is accepted, the fact that nobody anywhere, by any means, is seriously trying to bring about the political reunification of the country.' What he dubbed the 'bourgeois, bread and butter terms' of the country's actual polity, he saw as a necessary flouting of the ideals of 1916 consequent on the fact that 'it was the primary misfortune of the Irish State that from the very beginning of its existence constituted a violation of the principles of its formation'. As a result, he argued, his generation was burdened by a sense of failure, for, as he put it, 'we were bred to be patriotic, only to find there was nothing to be patriotic about; we were republicans of a republic that wasn't there'. For O'Brien, the Irish State was 'culturally part of Britain, distinguished from the rest of the archipelago mainly by its practice of a Puritanical form of the Roman Catholic religion and a marked deference to ecclesiastical authority'. And 'In Dublin this week,' he could not resist announcing, 'are held the funeral ceremonies of the Republic declared 50 years ago.'

On the face of it such an assault on national piety could easily have been dismissed by readers as an attempt by an intellectual maverick to épater la bourgeoisie. The fact was, however, that O'Brien, in writing in this way, was engaging in what many would have considered gross sacrilege. What a few might have considered healthy revisionism, many others would have seen as the objectionable breaking of a taboo.

O'Brien's article attracted some critical correspondence, but these letters concentrated in the main on his attack on clericalism in a deficient education system, which his article had also contained. One correspondent, however, surmised that epistolary silence on his major theme signalled that he had in truth touched a raw nerve. Ethna Viney commented: 'It would seem that the closer a writer gets to the heart of our national problems, the more reluctant is the public to commit either for or against' (Irish Times, 20 April 1966). On 24 April, as the paper reported the next day, President de Valera consecrated the Garden of Remembrance in Dublin as 'Holy Ground'. Curiously, as if a fortnight of nationalist self-regard had soured it somewhat, the Irish Times chose to dedicate its leading article to a defence of the novelist Edna O'Brien (one of Mrs Grundy's recent Irish victims) and to remind readers of how his fellow countrymen and the state had treated James Joyce. 'Is not this,' the editorial queried, 'and the story of the treatment of other writers, a damning criticism, as damning as any made on the grounds of present inequality and lack of opportunity, on a State which owes its existence (as we have heard again and again in the last fortnight) to the sacrifice, above all, of a group of writers and poets?' (*Irish Times*, 25 April 1966). Proof indeed, if proof were needed, that Gageby's newspaper had sharp liberal teeth and was still willing to bare them.

True to his anti-partitionism, Gageby, from the earliest days of his editorship, had focused the *Irish Times* more intently on events and developments north of the border than any of his predecessors had done. He took seriously that the country was geographically and historically one entity, partition being a temporary infraction of that reality. An Irish newspaper should, therefore, be consciously anti-partitionist in its all-island mindset and purview. One of Gageby's innovations was to give more than ample space to parliamentary reports from Stormont, where debates did not scintillate and the topics discussed in a body that reflected a unionist hegemony were often picayune. Questioned about this in 1984, Gageby told how he had been challenged by a Northern businessman about the fact that 'the North' became newsworthy for the *Irish Times* only 'when it concerned a rise in unemployment, or some particularly virulent outbreak on the part of a politician' (Kearney 1984, p. 14). His determination to report on proceedings in Stormont, despite warnings from several Belfast journalists that '"There is nothing coming out of this place ... It's not much more than a county council"'(Kearney 1984, p. 14), was based on his conviction that 'It was part of trying to say: this is a paper for the whole of Ireland. Stormont was an Assembly of Irish men and women debating on Irish soil. We were inviting people to read what they had to say. It was slice of Irish life' (Kearney 1984, p. 14).

To give effect to his determination that the paper should cover Northern Ireland in depth, Gageby appointed Fergus Pyle as northern editor in 1967. Pyle was the Trinity College-educated son of a English literature don in that university. He himself had graduated in modern languages, with German as a principal subject. A period at Freiburg University had made him fluent in that language. In 1961, after a period working for Aer Lingus (Mark O'Brien 2008, p. 335), Pyle joined the staff of the *Irish Times*. It was he who had put together, as special features editor, the paper's 1916 supplement and co-edited the subsequent book with the historian Owen Dudley Edwards. Gageby, in the interview cited above, claimed that Pyle and he 'had very similar views on the north' (*The Crane Bag*, 1984). Be that as it may, Pyle brought to reportage and the analysis of political and social life in Northern Ireland a journalist's insatiable curiosity, along with an academic's capacity to understand a situation in a larger historical context. He had the instincts of the reporter for a story, yet his writing was sometimes marked by an earnest thoroughness that was off-putting for *Irish*

Times readers south of the border, for whom 'the North' was terra incognita and who wanted it to stay that way (Gageby had included among his reasons for emphasizing Northern news a desire 'to show the so-and-sos down below what was going on'. In his persistent way Pyle would rub their noses in it.

Nobody in 1967, when Pyle took up residence in Belfast, could quite have realized how quickly (though Seamus Heaney, like others, was issuing his warnings) Northern Ireland would become a place with more than enough going on to make it an international news story, that in sporadic fashion would demand the attention of the world's media for more than three decades. Pyle's early reports gave copious details about matters discussed at Stormont, such as cross-border electrification and drainage schemes, but there were also more concerning developments to record. Questions were raised about the Northern government's housing policy. A ban on parades was announced to prevent commemoration of the 1867 Fenian Rising. They went ahead anyway, as Pyle reported. The visit of Princess Margaret, sister of the Queen of England, along with her photographer husband Anthony Armstrong-Jones, the Earl of Snowdon, in May 1967 gave the northern editor the chance to try a little colour journalism among his sober reports. He painted a telling picture: 'However it was worked – it was cautiously felt in official quarters that the sun came out in answer to prayer – the lawns at Government House at Hillsborough had all the qualities of Edwardian sunset that are evoked by a garden party' (*Irish Times*, 25 May 1967). But like a summer party in 1914, there was anxiety in the air and disturbing noises off when a lorry backfired, to the consternation of the police and guests. A sense of normality was restored in Pyle's report by the less than riveting information that the royal couple would that day be visiting a shoe factory in Banbridge.

By the autumn, however, the Minister of Home Affairs in the North was insisting in parliament that all was not 'as quiet as it seems', for subversive activity was still being carried out, and Captain O'Neill felt it necessary to defend the Union in no uncertain terms. He was adamant, aware of dissenting, suspicious unionist elements within and without his own party, that entry into the EEC could not affect the border between North and South. Haughtily dismissive of the 'Republic's tariffs on cat-food and cardboard boxes', he assured the faithful, in a debate on the implications for Northern Ireland's putative membership of the Common Market: 'those who saw Europe as the setting for a united Ireland were following an old time-worn path of self-delusion. Let me say it quite clearly and firmly, for all the world to hear and understand: Ulster – whether within the European Community or outside it – will remain British' (*Irish Times*, 15 November 1967). Readers in the Republic could have noted the confident tone, but could also have wondered about the speaker's certitude.

Nineteen sixty-eight was a year in which certainties everywhere would be disturbed, testing a newspaper's ability to report on a global scale and challenging it to hone its political responses. The Tet offensive at the end of

January raised disturbing questions about the US role in Vietnam which came to the fore in a presidential campaign in America in a year that saw the assassination of the civil rights leader Martin Luther King and of the presidential candidate Robert Kennedy, brother of the president slain in 1963. In France, in the spring, de Gaulle's presidential authority was challenged by enormous student protests and a nationwide strike, while later in the summer the experiment of 'communism with a human face', was crushed by a brutal invasion of Czechoslovakia mounted by the Soviet Union.

The *Irish Times* saw the Tet offensive as near-definitive evidence that US policy in Vietnam would lead to costly failure. An *Irish Times* editorial entitled 'Naked Power' on 1 February advised: 'The assumption that American material resources are bottomless is one of the most notable casualties of the present ordeal' (*Irish Times*, 1 February 1968) and judged, that although the offensive had been repelled, 'there is no doubt that, at the moment, the Communists are psychologically and militarily the masters of Vietnam. At no stage, since the war began, could as much be said for the baroque combination of the South Vietnamese soldier-politicians, the Americans and their allies.' This acerbic commentary on the progress of the war was accompanied by a certain almost amused condescension about the United States itself. Not exactly anti-American, the editorial could appear to be taking a certain anti-imperial pleasure in seeing a super-power discomfited: 'The British lion – now retired – knows what it is like to have his tail twisted: and now the American eagle is having a few of his pin-feathers plucked. It is a disagreeable experience but, for that reason, it may be salutary.' And the writer (the style, combining high sentence with near jocularity, suggests that it was Gageby himself) even had a cultural explanation for America's anti-communist zeal that had brought it to near-defeat in South-east Asia: 'The American conscience, by and large, is a Puritan conscience: salvation comes through suffering, and the Plymouth Rock is the foundation stone on which a national and international concept of morality is based.' A further leading article on the imbroglio in Vietnam took up this theme two weeks later, though in wholly censorious tones. Entitled 'The War of Morality', the leader took the US president to task:

> President Johnson still sees the Vietnam war as a moral crusade. This is the concept that has twisted the American intervention from the beginning. It is what is responsible for the crisis with which the United States is now faced, and which will end by destroying a country and a people for their own 'good'. In addition, the war in Vietnam has involved the progressive discrediting of American judgment along the entire chain of political and military command. (*Irish Times*, 14 February 1968)

An editorial of 26 February, however, 'Where Do We Stand?', abandoned tones of European condescension and condemnation of a simplistic transatlantic world-view, for a blunt demand that the Irish government should make its position clear on continued American belligerence against North Vietnam. Government and citizen alike should shake off pusillanimity in respect of US power and vociferously protest against Johnson's war.

In its editorial on 'Naked Power' of 1 February, the *Irish Times* had observed how the Russians had been humiliated over Cuba and that it was 'no coincidence' that there had 'been more realism in their behaviour since then' (*Irish Times*, 1 February 1968); this implied that the writer nursed the hope that a humiliation in Vietnam might subdue America's dangerous idealism. The Soviet invasion of Czechoslovakia in August 1968 tragically indicated there were strict limits to Soviet realism, however acquired.

An editorial the day after this shocking event on European soil could not but denounce Soviet folly: 'The invasion of Czechoslovakia by the Russians and their East European bondsmen must be condemned' (*Irish Times*, 22 August 1968). It must also be 'interpreted', the editorial entitled 'Claws Out' insisted. Concluding that the Russians had 'made fools of themselves at the cruel expense of the Czechoslovaks', the *Irish Times* considered the effect the invasion might have on Western opinion. The writer regretted the ammunition Soviet stupidity had given to reactionaries everywhere. They were acting in self-defence because it was necessary to do so. On 23 August the paper gave extensive space to an analysis by Owen Dudley Edwards to reinforce this point on how the Soviet action would adversely affect world politics. The day's front-page headline reported that the Soviets might already have decided on the membership of a Czechoslovak puppet government. Edwards's main concern was the effect of Russian folly on 'the World Left'. Like his editor, he feared that it would give comfort to reactionaries: 'It strengthens the appeal of right-wing elements in the United States' (*Irish Times*, 23 August 1968). Nonetheless, Edwards believed that the exemplary courage of the Czechs in the face of repression would inspire what he identified as the New Left generation of young activists in many countries, with students to the fore, who had been radicalized in part by the capacity of television quickly to spread disillusionment about authority. 'Television,' he observed, had 'proved a Frankenstein to the power elite'.

The *Irish Times* had already stated its view on student protest as a contemporary phenomenon, when in May it had greeted the riots at the Sorbonne in Paris with sympathetic understanding:

> Student power, wherever it shows its muscles at present, has some recurring elements: a desire for more responsibility in academic administration, a distrust of the authorities from the Government downwards, the pain of frustrated idealism ... it would be a mistake to interpret these eruptions as signs of an integrated international conspiracy ... Basically, they are

expressions of protest against things as they are, and of hope turned in on itself. (*Irish Times*, 13 May 1968)

Its own report of *les événements* in Paris had, indeed, highlighted how the riots pitched 1960s' youth, with its uninhibited aspirations, in conflict with inflexible state power, in a scenario made for television: 'As they were bombarded with tear-gas grenades, the students, at least half of them mini-skirted girls, replied with bricks, cobbles, firecrackers and chairs snatched from the cafés' (*Irish Times*, 7 May 1968). The paper's Paris correspondent, Dermot Mullane, deprecated the 'seemingly unnecessary and brutal manner in which the police [had] sought to crush the demonstrations' (*Irish Times*, 13 May 1968).

Similar reports of student unrest in 1968 came from West Germany and Japan. In the United States the Democratic Party's Chicago Convention in August brought the hippie and yippie phenomena, with their counter-cultural flourishes, to international attention. On 30 August, under the headline 'Michigan Ave. is Running with Blood', the paper carried a report of how 'An estimated 3,000 young demonstrators – New Leftists, college enthusiasts, yippies, hippies, Black Panthers – sprawled in the cold grass of Grant Park while 800 guardsmen with guns at port arms formed a line between them and the Conrad Hilton across Michigan Avenue' (*Irish Times*, 30 August 1968). Reports, too, of student participation in the Civil Rights movement in America increased the sense that there was a new generation on the move, at one in its instinct for personal and political freedom, opposed by implacable state power.

In 1956 the *Irish Times*'s astute radio and television critic G. A. Olden had identified television's unique capacity, as a bearer of information, to deliver an illusion of unmediated reality. He pointed to the interest in 'seeing things happening' as the medium's 'unique strength' and noted how in interviews with refugees at the Hungarian border during the crisis of that year, 'ruthless television cameras missed nothing, expatiated nothing'. 'Nothing but television,' he accepted as a print journalist, 'could have given so vivid a sense of the immediacy of these Hungarians' plight' (*Irish Times*, 15 November 1956). In 1968 and early 1969, as television flashed images of youth in rebellion around the world, Ireland would also find itself caught up in a media revolution, whereby the television camera became almost integral with the events it covered, challenging the other media by its apparent capacity visually to serve up raw experience. Northern Ireland was where such televisual reportage would have international impact as the issue of civil rights entered the public arena there in radical ways.

In the mid- to late 1960s opposition to the unionist hegemony in Northern Ireland became less focused on the border and on the demand for reunification of the country than on the achievement of full civil rights in the six counties themselves. On 5 October 1968 a banned civil rights march in Derry went ahead in spite of its prohibition. It met with a violent police response, television images of which became almost instantaneously available to TV screens in many countries. Soon after this, an attack in January 1969 by loyalist thugs on a poorly policed civil rights march by a radical student group, named People's Democracy, made the Northern statelet seem televisually the repulsive equivalent of racist Alabama or Arkansas. By August 1969 significant sections of the Northern Catholic minority were in open insurrection, with the local police force unable to enter the Bogside district of Derry, where young men and women confronted them with barricades and waves of stone-throwing. The images of a working-class community defying the armed Royal Ulster Constabulary, that defiance led by a mini-skirted firebrand in the person of Bernadette Devlin, ex-psychology student, People's Democracy founder-member and recently elected socialist member of the Westminster parliament at the tender age of 21, completed a quintessential 1960s' image of state power arrayed against the youthful vanguard of a necessary rebellion.

The *Irish Times*'s response to the RUC suppression of the civil rights march in October 1968 drew attention to how television was changing the context of newspaper reportage. Its editorial of 7 October observed: 'The B.B.C. is but one of the news disseminators which has brought home to the people of Britain that there is something rotten much nearer home than Rhodesia [then the focus of British government concern]' (*Irish Times*, 7 October 1968). The next day a 'London Letter' commented on how, through television, it was implied for 'the very first time, the average person is being made aware of conditions in Northern Ireland'. On 10 October Ken Gray in his television review column described how 'The most nauseating moment of the week' was the images coming from Derry on to the nation's screens. He caught the visceral intensity of on-screen violence as he wrote: 'The closer to home these brutal incidents, the more revolting they seem. Almost more unbearable is the sound track with its wailing and screaming, its half-heard shouts and curses and grunts of pain' (*Irish Times*, 10 October 1968). And on the evening of 11 October, television audiences in Britain had the opportunity to see how the passions of the street translated to the studios of the chat show, providing the kind of dramatically immediate commentary on events print could not match. ITV's *Frost Show* was devoted that evening to the emerging Northern crisis. The normally adroit host David Frost, in Ken Gray's words, was confronted by 'a studio full of partisans all literally shouting for attention'. He commented that the programme 'must have been one of the noisiest and most argumentative 45 minutes ever watched by British audiences' (*Irish Times*, 12 October 1968). Only an Irish journalist named Mary Holland, who worked for the *Guardian* newspaper, seemed capable of informed coherence. That Saturday, a week after the events north of the border, Backbencher with ponderous irony observed: 'I loved the general picture of strong government which we witnessed' (*Irish Times*, 12 October 1968).

Reports filed from Derry by Fergus Pyle on police brutality suggest that he was aware that TV was supplying vivid imagery of events in the city. The measured earnestness of much of his Northern coverage gave way to frank description and blunt disgust at what he had seen. In a report entitled 'An Old City Faces a New Sorrow' he described how for 'a quarter of an hour on Saturday afternoon, police in a Derry Street punished, batoned and pursued civil rights demonstrators in a brutal and sickening display of what can only be called concerted violence' (*Irish Times*, 7 October 1968). The force's handling of the march's aftermath Pyle condemned as 'a gratuitous and, although one hates to say it, sadistic attack on people still in the streets'. And when People's Democracy was savagely attacked in January 1969 at Burntollet Bridge (near Claudy, Co. Derry) the paper published two pages of compelling photographs as if to compete visually with television's powers. By this time 'the North' had become a major story and Pyle was joined by journalists such as Henry Kelly, who would succeed him as northern editor, when Pyle took up a post as Paris correspondent for the paper in 1971.

The recrudescence of the 'troubles' in Northern Ireland (an *Irish Times* editorial used the term 'troubles' in the opening sentence of an editorial on the Northern situation on 12 October 1968) in 1968 and early 1969, which would intensify as the decade ended, posed significant challenges for the press in the Republic. Not only were they competing with the electronic media to which people turned for news and images of the latest atrocity, with television supplying the illusion of a grandstand seat at history in the making, they had to determine how they should address the issues involved. For television had the capacity to inflame public opinion in ways that could run counter to the country's interests; newspapers had a duty not only to report accurately but to analyse and inform (and there were those ready to stir the pot; on 9 October 1968 the *Irish Times*'s own columnist Claud Cockburn, doyen of the old anti-Fascist British Left, suggested that police action in Derry was part of an international pattern of such behaviour).

Gageby took it on himself to write major editorials on the Northern crisis as it intensified in late 1968 and early 1969. They were curious exercises in committed engagement combined with restraint, couched in his distinctively lapidary style. There was no doubting where the writer's sympathies lay (he had taken part in at least one civil rights march in Derry himself; Mark O'Brien 2008, p. 186) but a sense of historical perspective and man-of-the world *sang-froid* usually gave them an air of mature, even military, judiciousness being brought to bear on a dangerous situation. He could be blunt too. When the civil rights marchers were confronted by the RUC in Derry in October 1968 Gageby stated that an inquiry into police behaviour 'will help to uncover "the political cesspool"' (*Irish Times*, 7 October 1968) in that city. The editorial ended, however, with a plea that the Northern Ireland premier, Sir Terence O'Neill, would rise to the occasion:

It may not be easy for the Premier to ride roughshod over the sort of supporters upon whom he relies in Derry and elsewhere; but he is a civilised man, and he must be aware of the real significance of last Saturday. He has had a chance ... to go down in history as a great Irishman. Is it now too late?'

A further editorial, entitled 'Time to Give', saw the events in Derry that month as likely to revive violent anti-partitionism in the country and warned: 'If the present moment accelerates, we may indeed be back with bloodshed and tears, and there is no pretending that this is not so' (*Irish Times*, 10 October 1968). Gageby sensed, presciently as things tragically transpired, that what many at the time thought could be contained by resolute security policies and minor reforms, could develop into bloody conflict – 'a prospect ... too savage to contemplate'.

The loyalist attack on the People's Democracy march in January 1969 brought that prospect disturbingly close. It drew from the *Irish Times* an anti-imperialist, anti-Orange, Anglophobic broadside that should have dispelled finally any impression that the paper harboured pro-unionist sympathies. An editorial entitled 'Throw-Back' described how:

> The entry into Derry of the remnants of the student marchers was a sight to touch any heart; the slow grind of the police vans, the rows of steel-helmeted R.U.C., and then the students bloodied, bandaged, limping. Moral courage is rare enough in Northern politics; the positive lesson of the march – and there are others on the debit side – is that these representatives of the new generation were not afraid to stand up in the most adverse circumstances; then down the precipitous streets there came leaping, like hill tribesmen out of Kipling, a posse armed with clubs and flags; and the stone-throwing began again. (*Irish Times*, 6 January 1969)

Those who saw anarchists, revolutionaries and republicans among the students were reminded: 'Anarchy is an old word in the Orange handbook'; and that the origin of what had happened was to be found in nineteenth-century political opportunism in England:

> ... the last few days have ... been a sickening throw-back. Sectarian strife is not ... the result of partition. It has been there for a much longer time. Sectarianism was given its modern momentum with Lord Randolph's famous Orange Card. The lords and lawyers made their speeches on Irish soil and then went back to swap stories over the brandy and port. The respectability they gave to the old slogans helped to bring us decades later to the shameful attack on unarmed and unresisting boys and girls at Burntollet Bridge and elsewhere on Saturday.

Yet even this emotionally charged, accusatory broadside, restrainedly stated: 'The gun solves nothing. Northern Ireland needs people to work for the

country, not corpses', and concluded by advising continued nationalist participation at Stormont. It carefully advised:

> The fear that active participation in Stormont politics will bring forget-
> fulness of the ideal of a united country where all will enjoy the common
> name of Irishmen, irrespective of origin and religion has perhaps been
> over-emphasised ... At no time has the North more needed all the intel-
> ligence and effort that the opposition can muster ... Serious strife can most
> easily be taken out of Northern life by Government action.

When in August 1969 the Battle of the Bogside and serious civil disorder, riot
and attacks on domestic dwellings in Belfast brought British soldiers on to the
streets to aid the civil power in Northern Ireland, the *Irish Times* responded
with similar moderation, despite evident outrage about what had occurred. It
argued that events there (which would quickly result in deaths and injuries)
had become a national issue which demanded international attention through
the good offices of the United Nations. On the evening of 13 August the
Taoiseach Jack Lynch, leader of the Fianna Fáil government, had addressed the
nation on television in ambiguous terms when he stated:

> It is evident that the Stormont Government is no longer in control of
> the situation. Indeed the present situation is the inevitable outcome of
> the policies pursued for decades by successive Stormont Governments.
> It is clear, also, that the Irish Government can no longer stand by and see
> innocent people injured and perhaps worse. (*Irish Times*, 14 August 1969)

There were those, in the heated atmosphere of that August, ready to read in
Lynch's address a threat or promise of military action (though Lynch at the last
moment had removed the word 'idly' from his speech to read simply 'no longer
stand by'; this inevitably became known as his 'stand idly by' statement) by the
Irish state north of the border and an encouragement for independent action
in defence of Northern Catholics. Others wanted support for a more general
assault on the Orange state. On 15 August, for example, a London correspondent
reported that that city's Regional Executive of the Northern Irish Civil Rights
Association had demanded that Lynch 'open the arsenals of the Irish Republic to
the people of Northern Ireland' (*Irish Times*, 15 August 1969). On the same day
the call from the Union of Students in Ireland for young people and students,
if they were free, to go north to join 'this first stage of the struggle for the final
settlement of the Irish question', received coverage in the paper.

An editorial, 'Another Plane', on 14 August rightly discerned that Lynch's
television address was no call to arms, but expressed a determination on his
part, which Gageby himself supported, to keep political options open with
Harold Wilson's British government which might be receptive to a negotiated
'settlement to the Irish question'. In an editorial the next day, entitled 'Sign of

Concern', the editor sought to scotch rumours (which north of the border Ian Paisley had fallen upon as proof of southern pervidy) of Irish troops massing for action. Such manoeuvres as were taking place, the old army man told his readers, could easily be attributed to the decision to place field hospitals south of the border to receive any injured victims of Northern strife as might present themselves. And the editorial asserted: 'It is ... the hope of everyone who wishes to see this country united again that Irishmen will not take up arms against each other' (*Irish Times*, 15 August 1969).

Reading Gageby's editorials written at the outset of the Northern troubles, one is struck by how they express fervent national feeling and republican inspiration, and exhibit a penchant for 'undiplomatic' frankness (on 16 August Gageby dubbed the suggestion that Ian Paisley might be included in a Northern Irish cabinet a 'lunatic possibility' and accused Harold Wilson of bearing responsibility for 'inequalities and injustices which would shame a Franco'). A recurrent theme of his in August and September 1969 was repugnance at the spectacle of unionist folly as it sought to respond to the crisis it faced. On 26 August an editorial, entitled 'What the Taoiseach Could be Saying' uttered the following judgement: 'The Unionist game is up – at any rate, in its more blatant aspects. This became evident as soon as the civil rights campaign got well under way. A government which could not accommodate itself to reasonable, humanitarian demands except under pressure was an anachronism' (*Irish Times*, 26 August 1969). However, accompanying expressions of concerned national feeling, distaste for unionism and for the malign influence of the Orange order on Northern politics (which at this time effectively caught the confused public mood south of the border about 'the North') was a scrupulous, principled opposition to the use of arms as a means to attain an all-Ireland republic.

In May 1970, arms, their alleged illegal importation and possible use, would seem to pose a direct challenge to Ireland's democracy greater than anything that had occurred since the Civil War. That apparent challenge proved that standing by, idly or otherwise, was not a possibility for the Irish state as the Northern crisis intensified, for developments in Northern Ireland were directly affecting politics in the Republic at the highest level. It also posed the question in stark terms as to what actions the state should take in relation to events dramatically unfolding north of a shared border.

On 6 May 1970 readers awoke to *Irish Times* headlines that Jack Lynch had dismissed two of his most powerful cabinet members, Neil Blaney and Charles Haughey. A subheading to the front-page story filed by Andrew Hamilton indicated that 'deep differences over policy on Northern Ireland' (*Irish Times*, 6 May 1970) were the cause. Kevin Boland, another minister, had also tendered his resignation and it had been accepted. The editorial of that day, entitled 'The Breaking Point', sketched a picture of near-chaos at the heart of government. The news had come to the newspaper from the Government Information

Bureau in the early hours of the morning. A member of the Dáil had earlier visited the editorial office 'under the impression that the news had already been broken'. The *Irish Times* sounded a grim warning about a meeting of Fianna Fáil parliamentarians scheduled for that day, thinking that it could be 'as decisive as any similar gathering held since the end of the Civil War. Not alone does the discarding of three of its most powerful ministers have a devastating effect on the Government party: it has most serious implications for the peace of the whole country.' On the morning of a day in which rumour would run almost uncontrollably through Dublin (some even talked of a possible army coup), Gageby sought to give the impression of a man keeping a cool head. He commented: 'The effect of these resignations on the peace of Northern Ireland must be damaging; it need not be catastrophic.' And aware of Blaney's bellicose attitude to what Gageby termed 'the unity problem', and evidently surprised that Haughey (Backbencher's 'Golden Boy') was associating himself with that Donegal deputy's openly expressed, aggressive irredentism, Gageby gave a cautious endorsement to Jack Lynch. Lynch, advised by T. K. Whitaker, and after the summer of 1969 by two far-sighted officials, Eamonn Gallagher and Séan Ronan, had maintained since the outbreak of the 'troubles' that unity could be achieved only by peaceful means and unionist consent. Gageby stated at this moment of high drama and danger: 'The Taoiseach has acted – some will say at last, or almost too late. The Government approach to the Northern problem has, to all appearances, been generally welcomed in the country. He has the support of the other parties: he deserves sympathy.'

Sympathy for Lynch was in shorter supply in Gageby's editorial, entitled 'Loyalty', the following day. The front page on the morning of 7 May had informed readers that two government ministers had been party to an 'arms plan'. The Dáil had met the previous evening, and, as John Healy vividly put it, the assembly 'was crisis-crowded from Chamber floor to ceiling' (*Irish Times*, 7 May 1970). Elsewhere in the paper Andrew Hamilton reported how 'The Taoiseach, Mr Lynch, last night with emotional frankness accused his two former ministers, Mr Haughey and Mr Blaney, of the attempted illegal importation of arms from the continent.'

For decades the vexed questions as to who knew what about this decision to import arms and for what use they were intended have preoccupied journalists and historians, and public reputations have been profoundly affected by what people choose to believe about these matters as more and more evidence becomes available. The nub of the thing is how much Lynch and his Minister for Defence, James Gibbons, knew about what ministers were doing and whether he or Gibbons had in fact authorized their actions. Secondary to this were the questions of whether the arms were intended only for defensive purposes in the Northern Catholic areas of Derry and Belfast, or was something more sinister afoot whereby a revived IRA was to be given military hardware by a faction of the Dublin government. In January 1970 the Sinn Féin party had fractured into what became known as the 'Official' and 'Provisional' movements. The latter believed in strict parliamentary abstentionism and favoured armed struggle to end partition. As inter-communal strife intensified in Northern Ireland in the early months of 1970, it was attracting more and more members and volunteers to its armed wing which became the powerful and impressively effective paramilitary force known as the Provisional IRA. The fact that the weapons and munitions which the gardaí had intercepted would have been sufficient to support really effective military action in the North by the IRA added to the impression of something truly dangerous at work.

Gageby's editorial on 7 May about the 'arms plot' was a curiously ambiguous one. As on the day before, he continued to affect an even-tempered *sang-froid* in response to the shocking news of alleged gun-running Lynch had broken in the Dáil the previous evening, when Fianna Fáil had been roused to his support in the name of party unity. He reflected:

> No one is sorry that what might have been a serious crisis, with perhaps violent sectarian repercussions in the North, has passed off quietly. Dublin, despite a flurry of highly coloured rumours yesterday morning, went about its business with fair aplomb. The Army was never, in the slightest, in doubt. The gardai, who have been placed in a ludicrous position by denials which were more incredible than the stories they purported to discredit, were untouched.

The *Irish Times*'s sanguine view that the security of the state had been assured was not universally shared. There were genuine fears that those in the country who favoured the sacked and departed ministers could be a force for instability, as even Gageby admitted in his affectedly calm editorial. Gageby's editorial, for all its air of almost breezy confidence, had been affected by the febrile emotions of the moment; for they stimulated in him a burst of outspoken republican impatience. He was at pains to point out how disavowals of force, by such as Lynch, as a means of uniting the country lacked substance in the absence of a credible alternative strategy. He insisted of Lynch and his eschewal of force: 'Neither he nor his Ministers show in their words or deeds that they have any appreciative conception of how to advance from there.' And Gageby even went so far as to suggest, in a way that went close to the heart of issues that would emerge at the trials that followed the unmasking of the alleged 'arms plot': 'The motives of those who seek to arm the Catholic people of the North are not, of course, necessarily or at all, conquest by arms of the Unionist majority.' The weapons could have been for the surely legitimate cause of nationalist self-defence. Then, as if seriously discomfited by his own republican sense that arms could well be needed in the event that the Unionist government could or would not protect its minority population if trouble broke out again, Gageby concluded his editorial by berating Lynch for allowing the Department of Justice apparently to turn a blind eye to the activities of 'illegal organisations' (a state euphemism for the IRA and its splinter groups). The editorial ends with Gageby as stern defender of the state's monopoly on lethal force.

It is clear from Gageby's editorials on the Northern troubles from 1968 onwards that his fundamental loyalty was to the Irish state, in whose uniform he had served in wartime, however inept and ineffective it had been in promoting the cause of Irish unity which also lay close to his heart. One recognizes, too, in his editorials that his hopes for Irish unity were not as they had largely been in John Healy's and Robert Smyllie's days, because in a united country Protestant influence on the polity would be the greater by dint of a larger numerical presence in a united country. Rather, he wrote as a convinced republican who believed devoutly in Wolfe Tone's terms that only in an all-Ireland republic could the common name of Irishman be substituted for that of Catholic, Protestant and Dissenter in an equality of citizenship. Furthermore, Gageby was wholly committed to seeing as much as it lay in his powers that the Northern minority was treated fairly by the unionists of Northern Ireland and by the British government before the happy date of national reconciliation in a reunited, sovereign country arrived. Gageby's holding and expression of such views must have raised the question of his relationship with the *Irish Times* board and with Major Thomas McDowell, as the Troubles took hold and intensified. For readers could not but have noted how Gageby was setting the paper on an entirely new political path and, in the small world of Dublin clubs and Masonic meeting halls (the Masonic Order had its members among the paper's hierarchy), the matter could not have gone unremarked. It must surely have been presumed that McDowell and Gageby did not see eye to eye on the Northern question. Revelations in 2002 have made the question of McDowell's actions at this time perhaps the most vexed in the history of the newspaper.

In 2002 correspondence became available which showed beyond doubt that in 1969 McDowell had been in contact with representatives of the British government, seeking guidance on how he, as a member of the *Irish Times* board, of which he was vice-chairman, could be useful to it 'with regard to the situation in Northern Ireland' (Mark O'Brien 2008, p. 188). A lunch had been arranged in Dublin with the British ambassador to Ireland, Andrew Gilchrist, at which it was discussed what he might do. It was Gilchrist's letter reporting on this meeting, to a Foreign and Colonial Office official in London, Kelvin White, that casts a troubling shadow over McDowell's acts and motivations at this time. In this letter Gilchrist quoted McDowell as describing Douglas Gageby as a 'renegade' and a 'white nigger' on 'Northern questions'. What was being expressed in these vulgar terms was that Gageby as a Belfast Protestant had gone native in a fashion alarming to McDowell and one or two others of the entirely Protestant board. McDowell, it seemed, along with some of his board, would be willing to receive 'guidance' on what kinds of viewpoint in the paper might be helpful or unhelpful to British interests, the inference being that they would seek to have those represented in the paper, in the interest of 'moderation'. Subsequent meetings in London between McDowell and White sought to refine what role McDowell might perform in this regard, but by December these discussions seem to have petered out, with McDowell offering the good offices and financial support of the Irish Times Ltd for meetings of a cross-border type which would bring together influential people from both sides of the border to discuss politically uncontentious ways of co-operating.

Following the revelation in 2002 of Gilchrist's letter to White, McDowell repeatedly denied that he had ever used the terms 'renegade' and 'white nigger' of the *Irish Times*'s editor. He claimed that in 1969 the concept of the 'white nigger' (associated with the struggle for civil rights in the American south) was unknown to him and that he could not have spoken of Gageby as a renegade since he 'was never a renegade. He was what he always was' (McDowell interview with Geraldine Kennedy). He even claimed he had taken a fellow Northerner to task for describing his editor as a renegade. In this same interview, given shortly before his death in 2009, McDowell was anxious to reaffirm his respect for Gageby and to give the impression that in the aftermath of Lynch's 'stand idly by' speech he was keen simply to do something in the cause of peaceful relations between North and South and had approached the British through Marcia Williams, Harold Wilson's right-hand woman at Number Ten Downing Street, since as a former British Army major he was more likely to gain attention there than in Government Buildings in Dublin. McDowell emphasized, too, that it was the proposed North–South meetings that were his primary concern.

On McDowell's quoted terminology one can perhaps offer an explanation. It is not impossible, though unlikely, that Gilchrist was glossing what had been said in colourful, in-house shorthand (perhaps diplomats are not always diplomatic). However, McDowell, according to John Martin's account, which cites a senior *Irish Times* source (John Martin 2008, 142), was not averse to barrack-room vulgarity and may well have spoken so crassly. However, that he considered doing more than helping to bring Northern and Southern opinion-formers together, from the textual evidence, remains a troubling possibility. Nor can it be denied that the British seriously considered how McDowell could be an 'asset' in intelligence terms in the Irish capital. These are far more serious matters than an ex-soldier's vulgar lexicon. For John Martin in his book *The Irish Times: Past and Present* (2008) McDowell's actions and the British response are taken as evidence that his known loyalty to the British state in whose army he had served as an officer may even have extended to membership of MI5. Martin makes the 'white nigger' episode the basis of an argument that from this date on the paper was unduly respectful of British sensitivities. Less inclined to credit an effective conspiracy, James Downey, in his memoir

In My Own Time: Inside Irish Politics and Society (2009), admits the force of Martin's analysis of the documentation but doubts that McDowell had any appreciable undercover significance. Nonetheless, he postulates that it was 'grotesque to imagine that the *Irish Times* should be influenced, contrary to the editor's opinions and his independence in editorial policy, by "guidance" from the British Foreign Office' (Downey 2009, p. 161). Downey concludes, as does Mark O'Brien (2008) in his history of the paper, that, 'in the period 1969–1974 there was no evident effect on the line pursued by the paper' (Downey 2009, p. 163), nor have I detected any such evidence in my reading of the *Irish Times* editorials during the period.

McDowell's motivation in all this may have been a compact of naivety (Downey tells us Irish officials fed McDowell misinformation on the assumption that it would be passed on to the British) and vanity mingled with genuine anxiety shared by many that the country was on the brink of civil war. Although he had proved himself a successful businessman in Dublin, his career to that date, that of an upwardly mobile British provincial, did not suggest a man who could be at ease in the upper circles of English society which his mannered cultivation of a military image seemed designed to allow him to be. The three-piece suits, fob-watch, monocle and trimmed moustache may have convinced at the bar of the Kildare Street Club in Dublin (to which he had quickly gained entry when he moved to the city in 1950), but they were the affectations of a man who resolutely carried his British military title into civilian life, although he had seen only limited action. His 'war wound' had been acquired on an exercise near Omagh, Co. Tyrone, when he had fallen down a cliff at night. He had married the Dublin-educated physiotherapist who had helped treat him after this accident. All in all, the only-child son of modestly placed parents in Belfast (Dennis Kennedy, another Northerner, recognized that McDowell's background was 'ordinary Ulster rather than Anglo-Irish'; Kennedy 2009, p. 84), he must have felt he was truly making a mark in the world as he talked with Foreign Office officials in London discussing affairs of state. In 1950 McDowell had drawn a graph of his promotion prospects in the British Army's legal service and had resigned his commission as he reckoned on ambition thwarted. In 1969 he apparently had the ear of a prime minister.

If McDowell attempted to influence Gageby in the interests of 'moderation' (and it must have been indirectly if it was attempted at all, for one cannot imagine Gageby being other than furiously obdurate on any direct approach), there is, as Downey and Mark O'Brien have stated, no evidence of Gageby trimming his republican sails to satisfy members of the *Irish Times* board. There is, however, evidence that Gageby at this fraught time was capable, if less riskily for the paper's reputation, of naive foolishness of his own.

In February 1969 Terence O'Neill, under attack in his own party for his policy of reform and assailed from without as a Lundy (the traitor of the besieged Protestant Londonderry in the seventeenth century) by a rampant Ian Paisley, called a snap election. Gageby, usually clear-eyed about Northern Orange recalcitrance and sincerely repelled by sectarianism, also nursed a simplistic, sentimental notion (although by this point he was being advised by a young Derry man, John Hume, who certainly knew better) that somehow in the ear of the unionist community beat the sound of a different drum, a drum that had mustered the United Irish rebels of 1798. Their modern avatar, the Presbyterian minister J. B. Armour of Ballymoney, Co. Antrim, who in 1913 had opted for Home Rule, was frequently advanced in the paper by Gageby and his commentator on social affairs and policy, Eileen O'Brien, as the epitome of Northern Protestant virtue. And John Healy had been encouraging a benign view of the individual Northern Orangeman as 'racy of the soil', fundamentally Irish in a demotic, colourful fashion. They both believed O'Neill would carry the day and wrote accordingly in face of mounting evidence that he was in electoral difficulty. In the event, O'Neill was trounced in the election and his party reverted to its default position: increased security and a hard line against reform. Shortly thereafter Captain O'Neill was replaced as prime minister of Northern Ireland by Major James Chichester-Clark.

So both MacDowell and Gageby had their foibles and blind-spots. As effective partners they probably both recognized that they needed each other. McDowell had taken the tiller of the *Irish Times* as a commercial enterprise, leaving Gageby free to concentrate on making the paper an editorial journalistic success. McDowell must have realized that Gageby was central to the paper improving its fortunes. And as ex-army men, they no doubt appreciated the other's abrupt management styles. Though McDowell was alarmed by some of Gageby's editorials at the outset of the Northern troubles, he was probably astute enough to sense, too, that his editor was uncompromising where it really mattered. The security of the Irish state was non-negotiable for a man who insisted there was only one army in Ireland, that which served the legitimately constituted Irish state, and who was adamant that the term 'execution' could be applied only to state action (personal communication), and never to the paramilitaries who used murder as a tactic. When in October 1969 a second arms trial found the accused innocent, exonerating among other Charles Haughey, who immediately made a speech addressed to 'fellow patriots' (the case against Neil Blaney had been thrown out before it could come to the first full trial, which had failed to reach a verdict), McDowell must have been relieved to read a measured *Irish Times* editorial, entitled 'Counting the Cost' which wisely counselled: 'The fact that a trial was held at all is some reassurance. We know at what cost we can short-cut the institutions which have been built up' (*Irish Times*, 24 October 1970).

Although Gageby disliked Lynch, whom he thought had sacrificed the intelligence officers involved in the case with cold, hypocritical pragmatism, the *Irish Times* was unequivocal about where accountability must lie: 'however powerful or charismatic some figures may be in Irish society, they are to be made accountable to the law of the land'.

Events over the next two years gave ample opportunity to Gageby to display his independence of mind on the Northern question. Chichester-Clark was unseated and succeeded as Northern premier by the more aggressively unionist Brian Faulkner, who in 1971 introduced internment without trial in an attempt to put an end to intensifying violence from the Provisional IRA. Ineptly performed, this action merely increased opposition to the Unionist regime in the nationalist community and brought recruits to the IRA. The terrible atrocity of Bloody Sunday in Derry on 30 January 1972 further acted as recruiting sergeant among the Catholic young in Northern Ireland, bringing many who would not otherwise have contemplated violence to support for or participation in 'armed struggle'.

Gageby's editorial the day after Bloody Sunday suggested that he was hardly inhibited by what members of his board might think, as he indicted the British government as an imperial overlord. Yet in the feverish, horrified week that followed, which saw a national day of mourning culminate in the burning of the British embassy in Dublin, to the evident satisfaction of a large crowd, Gageby's deeply engrained concern for constitutional order made his a steady hand at the editorial tiller. By 3 February Neil Blaney was sufficiently emboldened by irridentist sentiment to state in the Dáil: 'The House ... must lead or be overwhelmed. If they gave the right leadership, the Six Counties was there for the taking, and all Irishmen and women would be brought back to the fold' (*Irish Times*, 4 February 1972) – whether they wanted to be, or not, was his belligerent implication.

On 31 January Gageby had written with icy anger of the dreadful occurrences of the previous day in Derry. The paper itself, through eyewitness reportage, had supplied graphic descriptions of a period of 'intensive shooting' which lasted over three-quarters of an hour, which had been the Parachute Regiment's response to an anti-internment march that had the support of much of the city's population. The British Army's 'withering fusillade' had left 13 unarmed citizens dead and many injured. The *Irish Times*'s Dick Grogan reported that he had seen people who went to help the wounded fired upon. He also referred to how a priest (the subsequent Bishop of Derry, Edward Daly) had braved such fire to give succour to the dying. In the television footage that recorded the day's horror this act of bravery would gain iconic status, like some of those which had helped turn American opinion against continued involvement in the Vietnam War.

Gageby in his Monday morning editorial was appropriately vitriolic. He observed that television, through the BBC's coverage of 'the carnage', had vividly placed the responsibility for what had happened on the shoulders of

Bomb damage in Belfast after German bombing

Damage caused by German bombing
of the North Strand, Dublin

President John F. Kennedy arrives at Dublin Airport and replies
to President de Valera's speech of welcome, 1963

The opening of the Second Vatican Council, led by the new pontiff
Pope Paul VI in Saint Peter's Basilica, Rome, 1962

The Beatles arrive at Dublin Airport, November 1963

Pope John Paul II waves to the huge crowds turned out
to greet him in Phoenix Park, Dublin during his visit to
Ireland, September 1979

Police battle with rioters in the Bogside area of Derry, 1969

A funeral mass for eleven of the thirteen Bloody Sunday victims taking place in St Mary's Roman Catholic Church, Creggan, Derry, 1972

A British soldier looking out for snipers as he patrols the Falls Road in Belfast, May 1981; the graffiti in the background is in support of Bobby Sands and his fellow hunger-strikers in Maze Prison

Prime Minister Margaret Thatcher and the Irish Taoiseach Garret FitzGerald signing the Anglo-Irish Agreement, Hillsborough Castle, November 1985

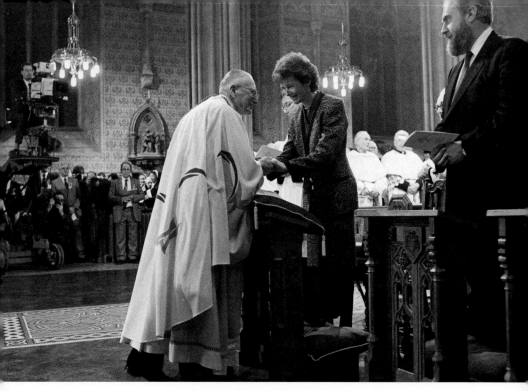

The Archbishop of Armagh, Dr Cahal Daly, greets President
Robinson in St Patrick's Cathedral, Armagh, December, 1990

Sinn Féin President Gerry Adams addresses the crowd gathered
at Connolly House following the IRA Ceasefire Announcement,
watched by Martin McGuinness (*foreground right*)

The *Irish Times* 'X case' cartoon from 1992, by Martyn Turner –
angry protests followed the court ruling prohibiting Miss X from
travelling to the UK for an abortion

one man, the British prime minister Edward Heath; the editorial, entitled with Shakespearean foreboding, "'In Blood Stepped In So Far'", had already judged that his name, along with that of England's, 'must spell shame around the world'. But it would not be as a harried Macbeth, but as the representative of a decadent, fading empire that Heath (dubbed a 'cold unfeeling man in Downing Street') would be universally execrated: 'It is as if Britain, shorn of her empire, has been able to concentrate in the small area of the six north-eastern counties of Ireland all that talent for arrogance, blindness and malevolence that an imperial Power in decline manifests when faced with a small but determined people.' Bloody Sunday 1972 was to be set in a litany of dishonour along with Bloody Sunday of 1920, Amritsar and Sharpeville.

On Thursday of the week following Bloody Sunday, with the British embassy a smoking ruin in Merrion Square at the heart of Dublin and reports coming in from various parts of the country of attacks on British-owned businesses, the *Irish Times* advised caution in dealing with a British government long used to exercising colonial muscle when confronted by 'recalcitrant small nations' (*Irish Times*, 3 February 1972). Gageby warned in the editorial, entitled 'War Talk': 'War psychosis is a dangerous tiger to ride' and while it called unrealistically for intervention by the United Nations, the writer gave his republican support to one Irish trade union's even-handed expression of sympathy to '"the relatives of all killed or injured since August, 1969, in North-east Ulster"'.

The Provisional IRA in 1972 was not in the mood for talk. After the breakdown of a brief ceasefire, it announced by an attack on Belfast that it was willing to risk civilian lives on a shocking scale in its determination to drive the British from Ireland once and for all, completing thereby the unfinished business of the War of Independence. On a perfect summer Friday afternoon in late July, when the city was crowded with shoppers as well as office workers, the Provisional IRA exploded more than 20 bombs in Belfast in the space of about 65 minutes. Nine people died, including two British soldiers. Among the 130 injured (some of them horribly mutilated) were 77 women and children. By midnight on Bloody Friday (as the day became known) there had been 39 explosions in the province as a whole (Bardon 1992, p. 697). The *Irish Times* the next day published a map of the city with the bomb sites marked, which could have reminded older readers of the wartime practice of mapping European war developments. An incandescent editorial set its face irrevocably against a 'war' that was to rage for more than three decades. Gageby wrote, employing the term 'holocaust' with evident deliberation, as he reflected:

> Throughout the 32 Counties Irish men and women should ponder how a virulent Nazi-style disregard for life can lodge in the hearts of our fellow-countrymen; all the more virulent in that, once again, the innocent have been the main sufferers.

> Hitler in his bunker decided that the German people were no longer worthy of him and deserved not to survive. Yesterday's dead and injured are testimony to something similarly rotten in our philosophy of life ...
>
> Anyone who supports violence from any side after yesterday's events is sick with the same affliction as those who did the deed.
>
> Can anyone now believe that anything worthwhile can be established by these methods? (*Irish Times*, 22 July 1972)

Tragically, there were sufficient numbers in Ireland north and south prepared to sustain a 'long war' in face of sustained condemnations from many sources, in which atrocity would follow atrocity over three decades, until all hope of ultimate success was lost and the IRA settled for substantially less than its declared 'war' aims.

An inevitable upsurge of anti-British feeling in the country provoked by 'Bloody Sunday' was not, it soon transpired, so intense that it weighed with the populace when it was asked to vote in May 1972 in a referendum on membership of the European Economic Community. The United Kingdom was on the point of entry and the fact that Britain was Ireland's major trading partner meant that economic self-interest should involve Ireland joining the EEC with her. However, there was the possibility that inflamed feeling about the British Army's actions in Derry could have derailed the smooth journey along the route of free trade which had been laid out for the country during Lemass's premiership. In the event, pragmatism won the day. A consensus emerged, with the farming community to the fore in the campaign, that Ireland had little choice but to join the EEC alongside the United Kingdom. The electorate voted for membership by a five-to-one majority. Nationalist *amour propre* in the matter was gratified by the argument that, in the wider European context, Ireland's dependence on Britain would be diminished and her standing as an ancient nation with close links to the Continent would be enhanced. The running sore of Northern Ireland could perhaps be salved by the balm of co-operation that had brought Germany and France together after the war in the mutual self-interest enshrined in the Treaty of Rome.

The *Irish Times* gave its unqualified support to the European project. On 12 May, the paper asserted of the referendum held two days earlier: 'The result is clear cut and a declaration of the self-confidence of the Irish people' (*Irish Times*, 12 May 1972). 'We are going,' the editorial declared, 'into Europe with our head up ... We are not shuffling into Europe with head in hand or our head down.' And the vote was not only a vote for EEC membership but one for democracy itself, a slap in the face for the IRA which was firmly told: 'the Irish people still likes democracy' (Sinn Féin as political supporter of the IRA had vociferously opposed entry). High hopes were held by the editor that the reunification of the country could take place within the developing European order. It was left to Garret FitzGerald on the same day to spell out in an article what he thought were the principal benefits for the Republic of Ireland that could flow from such a historic decision.

FitzGerald judged the vote historic since it would reset the Irish nation's relationship with Britain. He believed that Ireland's economic interests were 'secured for the first time in history'. No longer would Ireland be an economic dependency of Britain, for 'on Wednesday last ... the Irish people voted ... to end the humiliating bi-lateral relationship with Britain which began many centuries ago and which continued even after political independence was secured in 1922'. It was historic, too, in social and political terms, FitzGerald reckoned, since strategic alliances with other European nations would infuse new ideas about governance and social policy into the country. EEC membership would be a catalyst for change:

> The Anglo-centricity of Irish life, so carefully fostered by Britain after the end of the 18th century (starting with the Government grant to Maynooth College designed to cut Irish educational contacts with the Continent), will be weakened, and the rich and diverse culture of the Continent will become more accessible to us ...
>
> Last Wednesday our people, by a clear majority, opened a window on the world beside us – the world of Western Europe. From now on a cold draught will communicate a chill to many stale ideas we have too long cherished – a chill hopefully fatal in some instances at least. A healthy breeze will blow in on us also, forcing us to bestir ourselves to keep warm.

Upon accession on 1 January 1973, one stale idea and practice was almost immediately blown away. The state was obliged that year under EEC law to pass legislation ending what was known as the 'marriage ban'. This was the requirement that women in the civil service resign their positions on marriage. That one of the earliest effects of Ireland's EEC membership was a change of the law in respect of women's rights was telling. For in subsequent decades European law would often be a powerful influence for Irish change in matters affecting family and personal life. In the early 1970s it was one further element in a congeries of things that was making feminism a force that legislators could not ignore. The media, with the *Irish Times* as a leading voice supporting the 'women's movement', became heavily invested in this highly significant development in the country's social and cultural history. One activist recalls of the period, when 'the inimitable relationship between the women's liberation sector and the media in Ireland was a critical factor in advancing the movement, as a whole, in the early 1970s' (Connolly 2003, p. 125): 'The two key resources were RTE and the *Irish Times*. They recruited very independently minded women who "got away with murder".'

Since the mid-1960s the *Irish Times* had, indeed, been recruiting a cohort of women journalists, discovered and given their head by Donal Foley (they were often referred to quite admiringly as 'Donal's babes'). His sensitivity to social change was acute, as his determination to have skilled women writers on the *Irish Times*'s team certainly proves, but he cannot quite have realized as the paper recruited such figures as Mary Maher, Maeve Binchy, Mary Cummins, Elgy Gillespie, Christina Murphy and Nell McCafferty, that they would make columns of the newspaper sometimes serve almost as the house journal of the Irish women's liberation movement.

Various factors were at work to make feminism a force for change in the Irish media in the early 1970s. Accession to the EEC, with its progressive social legislation, certainly inspired women to demand equality of European citizenship. However, the impetus for change was already having its effects by the time Ireland joined the EEC. The papal encyclical *Humanae Vitae*, issued in 1968, with its proscription of artificial methods of contraception, had had the effect of making the topic of human reproduction and the female role in it widely discussed in the media with a frankness that would have been unimaginable a decade earlier. The liberalization of the Irish censorship laws in 1967 had signalled a freer social atmosphere in which such debate about contraceptive methods could uninhibitedly flourish. The government's establishment in 1970 of a Commission on the Status of Women was a response to this widespread shift in consciousness about what became known as 'gender politics'.

The roles played by women in the *Irish Times* in this period reflected the social changes that were at work. In 1965 the American-born Mary Maher was appointed to the paper and was soon producing, at Foley's behest, a Women First section, a half-page of the paper that confronted the kinds of social problems that Michael Viney and John Horgan had been writing about earlier in the decade (with increased awareness of the conditions endured by the Irish poor, but with a distinctly female slant). When in 1968 Maher returned to her first love, the newsroom, Maeve Binchy was appointed women's editor and was at this post when the Irish Women's Liberation movement became a story in itself, with some of the *Irish Times*'s journalists personally active in the cause. The fact that this was also the moment when the New Journalism of 1960s' America, in which the journalist is a protagonist in her/his own story, was a style to be emulated made the copy submitted by Donal's babes some of the most immediate and vivid in the paper. The vital impression that they were writing out of convictions rooted in personal experience gave their contributions an edge and authority that could not easily be set aside. The concept of the patriarchy was being made a near-unassailable category of thought in the public domain.

Women writers, too, in the paper were able to pose questions to their society in a way that many men would have found off limits. Indeed, Irish literature in the twentieth century not only had been restricted in its exploration of human sexuality by the rigorous literary censorship, but had struggled to represent the erotic outside the context of Catholic guilt. So there was something beguilingly and creatively subversive about freelance Mary Leland's 'In Defence of Eroticism', with its question, 'What is so terrible and calamitous about eroticism?' (*Irish Times*, 19 December 1973, cited Gillespie, 2003 p. 157). In this article, Leland, subsequently a distinguished writer of fiction, allowed herself to surmise: 'I do believe that some sexual experience before marriage can only help the relationship of a married couple', before going on to affirm:

> Eroticism, of course, is awareness. It is a conscious delight in sexuality, and without its common and unhappy abuses, should be a power for good. It should reveal our common physical structure and make it easier to express concern, sympathy, pleasure, and the love that is called charity in simple physical ways.

In his memoir James Downey tells us that Douglas Gageby was not really in sympathy with the 'feminization' of the paper that Mary Maher had set in train. He recalls: 'On rare occasions Gageby permitted his exasperation with the emphasis on social conscience to break out. He once said to me angrily, "Those women Mary Maher writes about they're all LOSERS"' (Downey 2009, p. 106). He was probably irritated as well by Nell McCafferty (from Derry's Bogside, appointed to the paper in 1970), who in her idiosyncratic column in the early 1970s made all too clear how the Irish courts served out rough justice to men and women, many of them the victims of circumstance whom Gageby might have dismissed in such impatient terms. In so speaking, it must, however, be said, he was exhibiting a degree of obtusemess at how his own paper was changing and was itself helping to change Ireland. The Women First feature had expanded not only the kinds of subjects women could write about, but had invigorated journalistic style and had served as a forum for the burgeoning feminist movement. And so successful, indeed, was that movement that by 1974 the idea that women required a separate section of the paper simply to accommodate their interests had long become outdated. For in the early 1970s women were taking their place alongside their male colleagues as writers about most spheres of life, sometimes at the front line, as it were. Renagh Holohan, for example, was appointed northern editor in 1973 (with bombings to cover, including the destruction there of the *Irish Times*'s Belfast office) and London editor (with the ongoing Northern crisis a major story) in 1974.

Probably the editor's mind was more firmly fixed on Northern Ireland and, along with his coadjutor John Healy, on the EEC, to which both of them were enthusiastically committed, than on the changing role of women in Ireland. European affairs were given extensive coverage after 1973 and a weekly page on 'Europe' introduced the Irish public to the workings of the institutions they had voted to join. Fergus Pyle from Brussels contributed lengthy expositions about the various roles of the Commission, the Parliament and the European Council of Ministers. His column 'Here in Brussels' tried to put human faces and give a sense of reality to the complex bureaucracy with which Irish diplomacy was engaged.

The paper's European editor, Dennis Kennedy, a Northern Protestant of the liberal unionist persuasion, who would later go on to a distinguished career as a European Union official, while reporting conscientiously on Community affairs, also provided thoughtful opinion pieces on the new context in which the Irish state was operating. More inclined to strategic reflection than Pyle, his take on Irish entry was positive, yet salutary in its realism. The month after entry, for example, he published an article entitled 'Developing a European Philosophy'. Kennedy noted how the referendum the previous year had been 'a beef-and-butter' affair (*Irish Times*, 6 February 1973) and commented: 'Ireland, despite its claim to have given Europe its major cultural impetus in the form of what was known as Christianity, has managed to become a full member of the European Community, in the 20th century, without evolving any explicit philosophy of Europe itself.' He observed that all other members were involved in transnational security arrangements and that the Irish government seemed to have nothing to say on the policy of European integration. Perhaps influenced by his Northern background, Kennedy warned that Ireland could be impeded in Europe by a tradition of isolationism and self-absorption, given added valency by the current 'troubles':

> We were not directly involved in the war that started it all, nor in the post-war reconstruction. We opted out of the practical side of the cold war. Ironically, now that we have joined the integration process, we have, as we did not have then, real reason to be preoccupied with national problems.

In 1974 those national problems became acute as shocking events occurred that would shape Irish history for decades to come. For the *Irish Times* itself, 1974 was also a watershed year in which not only would Douglas Gageby resign his editorship, but the conditions of ownership of the business and its institutional governance would change in remarkable ways. So readers awoke on 5 April to find that the paper they were reading had as a front-page headline 'The Irish Times Now a Trust', with the subheading 'Decision to Preserve Independence'. A first paragraph of the subtending article informed them that 'A Trust has been set up to maintain the *Irish Times* "as a serious and independent newspaper"', and 'a charitable foundation has been established which will ultimately benefit from the profits of the newspaper' (*Irish Times*, 5 April 1974). Much of what followed involved high sentence as the article quoted from the memorandum of the trust company, which committed the paper to strict independence 'as a benefit of the community throughout the whole of Ireland', to an editorial support for 'constitutional democracy expressed through governments freely elected' and to 'The progressive achievement of social justice between people and the discouragement of discrimination of all kinds.' Further statements quoted from the memorandum indicated an attempt to encapsulate the values of what was becoming known, in public debate in the 1970s, as 'pluralism' (though an earnest hope, expressed in masculinist terms, that the paper should help 'each man' to 'live in harmony with his neighbour, considerate for his cultural, material and spiritual needs' indicated that the framers of the document may have been neglecting the 'Women First' columns). A distinct air of liberal high-mindedness permeated the quotations from the document, as if its authors were situating themselves above the exigencies of the real world (an attitude that has survived to a degree when the paper refers from time to time to its trust status). Editorial practice was to promote a 'friendly society where the quality of life is enriched by the standards of its education, its art, its culture, its recreational facilities, and where the quality of spirit is instinct with Christian values, but free from all religious bias and discrimination'. An editorial on the same day trumpeted the new order as a manifestation of independence and social inclusiveness:

> In recent years, as all Ireland changed, so the staff of the *Irish Times* changed and the newspaper itself changed. Today's *Irish Times* staff is a fair microcosm of the people of this 32-County Ireland – from the Bogside to the Ring of Waterford, from the middle-class Dublin suburb to the poor acres of Mayo. The *Irish Times* was always a national paper. And one of the marks of it today is the composition of the Governors of the trust and foundation.

Oddly, this paean to pluralism was entitled 'New Every Morning'. One wonders how many, beyond those schooled in Holy Scripture, read this as a quotation from Chapter 3 of the Book of Lamentations. Those who did must surely have wondered how the declarations of an Old Testament prophet (words traditionally attributed to Jeremiah), as he contemplated the ruin of his life and the sufferings of his people, were germane to what was being spun as a triumph of renewal. The less exalted sections of the front-page article, which informed readers of the complex commercial, administrative and financial manoeuvres that had borne fruit in the trust, would have alerted them, however, to the fact that key figures in the *Irish Times* leadership had not been immune to Jeremiah-like forebodings about the long-term survival of the paper as an independent entity. A lengthy article on these arrangements by the *Irish Times*'s financial and business editor, Andrew Whittaker, published on the same day, could also have helped readers to understand that astute business judgement as well as moral idealism, were involved in this decision to place overall governance of the title in the hands of a trust.

Although the *Irish Times* was a publicly quoted company on the Irish stock exchange, Whittaker explained, the Irish Times Ltd. appears to have run into the sort of situation that commonly confronts private family concerns. The directors had an agreement among them to purchase the shares of any of their number who wished to sell: but the advancing ages of some directors, and the sums of money involved appear to have convinced the board that such an arrangement could not survive. (*Irish Times*, 5 April 1974)

The risk was that because they were making good profits and the paper had reached a record circulation figure of 63,128 copies in 1972 (Mark O'Brien 2008, p. 199) they might become an attractive takeover proposition to such newspaper moguls as Lord Thomson and Anthony O'Reilly. As the company was then structured, three of the older members of the board, in time, might be tempted to sell their shares to such a figure, placing the remaining two, McDowell and Gageby, in a minority position on any new board. The trust and suite of satellite entities it involved, in a series of carefully planned, impressively adroit moves, were established, in the best interpretation of these manoeuvres, to obviate such a possibility. In his history of the *Irish Times*, Mark O'Brien carefully examines an operation that was planned and set in motion over many months. He concludes, with eminent fair-mindedness: "The trust system was, it seems, the most efficient way to allow Hetherington and the Walker brothers [the directors who wished to depart] to leave and enable McDowell and Gageby to maintain control' (Mark O'Brien 2008, p. 203). Others were and have been less inclined to accept that probity was to the fore in all the tactics and transactions involved in setting up the trust (one commentator, indeed, has accused Gageby of malfeasance). The problem was that there were obvious grounds for suspicion that expressed high-mindedness masked straightforward cupidity.

The establishment of the trust was made possible by funds advanced by the Bank of Ireland to purchase, by means of an intermediary entity, Irish Times Holdings, the ordinary shares of the company. This resulted in a windfall of the very considerable sum of £325,000 going to each of the directors. The directors, it is true, had each to invest £76,000 to buy out the company's preference shareholders; but they would be entitled to a dividend on this investment and it was assumed that these shares could be redeemed in the future by profits raised by Irish Times Ltd. It was a good deal for all the directors.

That the founding of a trust similar to that which controlled the liberal/ Left *Guardian* newspaper in Britain, should have benefited Gageby so very handsomely (when an annual professional salary stood at about £1,500) grated with many of his paper's readers, who instinctively disliked the commercial world and capitalist rewards for business acumen. Gageby seemed to be functioning at a level far above that of those unfortunates who appeared in the courts, as described by the Bogsider Nell McCafferty, one of the paper's cohort of progressive young journalists, who had been invoked so readily in the editorial of 5 April.

Over the years further suspicion was directed at the complex restructuring process that resulted in the establishment of the trust, since the timing seemed improbably fortuitous: the directors narrowly missed the possibility of assessment for capital gains tax which, backdated to 5 April 1974 (the day after the trust arrangements came into force), was introduced by the government in 1975. The paper's defenders have pointed out, though, that in the complicated offsetting of expenditures legislation permitted, no tax liability would have arisen had the directors waited a day or more to inaugurate the new dispensation in D'Olier Street.

The Bank of Ireland's involvement in constructing the elaborate edifice that was to protect the *Irish Times* from hostile takeover bids also aroused suspicion, particularly since the structure required a financial injection by the bank of almost two million pounds (then a *very* substantial sum). In 2006 Andrew Whittaker, who had severed his connection with the *Irish Times* in 1974, revealed that he had been told in 1977 by the then managing director of the bank that the decision to support the paper in 1974 had been influenced by political considerations. The banker admitted to Whittaker: 'The directors had feared the conjunction of high interest rates and the activities of the IRA. They had wanted the *Irish Times* to be there as "at least one voice of sanity", even though the paper was not controlled by the bank (Whittaker 2006, p. 176). This revelation was grist to the mill of those who suspected that much more was afoot in the purlieus of the *Irish Times* in the mid-1970s. For John Martin in his book *The Irish Times: Past and Present* (2008) this amounted to a conspiracy among West Brits and the Anglo-Irish (the Bank of Ireland was a distinctly Protestant institution) with MI5's McDowell at its apex, in which Freemasonry played a noxious part, to maintain the *Irish Times*'s traditional sympathy for British concerns and to outface the energetic nationalism represented by Anthony O'Reilly's Independent Newspaper group. That the trust structure placed Major McDowell in a position of overall power in the new set-up could be read as further evidence of reprehensible non-national forces at work in the *Irish Times*. For such critics, the version of sanity which the paper could be trusted to express, with its high-flown foundational document, was that of the old imperial wolf in ostensibly liberal sheep's clothing, innately antagonistic to Irish national interests and prepared to work against them. In 1974 the *Sunday Independent* (a horse in O'Reilly's stable) had in fact categorized the establishment of the trust as the creation of a 'self-perpetuating oligarchy answerable commercially and financially and in every other way only to themselves' (cited Mark O'Brien 2008, p. 201). Presumably the Bank of Ireland, until the loans that were part of the arrangements of 1974 had been paid off, could have made the *Irish Times* jump a little to its tune, for it certainly had paid the piper. Otherwise, though stated in unfriendly fashion, there was an essential, commendable truth in the *Sunday Independent*'s assessment that by 'an extraordinarily ingenious financial exercise' the *Irish Times* had established an unusual degree of independence that could be deployed for good or ill. For such as John Martin, all this was a crucial step in Major McDowell's Machiavellian campaign on behalf of his masters in London. For most readers, it proved a journalistic asset which the paper under its various subsequent editors has exploited tolerably well.

The new order at the *Irish Times* had almost immediately to respond to very challenging events in the political arena, which would shape the Irish future for decades to come. In 1972 the British had abolished the Northern Irish parliament at Stormont and had imposed direct rule from Westminster. An election was held to a new Stormont Assembly in Belfast, which after negotiations agreed that an executive could be elected by the assembly itself on a cross-party, cross-community basis. Negotiations were then held in Sunningdale in England, which brought together members of the Northern Assembly with representatives of the British and Irish governments. The Sunningdale Agreement of 1973 envisaged that a Council of Ireland would reflect the Irish dimension of the problems in Northern Ireland which the new political arrangements were intended to solve. In early 1974 a new power-sharing executive took office at Stormont. This body was in office for only six weeks when the British prime minister Edward Heath, who had driven the negotiations which had resulted in the Sunningdale Agreement, called a snap general election in face of serious industrial unrest in Britain. Consequently, not only did Heath lose power to Labour's Harold Wilson, who had no personal investment in the Sunningdale Agreement, but the leader of the Unionist Party of Northern Ireland, Brian Faulkner, saw support for his party at Westminster diminish significantly. It was hard not to see that result as a vote against the new executive and the Council of Ireland.

The *Irish Times*, with Gageby attending closely to the views of the Northern nationalist leader John Hume, whose ideas on how the Irish question could be resolved were broadly reflected in the arrangements for the Stormont executive and the Council of Ireland, gave unqualified, enthusiastic support to the new administration north of the border. For Hume and his willing pupil Gageby, the structure established by negotiation between democratically elected politicians was a vehicle that would carry Northern unionists into what Hume liked to term an 'agreed Ireland' (one of his party members let a cat out of the bag in early 1974 when he spoke of unionists being trundled down a road that would lead to Irish unity). In the early summer of 1974 it became all too clear that the unionist community was not minded even to start on such an uncomfortable journey. It was obvious, too, that many of them did not support the concept of power-sharing (some of these unionists were wary of sharing power with those who thought the Northern Assembly a transitional arrangement, others of them simply could not stomach their representatives sharing power with representatives of the despised Catholic minority). On 15 May a group calling itself the Ulster Workers' Council (with members in key sections of the utilities infrastructure) called a general strike to bring down the executive and to destroy the Council of Ireland. At the outset it seemed that the executive might weather this storm but by means of intimidation led by the Protestant paramilitary Ulster Defence Association and as a consequence of serious reductions in power supplies owing to the action of strikers, together with the tacit support of large swathes of the unionist population, the province almost ground to a halt in an enormous display of direct political action. Initially, the British Army might have been able to suppress what became effectively a rebellion by much of Protestant Ulster against the British government, but by 21 or 22 May that task was probably beyond the capabilities of the force without very considerable bloodshed. On 28 May Faulkner and his Unionist colleagues resigned from the power-sharing executive, which was thereby consigned to history.

On 17 May a series of powerful car bombs was exploded without warning in Dublin and Monaghan, killing 33 people, with about 300 injuries. It quickly became clear that two of the vehicles used in this brutal attack on civilians had been stolen in Belfast, arousing the suspicion that the carnage wrought on a summer day in the streets of the Irish Republic was the work loyalist paramilitaries (perhaps with British secret service collusion; the logistics of the operation seemed to be beyond the estimated capacity of the Ulster Defence Association (UDA) and the, admittedly more lethal, Ulster Volunteer Force). As the North tottered on the brink of social collapse (with depleted power supplies even putting sewage systems at risk), it seemed there were those warning off a state that sought, through the Council of Ireland, to exercise a degree of jurisdiction over the six counties.

The *Irish Times* on 18 May, like all the national dailies, gave full coverage to the atrocities of the day before. A full page of photographs brought home how a city going about its peaceful business could instantly be turned into a war-zone with its pitiful victims. An *Irish Times* editorial entitled 'Bloody Ireland' reflected on those unfortunates – 'the young, the eager, the busy, the beautiful, the worried, the ordinary Irish men and women – and children, of today' (*Irish Times*, 18 May 1974), and attributed their fate to a deep-rooted intransigence on both sides, implicit in much unthinking talk about 'the people' and 'freedom', in a dispute that had the means of reconciliation to hand. The *Irish Times* was keeping faith with the Northern executive and the Sunningdale Agreement:

> A model has been worked out by which Irish men and women of
> different traditions might, without achieving all they have dreamed of,
> nevertheless live in dignity and harmony with their neighbours. It is fair,

it is Christian, it is Irish in conception. It could be improved upon. But not by mangled flesh.

On 25 May the newspaper published a poem by Eavan Boland: an elegy for a representative victim of the terror of 17 May, entitled 'Child of Our Time'. The poem could be read as endorsing Gageby's editorial imagining of a peaceful way forward, grounded in dialogue, for Boland concluded her poignant yet powerful poem with a plea for a new language of politics.

In contrast, two days later the *Irish Times*, which earlier in the month had pointed out that the British Army had had no compunction about shooting civilians in Derry on Bloody Sunday, seemed to call for armed action against what by that date had become an expression of the settled will of the unionist majority in Northern Ireland about the executive and the Council of Ireland. Ignoring the fact that that would have required a major military intervention, the *Irish Times* commented:

> To commit any army to what might be a bloody conflict is not a decision that any Prime Minister can be expected to take lightly. But an army is there for certain purposes and one of these is to head off an armed *coup*. It is not fanciful to see in the present Loyalist movement just such a *coup*. and if Mr Wilson had been firm earlier, matters might not have reached such a peak.

Perhaps pressure of events was telling on the *Irish Times*'s redoubtable editor (and they were, indeed, anxious times). He had poured energy and much emotional and intellectual capital into the process that had climaxed with the coming to power of the Northern executive. That had been a contemporary version of the kind of United Irish patriotism that stirred his soul as it utilized the talents of Catholic, Protestant and Dissenter. Its threatened demise in what Gageby thought was a near-fascist putsch must have affected him deeply. He felt particularly close to John Hume and was scarcely prepared to contemplate his friend's work coming to naught.

The *Irish Times* team of journalists in Belfast at this historic moment (the newspaper on 25 May had stated: 'There is no doubt that the crisis in the North is the biggest political event to hit the country in decades') was acutely aware of what was going on in the North. Such figures as David McKittrick, Walter Ellis, Conor O'Clery and Fionnuala O'Connor (all Northerners at the beginning of distinguished careers as journalists and writers) had excellent contacts, official and distinctly unofficial. They knew that the executive was in all probability doomed. So O'Clery filed a story to be published on Tuesday, 28 May, that would make this clear. Extraordinarily, Gageby, using deputies, persuaded O'Clery to change his copy (Mark O'Brien 2008, p. 195; Whittaker, 2006, p. 104). The paper ran that morning with the front-page headline:

'Executive Shows United Front after Action by Troops'. The British Army had begun to distribute fuel to petrol-starved garages. So the paper could editorialize under the headline 'Standing Firm', in direct contradiction of what its Northern team of journalists believed was the almost certain outcome of the Workers' Strike. 'The Executive is holding, despite predictions of an untimely end' (*Irish Times*, 28 May 1974). It concluded: 'The Executive is sitting it out.' That very morning the Executive collapsed.

The demise of the executive and of the Sunningdale Agreement was no real shock to anyone, for the writing had been on the wall for days. The editorial of that Tuesday had been a concession to wishful thinking and an expression of loyalty to an ideal and to those who had tried to put it into practice. It did not, however, sit well in a paper that had commended the establishment of the trust in April by assuring its readership: 'Those who read the *Irish Times* are in danger of getting all the facts, which may not please them' (*Irish Times*, 5 April 1974). Arguably, on 28 May certain 'facts' had been withheld, at a momentous juncture in the country's history.

Within the month Douglas Gageby had resigned as editor of the paper he had over 11 years so successfully steered to national prominence. Dennis Kennedy, reflecting on how the fall of the power-sharing executive in Stormont had affected Gageby, recalls: 'that spelled the end of the Sunningdale initiative, and also the eclipse of his own fond hope that a settlement had been found which could lead to the North, at last, "coming in"' (Kennedy 2009, p. 167). In the light of this, it is hard not to detect a valedictory note in the editorial the *Irish Times* published the day after the executive collapsed in Northern Ireland. Under the headline 'God Save Ulster!' the paper was in a kind of mourning: 'A great experiment has ended; but there will be another day. It will be difficult this morning for the brave politicians who formed the Executive to lift up their hearts. Yet they have before now weathered almost incredible set-backs. The long road to ultimate sanity and reconciliation may have to be paved with further failures and checks' (*Irish Times*, 29 May 1974). One senses that the writer's own heart was low and that he was appalled by what the future could hold for the province he loved. There, two parliaments had been brought down by the actions of opposed camps. All he could do was hope that 'Out of this knowledge must surely grow the belief that only the creation of a Parliament mutually acceptable and firmly rooted in both communities will save the North from a merry-go-round of stagnant politics, death and destruction.'

9

THE *IRISH TIMES* AND THE IDENTITY OF IRELAND

On 4 July 1974 the *Irish Times* published a two-part symposium conducted by the poet Eavan Boland, under the rubric 'The Clash of Identities'. This brought together four writers, two from the Republic (novelist James Plunkett and poet Thomas Kinsella) and two from the North (poet John Hewitt and novelist Francis Stuart, the latter then resident in Dublin), along with two members of the Ulster Defence Association which had been centrally involved with the Ulster Workers' Strike that had brought down the executive in Belfast, and the president of the section of Sinn Féin that gave support to the armed struggle of the IRA. Boland indicated that she had proposed such a conversation between writers and key figures involved with a crisis that threatened to engulf the whole island. She wrote that she had in mind such a discussion 'held during the Spanish Civil War when concerned forces and writers met to discuss the conflict and the culture out of which it had come' (*Irish Times*, 4 July 1974). Boland reported that a member of the UDA had said to her: 'I wonder whether this whole conflict is not one of identities', a remark she had found both 'perceptive' and 'striking'.

John Hewitt's contribution to the symposium was a notable addition to a debate about national identity in Ireland which had continued since the outbreak of the 'Troubles' in 1968 and was given added significance following Ireland's accession to the EEC in 1973. Hewitt stated with the kind of certitude unavailable to less confident souls: 'I'm an Ulsterman, of Protestant stock. I was born in the island of Ireland, so secondarily I'm an Irishman. I was born in the British archipelago and English is my native tongue, so I'm British. The British archipelago are offshore islands to the continent of Europe, so I'm European. This is my hierarchy of values and so far as I'm concerned anyone who omits one step in that sequence of values is simplifying the situation.' Nobody in the ensuing discussion challenged Hewitt as to how he acted when one of his hierarchy of values was in conflict with another; rather, there was an acceptance, with only Kinsella implying in his contribution that identarian politics could be pursued to the detriment of justice, that the concept of identity was germane to the Northern Irish imbroglio. Throughout the 1970s, as they continued to do until the signing of the Good Friday Agreement in

1998, ideas about identity, indeed, would colour a great deal of public debate as Ireland reflected on and sought to define how it wished to make progress as a small European state challenged by the political instability that continuing violence in Northern Ireland recurrently threatened. The *Irish Times* played a prominent part in this process of self-examination and questioning, in which Boland's symposium on 'The Clash of Identities' was a stimulating intervention. That the symposium involved writers was itself an indication that some residual sense of how literature had helped to inspire the independence movement earlier in the century still obtained as an aspect of national identity for the kind of people who took the paper.

It was the writer, journalist and Labour Party politician Conor Cruise O'Brien, in his 1972 book *States of Ireland*, who had most tellingly managed to make the concept of culture as integral with the idea of national identity part of the intellectual climate of the 1970s. That work of mingled autobiography, family history and political commentary had laboured to show how Irish nationalism in its various guises had never taken seriously the degree to which Northern Protestants were a distinctive people with their own sense of themselves and their own history, their own sense of identity. O'Brien's treatment of his theme by reference to family traditions had cleverly given readers to feel how personal inheritance constituted a culture that was powerfully at work in determining political ideology and allegiance. Family, in complex ways, was destiny. And a clash of competing cultures and identities could lead to actual civil war.

The *Irish Times* had given O'Brien's book to the SDLP's John Hume to review. He noted that there was 'no doubt that the family connections revealed ... cover practically every aspect of the political spectrum in Ireland through the past century, with the significant exception of the northern majority' (*Irish Times*, 9 October 1972). Hume accepted that this approach, with its emphasis on how memory could stultify politics, was 'of great value'. However, he strenuously resisted O'Brien's fundamental thesis: that given how little Irish nationalism understood the culture and identity of Northern Protestants, it was dangerous currently to press for Irish unity. Hume insisted it was dangerous not to, essentially insisting that the Irish question remained a political one, not a clash of cultures and identities. He insisted that 'O'Brien's case is a more subtle and effective defence of Unionism than any that has come from any Unionist quarter', setting aside social and cultural matters by stating: 'no-one today is asking for immediate unity nor [*sic*] for a narrow concept of a Gaelic Catholic Ireland intended to dominate the Northern Protestants'.

Hume's tough-minded insistence that the Irish problem was a political one, even if it involved cultural aspects and 'family connections', was echoed by other commentators in the 1970s who suspected that an emphasis on cultural differences on the island was a way of deflecting the public mind from the degree of discrimination endured by the Northern minority and the injustice of partition. And the claims made for cultural differences were in themselves, some argued, tenuous enough. A particularly acerbic example of such iconoclasm about culture and identity being at the heart of the matter was supplied in the *Irish Times* on the day the paper published the second section of Eavan Boland's symposium. On that day, the poet and critic Anthony Cronin, whose regular 'Viewpoint' column had established itself since 1973 as the disenchanted voice of sceptical realism about Irish and world affairs, reduced the vaunted and distinctive cultures of Ireland to insignificance. He referred impatiently to 'Northern atavisms and tribalisms' (*Irish Times*, 5 July 1974) and stated of Northern Protestants: 'The truth is that they belong, as most people down here do, to the fringe culture of cosmopolis.' Any claims to their being ethnically unique scarcely amounted to much. Of their identity, pronounced Cronin: 'Insofar as it is separate from the rest of the people of Ireland, [it] has, in the three hundred years of its history, produced no major cultural manifestations of any kind in the way of literature or anything else.' What others might claim to dignify as cultural traditions, Cronin disdainfully thought of as tribalisms, 'important all right in so far as they lead to horror and bloodshed, but ... not of any further moral or intellectual interest.'

In the intellectual conflict between Conor Cruise O'Brien and John Hume, manifest in Hume's review of O'Brien's *States of Ireland*, Gageby had robustly taken Hume's part. Politics, not social and cultural difference, were the nub of the problem, as an editorial entitled 'Unity and Disunity' had insisted in October 1972. 'Mr Hume and the S.D.L.P.,' this asserted, 'are unlikely to be shifted from their view that Northern Ireland, as it stands, is an unworkable unit. They claim, and many will agree, that to pretend that unity is not in their minds is a useless and despicable ruse. Unionists will not be deceived or placated if the word unity is expunged from the political vocabulary' (*Irish Times*, 16 October 1972).

It may well have been a hope of Major McDowell and some other members of the *Irish Times* trust that Fergus Pyle, who succeeded Gageby as editor in July 1974, would give greater credence than Gageby had done to Ulster unionist opinion. Pyle, as we noted earlier was a product of Dublin's secure academic and professional middle class. As northern editor, he had filed eminently fair-minded if sometimes prolix copy on the developing crisis in Northern Ireland which had avoided obvious partisanship (his schooling at Campbell College, Belfast, had given Pyle insight into the mindset of the unionist middle class in Ulster). His sterling work in explaining the EEC to Ireland in the period before and after Ireland's accession indicated that his imagination was more stirred by the vision of continental union than by the thought of the six and the 26 counties of Ireland uniting. As it was for most southerners of his class, that was an aspiration that could be postponed indefinitely as more evidently realizable objectives were pursued.

Pyle's three-year occupancy of the editor's chair proved so unsuccessful that commentators and historians have sought to account for his appointment. He had exhibited as a journalist no special managerial skill or capacity for leadership. There was even suspicions at the time, which grew for some as Pyle failed to develop necessary managerial skills when in the editorial chair, that his Protestantism had been a factor that had catapulted him into office above the claims, for example, of Donal Foley, who had done so much to make the newspaper expressive of Irish life in the round.

To what degree religious persuasion ever played a decisive part in the appointment policies of the *Irish Times* is a delicate and moot point. As Kurt Bowen has shown in his study of the Protestant community in independent Ireland (*Protestants in a Catholic State*, 1983), until the 1960s at least the Catholic and Protestant communities essentially lived apart in the Republic in a kind of mutually agreed apartheid. When, in the course of business life, they found themselves thrown together in co-operative activity, it would have been hard not to be aware that confessional differences were cultural and social markers in a society divided by religion (separate schooling and university education, for the small numbers who went on to tertiary level, were the norm). In the rough and tumble of daily journalism in a capital city, such division probably counted for little. And the fact that the highly effective and influential general manager of the paper from 1907 until 1941, John J. Simington, during both Healy's and Smyllie's editorships, was a Catholic, could be adduced as evidence that no overt sectarianism ruled at D'Olier Street. One can be sure, too, that the large-minded Gageby would have deprecated attitudes offensively reminiscent of those aspects of the Northern Protestantism he thought defaced the Belfast he otherwise loved.

Nonetheless, one Catholic, Horace Denham, who cut his teeth as a member of the clerical staff on the *Irish Times* in the 1930s, and who rose to become, after a stint with the Press group of papers, heavily engaged for the paper on the advertising side in London from 1963 to his death in 1985, told his son (personal communication) that he thought his open faithfulness to his Church was something that he felt at times may have discomfited some of the senior management in the paper. John Healy's *Irish Times* eulogy for Denhman – 'He had a cheerful Christianity we all loved' (*Irish Times*, 4 February 1985) – may, accordingly, have put too positive a gloss on what Denham himself experienced as a business environment overseen by the formidable Major McDowell, in which confessional distinctions did not always go unremarked.

Whatever criteria were in McDowell's mind when he precipitately brought Pyle back from Brussels to serve as editor in Dublin, commonplace efficiency, which in Ireland, by popular mythology, Protestants are supposed to possess, cannot have been among them. A man of exceptional energy and possessed of a vigorous, well-stocked mind, with an eye for detail, he, nonetheless, came to his new post with a reputation for filing complex reports at the last possible moment. Indecision and an incapacity to command respect (although most staff found him agreeable on a personal level) quickly frustrated a workforce used to Gageby's sure-footed blend of editorial authority with trust in his journalists. And if his own appointment had been a surprise to himself and others, he continued, certainly in one case, the paper's tradition of what seemed almost whimsical appointment and promotion policies. Walter Ellis in his memoir, *The Beginning of the End: The Crippling Disadvantage of a Happy Irish Childhood* (2006), has left us a drolly comic record of how Pyle plucked him, a man who knew no language but English (apart from rudimentary schoolboy French), from his native Belfast to serve as the *Irish Times*'s correspondent in Brussels. Ellis, as we noted, was one of O'Clery's team which had reported the Belfast Troubles. He met with Pyle and Dennis Kennedy (Pyle in due course appointed the Northerner Kennedy, along with Leitrim-born James Downey, as his assistant editors) in one of Dublin's few decent restaurants to be briefed: 'When I explained to [Pyle] that I knew nothing about the E.E.C. ... he dismissed my confession as if it was of no account. All he did, in between selecting wines, was stress to me the importance of keeping well-in with the Irish delegation in Brussels and the farming lobby' (Ellis 2006, p. 232).

As editor, Pyle was determined that the *Irish Times* would situate Ireland in a European context. Ireland's identity was to be realized in the EEC and the paper he was editing took as its models serious continental dailies such as *Le Figaro*, with earnest, dense articles on Community affairs often occupying the front page. On a Thursday in October 1976, for example, readers would have awoken to a by no means untypical *Irish Times* headline – 'Two-year plan to scrap Green £ urged by Lardinois' and to a report by no other than Walter Ellis writing from Strasbourg – all very instructive.

James Downey's damning view of Pyle's editorship was that he

> ... must have been one of the worst editors ever to preside over any considerable newspaper. He laboured from the beginning under several handicaps. At first, he enjoyed the good will of the staff. Then he forfeited the good will. He had always been an amiable colleague, but now he showed himself petty, unreliable, a fatal mixture of tyranny and uncertainty ... (Downey 2009, p.163)

Others, such as Dennis Kennedy, were inclined to be less severe in their judgements, but most doubted that Pyle had the ability to make a success of the job. Kennedy pointed out in his memoir (published in 2009): 'One monument to [Pyle's] credit still stands – he brought Martyn Turner into the paper as a full-time cartoonist, something it had never had before' (Kennedy 2009, p. 156). Turner's politically acute cartoons, appearing opposite the editorial and letters page, over succeeding decades would add to the paper's reputation for sharply expressed and hard-hitting commentary. And it was such long-standing features as Turner's daily cartoon which would help over the years to give the *Irish Times* the distinctive flavour of a well-liked miscellany which by its idiosyncratic charm appeals to its readers' loyalties. Among things that added to this were the daily Crossair and Simplex crossword puzzles, a column on chess, Brendan McWilliams's 'Weathereye' column on meteorology and Diarmaid Ó Muirithe's learned 'Words We Use' column on etymology and derivations.

However much Pyle as editor had his attention directed towards Europe, events in Northern Ireland, where Conor O'Clery remained as northern editor, could not be kept off the front page. Reports on the violence of what had the potential to become a long war thrust themselves with distressing frequency on readers' attention in the Republic, even as they might have wished to ignore them, as if they were happening far away. In a curious fashion, *Irish Times* editorials at this time may have helped people in the Republic to adopt what amounted to a partitionist attitude to the Troubles, that saw them as really affecting only the populace north of the border, even when, as we now know, the British government was considering precipitate withdrawal from Northern Ireland that would have destabilized the Republic as well as Northern Ireland. For where Gageby's editorial style reflected his instinctive engagement with Northern issues and problems, Pyle's discursive prose, his considered reflections, tended to suggest that faults lay on both sides of the dispute in Northern Ireland and that the conflict there could be held emotionally at bay in the way similar editorials on other world trouble-spots could also be. However, when the actions of the Provisional IRA directly threatened the interests of the Irish state, the *Irish Times*, it was crystal clear, had no doubt about where its loyalties lay. No more so, indeed, than when the newly appointed British ambassador to the Republic, Christopher Ewart-Biggs, was assassinated by the Provisional IRA 200 yards from the gates of his south County Dublin residence on 21 July 1976. While the headline in the *Irish Times* on the front-page story the next day referred to the 'killing' of Ewart-Biggs, there was nothing remotely equivocal about the first leader's heading: 'Murder'. This forthrightly denounced the IRA perpetrators of a dastardly deed, who had also murdered a young female secretary, while seriously injuring a senior civil servant and the driver of the car in which all four were travelling:

> Murder is always vile. There are people, however, whose moral sense is atrophied, or has never existed. They were at work yesterday in the Dublin suburbs, however, where they killed the new British Ambassador ... It was a terrible mindless crime, a source of personal grief to every honourable citizen of the Republic ...
>
> No matter how sincere the apologies or how deep the grief, the nation's self-respect will continue to suffer until Ireland, North and

South, forgoes – and is seen to forgo – every conceivable ambiguity and ambivalence concerning the use of violence as a political weapon ... This is a time for grieving not alone over what Ewart-Biggs' murderers did to the Ambassador and his colleagues but over what they have done to Ireland. (*Irish Times*, 22 July 1976)

The assassination of Ewart-Biggs was undoubtedly a grave blow to Ireland's standing as a peaceable European nation state. (The newspaper, in its issue of 22 July, published details of international reaction to the event, specifically including a Reuters report on opinion in France, where the ambassador and his wife had been popular members of the diplomatic circuit.) However, it was the actions of the state itself, in response to the activities of the IRA and other paramilitary groups, that were, even more importantly, soon to put in question Ireland's credibility as a fully democratic, law-abiding entity. Pyle's *Irish Times* had played a signal role in uncovering and publicizing this discomfiting fact.

Regular readers of the paper during Pyle's editorship (which began during the second year in power of a coalition government comprising Fine Gael and the Labour Party) could have been in no doubt about its firm opposition (at its most robust in its response to Ewart-Biggs's assassination) to the armed subversion of state authority by paramilitaries, and its commitment to the security arms of that state. For example, when the police effected the release of Tiede Herrema, a Dutch executive of a company that had brought employment to the city of Limerick, the paper was unstinting in its praise. Herrema had been kidnapped by a republican splinter group. The paper expressed its uncomplicated regard for the force: 'the patience and perseverance of the gardaí and military of all ranks, and the courage of those, who, in the line of duty, made themselves targets for the unpredictable kidnappers, deserve the highest praise' (*Irish Times*, 8 November 1975). A year later, however, the *Irish Times* acquired information that the gardaí were not all the paragons of virtue as painted in that editorial.

Two members of the force had individually approached a senior *Irish Times* journalist in late 1976 (O'Brien 2008, p. 214) and informed of him of serious allegations of police brutality directed against suspects in custody. The government's response to intensifying violence by militant republicans had been to enact the Emergency Powers Act 1976 (replacing, while retaining in force, elements of a similar act that had vested the state with powers thought necessary during World War II). The new act allowed suspects to be held in custody for seven days (previously it had been two). This certainly would have offered ample time for such mistreatment. Pyle bravely decided to investigate what his journalist had been told, assigning that task to a group of experienced staffers. By mid-February they had confirmed the truth of the allegations that had been made and the paper published, with some trepidation on Pyle's part, the facts as the team had established them. The front page led on 14 February

1977 with the headline 'Gardaí Using North-style Brutality Interrogation Techniques'. The story attributed to Don Buckley, Renagh Holohan and Joe Joyce stated bluntly: 'Brutal interrogation methods are being used by a special group of gardaí as a routine practice in the questioning of suspects about serious crimes. This group uses physical beatings and psychological techniques similar to those used in Northern Ireland, to obtain information and secure incriminating statements.' The report told how the group, dubbed by the Garda Síochána itself, 'the heavy gang', employed, as well as brute force, sleep and food deprivation to disorientate suspects. Information derived by these methods was being presented in the courts. On that day and the following two days the paper published details of case histories that made what was allegedly afoot all too believable. One edition carried a story of how a pregnant Northern woman had been assaulted by male garda officers in Dublin.

In editorializing on this matter the *Irish Times* was at pains to remind readers of the Garda Síochána's long record of unsullied service to the community, to insist on the research that had gone into its reportage, and to affirm that only a small minority of the force was engaged in this reprehensible ill-treatment of suspects. Most importantly, an editorial made clear: 'This investigation does not in any way align the *Irish Times* with the political views of any person who has been subjected to ill-treatment' (*Irish Times*, 14 February 1977). However, this leader was straightforward in its condemnation: 'Brutality is always brutality, regardless of whom it is practised by or upon.' The heart of the editorial did, however, pose the hard question as to what extent the existence and actions of 'the heavy gang' had been 'condoned or ignored by people in authority over the force'. The roles of the Garda Commissioner and of the Minister for Justice were raised in this regard. A hard-hitting conclusion stated: 'Subversion and violence must be put down; but not by brutality and the illegal use of force. The Gardaí ... cannot take it upon themselves unilaterally to extend their powers beyond those set down by the elected representatives of the people.'

In setting the paper so starkly against what some of the police were doing, Fergus Pyle was at odds with the outlook of at least one powerful figure in the governing coalition. For in his *Memoir: My Life and Themes* (1998), Conor Cruise O'Brien, Minister for Posts and Telegraphs in the 1973–7 coalition government, and authorized by the Labour Party to speak on matters pertaining to Northern Ireland, was unapologetic about his attitude to police brutality then. He tells how the police discovered the whereabouts of Tiede Herrema, about whose release the *Irish Times* had editorialized so effusively. O'Brien had been told by one of his own Special Branch protection officers how that information had been beaten out of one of the gang whom they suspected was responsible. O'Brien recollects how he had refrained from mentioning this to two of the more liberal-minded cabinet ministers because he thought it would worry them. He provocatively admitted: 'it didn't worry me' (Cruise O'Brien 1998, p. 35).

O'Brien does not inform us if he told any other of his ministerial colleagues about this particular example of the end justifying illegal means. Perhaps he shared his knowledge with the Minister for Defence, Patrick Donegan. The latter's attitude to legal nicety had been revealed when President Cearbhall Ó Dálaigh signed the Emergency Powers Act (1976) into law in October 1976. At that very moment Fine Gael's Donegan chose to denounce in vulgar terms the president's earlier decision to refer the legislation to the Supreme Court to test its constitutionality; this, which had arguably involved perilous delay in putting the legislation on the statute book, was, Donegan fulminated, 'a thundering disgrace' (a journalistic euphemism for his actual choice of words). The upshot was the resignation of the president, when the Taoiseach Liam Cosgrave refused to accept Donegan's tendered resignation.

The *Irish Times* had editorially excoriated Donegan when the minister's intemperate intervention had seemed to show scant respect for institutional due process (the right to submit legislation to the Supreme Court is one of the Irish president's few prerogatives). In the week of 18 October, editorial followed editorial attacking Donegan as being unfit for office, for 'The Minister's remarks ... displayed contempt for the office of President' (*Irish Times*, 21 October 1976). Even the Taoiseach was contaminated: 'One of the most shabby aspects of the affair is the apparent inability of Mr Cosgrave to understand the full implications of Mr Donegan's disgraceful behaviour.'

Pyle's *Irish Times*, it can be argued, in 1976 and especially in early 1977, when the 'heavy gang' reports appeared, was becoming, almost despite its temperamentally cautious editor, at a time when the state faced a serious threat to its authority, a voice insisting that Ireland in Europe must be a nation of laws. It accepted that this must involve the risky business of holding the executive to account, when such an ideal did not seem at the forefront of certain ministers' minds. When Conor Cruise O'Brien deployed Section 31 of the Broadcasting Act to banish interviews with Provisional Sinn Féin and representatives of both wings of the IRA from radio and television broadcasts, the paper protested vigorously in the name of law. It advised that O'Brien's démarche was 'irrational' and that 'confidence in the operation of the law could be undermined' (*Irish Times*, 19 October 1976) by anomalies such a proscription could provoke, and concluded: 'Dr O'Brien's plan raises the fear of arbitrary Government interference in a new and acute form, and the attitude of any responsible news-gathering organisation must be that, when terrible things are being done in our country, it runs counter to reason to hide them under the mat.'

During Pyle's editorship the *Irish Times* had occasion to feel the force of Irish law it was so zealous in upholding. In 1976 a report had inadvertently impugned the integrity of the Special Criminal Court (the non-jury court established to try individuals charged under emergency powers). Itself charged with contempt of court, a presiding High Court judge had accepted that no malicious intent had been involved. However Pyle's colleagues were disconcerted when, in the witness box, he had not taken overall responsibility for what had happened (Mark O'Brien 2008, pp. 213–14). Further discomfiture ensued in 1977 when, served notice that the paper might be prosecuted under the Official Secrets Act if it published details about independent valuations put on a zinc and lead mine of which the government wanted to purchase part, Pyle folded under the threat, against the views of senior colleagues (Mark O'Brien, 2008, p. 214). Apparent weaknesses like these, when added to the kinds of personality traits that James Downey characterized so negatively, meant that Pyle's unquestionable bravery in exposing the misdeeds of a section of the gardaí and in his defence of the rule of law, were not enough to convince his critics that he should hold on to his job. Even more persuasive was the fact that the financial security of the paper was being disturbingly undermined during Pyle's tenure. There was little point aspiring to be a paper of European style and status if the very existence of the title was in financial question.

Pyle had unquestionably been unlucky in taking office just as the first oil crisis put the world economy into recession. Advertising revenue dropped, the cost of newsprint rose alarmingly, sales figures fluctuated, adding to uncertainty, and profits fell to crisis levels. As Mark O'Brien succinctly states it: 'Cumulative losses for 1974 to 1976 stood at £1 million and this, combined with the debt the company had assumed to establish the trust, made extinction a distinct possibility' (O'Brien 2008, p. 211). The Bank of Ireland, which had bankrolled the arrangements that had put the trust in place, naturally became concerned about the threat to its financial position with respect to the newspaper. With the staff and board alike concerned for the future, Fergus Pyle was induced to resign and Douglas Gageby to take up the reins of editorial power once again. Pyle's resignation became effective on 30 June 1977. He had been in office for just short of three years.

Gageby's 'second coming', as it became known, meant that the *Irish Times* would offer different answers to questions about what kind of country Ireland should be in its new European context and about what kind of paper would best reflect and influence it. Issues that bore on Ireland's national identity had, indeed, become a staple in the paper's subject matter during Pyle's incumbency and this would intensify during the restored Gageby's regime.

For the country in the mid-70s and early '80s was engaging in a protracted debate with itself about identity, whatever sceptics like Anthony Cronin might interject, in which Pyle's attempt to Europeanize his paper and to valorize the concept of law was only one contribution. For others, entry to the EEC prompted a determination to re-examine Irish origins and history in the light of the nation's European, as distinct from British, links, while uncovering the riches of the indigenous tradition. University College Dublin archaeologist Liam de Paor's 'Roots' column in the *Irish Times* was a notable example of this cultural phenomenon. In March 1975, for example, writing about a review of the Broadcasting Authority Act (1960), de Paor noted how in its section on 'The Culture of Ireland'

> ... we have in it not only a reflection of the revisionist thinking on our cultural history and cultural objectives which has been so marked a feature of the past few years, but an instrument which may have a very great effect indeed in the near future on the whole character of our national culture. (*Irish Times*, 11 March 1975)

By employing the term 'revisionist' here, de Paor was referring to the way in which in the 1970s the idea of culture had been linked with the concept of a 'pluralism' which was challenging Irish Ireland claims that the authentic culture of Ireland was exclusively Gaelic and Catholic. He noted how the report struggled with 'the contradictions in the view which sees Irish culture as essentially pluralistic while at the same time seeking to retain the Irish language and its tradition at the centre of things' (de Paor thought a genuine cultural pluralism was implicit in the establishment in 1972 of an Irish-language radio station in Galway; this was to be preferred to the bland anglicization television then being propagated). The concept of revisionism in the 1970s also involved questioning the validity of the violence that had brought about Irish independence (Conor Cruise O'Brien was in the vanguard in this). The apparently insensate actions of the Provisional IRA were raising such questions. In the wake of the assassination of Ewart-Biggs, de Paor reminded readers, while dissociating himself from that dreadful deed, that there were still 'a great many people in the country, although they are for the most part sadly perplexed and confused at the moment, who believe that our fathers and forefathers were right to struggle for and ultimately achieve an independent Irish state' (*Irish Times*, 27 July 1976). He tried to steady the ship of national feeling by identifying the roots of Irish republican democracy, highlighting its European provenance, with origins in the 'classical Greek world' in which there 'are to be found so many of the intellectual roots at least of all European cultures' (*Irish Times*, 27 July 1976). The kind of ethnic nationalism that drove the Provisional IRA was an aberration, a betrayal of true republicanism.

Early in 1977 de Paor, in a column entitled 'A Time for Change', argued that a 'change, almost certainly of historic proportions, has been taking place in the political culture of the Republic over the past few years' (*Irish Times*, 8 February 1977). The country's decision to seek entry to the developed world of advanced capitalism had caused 'a great many people' in the Republic to wish 'that the North and its troubles would simply go away'. It acknowledged, too, that a change was taking place in the nation's sense of itself, under the pressure of events in the North: 'We are viewing our history differently.' Irish history was no longer simply the story of 'the struggle of the historic Irish nation against repression and foreign rule'. However, despite this revisionism, de Paor insisted that the problem of the North, where profound change was also occurring, would not go away. Nor, he said, 'will history go away, even if looked at through different-coloured spectacles'. What was needed was a reconfiguring of 'relationships' on the island of Ireland 'before the words can be found to fit them'. On St Patrick's Day in 1977 the *Irish Times* added significantly to the continuing debate about national identity, political, social and cultural change in relation to EEC membership and the Northern crisis by republishing a lengthy article Garret FitzGerald had contributed to a French journal concerned with Irish affairs.

In this article, headlined 'A Hope of Solving Ireland's Identity Crisis', the serving Minister for Foreign Affairs in the coalition government offered an analysis of what he termed the 'double identity crisis' that history had bequeathed to twentieth-century Ireland. FitzGerald admitted that the concept of 'pluralism' had yet to strike deep roots at a popular level in the Republic; nevertheless, he concluded optimistically: 'there is at least a fair chance that in a perspective of history the recent tragic years in Ireland will come to be seen as a period in which a new and wider concept of "Irishness" began to emerge, providing a looser but stronger basis upon which Irish society may eventually achieve a measure of reintegration.'

The *Irish Times* chose to publish a St Patrick's Day leader, entitled 'Thought for the Day', on the minister's argument, noting that he had been propounding his thesis on a new idea of Irishness not only in a French journal but, the evening before, in a speech in Washington. The editorial especially welcomed FizGerald's interesting comment in his article that the 'ideal of a Catholic, Gaelic Ireland has quite possibly never been shared by a majority of the people in the island' (*Irish Times*, 17 March 1977) but expressed irritation that the current Irish government had entrenched rather than challenged such thinking. It was also impatient that years of discussion on such matters had brought little change. The editorial pointedly stated: 'it is this Catholic, Gaelic tradition that is enshrined in the Constitution and laws of the country', and acerbically went on:

> ... there has been little to show for all the debating of the past decade. Few,
> if any, nettles have been grasped, and there is a growing note of frustration
> in the voices of those who continue to argue for liberalisation of the
> position on divorce, contraception, censorship, integrated education and
> so forth. Dr FitzGerald writes that the concept of a pluralist society has
> yet to strike deep roots at a popular level in the Republic. He might have
> said it has yet to strike any roots at all at the highest levels of Government.

It is telling that this editorial concentrated, in its critique of FitzGerald's article, on matters of religious and ethical import. This emphasis can be seen as of a piece with the way religion and its relationship with national identity and social practice had been a recurrent topic of report and analysis in the newspaper's pages to that date in the 1970s. To the fore in making religion a subject of vigorous discussion and controversy in the period was the paper's religious correspondent, John Cooney. This Glasgow-born, radically minded Catholic (appointed from the ranks of reporters as 'Religious Affairs Correspondent' at the end of 1973) brought to the *Irish Times*'s coverage of religious affairs a spirited, undaunted outlook compacted of commitment to the Church's mission and a probingly intelligent scepticism about how that mission was being accomplished.

The role of the Catholic Church in Ireland had come under serious question as political instability in Northern Ireland created the possibility of Irish reunification less remote. How, it was increasingly asked, could Northern Protestants be expected to live in an all-Ireland state that afforded them fewer rights on matters such as divorce and contraception than they enjoyed as citizens of the United Kingdom. In 1972 the clause in the constitution that acknowledged the special position of the Catholic Church in Irish society was removed in a referendum. The intent was to reduce an impression given by that clause that Ireland was a confessional state. Furthermore, the catalyst given to ecumenism by the Second Vatican Council in Christendom generally was given added impetus in Ireland by the political violence in the North which seemed to pit Catholic against Protestant in a disgraceful religious war. In the Republic and on an all-island basis, the ideal of ecumenism became linked to hopes for a peaceful political settlement. In this context, reports on Church affairs and especially on ecumenical dialogue accordingly were matters of political as well as religious import. Cooney had a great deal to write about. At issue, essentially, was the question as to whether a new Ireland could accommodate religious pluralism of the kind Garret FitzGerald would comment upon in his 1977 article.

There were straws in the wind that an ecumenical movement was truly being born in the country as 'ecumenism' itself became a recurrent word in the *Irish Times*'s lexicon. On 6 November 1972 John Cooney reported that the Catholic Archbishop of Dublin, Dermot Ryan, had attended a service in the Protestant Church of Ireland's Christ Church Cathedral, breaking ice that had been frozen since the Reformation. On 19 January 1973 prayers for Church unity were said in the Catholic pro-Cathedral in Dublin by six churchmen from differing denominations, in what Cooney assessed as 'A new and positive stage in the history of Church relations in Ireland' (*Irish Times*, 19 January 1973). The ban on Irish Catholics attending Trinity College Dublin had been lifted in 1970 and Cooney could report in November 1973 that agreement had been reached to make the college chapel multi-denominational. Mass would be said there for the first time.

The *Irish Times*'s focus on ecumenism at this time was given clear definition by its weekly 'Thinking Aloud' column, supplied by a Church of Ireland scholar/priest, George Otto Simms (Archbishop of Dublin, 1956–69 and subsequently Primate of All Ireland). Simms was courteously persistent in support of ecumenical dialogue (eventually this long-established Saturday feature came to be contributed by alternating Catholic and Protestant writers).

Yet Cooney, whose reports were notable for their challenging blend of fact, hard-hitting commentary and personal observation, remained dubious about the pace of change. Reporting on the general election campaign in February 1973, an election that dismissed Fianna Fáil from government and brought the coalition of Fine Gael and Labour to power, he noted how 'pluralism' was 'the missing word at the hustings':

> Unfortunately, all political parties appear unprepared to pursue the impli-
> cations of what a 'New Ireland' means in terms of socio-religious change.
> Cynically, it might be said that if any party used the word 'pluralism',
> the others would seize upon it as associated with the permissive society,
> and would reduce the word to an emotive football. 'Pluralism' would
> become the scapegoat successor of the word 'Communism'. (*Irish Times*,
> 20 February 1973)

While the body politic was innately conservative, churchmen, despite ecumenical dialogue and goodwill gestures, were in fact locked in theological disagreement. So, in an article in January 1974, Cooney inquired as the annual Week of Prayer for Christian Unity began, whether 'Church Unity' was a 'Real Goal or Window Dressing?' (*Irish Times*, 18 January 1974). Considering the stance taken by the Vatican in a document issued by the Congregation for the Doctrine of the Faith (which re-emphasized papal infallibility and the uniqueness of the Roman Catholic Church), Cooney supplied his own implied answer: 'Despite the veritable ecumenical industry that has grown up in recent years, church unity seems no nearer and church union appears to be even more elusive.' Indeed, one local branch of that industry, the 'summit meeting' of churchmen in Dundalk the previous September, had indicated that the issue of 'mixed marriages' was a bitter bone of contention for the Presbyterian Church in Ireland. Cooney advised: 'It does seem clear that the issue of mixed marriages symbolises for many Protestants in Ireland the test of the Catholic Church's sincerity on ecumenical dialogue in this country' (*Irish Times*, 18 January 1974).

Cooney soon got a formal answer to his question. In February 1974 he hailed a report on an international conference on the issue of mixed marriages, which had been hosted the previous September by the Irish School of Ecumenics (founded in 1970 by an Irish Jesuit earnest to give substance to hopes raised by the Second Vatican Council). He enthused that its liberal recommendations could prove a 'Magna Carta on the most tense inter-Church issue in Ireland' (*Irish Times*, 1 February 1974). A year later Cooney was obliged to report a statement from the Irish hierarchy that indicated that it would 'continue to stand firm in support ... of a strict interpretation of Vatican regulations on mixed marriages – despite the present public debate about the need for ... a more flexible system of inter-church marriage' (*Irish Times*,14 February 1975). He judged: 'While claiming to respect the conscientious position of the Protestant partner, it does not recognize the rights in conscience of that partner.'

In articles in the mid-1970s, Cooney in fact had to report how the Roman Church was checking the momentum for reform set in motion by the Vatican Council as tight centralized control was being resumed. An article headlined 'As You Were' in October 1975 (written after a time spent in the Holy City), reflected: 'ten years after Vatican Two it is clear that, despite a period of religious upheaval, unrivalled since the 16th century Reformation, Rome has again resumed the role of centraliser and controller. To oppose policy is to provoke Papal umbrage' (*Irish Times*, 31 October 1975). Cooney quoted, to confirm his argument, the views of a Swiss theologian that 'the ecumenical movement between the Roman Catholic Church and other Churches has come to a halt'.

On this climate of reaction in Rome and at home, Cooney was not inclined to hide his own progressive light under a bushel. He seldom missed an opportunity to highlight in the *Irish Times* occasions that the conservative faithful might find discomfiting. In 1973, reviewing a book about episcopacy and women, he waspishly pointed out: 'there are two Episcopal vacancies in Ireland at the moment (Derry and Limerick) – why not women bishops in Ireland?' (*Irish Times*, 20 November 1973). In February 1975 he gave publicity to how opposition to the official teaching on contraception was gathering in the Catholic world since 'Catholic scholars and laity remained unconvinced by the arguments of *Humanae Vitae*' (*Irish Times*, 20 February 1975). In March the same year he reported the conclusion of an article in an American journal that had contentiously claimed that 'The substance of the Orange charge that "Home Rule means Rome Rule"' could 'not be easily dismissed' (*Irish Times*, 18 March 1975). Then, in the autumn of 1975, during what was in fact International Women's Year, Cooney wrote of how the Irish hierarchy had set its priests the challenge of preaching on a September Sunday on the ideal of womanhood. Cooney commented that 'while some priests faced the daunting task of assessing women's liberation and the changed social position of women with some sensitivity and understanding, others presented a normal stereotype picture of the docile little domestic woman' (*Irish Times*, 8 September 1975).

Cooney's report from Rome in October 1975 had astutely recognized that, as Pope Paul VI aged, the 'question of the Papal succession' was 'crucial to the future development of the Catholic Church'. By the time Pope John Paul II ascended St Peter's chair, after John Paul I's brief occupancy of that seat, Cooney had departed his post as religious affairs correspondent. He had been replaced by the altogether more conservatively circumspect Pat Moran, who welcomed Karol Wojtyla's elevation to the papacy in 1978. He reported that the new Pope was 'regarded as a middle-of-the-road progressive churchman' (*Irish Times*, 17 October 1978). It would not be long before that assessment of a remarkable man would seem hopelessly bland. The editorial of that day was also bland enough, but did foresee that the appointment of a Polish Pope could affect the power-relations of the Cold War. The force of nature that was Pope John Paul II was soon fully to reveal itself.

By the end of September 1979, when Pope John Paul II made history by visiting Ireland (the first Pope to do so in the long years of Irish loyalty to the see of Rome), the momentum of his reign had been established. Visits to the Dominican Republic, to Mexico and to Poland had served notice that this was a man who would personally take his message to all parts of the globe and who would use his powerful theatrical and homiletic gifts to rouse large crowds to high levels of religious fervour. Nor would he hesitate to enter the political domain (though he was adamantly opposed to clergy who had any truck with Marxism). His June 1979 visit to his native Poland had been unambiguously an intervention that was likely to challenge the dictatorship of the ruling communist party in the name of dissidence and a nationalism in which Catholicism played an integral part. His visit to Ireland immediately preceded a journey to the United States where he would meet the 'born again' southern baptist president Jimmy Carter.

Religious and political issues were compacted in the papal visit to Ireland too. The Pope could not, for example, go north of the border to Armagh, in British territory, where the national cathedral is situated. Security issues could be cited as preventing a visit that would have raised difficult diplomatic problems for Ireland, the United Kingdom and the Vatican. Furthermore, what seemed to the outside world to be a nasty sectarian conflict between religious factions, shameful in a Christian land, was something the Pope could not ignore during his visit. In the event, he made an impassioned plea (unheeded then, sad to say) in Drogheda, some twenty miles south of the border with Northern Ireland, for the laying down of arms. A meeting with representatives of the Protestant Churches was also scheduled and took place.

Douglas Gageby, more than two years into his reinstatement as editor of the *Irish Times*, was not inclined to be analytical about the papal visit. As Mark O'Brien informs us, he demanded that the visit be enthusiastically celebrated by his paper. O'Brien writes, citing one contemporary journalist, that Gageby was determined 'to bury any memory of the *Irish Times* as a voice of Protestant Unionism. He wanted us to be liberal but also to be part of the mainstream of Irish life' (Mark O'Brien 2008, p. 221).

The front-page banner headline on 1 October read 'Out-pouring of Joy and Fervour', and 12 pages were devoted in the edition to exuberant reportage of a weekend that had seen a million people assemble in the Phoenix Park in Dublin to hear the Pope say Mass and many thousands of young people gathering at Galway's racecourse to hear him assure them that he loved them. The warm-up session in Galway, at what had something of the atmosphere of a rock-concert, was handled by the Bishop of Galway, Eamonn Casey, and the 'singing priest', Rev. Michael Cleary. The *Irish Times*'s editorial that Monday morning was entitled 'JOY'. Joy, indeed, was what Gageby thought the Pope had brought to Ireland. In an oddly Chestertonian touch, he waxed lyrical about the great man's arrival on Irish soil:

> Who could forget the gales of laughter from the most reverend doctors as the Pope went along the line of bishops at the airport making jokes not everyone overheard. Connoisseurs of episcopal lore must be the first to admit that this captivating incident perhaps told the country that something new was happening. (*Irish Times*, 1 October 1979)

More seriously, if unconvincingly, the editorial sought to make the papal visit speak to the fundamental unity of the nation, Northern Protestants and unionists included. 'It must move', the editorial claimed, in a passage expressive of Gageby's pan-national outlook,

> any Irish man or woman with the minutest historical sense to see, for the first time in two thousand years, a Pope walk the soil of Ireland. In general John Paul tapped deep roots for all those on this island who believe in the one way of life. Irish history is one fabric, made up of many (and sometimes clashing) strands; but it is one. And John Paul at Clonmacnoise can be as much a source of retrospective pride to any Northern Protestant as to all those who stayed with the old faith. Yesterday he made something of a reality of our occasionally romantic and exaggerated view of the past.

Gageby had not wanted any 'fashionable liberals sneering at the pope' (Mark O'Brien 2008, p. 221). Ironically, it was the conservatively minded John Healy (whom Gageby had re-employed after Healy's brief unsuccessful sojourn at the Independent Newspaper group during Pyle's editorship), who interrupted the joy-fest with a column that doubted the papal visit would have much effect on what he termed 'the Old Foolishness which all of the merchants of power have accumulated over the centuries' (*Irish Times*, 1 October 1979). 'What, in Christ's name', Healy bitterly queried, 'have we learned about ourselves, and our miserable strife-torn island?' His editor had thought the Pope's pastoral visit had 'become a potential illumination for everyone on the island'. Healy feared that light had simply revealed how power and religion were inextricably linked in a country Christian in name only.

This was a rare instance of public disagreement between Gageby and his robust columnist (who now contributed under the rubric 'Sounding Off'). For they shared a vision of improvement in Irish economic life, which had begun in the 1960s, being consolidated and developed under the powerful leadership of Charles Haughey. With Haughey at the head of Fianna Fáil (no mere political party, in their view, but a national movement expressive of the resurgent energy of the Irish people), the country could fulfil its destiny as an economic power-house to be reckoned with.

Such economic confidence was not easy to sustain as the 1970s ended, although Ireland was then enjoying rapid growth. The decade had seen the economic global expansion of the post-war period falter, as the first oil crisis, which had, we noted above, played havoc with the *Irish Times*'s own finances, brought with it stagnation and inflation to many countries. For the neighbouring island of Britain the 1970s had been a decade of profound crisis. This came to a head in the autumn of 1976, when the British government was forced to seek a loan from the International Monetary Fund to check a threatened run on the pound sterling. The sum required was so large (the biggest to that date requested from the fund) that additional resources were sought from the EEC and the United States. For a former imperial power that still held a permanent seat on the UN Security Council, this was a shocking humiliation and would prove a death-knell for the Labour government. In the final months of 1976, news from Britain that the *Irish Times* published was, unsurprisingly, dominated by the economic crisis there. On 15 October, for example, the paper took from the *Financial Times* service an extended article entitled 'A Government Living from Hand to Mouth' which spelled out the severity of the problems facing the British economy. It concluded that the fact that the government was bizarrely taking comfort from how inflation in 1977 would amount to 15 per cent (thereby reducing national indebtedness) was a 'fitting commentary on Britain's present state of affairs' (*Irish Times*, 15 October 1976). On 12 November an editorial reckoned that the British prime minister, James Callaghan, had little option but to soldier on, even as difficulties increased daily and his government's prestige constantly dwindled. And it saw little profit in a change of governing party in a situation where austerity would have to be applied rigorously by whomever was in power:

> A Tory Government under Mrs Thatcher is not an appetising proposition. Her front bench is not over-laden with administrative talent or economic expertise; the policies it favours are class-based and provocative and could well lead to a confrontation with the unions even more damaging than that which brought down Mr Heath. The Callaghan guillotines, however painful, may be preferable to the Thatcher knitting needles. (*Irish Times*, 12 November 1976)

An acerbic article by the *Irish Times*'s resident socialist 'stormy petrel' Claud Cockburn reminded *Irish Times* readers in November 1976 that they, too, could be affected by the cries for austerity sounding so loudly across the Irish

Sea. In this he recalled how governments more generally in Europe and in Britain had, in the past, used fears of rampant inflation to impose swingeing cuts in living standards. 'All this,' Cockburn reflected,

> affects one with an unpleasant sense of *déjà vu* as one listens to Richie Ryan and other Government ministers here, and – still more acutely – as Mr Callaghan and Mr Healy [Chancellor of the Exchequer] in Britain seek to prepare the public mind, and in particular the minds of organised trade unionists, for the moment when the visiting team from the International Monetary Fund comes down from Sinai with whatever stony Commandments they are about to disclose. (*Irish Times*, 16 November 1976)

Cockburn's reference to Richie Ryan was to the coalition's Minister for Finance. Dubbed 'Richie Ruin' by a popular RTE satiric show and 'Red Richie' by the tabloid press, on account of his introduction of a wealth tax, as the economy worsened following the oil crisis. Ryan was in fact a fairly conservative member of the fundamentally conservative Fine Gael party. His instincts were those of a fiscally responsible accountant (by profession he was a solicitor). In the opposition Fianna Fáil party there were those less inclined to pay attention to the tiresome rigours of accountancy. When the Taoiseach Liam Cosgrove called for a general election to be held on 16 June 1977, he was hoping that, despite the obvious unpopularity of his government as austerity bit hard and its law-and-order face became increasingly unappealing, the recent redrawing of the electoral boundaries would work to his advantage. He could scarcely have imagined that the customarily prudent Jack Lynch would authorize a 'give-away' manifesto that would deliver his party the largest electoral success in the country's history. It promised the abolition of domestic rates, of the wealth tax, and of the annual road tax on cars. The electorate found this irresistible and Fianna Fáil was put back in power with a twenty-seat majority in a historic electoral coup that would eventually cost the country dear. In effect, an enormous wager had been placed, in economically perilous times, that such actions would stimulate swift recovery (Lynch promised to reduce unemployment substantially). As early as 1980, when a second oil crisis took hold internationally, Lynch's wager had already proved foolhardy; but more serious was the way in which the implementation of the election promises of 1977 would make it almost impossible for future administrations to replace the traditional system of rates by an efficient tax on privately owned homes.

The day before the election, the *Irish Times*'s leader managed the peculiar feat of neither referring to how the coalition had offended many by the heavy-handed attitude to state security of some of its ministers nor to the tantalizing tax and rates proposals in Fianna Fáil's election manifesto. Rather, the leader, entitled 'Vote for Tomorrow', was a convoluted attempt to discern which exact parliamentary balance of power would best fortify the 'various strands of liberalism already in the Dáil' (*Irish Times*, 15 June 1977). We know from James Downey's memoir that the newspaper had commissioned its own pre-election opinion poll (the practice of such polls was in its infancy in Ireland in 1977), which indicated that Fianna Fáil was heading for victory. Fergus Pyle did not believe this was possible and, furthermore, thought the paper might lose credibility if it published something he contended was unbelievable, which would quickly come to be seen as having been so. The editorial of 15 June, inasmuch as it committed itself, opted for continuity. It opined:

> Apart from one or two bright new faces, Fianna Fáil is still very much the tired old team of 1973. In addition to his security connotation, Mr. Haughey personifies the Taca image of Fianna Fáil, which is hardly progressive. The party would benefit substantially by another few years of reconstruction out of office.

On election day the *Irish Times*'s front page carried a prognostication by its political correspondent, Dick Walsh, that the coalition was 'set to win' (*Irish Times*, 16 June 1977) the general election, 'although by a much smaller margin than politicians and observers anticipated before the campaign began'. It was far from the paper's finest hour and would prove a serious blow for the hapless Pyle, who was shortly to lose his job, to allow for the return of Gageby as editor.

The reference to Haughey, security and Taca in the *Irish Times*'s editorial on the forthcoming election, it is necessary to explain, was an indication that the writer for all his circumspection was fully aware of tendencies in Fianna Fáil of which he could not approve. Taca (Support) was an organization that had been established in the 1960s to enable builders and developers to contribute to the party's coffers and which began an association between thrusting young ministers like Haughey and the movers and shakers in an economy embracing the free market in a red-blooded fashion, well-tailored mohair suits covering naked greed. The 'Taca image of Fianna Fáil' was short-hand, therefore, for suspicions entertained by many that this involved conflicts of interest and opportunities for corruption. Allusion to 'security' not only brought to mind Haughey's indictment and trial on a charge of illegally importing arms at the beginning of the decade, but reminded readers how, by dint of an assiduous courting of the party's grassroots, that inveterately ambitious politician had re-established a personal power-base and could expect a ministry in any new Fianna Fáil cabinet. The writer would have known, too, that Haughey had the support of that wing of the party which thought a more overtly green nationalism should drive Irish policy in respect of Northern Ireland. Best vote to keep him on the opposition benches.

In the event, Lynch appointed Haughey as Minister for Health and for Social Welfare when the new government was formed. Lynch had indicated that he would not serve the full term in office, intending to resign in 1980 to allow a chosen successor the best chance to take up the reins before the government's term of office expired. However, discipline in a party with a large parliamentary majority loosened in 1979, and the resulting fractiousness, especially about co-operation with the British in the fight against the Provisional IRA, convinced Lynch that he should resign both as Taoiseach and as party leader slightly prematurely, in early December. In the ensuing election for his party's leadership, Haughey triumphed, with the obvious backing of a group of outspokenly republican deputies. He was proposed as Taoiseach in the Dáil and duly elected on 11 December 1979.

Haughey Redux was greeted with no little alarm in some quarters. The leader of the Labour Party, for example, implied that he would question Haughey's fitness for office, when his name was proposed in the Dáil, drawing censure from Gageby's *Irish Times* in an editorial entitled 'Rancour and Reason'. The writer insisted that any rerun of the debates on the Arms Crisis, which took place 'so many years ago' (*Irish Times*, 11 December 1979) would breed only unnecessary rancour, and he portentously concluded: 'Mr Haughey is more than the new leader of the Fianna Fáil Party, the new Taoiseach; he is also Leader of the House and of the people of this State for the time remaining to this Dáil ... It will be well for deputies to bear this in mind.' Naysayers, it implied, should cease their cavilling.

In the Dáil the next day Fine Gael's Garret FitzGerald was not inclined to any such forbearance. The *Irish Times* reported his speech on Haughey's nomination as Taoiseach under the headline 'FitzGerald launches slashing personal attack on Haughey'. The headline writer was obviously focusing on FizGerald's claim that Haughey came with '"a flawed pedigree"' (*Irish Times*, 12 December 1979) – an ill-chosen phrase, given that Haughey's family was in the chamber to observe his elevation to high office. In fact, FitzGerald's speech was a political assault on a man he believed could pose a threat to Irish democracy. The events of 1970 could not, in FitzGerald's view, be relegated to history, especially since Haughey had kept totally silent thereafter on the Provisional IRA's campaign of violence until he had achieved the leadership of Fianna Fáil. His credentials as a democrat were, therefore, in question, since he could apparently exploit the issue of paramilitarism so opportunistically. FitzGerald warned that members of his own party, as well as others, 'attribute to him an overweening ambition that they do not see as a simple emanation of a desire to serve, but rather as a wish to dominate, indeed to own the state'.

The *Irish Times*'s leader 'Rancour and Reason' had been criticized in the Dáil in the debate on Haughey's nomination by one of FitzGerald's colleagues, who had objected to the suggestion that bygones should be bygones in the matter of the Arms Trial. So the paper was duty-bound to respond to the debate of the previous day, in which it found 'a great deal of spark and bounce

THE IDENTITY OF IRELAND 311

... likewise malevolence, envy, and frustration, as Opposition speakers had their say about Charles J. Haughey' (*Irish Times*, 12 December 1979). FitzGerald's colleague, in censuring the *Irish Times*, had remarked 'This is not the Reichstag.' 'No,' replied a second leader that followed a judicious enough analysis of the newly appointed cabinet, 'nor is it a Volksgericht, the Nazi court which ended up with its victims hanging from meat hooks' (the style and field of reference that suggests Gageby was the writer). In a curious turn, in a piece the drift of which was that Haughey was being ill-used by his critics, the editorial admitted, 'There is, without any doubt, more of the aura of the dodgy around Charles J. Haughey than around any other occupant of his chair since 1922'; but it soon becomes clear that this is a rhetorical device to allow the writer to compare FitzGerald (also ambitious, also capable of political opportunism, and able to seek democratic endorsement by the people at an election) with Haughey, to whom the *Irish Times* can give its apparently well-judged support as one who 'has never denied his ambition' and who 'has worked openly and without concealment for the office he holds today, in the belief he will be good for his party and his country'.

In its 12 December editorial on the Haughey for Taoiseach debate in the Dáil, the *Irish Times* had affected to be particularly affronted by the way FitzGerald and others, protected from the libel laws by parliamentary privilege, had not provided 'the substance of their complaints [about Haughey], be they financial, sexual, political, subversive in any way'. FitzGerald, willing to wound and yet afraid to strike with hard fact, had hinted at rumours which could not be substantiated: 'Newspapers do not have the privilege of indulging themselves in this way.' They could, however, publish truthful material that might help readers to form their own opinions about their new Taoiseach. Despite such high-mindedness in this editorial about politicians and the substantiation of rumour, it seems that Gageby was not always keen to follow his own paper's counsel. For Frank McDonald, one of the paper's young journalists, had been trying to trace the sources of Haughey's wealth, and, as he has subsequently informed Mark O'Brien, he thought that Gageby 'buried' his well-researched article on the matter on page eight of the 14 December 1979 edition (it was actually on page seven),'basically' because he 'didn't want stuff that was "damaging" to Haughey to appear in the paper other than the usual political stuff' (Mark O'Brien 2008, p. 223).

McDonald, in the article alluded to above, painted a picture of the opulence enjoyed by the 'richest man to hold the office of Head of Government since the foundation of the State, far outstripping in wealth any of his six predecessors' (*Irish Times*, 14 December 1979). A connoisseur of art and fine champagne, the Taoiseach led the life, McDonald implied, of a chieftain, to which he believed he was entitled. How he came by the wealth that sustained it, Haughey, when questioned on the matter, chose not to divulge, though

McDonald's careful sifting through the available evidence could be read to suggest that 'dodgy' land deals had played their part in Haughey's spectacular rise to fortune. McDonald summed up with nicely honed irony:

> Life has been good to Charlie Haughey, and he clearly enjoys it. With his estimated wealth of £3 million, he has come a long way from his Donnycarney days when he was the scholarship boy who had nothing. But there is persistent speculation about his involvement in business deals in Dublin and other parts of the country. However the truth will probably never be known, at least not until there is a provision obliging Government Ministers and even Dáil deputies to disclose the extent of their wealth and income, and declare their interests in any activities outside parliament. Certainly, Mr Haughey, himself, seems to be in no rush to make a full declaration. All he would say on the subject of his wealth at his press conference last Friday was: 'Ask my bank manager'.

Haughey's suave truculence about the sources of his flaunted opulence was bred, it is fair to say, of a conviction that in some degree the state did belong to him as leader of a formerly dispossessed people who would brook no interference in their rise to the power wealth can help command. His emulation of the Protestant Ascendancy's lifestyle was an ebullient, self-aggrandizing statement of who was now in charge. And Ireland, with Charles J. Haughey as Taoiseach, could happily abandon any illusion that national identity was bound up with de Valera's vision of frugal comfort as a desirable ideal. So if the brash release of a long-denied materialism in Haughey's Ireland meant that developers and property speculators could cut corners here and there in the planning regulations, the strong suspicion that Haughey's enrichment was itself 'dodgy', in the *Irish Times*'s term, gave a kind of licence to the unscrupulous. For the more civic-minded, who hoped for an Ireland properly answerable to the public good, Haughey represented the embodiment of an unbridled will to personal power and wealth.

There was indeed a sad irony in the image of Haughey living in the splendour of a renovated Palladian mansion on the outskirts of a Georgian city that since independence had fallen into near terminal decrepitude, supinely open to the depredations of speculative building. In November 1979, just before Haughey came to power, Frank McDonald had published in the *Irish Times* an important series of articles that registered how far things had in gone in the city centre. In advertising the series, the paper regretted how 'Dublin, once beautiful, is now probably one of the ugliest capitals in Europe' (*Irish Times*, 10 November 1979). McDonald's first article, which evoked Dublin as 'a shabby city rotting to the core' (*Irish Times*, 12 November 1979), confessed 'The sad truth is that one can no longer be proud to call oneself a Dubliner. The condition of the city is a cause for shame, a cause for outrage.

There is degradation almost everywhere.' He was especially appalled by how developers had been demolishing buildings and then erecting structures with fake Georgian façades, and how the city fathers had passed no by-laws to prevent the altering of interiors in listed buildings. 'And what,' he asked, of 'Dublin's new buildings, the glass and office blocks of the 20th century? To many people, they are the creation of the "architecture of avarice".'

An editorial in the *Irish Times* on 17 November 1979 accepted McDonald's grim verdict on the fabric of the capital city; even Belfast, it was suggested, had done better with poorer resources. In comparison, Dublin was 'a heartbreak ... For all its past inequities, it had a certain nobility of mien, a dignified bearing, and now is reduced architecturally almost to the provincial squalor of one of England's scrap-heap towns. And all done by ourselves' (*Irish Times*, 17 November 1979). In all this Dublin Corporation was inert or complicit, with its road-widening plans, alongside 'get-rich-quick builders'.

In fact, 1978 and 1979 had seen a significant demonstration of a developing civic spirit in the nation's capital, as people rallied to save what they could of their urban inheritance. Dublin Corporation announced its intention to build offices for itself on the south bank of the River Liffey. The plans showed that the proposed tower blocks would interfere disastrously with one of the city's most attractive vistas, the view of the two medieval cathedrals from the Liffey's north bank. This was disturbing enough for many Dubliners, but when initial work on the Wood Quay site unearthed the remains of the early Viking city that was Dublin's foundational settlement, a protest movement quickly developed, drawing support from many parts of the country to oppose the Corporation's intentions. Led by a redoubtable priest and medieval historian, F. X. Martin of University College Dublin, through marches, occupations of the site and sustained propaganda activism, this managed to force a design rethink and to delay the construction of the office blocks for a sufficient time so that archaeologists could salvage some impressive artefacts that might otherwise have been lost beneath twentieth-century concrete.

It was strikingly apt that a decade in which the country had been reflecting on its national identity should end with archaeology highlighting the complex origins of its capital's past. For archaeological remains and the human past preserved in the rich loam of memory had been a trope explored in some of the finest Irish poems of the decade by John Montague in *The Rough Field* (1972) and Seamus Heaney in *North* (1975). Indeed, this latter volume, which set the island of Ireland in an imaginative cosmos that encompassed Icelandic and Viking perspectives, contained poems such as 'North' and 'Viking Dublin: Trial Pieces' which seemed like eerie premonitions of the Wood Quay finds. The poet Michael Hartnett, who reviewed Heaney's *North* in the *Irish Times*, astutely sensed, too, how the future Nobel Laureate in this volume was employing metaphors of exhumation and unearthing, the better to comprehend how the past bore on present political distresses. Hartnett perceptively wrote: 'His green world, beautiful but barbaric, was enriched by the attention he gave to a deeper and more ancient world, the bog, which is not only our timekeeper, but a graph of our consciences as well' (*Irish Times*, 14 June 1975). In June 1979 the novelist and historian of Dublin's language and lore, Bernard Share, drew a more humdrum, sardonic lesson from the Wood Quay affair, when the *Irish Times* published his poem 'Wood Quay'. It ran:

> Rogues' galleries are out of fashion: pity
> the ranks of minor villains unremembered –
> the greedy and the foolish who dismembered
> a heritage to raise their get-rich city.
> There's no encapsulation in the witty
> vehemence of Dublin or the embered
> ruins of a Rising: none remembered
> save as a paradigm of plasticity.
>
> And those dead Danes? Amongst them, sure as fate,
> some fly-boy seeing in the Hurdle-Ford
> a civic speculation. What walls burned
> to mulch the ground-plan of a city gate?
> A blindness no one bothered to record
> buried what Sitric's bulldozer upturned.

Change is the law of urban life and those who effect it have names writ in water; even their disgrace does not outlast them.

The *Irish Times* itself was aware that the Wood Quay finds were sermons in stones, bricks, shards and in intact objects that spoke to a country adjusting to a new European identity and to layers of indigenous traditions that must all be recognized. In an editorial entitled 'Father Martin's Ireland', on F. X. Martin's achievement in spearheading opposition to Dublin Corporation's plan for Wood Quay, the leader writer reflected:

> Now that we know more clearly the facts of our past, all the greater is the onus on us to respect that which has been left to us. Whether the remains are Viking or Celtic or Anglo-Irish (or Shankill Irish), in bulldozing them as if they were Sunset Strip hamburger joints, we are leaving a miserable, craven, cheap inheritance to succeeding generations. (*Irish Times*, 4 June 1979)

There were those, however, as the decade ended, ready to view the EEC, not the Americanization alluded to above, as the greater threat to Irish identity and cultural distinctiveness. The *Irish Times* would have none of it. An editorial 'Lest We Forget' in June 1979 responded to such claims by reminding readers of how the European ideal was of peace that allowed the people of the Continent to 'associate in amity, each country or people, keeping its identity and customs' (*Irish Times*, 5 June 1979). The writer argued, indeed, that the opportunities for travel afforded to young people by the Community had seemed 'to stiffen their resolve to maintain and even foster what we have'. Yet in this editorial, fired with enthusiasm for the European project that 'one day' might 'lead to an association bordering on unity', the question of Irish identity is, nonetheless, treated as problematic. Partition is still thought of as a bar to the full cultural realization of national destiny. 'This part of Ireland –,' the writer stated, 'the 26 County State – has no lasting identity of its own, but in a hopeful way, stands for all the Irish nation.' The truth may rather have been that in the 1970s the 26-county Republic of Ireland was coming into a sense of itself as a small independent nation state, which despite the continuing conflict in Northern Ireland, was increasingly gaining confidence, as it co-operated confidently with EEC institutions, in an identity being made actual in action.

There was much in the paper's columns in the 1970s to suggest that this was a process in the making. The Northern 'Troubles' often forced their way on to the front page (and a decade of atrocities was epitomized on one day in August 1979 when Earl Mountbatten of Burma was assassinated while on holiday in County Sligo, and 18 British soldiers lost their lives to IRA bombs beside Carlingford Lough in County Down), but inside pages carried regular, thoroughly researched reports, articles and opinion pieces by specialist correspondents on such things as education, economics, industrial development, business and finance. The focus of these was predominantly the independent Irish state and society, serving a readership that found this subject matter more germane to their everyday lives than appalling front-page stories of lives interrupted or ended by soldier's bullet or terrorist's bomb.

Education was a major topic in the 1970s' *Irish Times*. The introduction of free secondary education for all in 1967 was bearing fruit as the country began to pride itself on its well-educated young people. The newspaper had responded to this proritizing of universal secondary education as national policy by founding the weekly *Education Times* (emulating the London *Times Educational Supplement*) in 1972 with John Horgan (who had left the paper's staff to serve as a senator in the state's upper house) as editor. Although education was a growth industry in the 1970s, this experiment was hampered from the start since it could not depend on revenue from advertisements for teaching posts being placed in its pages (as the *Times Educational Supplement* could). Unable thereby to pay its way, the *Education Times* was closed in 1976, but not before it had established such concepts as curriculum reform and ideas on community and comprehensive schools as integral to progressive thinking about education. In 1975 Christina Murphy, who had succeeded Maeve Binchy as the editor of the 'Women First' section (until such material was subsumed into the paper as a whole), became education correspondent and quickly established herself as the country's foremost educational journalist.

Murphy's distinction as a writer on education matters in the 1970s was rooted in her enthusiastic respect for what was being achieved in Irish schools, together with a willingness to raise controversial and sensitive issues in a thoughtful way (when in charge of 'Women First', she had not hesitated to report on the embryonic gay rights movement).

In March 1976 on no other than St Patrick's Day, Murphy pleaded for sex education to be made universal in Irish schools. She stated frankly: 'there is very little sex education being undertaken here and there is hardly a teacher, agony columnist, youth or social worker – not to mention marriage guidance counsellor – who will not agree that there is need for some form of education in this area' (*Irish Times*, 17 March 1976). Against some religious, who contended that sex education should be confined to the home, Murphy argued for a 'good sex education programme' in the schools. She was forthright about what the denominational debate in the education field actually concerned. She firmly insisted that it was 'power and control' at stake when a 'desire' emerged 'among a majority of Catholic parents for a more secular type of education for their children and for an involvement of community groups in the provision of schools' (*Irish Times*, 31 March 1976). Murphy identified the 'nub of the matter' thus: 'If national schools [primary level schools] start going multi-denominational, the main power basis of the Catholic Church in Irish education will be eroded. It is their patronage and management of the school which is at issue rather than the religious affiliation of the attendance.'

There was a polemical edge to Christina Murphy's article on the Church control of the Irish schools and on the emergent demand in a few places for multi-denominational schools. It was also informed, as was the case with a good deal of her work, with an impulse to inform and to explain to the parents and pupils beginning to participate in a mass-education system, in construction since the late 1960s, how it operated and what could be expected from it. A similar pedagogic, explanatory intent was evident in the writings of the *Irish Times*'s cohort of analysts and commentators on the Republic's financial, business and industrial life in the 1970s. Like the focus on educational developments, their work contributed to the formation of a settled conviction in the decade that the 26-county state was the now a stable entity in which most citizens found their national *raison d'être*.

Nineteen seventy-nine, for example, was a year in which there was a good deal of economic explaining to be done and the *Irish Times* rose to the challenge. In September Paul Tansey, a recruit from student politics to the paper's finance columns, was obliged to explain to readers why, in John Maynard Keynes's arresting formulation, the world's economy was once again 'crucified on a cross of gold'. For the precious metal was re-emerging as 'a store of value against inflation' (*Irish Times*, 24 September 1979). Furthermore, in this period of international uncertainty, Ireland had chosen, in March 1979, to break the link with sterling to which its currency had been tied since independence. So the same journalist, nine months after this financial divorce from the former imperial master, sought to account for this: 'Lying behind the decision to break the link with sterling,' Tansey argued, 'was an implicit assumption that the British economy was slowly subsiding. It was therefore thought opportune to cut the umbilical cord binding us to Britain' (*Irish Times*, 19 November 1979). Tansey noted that this was affecting relations with Northern Ireland as the land border became a currency border too.

Throughout the year the newspaper had devoted much space to reports on and analysis of the parlous state of the British economy. For example, a review of three books on post-war political developments there by one of the paper's leader writers, James Downey, was entitled 'Britain's hour of reckoning'. Downey wrote:

> ... decline is concealed by two factors: North sea oil and the country's unique stability and continuity. But the oil will run out and the tradition of good government and civilised living is threatened by pessimism and loss of nerve on the part of the lower echelons of the ruling class. Britain can hobble along for decades or even generations, propped up by tradition and the income from foreign investment, but the day of reckoning has come to look very close. (*Irish Times*, 13 October 1979)

At the end of the year in an article simply entitled 'Britain', Vincent Cowley painted a depressing enough picture of a neighbouring country whose economic well-being was under serious threat: 'In line with Ireland's young people, those in Britain are confronting a future pockmarked with economic constraints and even greater, and more threatening, financial uncertainties' (*Irish Times*, 28 December 1979).

An editorial of this year also commented on the apparent diminution in British economic and political power. 'There is no satisfaction,' it read, 'on any score, for Irish people in seeing Britain in decline. From the selfish point of view, too, misery in any major British industry can hit our own people, for so many Irish live and work there' (*Irish Times*, 30 November 1979). The main point of this editorial, nonetheless, was that the British government was in no position, with its depleted industrial production and moribund parliamentary machinery, to make too much of a fuss about its contributions to the EEC at the European summit shortly to be held in Dublin. The editorial was entitled 'Thatcherism' (Margaret Thatcher had been appointed prime minister in May). Its patronizing tone suggests that the writer had not yet grasped what a forceful personality and how committed an economic ideologue lay behind the new concept of 'Thatcherism'.

If the term 'Thatcherism' was yet to acquire its full meaning as an economic doctrine and style of leadership, other terms by the end of the 1970s had become so common in debate about public affairs in the Republic that the *Irish Times*, in its pedagogic mode, thought it necessary in 1979 to supply a layman's guide to the economic thought that was coming to dominate the national conversation. On 27 November that year Ken O'Brien, Paul Tansey and Eoin McVey supplied a special report that amounted to a crash course in the subject. The paper accepted that a certain demystification of terminology was necessary if the populace was to keep up to speed in this field, and was keen that it should do so:

> The economic revolution in Ireland over the last 25 years has brought dramatic changes in prosperity, in the Government's role in the economy, and in the role of unions, employers and banks in determining our material fortunes and standards of living. The changes have been accompanied by an increase in the usage of sometimes bewildering words and concepts, such as 'deficit budget', 'external reserves', 'Keynesian', to name but a few. In this supplement you will find explanations of both the words and the concepts, and what they mean to this country.

Ireland, the identity of which had been the focus of so much debate throughout the decade, was becoming in many respects thought of as an 'economy' whose present and future could be understood in the deployment of terms of art derived from the dismal science.

However much the issue of Ireland's complex identity was reflected upon in the 1970s in the columns of the *Irish Times*, the decade also saw the country becoming more and more permeated by the mass culture of the Anglophone world. In an astute recognition that this was an undeniable fact of the contemporary moment, the paper had, in 1970, recruited the young Northern Irish playwright Stewart Parker to write a fortnightly article on pop music. Entitled 'High Pop', this gave the kind of informed attention to the international phenomenon of pop music, which the paper had lacked in the 1960s when the era of touring rock bands, pop music radio stations and the counter culture had shaped the experience of many millions of young people in North America and the British Isles. For six years Parker (who shared an east Belfast background with a coming megastar in the pop firmament, Van Morrison) was a voice in the *Irish Times* that made contact with those in Ireland who valued his guidance through the mazes of pop groups, record labels and the latest trends, local and international. Parker brought to his column not only the aficionado's zest for a wide variety of musical forms (his critical range extended from Leadbelly to Stockhausen) but a thoughtful awareness of the cultural implications of the phenomenon of pop. In an article published in February 1972 (less than a month after Bloody Sunday in Derry) he reflected how:

> There's nationalism and there's international urbanism. While the first continues to motivate real politics, the second has long since dominated real culture. So far as vital forms of expression go, from sport to the higher mathematics, the global village is a fact of life ... It's a small spaceship, earth. (cited Dawe and Johnston 2008, p. 122)

Parker's articles, therefore (witty, opinionated, iconoclastic about such figures as Bob Dylan and John Lennon, but consistently generous in spirit), inscribe Ireland in the context of that international urbanism (later in the decade the serious-minded Fergus Pyle's concession to a readership anxious to be au fait with all things chic in the global village, from gardening, travel, cuisine to the latest theory in history or philosophy, was to inaugurate a magazine-style Weekend section each Saturday that joined the book page with three others devoted to feature articles, colour pieces and entertainment guides). Parker argued, furthermore, that this ubiquitous urban music had it sources in the Blues, the 'downhearted heart of all modern popular music'; but since 'the history of culture is a saga of the migration of art forms', pop music, he implied, can serve as a reminder of how national identity is never mono-cultural and can be the local expression for good or ill of international modes. He observed:

> I think music has to be considered as an international medium, in the same sense that neoclassical architecture was international in the eighteenth century. The roots of the music are all in America – most of them in Black America – but the electric guitar, after all, is no more 'American' than television. The best groups are those that accommodate this international medium to their own idiosyncratic sense of reality.
>
> (Dawe and Johnston 2008, pp. 35–6)

Yet for all his confidence that rock music, as he put it in 1972, had been 'pre-eminent among the lively arts in the past decade as a form of lyric expression, assuaging and defining the content of personality and personal relationships', Parker admitted, 'it can't handle large-scale public or political emotions or ideas' (Dawe and Johnston 2008, p. 126). Its cultural hybridity could not encompass, indeed, a clash of national identities on a small island, where nothing had come out of the Northern Ireland troubles except 'death, agony and a murderous hatred which our forms of expression have shown themselves unable to assuage or define' (Dawe and Johnston 2008, p. 126).

10

THE *IRISH TIMES* IN UNCERTAIN TIMES

O n 23 September 1980 a play entitled *Translations* was premiered in the Guildhall in Derry. It was the first production mounted by a new theatrical and cultural ginger group that styled itself the Field Day Theatre Company. The author of *Translations* was the dramatist and short-story writer Brian Friel.

Friel had made his reputation as a dramatist in 1964 with a play that had poignantly expressed the ambivalence many Irish people felt about emigration. His play about Bloody Sunday, *The Freedom of the City*, had in 1973 challenged the findings of a British inquiry into that atrocity perpetrated by the British Parachute Regiment. He was a writer who addressed the condition of the nation in his drama. Accordingly, Friel's new play, with its nineteenth-century Donegal setting and its imagining of a moment when British troops, representing imperial power, were at work in anglicizing Gaelic Ireland (in fact anglicization in Ireland was a more complex process as the play does, indeed, allow), could readily be interpreted as a kind of parable on the contemporary Northern situation, where many nationalists viewed the British Army's presence as that of an occcuping power.

However, the play's impact on audiences in the Republic, where it was widely and successfully toured by the new company (as it was in Northern Ireland too), suggests that its significance bore on deeper issues than a desire to repossess the fourth green field. Friel's subtle exploration of the various attitudes of his play's characters to a linguistic transition that involved the possibility of economic modernization at the expense of cultural identity seemed to touch a chord in contemporary Irish feeling. For since 1959 the Irish state had been intently focused on economic development and by 1980 many citizens were unsure about whether the cost of the project had been too high in cultural and even in political terms. Perhaps the concentration on economic advancement in the Republic had distracted from the urgent need to confront the injustices being endured by nationalists in the North. What compounded the mood of national uncertainty (to which Friel's play spoke) as the new decade began was an awareness that the economic upturn of the 1960s was seriously at risk and that the 1980s could put in doubt such material gains as the country had made. At the end of Friel's play, one character, who understands how discourse in which emotion is implicit can be out of alignment with 'the landscape ... of fact', delivers himself of the resonant observation: 'confusion is not an ignoble condition'.

The landscape of fact in the early 1980s quickly revealed itself as a rocky terrain where economic growth could not easily be sustained. The uncertainty bred of rapidly deteriorating public finances and alarmingly raised national indebtedness found expression in several years of political turmoil which gave electors and citizens ample opportunity to test the truth of *Translations'* apothegm about confusion. Who to vote for was itself confusing as general election followed general election.

Charles Haughey, on his election as Taoiseach by the Dáil in December 1979, had addressed the nation in terms that made quite clear that the wager placed by his party in the 1977 general election had already been lost. The second oil crisis and international recession had meant that the gamble that Ireland could trade its way to greater prosperity as concessions on domestic rates and motor tax kept wages competitively low, was now revealed to be a failed strategy. On 9 January 1980, in an address to the nation, Haughey informed his television audience that the country was living beyond its means and promised a period of belt-tightening. In the event he did little to ameliorate the situation and by the time an election was called for June 1981 a full-blown economic crisis had unfolded. Unemployment had risen swiftly and would stand at 160,000 people by 1982. In 1979 foreign debt was already rising. Between 1980 and 1981 it doubled since the state was forced to borrow simply to pay its way and to service the debt that had already accrued.

In this economic tempest the *Irish Times* was well placed with its expert team of economic, industrial and business writers to analyse how a perfect storm was battering the Irish economy and state. Most crucially, Paul Tansey, in an article entitled 'Caught in Our Own Trap', published in October 1980, identified how the economic crisis posed a major problem for the political process in Ireland. He succinctly argued:

> Irish governments are now caught in a trap of their own making. Having allowed borrowing to soar since 1975, no Irish government can now prise itself free of heavy annual borrowing without extremely painful consequences. The real problem faced by this and future Irish governments centres on the fact that the economic necessity of reducing dependence on loan finance conflicts directly with the political imperative of retaining power. (*Irish Times*, 22 October 1980)

In this article Tansey suggested that a tipping point might soon be reached in which the state would be forced into the arms of the International Monetary Fund, for he saw all too well how the 'slippery slope of deficit budgeting leads quickly to a quagmire from which governments find it extraordinarily difficult to extricate themselves'. He was not sanguine that the Haughey government would rise to the economic and political challenge: 'Presented with ... stark and unappetising choices and with an election on the horizon, it is likely that the government will duck the issue and continue to run a very high level of borrowing.'

The general election of June 1981, despite Haughey's cynical U-turn on the stark warnings of imminent austerity he had delivered in 1979, saw Fianna Fáil give way to an insecure coalition led by Garret FitzGerald which comprised Fine Gael, Labour and a number of independents. This administration struggled to tackle the economic mess Fianna Fáil had left it. When the coalition government fell over a mismanaged budget, Haughey regained power in February 1982 (depending on a deal struck with a demanding Dublin inner city independent deputy). Haughey survived for less than a year before he was succeeded once again as Taoiseach by Garret FitzGerald in a Fine Gael/Labour coalition.

Such governmental instability was scarcely conducive to coping with the economic crisis in a systematic way. In the midst of this political less than merry-go-round, Paul Tansey was moved to warn that 'Ireland is well on the way to becoming ungovernable' (*Irish Times*, 4 January 1982) since governments, fearful of the electorate, would probably 'continue to evade dealing with the basic economic problems'. He feared the 'likely outcome is that the country will drift aimlessly along the road to God knows where'. The paper's financial and economic writers were aware, too, as they combined detailed analytical articles with reportage, on how the financial crisis was affecting Irish society. For example, in January 1982 Ken O'Brien published a four-part series of articles on the black economy which he identified as 'the most rapidly developing area of the Irish economy' (*Irish Times*, 18 January 1982); tax evasion was both easy and commonplace.

It was not surprising that, in the midst of the economic storm, the *Irish Times* began to publish columns of financial advice with headings like 'You and Your Money'. This marked tendency of the early 1980s culminated towards the end of the second year of the second coalition's term of office, in a six-part series in the paper in November 1984 on 'Keeping Your Balance in the Uncertain Eighties'. In the first of these, Ken O'Brien assured readers that they could be helped to make 'the most of their money' (*Irish Times*, 26 November 1984) by reading the paper's explanation of 'the background to the present state "of uncertainty in Ireland and abroad"'. However, O'Brien also admitted, 'The present decade is more uncertain than any since the Thirties.'

Nor was it surprising that in such a climate of uncertainty both citizens and commentators sought for signs of recovery in a winter of discontent, and auguries of a better future. In September 1983 Ken O'Brien himself, in a series of articles on the United States and investment in Ireland, had observed how 'American firms in this country accounted for more than half of Ireland's industrial exports. Fast-growing technology industries, most from the United States, have eclipsed

UNCERTAIN TIMES   323

what was the country's most important economic activity, the cattle trade' (*Irish Times*, 26 September 1983). Also in 1983 the prospect that substantial oil reserves might be discovered off the coast of County Waterford aroused such a mood of expectation that O'Brien had to counsel against 'economic euphoria' (*Irish Times*, 16 August 1983). A find by British Petroleum in 1980 off County Galway had proved uncommercial and O'Brien warned that the same thing could happen again in the new drilling area. Yet even the cautious commentator could not resist imagining Ireland as an oil-producing nation. The discovery of oil 'could, if properly used, turn out to be the event that transforms the economic outlook for Ireland for the next decade'.

For the editor of the *Irish Times* and his coadjutor John Healy, the appointment of Charles J. Haughey as Taoiseach in 1979 had been supposed to be a transformative event, if not quite on the same scale as the discovery of an oil-field of North Sea proportions in Irish territorial waters. That the Irish economy almost went into free-fall on Haughey's watch was at the very least an embarrassment for those who had vaunted him as the man who would stave off disaster. With the paper's economic, financial and industrial correspondents laying out in extensive detail how close Haughey had brought the economy to a cliff, the editorial line could not credibly continue to afford the Taoiseach unqualified support. Nor did it. On 29 January 1982 an editorial warned Haughey not to sing economic lullabies to the electorate since the Republic did need 'a rescue job' (*Irish Times*, 29 January 1982). It, nonetheless, still expressed faith in Fianna Fáil, in comparison with a Fine Gael with its 'eyes ... too fixedly aimed at the stars. Fianna Fáil, in a good Ulster Scots word, was more aware of the clabber underfoot.' And as Mark O'Brien (Mark O'Brien 2008, pp. 222–3) has told us, the lukewarm credit for honest effort the paper gave to Fine Gael and Labour on election day in February 1982 was at the prompting of an editorial team that was strongly anti-Haughey.

Yet when Haughey formed his second administration, the *Irish Times* issued an editorial of bizarre ambivalence. The editorial, entitled 'To Work', was all too conscious that Haughey was in power again through a piece of costly opportunism (his deal with an independent Dáil deputy would direct support to one section of Dublin in isolation: *Irish Times*, 10 March 1982). Nor could he fail to admit that 'Haughey's first period as Taoiseach was a disappointment', as it observed, 'The onus of having to excel this time will lie heavily on his shoulders.' However, the writer prefixed this must-do better report card with a quotation from an ancint Irish epic that recounted how its hero Cuchulain bested his numerous foes in battle: "'The warp-spasm overtook him ... The hero halo rose up from the crown of his head'". The editorial proper began in a similar high-flown vein: 'In such heroic terms might some of Charles Haughey's admirers think of him today; the man who like Cuchulain, overcomes all obstacles. Rejected, restored, then toppled, assailed from without and within, he is again on the attack.' The effect of this blustering was to suggest, in denial of the evidence, that Haughey still had the stuff of effective leadership in him, though the task he faced was daunting enough.

Haughey's second premiership was marked by controversy and scandal which brought him to electoral defeat before the year was out. The most serious of the scandals that dogged his administration was the revelation by the *Irish Times*'s Peter Murtagh that the Minister for Justice, Seán Doherty, had been interfering in Garda business, to the apparent benefit of private individuals. Even in the face of such damaging indications of governmental malfeasance, and in the knowledge that Haughey was in fact opposed by a substantial part of his own party, the *Irish Times* on election day in November 1982 affected a studied neutrality as it called for a decisive leader who would make the state 'a better place to live in' (*Irish Times*, 24 November 1982). Nonetheless, it could not help boosting Haughey as a man 'born to be chief': 'Haughey's spirit cannot be denied. Such racking ambition would be burden and a source of anguish to another man; he carries it lightly and even enjoys it.' And it was only after FitzGerald had formed a new administration with Labour and had passed a swingeing budget that an editorial took the full measure of the country's economic condition.

Entitled 'Newly Broke', the leader conceded: 'In one generation, it seems we have gone from being a poor society to being a newly broke society' (*Irish Times*, 10 January 1983), without any mention of the party and of the leader who had been ineffectively at the helm for much of the time when the economy almost foundered. Rather, the writer predicted that the new government would probably be 'the most unpopular government in living memory'. And this when just opprobrium was in fact being focused more intently on Haughey's dismissed administration. For FitzGerald's government had revealed how the intelligence services had been tapping the phones of two journalists, Geraldine Kennedy and Bruce Arnold, to gain knowledge of Fianna Fáil plotting against Haughey's leadership of the party when he was Taoiseach. As Mark O'Brien has further enabled us to grasp (Mark O'Brien 2008, p. 224), Gageby's editorial response to this was concern more for the integrity of the intelligence services than for the infringement of civil liberties. When he did get around to apportioning some blame, it was Fianna Fáil, 'reckless beyond belief', rather than Haughey, the presumed beneficiary of such activity, whom he incited.

Gageby and Healy, it seems, found it hard to break the umbilical cord with Fianna Fáil and a fraught fascination with 'the boss', in the person of Charles Haughey. In the early years of the 1980s they certainly found various reasons to commend and upbraid both party and leader, but for both men there was something deeper than mere politics at work in their attachments. Gageby possessed an intense dislike of Fine Gael that vied with his Anglophobia as a controlling passion, and he probably nourished hopes that Haughey was the kind of man who could, in the right circumstances, effectively challenge Britain to agree a negotiated settlement to end partition. Healy was convinced that in the past Fianna Fáil had been the 'moral community' of the Irish nation, with its roots in the village life he admired. The new consumer society, as he expressed it in a considered if simplistic piece of historical reflection in the paper in 1984, had substituted the idea of 'the economy' for that old way of life where you 'were authentic: every man and woman in the village had a place, everybody was somebody and everyone had a place in the hierarchy of the village. It was reassuring, no matter how lowly the place in the pecking order' (*Irish Times*, 14 March 1984). In the new consumerist dispensation, economists had replaced the priesthood, Healy opined, preaching the grubby values of the marketplace where communalism (the concept of the *meitheal* figured large in his 'philosophy') had once held sway. It was economists who were intent on 'making us citizens of an economy', rarely treating 'the Irish as being citizens of a State, an old nation'. The proof of this depressing condition, which was impeding Ireland from becoming a second Japan (where traditional values of the village apparently coalesced with technological modernity) was Garret FitzGerald's premiership, then in its second year. Of FitzGerald and the new economic priesthood, Healy dismissively inquired: 'is not one of them, the first of them, now elevated as leader of the Economy, a man who talks and acts like The Taoiseach of the Economy he is?' For Healy, Haughey, for all his faults, was the antithesis of FitzGerald (whom he had satirically dubbed 'Garret the Good', in implied contrast to the interestingly 'wicked' Haughey), inasmuch as he aspired to epitomize in his person the spirit of a nation at the apex of Fianna Fáil's residual 'moral community' ('There is a fair residue left in us still').

In 1980 Haughey had challenged Margaret Thatcher's government on the issue of partition in a forceful if unproductive way, to the satisfaction of the *Irish Times* editorialists. Early in his first term of office he had sought to woo Mrs Thatcher herself to consider a new approach to the problem of Northern Ireland. Since the fall of the Northern executive in 1974, the main Irish political parties, Fine Gael, Labour and Fianna Fáil under Jack Lynch, had shared the view that politicians in the North should be encouraged by the British to re-establish a power-sharing administration there with some links of association with the Dublin government. Haughey took a very different view, judging, as he did, that the problem was a territorial dispute between two sovereign governments over what he termed in February 1980 'a failed political entity', which must be solved at an intergovernmental level, essentially over the heads of the Northern parties and population. In adopting this approach, he was willing to break with the near-consensus that had developed in the Republic that inter-party agreement in the North was a prerequisite of a settlement.

In December 1980 Haughey played his hand in the diplomatic poker game that he intended would alter the terms of engagement between Britain and Ireland on the matter of partition. In the context of a hunger strike in the Maze

Prison, Long Kesh, just outside Belfast, which housed republican prisoners who were demanding political status, Margaret Thatcher agreed to meet Haughey in Dublin. The encounter in Dublin Castle, former seat of British rule in Ireland, in the seventh week of the hunger strike, was treated in Dublin as a summit, and the fact that Thatcher brought senior ministers with her catered to that interpretation of the event. Moreover, a communiqué that announced that the 'totality of relationships within these islands' was to be the subject of a series of studies was seized upon by the Irish side in the conversation as a reopening of the Irish question that had been left in abeyance in 1920 and 1922.

The *Irish Times* thought this meeting and its outcome so important that it devoted three editorials in a week to it in terms that suggested that the newspaper basically shared Haughey's ideological position. Its editorial the day after the meeting welcomed the presence of Thatcher in Dublin. On 9 December an editorial entitled 'The Right Context' unequivocally insisted that 'It can hardly be stated too often, or too strongly, that problems of Northern Ireland are the inescapable problems of all Ireland' (*Irish Times*, 9 December 1980). The editorial was not fully certain that the outcome of the mooted studies would be as profound as the phrase about 'totality of relationships' suggested they might be. The editorial was certain, however, that Haughey had set the Northern question in the correct context:

> ... however difficult the working out may prove, Mr Haughey can claim a
> substantial gain in having placed the problems affecting the two islands in
> the context in which they belong: the context of the relations of the Irish
> and British Governments, and the Irish and British peoples. A good day's
> work was done in Dublin Castle yesterday.

The next day, reflecting on the fact that Mrs Thatcher, at a press conference held on her return to London, had not seen the resonant phrase about 'totality of relationships' as presaging a tectonic shift in British policy towards the North, an editorial expressed a conviction that, though 'the phrase sounds a bit pompous ... there is no dodging what it means. Everything is up for consideration' (*Irish Times*, 10 December 1980). Tellingly, this editorial, entitled 'Threat and Promise', welcomed the discomfiture being felt by Northern unionists as proof that something fundamental was afoot, as it dismissively referred to the British guarantee that the status of Northern Ireland would not be changed without the majority consent of its people: 'The Unionists have had a reiteration of the old guarantee, but they may feel like Liam Cosgrave, who inelegantly puts it that the British always sell their friends down the river.' It was clear that the leader writer would be happy enough to see them suffer that unhappy fate: 'The implicit threat to Unionists stands. What is more important is that something more than implicit has been entered on the positive side for all the inhabitants of these islands.' An editorial on 12

December circumspectly described the divergence of opinion on what had been agreed to in Dublin as a contretemps that did not alter the significant substance of what had transpired: 'It would be hard for any nationalist to maintain that the meeting had been other than a very welcome step forward.'

Little came of this meeting in Dublin. Thatcher was unhappy at the way Haughey and his foreign minister had seemed to overplay their hands in the immediate aftermath of the Dublin Castle encounter. The ghastly outcome of a second hunger strike in the Maze Prison in 1981 was also to reconfigure the problem in a way that meant neither government could impose a settlement on Northern Ireland without taking due regard of the attitudes of the republican movement, whatever about those of Northern unionists.

The first of the hunger strikers to die, the leader of the Provisional IRA hunger strikers, Bobby Sands, passed away on 5 May 1981, to the widespread sorrow of nationalist Ireland at home and abroad. His death was widely reported on by the world's media. The next day the *Irish Times* published a moving editorial that suggested that the British government was playing with fire in refusing to compromise on the matter of political status for republican prisoners. It asked 'Does no-one in Westminster read Irish history?' (*Irish Times*, 6 May 1981) and reminded readers of how the executions of 1916 had been the catalyst of a more widespread rebellion against British rule. The writer sensed that Ireland was approaching a similar watershed that would present a major challenge to nationalist Ireland as well as to the British government. In face of demands that a national day of mourning be declared, the leader writer counselled:

> However widely support is given to the obsequies for Bobby Sands, it can in no sense be said that there is a process of national mourning going on. For one million people in the North are mourning their own dead. The population of this island without that one million people in no way constitutes the nation.

The subtext of this editorial was, accordingly, expressive of an anxiety that the deaths of republican hunger strikers could make partition a powerful one of sorrow, with nationalist Ireland at one in its mourning for Sands and his starving companions and the unionist North at one in mourning its own victims of the republican 'war'. The editorial accepted that 'small Protestant people' had in the last few years been enduring a 'process of decimation'. In two such congeries of feeling, it was implied, could be sown the seeds of an Irish civil war.

Garret FitzGerald, on his return to power in June 1981, was abruptly thrust into the intensifying political and security crisis fomented by the hunger strikes. On 18 July, less than three weeks after he had become Taoiseach, with the deaths of five more martyrs to the cause stirring up public feeling in the Republic as well as in the North, FitzGerald was confronted by a direct challenge to the Irish state. A huge protest march was directed at the new

British embassy building in Merrion Road, Dublin 4 (where it obtruded as a formidable redoubt in a settled middle-class suburb). Many of the crowd were possibly intent on repeating what had happened after Bloody Sunday in 1972. The police stood steadfastly against them, with 120 officers suffering injury in the riot that ensued when the marchers' progress was blocked. The front page of the *Irish Times* reported in terms that suggested that some kind of attitudinal climax was being reached in the country, stating 'the most serious street violence ever to break out in the Republic as a result of the Northern troubles' (*Irish Times*, 20 July 1981) had taken place.

The editorial of 20 July made clear that the *Irish Times* stood alongside the country's police force. 'Nothing,' it said, could 'condone the abominable thuggery which occurred on the Merrion Road on Saturday' (*Irish Times*, 20 July 1981). But more than thuggery was involved. The editorial continued:

> Doubtless some of the rioters did what they did out of sheer wanton love of hooliganism. But in the background, in the shadows, can be discerned the figures of the 'godfathers' of the Provisional IRA, manipulating them for their own ends. These ends include nothing less than the destruction of Irish democracy. They cannot be allowed to succeed.

The editorial also feared that anti-British feeling was being provoked by inflexibility on Thatcher's part. A 'poison,' the paper advised, was 'weakening good relations within these islands'. Only an immediate settlement of the hunger strike could begin to drain it away. Next day an editorial reaffirmed the *Irish Times*'s unambiguous commitment to the police: 'There will be allegations of over-reaction ... But they did their duty, which was to protect the embassy' (*Irish Times*, 21 July 1981).

By the time the hunger strike was called off in early October 1981, four more names had been added to the roll-call of the republican martyred dead. At the last the British government ceded to republican prisoners the right to wear their own clothes during incarceration, but continued to refuse them political status (though effectively that was what they would experience). Thatcher could claim a victory of sorts, but it was a pyrrhic one. For the hunger strikes, with their ten heroic martyrs, gave a legitimacy in the eyes of many to the Provisional IRA's armed struggle that, North and South, they had hitherto refused to grant it. To add to this, electoral successes achieved by republicans while the strike was in progress helped to persuade the wing of Sinn Féin which supported the Provisional IRA that henceforth it would put up candidates for British and Irish elections, even if victors would not take their seats at Stormont in Belfast, at Westminster in London, or at Leinster House in Dublin (they would sit at local level in Northern Ireland). A new and powerful phase in the separatist struggle was in the making which threatened to wrest the initiative in the matter of Anglo-Irish relations from the Irish government and set in question electoral support for the constitutionalist nationalist party in the North, the Social Democratic and Labour Party, led by John Hume.

Garret FitzGerald's response to these developments was a very curious one which made abundantly clear how much he differed from Haughey on the vexed issue of how to end partition. Where Haughey basically thought it was the responsibility of the British government to come to the table to discuss how a final disengagement from Ireland could be managed, FitzGerald accepted that the Irish state should effect certain changes in the 1937 Constitution which would make it more acceptable to Northern unionists as a basis for national unity. In September 1981 he embarked on what he called a 'Constitutional Crusade' to remove those articles in the 1937 Constitution which laid claim to Northern Ireland as an integral part of the national territory, as well as the article that proscribed divorce.

FitzGerald's announcement presented the *Irish Times* with a dilemma. As a 'liberal' paper it had long argued that divorce was a right that should not be withheld from the people of a republic. Yet it was not inclined to be too sensitive about Northern unionist fears of being dominated by Rome in a united Ireland, since it reckoned these were trumped up as an excuse for avoiding dialogue on national reunification. On 25 September the newspaper gave its view in an editorial entitled 'The Constitution', stating unequivocally about what it characterized as 'a minor spat of argument' set in motion by the radio broadcast in which FitzGerald had laid out his plan: 'Whether any further tinkering with the Constitution will have the slightest effect on Unionist attitudes is to be doubted. Anyway, if the Constitution needs amending for reasons, it should be amended. Right is right' (*Irish Times*, 25 September 1981). The editorial went on to suggest that Fianna Fáil, which had summarily condemned FitzGerald for speaking as he had done of de Valera's 1937 document, should lay out what kind of terms it might offer unionists in a united country, which directed readers' attention to Haughey in opposition. But the editorial studiously avoided reference to Articles 2 and 3 which were the crux of the dispute between nationalists and unionists and in truth between the Irish and the British governments. A report in the paper on 29 September quoted Haughey as claiming that FitzGerald had 'sold the pass as far as the claim for national unity was concerned and had given enemies of unity countless propaganda sticks with which to beat the south for a long time to come' (*Irish Times*, 29 September 1981).

What the *Irish Times* had characterized as a 'minor spat' about the validity of the 1937 Constitution did in fact stimulate an extensive correspondence in the paper's letters columns as the pros and cons of the FitzGerald crusade were vigorously mooted. Yet by mid-December John Healy, in his 'Sounding Off' column, felt confident in declaring that the crusade was grinding to a halt. For all that letter-writers to the paper were exercised by the issue of constitutional change, Healy reminded readers that such change could be effected only by referenda and that no popular will existed to make the kinds of changes the crusading FitzGerald envisaged. He warned his 'Northern friends of the middle ground', who had been expressing pleasure at the prospect of such change in the Republic, that they should not 'confuse the speech for the deed' (*Irish Times*, 14 December 1981). There was, he implied, no real appetite for the referenda such changes would require.

Haughey's return to power in February 1982 put an abrupt end to FitzGerald's attempt as Taoiseach to generate a groundswell of support for changes in the Republic that could soothe unionist anxieties about their future in a united Ireland. There had always been something quixotic about his crusade at a moment when nationalist feeling was still primarily focused on Thatcher's government, which had allowed, so it was believed, the hunger strikers to die. Haughey's insistent determination to confront the British with their responsibility for sustaining a failed political entity on Irish territory was, by contrast, expressive of the views of a significant proportion of the electorate, not minded to give much credence to unionist fears.

It was not likely that Haughey could make much headway on the Northern issue with Mrs Thatcher. She had resented how he had, in her view, falsely claimed a constitutional breakthrough at the Dublin summit of December 1980. The Falklands War in the summer of 1982 was to plunge Anglo-Irish relations into waters as chilly as those of the South Atlantic.

We now know that Ireland was one of the countries Thatcher asked for support when the Argentine junta invaded the Falkland Islands. Just before British forces landed there to repel the invaders, a British submarine sank the Argentine battleship *General Belgrano*, with great loss of life. In response, Haughey ordered Irish diplomats at the United Nations (where Ireland was a temporary member of the Security Council) immediately to seek a meeting of the council which could demand the deferral of hostilities and the opening of negotiations to prevent the imminent war. He also indicated that he was seeking an end to EEC economic sanctions on Argentina. However much such actions could be nuanced as a useful expression of Irish neutrality on the international stage, it was inevitable that Thatcher would see them as a serious hindrance, not a help, as British soldiers and sailors risked their lives 8,000 miles away. What it certainly meant was that Haughey could no longer be an effective interlocutor with Thatcher on matters closer to home. Where FitzGerald's crusade (of which Thatcher approved) was impractically idealistic, Haughey's stance on the British action in the South Atlantic was of a piece with an anti-British national mood in the country and a boost to his popularity in some quarters. The *Irish Times*, despite the fact that it could only damage the Irish government's relations with the United Kingdom and with Northern unionists (the latter of whom saw Ireland as siding with Britain's enemies; Haughey's Minister of Defence had dubbed the British the 'aggressors'), was inclined to indulge this instinctive and self-serving Anglophobia, even when it deprecated Argentina's act of aggression. It was, indeed, a confusing and confused time.

Throughout the course of the invasion and war, the newspaper used the formulation Falklands/Malvinas in its editorials and letters pages, arguably to indicate its own support of Irish neutrality but, in the context of an upsurge of pro-Argentine feeling in Ireland, a coded marker of intense editorial distaste for British policy. On 3 May, in an oddly minimizing phrase, an editorial entitled 'Blunderers' did, it is true, concede: 'Of course Argentina had no business carrying out an armed invasion in the first place' (*Irish Times*, 3 May 1982). Britain, though, was guilty of abandoning 'a sense of proportion' in its forceful reaction. The next day, in an editorial entitled 'Blood Up', the writer, while acknowledging the noxious nature of the Argentine military regime, aggressors in the matter, claimed, 'The British are going to be insufferable in their pride after this. They have set up in the south Atlantic what is almost a no-contest situation' (*Irish Times*, 4 May 1982). Considering the sinking of the *General Belgrano*, with its disturbing death-toll, the paper editorialized on the 'daft momentum' of war. The writer's own sense of proportion wobbled somewhat, as the role of propaganda in wartime reminded of how a 'huge literature [had] grown up' on the 'war of deception' fought 'alongside the shooting war from 1939 to 1945' (*Irish Times*, 5 May 1982). It seemed to the leader writer that British folly threatened the world order as that oddly identified cataclysm had done. There was no reference to the more immediate risk Haughey was taking: that his intervention would sour Anglo-Irish relations seriously, making resolution of the issue of Northern Ireland significantly more difficult. And peace in the North was a key national interest of the Republic of Ireland. Reporting from Buenos Aires, Olivia O'Leary, who had been dispatched to Argentina by the *Irish Times*, described how the Argentine government 'accepted the Irish stand with relief' (*Irish Times*, 5 May 1982).

The election of December 1982 that brought FitzGerald back as Taoiseach in a coalition with the Labour Party, led by Dick Spring, would administratively settle the country, for it would stay in power until January 1987. It soon took steps, however, to bring about a constitutional change that in its intentions and consequences was the direct opposite of what FitzGerald had argued for in his ill-fated constitutional crusade. In this episode, which amounted to a moral civil war which convulsed the country, Haughey had played and would play a part that not even Gageby and Healy could find other than disreputable.

Since the papal visit in 1979, with John Paul II's resounding call for Ireland to uphold traditional Catholic values echoing in their ears, a number of lay Catholic groups had been lobbying politicians to hold a referendum to enter a clause in the constitution proscribing abortion in any circumstances. A skilful Pro-Life Amendment Campaign (PLAC) was mounted by committed individuals. In the volatile political climate of the early 1980s, neither of the major parties was inclined to permit its opponent to claim the high moral ground on such an issue (though there was no real chance any Irish government would pass legislation permitting abortion). FitzGerald first took the bait and Haughey, not to be outdone, followed suit. Late in his second term of office as Taoiseach, indeed, his government drafted the wording of the amendment that was eventually (though not without FitzGerald unsuccessfully trying to amend the wording to make it more securely anti-abortion) put before the people by the coalition and passed on 7 September 1983. In a perplexing complication, the wording FitzGerald sought to substitute for that which Haughey had brought forward was found less objectionable by the Protestant churches. In the end, the electorate, was confronted by the bizarre spectacle of FitzGerald campaigning against an amendment proposed by his own government, to be put before the electorate to vindicate a promise that he would hold such a plebiscite. In June 1981 the *Irish Times* had published a strongly argued article on the dangers of enshrining a proscription on abortion in the Irish Constitution. It was contributed by an *Irish Times* staffer and at that time assistant editor, Dennis Kennedy, who was introduced in a byline as 'a Northerner who came to live in the South in the late '60s when a liberal wind was blowing in the country' (*Irish Times*, 11 June 1981). In the article, 'Wholly Catholic Ireland', Kennedy argued that it was quite legitimate, where a strong majority existed in a democratic society who opposed abortion, that it should be illegal. Those who favoured change would argue their case. However, he went on:

> ... the Constitution is meant to embody the ethos of the nation – to say what Ireland, and being Irish is all about ... .
>
> To put a ban on abortion into the Constitution is to say that here is something fundamental above and beyond ordinary political and social debate. It is to say those who do not accept the Catholic view on abortion that their opinion is somehow 'unIrish'.
>
> It is not necessary to be pro-abortion to be appalled by this; one could fully accept the Catholic view of abortion and yet deplore a Constitutional ban on it as sectarian.

Kennedy summarized things bluntly enough, as the general election of that month put the constitutional proscription of abortion on the agenda:

> The politicians will argue in their defence that there is an election on, and that to resist the anti-abortion lobby would be suicide. Maybe so, but that simply confirms how Catholic society is in the south, and the extent to which the Catholic view must be the state view.
>
> Anyone prepared to accept that should also be prepared to accept Partition ... and should stop pretending to Republican principles.

As the process unfolded which would culminate in the eighth amendment of the Constitution, it became clear that the *Irish Times* could not deny the unassailable logic of Kennedy's argument. For Gageby and John Healy joined in opposition to the abortion amendment, as the public atmosphere deteriorated in rancorous exchanges on radio and television, reserving, in Healy's case, especial opprobrium for his erstwhile hero, Charles Haughey. In January 1983, when it was clear that a referendum on the issue was unavoidable, given FitzGerald's insistence that he would honour his earlier commitment, Healy expressed himself with the countryman's characteristic forthrightness: 'I have watched the Anti-Abortion Amendment Campaign progress from a lunatic fringe on the way-out Catholic right, a sperm of an idea which was planted in the ovum of the body politic, fertilised by vote-seeking politicians, and now we are well and truly up the pole with a bastard referendum on our hands' (*Irish Times*, 10 January 1983). Healy said he would 'take the greatest of personal pleasure' in voting against an amendment as envisaged, which Haughey had opportunistically exploited as a election gambit ('We all know Haughey would do anything to stay in office').

As the date of the plebiscite approached, the *Irish Times* published an editorial that unequivocally endorsed what Dennis Kennedy had argued in 1981. Entitled provocatively 'The Second Partition of Ireland', the writer (undoubtedly Gageby himself) berated FitzGerald as author of a new partition: 'We are copper-fastening Lloyd George's work every day' (*Irish Times*, 30 August 1983). Enshrining an anti-abortion clause in the Constitution when unionists in the North and Protestants in the Republic had expressed their objections to such an action, the writer insisted, would betray the cause of true republicanism:

> ... it is not just the Unionists we are abandoning. We are closing off the one-third of our people in the North who represent Nationalism. There won't be a civil war over the Second Partitioning of Ireland, as there was over the First Partitioning.
>
> It may be a new beginning, but it is, among other things, the burial of an ideal that set the nation alight in the last decades of the eighteenth century.

At the local level, Gageby presciently warned: '... if this amendment goes through there will be legal arguments for ever, and civil war among the doctors, especially the paediatricians and gynaecologists. What an appalling prospect for the future generation.' And a series of articles the *Irish Times* published on how the amendment was affecting both individuals and the various professions was a sharp reminder of how divisively the current referendum debate was being conducted. On 23 August a Dr Maire Woods, speaking for the anti-amendment campaign, wrote of how doctors at hospitals with bishops' contracts were afraid of losing their jobs if they declared for the anti-amendment campaign (though the Catholic hierarchy had indicated that the faithful could vote according to conscience). On 25 August Dick Walsh, in an opinion column entitled 'At Each Others' Throats', wrote of how 'not for decades has there been such corrosive disagreement ... according to some commentators there has been nothing like it since the Civil War'. The paper's medical correspondent, David Nowlan, reported that in his experience 'the differences between Irish doctors' had never been 'as deep or as bitter or as disagreeable' (*Irish Times*, 30 August 1983). He wrote of 'intimidation and character assassination which have been prevalent in Irish medicine in recent weeks'. The amendment was carried by 66.9 per cent to 33.1 per cent, an apparent triumph for PLAC and its various outriders (though, as we shall see, with serious unintended consequences). However, the debate it had generated gave evidence that a substantial minority of Irish people did not view the world as starkly as PLAC wished it to do. Moreover, the airing of the issue, in which the *Irish Times*, in articles and in its letters pages, played a signal part, helped to give the lie to those who liked to pretend that the Irish people were unanimous on the matter. In a paradoxical way the pro- and anti-campaigns had put medical ethics, personal morality and the role of the state in relation to them on the agenda to a degree they had never quite been before. Afterwards it became harder to silence dissenting voices in the complex fields of gender and sexual politics, especially where the law bore on these. By opening its columns to a range of voices during a heated debate on a highly sensitive, even intimate, topic, the *Irish Times* had helped to make the idea of national debate itself and uncomfortable disagreement in the public sphere fully acceptable (television and radio also played a crucial part in this process). A genie was out a bottle that would in time come to make Pope John Paul II's 1979 vision of an Ireland loyally at one in unquestioning obedience to papal ordinance seem anachronistic rather than prophetic.

A number of correspondents to the *Irish Times* on the abortion amendment campaign spoke of the 'confusion' that had been introduced as theology vied with biology to determine when life began and when the 'unborn' (the neologism entered in the constitution) acquired human rights equal to those possessed by mothers. FitzGerald, who, of course, had inherited the wording from Haughey's administration for the amendment, with its less than clear formulation, had also been bequeathed the difficult conundrum of how he might reopen dialogue with Margaret Thatcher on the confusing question of Northern Ireland, where Haughey had sown seeds of discord. The alarming rise in the electoral potential and military strength of armed republicanism made action by the coalition government imperative.

How urgent a problem Northern Ireland had become was violently proved in October 1984. On the 12th of that month the Grand Hotel, Brighton, on the south coast of England, was bombed by the Provisional IRA during the British Conservative Party's annual conference. The attack came close to killing many of the British cabinet (the consequences of such a massacre for

Anglo-Irish relations would certainly have been profoundly damaging). It was horror at what might have been which dominated the *Irish Times*'s editorial the next day (though it condemned the death-toll that then stood at four; a fifth person died later). The paper damned an action that it found 'remarkable and astonishing and in its implications ... terrifying' (*Irish Times*, 13 October 1984). For 'the might-have-been was an enormous political crime' committed by an organization determined to impede 'hopes of constitutional political progress'.

In this editorial the paper vested such hopes in the findings and proposals of the New Ireland Forum FitzGerald's government had established in Dublin in 1983 to chart possible ways forward in Northern Ireland and in Anglo-Irish relations. It fully understood that the Brighton bomb had made conversation with the British on the subject very difficult, for it would 'take a great deal of persuasion to find the right road forward to a lasting and peaceful settlement'. That 'right road', however, even in the chastening aftermath of the attempted mass assassination of a democratically elected government in peacetime, for the *Irish Times* still involved the confronting of what it dismissed as 'the unionist veto'. For in the nationalist lexicon the phrase was a dismissive way of referring to the British government's guarantee to British citizens in Northern Ireland that there would be no change in their status without the consent of a majority in the province. Certainly, constitutional nationalists in Northern Ireland and in the Republic granted that the desired national unity could be achieved only with unionist consent, but when they spoke, as this editorial did, of the 'unionist veto', they were indicating that they believed the unionists should be manoeuvred by political and diplomatic pressure to a position where they could do no other than consent. FitzGerald, by his Forum Report which outlined possible scenarios for an independent Ireland, and, when these were peremptorily rejected by Thatcher, by his patient unwavering pursuit of a new agreement with the United Kingdom which would give Ireland an advisory role in the governance of Northern Ireland which could evolve into joint authority and eventual Irish unity, was seeking to effect by incremental steps what Haughey had hoped to achieve more swiftly in direct talks with the British, though FitzGerald undoubtedly believed in a sincere way that unionists should not be compelled to give consent; they should rather be helped over time to see the error of their ways. At the very least, by its undaunted consistency FitzGerald's strategy was an improvement on the confusion of the early years of the decade, when political instability and Haughey's volatility made co-operation with Britain on Northern Ireland almost impossible. The Anglo-Irish Agreement of 1985 also began to wrest the initiative from the Provisional IRA and a newly empowered Sinn Féin, as the two governments reasserted their authority together.

The *Irish Times* marked the signing of the Anglo-Irish Agreement in Hillsborough near Belfast on 15 November 1985 by publishing the text and affording a good deal of its Saturday extended edition to the subject (it would republish the text several times). The leading article was circumspect in the welcome it gave to what it termed 'a reasonable deal' (*Irish Times*, 16 November 1985), identifying it as 'a beginning' which had to be welcomed since 'two of the chief protagonists in the North have welcomed it – John Hume and Seamus Mallon, leader and deputy leader of the SDLP'. Tellingly, the main theme of the editorial was unionist reaction to the agreement. Neither of the two Unionist parties in Northern Ireland had been consulted about or even officially informed in advance of the contents of the agreement, and the editorial quoted the leader of the Ulster Unionist Party as saying 'this is the end of the Union'. It reckoned that many in the Republic might be 'confused by some of the detail' in the agreement, but the writer was more concerned that 'the confusion of the Unionists could not quickly be dispelled'. It warned: 'Unionists are capable of great mischief in their confusion and in what they see as their rejection by Britain'. The editorialist's contribution to helping them in their unhappy state was to quote from the Ulster Protestant poet John Hewitt's poem, 'The Colony' (printed in its entirety on a separate page of that day's edition), which speaks in an extended parable of Roman colonists abandoned by Rome to their fate in some far-flung province. The force of this was to suggest that their 'rejection by Britain' was no mere matter of appearances. An article by John Healy on the agreement put it more directly. This declared, with a certain sadness, that unionism had been so badly led that:

> It is the writing on the wall for Unionism, a verbally disguised moment of truth, but a moment of political and constitutional truth all the same ... Shout as they must, bray as they will about betrayal, bluster as they may about the South and Maggie Thatcher, the thinking, quiet-spoken men of the majority faith must look at the day's work and ask what led to this impasse.

On 30 November the *Irish Times*'s London correspondent, Conor O'Clery, reported on the isolation of the Unionists in Westminster when the agreement was debated and passed. He referred to the 'routing of the Unionists' when the vote took place, reporting how one Labour Party speaker had argued '"Almost everyone in the House ... is a conditional Unionist. The people of Northern Ireland understand us to be saying that they are only slightly part of the United Kingdom"'. O'Clery commented: 'No one challenged [his] basic analysis. His words went to the heart of the debate. The Unionists showed they knew them to be true.' He reported, too, conversations among MPs that the unionists would 'come to heel' when they thought about the United Kingdom's financial support for the province: 'There was more than an echo of the spongers jibe of Harold Wilson in the endless conversations in the corridors about what might happen when the crunch came.'

If the general tendency under Gageby's second editorship was to promote an editorial line in support of the traditional nationalist attitude to partition, how deeply it went as a settled imperative of the people is another matter. However abrasively it had been expressed by a Haughey after a brief diplomatic courtship of Mrs Thatcher, or with more sustained finesse by a FitzGerald, the paper did in a principled way allow for dissent about Irish national ambition. Chief among those dissenting voices to which the newspaper allowed free expression in its columns was that of the former Labour Party minister and internationally renowned author and critic Conor Cruise O'Brien. In his memoir O'Brien makes clear that he and Gageby were close neither on the ideological nor on the personal level. But when Gageby invited him to write a regular column for his newspaper, O'Brien took it 'as the greatest implicit compliment' (Conor Cruise O'Brien 1998, p. 380) that had ever been paid to him professionally. Granted complete freedom by Gageby from editorial direction provided he did not attack 'any of his other contributors', Conor Cruise O'Brien set to with a will.

He differed from Gageby and from Healy, indeed, in holding Charles Haughey in complete disregard. For O'Brien viewed the Fianna Fáil leader as a sinister threat to Irish democracy who would stop at nothing in the interests of personal power. In an article on the phone-tapping of journalists when Haughey was Taoiseach, O'Brien wrote in the *Irish Times* that there had been a 'drift ... away from the rule of law, and towards personal rule' (*Irish Times*, 25 January 1983). He warned that Haughey, whom he argued must have been responsible for the tapping of phones of journalists deemed 'non-national', 'should have no political future in a democracy that respected and cherished its institutions, or even values its life' (*Irish Times*, 25 January 1983). It was on the issues of Northern Ireland and partition, however, that O'Brien disagreed most fundamentally with Gageby, who was able from time to time, as we have seen, to consider Haughey not wholly estimable.

O'Brien's abiding concern in the time he wrote on a regular basis in the *Irish Times* until, at the end of 1985, he transferred to Anthony O'Reilly's Independent Newspaper group, was that in not taking seriously the Northern Protestant determination to avoid incorporation in an all-island polity, the Republic's government was failing to tackle how peace in Northern Ireland could actually be established in the present and storing up great trouble for the future. As he argued of the Anglo-Irish Agreement (alarmed as he was that what had been negotiated over the heads of the unionists would not be accepted peacefully by them as a fait accompli):

> Mrs Thatcher's celebrated intransigence, so loudly deplored in the days
> of the hunger strikes, is now seen as her most endearing characteristic.
> Because this time it is the Prods who are expected to get it in the neck.
> She'll reconcile the two traditions for us, by screwing the other one.
>
> I wouldn't bet on it. I think we are unwise if we put our trust in a
> political personality, as against the aroused feelings of a people. I fear we

are in for years of increasing turmoil, tending towards a terrible climax.
(*Irish Times*, 19 November 1985)

O'Brien, in his memoir, recalls being told that Gageby often swore when he read his copy; however, the editor dutifully published what arrived on his desk from the well-practised polemicist he had recruited. He must have accepted with ambivalent feeling that O'Brien could be maddeningly controversial as he subjected received opinion to an analytic scalpel that did not baulk at cutting in certain tender parts. His suavely conducted exercises in skilful dialectics in a style of cheerful self-confidence could be depended upon to keep the letters page well stocked with offended counter-argument. Conor Cruise O'Brien in the *Irish Times* was both a weekly litmus test of the paper's liberalism, of its vaunted tolerance, and a heavy-hitting presence always ready for a fight with all-comers. In short, well worth letting him have his head. People loved to hate him.

As Gageby's second editorship of the *Irish Times* drew towards a close (he would vacate the position in August 1986) there were other things likely to cause intemperate reactions. Foremost among these was the defeat of the referendum to change the Constitution in a way that would permit the state to enact divorce legislation. The Fine Gael/Labour coalition put this before the people in June 1986. It was defeated by a majority of almost two-to-one (fears about property rights in agricultural Ireland were decisive in swinging the electorate – contrary to earlier opinion poll predictions – firmly against change). It was a bitter blow to Gageby, who could not fail to see how this declaration by the Irish people that they were at ease with denying to Protestants in the Republic what was considered a human right in Northern Ireland could be a body-blow to his hopes for an end to partition.

On 16 June the *Irish Times* carried an editorial that signalled how very seriously its editor was taking the forthcoming plebiscite. It was clear that the possibility that the amendment could be rejected was unsettling Gageby. For having made the unremarkable observation that 'It is reasonably certain that a "no" vote would cause Unionists to repeat with satisfaction their charge that Home Rule is Rome Rule' (*Irish Times*, 16 June 1986), the editorial went on improbably to argue that 'many constitutional nationalists' could 'see in that vote the fading of the prospect of a new deal in Ireland'. 'Some,' it continued, 'would merely retreat into themselves; others could fall into the arms of Sinn Fein and the IRA. The south they would say is playacting; is not and maybe never was genuine about a New Ireland, about one Ireland. This could lead to more anarchy, more killings on both sides.' This bizarre prognostication suggested that Gageby was losing his formerly fairly secure hold on popular feeling in the Republic (James Downey certainly thought that he was, in seeing it as so imbricated with the Northern question; Downey 2009, p. 212). On voting day the *Irish Times* advised a 'yes' vote in more measured terms, making a plea for generosity of spirit since the electorate was 'being asked to prove that ... we can deal fairly with minority rights' and with those 'who are in marital straits' (*Irish Times*, 26 June 1986).

When the vote went decisively against change, and the *Irish Times* could not but describe the outcome as a decisive rejection of even the limited form of divorce legislation the coalition had had in mind, the leading article of the day was aghast in its disappointment that the majority of the electorate was apparently unconcerned about how its action bore on the national question: 'So the votes are saying: "we have two countries". It may well be' (*Irish Times*, 28 June 1986).

The defeat of the divorce referendum in June 1986 can scarcely be compared as a cause of distress with the collapse of the Northern Ireland executive in the early summer of 1974. That put paid to the Sunningdale Agreement, with its envisaged Council of Ireland; and Gageby's consequent depression at these developments had probably helped to precipitate his resignation shortly thereafter. His sense in 1986 that the Republic was unwilling to adapt to accommodate Northern Protestants, even when the ongoing violence made imperative a political breakthrough on the future of Northern Ireland, may, however, have added to a more general loss of enthusiasm for the day-to-day work of the newspaper as he grew older. By the mid-1980s much of that daily responsibility of making sure the paper appeared was being taken by deputy editors. On the practical level, production methods in the newspaper industry were undergoing rapid change and James Downey, not the editor himself, was bearing the brunt of a difficult but necessary transition. The *Irish Times* board believed it must install a new printing press that could handle colour, especially in advertising, supplements and special editions. The era of hot metal was giving way to that of electronically generated printable copy. So the clatter of typewriters would in time give way to the near-silence of the desk-top computer and laptop. By the summer of 1986, though Gageby declared his wish to continue in office, he apparently lacked the will for a fight and when he was prevailed upon by senior figures to resign, he did so that August. It was not the happiest of endings for a man who had given the paper so much.

At the basic level of maintaining the newspaper as a going concern, Gageby's 'second coming' in 1977 had been vital. As Mark O'Brien reports it, advertising campaigns on radio in 1977 had helped to give an initial boost to circulation and in the years between 1977 and the second half of 1982 sales figures rose to the highest ever at 87,433 (Mark O'Brien 2008, pp. 220–1). The early 1980s had posed significant challenges to profitability as a high VAT rate and falls in advertising revenue meant that the price of the daily paper almost doubled between 1981 and 1984 (Mark O'Brien 2008, p. 221). Nonetheless, when Gageby took his leave, the paper was still selling about 80,000 copies a day (even in straitened times, it had its loyal constituency of readers), a reasonable foundation for his successor to build on. A substantial sum which the company received when Reuters news agency (in which it held shares) was floated on the stock market was used to arrange a settlement with the Bank of Ireland in 1984 that removed the threat to the paper that serious indebtedness to a bank had represented since 1974.

Gageby's retirement in 1986 brought to an end the professional relationship that had existed between him and Major Thomas McDowell over many years. As two Northern Protestants who had made their careers in Dublin, despite their political differences they had, perhaps almost unconsciously, shared the kind of appreciation of one another's sensitivities and attitudes that the experience of Belfast grammar schools and service in the armed forces during the war had given them. With Gageby gone, McDowell would find himself in new territory, for it was likely the next editor would be Catholic by social formation and a product of the Irish mainstream in a way that not even Fergus Pyle had been. Possibly aware that he could no longer depend on the instinctive understanding of his editor, despite their contrasting politics, McDowell was no doubt happy that in June 1986 changes to the articles of association of the Irish Times Ltd and to the trust further consolidated his power as supremo in the governance of the curious institution the *Irish Times* was. The new arrangements essentially confirmed him as chairman for life of the company, with an equivalent status in the trust.

If these complex business agreements were effected with efficiency, the appointment of a successor to Gageby was not managed with the same sure-footed dispatch. It was clear in 1974 that the way Pyle had been parachuted into the editor's chair would not do, in a country that was anxious to burnish its new credentials as a progressive European place to do business. Hence an appointments procedure had been devised. The problem was that, when put in motion, it took more than three months to give it effect. This allowed ample time for rumours to circulate among the paper's staff, with supporters in the wider community ready to give the mooted candidates backing. In the event, only two names comprised the short-list: that of James Downey, an internal candidate whom many of the staff would have been pleased to see appointed, and that of Conor Brady, a former employee, who also had his in-house support. On 15 December Gageby announced that Brady had been appointed as his successor. As Brady himself has admitted, his success was greeted in the newsroom, where Gageby had gathered the staff to meet their new boss, less than wholeheartedly: 'There was applause. But it was muted and I could see disbelief, not to say dismay, on some of the faces around me' (Brady 2005, p. 58). Unfortunately, Gageby also told the assembled journalists that the absent Downey (who was being apprised elsewhere of his fate by Major McDowell about the same time that afternoon) would be well looked after. This must have upset Downey's friends and it certainly enraged him when he learnt of it afterwards. Brady's path to the editor's chair had not been made an easy one by this less than adroit handling of a very emotionally charged situation. McDowell had told Downey that 'the younger man' was being appointed (Downey 2009, p. 219).

Conor Brady became the eleventh person to serve as editor of the *Irish Times* but he was the first Catholic and the first graduate of a university other than Trinity College Dublin to do so. At one level this meant very little, though his appointment was bound to be remarked upon as breaking the long-established mould. Individuals like Downey himself and Donal Foley had both been highly influential figures in the newspaper and they were both Catholics by social formation. And in the normal workings of a busy newspaper, where one worshipped (if at all) was of little account. However, at a more significant level Brady's appointment brought to the leadership role in the paper a man who came from what may be termed middle, mainstream Ireland in a way none of the previous ten editors had done. He was a native of Tullamore, Co. Offaly, had been educated by the Cistercians at Roscrea, where, after his father's early death, he had been a boarder. A degree in history and politics followed at University College Dublin. So he was very much a gifted product of the confident Irish provincial Catholic middle class, with 'teachers, doctors, religious and lawyers in the family' (Brady 2005, p. 32). His father had trained as a teacher of modern languages but had also served at a senior level in the new police force after the Civil War. Some in the family connection had made their way in the newspaper world.

Brady's progression to the editorship had involved experience not only as a reporter in the paper itself, but he had worked as an interviewer and presenter on RTE radio. He had edited the *Garda Review* and he had been editor for a short time of an undercapitalized Sunday newspaper, the *Sunday Tribune*. He was also a published author, with a book on the early history of the Irish police to his name and had found the time to burnish his academic credentials with a University College Dublin Master's degree in politics. When he took over at the *Irish Times*, he was entering his prime at 37 years of age.

From the start Brady demonstrated that he was going to be very much his own man. Shortly after his appointment, when it was clear that the Fine Gael/ Labour coalition had run its course and a general election was imminent, Brady agreed to a suggestion that he should meet Charles Haughey at the Fianna Fáil leader's home. John Healy, despite times when he felt obliged to criticize Haughey (for example, on his cynical opportunism on the abortion issue, as we saw above), remained his principal devotee among the *Irish Times* staff, many of whom distrusted him and some of whom had been assiduously trying to discover the source of his wealth. Brady was concerned by how Haughey had attacked the Anglo-Irish Agreement in 1985 and, though assured by Healy that Haughey would work it pragmatically if he gained power, Brady was repelled by such a blatant example of *realpolitik* on a matter of basic national interest. Nonetheless, he was ready to consider that Haughey, who outlined for Brady his plans for a financial centre in Dublin and for a regeneration of a central city area beside the Liffey as a cultural quarter, could be given another chance to prove himself. He knew that Haughey had been the focus of intense divisiveness in his party (Desmond O'Malley, who split from the party in late 1985 to form the Progressive Democrats, had taken some key Fianna Fáil deputies with him) and was unlikely, therefore, to command a really solid majority. Albeit, Brady wrote strongly worded editorials before and during an election campaign castigating the coalition's economic record, which implicitly seemed intended to help its principal adversary, Fianna Fáil, and its leader. There were those on the paper's staff who were outraged, but the editor was the man in charge and was both expressing his carefully formed conviction (in the depths of the economic crisis there was to be no more 'confusion') and putting down a marker. He had, he explains in his memoir, resolved that on matters of such national import he would write the necessary leading articles himself and not leave them to deputies, as Gageby had sometimes done. His editorial on 21 January 1987, entitled 'Whose Chance Now?', offered readers the kind of direct speaking on the coalition's record he believed they deserved:

> ... it was not a good government – for all its striving ... For all the intel-
> lectual firepower of some of its members, for all the dedication and
> undoubted hard work, the Government's failures outweigh its successes.
>   ... the Government did not halt the economic slide as it promised to
> – and as it was expected to. (*Irish Times*, 21 January 1987)

While Brady was circumspect about the lack of forthrightness in what Haughey was offering the electorate, such an editorial was an invitation to consider giving him 'a second chance', even if his opponent, Garret FitzGerald, could arguably have been afforded the same indulgence.

Haughey's 'second chance' was a slim enough one, for following the general election he was elected Taoiseach in a minority government only by the casting vote of the chair of the Dáil. However, his position was bolstered by the support given to his minority administration by the new leader of Fine Gael, Alan Dukes (FitzGerald had resigned as party leader following the unsuccessful election campaign). Dukes, in a spirit of national solidarity, announced in early September, as Haughey and his Minister for Finance, Ray MacSharry were beginning work on a budget for 1988, that would impose swingeing cuts in public spending intended to save the Irish state from insolvency, that Fine Gael would not seek to obstruct (as was the usual way of things for parties in opposition) the delivery of the necessary surgery. Brady and his political staff strongly approved of this stance, which gave the new government some breathing space in a very challenging situation, to try to rescue the public finances. In its leading article, the day after Dukes announced his strategy in the west Dublin suburb of Tallaght (a large working-class area of the city that would be seriously affected by intensifying austerity) the writer argued that what Dukes had pledged himself to was 'a rare display of political maturity' (*Irish Times*, 3 September 1987). It acknowledged that 'something of a landmark' had been reached in Irish politics, for Dukes had 'in effect, abandoned adversarial politics (temporarily, at least) in favour of a policy of constructive opposition'. In his memoir Brady described it as 'one of the most radical initiatives in the history of Irish public life' (Brady 2005, p. 93).

So Brady gave general support to Haughey in his first year in office, though on matters of education, especially at primary level, he encouraged those on his staff who sought to help to mitigate the most severe of the cuts being effected. In the autumn, with Brady's approval, the paper mounted a campaign (in which other papers and media were also involved) to highlight the threat the cuts posed to the very existence of primary education. Savings were necessary but the *Irish Times* was to remain as true as possible to a liberal pragmatism by encouraging the government to find its necessary savings in a way that did not concentrate fire on easy and vulnerable targets. John Healy found this insufficiently robust a support of Haughey and soon quarrelled with the new editor, abandoning his column in the newspaper.

Brady had impressed the appointment board, which preferred him as editor to the older James Downey, with a detailed prospectus for change he had presented as part of his application for the post. He was ambitious that the paper would raise its standards and its circulation by deepening its coverage of key subjects such as science, society and culture. Perhaps most importantly, the coverage of international affairs required the appointment of a team of the paper's own foreign correspondents in important locations. It was fortuitous, therefore, that the requirement to create a place for James Downey (who understandably was anxious to leave the Dublin office) in London meant that a new posting could be created for the incumbent there, Conor O'Clery. Brady had been of a mind to open a Moscow office (the old *Irish Times* hand Bruce Williamson had alerted him to how history was in the making in the Soviet Union). O'Clery was a Northerner who had served as the *Irish Times*'s editor in Belfast and as news editor in Dublin. In March 1987 he took up residence in Moscow, where he would make his name as an international correspondent of the first rank.

It was an extraordinary time to be in that city. The permafrost of the Cold War was beginning to thaw, but even more surprisingly, the edifice of Soviet power itself was beginning to exhibit cracks. The bipolar world that had defined the post-war era could no longer be taken for granted as a restive eastern Europe began to sense that its hour could come again. O'Clery's reports from Moscow (along with those by Helen Womack in the London *Independent*) became essential reading for those who wanted to discern the emerging shape of a new architecture in world affairs.

O'Clery's gift as a journalist in Moscow in the late 1980s was his capacity to write informative, thoughtful analyses of Soviet politics in the period of *glasnost* and *perestroika*. Vivid reports about the political scene in Russia made Mikhail Gorbachev and his future nemesis Boris Yeltsin seem larger-than-life players in an unfolding drama of reform and reaction. O'Clery combined this in his 'Moscow Letter' with a good deal of colourful reportage of events (Russia was becoming *the* story) as he cast an astute eye on society in flux. He made a world which had been a closed book to most Irish people seem fully human, a place where lives ran their courses as they did elsewhere. The Soviet reality was being demystified. Early articles, in April 1987, noted how faith in atheism was in retreat as 'a cornerstone of Soviet education' (*Irish Times*, 8 April 1987), was attacked in influential journals, and how art that would previously have been suppressed was being displayed by artists at weekends 'among the silver birch trees of the forest. Sunday skiers would pause to examine their samples' (*Irish Times*, 6 April 1987). It was an encouraging sign that a new law permitting small private businesses, from car repairs to hairdressing and toy-making, would unleash an entrepreneurial spirit. An article by O'Clery the following month explained how queuing was the curse of the drinking classes in Moscow, since 'the abuse of alcohol, the Communist Party had decided was one of the main impediments to the reconstruction of the Soviet economy' (*Irish Times*, 28 May 1987). An article in June helped readers to understand how profound an economic crisis the Soviet Union faced. O'Clery reported that an article by a respected economist in the popular journal *Novy Mir* (*New World*) had published a 'devastating indictment of the present state of the Soviet system' (*Irish Times*, 13 June 1987). O'Clery explained how the article was part of an intense debate at the highest levels of the Soviet state about the role the market should play in reconstruction. In this, Gorbachev was walking a tightrope since socialist purists were opposing those who hoped market forces could generate renewal in a society, which the *Novy Mir* article stated, had 'one of the lowest productivity rates in the industrial world'.

O'Clery was deeply impressed at how adroitly Gorbachev was managing not only the transition from dictatorship in the Soviet Union at the same time as he was negotiating with the US president about arms control, but was holding power in the Communist Party as economic reform was set in motion. At the end of 1987, in a reflective piece that took account of the history of Soviet–US relations, O'Clery posited a new stage in their interaction, more fundamental than mere détente. He judged that 'a slowly developing new appreciation of each other by the people of each superpower' was in train and a 'curiosity about each other unparalleled in Soviet-American history' (*Irish Times*, 4 December 1987) was emerging. Ten months later he was saluting how Gorbachev had seen off a challenge in the Central Committee of the Communist Party 'with consummate skill' (*Irish Times*, 3 October 1988) as he 'moved into the position of perhaps the most commanding Soviet leader since Stalin'.

Events in 1989 in central and eastern Europe unfolded with a rapidity and a social impetus that only the kind of military force that a Stalin might have been prepared to unleash could have kept back the anti-communist tide. Happily, Gorbachev was no Stalin. When the Catholic and worker-based Solidarity party won a landslide election victory in Poland in June 1989 and the Soviet Union did not intervene to restore socialist hegemony, the floodgates opened. On 7 June the *Irish Times* greeted Solidarity's election victory with an editorial entitled 'Poland the Brave'. It warned that the apparatus of the 'State within the State' was still in existence and prophesied that what happened next in Poland might 'decide the future of the reform movement in Eastern Europe as a whole' (*Irish Times*, 7 June 1989). The front pages of the *Irish Times* that week, like the global media in general, were carrying graphic images and reports of the brutal slaughter of pro-democracy demonstrators in Tiananmen Square, in Beijing. It might almost have been staged as a terrible object lesson on what the state within the state could do in the communist bloc, if it chose to emulate the actions of the Chinese Communist Party. Paul Gillespie, the paper's foreign editor, on 10 June, as he reported how 'The old guard, the gerontocracy, the hardliners, the Stalinists, are back in control after a tumultuous and bloody week' (*Irish Times*, 10 June 1989), observed that the horror unleashed by a murderous regime 'had engraved itself on the consciousness of people all round the world made smaller by the immediacy of mass communications'. He was astutely recognizing how television's instant, global reportage was creating a sense of disparate events in widely separated locations constituting a moment in living history. When in July the paper printed an article entitled 'Why Solidarity Should Govern Poland' by the Polish philosopher and politician Adam Michnik, then in Moscow for talks with the Kremlin, it was striking how he claimed, despite the evidence of Tiananmen Square, that 'we can see how the epoch of totalitarian systems is coming to an end' (*Irish Times*, 12 July 1989). Television coverage, with the printed media adding its own reporting and analysis, was generating the globally shared international event, compacted of spectacle, excitement and a frisson of terror. News and the sense of hope-filled drama being enacted in a public sphere dominated by mass entertainment combined in 1989 in a way that it had never quite done before.

The fall of the Berlin Wall was perhaps the defining event in a year that would change the world. The *Irish Times* proved itself well able to deal authoritatively with the momentous days when history was shifting gear. On 11 November (by chance, Armistice day, on which the guns of the Great War had fallen silent), Seán Flynn sent a stirring report from Berlin that evoked the euphoria there, as the city so long divided enjoyed its sudden coming together:

> There were vivid historical images around every street-corner in the city
> yesterday. The Berlin Wall may have been a symbol of Cold War; yesterday

the East Berliners wished to symbolise their new-found freedom. At Checkpoint Charlie an elderly man strode back and forth on numerous occasions across a white line which separated East from West.

In Dublin on the same day, the paper's left-wing political correspondent, Dick Walsh, sounded a socialist's warning that the meeting of East and West could not be seen simply as a triumph for the capitalist West over the communist East and the end of history. He counselled against being so 'fascinated by the theatre of events that we may miss their real significance'. And from Moscow Conor O'Clery sent a magisterial analysis of how the threatened demise of the German Democratic Republic was being viewed by the political elite there. Moscow had 'welcomed the opening of the Berlin Wall, but for the first time expressed some anxiety about the bewildering changes in East Germany'. An editorial entitled 'A Peaceful Revolution' strove effectively to put the bewildering events in Germany in historical context. From such a perspective, it saw the European Community as providing the framework for a future reunification of the central European power: 'The democratic perspective opened up by this week's momentous changes in East Germany should be an inspiration for this task'. (*Irish Times*, 11 November 1989)

There were those in the last decade of the century, as these remarkable events unfolded, whose eyes were set on a long hoped-for, swift reunification of the island of Ireland. The Provisional IRA, apparently wedded to its campaign of violence, intended to bring the British government to the negotiating table so that it might set a schedule for the abandonment of its claim to sovereignty over Northern Ireland. Events revealed both its formidably increased military capacity and its continued ruthlessness. For the Army Council of the IRA and key figures in Sinn Féin still hoped that outright victory was attainable, whatever constitutional politicians might promote by way of incremental co-operation in the terms of the Anglo-Irish Agreement. The interception by French authorities in November 1987 of a ship (the MV *Eksund*) carrying a substantial cargo of Libyan-supplied weaponry for use by the IRA was in itself an alarming indication of the level of terrorist ambition, for it quickly became clear that four earlier shipments had been brought ashore in County Wicklow, to be dispersed to arms dumps around the country awaiting their use in a frighteningly raised level of military activity. The bloody nature of the IRA's long war with the British Army in Northern Ireland had been savagely highlighted earlier in the year when an eight-man active service unit had walked into a carefully planned British ambush in Loughgall, Co. Armagh. The entire unit was wiped out in a hail of bullets that May evening. On Sunday 8 November, shortly after the discovery of the IRA's arms importations, a unit of the organization placed a bomb to explode during an Armistice Day service at the cenotaph in Enniskillen, Co. Fermanagh. Eleven people perished, six of them women.

This ghastly event brought home to many how terrible the Troubles had become. In November a tremor of fearfulness ran through the Republic where it dawned that the whole island could quickly be engulfed in violence if the conflict intensified. On 3 November the *Irish Times*'s leading article questioned with alarm what the arsenal which had been en route to Ireland on a vessel was meant to unleash. It understood that 'Weaponry on the scale and of the variety uncovered on the *Eksund* is suited for a Beirut-type situation. Deployed among trained and experienced forces, it would wreak a terrible toll of destruction ... Death and injury would have to follow on a scale that has hitherto not been known' (*Irish Times*, 3 November 1987). Later in the week, the paper, listing the 150 tons of arms and ammunition on board the intercepted vessel, stated: 'what would have happened', had the cargo been undetected, 'is almost unthinkable' (*Irish Times*, 6 November 1987).

The following week, with the horror of Enniskillen deeply affecting the majority of the Republic's population, the *Irish Times* published strongly worded editorials that sought to steady the ship of state in a perilous time. There could be no confusion. The constitutional road must be followed to 'peace, confidence and reconciliation, because there is no other way' (*Irish Times*, 9 November 1987). The newspaper reaffirmed its commitment to the Anglo-Irish Agreement as the instrument that must be made to give the nationalists of the North a 'strong constitutional voice', thereby draining support from violent republicanism. On 12 November, in an editorial entitled 'Terrorism', the paper caught the public mood when it observed: 'Not perhaps since the Dublin and Monaghan bombings of 1974 have the citizens of this State felt themselves so close to the realities of terrorist violence as in the past week' (*Irish Times*, 12 November 1987); a kidnapping by a republican splinter group had also run a grisly course during the same week. The writer was unequivocal: 'A people which must contend with ... evils in its midst cannot afford any ambivalence in its approach to violence; or to those who are prepared to apply it in order to achieve what they describe as political ends.' The fact that, for many in the Republic, the North over the years, though a mere two hours' drive away, had been as remote as 'the far side of the moon' (in the editorialist's telling image) could no longer be an excuse for indifference to or ambivalence about events there. The force of the law north and south should be used co-operatively to quell the terrorist threat.

It was not that *Irish Times* readers had had any real excuse since 1968 to plead ignorance about what had been occurring north of the border, for since the outbreak of the Troubles the paper had employed some of its most skilled reporters and journalists to cover the Northern question. And since 1985 readers had had the benefit of Mary Holland's weekly columns which frequently reported developments in the North with a depth of insight that surpassed most commentators in either Britain or Ireland. Holland since 1968 had made understanding of and reportage of Northern Ireland almost a lifetime avocation. She had brought to that subject an shrewd reading of political developments and a clear-eyed grasp of how state power was exercised, along with a compassionate awareness of how individuals in a divided society suffered grievously in a time of violence. Her writing was marked by an insistently analytic concern to get at the truth however unpalatable, warning, for example, that support for the Provisional IRA was gaining ground even after the Anglo-Irish Agreement, based as it was on alienated, unemployed youth in such places as Derry city and west Belfast. She also took the temperature of post-agreement unionism, recognizing how volatile the mood was among loyalists. Her writing bore the mark of a moral determination that a politics of exclusion could not bind up the wounds of a broken society.

Two articles that Mary Holland contributed in 1987 exhibit the power of her writing. In the aftermath of the Loughgall ambush, she wrote of how what seemed like a bucolic country village on a summer evening had been visited by terrible slaughter. The article, entitled 'The almost-written Ballad of Loughgall', reminded readers that those who died were members of a community in which, whatever others might think, they would not be seen as terrorists, for 'They are fathers and husbands, the sons of decent families, well respected in their own areas. The mother of one of them said she hadn't thought to ask where he was going. It was the end of the week, he'd been paid: she assumed he'd be going for a few drinks. Instead, he and his friends went out on a bright May evening and died for Ireland. The words of the ballad do, alas, almost write themselves' (*Irish Times*, 13 May 1987). And the hard questions got asked: did the incident mark a determination to treat the IRA in the future 'as an armed enemy to be ambushed and shot on sight?' If so, Holland warned, 'It would seem that the British Government has now acceded to the IRA's view that what is happening in the north is war.' Was what had happened a lawful response by the civil power to a paramilitary threat? The Enniskillen bombing later in the year brought from Holland an equally compelling response. She coldly pointed out that what had occurred was abominable (the *Irish Times's* Dick Walsh, himself a Left-wing republican, in another article later in the week accused the Provisional IRA of sullying the core traditions of anti-sectarianism it purported to serve). Under the headline 'Dragging Our Traditions Through the Mud' he wrote of the Provisionals: 'Their actions mock the traditions they claim to espouse: for the traditions of Republicanism and Socialism are democratic and theirs are not' (*Irish Times*, 12 November 1987). Affronted by the tragic loss of life, Holland was stimulated to ponder how nationalist Ireland had failed to acknowledge the part many Irishmen had played in the war against Hitler. Respectfully recalling her own father, who had served in the wartime British Army, and was no less an Irishman for that, she wrote: 'How much we limit ourselves and the part we have played in Europe's history by denying the Irish men and women who fought in both world wars. How pitiable that we think it will diminish the sacrifices made by those who died on Irish soil for independence if we recognise fully that other Irish people shed their blood in other fields' (*Irish Times*, 11 November 1987).

It was in fact the death of British soldiers on Irish soil that drew from Mary Holland one of the most remarkable pieces of journalism that the Northern troubles threw up. In March 1988 a republican funeral in Belfast had been attacked by loyalists. Two days later, two British soldiers strayed apparently inadvertently into a republican crowd in a funeral procession in the west of the city; they were dragged from their vehicle and delivered by the crowd to be dispatched by IRA bullets. Holland, in the face of widespread revulsion, bravely sought to account for the way a community could be overtaken by such animus. Not excusing what had happened, she, nonetheless, insisted, 'I am suggesting that the blame does not lie only on the crowd who ran amok last Saturday but on the many of the rest of us who have left this community increasingly abandoned in recent years' (*Irish Times*, 23 March 1988). An alienated community, she argued, would have to be drawn back into 'the mainstream of the nation' if the country was not to 'reap the whirlwind'. The cogent moral force of Holland's argument in this article was impressive, but what gave it traction on a deeper reality than political calculations was its unforgettable, pained account of how one of the soldiers went to his death. Helpless to intervene in any way, Holland recalled how 'a dark handsome lad in a chain-store sweater' (*Irish Times*, 23 March 1988) was hauled on to the pavement from the car: 'he passed within a few feet of myself and dozens of other journalists. He didn't cry out, just looked at us with terrified eyes as though we were all enemies in a foreign country who wouldn't have understood what language he was speaking if he called out for help.'

Brian Friel's play *Translations*, in which one character had made a plea for 'confusion' as not an 'ignoble condition', had been a play about language. In one scene a British soldier and an Irish girl seek to communicate in their respective tongues and seem to break through the barrier of language. The play ends, however, with the disappearance of the soldier and his presumed murder. Holland's article, entitled 'Could Any of Us Have Shouted "Stop"?', with its sense of linguistic worlds in an irresolvable conflict, was a like a grim coda to that haunting work.

11

THE *IRISH TIMES* AND THE
SHAKING OF THE FOUNDATIONS

In 1990 the fiction writer John McGahern published *Amongst Women*. This 184-page novel told the tale of how a former guerrilla leader in the War of Independence had tried to rule his family with a rod of iron but had failed to adjust to the conditions of peacetime Ireland. He had sought to govern his home and small farm as if they constituted a world of patriarchal permanence immune to the forces of change affecting the wider world. His second marriage to a sensitive but powerful woman and his dysfunctional relationship with his sons and daughters slowly undermine his authority until by his death the balance of power in the family has subtly shifted to its female members (the implication of the title, with its echoing of the 'Hail Mary' which has been the basis of the family's nightly devotions). A deeply affecting narrative, the novel was quickly seized upon by readers and critics as a kind of parable of contemporary Ireland. The life of the rural Moran family, with its children tied as if by chains to the paternal homestead even in economic exile, seemed to catch the public's mood as unemployment was once again scattering Ireland's young abroad to seek work. Moran could be seen as representative of the failed hopes of the Irish revolution, unable to adapt to a shift in social values that set in question all he sought to stand for. Most crucially, his patriarchal assumption that power is a male prerogative is interrogated in the novel by the way control is wrested from his hands over the course of the narrative. McGahern's novel, accordingly, was a measurement on the Richter scale of tremors that presaged unsettling events to come. For the last decade of the twentieth century in Ireland was to be the most remarkable since the period 1912–22, when the foundations of both society and state were to be shaken by repeated shocks.

As if to make *Amongst Women* seem almost prophetic, Irish society in the 1990s was rocked by a flood of discreditable revelations about the worlds of business and politics, and about the Church and its role as moral guardian of the community, which posed questions about the legitimacy of these, just as Moran in McGahern's novel had been shown to be vulnerable, for all his assumed strength. In a society that had hitherto been notable for its concern to keep things secret, in which strict libel laws had protected the wealthy and the powerful from press intrusion, the 1990s were a watershed, when the public began to demand that windows be opened on aspects of Irish life that had been hidden for decades from scrutiny of any kind. What exactly fed this public appetite for investigation, which made the 1990s a decade of the unmasking of powerful forces and the establishment of tribunals, it is difficult to say. Perhaps a few astonishing revelations early in the decade simply stimulated a public appetite that was felt as a lasting hunger for revelation. The newspapers were perforce bound to respond to the demand for transparency.

It was not that the *Irish Times* and other Irish newspapers had not been willing to break stories of past scandals, but they had understood how easily they could fall foul of the libel laws. In his memoir, Conor Brady gives a chastening account of how libel suits and threats of such had increased since the 1970s until by the early 1990s the *Irish Times* was receiving them at the rate of one every two weeks. And in this book he is much exercised at how the sources of Charles Haughey's wealth (raised, as we saw earlier, by Frank McDonald, and revisited thereafter from time to time, until Dick Walsh made it a personal cause) had been kept secret for so long. The 1990s, with its taste for revelation aroused, was, therefore, challenging for newspapers as it became expected, to a degree it had not been before in independent Ireland, that they should uncover scandalous matters. But editors knew the great risks involved as leaders in the Church, newly enriched entrepreneurs, developers and powerful politicians were perfectly prepared to bring down a newspaper if need be by litigation, in order to protect their reputations. It was both an exciting and worrisome time to sit in an editorial chair.

Brady at least could be assured that by the early 1990s the paper he had edited since 1986 had not only weathered the economic downturn of the 1980s but had increased profits. As O'Brien records, 'in the year ending December, 1988' the paper had 'made a profit of £1.2 million. The profits for 1989 and 1990 were £3.6 and £3.1 million' (Mark O'Brien 2008, p. 232). Moreover, the risk the board had taken in 1985 when it had sanctioned the transition to electronic production and had purchased a new printing press that could produce a 48-page newspaper and allow for full-page colour advertising had begun to prove its worth in the issuing of supplements on business, sport and the property cash-cow. To produce the enlarged paper with its widened focus, staff numbers rose and the *Irish Times* began to make its presence felt in Dublin and beyond as more than simply a newspaper, but as an institution of civil society with its sponsorship of annual awards in various fields. Science coverage once again, as in Healy's time, became a key feature of the paper, with its science correspondent Dick Ahlstrom (appointed in 1987) eventually responsible for a weekly page on scientific and technological matters. The paper gave generous coverage to the annual Aer Lingus-sponsored Young Scientist and Technology Exhibition, highlighting how the country's future depended on research and development. In February 1990, a historian warned that government cutbacks were driving gifted young Irish researchers abroad.

By 1990, many young people had been forced to flee the country since the near economic collapse of 1987, which was still being led by Charles Haughey, now very much projecting himself as the dominant power in the land, determined to get things done. His six-month occupancy in the first half of the year of the role of president of the European Union gave him ample opportunity, as he worked to help expedite the reunification of Germany, to act as someone who could perform on a world stage. The impression was deceptive, however, for his power-base was very insecure. In 1989 he had called a snap election and had failed to win an overall majority. Forsaking what had long been a core value of his party against sharing power, he had agreed to enter a coalition with the Progressive Democrats led by Desmond O'Malley, who had withdrawn from Fianna Fáil because of Haughey's leadership to found the new party. Haughey's taboo-breaking iconoclasm was to have profound consequences, but even in 1990 his position was precarious, dependent as it was on the good political relations with not only the formidable and principled O'Malley, but with one of the most impressive of the younger women politicians who were making their mark in the Dáil, Mary Harney, also a former member of Fianna Fáil who had left the party to help found the Progressive Democrats. The autumn of 1990 would give proof of how power was shifting to allow women an increased role in the body politic. In this development, the *Irish Times* would play a significant part.

In 1990 the presidency of Ireland was to become vacant after a period of 14 years in which Dr Patrick Hillery had held office with a reserved sureness of constitutional touch. Fianna Fáil had always considered the presidency as its prerogative and it was widely assumed that when the highly popular Brian Lenihan, who had substantial ministerial experience, allowed his name to go forward for election, he would win easily. Recent illness, together with his genial personality, would assure him of a sympathy vote over and above his considerable qualifications for the role of first citizen. It was not to be.

Lenihan was opposed by the Fine Gael candidate Austin Currie, a Northern nationalist who had served in Brian Faulkner's short-lived executive in Northern Ireland and in the Dáil, and by Mary Robinson, a civil rights lawyer who had served in the Senate as a representative of the graduates of Trinity College Dublin. She was standing as an independent, though, with the support of the Labour Party (in whose interest she had unsuccessfully stood as a candidate for Dáil Eireann and whose leader, Dick Spring, had invited her to consider running for president) and the more left-wing, and smaller, Workers' Party.

At the outset Mary Robinson's campaign seemed quixotic to many. By sheer assiduity, however, as she travelled the length and breadth of the country making contact with groups (especially women's associations) and organizations which comprised civil society that existed outside the main political parties, she established a constituency that made her credible as a candidate, even if Lenihan was still expected to win. Shortly before voting day Lenihan's candidacy was holed underwater by an article published in the *Irish Times*, at a press conference convened by the article's author and the *Irish Times*, and by the subsequent fallout.

Curiously, the issue turned on the institution of the presidency itself. Jim Duffy, a student of politics at work on a doctoral thesis on the subject for University College Dublin, had interviewed Brian Lenihan in May, when he had told the researcher in a recorded interview that he had phoned Patrick Hillery in 1982 at his official residence to pressure him to refuse a dissolution of parliament and to ask Charles Haughey to form a government without the need for a general election. On 27 September, in one of a series of articles commissioned by the *Irish Times* on the history of the presidency, Duffy hinted at this information, which in the event turned out to be a figment of Lenihan's false memory. Phone calls had certainly been placed to Áras an Uachtaráin (the president's residence) by Lenihan among others, on the date in question but had not been taken by Hillery. What in fact had occurred became the focus of a media frenzy amid which Lenihan denied he had even called the Áras. On a television programme he contradicted a claim made on air by Garret FitzGerald that he 'had heard Hillery remonstrating with the Fianna Fáil politicians'. This could not refer to him. He simply had not done so.

Denial became impossible for Lenihan when the *Irish Times* reported on 24 October that there was 'corroborative evidence' that Lenihan had, indeed, phoned Hillery (Duffy had played, for senior *Irish Times* personnel, his tape-recording, in which Lenihan certainly claimed that he had contacted Hillery; the doctoral student had been affronted by Lenihan's stance on the issue). The next day at a Duffy/*Irish Times* press conference, a roomful of journalists were given the opportunity to hear Lenihan's unmistakable voice make the factually incorrect, but career-ruining claim, that he had phoned Hillery in 1982. That evening on national television Lenihan was forced to admit that 'mature recollection' had allowed him to recall that what he had said to a tape-recorder earlier in the year was unfounded. He was in an impossible situation. Haughey, for whom Lenihan had performed many political services over the years, duly sacked him as Tánaiste, and he faced election day seriously damaged.

The whole affair generated speculation and controversy, which has lasted to this day. Throughout, Conor Brady has claimed (Mark O'Brien 2008, pp. 241–3) the *Irish Times* exercised caution in its reportage. It had risked derision, indeed, when it withheld a scoop by agreeing to hold a press conference on Lenihan's tape-recording with Duffy, rather than immediately publishing the fact of its existence. However, Brady was concerned that the paper, some of whose left-leaning journalists favoured Mary Robinson's candidacy, would be suspected of scheming in her interest (Lenihan was intensely suspicious of the newspaper's good faith in the matter), so he believed he was giving the candidate the chance to issue a clarifying statement. Others suspected that Fine Gael had sprung a trap for Lenihan, into which he had stumbled, perhaps confused by the medication he was taking to maintain his health following the liver-transplant he had undergone. Duffy, however, insists that he had no part in such a plot which Brady subsequently came to see as a plausible explanation for what had happened. If this is the case, it was only a partially successful ploy, for in denying Lenihan the presidency it opened the road for Robinson's success, with the party's candidate Currie coming in third and last.

The *Irish Times*, the day before the poll, effectively declared Lenihan unsuitable for office, and in fact in the same editorial had indicated that, on an individual basis, Currie was perhaps best suited to the office of president. It admitted, however, that the election had become a two-horse race, redolent with cultural significance. 'This,' it reckoned, 'is where the choice lies, where two cultures clash. We shall learn something about ourselves as a people when the votes to be cast tomorrow are counted' (*Irish Times*, 6 November 1990). On 9 November 1990, in an editorial entitled 'The Broadening of the Road', the newspaper enthusiastically welcomed the result of the mid-week poll. It noted the role women voters had played in the election as it judged:

> Mary Robinson's success, in Irish terms, is phenomenal. It is more than a milestone. It marks the point at which a narrow and often cruel road, journeyed by a society often narrow and cruel, gives the first sign of broadening out; widening into a more tolerant and accommodating carriageway, offering its users the choice of travelling at their own pace and in whatever company they wish ... The people have indicated that Ireland must change ... They have indicated that the old ways are not acceptable.

There was to be considerable evidence in the years ahead that the 'old ways' had a tenacious enough hold on many aspects of Irish life, where narrowness and cruelty could work their will. However, there can be no gainsaying the enlarging vision of Irish identity Robinson brought to her determination to be the catalyst of a more inclusive nation. The *Irish Times* was strong in its praise of Robinson's inaugural speech, which took place on 3 December 1990, highlighting its comprehensive ambition to enlarge what it meant to be Irish:

> In an address rich in detail – precision pinning down elusive ideas – she embraced both the values of local communities and of a common European home; Ireland's language, culture and environment and the international protection of human rights; the 70 million people of Irish descent across the world and the people of both communities in Northern

Ireland to whom she offered friendship – 'no strings attached, no hidden agenda'. (*Irish Times*, 4 December 1990)

There can be no doubt that Robinson's presidency, true to these words, was to be marked by daring steps taken to engage with the problem of Northern Ireland and with Irish–British relations. Meetings with Queen Elizabeth II in London and with Gerry Adams in Belfast were to be ice-breaking gestures in the complex political choreography that in the 1990s began melting the frozen landscape of failed initiatives that had threatened to make the 'Troubles' permanent. In the Republic, however, it was perhaps Robinson's evoking of the Irish diaspora that chimed most with the public mood. For the reality of the Irish diaspora had been brought home to Irish people in immediate ways in 1988 and 1990, not only because so many young people were once again being forced to emigrate but through the medium of sport. The *Irish Times* in its sports reportage both described this development and was affected by it.

The Republic of Ireland soccer team qualified for the European Championship finals held in the German Federal Republic in June 1988, for the World Cup finals in Italy in June and early July 1990, and for the finals of the latter competition held in the USA in 1994. The Irish soccer team had had occasional limited international successes before, but on these three occasions it exceeded anything achieved hitherto, giving the game a national popularity it had never hitherto enjoyed. The fact that the team was an object lesson in the complex nature of the Irish diaspora (in salute to whose far-flung members President Robinson placed a lit candle in a window of her residence) and living question mark about Irish identity and culture, made its exploits in West Germany, in Italy and the United States much more than sporting phenomena.

The Football Association of Ireland had taken a surprising step in 1986 in appointing the rough-hewn, Northumberland-born Jack Charlton, brother of the more famous Bobby Charlton, as manager of the Irish team. His great gift in this role was to assemble a consistently cohesive team that included Irish-born players who were playing in the English and Scottish leagues alongside players from the same leagues who, by reason of the emigration of parents or grandparents in earlier generations, could qualify for international honours in a green shirt. The team membership of the latter revealed how the Irish diaspora included people with regional English accents (like Charlton's own); that of the former posed challenging questions about culture and class in Ireland. For when the Gaelic Athletic Association spoke censoriously about 'foreign games', it was principally soccer it had in its sights. Mostly played in former garrison towns and in Dublin by working-class males, it had often been the focus of censure by enthusiasts of the Gaelic codes, who in Dublin schools in working-class suburbs judged playing the Sassenach game worthy of severe punishment (rugby football, almost completely the preserve of the middle class, except in

Limerick where it had mass appeal, felt itself remote from such opprobrium in private schools and clubs). Soccer was viewed as non-national by reason of its English origin and its urban following (the GAA believed that it expressed the best of nationally authentic rural values). Its working-class constituency also alarmed the Christian Brothers in their city schools, viewing as they did a love of soccer as an impediment to the social advance of their pupils. Suddenly, however, young men in the national colours were bringing honour to Ireland on the European and world stages, which in the era of global television broadcasts could put a small country on the map of success. So in 1988 and 1990 soccer became *the* story for the Irish media as the 'boys in green', led by an Englishman, with an army of fans, raised the country's profile.

For the *Irish Times* this was a special kind of challenge. Historically, its middle-class readers would have been most interested in field sports, in the fortunes of rugby clubs and of the national side, which comprised players from North and South (in the North most rugby players were Protestants). Those readers from a different perspective would have viewed Irish soccer and its international team with a condescension that mirrored that of the GAA. As the paper adjusted over time to reflect the concerns of Ireland's mainstream, its sports department had as well as such knowledgeable rugby men as Edmund Van Esbeck, employed such GAA aficionados as Paddy Downey (a brilliant, thoughtful writer on hurling as well as on football) and Seán Kilfeather (who covered boxing as well as Gaelic football in hard-hitting sportswriter prose). Peter Byrne, the paper's well-informed writer on soccer (he also covered athletics), had met head on the problem of the ambiguous position of the game in national life by treating the scarcely glamorous local league game with the same conscientiousness with which he wrote about the English upper divisions and international soccer. The effect was often enough to make the Irish League seem small beer in comparison with the exciting profile soccer enjoyed elsewhere. The events of 1988, 1990 and 1994 were to change all that.

From early in the Euro '88 competition Byrne grasped how Charlton's team was a product of the local game and of the diaspora. It was a 'motley Irish squad', in which accents of 'full-blown Dubs' mingled in the changing room with those who spoke with English accents. He profiled one of the players, Chris Morris, in this article entitled 'Born in England, Working in Scotland, Playing for Ireland' to explain how he had been 'born of a father who was evacuated to Cornwall during the war and a mother who hailed from Co. Monaghan'. Now he was a loyal recruit to the Irish sporting cause. When an Irish victory over England prompted some English commentators to query the right of such players to tog out for Ireland, Byrne rose to their defence. For nothing was to take away from a victory that had galvanized a nation, transforming many who had paid little attention to soccer before into avid supporters. Byrne, in a report of the game in Stuttgart, entitled 'The Longest Day and the Greatest Day', hailed the Irish win:

'It was the day that the Republic of Ireland took its place among the aristocracy of international football' (*Irish Times*, 12 June 1988). When the team was dismissed from the European competition, however, amid much euphoria at how well it had performed and expressions of goodwill, Byrne could not help sounding a contentious note: 'Unfortunately the reported cable of goodwill from the Gaelic Athletic Association was not among them' (*Irish Times*, 20 June 1988). In the event, the president of the GAA did send the team congratulations.

One of the newspaper's most astute cultural commentators pondered what all this might mean. Nuala O'Faolain, Dubliner, feminist, literary scholar and admired weekly columnist, devoted a column in June to the way the nation had been affected by the emotion of the week before Ireland was finally defeated by Holland. She wrote how the excitement and joy of the week had transcended the 'ambiguities' involved. O'Faolain felt that the 'success of the Ireland team' had indeed 'palpably improved the quality of life' (*Irish Times*, 20 June 1988) in the country, while it lasted. She noted, however, that the players had been welcomed 'home' to Dublin before they 'immediately left for their homes in Britain'. Unconvinced that sport really expresses much about society, she could only see the team as 'a gift, a fluke. We didn't do anything to deserve them so to speak.' Oddly, for one so sensitive to cultural nuance, O'Faolain seemed oblivious of how decades of dedicated soccer coaches in Dublin and other towns had fed working-class youngsters to the English and Scottish leagues. Nonetheless, for her the joy of the week *was* a gift of the diaspora: even if she failed to see how it also came courtesy of her own city: 'The team is a wholly unexpected return from the emigration of the Fifties, all we ever got back from that. That they are playing for us is somehow a reconciliation with all that loss – to me, anyhow.'

The fortunes of the Irish team in the World Cup finals in Italy in 1990 were unambiguously a national, almost a mythical, progress to elimination by the home team in the quarter-finals. A draw against England and victory against Romania in a penalty shoot-out transfixed the populace which identified fully with the team's exploits. The *Irish Times* issued extensive colour-supplements to compete with the television coverage and reported the games as epic encounters. Of Ireland's goal against England, Peter Byrne waxed poetic: 'The English silence was as deep as the ocean, the Irish delight caused the out-roared thunderstorm to lift up its skirts and flee' (*Irish Times*, 12 June 1990).

Before the World Cup finals in the USA in 1994 (at which there was an equally famous victory when Ireland defeated Italy in New York) Ireland's reputation on the international stage was to be set damagingly in question by profoundly serious developments in the worlds where business and politics met. An ITV television programme, *World in Action*, broadcast in Britain in May 1991 made very disturbing allegations about practices employed by Ireland's principal exporter of beef, Goodman International. The leader of Fianna Fáil's Progressive Democrat coalition partner, Desmond O'Malley, on coming to office as Minister for Industry and Commerce, had denied Goodman International export credit insurance which formerly had been available to it. Goodman's suit against the government on the matter still rested in the courts when *World in Action* made its allegations of 'fraud within the export credit insurance scheme, tax evasion through under-the-counter payments to Goodman staff, complicity in these by the regulatory authorities and inappropriate political influence by Goodman' (Mark O'Brien 2008, p. 110). Amid calls by the opposition to set up an inquiry and O'Malley's threat that he would withdraw his party's support for the coalition, the Taoiseach, Charles Haughey, had no alternative but to set up a tribunal, to be chaired by Mr Justice Liam Hamilton, president of the High Court, to investigate these matters. The Tribunal of Inquiry into the Beef Processing Industry (known as the Beef Tribunal) sat, with a preliminary hearing on 21 June 1991, and issued its report on 29 July 1994.

In her book *Political Corruption in Ireland, 1922–2010: A Crooked Harp?* Elaine A. Byrne writes:

> The Beef Tribunal of Inquiry (1991–94) was perhaps the most extraor-
> dinary political episode in modern Irish history ... the reciprocal
> relationship between politics and vested interests was placed under intense
> political, public, judicial and media scrutiny. This was a period when
> questions about political corruption, golden circles and the integrity of
> public officials were raised in a meaningful way. (Byrne 2012, p. 107)

Central to the media scrutiny referred to here was that of the *Irish Times* and the skilled reportage of its columnist Fintan O'Toole.

The *Irish Times* took the decision to cover the Beef Tribunal in a detailed fashion, sending O'Toole to its many sittings. At the outset this seemed a curious decision beacause O'Toole, who had been working for the paper since 1988, had made his reputation as a drama critic, who, from a generally left-wing perspective, contributed cultural criticism and social analysis to the newspaper. The complex arrangements of export credit insurance, one might have thought, would surely not interest him sufficiently to command his sustained attention. In the event, O'Toole made himself a principal expert on the doings of the Irish beef industry, on procedures in Hamilton's Dublin Castle tribunal and on its findings. This was evidenced not only in his newspaper reports from the castle but in his book *Meanwhile Back at the Ranch: The Politics of Irish Beef* (1994).

O'Toole, in his many reports in the *Irish Times* on the Beef Tribunal, managed the well-nigh impossible task of making the labyrinthine processes of the hearings and the irregularities it was uncovering not only comprehensible but interesting. He brought his experience as a drama critic to bear on the Dublin Castle sittings to present them as often as possible as dramatic encounters among a cast of formidable characters. Powerful figures such as Charles Haughey, Albert Reynolds (who had succeeded Haughey as Taoiseach in 1992) and Desmond O'Malley had their evidence sifted by O'Toole, to allow dramatic conclusions to be drawn. In June 1992, for example, O'Toole wrote of how 'For the first time the Beef Tribunal', in it sessions of the past week, had 'offered a glimpse into the hidden world of political lobbying and of financial contributions to political parties ... at least some indications of the complex connections between the worlds of commerce and politics began to emerge' (*Irish Times*, 6 June 1992). Just over a year later, as the tribunal neared the end of direct evidence, O'Toole wrote of how recent sessions of the tribunal had erupted in high drama: 'As if to compensate the long-distance runners for the hard slog of 220 days of evidence, the penultimate lap around the stadium was full of colour and intrigue. At times this week the evidence was like a script for *Dallas among the Drumlins*, a Cavan soap opera that made its Texas antecedent seem as dull as a self-assembly kitchen unit' (*Irish Times*, 26 June 1993).

When Hamilton issued his 904-page report at the end of July 1994, the *Irish Times* was itself drawn into the drama for, as senior figures in Fianna Fáil hurried to claim that Hamilton's bland, unfocused findings should be accepted, O'Toole wrote in the newspaper that:

> For all its complexity and its nuances, one simple issue emerges from the beef tribunal report, the issue of credibility.
>
> It is clear from the report that a number of statements by very senior political figures were somewhat economical with the truth. Since its publication, there has been more of the same. But the claims by senior political figures in the media do not sit easily with the actual contents of the report. (*Irish Times*, 12 August 1994)

O'Toole listed ten occasions on which claims made by Fianna Fáil ministers were, he believed, at variance with Hamilton's actual findings: 'The principle at work it seems,' he warned, 'is that enunciated by Lewis Carroll in *The Hunting of the Snark*: "What I tell you three times is true".' One of those named in O'Toole's indictment took on the role of protagonist in the drama, as if he feared that O'Toole was a dangerous antagonist, whose article must be challenged. Charlie McCreevy, Minister for Tourism and Trade, took to the stage on 22 August (the *Irish Times* encouraged the sense of personalities in conflict by accompanying McCreevy's article with large photographs of the minister and of Hamilton, Reynolds and O'Toole as if they were the dramatis personae of a play). And McCreevy struck the note of a theatrical rhetorician, condescendingly pretending to being disappointed 'by the quality of Fintan O'Toole's endless analysis of the beef tribunal', before accusing him of being 'reduced to unsophisticated "spin-doctoring" and distortion of the type he so frequently criticises'. In the body of his contribution, which mixed sarcasm with a robust defence of himself and Reynolds, McCreevy indicated he was ready for a fight and was not to be intimidated by a mere journalist.

In fact, McCreevy had not really needed to deploy the heavy guns of his sarcasm. For, despite all that had emerged since ITV had first broadcast its allegations, Irish public opinion was not significantly affected by alleged scandals in the beef industry. Some of the most serious findings of the tribunal had little impact. As Elaine Byrne has commented:

> Fintan O'Toole, the *Irish Times* columnist who observed and critized the workings of the Beef Tribunal more than any other commentator, noted on its tenth anniversary that: 'The bank [AIB] was at best turning a blind eye to a massive tax fraud, at worst colluding in organised crime ... Yet, when all of this was revealed, there was no Garda investigation, nor Revenue scrutiny, and little media interest. The idea that it might have ethical and legal responsibilities didn't arise.' To all intents and purposes, there were no consequences. (Byrne 2012, p. 113)

So what Byrne characterized as 'perhaps the most extraordinary event in modern Irish political history' and O'Toole's reportage, which his editor thought 'one of the most telling exercises in Irish journalism in [his] professional lifetime' (Brady 2005, p. 232), quickly became history. The foundations of the state felt a tremor but the moment quickly passed.

It was probable that few citizens had had the stamina and the patience of an O'Toole to follow the saga of the Beef Tribunal through its many turns of plot and changes of supporting cast. Nor did even its most extraordinary revelations (that Irish tax payers had helped to provide export credit insurance to Northern Irish and British produced beef, for example) have the kind of startling human interest that other disclosures of the 1990s had, which made them compelling media stories. Among these were revelations about the Catholic Church in Ireland.

When Neil Belton, the editor who worked with Fintan O'Toole to produce *Meanwhile Back at the Ranch*, recalled a meeting with the editor of the *Irish Times*, he wrote:

> I remember sitting at a dinner for the nominees of the Irish Times Literature Prizes beside Conor Brady, then editor of the paper, who passionately admired Fintan's work. When I mentioned that I was publishing the book – which touched on Haughey, his successor Albert Reynolds and other big fish in the stagnant pool of Irish power – Brady told me with great emphasis that I was taking a huge risk. 'These are people who will spend a hundred pounds to take a penny off you', he said. This was the received wisdom from the school of hard knocks. Few knew better how determined 'these people' could be. (Belton 2013).

If the big beasts of the Irish political jungle could induce such consciousness of risk in a confident, successful newspaper editor, it can readily be imagined how the power and resources of the Roman Catholic Church, with its immense capital of public respect, could induce even greater caution. So when in January 1992 the *Irish Times* received remarkable information about a senior and very popular Irish Catholic churchman, it proceeded with the utmost circumspection.

A decade and more of revelations about the sins and misdoings of Irish clergy and of the Church's lack of civic responsibility, which would undermine ecclesiastical authority in fundamental ways, began with a phone call. A duty-editor at the *Irish Times* first heard a claim that would shock a nation. Within the hour Brady had been informed that the caller was the male partner of an American woman called Annie Murphy, whose 17-year-old son, it was claimed, had been fathered by the Bishop of Galway, Eamonn Casey, with whom she had had an affair in the 1970s. Conor O'Clery, recently settled in the United States as the newspaper's North American correspondent, was instructed to investigate. Having met Annie Murphy, her partner and her son, O'Clery reported back that he thought the story stood up. When Brady heard the tape-recording of a formal interview with the three people, he agreed their story was probably true (Brady 2005, p. 145). As Brady describes in his memoir, possession of this information was both the chance to break a major story and a burden freighted with high risk and ethical dilemma. If the *Irish Times* published what it knew without foolproof corroborative evidence, the newspaper could be accused of seeking to undermine the Church, that it was driven by ideological venom. There was even the chance that the entire story had been manufactured to expose the newspaper to fatal obloquy. And the ethics of invading a man's privacy weighed heavy too. When Brady consulted a canon lawyer about his concerns, without mentioning the cleric in question, he was advised, as he recalls: '"You may have difficulty proving this, you know," he told me as we parted. "And if you're wrong or if you can't prove it, the church will destroy the *Irish Times*." That's got to be part of the moral calculus too. In the long term, wouldn't this society be much worse without it?' (Brady 2005, pp. 146–7).

After 12 weeks, as Murphy and her partner became impatient at the delay in breaking the story, evidence was supplied that Casey had been making payments to Annie Murphy that certainly provided evidence that there had been a relationship of some kind between them, if not the paternity of her son. The newspaper contacted the bishop and asked for a meeting so that he could respond to Murphy's allegations and to questions about his payments to her. He failed to attend an appointment with two senior *Irish Times* journalists. That evening the Vatican announced his resignation, citing personal reasons. Cautious to the last, over the next few days Brady issued editorials that called on Casey to clarify his position in respect of the money allegedly paid by him to Murphy and to respond to her as yet publicly unrevealed allegations about him. When Casey admitted paternity of Peter Murphy, the paper felt free on 12 May 1992 to splash the whole sorry tale on its front page. More truly terrible stories about the Church and its Irish servants were to appear there soon, but it is difficult to underestimate how shocking, even if titillating for some, the Irish public found the story of Casey's downfall. He had been perhaps the hierarchy's most colourful and admired personality. His commitment to the developing world and to the poor had won him wide respect. He was genuinely liked by many. There seemed something tragic and perhaps unjust in the way the Vatican swiftly dispatched him to safe anonymity in South America. What is certainly true is that no story like his had ever appeared before in the Irish media. A taboo had been broken that could not be restored.

That taboos would increasingly lose their power to silence in Catholic Ireland was evidenced on the very day that the Casey story was broken by the *Irish Times*. For the paper published an outspoken riposte by a feminist theologian Mary Condren, to Cahal Daly, Cardinal and Archbishop of all-Ireland, which took issue with how he had claimed of Casey 'a bishop's personal life is very much his own. His personal ordering of his diocese is a matter between his conscience, God and the Holy See' (*Irish Times*, 12 May 1992). She directly asked the prince of the Church, without customary deference: 'How can the church credibly speak on issues of sexual morality when one of its most popular, distinguished and influential leaders is alleged to have acted in such a sexually irresponsible and exploitative way while simultaneously preaching sexual social responsibility to others?'

In the 1990s religious news became a headline story in a way it had not been since the 1960s when the Second Vatican Council in Rome was covered by John Horgan. The paper's religious correspondents, Joe Carroll, who was succeeded by Andy Pollak and then by Patsy McGarry, rarely lacked for fascinating, sometimes explosive copy, as the Irish hierarchy entered a period of intense controversy and its dark night of the soul when the role of clergy in numerous acts of child abuse was revealed and the Church's efforts to conceal these crimes attracted public outrage far greater than the follies of the egregious Casey had ever done.

It was the issue of abortion, and of 'a woman's right to choose', which in 1992 agonizingly confronted Irish society with how the absolutist teaching of the Catholic Church on abortion could have shocking implications for individuals. The case in question involved not a woman but a young girl, which accounts for the way in which what became known as the X-case struck at the heart of the nation's value-system. It was the *Irish Times* that broke a story that quickly engulfed the media and convulsed public opinion.

The newspaper had got wind of an impending court case involving a pregnancy and a possible abortion. Carol Coulter, subsequently the paper's legal correspondent, quickly ascertained most of the facts and these placed the editor in a real quandary. A minor of 14 years old had been raped by a family friend and had gone to England to seek a termination there. The girl's family had contacted the Garda Síochána about the harvesting and protection of DNA evidence, which could help to convict the perpetrator in any subsequent trial. The guards, uncertain of the implications of this, had approached the Attorney General, Harry Whelehan, for advice, who, on the basis of the constitutional amendment of 1983, had sought an interim injunction restraining Miss X (as she was referred to in court) from leaving the jurisdiction to seek an abortion.

Alarmed by this, the girl and her parents returned to Ireland to await the High Court's determination on the interim restraint order, which was duly granted at an *in camera* hearing, effectively making a teenage girl a prisoner in her own country.

Brady was aware that to publish the findings of an *in camera* hearing of the High Court risked a charge of contempt, a large fine for the newspaper and possible imprisonment for himself as editor. He sought legal advice and consulted Major Thomas McDowell, who asked for the opinion of trust members. The editor was assured of McDowell's firm support if he decided to publish and damn the consequences, so serious was the issue at stake. On 12 February 1992 the *Irish Times* broke the story with an unsensational front-page report: 'State Attempts to Stop Girl's Abortion'. The outcry in the media in general and in the country was immediate and vociferous. The question of whether the *Irish Times* and its editor would be prosecuted had become academic within twenty-four hours. For the courts could not have coped with the numbers who were uninhibitedly publishing and commenting on what had become the focus of an anguished national debate.

On 17 February the *Irish Times* published a devastating cartoon by Martyn Turner which linked the predicament of Miss X with the idea of internment. While there were those who thought Whelehan had done right in seeking to prevent an abortion and Whelehan himself certainly believed he had done his duty in trying to uphold the constitution, Brady's editorial on 18 February caught a wider sense of unease that the amendment of 1983 could result in so harsh a decision as that of the High Court. Entitled 'Descent into Cruelty', the editor asked:

> What has been done to this Irish Republic, what sort of state has it become that, in 1992, its full panoply of authority, its police, its law officers, its courts, are mobilised to condemn a 14-year-old child to the ordeal of pregnancy and childbirth after rape at the hands of a 'depraved and evil man'? With what are we now to compare ourselves? – Ceaucescu's Romania? The Ayatollah's Iran? Algeria? – there are similarities. (*Irish Times*, 18 February 1992)

The paper urged the grounds upon which an appeal should quickly be taken by the Supreme Court.

To vast relief, the Supreme Court threw out the lower court's decision and Miss X was released from her obligation to remain in Ireland to bring her pregnancy to term. Brady has written in his memoir that in time he received a letter from Miss X, telling him of her current well-being and appreciation of the fact that he had placed her plight in the public domain. He recalled: 'It was probably the most valuable and affirming letter I ever received in 16 years of office' (Brady 2005, p. 163).

In a year which saw the resignation in disgrace of Bishop Casey, the X-case was bound to have had a more unsettling impact on the authority of the Catholic Church in Ireland, for not only had a senior cleric's fate revealed how principle and practice could come into conflict but, by year's end, the populace had to go to the polls in a referendum that sought to give effect to what the Supreme Court had determined about abortion when it had delivered a judgement on the X-case: that an abortion could be performed in Ireland when the mother's physical life or mental health was threatened, and that the right to travel, even when an abortion abroad was the intent, could not be restricted. It was being demonstrated that the absolutism of Church law could not but raise almost intractable problems for the state and the individual when they had to deal with real-life situations.

It was in such a context of increasing doubts about the exercise of Church power that in the mid-1990s the scale of the abuse of minors in Catholic Church institutions was revealed, as was the fashion in which the Church authorities had sought to hide these facts from the civil power. The effect was a devastating loss of Ireland's almost unanimous traditional respect for its religious and a revulsion at crimes perpetrated by some of them and the apparent collusion of others in what was perceived as a cover-up.

Like the foreign television programme that broke the beef scandal, it was an Ulster Television *Counterpoint* broadcast that brought the attention of the Irish public to the case of Father Brendan Smyth, a member of the Norbertine Order, who had been charged in Belfast in 1991 with sexual offences against minors. He had fled that jurisdiction for his home abbey in County Cavan and had surrendered himself to the Northern Irish authorities only in January 1994. His subsequent guilty plea to 17 charges of indecent assault and four-year prison sentence had been reported by the *Irish Times* on 25 June 1994, but it was Chris Moore's documentary on 6 October that opened a floodgate of reportage of clerical sexual crime in the newspaper that has flowed almost unabated to the present. In a review of Moore's investigative work, Fintan O'Toole understood that the Smyth case was a watershed. He wrote in a piece entitled 'Tracing Fr Brendan Smyth's 40 Years of Child Abuse': 'The affair of Bishop Eamon [*sic*] Casey and Annie Murphy, so traumatic for Irish Catholics, may in retrospect be bathed in a warm glow of nostalgia' (*Irish Times*, 8 October 1994). For in comparison with Casey's all too human fall from grace, Smyth's life of sexual depredation was an abomination and one that had been conducted within sight of his some of his superiors: 'Smyth's career as a paedophile, though it was an "open secret" within the church, was allowed to continue over 40 years and two continents.' There was even the possibility that 'awareness of Father Smyth's crimes went all the way to the heart of church power'.

The new concept of the 'Paedophile Priest' was unapologetically entered in the newspaper's lexicon, as letters on Father Smyth were published under that shocking heading. Taboos were, indeed, being shattered as deference to clerical eminence melted away. One woman correspondent wrote of Cardinal Cahal Daly, whose role as Primate of all-Ireland in Armagh in the Father Smyth affair had been questioned: 'The fact that he appears to have been following Church policy in covering up the activities of Brendan Smyth, and others like him, is still not sufficient reason for him to stay in office' (*Irish Times*, 1 November 1994). It is hard to envisage such a letter appearing before the public furore fomented by the TV documentary.

A lecturer in social studies published an article in the paper advising that it would be wrong to think of Father Smyth and his activities solely in a Church context. He stated: 'Smyth is very much the embodiment of previous public neglect coming back to haunt us' (*Irish Times*, 18 October 1994). The body politic, it was being stated, was not guiltless in the matter. With a terrible irony, it was the body politic that was to be unnerved by such a spectral revisitation.

The *Counterpoint* television broadcast in 1993, among its disturbing revelations established that the extradition warrants for Father Smyth to be sent to Northern Ireland for trial had lain in the Attorney General's office in Dublin for seven months. When Smith surrendered himself to Northern justice, the warrants were overtaken by events and were no longer relevant. They might well have been forgotten about had not the Taoiseach, Albert Reynolds, in October 1994, wanted to elevate Harry Whelehan, the Attorney General to the presidency of the High Court, when the Smyth warrants had been awaiting a decision about their validity in Irish law. It would eventually become known that the apparent delay in addressing the question of Smyth's possible extradition had been because of pressure of business in the Attorney General's office and to the way work had been prioritized by officials there. Reynold's coalition partners in the Labour Party opposed Whelehan's appointment unless there were to be an explanation of the seven-month delay in 1993. Reynolds went ahead in defiance of the leader of the Labour Party Dick Spring. For Spring and his senior colleagues this was unacceptable and a full-blown political crisis erupted in November 1994. It became clear that another case involving a religious had been treated in similar fashion to Smyth's. Consequently Spring would be satisfied only by Reynolds's resignation and by that of the newly appointed president of the High Court as the price of remaining in government with Fianna Fáil.

How unsettling this was for the country at large (where some were ready to indulge conjectures about right-wing Catholic interest groups affecting decision-making at the highest level) was suggested by the *Irish Times*'s editorial of

17 November. The newspaper categorized recent events as 'a saga of unprecedented shabbiness, deceit and ineptitude' (*Irish Times*, 17 November 1994). How seriously it viewed what had transpired was expressed in a blunt paragraph:

> It has been a humiliating and shameful passage in Irish public life. Leinster House has seen its fair share of dark days, perhaps memorably in the wake of the arms scandal and subsequent trials in 1970. But even that critical drama did not yield up the sleaze, the cringing efforts at self-exculpation, the cowardly attempts to transfer blame to paid officials which have characterised this affair. And the arms crisis did not draw in either the office of the Attorney General or the legal system.

The newspaper was in no doubt that the Taoiseach must resign.

On 17 November both Reynolds and Whelehan bowed to the inevitable, drawing from the *Irish Times* the pained observation that 'Words can only inadequately describe the mixed emotions of anger, bafflement and shame which have been aroused by the chain of events which started with the revelations in the Brendan Smyth extradition case' (*Irish Times*, 18 November 1994). Early the following month the newspaper itself was to add its own crucial link to that chain. Its intervention would help to bring about a new government, following a month when the foundations of the state had seemed to rock dangerously (on Friday 18 November the *Irish Times*'s editorial had commented: 'by Thursday night, with ripple effects of the affair touching Leinster House, the Attorney General's office and the law courts, public opinion had been conditioned to expect almost any shock') .

Among the reasons the *Irish Times* had given in calling for Reynolds's resignation was the suspicion that he had misled the Dáil about another case that had been delayed in the Attorney General's Office. With Reynolds gone, Spring was willing to negotiate with his successor Bertie Ahern, the new leader of Fianna Fáil, about forming a new administration without the need to go to the country. In early December the *Irish Times*'s experienced political correspondent, Geraldine Kennedy, discovered that other members of Ahern's party had known full well about the second case too, but had kept silent about it. When the *Irish Times* broke this story, it made it impossible for Spring to contemplate being in office with such apparently untrustworthy colleagues. The Labour Party, less than willing to face the electorate, having been close to supping for a second time with the Fianna Fáil devil, turned its attention elsewhere, agreeing to form a coalition with Fine Gael and a smaller party, Democratic Left.

For the *Irish Times*, the fallout from this extraordinary set of events, in which it had played a significant part, was less that it attracted ire from members of the political class (Fianna Fáil and especially Bertie Ahern, who saw the premiership slip from his fingers to Fine Gael's John Bruton, certainly had reason to feel sore), but that it became increasingly the object of anonymous venom directed against its policy of publishing emerging details of cruelty against children in Church-run orphanages and reformatories, and legal cases taken against Catholic clergy for the sexual abuse of children. The X-case in 1992 and the Smyth case in 1993 opened a spate of these and the *Irish Times* was determined to report them alongside its other coverage of social affairs and court proceedings. Conor Brady has recalled:

> It was never easy nor [*sic*] pleasant to report these matters. But we reported them in full. For that – especially for our court reporting of the sexual abuse cases – we drew a lot of hostility. The *Irish Times* was frequently accused of seeking to destroy the moral fabric of the country. Abusive telephone calls and threatening letters were not infrequent. Envelopes containing excrement were posted to me. On two occasions members of extremist pressure groups picketed the offices. One group threatened to picket my home but it never materialised. (Brady 2005, pp. 162–3)

There was a sad irony that such noxious behaviour was directed at Brady's *Irish Times*. For not only was the editor giving, as we noted above, ample space in the newspaper to his well-informed religious correspondents, who created a sense, despite the misdeeds of some clergy, that religion was a vital aspect of Irish life, where exciting change was afoot, but he himself wrote sympathetically and well about religious matters. For example, he clearly understood how demanding was the role of a Catholic bishop and the stresses under which such figures worked. When, for example, Bishop Brendan Comiskey questioned the Church's teaching on priestly celibacy, the *Irish Times* published a concerned editorial that expressed the widespread view among the laity in Ireland as elsewhere that 'the issue of a married priesthood, and the end of priestly celibacy it would entail, was a live one throughout the Catholic world'. The editorial, entitled 'Bishops, Priest and People', envisaged a time when the Church, in light of falling vocations, would have to face not only the issue of married clergy but the role of women as priests. It saluted Comiskey as 'a courageous' man who, along with a fellow bishop Willie Walsh of Killaloe, was a harbinger of a great debate 'about opening up the Catholic Church in the 21st century' (*Irish Times*, 13 June 1995).

The paper's religious correspondent, Andy Pollak, that same month supplied a pen-portrait of Comiskey, who was angry at being swatted down by Cardinal Daly. He presented the Bishop of Ferns as 'a charismatic and convivial figure', 'but he can also be an angry and authoritarian one ... a worldly man in a hierarchy of unworldly farmers' and rural shopkeepers' sons' (*Irish Times*, 28 June 1995). By early autumn, when it was announced that Comiskey was to take a three-month sabbatical in the United States from his post in the Ferns diocese, Brady, without any mention of conviviality bringing him to this pass, defended the bishop on the grounds that the pressures of office and his outspoken position in the hierarchy had placed him under enormous strain. His editorial of 19 September was a notably humane consideration of the bishop's plight: 'The lay person, accustomed to processes of dialogue and open discussion of ideas in secular society, cannot fully empathise with a churchman who challenges the system' (*Irish Times*, 19 September 1995).

Brady concluded, as if in personal testimony:

> Bishop Comiskey's contribution to the debate in his church has helped to restore for many Irish Catholics their sense of participation in shaping its future after it has gone through a particularly difficult period. It is for this reason that they will hope this sabbatical will bolster his return to the debates as well as alleviating the stress which has made it necessary.

Tragically, it quickly became clear that an epicentre of the Church's problems with sexual abuse was the diocese of Ferns itself. For in November 1995 an egregious paedophile priest there, Father Seán Fortune, was charged with crimes of gross indecency and indecent assault against six male youths over an extended period. Comiskey's possible part in any cover-up of his priest's depredations on the young was bound to surface as an issue.

Even when by February 1996 a great deal discreditable to Comiskey had emerged, Brady could not bring himself to be other than compassionate. There certainly were questions to answer and for a man who had prided himself on public relations expertise, the Comiskey story was the stuff of personal ruin:

> Amidst a welter of rumour and counter-rumour he flees the country in secret. His drinking problem, first denied, is then confirmed. Questions are raised over diocesan finances, his handling of sex abuse cases and his own lifestyle. A friend and adviser is found dead in a Wexford apartment. And those who are left behind to face the music on his behalf have no answers to give, no information on his plans, and no clear idea of his whereabouts. (*Irish Times*, 17 February 1996)

To counter such a 'story', Brady recalled the 'most wonderful of parables – the Prodigal Son'. He hoped that Comiskey on his return might even give 'contemporary embodiment' to the gospel tale.

The difficulty was that the bishop had fled to a far country and the problems he faced were at home. In this he was not very different from the many figures in public and political life in Ireland in the 1990s who found their past 'sins' damagingly uncovered to a populace with an aroused appetite for scandal. Undoubtedly the media were prepared to feed this appetite, when hard facts became visible, frustrated as they had been for so long by strict libel laws. Among those primed for a fall was Charles Haughey, whose wealth and its sources had fascinated and bemused for so long. When in January 1992 Haughey was forced from office, following the revelation that he had known of the tapping of two journalists' phones a decade earlier, the *Irish Times* treated the event as the end of an era, the fall of a Titan (the Irish response to Haughey's political demise was not unlike that of the British to Margaret Thatcher's enforced resignation from her premiership in November 1990).

In the special supplement the *Irish Times* published to mark Haughey's exit from political power, Nuala O'Faolain contributed a challenging article that sought to explain how such claims were warranted. She accounted for much of the disdain and 'moral indignation' Haughey aroused among Ireland's bourgeoisie as mere snobbery about a man who had gone to the wrong school on Dublin's unfashionable north side and had merely studied Commerce at University College Dublin. And she saw Haughey, like her late father, the influential social columnist for the *Evening Press* newspaper, Terry O'Sullivan, as members of the generation in the country which had managed 'to fully escape the austerity and puritanism and bitterness of the first decades of the state' (*Irish Times*, 31 January 1992). In 'Why Shouldn't a Free-born Irishman Do Exactly What He Wants?', O'Faolain defended Haughey's aristocratic tastes, especially in the arts, and observed that his working-class constituents were 'not even remotely alienated by his wealth'. They knew a Taoiseach when they saw one: 'Like all the great TDs, Charlie is not a politician to his own people, but a chieftain of its concrete-dwelling tribes.' On 3 February she devoted her customary column to the range of Haughey's knowledge of the Ireland he loved and of his international contacts. In both pieces she was adding, even as he apparently was leaving the scene, to the myth of Haughey's grandeur that before the end of the decade would lie in tatters. Like others in the capital's journalistic world, O'Faolain was helping to give Haughey's fate the aura of a tragedy (Haughey himself quoted Othello in his final speech in the Dáil).

Dick Walsh (who had long pursued the mystery of Haughey's finances) was not of the myth-making party. He concluded, in the *Irish Times's* special supplement, his measured account of Haughey's career by claiming: 'He contributed more than any other politician of his age to the erosion of confidence in politics, the diminution of the Dáil and a rising tide of frustration among the electorate.' The leading article of the day by Conor Brady, entitled 'The Haughey Years', manfully tried to give the departing leader his due as one who 'worked like a Trojan for his Ireland'. There had been 'periods of great statecraft. There were occasions of the most graceless opportunism.' He had been a transitional figure who may well have been crucial to helping a traditional Ireland on its path to modernity. However, over all hung suspicions that there were things about Charles J. Haughey that defied explanation:

> It is easier to comment on his style than to judge his substance. The mansion, the island, the yacht, the paintings and all the rest – take them together with his contemptuous refusal ever to make any explanation as

to how he acquired this great wealth – and it is clear that one is dealing with an extraordinarily complex character. That he was capable of the most profound misjudgements about the people he placed around him is certain. That he encouraged the cult of the adventurer and then failed to control those who took adventurism to its ultimate and unacceptable limits is also now clear. (*Irish Times*, 31 January 1992)

None of these writers, when Haughey took his leave, could have imagined that damning and simple truths about this 'complex character' would emerge following as bizarre a chain of events as that which had brought down Albert Reynolds. Haughey could have drifted into a comfortable retirement had not a scion of the grocery empire founded by Ben Dunne Sr in 1944 indulged in February 1992 in a night of cocaine-fuelled excess in a Florida hotel. The resulting court case, in which Ben Dunne was found guilty of possession of an illegal substance, provoked conflicts about his behaviour in what was still a family business. Dunne's sister commissioned a study of her brother's finances which indicated that he had made payments to two politicians. At two government-appointed tribunals (the McCracken and the Moriarty tribunals) it became known that Haughey had received substantial sums from Dunne and other businessmen and that Haughey's accountant, Desmond Traynor, probably with Haughey's knowledge, had placed considerable sums beyond the Revenue's view for his client's use. It was also clear that the former Taoiseach had come close to perjuring himself at the second of the tribunals.

Haughey had lived by a kind of cult of personality. In a decade when the media liked to cast individuals as heroes and villains (with Father Brendan Smyth a kind of demon out of hell in a frequently published and broadcast visual image), extracts from Haughey's televised appearance at the Moriarty tribunal were calamitous for his reputation. Of the flood of revelations at the tribunals and of the damaging information supplied by a government inquiry into Traynor's scheme, one analyst commented in 2002:

In the court of public opinion ... Haughey the young and able minister who promised so much, has been reduced to a pathetic figure. His once great persona has been diminished to that of a man scrounging off the rich, devoid of moral character and engaged in a determined, futile attempt to gain acceptance by the monied elite who regarded his osten-tation as vulgar pretension' (Justin O'Brien, p. 169).

Columns in the *Irish Times* expressed a similar severity. In 1999 Fintan O'Toole summed up what all the shocking revelations of malfeasance among the nation's elite had shown: 'we know that key parts of the establishment in Ireland have been covered by little more than a veneer of legitimacy' (*Irish Times*, 25 September 1999). He noted how Haughey had been a 'central figure' in the scandal of Traynor's manifestly dubious investment scheme and he identified 'Haughey's golden circle' as obviously compromised. Damningly, O'Toole was forced to an unsettling conviction:

> We have to adjust our understanding of contemporary Ireland to take account of two startling facts. One is that, at least from the early 1980s onwards, a large swathe of Ireland's ruling elite silently withdrew its allegiance from the state. The other is that organised crime in Ireland, which we used to imagine as the preserve of shifty working-class men ... is also carried on by respectable, beautifully tailored members of the upper-middle class.

For Colm Keena, writing in September 2000, after a week in which Haughey had been subjected to forceful interrogation at the Moriarty tribunal about his extravagance being dependent on the generosity of prominent businessmen (Keena's piece was jocosely headlined, with a nod to the Beatles, 'Getting by with a little help from my friends'), the truth was clear-cut: 'Low standards in high places upset the whole body politic and all of civic society' (*Irish Times*, 30 September 2000). Keena also observed of the Flood tribunal – uncovering, at the same time as Moriarty was about his work, the irregularities in the planning process in north County Dublin, that Frank McDonald had long argued was endemic in the city as elsewhere:

> Many of the people who are the focus of the Flood tribunal's enquiries were prominent figures during Mr Haughey's stewardship of Fianna Fáil. The rumour and suspicion – and knowledge – concerning Mr Haughey's personal ethics which existed during his years in power set the tone for many of the matters now being examined by Flood.

If the revelations at tribunals in the 1990s administered tremors to the edifice of the Irish state, they did not constitute an earthquake. A marked improvement in the country's economic condition after the crisis of the late 1980s, with rapid improvements in the standard of living for the majority of the population, meant that an essentially conservative society managed to absorb what it had come to know about itself without demanding any radical transformation. The foundations shook but stood firm, even in a decade of extraordinary change internationally.

In February 1990, Seamus Martin, an experienced and resourceful *Irish Times* staffer, was dispatched by the paper to South Africa to cover the immediate aftermath of the release from prison of Nelson Mandela, where he managed, in a notable coup, to gain an interview with the ANC leader on the 22nd of that momentous month (Seamus Martin 2008, pp. 90–102). On this and other visits to the country that year, he managed to meet and interview some of the main figures who would expedite a transition which in 1994 would see the end of apartheid and the installation of an ANC government. Mandela's triumph was greeted with exhilaration in many parts of the world, but Dublin felt it had a special claim on him, having given him the freedom of the city in 1988 and Mandela had visited to receive the honour in person at the end of 1990. The anti-apartheid movement in Ireland had been vigorously led by a South African, the Trinity College Dublin law lecturer, Kader Asmal. In an editorial in January 1994 the newspaper saluted the fact that the campaign against apartheid had had 'a long and tenacious history' (*Irish Times*, 13 January 1994). In December, with Asmal a minister in the new government, the paper acknowledged 'the special links of solidarity and engagement between Ireland and South Africa' (*Irish Times*, 3 December 1994).

In mid-1991 Conor O'Clery was posted to Washington to become the newspaper's correspondent there; Seamus Martin took his place in Moscow where the communist regime collapsed even more quickly than it had taken the apartheid government to fall in South Africa. Martin was witness to some of the most significant events in world history to take place since the ending of World War II. He sent the *Irish Times* insightful reports on the chaos and confusion and on history in process that followed the attempted coup against Gorbachev, the disintegration of the Communist Party, the dismantling of the Soviet Union and the grotesque Yeltsin presidency of the Russian federation. What gave Martin's work its edge was his acute sense that what was occurring was no simple triumph of western values in an evil empire, but a complex, difficult new phase in a nation's history. He brought to his analysis an Irishman's fatalistic sense that politics were both intensely personal and cruelly indifferent to the individual's fate. And he reported on what he saw with a keen awareness of how the ending of socialism affected the daily lives of ordinary citizens, as emerging oligarchs seized immense wealth.

Actual links with Ireland, less obvious than those with South Africa, were real enough, it seemed, and politically highly sensitive. For in 1992 Martin unearthed in Soviet archives what appeared to be evidence of contact in 1986 between Ireland's Workers' Party and the Central Committee of the Communist Party of the Soviet Union, in which financial support for a 'party school' had been sought (Seamus Martin 2008, pp. 193–7). Though the *Irish Times* published details about the contents of this letter and invested a considerable amount of journalistic time in trying to authenticate it, before long its provenance became so much in doubt that the paper abandoned the story. What had made Martin's discovery of this document so potentially explosive and the need to prove its authenticity so crucial, was not only that such a contact might have been part of a more extensive relationship between the Workers' Party and the Soviet Communist Party (the letter, as it was reported, referred to previous, discontinued support for 'special activities') but that it could remind the Irish public of how recently the party had espoused democracy. Furthermore, the Workers' Party could ill-afford to have its evolution from Sinn Féin (the Workers' Party), which had given political support to the illegal Official IRA (some of whose activists included members of the IRA who had not joined in the Provisional IRA's campaign of violence), into a party that gave full loyalty to the state, revisited as the new story appeared to conjure up a murky past. For any close analysis of its history would remind the Republic's electorate that the Workers' Party was the adult form of a child born in the crucible of the Northern conflict, sensible voters did not wish to have life in the Republic

News from eastern Europe in the early 1990s was giving readers in western Europe a terrible opportunity to understand how quickly societies could collapse into barbarism fed by the forces of territorial ambition and ethnic hatred. The dismemberment of the Yugoslav federation and the violence in Croatia and in Bosnia were given heart-rending coverage in the *Irish Times* as the concept of 'ethnic cleansing' gained explanatory purchase to account for atrocity. In August 1992 the paper published a chilling report on how 'a hatred that stretches back through the centuries' had resulted in a mostly Muslim town of 10,000 people (one of many such) being claimed as Serb territory, its residents killed or forced from their homes and their businesses destroyed. The article reported that a mass movement of some 2.3 million people had taken place since armed conflict began in the former Yugoslav republics a year earlier. The fighting had compelled many to flee their homes, but 'vast numbers' had 'been deliberately expelled as broad swathes of Bosnia were cleared of Muslims and Croats by Serb forces in what is being termed "ethnic cleansing".' An article by William Safire published in the paper on 23 April 1993, taken from the *New York Times* service, explained the recent etymology of that 'euphemism for murder', of a 'big phrase that is likely to be with us for a while', as he warned:

> If the practice is not stopped, the term will continue in active use; if the world forces the forcible separation and killing to end, the phrase ethnic cleansing will evoke a shudder a generation hence much as the final solution does today – as a phrase frozen in history, a terrible manifestation of ethnocentrism gone wild.

Earlier that April the *Irish Times* had joined with 34 newspapers in 33 countries in publishing, to mark the first anniversary of the siege of Sarajevo by Serb forces, a facsimile of *Oslobođenje*, a daily newspaper there. It was an act of journalistic solidarity with brave, beleaguered colleagues.

In reporting the horrors of the break-up of the former Yugoslavia, the *Irish Times* could draw on the vivid reportage of an intrepid young Irish war reporter, Maggie O'Kane, whose material for *The Guardian* the paper could copy as part of a European-wide exchange agreement. O'Kane had covered the First Iraq War in 1991, but she made uncovering the horrors she believed that Slobodan Milosevic had unleashed on Bosnia almost a personal crusade.

The years 1992 and 1993, while the former Yugoslavia was being broken apart, saw Northern Ireland's own long-standing conflict threaten to descend into widespread inter-communal violence, if not on a Bosnian scale, then with similar destructive energies being released. Although the SDLP leader and the leader of Sinn Féin had been engaging in protracted talks (which became public knowledge in April 1993) in an effort to establish how a settlement might be achieved, and the British and Irish governments were setting in place agreed positions on the issue which resulted in the Downing Street Declaration of December 1993, in those two years atrocities were perpetrated which suggested that society was falling over an abyss. By early February 1992 the *Irish Times* was reporting that the death-toll in Northern Ireland was its highest to that date in the year since 1976 as its northern editor told how the province was undergoing 'one of its most appalling phases of violence for years' (*Irish Times*, 6 February 1992). A new wave of recruits was joining the loyalist UDA, which was determined to take the 'war' to the IRA and the Catholic community. An editorial sounded an ominous note:

> This is now a primal blood lust without rhyme or reason or political warranty. It is killing gone out of control whose only explanation appears to be that the old leaders have been replaced by new ones whose appetite for blood must be assuaged.
>
> Over the last 20 years the hope of some political movement put a break on the periodic cycles of tit-for-tat killings. That bleak and limited control now seems to be gone. (*Irish Times*, 6 February 1992)

By the autumn of 1993 what this editorial termed a 'circle of blood' was nearing a terrible completion. When an IRA unit on 23 October bombed a fish-shop on the Shankhill Road in Belfast on a busy Saturday afternoon, in the mistaken belief that some of the UDA leadership was meeting in a room above, eight Protestant civilians died, along with one of the bombers. The *Irish Times*'s editorial the following Monday was blunt. Entitled 'Aftermath of Murder', it related what had happened to the Hume–Adams talks: 'At the heart of the developing debate is a question about the long-term intentions of the Provisional IRA. About their short-term intentions there seems to be no doubt: the attack, whatever they may say, was blatantly sectarian' (*Irish Times*, 25 October 1993). It was likely, too, to lead to revenge attacks by loyalists, 'given the IRA's declared aim of wiping out the leadership of an equally murderous loyalist group'. In the same issue the *Irish Times* published an interview with Gerry Adams; the editorial that day insisted that he had yet to prove his bona fides as a peacemaker.

The next days brought the feared reprisals, culminating in a massacre of mostly Catholic customers in a public house in Greysteel village in County Derry on 30 October. This raised the number of violent deaths in eight days in Northern Ireland to 23. It was hard, as the *Irish Times* supplied a map of the province which showed the pattern of killings in Belfast over the years and of the recent province-wide murders, not to think of how similar maps had supplied the locations of the killing fields of Bosnia. On 2 November the *Irish Times*'s reporters in the North wrote: 'Northern Ireland reels under the shock of another mass killing'.

It was a credit to the *Irish Times* that, at such a perilous time, it kept its nerve as it nailed its colours firmly to the mast of what at the beginning of the decade was being thought of as the Irish 'peace process'. The term 'peace process' had been ubiquitous in the paper's columns in the late 1980s in reference to attempts to broker a settlement between Israelis and Palestinians and in the conflict zones of Central America. In November 1989, when the British Secretary of State for Northern Ireland, Peter Brooke, suggested that Sinn Féin might have a role to play in future negotiations, an *Irish Times* editorial adverted to the achievement of peace and the risky 'process' it would involve. By March 1990 Gerry Adams had made the term his own. An *Irish Times* report had him addressing Brooke in a rhetorically adroit speech: '"With a new and imaginative approach he can begin the peace process"' (*Irish Times*, 26 March 1990). In its editorial of 1 November, entitled 'Beyond Greysteel', the *Irish Times* argued forcefully that what was a discernible, widely shared aspiration for a settlement must be sustained, even in the face of recent atrocities. It insisted, taking a long view: 'The Reynolds-Major initiative will not be an easy passage. The stakes are high. How it fares will have an impact on the fortunes of political leaders in Dublin, Belfast and London. It has the potential to have a profound influence on the future of these islands.'

There were senior journalists on the *Irish Times* who thought that the greatest risk posed by the peace process which gathered pace after the Provisional IRA declared a total cessation of violence in August 1994, was that the republican movement could never be trusted to truly abandon militarism. And the scepticism of Dick Walsh – whose sympathies had been with the wing of the republican movement that had evolved to form the Workers' Party – and of Kevin Myers, principal contributor to 'An Irishman's Diary' since 1980, whose experience as a young RTE reporter on Bloody Friday in Belfast had confirmed in him a detestation of the Provisionals, in 1996 seemed well founded. For as negotiations appeared to stall, the IRA exploded a huge bomb at Canary Wharf in London, which killed two civilians, as if to prove the worst suspicions of those who thought the 'total cessation' of 1994 was a tactical ploy that could be reversed. At the least it was a lesson, if lesson were needed, that the IRA was a ruthless organization, prepared to risk the taking of life as a negotiating card.

Conor Brady, in his memoir, recalls how in these difficult years, when the *Sunday Independent* in particular was vocal in its criticism of how both governments were seeking to bring the untrustworthy republican movement into the political arena: 'The *Irish Times* adhered to the view that the only way forward was a negotiated settlement supported across both communities, with full demilitarisation and an unqualified acceptance of constitutional means' (Brady 2005, pp. 86–7). Brady himself, as editor, had given practical expression to his sense that any progress towards that goal must involve both Northern communities, when in 1989 he had asked Frank Millar if he would like to contribute to the newspaper. Millar, a Northern Protestant and former Unionist Party politician, was working in British television when Brady issued his invitation. Millar quickly accepted and began regularly to submit copy on the Northern issue to the paper. In January 1991 he was appointed London editor. Among his early contributions was a 1989 series of in-depth interviews that took the current thinking on the matter among key figures across Northern Ireland's political divide (in his role as a Unionist politician, Millar had worked on a document that recommended power-sharing as an aspect of a settlement). Readers of this valuable series could have been in no doubt that for unionists and their Unionist leaders the existence of Articles 2 and 3 of the Irish Constitution, which laid claim to the six counties of Ulster under British rule as part of the national territory of Ireland, were deeply objectionable. Peter Robinson, then Ian Paisley's deputy in the Democratic Unionist Party, bluntly dismissed the articles as an 'arrogant claim' (*Irish Times*, 20 March 1989). When in March 1990 the Irish Supreme Court judged, in a test case taken by a two Northern unionist politicians, that the clauses were a legal imperative and not simply an aspiration, it was clear that they were integral to the very construction of the Irish state, part of the foundation upon which it rested. Removing or changing them could require the Republic to build a new constitutional structure upon which future relations between the two parts of Ireland could peacefully rest. That was not likely to be an easy task. The *Irish Times*, in its editorial of 26 March 1990, accepted that 'in any possible settlement, Articles 2 and 3 will have to be on the table' and that the Supreme Court had left the state 'with a profoundly serious issue of principle which has to be addressed'. That there were those ready to countenance such a change of national principle was evidenced later in that violent year in a moving, even visionary, *Irish Times* article by Nuala O'Faolain. With the dead of Greysteel still unburied, she invited *Irish Times* readers to imagine what an Ireland at peace might be like.

O'Faolain was direct about why she had hitherto supported the constitutional articles in question. She wrote:

> I never would have signed away Articles 2 and 3. I feel the symbolic import of the words. They seem to tell the people on the earth nearest to my own culture that I regret that they've been trapped by history in an alien environment. They were a bargaining counter on behalf of those people. (*Irish Times*, 1 November 1993)

Now, despite the horrors being covered in other sections of the newspaper, O'Faolain grasped that there was a feeling abroad that was 'the chance of real change'. She concluded powerfully:

> We ordinary people are mired in our own histories and prejudices, and the more bitter we are, the more blind. We cannot see our little island with all its people as it sits in the world. We can hope, however, and we can make it clear what we want, that up there, where politicians are also statesmen, the forces are being marshalled that will be sufficiently powerful to change the paramilitaries, change the unionists, change Britain, and, by no means least, change us. Not so much to change them by strength, as be strong enough to open up ways for the combatants, especially the IRA, to express their own change.
>
> If I saw signs of that, do you think I'd cling to Articles 2 and 3? I'd *run* to vote them away. *Run.*

The steps towards the removal of Articles 2 and 3, and their replacement by new clauses, were slow and painful. It was following the Good Friday Agreement of 1998 which laid out how Northern Ireland would be governed by an inclusive power-sharing administration with links to the Republic, that new clauses could be put to the people of the Republic in a referendum. Key phrases in this were to be the coping stone of a new Ireland, that removed what the Supreme Court had defined as a legal imperative to seek reunification of the national territory, with the implication that the will of the people in either jurisdiction was of no account:

> It is the will of the people of the Irish nation, in harmony and friendship, to unite all the people who share the territory of the island of Ireland, in all the diversity of their identities and traditions, recognising that a united Ireland shall be brought about only by peaceful means, with the consent of a majority of the people, democratically expressed, in both jurisdictions in the island.

On the Saturday after the plebiscite, when it was clear that the constitutional amendment would be passed by a huge majority in the Republic (on the same day, a much slimmer majority in Northern Ireland agreed to the implementation of the Good Friday Agreement), the former Taoiseach, Garret FitzGerald, warmly welcomed the result as 'clearing the way for a constructive relationship between North and South' (*Irish Times*, 23 May 1998). Dick Walsh declared in his article on the result: 'Today we celebrate democracy and the principle of consent.'

On 25 May the *Irish Times* published an editorial that marked a watershed in Irish history. It endorsed Taoiseach Bertie Ahern's claim that Ireland had been redefined, and continued: 'It is a simple statement; but of the most profound implication. The two great political cultures of nationalism and unionism have committed themselves to a new accommodation with each other and that commitment has been solemnised by votes of a majority of both traditions' (*Irish Times*, 25 May 1998). The tone rose to a kind of panegyric:

> Ireland is being made anew, as if the Fates or the divine arbiter had at last decided to take pity on a country long scarred and riven by violence and hate. We have witnessed a commitment to compromise by Irishmen and women of all traditions and denominations. It marks the end of a period – stretching over centuries – in which relationships have been defined by mistrust and aggression and by staking out local hegemony or dominance. In its place there is now a commitment to an agreed sharing which many believed could never become a reality, much less that it would happen in their own lifetimes. In this State, the people have voted overwhelmingly to replace an inherently threatening territorial claim with a simpler aspiration, grounded on the principle of consent. Truly seismic changes have been taking place.

So a decade in which the underpinning Church and state had historically given society in the Republic of Ireland had been shaken by serious scandal, 'seismic changes', as the *Irish Times*'s editorial put it, had now laid the basis of an agreed Ireland to be built on a new constitutional foundation.

Undoubtedly the national self-confidence that was engendered by the remarkable economic boom that the Republic of Ireland experienced in the second half of the 1990s made it easier for the country to make this basic adjustment in its political outlook. A new national sense of achievement and the international respect increasingly being afforded Ireland meant that maintaining an irredentist claim on Northern Ireland became more and more irrelevant to *amour propre*. For success on the football field in the early 1990s had inaugurated a decade in which an economic miracle, the envy of the world, was accompanied by cultural achievements which also raised Ireland's profile internationally. Paradoxically, as it became less important to national pride to resolve the Northern question in the terms in which it had been traditionally formulated (there being other substantial successes in which that could be vested) meaningful progress could be made on the issue.

In December 1994, in the year in which the IRA had declared its 'complete cessation' from military action, the *Irish Times*'s Cliff Taylor reported that the 12 months past were 'the first year of the recovery' (*Irish Times*, 29 December 1994). That autumn, in a speech in Atlanta, Georgia, President Mary Robinson had referred with pleasure to how a Morgan Stanley analyst had recently referred to the Irish economy as 'a Celtic Tiger' (*Irish Times*, 26 October 1994). Within a few months the phrase would dominate reportage on the Irish economy, at home and abroad, with the *Irish Times* no exception. In his

December 1994 article Cliff Taylor had observed how economists had been arguing whether Ireland was in fact a '"Celtic Tiger" or an artificial inflation of economic growth by multinational accounting'. By January 1996 the Taoiseach John Bruton could confidently assert that Ireland had 'earned its title "Celtic Tiger"' (*Irish Times*, 25 January 1996).

The *Irish Times*, as the boom took hold, played no small part in recording its progress and noting its effects on the quality of Irish life. In June 1996, for example, Cliff Taylor published a four-part series on the Economic Boom. He prefaced the series by outlining how 'For many these are the best of times in Ireland. Demand in the shops, even for the most expensive items, has never been so good. House prices are surging ahead. Ireland, for so long in the economic second division, now stands as a role model for the rest of Europe' (*Irish Times*, 3 June 1996). In April 1997 an *Irish Times* supplement entitled 'Towards the New Millennium', edited by Seán Flynn and Cliff Taylor, with Garret FitzGerald as an associate editor, put a kind of imprimatur on the boom. It was real and would continue. 'Since 1987 there had been a decade which had made a huge difference' (*Irish Times*, 30 April 1997). Headlines in the supplement reflected a buoyant mood – 'Ireland's Coming of Age'; 'The Birth of the Irish Tiger'. The paper's political correspondent Denis Coghlan wrote:

> Politicians from the major parties are salivating quietly at the prospect of running the government for the next five years, because of the latest social and economic projections. It would seem that the good times are only beginning to roll as a youthful and highly educated workforce gears up for the new millennium. Citizens of the hungry 1950s and 1960s will never have it so bad again. And whatever government controls this miracle-that-is-taking-place can anticipate a benign future.

However, not everyone was caught up in the general mood of optimism. Fintan O'Toole sounded a warning note. Acknowledging, in the same supplement, that since the late 1980s an 'astonishing' economic transformation had occurred in Ireland, he pointed out, in an analysis of the sources of Ireland's current economic success entitled 'A Disturbingly Pleasant Prospect', that success brought its own problems. An Economic and Social Research Institute review had highlighted how a well-educated workforce was crucial to attracting foreign inward investment by multinational companies and that one of the assumptions of the review was that 'the proportion of young people leaving school without qualifications [would] remain unchanged'. O'Toole feared: 'As the successful become more so, the gap between them and the marginalised will become a huge chasm. And the more spectacular the leap forward, the more bitter will be the experience of being left behind.' He presented the politicians anxious to enjoy power in good times with a challenge: 'The big task that faces them is to make the social fatalism of the late 1980s look just as misplaced in 10 years time as the economic fatalism of the 1980s looks now.' He sensed 'all of this bounty could well create a society that is worse off'.

Other, even more contrarian, voices were raised in the newspaper to question the very existence of a Celtic Tiger, or, if it existed, to bewail its feral effects on the social fabric. Kevin Myers, in 'An Irishman's Diary', harrumphed of the putative creature as he contemplated the state of the nation's roads: 'this spurious, ridiculous confection called the Celtic Tiger'. Again he roundly complained: 'You hear all this stuff about the Celtic Tiger, but often enough it can seem no more than the old ineffectual Hibernian sloth dressed in the raiments of oriental felinity. Has a plumber ever arrived on the day – never mind the hour – of the fixed appointment?' (*Irish Times*, 2 October 1997). Frank McDonald, so long a defender of Dublin's architectural heritage, bewailed how rampant development in the city was sweeping away 'favourite haunts' of the citizenry. The losses were 'almost relentless' (*Irish Times*, 11 October 1997). He was appalled at how they were 'falling like ninepins in the path of the "Celtic Tiger"'. The columnist and author John Waters, convinced that Ireland was still a country deeply wounded by colonialism, its spirit beyond healing by mere consumerism, wrote dismissively of 'the "Celtic Tiger" fantasy' (*Irish Times*, 27 August 1996).

Despite such misgivings, however, it is scarcely to be denied that the remarkable upturn in Ireland's fortunes (growth rates had been between 6 and 8 per cent over recent years) gave a strong boost to the national self-confidence that was necessary to reach a settlement of the Northern question. The editorial the *Irish Times* published on the 75th anniversary of the founding of the Irish Free State was a testament to the way the condition of life in the Republic was bound up with the fact that real progress on the national question was at hand. 'Now we dare to hope that we stand on the threshold of a final and full transition to peace' (*Irish Times*, 6 December 1997) The leading article, entitled 'The Making of a State', quoted an editorial published 75 years earlier when the Irish people in the 26 counties had embarked on independence: '*Today all things are made new*.' The 1997 leader imagined what the writer of that editorial, penned when 'anything approaching today's economic success would have seemed an impossible dream', would make of the Ireland of the 1990s: 'He would surely stand amazed at the phenomenon of the Celtic Tiger economy.' In October 1997 the *Irish Times*'s media correspondent, in an article entitled 'Catching the Tail of the Celtic Tiger', wrote of how the Republic was attracting the notice of international journalists. He reported that there were about 50 plying their trade in the country and remarked: 'Their presence illustrates a change in the world's attitude to Ireland, not just mist and reels, but success big time' (*Irish Times*, October 1997). Where in the past the *New York Times*'s coverage of Ireland involved only reports on Northern violence, 'Now [the newspaper] is publishing about two stories a week from Ireland – on a whole range of subjects,' that newspaper's man in Dublin told Michael Foley.

In September 1988, when the inauguration of the *Irish Times*/Aer Lingus Irish Literature Awards was held in London, Conor Brady commented of the newspaper he was editing: 'over the last 125 years, many editors had noted the distinct tension between hard news and the particularly strong literary slant of the paper' (*Irish Times*, 24 September 1988). This was noted by one literary editor, Caroline Walsh, who remarked that Irish 'poems are linked to the newspaper's lifeblood: News' (cited Ramazani 2012, p. 550). On that occasion Walsh surely recalled how, when the IRA had called a cessation of violence in 1984, the newspaper had published Michael Longley's remarkable poem 'Ceasefire' (3 September 1984) which by a Homeric analogy addressed how peacemaking involves painful sacrifices. This was reflected in the fact that at different times such distinguished writers as Brian Friel, John Montague, Derek Mahon and Kate O'Brien had all been regular columnists. That was to continue in the 1990s in a decade in which an international reputation for literary excellence, of the kind the country had enjoyed during the Irish Literary Renaissance in the late nineteenth and early twentieth centuries, was being revived. Irish names began to seem normal in the short-lists of international literary competitions. The Booker Prize was awarded to Roddy Doyle in 1993 for his novel *Paddy Clarke Ha Ha Ha*. And as if to confirm this resurgence of literary attention directed towards Ireland's novelists, dramatists and poets, Seamus Heaney was awarded the Nobel Prize for Literature in 1995, inspiring an outbreak of national jubilation in which the *Irish Times* enthusiastically joined. 'It will be a source of particular pleasure for many people,' the leader of the day affirmed, 'that the Laureate this year should be Seamus Heaney, one of the most popular and genuinely loved poets now at work in the English language' (*Irish Times*, 6 October 1995).

As well as editorial space, the *Irish Times* devoted two full pages to reports and commentary on Heaney's honour. Brian Fallon, the paper's chief critic (a role he had occupied since 1988), rightly praised how the poet had comported himself during years when Ireland was often in the news for unhappy reasons: 'Ireland never had a better cultural ambassador abroad than he, and at a time when she badly needed one.' Eileen Battersby wrote a thoughtful piece on the country's three previous winners – Yeats, Shaw and Beckett – while the paper's literary editor, John Banville, reminded readers that for all the 'decency' of Heaney's aesthetic, the fact that the 'commonplace world' was where he had 'chosen to work' meant he was a more complex poet than was often credited: 'some of his finest work comes out of darkness, hewn from the black stuff that lies in every human heart'.

That the *Irish Times* on this auspicious occasion could draw on the in-house critical expertise of Fallon, Banville and Battersby (Battersby was a staff journalist on the paper) is indicative of how the newspaper's historic 'literary slant' remained as pronounced as ever. For each of them brought a distinctive critical edge to the paper's coverage of literature in a decade when in the academy and in the media the concepts of post-modernity and literary theory were challenging the status of literature as a privileged discourse. In their varying ways the three writers were each in thrall to the power of the word, of the literary and artistic, which made them countervailing voices in the ironical, reductionist, often politicized, arena of literary and cultural commentary in the Anglophone *fin de siècle*.

John Banville was appointed literary editor of the *Irish Times* in 1988 to succeed Brian Fallon, who had been in charge of the literary pages since 1977. Banville knew the world of journalism, since he had worked for the Irish Press group and in 1988 was a sub-editor for the *Irish Times*. His claims on the post were his work as a novelist, with a body of work beginning to receive critical admiration for its high style and conceptual ambition, and his polished book reviews. He would hold the post with distinction until 1999.

Unlike some newspaper literary editors, Banville was not shy of supplying book reviews himself to the literary pages. He brought to these contributions a commitment to the humanistic value of literary and artistic endeavour and to the power of critique, which was always tonic. Early in his occupancy of the post, his sonorous, contemplative eulogy for Samuel Beckett, who died in December 1989, was a kind of apologia for his own aesthetic. Recognizing that Beckett's work was 'the shattered song of our time' (*Irish Times*, 25 December 1989), Banville counselled:

> It is a bad mistake, it is the worst mistake, to treat art as commentary upon the life and times of the artist. Relevance is always an accident. It is no more inevitable that art will represent life than that mathematics will represent reality: it just happens that the case is so ...
>
> It has been a wholly *literary* adventure. The falling of the light and encroaching silence, the tedium and laughter and sorrow, these are not things transposed raw from life into the work, but, rather, they are the processes of the work itself.

True to this credo, Banville as literary editor, chose when occasion presented itself, to write considered review-essays on major figures and topics: on Henry James, Philip Larkin, on Michel Foucault and Martin Heidegger, on the *New Shorter Oxford Dictionary*. Committed to literature, as he was, and to the power of language to evoke a possible transcendence (he wrote an admiring review of George Steiner's book *Real Presences*, 1991), with its claim, contra the literary theorist's and deconstructionist's doubts, that art provides real food for the spirit), the responsibility of the writer in the face of evil consistently troubled him. No aesthetic bystander, he was robust in defence of Salman Rushdie when the Iranian fatwa was issued against him. His open letter to 'The Journalists of *Oslobođenje*, Sarajevo', published on the day his newspaper printed the facsimile of that paper, was unequivocal about the duty of those who work with words: 'We journalists, like you, can do no more than bear witness to what we believe to be the truth.' The case of Heidegger clearly troubled Banville, for in a review-article (which stimulated some vigorous responses in the letters page) he acknowledged how the philosopher's work, with 'its particular mixture of high rhetoric and deep seriousness', was 'hard to resist' (*Irish Times*, 31 July 1993). Nonetheless, the question remained how such a writer could have had any truck with National Socialism. Banville concluded that it was 'profoundly disturbing' that a thinker who had had the courage, like Nietzsche before him, 'to discard the shibboleths of organised religion and deny our craven desire for a personal God', had 'thrown in his lot with the monsters of Nazism'. For Banville, the case of Heidegger was 'of continuing relevance to our conception of present-day culture and society'. As if to buttress his own trust in his avocation as writer, in face of the terrible facts of Heidegger's career, Banville took heart from the poet Michael Longley. Reviewing a short memoir by the Belfast writer, whom Banville nominated as 'one of the finest poets now writing in English' (*Irish Times*, 30 July 1994), he quoted his subject, on the challenge of being a poet in a time of trouble: 'in the "context of political violence the deployment of words at their most precise and most suggestive remains one of the few antidotes to death-dealing dishonesty"'. To which Banville responded: 'Surely all artists, Irish or not, should have that ... sentence engraved in marble above their desks.'

Eileen Battersby, a young Californian who had settled in Ireland, brought to the book pages in the 1990s (as she still does at the time of writing, as the paper's literary correspondent) a voracious appetite for fiction from all parts of the globe and enthusiasm for the simple/complex joy of reading. Opinionated, forthright, unintimidated by reputation, her reviews, articles and interviews with authors were an open, refreshing invitation to broaden one's perspectives, even when her judgements could sometimes infuriate. At her best as a critic, there was a kind of readerly vulnerability about her responses to the undeniable force of fiction in her daily life (how could she have one, apart from the obsessive reading?) which made her a most uncommon common reader, urging that we should read the books she praised. Her extensive knowledge of contemporary prose fiction also made her an astute observer of the Irish literary scene, as when she observed in 1992 the increasing number of women writers in the country, and the quality of their work. Noting how some recent Dublin fiction by men had had their work 'elevated to the status of sociological tract,' she observed: 'This brings us to the issue of the good versus the important. A point which is relevant when discussing much of the fiction being written by Irish women writers. It is difficult to separate a still campaigning feminist voice from their actual storytelling while a socio-political sexual transition is still in progress.' (*Irish Times*, 11 March 1992) Battersby was never afraid to step in where angels would fear to tread.

Nor in his quiet way was Brian Fallon. Fallon was the son of the poet Padraic Fallon. The poet's son, a man of polymathic interests in literature and the fine arts, had, on Banville's appointment as literary editor, concerned himself principally thereafter with contributions to the paper on the plastic arts (he had in fact, among his various roles, served as art critic for many years). The result was increased coverage of these as Fallon wrote with his usual discernment on the international art scene and on Irish and European painting. His tone was consistently that of a man who knew his own mind, unimpressed by mere reputation, but prepared to back his convictions. An extended review of two centennial exhibitions of the work of Vincent van Gogh, mounted in Amsterdam in 1990, show Fallon at his distinctive best as the judiciously informed art critic who can also capture the larger significance of an oeuvre. Fallon tells us that van Gogh's 'development was terribly condensed and hurried and he reacted to a whole medley of influences, many of them only half-assimilated' (*Irish Times*, 28 April 1990). Furthermore, his 'taste was often bad' and even 'some of the works which the world knows and loves best are rather disappointing to see in the original – crude in technique and terribly overstated and unsubtle in colour'. He confessed to disliking 'the queer greenish-brown tone' of the famous 'The Potato Eaters', but he understands that van Gogh is an artist the public have, rightly, taken to their hearts and that he 'is one of the great democrats of art and a prophet and "primitive" of 20th-century sensibility'. As draughtsman, however, van Gogh was no primitive; for Fallon includes himself unambiguously among those who reckon he excelled as a graphic artist in the company of Rembrandt and Dürer.

In July 1990, reviewing a Royal Hibernian Academy exhibition on Irish art produced between 1860 and 1960, Fallon observed, 'Irish art has established itself both with scholars and salesrooms'. It had also begun to be popular as an investment for a newly prosperous middle class (in the 1990s, as the economy boomed, the newspaper's weekly reports on the art and antique auctions and sales expanded appreciably). New artists, many of whom were women, were emerging from the country's art colleges, eager to market their work. On the same day as the *Irish Times* had published Fallon's assessment of van Gogh, the critic had ventured on the same dangerous ground on which Eileen Battersby had entered when she had questioned the quality of Irish women's writing. He dared to suggest, reviewing a book on *Woman, Art and Society*, that the times seemed 'ripe to talk no longer about woman and male artists, but simply to class them as good and bad'. Within the week, Fallon was proving that this was a fond hope. In an article entitled 'The Female Vision', he argued that Irish women had always been strong in the visual arts and in sculpture since those had existed in the country 'in the modern sense' (*Irish Times*, 1 May 1990). Now, when there were more artists in Ireland, male and female, than there had ever been before, many of the younger women graduates from art colleges in Dublin, Belfast, Cork and Limerick were seeking 'what they see as their proper place in the sun'. In the highly competitive field Fallon surveys in his article, it was unlikely that the issue of gender would recede. Indeed,

Fallon himself concluded his piece by commenting on how role reversals were currently taking place, in which bread-winning husbands were 'quite content at times to play second fiddle' to their successful artist wives.

It was inevitable that the *Irish Times* would be drawn into the intense debate that flourished in the 1990s about the distinctiveness, standing and quality of Irish women's writing. Indeed, a column in the newspaper by Nuala O'Faolain on the *Field Day Anthology of Irish Writing* (1991) was a key intervention on the matter, which to a large extent set the terms of subsequent discussion in the media of that work in general. The Field Day Theatre Company in Derry had in the 1980s, as we noted above, been a lively artistic collective which through drama and pamphleteering had sought to raise awareness of how Ireland had been deformed by its experience of colonialism and how resolution of the 'national question' must take account of that fact. Its board included some of the country's best-known writers and academic critics. Much was expected of the anthology it decided to publish under the general editorship of Seamus Deane, for it promised a reimagining of the Irish literary inheritance that would, by displaying its rich variety, underpin an inclusive appreciation of the many cultural strands that constituted a nation as yet to achieve its full freedom. The anthology when it appeared in November 1991 was launched by the Taoiseach Charles Haughey, investing the occasion with national import. Brian Fallon provided a lengthy review for the *Irish Times*, combining a grateful sense of the task Deane and his team of assistant editors had performed, along with thoughtful, critical observations about the anthology's contents, exclusions and structure. He saluted it as 'a major achievement of planning and scope' (*Irish Times*, 20 November 1991). However, before his review appeared, Nuala O'Faolain had definitively altered the conditions of the work's reception in Ireland when she published her article 'The Voice that Field Day Didn't Record' (*Irish Times*, 11 November 1991). Like Fallon, she found much to admire in the anthology and recorded her fair-minded sense of its 'sheer scope' ('For much of its length, this anthology really does constitute an act of national memory retrieval'). This made her overall critique all the more devastating. For she feared, 'The male editors failed to find women interesting.' So that while female writers, in her view, were under-represented in volume three of the anthology, which concluded with selections from current writers, more fundamentally, women's history and experience as explored in Irish writing had been disregarded. While the anthology was 'enormously sensitive to the "two traditions" in Northern Ireland ... the transformation of women's lives, the beginning of the shattering of their traditional bonds, is not important'. It was not that women's voices were excluded from the work (defenders of the enterprise could point to the women included) but the voice of women.

O'Faolain's article provoked a wave of support in the media and at a public meeting. One letter to the *Irish Times* demanded that the anthology be withdrawn. A contributor to *The Bloomsbury Guide to Women's Literature* (1992) damned it as 'the most disgracefully damaging insult to the history of women's writing'. And in 1998 the poet and critic Eavan Boland remembered that the debate the anthology provoked, as Eileen Battersby recorded in an interview with her, was the one of the many debates in which she had engaged that became the 'most clouded by bitterness' (*Irish Times*, 22 September 1998). Yet in another interview, published in the *Irish Times* in 1992, following the controversy unleashed by the *Field Day Anthology*, Boland made her own distinctive contribution to the debate. She told Kevin Myers:

> Field Day sees through a nationalist lens; that lens has shown women up traditionally as passive parts of the poem, the fiction, the oratory, and I do not think they can figure women's literature as Irish writing. They can figure women's writing as women's writing, and the problem psychologically for them is to accept that women write Irish literature (*Irish Times*, 17 April 1992).

Yet, interestingly Boland's response was not that of a self-consciously feminist poet, for she argued '"You couldn't have a feminist poet any more than you could have a Marxist poet. Poetry begins where all those isms stop, it begins in all those ambiguities and powers of human feeling that the isms don't go that far"'. It was such a resolute commitment to poetry as an art that could not be recruited to serve any cause that made Boland one of the best literary journalists in the paper's history. Her occasional reviews in the 1990s and thereafter, especially on poetry, helped to make the *Irish Times*'s book page essential reading. Reading her, for example, on the fraught issue of the poet Ted Hughes as executor of Sylvia Plath's estate, was a lesson in critical honesty, historical perspective and forthright judgement. In face of many attacks on Hughes as Plath's errant husband, she stated in a review of his selected prose writings: 'it is fair and right to record that he was a wonderful influence on Plath and a wonderful friend to her poetry in her lifetime' (*Irish Times*, 5 March 1994). But Hughes's belief that he could choose, as executor, which of her poems should see the light of publishing day, Boland judged, was unconscionable: 'They were written by a woman,' she insisted, 'who had, when she wrote them, the prior rights and freedom any poet has to explore her or his imaginative worlds. Every poet is bound, by her or his art, to sustain that freedom in every other poet. It is the cornerstone of the enterprise, and is perfectly well understood.' As, it may be inferred, for men to live honourably 'amongst women' (as McGahern had entitled his novel which had honoured female empowerment at the outset of the decade) must involve a similar respect for human agency.

12

THE *IRISH TIMES* AND A MODERN IRELAND

If Eavan Boland had helped to bring critical flair to the literary pages of the *Irish Times* in the 1990s with perceptive reviews and articles, it had been the volumes of poetry she had published since the 1960s which had established her international reputation as one of Ireland's most admired poets, whose work had treated of the nation's history and women's role in it. To a marked degree her poetic oeuvre had been responsive to the social and cultural shifts the country had undergone in her lifetime and by writing women into the national narrative in her poetry, she had been instrumental in making ordinary life in suburban Ireland seem to her readers to be the normal condition of the modernity the country had been striving for since at least the 1960s. With the economic boom of the late 1990s and the early years of the twenty-first century, it was widely believed that the country had reached a point in its history when a store of national wealth had been amassed which could sustain a secure future for the majority of its citizens. It seemed apt, therefore, that a new collection of poetry by Eavan Boland in 2001 should include a poem entitled 'Code' which from an Irish suburb saluted the American computer-program writer Grace Murray Hopper, the mother of COBOL, the business-orientated computer language. For information technology, the product of inward investment, particularly from the United States, was a main driver of the economic growth in Ireland which underpinned the country's novel experience of an Irish modernity to believe in. In her poem Boland addressed Hopper, 'west' of her 'and in the past', as 'Maker of the future':

> There is still light
> in my suburb and you are in my mind –
> head bowed, old enough to be my mother –
> writing code before the daylight goes.

That information technology was serving as a kind of magnet for employment in the early years of the new century in Ireland was evidenced in the jobs vacancies sections of the newspapers. The *Irish Times* had carried a regular column on computers and computing since the mid-1980s. Each Friday, for example, even after the severe downturn in the field following the dot.com

387

stock market collapse in 2001, in the *Irish Times* scores of posts were advertised in that field, many of them offering substantial salaries. The worlds of
business, finance and accounting were keen to recruit graduates in computer
science (knowledge of COBOL and its offshoots was in demand by employers).
In fact, information technology in the 2000s became a major news story in
itself, reported on expertly in the *Irish Times* by Karlin Lillington, a young
Californian who had come to Ireland to study its literature, who had carved
out a career for herself explaining the communications revolution to the Irish
public. Middle-aged readers were familiarized in her lively columns with the
argot of a new field: 'spam', 'identity fraud', 'downloads', 'search engine', 'aps'. An
article Lillington wrote for the paper in May 2003 sought to understand 'the
truly transformational nature of the technology industry on the Irish economy'
(*Irish Times*, 23 May 2003). In her article entitled 'Our Past Is Not So Far
Behind Us', she reminded readers that in 1988 70,000 people had emigrated
from Ireland: 'That's as if the entire city of Limerick emptied in a single year.
No other country could boast, as the Republic of Ireland could, of more than
3,000 communications and technology firms' contributing in this crisis 16 per
cent of GDP, 'a third of their goods and services we export every year'.

And all this was not simply dependent on the multinationals which were
using Ireland as a base from which to sell products manufactured in Ireland
to countries in the European Union. Of the 55,000 Irish men and women
employed in the ICT industry, 11,000 were working for indigenous firms.
Indeed, Ireland was weathering the downturn in the industry being experienced
elsewhere. A sign that the future remained promising was the fact that 'the State
won a valued and high profile project' when 'internet search engine kingpins
Google' decided to base a European centre in Ireland. Yet Lillington also issued
a warning when she noted: 'While the State's international internet connectivity
might be top-notch, the reality in our homes, schools and public places is dire';
in a recent international comparison of domestic broadband usage, Ireland had
found itself 'trailing even developing nations such as Peru and Nigeria'. This was
a matter of concern to the newspaper because the internet was having an impact
not only on the way business in general was being done in modern societies,
but specifically on the newspaper industry. This development was discussed
in another of Lillington's articles. In August 2002 she considered the new
phenomenon of the blogger, arguing that journalists should consider him or her
a friend, not an enemy. In a column in which Lillington announced her own
blog site, it was clear that there was just as much room for conflict as friendship
between traditional journalists and bloggers. 'There have been,' she reported,
'some well-publicised verbal battles between traditional press journalists, who
earn their crust writing, and bloggers, who feel they don't get enough respect
for their alternative to the mainstream press' (*Irish Times*, 23 August 2002). At
a discussion on blogs, held in London, in which Lillington had participated,

agreement had been reached that, although the two forms of journalism could be complementary, 'blogs pose, if not exactly a threat, then a huge challenge to traditional journalism because they are so immediate and often so informed'. She summed up the situation: since journalists write for a broad audience, they have to be 'generalists' – 'they are trying to summarise perspectives, and give multiple views of a story ... Bloggers are often specialists and deeply knowledgeable about their areas of interest. They can delve more deeply into detail; they have the endless room of a webpage in which to do this.' Lillington did not mention in this article that traditional newspapers had had in the past the kind of resources to dedicate teams of investigative journalists to a particular issue over many months. The contemporary blogger could not begin to emulate that.

In fact, the *Irish Times* had realized almost a decade earlier that the internet was creating a new context for the newspaper industry. In 1994 the paper was the first in Ireland or Britain to publish an online edition. This was made available free of charge until 2002, when it became a subscription-based site. As for most newspapers in the English-speaking world, the internet was both an opportunity for and a threat to the *Irish Times*. It made it internationally visible in a new way and allowed for the creation of associated sites which could attract advertising revenue. The culmination of this was the purchase in 2006 of the Irish property website Myhome.ie and in 2007 of Entertainment. ie, in Mark O'Brien's words, 'as a part of its strategy of protecting advertising revenue and developing itself as a major digital media business' (Mark O'Brien 2008, p. 251). However, newly established electronic newspapers, with their substantially lower costs, could undercut advertising revenues. And perhaps most alarmingly, an online survey showed that by 1999 two-thirds of site visitors were aged under 35 years (Mark O'Brien 2008, p. 250). There was a distinct risk that the internet site was being preferred, even in Ireland, to the printed version, where half the visitors were located. In 2008 the *Irish Times*'s daily newspaper was once more offered to readers online free of charge.

Jobs vacancies advertised in the *Irish Times* indicated in the first five years of the twenty-first century that the country was undergoing an employment revolution. For not only were IT graduates being sought in diverse fields, but graduates in science subjects were in high demand in pharmaceutical and biotechnology companies. By 2000 the state had recognized that to make secure the inward investment that had been won would involve a major investment in research and development by Irish universities. That year Science Foundation Ireland was founded to support research in biotechnology and information and communications technology. It was envisaged that €2.5 billion would be earmarked for such research, a multiple of five of what the state had invested in research between 1994 and 1999. Developments in science accordingly provided important stories for the newspaper in an expanded weekly page, entitled 'Science Today', with Dick Ahlstrom, science editor, judiciously selecting international science news and supplying accessible articles for the interested general reader. Commentators had long argued that Ireland as a predominantly literary culture had disregarded science since the nineteenth century. We noted earlier how John Edward Healy as editor had tried to give due credit in his paper to scientific achievement. He would, one surmises, have been gratified by the fact that in the twenty-first century the *Irish Times* was to the fore in the country in highlighting science as a crucial human activity upon which socio-economic progress in the modern world depended. In 2006 the Royal Irish Academy, with the support of the Industrial Development Authority, published Ahlstrom's book *Flashes of Brilliance – The Cutting Edge of Irish Science*, which collected 60 of his *Irish Times* articles written over the previous four years. Reviewing this book in the newspaper, Mary Mulvihill, herself a noted science writer, commented that the collection provided an overview of 'the richness of current Irish science' (*Irish Times*, 8 April 2006). She remembered how in the 1980s 'science was a foreign place – news reports from journals such as *Nature* would appear on the *Irish Times*'s foreign pages'. Now she could report that Ahlstrom's writings were a 'perfect antidote to the usual clichéd images' of Ireland as a scientific backwater, 'with its portrait of a very modern, 21st-century scientific Ireland'.

The greater part of 'Science Today' in the *Irish Times* dealt with scientific discovery, its technological potential and economic impact. However, on these pages the question of how science was affecting the human prospect was raised in ways it had scarcely been in the recent past in Ireland, where religious dogma had been afforded widespread, often uncritical, respect. In the early years of the new century, articles in 'Science Today' informed readers about how a modern scientific Ireland would in the near future be confronted by complex ethical issues. As Ahlstrom wrote of the human genome project in 2000:

> Scientists are searching uncharted territory as they slowly but relentlessly delve into the hidden chemical world that exists within the human cell. Discoveries are coming thick and fast, and each offers great promise in the effort to overcome disease.
>
> Yet if ever the hackneyed Pandora's Box analogy was appropriate, this surely is apt in the case of leading-edge medical research. Our technical understanding of the cell's inner processes is rushing ahead of social and ethical controls to oversee the applications of these discoveries. (*Irish Times*, 29 December 2000)

Ahead lay such things as human cloning, the genetic engineering of body organs, 'designer babies', the possible understanding of consciousness itself. Furthermore, readers of the *Irish Times*'s science coverage could not have failed to appreciate how contemporary science was conducted on the assumption that evolutionary theory was a guiding precept. In February 2001 Ahlstrom reported that one scientist working on the human genome project had recently stated: "'We are confirming Darwin ... It's great to be getting the molecular correlates of what Darwin hypothesised 150 years ago. It is the unity of life, or nature being conservative, or the idea of the blind watchmaker – the notion of evolution as a constant reworking or random recombining of parts'" (*Irish Times*, 12 February 2001). In the same article Richard Dawkins was quoted as likening the accomplishment of the genome project, 'to other great human and personal endeavours. Along with Bach's music, Shakespeare's sonnets and the Apollo Space Program [it] is one of those achievements that makes me proud to be human.'

'Science Today' also included contributions by William Reville, Associate Professor of Biochemistry in University College Cork, where he was also public awareness of science officer (the *Irish Times* had published his book *Understanding the Natural World* in 1999). As a biologist, Reville was adept at explaining the workings of natural selection. As a practising Christian, he was ready to write about how the scientific world-view did not preclude religious faith. Improbable as it may seem, debate about the claims of religion as they are affected by scientific knowledge had simply not been conducted in the public domain in Ireland in the twentieth century. In his apparently small way Reville was changing that at the beginning of the twenty-first century. For in his columns he felt obliged to react to such challenging ideas as, for example, Richard Dawkins's concept of the 'selfish gene', and with the theory of inherited cultural 'memes', which Dawkins endorsed, in which religion is 'an exploitative meme, with believers under orders to pass on the belief under threat of damnation and the promise of salvation' (*Irish Times*, 1 June 2006). Although Reville's thoughtful articles on the conflict of science and religion made space for faith, the fact that he felt it important to deal with the evangelical atheism of such influential evolutionary biologists as Dawkins inevitably risked, though that was far from his intention, making religious convictions seem in some way out of tune with the dominant scientific secularism of the modern age.

The Irish government's commitment at the beginning of the new century to foster research and development (giving effect to the European Union's hopes that member states would invest up to 3 per cent of GNP in scientific research) involved the hope that research centres would become magnets for highly qualified scientists from abroad, to make Ireland the base for their activities. In consequence, Ireland would begin to establish a reputation as a first-world country in scientific terms. Science Foundation Ireland (SFI) was expected to bring internationally successful research teams and renowned scientists to work in Irish universities. As such, at its elevated level in what was becoming known as the 'knowledge economy', SFI was part of a remarkable change that was taking place in the nation's sense of itself. For centuries Ireland had been a country from which people emigrated. Suddenly, as it flourished economically, it was a country that was attracting immigrants from many parts of the globe, whether to work in such arcane fields as nano-technology, in the *Irish Times*, or the construction or service industries. The topic of immigration became a major theme in the national conversation, much of it conducted in the *Irish Times*. Writing in the newspaper in June 2001, Karlin Lillington made reference to the fact that she had heard the Tánaiste, Mary Harney, warn that the country would need 200,000 immigrants to fill necessary jobs, particularly in the technology sector. She wrote that this had set her thinking about racism, which she stated was 'now ugly and visible' (*Irish Times*, 8 June 2001). She continued:

> In all my years in the United States and the Republic, I have never read such hate-filled graffiti on city walls, heard such appalling comments in public and private, or witnessed such ignorant reactions to people of different colour or cultures as I have seen here recently ... I think of my friends and relatives of varied ethnic backgrounds in the US and know I fear inviting them to visit the country that is my home ... And from a detached and cold economic viewpoint, how can we expect to fill 200,000 jobs from abroad in such a vile atmosphere?

Mary Harney had announced in March 2000 that the government was planning to bring 200,000 workers into the state to implement the National Development Plan formulated that year (it was envisaged that 100,000 of these would be Irish emigrants tempted back by economic opportunity). Reporting on her speech, the *Irish Times*'s Emmet Oliver thought that there had been 'a sense of unreality in the air' (*Irish Times*, 4 March 2000) as the Tánaiste outlined the country's future as a focus of inward migration. He commented, in an article entitled 'Facing the Challenge of Mass Immigrations':

> Here was one of Europe's former basket cases, renowned for exporting its young in droves, boldly telling the world it would be setting up a skills-based selection system, no less, to recruit young workers to fill gaps in its overstretched economy.

In what felt like one stroke, the word emigration, with all its haunting associations, was banished, to be replaced by the word migration.

'Migration' was a word that would recur frequently in the paper in the years to come. The fact that when a number of eastern European states acceded to membership of the European Union in 2004, Ireland did not set any limits on the rights of their citizens to seek employment in the country meant that the estimate of 200,000 foreign workers taking up residence was far too low. By 2006, as the census of that year revealed, around 400,000 'foreign nationals' (the term that became common usage for the country's immigrants) were living in Ireland, equal to about 10 per cent of the population. Of these the largest number were UK citizens, but the second largest group comprised Poles, followed by Lithuanians, and then Nigerians (for it was not only EU citizens who were entering the state as immigrants). There were over 11,000 Chinese, more than 8,000 Indians and almost 5,000 Pakistanis. In effect, Ireland had been experiencing the largest inward migration of people born outside the country since the sixteenth and seventeenth centuries. How this remarkable influx over a short period of time was affecting and would affect the country was highlighted in many of the articles the *Irish Times* published on the topic.

Emmet Oliver, in his 2000 article, had warned that inward migration could throw up a range of problems that other countries had failed to solve. He observed: 'the settlement of the immigrant workers will be vital. Mixed housing – where immigrants live side by side with Irish people – is a must.' Implicit in this assertion was the key issue that would stir debate in the coming years – how and to what degree the newcomers would be integrated with local Irish communities. He noted how governments in Britain and on the Continent had had to 'grapple with issues of dress and religion' and that language could be an even more vexing issue. Oliver suggested that it was 'sure to be one of the biggest mountains the government would have to climb'.

As the range of such mountains began to become visible at the start of a new century a small ginger group briefly made its voice heard. Calling itself the Immigration Control Platform, it pressed for the strict control of immigration and the rigorous vetting of asylum-seekers. Its statements indicated that it was concerned that Irish culture could be undermined by uncontrolled immigration. In his 'Irishman's Diary', Kevin Myers quickly made clear his contempt for what he called a 'self-appointed crackpot organisation' (*Irish Times*, 31 January 2002) (one member of the group had failed to condemn a recent racist murder of a Chinese student in Dublin). Her organization should be viewed 'with quiet, studied loathing,' Myers wrote. In obvious comparison with the members of such a group, he said:

> Far from being opposed to immigration, I welcome it. Normans brought their law, the English their parliament, the Huguenots their linen, the Scots their business acumen, the Germans their industrial method, the Americans their silicate vision, the Chinese, French and Bangladeshis their cuisine. Fresh forms of Irishness are being forged now as peoples of different cultures from Africa and Asia come here, and settle, and marry and bring their diet, their music, their wisdom with them: and of course their problems.

However, in his direct way, Myers was intent to make the point that, while the issue of immigration had been clouded by terminological confusion, since people who had the right to work in Ireland were being lumped in the general mind under 'the generic title "asylum-seekers"'. In such confusion, Myers counselled, lay the breeding ground for 'fantasists, hate-mongers and ranting fascists'. He judged that the country had to face up to the fact that its future involved legal immigration and that the problem of illegal immigrants masquerading as 'asylum-seekers' should be tackled with 'courage, determination and thought'. It was readily solvable, he argued, for the numbers were tiny – 'a few score thousand in a population of four million, in the least densely populated country in Europe'.

Two years later, as the state policy on immigration was bringing about significant demographic change in the country, it was numbers that did begin to concern Myers. In May 2004 he wrote an 'Irishman's Diary' that denounced in characteristically forceful terms the low quality of debate about immigration that had developed. He was keen to emphasize that contemporary Ireland was blessed since it offered a generation, for the first time, 'some sort of semblance of control over the real future of Ireland' (*Irish Times*, 20 May 2004). Failure to confront the issue of immigration in a frank way, when any suggestion that restrictions on entry to Ireland could be dismissed as 'racist' by unthinking commentators, risked, Myers feared, putting that new-found freedom of action in peril. The spectacle of how towns and cities in the north of England had become since the 1960s 'nearly 50% Muslim, as they are now' (*Irish Times*, 20 May 2004) was adduced as a portent for the Irish future. Admitting that 'more immigrants, more diversity will make Ireland a more interesting place' and that 'most Muslims will be what most Muslims are today – hard-working and law-abiding, and will be a cultural and intellectual asset', Myers, nonetheless, provocatively asked: 'Who actually wants Athlone or Portlaoise, 50 years hence, to be what Preston, Bradford, Huddersfield are now?' He believed the hard questions posed by such eventualities were being avoided in the 'mealy-mouthed evasions and vapid pieties' of the politically correct.

As with a good deal of Myers's writing in the paper, this column presented the author as an intrepid Mr Valiant-for-Truth, who dared to speak the unspoken, asking, for example, in combative tone: 'Have we the courage now to discuss the Islamic component in Ireland in 2054?' He continued: 'Weakness, inertia, liberal smugness and abject political cowardice allowed an army of self-styled "asylum-seekers" to drive a coach and four through the dismal charade of our immigration controls.' In his article Myers was particularly scornful of the way the country was being encouraged to contemplate the undoubted attractions of a multicultural Ireland, rather than to confront the 'complexities and the consequences of immigration'. Instead, he regretted, 'we ... waffle on (in *Irish Times*-reading circles especially) about the glorious benefits of immigration'.

Fortunately for its readers, the newspaper was supplying them with more considered material on the matter (and to be fair to Kevin Myers, he had the capacity to analyse things more dispassionately; a subsequent article counselled cogently: 'So even as we acknowledge that, on principle, immigration refreshes and renews, we must also consider the practical aspects: how many, and are they culturally assimilable?' (*Irish Times*, 11 November 2004)

In 2001 an Immigrant Council of Ireland was founded. This independent initiative was officially launched by the Taoiseach, Bertie Ahern, in March 2003, as an organization advocating for the human rights of immigrants and acting as a catalyst for public debate and policy change. Its executive chairperson was Sister Stanislaus Kennedy (who had a long record in the human rights field). In June 2004 she wrote in the aftermath of a referendum that had been held to remove the right of automatic citizenship to children born of two non-nationals on the island of Ireland (it was passed by almost 80 per cent to just over 20 per cent). Kennedy's article registered regret that the referendum had been 'shamefully rushed-through' (*Irish Times*, 28 June 2004), while reminding her readers that immigrants were working in every sector of the economy and helping to 'counteract [an] aging population which [was] under the replacement rate'. Sister Stanislaus argued that the country must have 'an informed and reasoned discussion about the issue of immigration', continuing, in terms that became the note the *Irish Times* would consistently strike in its coverage of the issue:

> We must have such a discussion now in order to develop a comprehensive and managed immigration policy, which is crucial if Ireland is to continue to thrive in the global economy and attract the workers our economy needs, and if we are to take our place among the nations that have embraced diversity and inter-culturalism.

In line with that approach, in the autumn of 2005 the newspaper began a weekly series entitled 'New Neighbours', which sought to give an insight into the daily lives of immigrants. Fintan O'Toole opened the series with an attempt to sort the fact from the fiction that immigration was generating. He pointed out, for example, that as regards the qualifications of the individuals entering the country that 'economics defines people's relationship with Irish society even more clearly than race and nationality do' (*Irish Times*, 7 September 2005) while, noting sadly, 'The Irish experience of what it's like to be a vulnerable migrant has not made us any less likely to be swaggering bullies.' Interestingly, O'Toole saw how migration was altering the homogeneity of Irish identity (plurality of national identity had been recognized as a possibility in the Good Friday Agreement):

> The old Catholic nationalist Irish identity was crumbling for the same underlying reason that the immigrants have come here: economic globalisation. The challenge posed by immigration – how to create an open society that integrates people with different intellectual, spiritual, and cultural identities or a common set of public values – is one already posed by both the collapse of the Catholic monolith and by the Belfast Agreement [as the Good Friday Agreement had become known].

Sticking to his last, Garret FitzGerald let statistics do the talking, when in June 2006 he warned: 'Even though we now have detailed figures of the flow of immigration into our State, as well as information on the scale and pattern of employment of foreign-nationals, the media continue to publish grossly exaggerated figures that seem designed to alarm public opinion on what is a sensitive subject' (*Irish Times*, 17 June 2006). He pointed out that the figures quoted in such reports often ignored how much migration was often temporary, with workers returning home, to Poland, for example, or to the Baltic states, after short periods in Ireland. FitzGerald acknowledged that the scale of the likely flow from eastern Europe had been underestimated in 2004, 'but also, happily, the amount of additional labour that we could usefully absorb'. An important article by Alan Barrett of the Economic and Social Research Institute, published in August 2006, demonstrated that to draw conclusions about the economic impact of immigration on a society was no easy task. It concluded that an 'overly liberal policy on immigration' could drive down wages in a disruptive way, but that 'the potential longer-run impacts of immigration point to the potential value of a continuing, moderate rate of inflow' (*Irish Times*, 4 August 2006).

In 2007 a young journalist named Ruadhán Mac Cormaic was awarded a fellowship, named in memory of Douglas Gageby, which allowed a journalist at the beginning of his or her career to work on a series of stories for the paper. Mac Cormaic's, entitled 'Migration and the Reinvention of Ireland', which appeared in May and June 2007 under the general heading 'Changing Places', gave added weight to O'Toole's claim that the old monolithic Catholic nationalist identity no longer had purchase on the social and cultural reality of a country that had become one of 'the rich world's magnet-states' (*Irish Times*, 27 June 2007). In the last article of the series (*Irish Times*, 27 June 2007), Mac Cormaic called for a new vision of national identity if migrants were to be enabled to become full members of society. The recent appointment of a government Minister of State for Integration, while in principle auguring well in this regard, could not disguise the fact that problems had been ignored – the influx of non-English-speaking children to school classrooms had been unanticipated and the probable ensuing difficulties unappreciated. Mac Cormaic made some devastating observations about how little modern Irish society had adapted to the new multi-ethnic and multi-cultural reality:

> Minority ethnic voices, in fact, are virtually unheard in most spheres of public life, from the arts and media to politics and the law. When the 30th Dáil convened for the first time recently, there was among the 166 TDs not one member of an immigrant or ethnic minority community that numbers over 10% of the population.

Mac Cormaic persuasively argued in this article that 'there are ... indications that the mental leap that will be required to fully absorb immigrants has yet to take place'. One such indication was the fact that politicians and other opinion-formers tended to speak of migrants as simply 'members of the workforce' and not as 'prospective members of the community'. He reported: 'One impression that has returned to me over the past four months is that huge numbers of immigrants are fully-fledged members of the economy but have no place in society, living their lives in parallel to (and unheeded by) the rest of the community.' He pointedly enquired: 'What does migration mean for our notions of citizenship, of the welfare state and reciprocity of culture, of nationhood? Or do we not trust ourselves to talk about it?'

Mac Cormaic's series prompted an editorial entitled 'Beneficial Impact of Immigration', published three days later. It recognized that Mac Cormaic had painted a picture which statistics could not, of how immigrants had 'changed the dynamic of social exchanges across so many spheres' (*Irish Times*, 30 June 2007). The writer was convinced that 'The economic and social well-being of this and future generations is ineluctably tied to our success in engaging with newcomers.' The editorial presented the government with a challenge, when it concluded: 'We must ensure that while working to defeat prejudice, inequality (and the resentment it breeds) is not allowed to assume an ethnic dimension. The experience of our European neighbours shows that the rewards of success are great, but so too the costs of failure.'

The *Irish Times* continued to give prominence in its columns to the subject of immigration. Indeed, Mac Cormaic was appointed 'Immigration Correspondent'. However his sense that minority ethnic voices were not being heard in the Irish public sphere was evidenced by the fact that the journalistic staff of the *Irish Times* itself seemed singularly lacking in the identifiable ethnic voices of migrants and the new Irish (though journalists of American or British background had often been recruited by the paper in the past). In July 2008 Mac Cormaic warned his readers that Ireland was at risk of losing its immigrants 'in a fog of vague intentions'. He was concerned that politicians still had not really confronted what the 'integration' of immigrants might involve and advised:

> Integration is a process as much as an outcome, a two-way exchange that will require not only Government action, but a reformulation of the way we think about fundamental ideas about identity and belonging. If it is to mean anything more than an empty mantra, it will depend on newcomer and native buying in. If politicians don't engage with it, how can they expect others to do so? (*Irish Times*, 3 July 2008)

The *Irish Times* in the early twenty-first century, by reflecting on how the country was raising its standing as a site for scientific research and development, on how Ireland was placing itself as a foremost participant in the IT and communications revolution, and on how it had become a magnet for immigration, was itself playing a role in the very modernity it was engaged in representing and analysing. For since the 1980s the newspaper had become a key element in Ireland in what constituted a powerful new modern phenomenon – 'the media'. In truth, newspapers, television and radio had come to constitute a congeries engaged in the gathering and dissemination of information in a globalized world that traded in knowledge as it did in goods and services. Editors, television and radio producers and the journalists who supplied the material they circulated had become the brokers in a marketplace of ideas and information which profoundly affected how influence and power were distributed in society. Who shaped the narratives in which information was both embedded and interpreted had become a key question for societies that purported to be both free and democratic.

In a thoughtful chapter, 'On Irish Journalism', in his memoir, Conor Brady suggested some of the ways in which Irish newspapers had sought to adjust to this recent shift in society's power dynamics, in which such things as government and a formerly respected Church hierarchy were in crucial ways beholden to the power of the media (and, in certain cases, perhaps to that of the financial moguls who owned them).

For a newspaper to operate convincingly in this context involved new degrees of professionalism and expertise. Accordingly, the *Irish Times* had increasingly sought to recruit new staff from the cohorts of graduates in a wide range of subjects whom the universities were producing each year. Journalism, indeed, had become an attractive career for the ambitious young person keen to deploy his or her knowledge of a subject – the law, political science, economics, cultural criticism – in the interesting world of the media. And the *Irish Times* in its appointment policies reflected the fact that newspapers could no longer depend only on journalistic generalists, as it had often done in the past, but needed individuals with specialist knowledge of particular fields. On Spanish politics and the Basque question, for example (with its parallels in the Northern Ireland problem), it required Paddy Woodworth with his sure knowledge of Peninsular history and politics, to supply well-informed analysis. He brought to that subject the kind of detailed reportage that had long characterized Michael Jansen's reports on the politics of the Arab world and the Middle East. Carol Coulter, who came to the paper with a Trinity College thesis on the politics of Sean O'Casey behind her, soon became the paper's legal correspondent, reporting on tricky matters of law with impressive clarity. In arts coverage Aidan Dunne, a graduate of Dublin's National College of Art and Design, established himself as the paper's reviewer of exhibitions, while the poet and travel writer Rosita Boland, who had graduated with a degree in English and History from Trinity, proved herself a skilled writer of human interest features and a sensitive conductor of interviews with creative people. Retired army captain Tom Clonan brought expertise on defence matters as the paper's security correspondent. Dr Muiris Houston wrote on medical matters, Conor Pope on consumer affairs. Newspapers needed, too, young recruits who appreciated how the media had acquired responsibilities with power, alert to media manipulation in the era of the spin doctor and floods of public relations material. Recognizing this, during his period as editor Conor Brady encouraged his journalists to take short courses at the Poynter Institute in St Petersburg, Florida, which was endowed by the *St Petersburg Times*, to keep them apprised of current journalistic best practice.

Brady was concerned, too, that the paper should become less Dublin-centred. He appointed staff reporters in Cork, Galway, Belfast, Limerick, Waterford and Sligo. In such posts individuals could carve out roles that challenged the metropolitan perspectives of the national media. Lorna Siggins, for example, a Trinity College Dublin history graduate, in time was appointed Western and Marine correspondent. A strong team of international correspondents reported from the world's major countries and cities during Brady's editorship. Conor O'Clery, as we saw, was posted in Moscow (where he was followed by Seamus Martin, who also covered the end of apartheid in South Africa). O'Clery also served in New York and in Beijing. Miriam Donoghue followed him to Beijing, Paddy Agnew served in Rome, Lara Marlowe in Paris and Washington. Paddy Smyth was Washington correspondent for a short period before becoming opinion page editor (Brady 2005, p. 265). Fergus Pyle, the former editor, found, until his untimely death in 1997, a new role in the paper as *Irish Times* German correspondent in Bonn and then Berlin, who covered the reunification of that country after 1990. In Dublin, Paul Gillespie acted as foreign editor, with overall responsibility for international policy and foreign news coverage. By education a historian and specialist in international relations, Gillespie wrote a weekly column on foreign affairs. In a period when post-communist Europe was reshaping itself and the United Kingdom was experimenting with devolution, Gillespie's deep interest in such topics as the constituents of national identity and in the necessary role of civil society in democratic societies, made his writings weighty contributions to thinking on Ireland's future in the European Union, as a state contiguous with a reconstituted post-devolution, post-Belfast Agreement United Kingdom. His edited book *Blair's Britain, England's Europe: A View from Ireland*, published in 2000 under the auspices of the Institute of European Affairs, evidences how his journalism was grounded in extensive reading of the relevant academic and other literature.

In a modern society in which information was a commodity that the media constantly circulated as narratives of one kind or another (the traditional journalistic notion of 'breaking a story', had accurately reflected how the media had always been engaged in a process of fashioning narratives by means of which the public could be enthralled by events as they occurred and by which they might seek to understand them). The risk in this context for the various media was always that, instead of telling the story, they themselves could become the story, with consequent implications for their authority and credibility as the gatekeepers of news. In the 1990s and in the first decade of the twenty-first century the *Irish Times* on a number of dramatic occasions itself became a story, in a period in which its survival would be cast seriously in doubt.

There can be little doubt that Thomas McDowell, both as chairman and as chief executive of Irish Times Ltd and as chairman of the Irish Times Trust, had played a pivotal role over many years in securing the commercial viability and reputation of the newspaper. On the commercial side of the operation, he had been ably assisted by Louis O'Neill, who had served as general managing director of the company since 1977. Furthermore, McDowell, as a formidable and self-assured man, had proved himself able to work productively with strong-minded editors without interfering in any way with their editorial freedom. As Seamus Martin stated in his memoir *Good Times and Bad: From the Coombe to the Kremlin: A Memoir* (2008), in a measured assessment of the man who had held the reins of power in the *Irish Times* for decades: 'The major, it should be said, had never in this long association with the paper attempted to interfere with its editorial independence. Also his undisputed business acumen had been of great benefit over the years' (Seamus Martin 2008, pp. 291–2). Given such a record, which bespoke both judgement and principle, it was a considerable shock, especially to the paper's editor Conor Brady, when in November 1994 McDowell suddenly informed him, in anticipation of Louis O'Neill's soon-to-be-expected retirement, that he had appointed his daughter, Mrs Karen Erwin, as deputy managing director and that she would be joining the board. It was to be assumed that Mrs Erwin was to be prepared to take over as managing director when O'Neill did in fact retire.

It was probably within McDowell's powers to make such a decision. The problem was that since Pyle had been replaced by Brady in an open competition, following the advertisement of the post of editor, it was certainly an expectation among the paper's employees that senior positions within the organization would be made according to a similar procedure. In that context it was inevitable as she undertook her new duties that Mrs Erwin's appointment at Major McDowell's instigation would cause consternation among those who would have to work with her. In the event, Erwin's courteous and considerate disposition, together with her skills acquired as a solicitor in a well-known Dublin law firm, meant that the business of the paper could be effected without serious contention (Louis O'Neill, though always the complete professional, never fully accepted what had transpired). Perhaps, too, McDowell's decision, no doubt based on an understandable wish to prolong his family's influence in a paper he had served so loyally for so long, helped to focus minds, among the staff, on the paper's governance, an issue that would emerge as salient in the financial crisis that erupted in 2002. More immediately, the Erwin appointment became a story that risked damaging the paper's reputation, however correctly it had been taken. Brady remembers his reaction when McDowell informed him of what he intended: 'The *Irish Times*'s editorial values proclaimed openness, transparency, accountability, equality of opportunity and fair play. It seemed to me that what Tom McDowell was proposing ran counter to all of this. A great chasm would open up between what the newspaper stood for editorially and how it went about its own business' (Brady 2005, p. 182).

The *Irish Times* had announced Karen Erwin's appointment in its own pages on 23 November 1994, noting her education (at one of Dublin's best-known private schools and at Trinity College) and her legal experience. Many readers would have recognized immediately that she was the boss's daughter. If the concept of nepotism, in respect of this appointment, did not then enter their minds, an editorial written by Conor Brady and published on 23 November 1994 assuredly meant that it would (though Brady is on record as saying that he had no such intent when he wrote what he did). The Labour Party, led by Dick Spring, then in discussions with Fianna Fáil about the possible formation of a new government, had been accused of that very activity in its appointments to public posts, during its recent period in power, of family members and supporters of the party. Under the headline 'A Dilemma for Labour', Brady on 23 November wrote, challenging Labour's and its leader Dick Spring's right to be regarded as standard-bearers for probity in public life.

Unsurprisingly, a Labour Party member reacted to this. Joe Costello TD, wrote from the seat of government, pointedly stating: 'I would like to ask Major McDowell to state publicly what special qualifications his daughter has for the job to which she was appointed, how the post was advertised and what selection process was followed?' (*Irish Times*, 29 November 1994). Costello's implication was obvious – nepotism had been involved in positioning Major McDowell's daughter to 'succeed the father in one of the most powerful and influential positions in Irish life'. It was sheer hypocrisy for the *Irish Times* to accuse the Labour Party of favouring its friends and family members in its appointments to public posts. It fell to Donal Nevin, vice-chairman of the trust and of the Irish Times Ltd, in McDowell's absence because of illness, to put the record straight, as best he might. He insisted in a letter, published in the paper on 29 November, that there was a crucial difference between appointing people to jobs funded from the public purse and to a post like the one to which Mrs Erwin had been appointed, which was not. Nevin continued in waspish tones:

> The Trust's decisions on commercial management matters are made exclusively in the best interests of the company. Deputy Costello would scarcely demand of any commercial concern that it satisfy his curiosity about the matter referred to in his letter. To seek such information from a commercial enterprise through the press seems to me an intolerable impertinence.

Despite his asperity, Nevin judiciously concluded: 'When a vacancy for Chief Executive of the Irish Times Limited arises it will be advertised.' It was soon agreed in house, with a committee representing journalists on the paper, that the post would be filled when it became vacant on essentially the same basis as the editor's job had been when Brady had been appointed. Paradoxically, the outcome of what could only be seen as an attempt by McDowell to sustain his family's influence in the newspaper, was that such an arrangement would ensure that Mrs Erwin could only be appointed to the top commercial position in the paper (the post Thomas McDowell thought he was preparing her for in 1994) following a competition she might prefer not to enter. In the event, when Louis O'Neill retired in 1999 and the post was advertised, Mrs Erwin did not apply (Mark O'Brien 2008, p. 258).

The *Irish Times*, though in a much more serious manner, since the continued existence of the title came into question, became a story once again in late 2001 and early 2002. The economic downturn in the world economy in which the collapse in what proved to be the dot.com bubble played its part, had a direct impact on the *Irish Times*'s difficulties at that time. Advertising from *Irish Times* companies fell away precipitously and projections of income and costs began to indicate a precarious future. The newspaper had seemed in rude financial health at the beginning of 2001. In 2000 it had made a profit of £7.15 million and had reached its highest ever circulation figure at 120,397 during that year (Mark O'Brien 2008, p. 264). It had been able, moreover, to order a new printing press and to plan to locate it at a site to the west of Dublin. Existing reserves, it had been believed, could safely be used to cover this expenditure.

There was a grim irony in the fact that post 9/11 2001 with the attacks on New York and Washington, difficulties in trading conditions intensified. So when in August 2002, less than a year later, Conor Brady announced that he would retire as soon as a new editor could be appointed, he was leaving an organization that had undergone the stresses of restructuring, with its internal affairs the stuff of unrelenting media interest. While the paper had been put on the path to rescue (it became profitable again in 2003), the new editor, Geraldine Kennedy, must have been hoping as she took up office on 11 October 2002, that the *Irish Times* would be less in the news than it had been and would soon be breaking the news rather than making it. Her early years in office were, however, to be punctuated by a number of difficult controversies that tested her mettle as the occupant of the editor's chair. And in 2005 the paper broke a major story that had very unsettling legal consequences. Perhaps most significantly, Geraldine Kennedy served as editor in years in which the slowing of Ireland's much-admired economic boom began to raise doubts, which had already surfaced when she took office (since the new printing press was proving less than cost-effective to run), about the newspaper's capacity to stay in business. The paper had been directly affected in a damaging way by the 9/11 attacks.

For three days after the dreadful events of that date in the United States, the paper had failed to appear. The Irish government had declared a national day of mourning for the Friday following. Brady himself was in the United States on 11 September 2001. In his absence, and given difficulties with transatlantic communications in the aftermath of the attack, the board took it upon itself to decide that no issue would appear on that Friday. It was the first time such a decision not to publish had been taken in the newspaper's long history since 1916 and during periods of industrial action. Employees of the paper, especially the journalists, were appalled. Their outrage could not easily be assuaged by the information that possible problems with the press and with distribution of an edition on such a day could also set at risk the Saturday edition, and even some editions the following week had weighed heavily with the board as it made its momentous decision. To fail to appear seemed to many an abnegation of a newspaper's primary responsibility to its public. The paper was missing on the news stands when the world's press was reporting on an earth-shattering event.

The *Irish Times*'s non-appearance on 14 September, when the other national dailies appeared as usual, can have done nothing to strengthen morale among the staff in general for what lay ahead, when in November the senior management began to restructure the operation of the paper in cognizance that, unless this could be achieved, it faced financial disaster and closure. On 6 November the company issued a statement outlining the crisis it faced and what was proposed to meet it. That evening RTE television carried the news that this would involve redundancies. Under the headline 'The Irish Times seeks 250 redundancies from staff', the paper's own industry and employment correspondent, Pádraig Yeates, told his readers the next morning that a group operating loss of £2 million had been forecast for 2001 and 'that failure to cut costs' would result in losses of £17 million in 2002. In an effort to rally the troops (of the 250 jobs to go, it was hoped by means of voluntary redundancies, 112 would be those of journalists), Conor Brady had said that the newspaper's 'character and ethos would remain the same'. Notwithstanding the proposed cuts, it would 'remain independent of all external interests, primarily concerned with serious issues. It would continue to provide the most comprehensive and most informed opinion and analysis' (*Irish Times*, 7 November 2001). The story reached national prominence that day and Brady agreed to be interviewed on an RTE radio programme about the crisis at the newspaper. In this interview, Brady held out the hope that two out of three jobs might be saved. His interviewer put a question to him that suggested how the troubles of the *Irish Times* were taking on the rolling energy of a full-blown, very damaging media story. He was asked if some of these redundancies could be averted if

...the featherbedding that, as I say, some of your own workers – some of your own staff talk about. They say, too many company cars, too many inflated salaries, maybe too many staff in some areas. Is this a fixed number of redundancies, could it be lower than this if you cut costs elsewhere, including in the upper reaches of the company? (cited Seamus Martin 2008, p, 275)

Brady unfortunately gave the story strong legs when he unguardedly referred in this interview to 'taking people out'. In an article published in the paper on 10 November 2001, Seamus Dooley, the Irish organizer of the National Union of Journalists, censured Brady for the use of this phrase which Dooley associated with a doomsday approach to the problems of the *Irish Times*. He provocatively asked:

Where has the chairman of the Irish Times Trust, the all-powerful Major Thomas McDowell, been all this week? He could have addressed the Dublin Printing Group of Unions and displayed a concern for the welfare of his staff, or at least attended as an observer, as a show of solidarity to his own management and workers.

It must have been galling for McDowell to read this in what he no doubt still thought of as his newspaper, but he could scarcely have failed to appreciate that the severity of the crisis the paper faced might well involve his own position in the organization. In an article published in the *Irish Times* on 21 December 2001, Joe Humphreys examined the changes in the management structures of the *Irish Times* which had been agreed with interested parties since Brady's bombshell announcement of 6 November. McDowell was to have no further role in the governance or management of the *Irish Times*. He was to be granted the honorary title of President for Life of the Irish Times Group. Humphreys indicated that McDowell's departure marked the 'beginning rather than the end ... of management reforms' (*Irish Times*, 21 December 2001) and he made clear that a decision to reduce the number of trustees, or 'nominated directors', on the board of the company from eight to three, represented 'a major shift in power on the board from nominated to executive directors'. Changes in the voting rights of board members, Humphreys continued, were explained by the chairman of the board, who would also retire shortly. They were 'designed to let the board of The Irish Times Ltd. take full responsibility for the operations and profitability of The Irish Times Ltd. and to keep the trust to a kind of oversight role to ensure we stick to the objectives, principles and ethos set out in the memorandum and articles'.

As is the case with most company restructurings brought about, as was readily admitted in this case, by financial crises, these changes had been presented as 'reforms' that would 'assist in the creation of a modern, "clean-cut, managerial structure" that would replace that established in 1974'. However modern the new structures put in place were, with a Trinity College Professor of Genetics, in the person of David McConnell, to serve as chair of the trust, the *Irish Times* at the end of 2001 and in early 2002 was uncomfortably caught in the modern media machine, when the issue of featherbedding became the focus of unfriendly commentary about the newspaper in rival publications. It was an easy case to make because the career grading system the company employed meant that the paper had on its books 18 people with the title of assistant editor. This apparent organizational imbalance could be presented as deriving from the hubris of a newspaper which, it was felt, liked to consider itself to be a cut above the rest. The newspaper's cadre of foreign correspondents was seen, too, as evidence of a misplaced ambition to ape its international betters. Arguably, however, Brady's determination to enhance international coverage in the paper had been a defining feature of his editorship. Indeed, symptomatic of how deeply the financial crisis of 2001 had bitten, was the fact that among the cuts that were enforced then were the closure of the Beijing and Washington offices, when awareness in Dublin of imminent disaster had begun to emerge. How the newspaper, under its new editor and with its new governance arrangements in place, dealt with the aftermath of this time of crisis in the newspaper's history, was to be a measure of its institutional strength and of its capacity to continue to comment on the condition of modern Ireland in relevant, independent ways.

When Conor Brady had been appointed editor, the fact that he would be the first Catholic to hold the post had caused some media comment. That Geraldine Kennedy in October 2002 was the first woman to be appointed editor of a national daily in Ireland caused surprisingly little comment (her religious formation was ignored). Some readers, long accustomed to letters to the editor beginning 'Dear Sir', may have been slightly taken aback when they saw for the first time a letter beginning 'Dear Madam', but it quickly came to seem simply the proper order of things. Perhaps the reason why Kennedy's appointment did not become a story that epitomized how modern Ireland was comfortable with the idea of female success can be attributed to the fact that she came to the post not only with substantial experience as a journalist but having served as a parliamentarian. Her appointment seemed an appropriate advance in a career in which she had already exhibited high levels of expertise and achievement.

Geraldine Kennedy, indeed, was well known to the public when she took up office as editor. In 1987, she and Bruce Arnold (another journalist), as we noted above, had successfully sued the Irish state for illegally tapping their phones. In 1987, too, she had stood successfully for election to the Dáil as a member of the Progressive Democrat party (the PDs). This party had been recently founded by former members of Fianna Fáil disillusioned with the leadership of Charles Haughey. It made much of the need for integrity in public life, efficiency in business and fiscal prudence in managing the economy. The party was pro-business and supportive of free markets. When Kennedy lost her seat in the 1989 general election, she returned to the journalism in which she had been engaged for most of her adult life. Appointment to editorship of the *Irish Times* set a seal on her career.

It was unfortunate that on two occasions during that editorship, the finances of the *Irish Times* once again became the subject of newspaper stories. What were alleged to be excessive payments to directors in 2002, when the company had been engaged in a painful downsizing, caused outrage among the remaining staff, who were engaged with the challenging task of rescuing the title, when payments became public knowledge in November 2003. The views on the matter of one of the *Irish Times*'s regular columnists, John Waters, may have struck a chord with at least some of these. He chose to express his opinions in an article he contributed to the paper in which he claimed that the *Irish Times* did not practise what it preached to others about accountability and transparency. Kennedy, on legal advice, decided against publication. Another paper, the *Sunday Business Post*, acquired Waters's article and duly published it. Waters himself gave an interview on national radio, when he explained: 'You would not meet a straighter person; you will not meet a more ethical person; but Geraldine Kennedy is compromised, I believe, by the situation she had inherited, by the structure and culture of the *Irish Times*.' Kennedy immediately wrote to Waters in terms that revealed the steel in the woman who had once sued the state. She wielded the rapier stylishly (her letter was included in the *Irish Times*'s own report on the contretemps):

> I had thought I might have heard from you in connection with your several public comments and selective disclosures this week about the *Irish Times* and me, personally, as Editor. You expressed the view publicly on RTÉ that I was 'compromised' as Editor of the *Irish Times*. Your challenge to my journalistic ethics cannot stand.
>
> You are clearly unhappy working for a newspaper where you believe that its structure, culture, and Editor, are 'compromised'.
>
> Accordingly, I would like to minimise your discomfort by relieving you of any further necessity to contribute to the *Irish Times*. I wish you well in finding a more congenial environment for your journalism. (*Irish Times*, 24 November 2003)

Following an intervention by the National Union of Journalists and Waters's withdrawal of his claim, the paper retained him as a columnist. On 26 November the *Irish Times* did publish the details of executive directors' remuneration in 2002. The amounts involved in certain cases, though properly at the discretion of the board, were such as were likely to provoke comment.

Levels of payment to senior staff in the *Irish Times* was certainly the cause of comment in 2005 when the *Sunday Independent* ran a story on what it termed an 'Irish Times staff revolt at the editor's and directors' "indefensible salaries"'. It reported that more than 50 senior staff had already signed a letter objecting to the level of remuneration enjoyed by the editor among others. The article pointed out:

> To put it in context, Kennedy is being paid almost as much as some UK tabloid editors and more than the editor of the market leader, the *Daily Telegraph*, in the UK. That title sells almost one million copies a day compared to the modest 115,000 sold by the *Irish Times* each morning. (*Sunday Independent*, 7 August 2005)

It was stated in the article that the letter of protest included the observation 'that the inflated salaries being paid to those at the top make a mockery of the paper's very identity'.

Arguably the public could have taken some satisfaction in reading about the high rates of pay some individuals were enjoying as an indicator of how Ireland had, indeed, become a rich and successful modern country. And revenue from property advertisements and of employment opportunities, as the Irish property market expanded, probably allowed the *Irish Times* safely to pay some of its staff impressive salaries.

The property supplement of the newspaper appeared every Thursday, becoming increasingly bulky as the market expanded. In 1995, on a Thursday at the end of April, for example, this section ran to 44 pages. By the end of 2005 the section had swollen to 67 pages. The advertisements in the property section were mostly for domestic dwellings, with much use of colour photography. Pages were devoted to foreign property, covering France, Spain, Bulgaria, and even more exotic locations. When on 27 April 2005 an ad appeared for apartments for sale in Beijing ('at the centre of the fastest-growing economy in the world') it was clear that the *Irish Times* was catering for a public in the grip of a property mania. A weekly designs section of the supplement made the house beautiful seem almost like a moral imperative of the modern economy. Sales results, with their tantalizing figures, encouraged restless trading-up. A clever entry each week allowed owners of quite modest Irish houses, now valued at bloated sums, to contemplate properties they could purchase for the same prices in various overseas countries. The sale of a Dublin semi could, it seemed, raise enough to buy a small French château. Orla Mulcahy served as property editor during the housing boom (when a banking crisis broke in September 2008, Irish banks had 106 billion euro loaned to the construction industry). During the boom many 'feel-good' property stories were published. The readership envisaged was, in the main, the newly rich Irish middle class, especially in Dublin, but it was also their children who were the imagined readers as well. Property writer Edel Morgan soon became a kind of guru of the property boom in her 'City Living' column. In January 2004 she posed the question, 'Are you obsessed with property?' identifying the FOP as a person fanatically obsessed with property (*Irish Times*, 22 January 2004), intent on making a fortune by investing in houses or apartments. In this piece she passed on the advice of an investment adviser, who reported how 'some younger investors are seeking to mirror what they see as the successful investment patterns of their older colleagues'. In an article entitled 'Trade-up for the Right Reasons', published in September 2005, Morgan considered how the prevailing attitude to property as investment and a house as a stepping stone to the dream home or trophy house was affecting community values. She wrote:

> The relative ease with which people can move onwards and upwards towards their ultimate property is a reversal of the situation faced by previous generations when financial institutions were less forthcoming – and often a person's first property was also their last. The upside of staying put was that people knew their neighbours, knew what was happening in the community and if they were not living in their ideal location, they made the best of it. (*Irish Times*, 8 September 2005)

She concluded this thoughtful piece by reporting how the Taoiseach, Bertie Ahern, an enthusiastic cheer-leader of the economic boom, had invited Harvard's Professor Robert Putnam (author of *Bowling Alone*, 2000) to speak at Fianna Fáil's annual parliamentary meeting on the 'importance of active community participation'. Edel Morgan judged that this invitation reflected a concern that, 'although Ireland has traditionally had a high level of social participation and neighbourliness, the demands of modern life have made us more focused on our own lives at the expense of the wider community. In our hunger to trade-up, the trade-off has been the support network a strong community can provide.' If Bertie Ahern was looking to a Harvard professor for counsel in the midst of the housing boom, Morgan introduced her readers in this column to the novel idea of a life coach, the kind of person who could tell us 'We don't know what is enough sometimes.' A later article by Morgan indicated that there were many young Irish people who were in no position to benefit from nostrums advocated by such a figure. It was Morgan who noted in April 2006 that, according to the most recent census, 'over 15,000 people between the age of 25 and 35 were living with their parents, and with property prices spiralling out of the grasp of many first-time buyers, this number is expected to be higher in the next census' (*Irish Times*, 27 April 2006).

It was early in 2004 that doubts about the housing boom began to be expressed by some Irish commentators. The *Irish Times*'s economics editor, Cliff Taylor, published an article in January of that year, entitled 'Room with a View', which asked 'Will it all end in tears?' (*Irish Times*, 6 January 2004). He adverted to the fact that the respected London-published *The Economist* magazine had concluded that Irish houses were overvalued by 40 per cent and were 'likely to fall by 20 per cent over the next four years'. He also reported that 'Similar gloomy warnings have come from no less an august body than the International Monetary Fund.' Taylor cast about for evidence that would encourage a hope that, in a term that would become ubiquitous over the next few years, 'a soft landing' might be achieved after years of spectacular growth in the property market'. Taylor advised: 'the period of rapidly increasing house prices is fast ending ...'

By the end of February 2004 the same writer was the author of another *Irish Times* article, headlined this time 'All Is Well in the Property Market ... for now' (*Irish Times*, 27 February 2004), which reminded readers that 'A house price boom and an associated surge in lending is a traditional indicator that trouble may lie ahead.' He mused: 'It would be a mistake to conclude that all this is going to end in tears.' Encouraging him in this view were the facts that Allied Irish Bank was comfortable that its 'Mortgage lending in the Republic rose by an extraordinary 34 per cent last year' and that the Irish Financial Services Regulatory Authority was not 'unduly concerned' by the big 'growth in household debt' which had taken place. A paper then recently presented to the Central Bank had taken 'a reasonably relaxed view' of the risk that mortgage-holders might default. Taylor did accept, however, that 'from being a relatively low-debt economy, we have moved sharply up the economic league and have a group of people with high debt-to-income ratios, many of whom, for example, would depend on continuing two incomes to be able to keep paying the mortgage'. He ended: 'Let's all hope for a soft landing in the soaring property market.' March 2004 brought further cause for concern, when, as the *Irish Times* reported, *The Economist* 'reiterated its claim that the Irish housing market and several global housing markets are teetering on the edge of a crash' (*Irish Times*, 18 March 2004). Yet other voices were less pessimistic and were seized upon by nervous readers. The *Irish Times*'s finance correspondent wrote at the end of that month, citing 'a new report': 'Consumers are no longer worried about a property market crash and believe there will be a "soft landing", with house price inflation slowing to modest levels' (*Irish Times*, 25 March 2004). In April, under the headline 'Soft Landing Likely for Housing Market', the *Irish Times* reported the view of the chief economist of a major bank that 'the housing market displayed no sign of a bubble about to burst, despite repeated speculation on an imminent crash' (*Irish Times*, 15 April 2004). When on 21 April the Central Bank presented its view on the Irish property market, the *Irish Times* itself felt obliged to publish an editorial on 'Property Prices'. It took a measured view of the situation, which, in global terms, had raised property values in Dublin to a level second only to those in London. It reckoned: 'There are no immediate reasons to fear a collapse in the property market' (*Irish Times*, 22 April 2004). The editorial ended by invoking a 'soft landing', the near oxymoron which was coming to seem like a mantra intoned to settle the nerves of those who (like the newspaper itself, with its property advertising revenue stream) had an interest in a healthy property market. The leader writer seized on the Central Bank's assessment that the 'rate of property price growth should soon start to slow' and stated: 'The hope must be that this will allow a "soft landing" in the market, rather than a rapid fall in prices. The longer the property boom continues, however, the greater the risks in the years ahead.'

Hopes for a 'soft landing' were entertained by many for almost a further two years, as property prices seemed to defy gravity. And there were those who expected the boom to continue. For example, in November, Cliff Taylor's successor as economics editor, Marc Coleman, in an article headlined 'House Prices Set for a "Soft Landing"' (*Irish Times*, 22 November 2005), reported on a meeting to mark the fifth year in business of a mortgage provider. Those present had heard a talk from an official of the Economic and Social Research Institute, who assured them that 'rising property prices had been justified by economic fundamentals and this would continue into the future'. The meeting had also heard from *The Economist*'s Pam Woodall, who, less sanguine than the ESRI's man, had said: '"housing market trends in Australia and the UK proved that housing prices could fall, even without sharp rises in interest rates, and that modest falls in house prices could impact on the economy ... This is the biggest financial bubble in history," she said.'

Irish Times readers more inclined to trust the benign prospect sketched by the ESRI speaker at this meeting could have taken encouragement two days later from one of Edel Morgan's 'City Living' columns. There she revealed that Pam Woodall had admitted that week that she had got it wrong two years earlier when she had predicted a 20 per cent fall in Irish house prices. Morgan reported that Woodall was still of the view that a fall in Irish house prices was imminent, but remarked of her: 'While she may be proved right, she's beginning to look like the girl who cried wolf' (*Irish Times*, 24 November 2005). Morgan in fact had herself contributed a 'City Living' column earlier in the month, which quoted various Irish analysts who discounted the serious import of an OECD assessment that the Irish property market was overvalued by 15 per cent. She reported an economist at a well-known Dublin estate agency as saying that the OECD's views were 'academic' unless there was 'a huge shock to the economy, something bigger than September 11th ...' (*Irish Times*, 10 November 2005). Other figures in the property business were cited as expressing similarly bullish opinions, despite the fact that the Central Bank in its 2005 *Financial Stability Report* had stated that the risk of a sudden fall in house prices could not be dismissed.

By June 2006, Edel Morgan was writing in a column entitled 'Soft Landing – or Hard Times Ahead?' of how with interest rate rises in the offing, first-time buyers – those she identified as 'both the most powerful property buyers in the Irish market and the most vulnerable' (*Irish Times*, 8 June 2006) – were delaying purchasing houses. 'The very prospect,' she wrote, 'must have builders and estate agents quaking in their boots.' This and the warnings of international agencies about a global housing bubble did not appear to inhibit the board of the *Irish Times* itself when in July 2006, the company purchased for the sum of 50 millon euro, Myhome.ie, a property website. It was bought, as we noted above, as part of its strategy of developing a major digital media business.

All thoughts that the housing market and the Irish economy could hope for a 'soft landing' (obviously things of immediate interest to a company that had ventured 50 million euro in a property-related business) were unsparingly dispelled in an article the *Irish Times* itself published at the end of 2006. It is certainly to the credit of the newspaper, with its significant dependency on the property market, that it was prepared to publish an article by Morgan Kelly, Professor of Economics at University College Dublin, (though its contents would surely find a wide readership), which as the headline had it: 'How the Housing Corner Stones of Our Economy Could Go into a Rapid Freefall' (*Irish Times*, 28 December 2006). Kelly had sent his uncommissioned article to the editor, who must have realized that she had a scoop on her hands when she read its opening paragraphs:

> Offering no evidence except wishful thinking, estate agents and politicians assure us that we have nothing to be worried about; the Irish housing market can look forward to a soft landing.
>
> If however, we look at what has happened to other small economies where sudden prosperity and easy credit drove house prices to absurd levels, we should be very worried indeed.

Geraldine Kennedy checked out the professor's credentials (private communication with the author) and put into the public domain an article that presented the evidence, which it was argued would 'show conclusively that our housing boom is a bubble, pure and simple'. There would be no 'soft landing' for it was 'not implausible that prices could fall – relative to income – by 40–50 per cent'.

Even more devastatingly, Kelly claimed that Ireland had been living in a kind of economic dreamland. He pointed out that 'Between building new houses and selling existing ones, housing generates almost one-fifth of our national income.' When the crash came, 'it will,' he ominously calculated, 'be from about 18 per cent of national income. We could see a collapse of Government revenue and unemployment back above 15 per cent.' What to most Irish people had seemed an impressive modern economy with its high-tech industries and its grateful immigrants was founded on sand: 'As our exports have stalled since 2000, our economy has come to be entirely driven by house building ... In effect, the economy is based on building houses for all the people that have jobs building houses.' Morgan Kelly contributed a further article in September 2007 (it had initially been rejected by the *Irish Independent*, which found it 'offensive'; Michael Lewis 2011, p. 95). In this Kelly raised the question of the stability of the Irish banking system which had helped to fuel the property boom. Contemplating the banks' role in the housing boom, he mordantly commented: 'Effectively the Irish banking system has taken all its share-holders' equity, with a substantial chunk of its depositors' cash on top, and handed it over to builders and property speculators' (*Irish Times*, 7 September 2007). Conscious that the Irish banking system was tottering on its foundations, Kelly waxed sarcastic:

> You will probably think that the fact that Irish banks have given specu-lators €100 billion to gamble with, safe in the knowledge that taxpayers will cover most losses, is a cause of concern to the Irish Central Bank, but you would be quite wrong.
>
> At a recent Irish Economic Association discussion of house prices, the Central Bank official in charge of financial regulation ... stopped the proceedings to announce that the view of the Bank was that, as long as international markets were happy to buy debts issued by Irish banks, there could be no problem with their lending policies.

Morgan judged this 'insane logic'. The credit crunch and the collapse of Lehman Brothers lay ahead.

The government that would have to deal with the effects of these global economic events on the already fragile Irish economy was formed following the general election of 24 May 2007. Reflecting on the election campaign in an editorial on election day, in which the *Irish Times* urged citizens to cast their votes, the writer concentrated on how the campaign had been fought by the various parties. In this, it reflected on how possible economic difficulties had not played a role in any party's pitch to the electorate. The editorial blandly advised: 'This is an important election because it coincides with a serious concern that the Celtic Tiger is slowing down. Is the outgoing government responsible for the slowdown? Will a change of government make a material difference? (*Irish Times*, 24 May 2007). When Fianna Fáil's Bertie Ahern (who in the face of questions about his personal finances had precipitated the election) managed to put together an unlikely coalition that comprised his own party, the Progressive Democrats, the Green Party, and a few independents, an editorial focused on how the horse-trading of the Green Party had managed to put an ecological imprint on the agreed programme for government. On 15 June an editorial about the political skills of Ahern was unequivocal: 'There is no gainsaying it. Bertie Ahern's achievement is awesome. It exceeds that of Eamon de Valera, who also held office for three terms' (*Irish Times*, 15 June 2007).

In the glow of his election victory, with the *Irish Times* likening him to de Valera, Ahern could have been forgiven for recalling that when de Valera forsook the office of Taoiseach, he also served two terms as president of Ireland. That no such future would be possible for Ahern can largely be attributed to the sequence of events that a story published in the *Irish Times* set in motion.

On 21 September 2006 the newspaper had run a front-page story by its political affairs correspondent, Colm Keena, revealing how the Mahon tribunal, established in 1997 to examine certain planning matters and payments, was investigating payments by businessmen to Ahern in 1993, when he had been Minister for Finance. Initially it appeared that this story would not damage Ahern. Indeed, an opinion poll indicated that his popularity, rather than diminishing, had actually increased following this revelation. On 13 October the *Irish Times* published a puzzled editorial entitled 'A Poor Reflection of Ourselves' which asked and answered a question: 'What sort of people are we? We know now' (*Irish Times*, 13 October 2006). The writer continued:

> The culture of nods and winks and looking the other way is alive and well in Irish democracy. Among a significant sector, however, it reinforces the case that the public interest requires vigilance, investigation and continued scrutiny.
>
> If the rest of us 'look the other way', it won't be long before the culture of corruption engendered by Mr Haughey will resurface. But, regrettably, this poll would indicate that this does not seem to matter.

The result of the election of 24 May 2007 certainly suggested that much of the Irish electorate was untroubled by the fact that the Mahon Tribunal would continue to investigate the payments Ahern had received. Initially, indeed, it had seemed that it would be the reporter who broke the story and the editor who published it who would suffer for their temerity. The story had come to the *Irish Times* by way of an unknown person, who had, unsolicited, made correspondence from the tribunal about such payments available to Colm Keena. When the *Irish Times* had ascertained that this material involved fact and not just allegations, the paper had little choice but to publish this story, whatever the consequences. The tribunal, concerned about confidentiality, issued an order requiring the journalists to hand over the material on which the story had been based. Kennedy responded, saying that the material sought had been destroyed (so in effect the tribunal was demanding the impossible). Keena and Kennedy were then summoned by the tribunal, which demanded they comply with its order. They had acted in the conviction that it had been their professional duty not to be part of a course of action that could lead to the identification of their source. Consequently the tribunal applied to the High Court to compel the two journalists to obey its order. The High Court judged that the *Irish Times* had been 'reprehensible' in destroying in the way it had done material germane to the matter and it instructed Keena and Kennedy to return to the tribunal to answer its questions. This judgement was appealed to the Supreme Court which on 31 July 2009 dismissed the tribunal's application, though later in the year the court awarded costs against the newspaper. Seamus Dooley, Irish secretary of the NUJ, had hailed the July judgement as a 'victory for journalism and for common sense' (*Irish Times*, 1 August 2009). In December 2009 an article by Dave O'Connell in the *Connacht Tribune* reported on a speech that Geraldine Kennedy had recently given in Galway in which she admitted that the robust defence of press freedom mounted by her paper had cost the *Irish Times* 600,000 euro. O'Connell quoted Kennedy as claiming that 'the decision of the Supreme Court ... was a landmark one that enshrined the principle of journalistic privilege and the protection of sources into Irish law for the first time'.

In saluting Kennedy, whose resolution, along with that of Keena, had been crucial in the achievement of this outcome, O'Connell highlighted how current economic circumstances in terms of legal costs in the country might inhibit other editors from taking similar financially risky stands in the interests of press freedom when the consequences could be so severe. He commented: 'there are very few papers who [*sic*] would risk exposure to this sort of punitive ruling at a time when revenues generally are in decline'.

Revenues were, indeed, in decline, for the *Irish Times* had found itself liable for costs in the case which had vindicated the right of journalists to protect their sources at a time when the Irish state was facing an economic crisis of existential proportions, one that was putting in question the continued viability of many national institutions, including the daily newspapers. The closure of the *Irish Press* and *Evening Press* in 1995 had served as a warning that no title was sacrosanct nor immune to market forces. In 2008 those forces had blown like a whirlwind through the country's financial system.

On 30 September that year the Irish public had awoken to the astonishing and perplexing news that, overnight, their government had agreed to guarantee the deposits and debts of Irish-owned banks and building societies since these could no longer access short-term funding on the money markets. Alarm bells had been ringing loudly the day before that the Irish financial system was in serious peril as the value of bank shares fell precipitously. The government had taken this momentous decision in the belief that a lack of liquidity threatened the banks' capacity to remain operational. On 1 October economist Alan Ahearne made clear the alarming implications of what had occurred: 'the financial exposure for taxpayers is enormous. The guarantee covers 400 billion euro in deposits and shares, equivalent to about 120 per cent of GDP' (*Irish Times*, 1 October 2008). The paper's editorial of that day was headlined 'Beholden to the State' and was generally supportive of a decision that had been taken to prevent a 'catastrophe' which the collapse of an Irish bank could have precipitated.

In Geraldine Kennedy's Galway speech, referred to above, in which she had said the costs incurred by the *Irish Times* had been a price worth paying to have a key aspect of the freedom of the press defined in Irish law for the first time, she had, according to Dave O'Connell's report in the *Connacht Tribune*, explained her paper's decision to destroy the documents that had first alerted Colm

Keena to the fact that payments to Taoiseach Bertie Ahern were attracting the attention of the Mahon Tribunal, on the grounds, as O'Connell reported her as stating: 'The reality is that if they didn't destroy those documents, the focus would have switched from the Taoiseach's money trail to an investigation into who spilt the beans'. It would have been surprising had Kennedy not felt some sense of vindication when the focus of the Mahon Tribunal in the spring of 2007 did fix on the issue of Ahern's finances. His appearances at the tribunal and his responses to its questions at that time generated so much adverse publicity and doubt about his probity in public affairs that on 6 May he resigned as Taoiseach disclaiming a connection (he subsequently resigned as leader of Fianna Fáil). Kennedy's resolution as editor of the *Irish Times* had resulted in a notable, though costly, advance for the profession of journalism, in the courts, while the *Irish Times*'s publication of Keena's story about Ahern and the Mahon Tribunal's knowledge of payments made by businessmen to him had demonstrated in dramatic fashion how in a democratic society the highest in the land could be held to account by a free press.

As the financial tempest battered Ireland in the autumn of 2008 and readers had to accustom themselves to stories involving many billions of euro and headlines such as 'How to Protect Your Savings', making Finance Minister Brian Lenihan's claim, reported on 24 October, that the bailout of the Irish banks would prove 'the cheapest in the world' ring unnervingly hollow. Questions naturally began to be asked about how the authorities had allowed such a crisis to overtake the country. An anxious public could easily recall how the airwaves in recent months had resounded to economic experts, some of them in the employ of the banks, assuring them that 'the fundamentals' of the banking system were sound (that phrase vying with 'a soft landing' as an economic comfort-blanket). Advertisements for financial products had been accompanied by the assurance that particular institutions were regulated by the Central Bank of Ireland. A sense swiftly developed that a hurricane had struck without warning and that the forecasters must have been asleep on the job.

At least the *Irish Times* had no reason to reproach itself that it had allowed the banking crisis of 2008 to arrive without issuing a warning, for a year earlier it had published the article by Professor Morgan Kelly which had added to his gloomy forecasts about the Irish property boom, that banking in the country rested on 'very shaky foundations' (*Irish Times*, 7 September 2007).

By publishing Morgan's articles, and that one in particular, the *Irish Times* had demonstrated its willingness to present its readers with unpalatable opinion, as the *Irish Independent* had not done.

During her tenure as editor of the *Irish Times*, Geraldine Kennedy had in fact consistently served notice that she was not averse to giving space to writers who would broach contentious subjects. Her decision in January 2006 to begin publishing articles by the conservative North American commentator

416 THE IRISH TIMES: 150 YEARS OF INFLUENCE

Charles Krauthammer was signal proof of that. That he was a renowned, Pulitzer prize-winning contributor to the *Washington Post* did not cut any ice with some readers. For example, a Conor MacCarthy wrote to the *Irish Times* complaining that Krauthammer, introduced by the paper as 'our new columnist', was 'a pundit from inside the Washington beltway, dubiously close to government, providing arguments "in the service of power"' (*Irish Times*, 9 January 2006). It did not seem to strike this correspondent that in a decade in which US military power had been and was being exercised in the Middle East, it might be instructive to be allowed to read the views on US policies of a well-placed columnist such as Krauthammer.

Irish public opinion in the 2000s was not in ready sympathy with the policies of the Bush administration in the United States. This had been evidenced in February 2003 when, on the 15th of that month, 80,000 people had joined a peace march in Dublin, swelling the number of those who protested around the world on that date against the imminent US attack on Saddam Hussein's Iraq. Accordingly, the readership of the *Irish Times* was unlikely to find Krauthammer's vigorously pro-American views sympathetic. He was, too, a robust apologist for the Israeli state in its dispute with its Arab neighbours and with the nascent Palestine, in terms that were unusual in the columns of the *Irish Times* where frequent letters from the composer Raymond Deane, founding member of the Ireland Palestine Solidarity Campaign, cogently argued the justice of the Palestinian cause (the paper consistently did give space to letters challenging Deane's viewpoint from officials at the Israeli embassy). Krauthammer was willing to foment controversy on the issue. For example, when what was perceived by the world's press as an especially egregious act by the Israeli military, he commented: 'The Palestinians prefer victimhood to statehood. They have demonstrated this for 60 years, beginning with their rejection of the UN decision to establish a Palestinian state in 1947, because it would also have created a small Jewish state next door. They declared war instead' (*Irish Times*, 19 June 2006). Just as provocative was Krauthammer's article of July 2006 in which he argued that the world had lost its moral compass in respect of the Israeli–Palestinian conflict. Once again he was prepared to indict a people's cause in defending Israel's right to use lethal force in self-defence. Krauthammer saw this as an intended consequence of the deliberate policy of the Palestinians' ally in south Lebanon: 'Hizbullah hides its fighters, its rockets, its launchers, its entire infrastructure among civilians. Creating human shields is a war crime. It is also a Hizbullah speciality' (*Irish Times*, 31 July 2006). Krauthammer had no patience with the view that the Israeli response to rocket attacks on its towns and villages from beyond its northern frontier should be 'proportionate'. He thought it was a measure of Israeli restraint that Israel had chosen not to attack civilian infrastructure in Beirut in response to 'perhaps the most blatant terror campaign from the air since the London Blitz' (*Irish Times*, 31 July 2006).

It was not that the *Irish Times*'s staffers were not as capable of controversial opinion pieces as anything a syndicated US columnist could produce. On Kennedy's staff were John Waters and Kevin Myers, both of whom were quite prepared to court controversy in their columns. Furthermore, Dick Walsh and Vincent Browne, both senior, experienced journalists on the paper, could be depended on in their columns of commentary on Irish affairs to subject the body politic and the economy to probing socialist analysis. Waters, for example, was prepared to question in a blunt fashion much of the conventional wisdom in the Republic of Ireland which had underpinned the peace process in Northern Ireland to which his own paper had given consistently firm editorial support.

The measure of Waters's frankly iconoclastic analysis of the peace process can be taken from an article he contributed to the paper in February 2000 in which he identified the means of exchange which that process depended upon as 'faith' (*Irish Times*, 15 February 2000); this he defined as 'a willingness to suspend scepticism'. Republicans and the people of the Republic had done this. Unionism, almost by definition, was incapable of such good faith. Waters argued, as Northern unionists kept up their vociferous demand that the IRA must disarm and disband, that 'unionisim was incapable of such faith. It is not possible to possess faith and demonstrate its confidence only when things are going your way.' Recalling the euphoria that had greeted the Good Friday Agreement in 1998, Waters wrote:

> Although the widespread euphoria suggested a 'South Africa moment', it now appears that the delight of the two governments and the Ulster Unionists was to do with belief that republicans had finally been tricked into the Orange trap, to be divested of military power and neutralised.
>
> The celebration, then, instead of announcing the transformation of the situation, signalled partisan triumphalism at the success of self-serving tactics. The agreement was a hoax, a sham, a carnival of bad faith.

Waters was even willing to indict his own newspaper as a victim of this unionist trap-setting for the republican movement, when he wrote in March 2000: 'Listening to TDs and reading editorials in this and other newspapers, you might not think the Belfast Agreement had represented no change at all in attitudes to the meaning of the conflict, or that it was a pretence to trick republicans into handing up guns' (*Irish Times*, 14 March 2000).

John Waters was not the only opinion columnist writer on the *Irish Times* to have entertained doubts about the Good Friday Agreement and to have expresssed them openly. Kevin Myers had served as the author of the daily 'An Irishman's Diary' since 1980 when he took up the post long occupied by Séamus Kelly, who had died in 1979. Myers had not hesitated to make the column, even in the face of his then editor Douglas Gageby's intense disapproval, a vehicle for the expression of his often controversial ideas and opinions. Myers had been in Belfast working as a reporter for RTE during the early phase of 'the Troubles' (his memoir, *Watching the Door*, is a brilliant account of that grim time). His experience there (which included reporting on Bloody Friday) seemed to have induced in him a settled loathing for politically inspired violence and for republican versions of Irish history. Readers quickly came to expect his regular denunciations of the republican movement from which, as far as Myers was concerned, no good could come. Certainly Sinn Féin (with its bloody tradition of support for armed force) could not be trusted to sign and adhere to any kind of peace deal. When the agreement was in fact struck in April 1998, Myers issued a characteristically forthright admission that he had misjudged the situation. In his retraction of much of what he had written on the subject, he confessed he had been 'gloriously, magnificently, totally wrong' (*Irish Times*, 15 April 1998).

Where Myers was not willing to consider any kind of retraction was with respect to how he regularly employed his column to urge that the Irish dead in the two world wars should be properly honoured and commemorated. Writing about his almost single-handed near-crusade for this cause, Myers recalled how Douglas Gageby had unsuccessfully tried to temper his diarist's zeal on this controversial topic. Myers had been resolutely determined to challenge a national narrative that had almost completely expunged from history the sacrifices of those who had died. He told Gageby that he would stop writing about the Great War only when the state formally recognized the tens of thousands of Irish who died and have been forgotten' (Whittaker 2006, p. 121). As a near-paradoxical consequence, in the first decade of the twenty-first century, while John Waters in the *Irish Times* was probing in forceful terms the weaknesses of unionism as a political philosophy, Kevin Myers was exploring a theme which had been dear to the newspaper in the 1920s, when commemoration of the Great War dead had been, as we saw earlier, a sacred duty conscientiously discharged by the paper. Moreover, Myers's frequently expressed antagonism to the Provisional IRA and to its nationalist ideology that made Easter 1916 a sacred myth of republican authenticity must have been as music to the ears of unionist Ireland. How provocative Myers could be on this subject is exemplified by a piece he wrote in January 2006, in commentary on a speech on 1916 by President Mary McAleese. He bluntly damned the speech as 'among the most imbecilic ever by any president, ever' (*Irish Times*, 31 January 2006). He continued: 'It's as if we hadn't just gone through a quarter-century of catastrophic 1916-inspired violence':

> Now I know this 'republic' that was declared in 1916 very well indeed.
> It *is* not a republic at all but the formal inauguration of a political cult
> of necrophilia whose most devoted adherents over the past 36 years have
> been the Provisional IRA. Each year during the 25 years of the Troubles

they rededicated themselves to this same Republic that 'guarantees the religious and civil liberty, equal rights and equal opportunities to all its citizens.' And each year, like Aztecs placating their heathen gods, they went out and killed more of its citizens. (*Irish Times*, 31 January 2006)

In his columns in this uninhibited fashion, Myers did not hesitate to challenge what he thought of as the pusillanimous circumspection of the politically correct. Even 'gender politics' were not off-limits to him, to his own undoing and to the great embarrassment of his newspaper. In February 2005 a well-known professor had queried the social wisdom of the state provision for unmarried mothers and their children. Myers took the opportunity this afforded to launch a broadside against how the delicate topic of illegitimacy was carefully treated by the politically correct. As was often the case when he courted controversy, the journalist presented himself as a plain-dealer willing to attract opprobrium by speaking frankly. In his piece (oddly appearing as 'An Irishman's Diary') Myers wrote of 'bastards' and imagined their mothers as living lives on state benefits that would be 'crushingly limited with little sense of achievement or personal ambition, and no career to speak of, other – that is – from cash-crop whelping'(*Irish Times*, 8 February 2005). Not content with that, Myers compounded his offence against a class of persons by suggesting that a future generation of crime-gang members was in the making. He concluded with a show of disdain for those who would deprecate his opinions and views, 'but of course in Dáil Eireann, we'll get some weepy sanctimonious bilge over what is "offensive"; while the rest of us reach for the ear-plugs'.

In fact, many of Myers's readers reached for their pens to write to the editor to object that the *Irish Times* had published such a piece. The newspaper over the next few days published a substantial sample of these very critical reactions to Myers's intemperate article. Mark O'Brien cites Fintan O'Toole as experiencing the day after Myers's article appeared as 'one of the worst days in the history of the *Irish Times*' (Mark O'Brien 2008, p. 270). One correspondent told the editor that the article was 'a new low in the history of [her] newspaper' (*Irish Times*, 9 February 2005). Others objected to Myers's 'continuous and gratuitous use of the term "bastard"'; it was pointed out that the legal concept of illegitimacy had been removed from Irish law in 1987, giving force to one claim that the article in question had been 'inaccurate, lazy and cruel'. One letter judged it 'plain nasty, attention-seeking name calling' (*Irish Times*, 9 February 2005).

On 10 February Myers used his 'Irishman's Diary' to issue an 'unconditional apology' for his remarks, and this on the same page as that day's leading article (entitled ' Regret for the Offence Caused'), in which the newspaper joined its columnist in unequivocal apologetic mode.

Myers insisted that his apology had been made on a voluntary basis and not under pressure from the editor. The editorial made a point of reinforcing how *Irish Times* journalists were free to express themselves as they wished when it stated:

> The *Irish Times* defines itself in part by providing a platform for divergent views. The opinions of one columnist will differ from another; they may at times conflict with the editorial policy of the newspaper, as in this case. However, it should be pointed out to readers that the whole editorial process tries to avoid undue interference in the opinions of columnists, except on factual and legal grounds. And when it does occur, the newspaper, more than any other, is criticised for censorship. (*Irish Times*, 10 February 2005)

Myers's apology was couched in terms that suggested real contrition since he acknowledged the authenticity of the reactions he had provoked; as he expressed bitter regret 'for using provocative, ill-thought-out and confrontational language', he recognized of those who had written to the paper: 'Their feelings are real, passionate and heartfelt' (*Irish Times*, 10 February 2005). The editorial of the same day suggested how shaken the newspaper had been by the furore Myers had aroused. In the paper's defence, the editorialist adduced a sociological argument to try to explain how such a piece had been allowed to appear, which read, it must be said, rather like special pleading:

> Irish society has changed hugely in recent decades and at a pace that has been breathtaking. Much of this change is for the good and has been led by the *Irish Times*. Stigmatising social differences is no longer as acceptable as it once was and rightly so ...
>
> But with these changes come challenges: Irish society, no less than some others, is being confronted increasingly with the consequences of dramatic social change – changing precepts about the family, about marriage and partnership, about children and their welfare, about rights and responsibilities, collectively and individually.

It seemed disingenuous for the *Irish Times* to suggest that it had sanctioned, in the spirit of freedom of expression, to which the paper had traditionally adhered, the publication of Myers's rebarbative article as a contribution to a debate about such social changes in modern Ireland, for the case was more troubling. In writing of single mothers and their offspring as he had, Myers had touched a very sore spot in the public consciousness. Unwed motherhood had long been treated censoriously by Irish society and it had not been unusual for unfortunate young women who gave birth outside of wedlock to be dispatched to effective servitude in what were known as Magdalen laundries, run by religious orders. How these orders had treated the girls and young women in their charge in these institutions, and children in industrial schools and reformatories they were also responsible for running, had been progressively revealed since the early 1990s. This had made attitudes to vulnerable women and children a litmus test of acceptable opinion in modern Ireland which Myers, whatever his intentions, had clearly failed.

On 20 May 2009 the grim truth about how religious orders and the state had treated vulnerable children in their care was revealed to an appalled Irish public. For on that day the Ryan Commission on child abuse in reformatories and industrial schools was published. The stories it had to tell, even for those who remembered Michael Viney's *Irish Times* articles in the 1960s which had broken silence on the subject, were beyond shocking for they raised questions about the legitimacy of a state which, arguably, had colluded with religious orders in the torture and enslavement of children. The *Irish Times* did not shrink from using such terms in the excoriating editorial it published on 21 May 2009, under the headline 'The Savage Reality of Our Darkest Days'. The editorial struck a tone of uncompromising, unvarnished truth-telling:

> The Report of the Commission to Inquire into Child Abuse is the map of an Irish hell. It defines the contours of a dark hinterland of the State, a parallel country whose existence we have long known but never fully acknowledged. It is a land of pain and shame, of savage cruelty and callous indifference. The instinct to turn away from it, repelled by its profoundly unsettling ugliness, is almost irresistible. We owe it, though, to those who have suffered there to acknowledge from now on that it is an inescapable part of Irish reality. We have to deal with the now-established fact that alongside the warmth and intimacy, the kindness and generosity of Irish life, there was for most of the history of the State a deliberately maintained structure of vile and vicious abuse. (*Irish Times*, 21 May 2009)

In the wake of the publication of the Ryan Report, the *Irish Times* sought conscientiously in the spirit of this editorial to confront the dreadful reality the report had uncovered. It published hard-hitting articles, such as one by Mary Raftery, whose television documentary *States of Fear* had a decade earlier prodded the national conscience on the mistreatment of children in industrial schools. Entitled 'Report a Monument to Society's Shame', her article was an implied indictment of the society so many had worked to build since independence. She wrote: 'it is quite simply a devastating report. It is a monument to the shameful nature of Irish society throughout most of the decades of the 20th century and arguably even today' (*Irish Times*, 21 May 2009). The political commentator Noel Whelan observed: 'The younger generation reading the Ryan Commission report are entitled to ask their elders why they did nothing to help children' (*Irish Times*, 23 May 2009). He continued: 'in careful but clear language the report concludes that the communities surrounding those institutions knew that something horrific was going on'.

In an effort to register the national impact of the Ryan Report, the newspaper opened its letters column to correspondents, who in the week following the report's publication conducted what amounted to a public forum on the report and its findings. It made for compelling and affecting reading (some writers wrote of their own experience of abuse). Others attested to the kindness of individual religious and defended the orders' contribution to Irish life. Several themes emerged in the correspondence: it was the Irish poor who had been subjected to mistreatment because they were poor; it was past time for Church and state to be definitively separated. Correspondents wondered how it had been possible for such abuses to remain hidden from the public for so long. Was the populace really ignorant of the wrongs that were being committed in the industrial schools? One writer reminded Dublin readers: 'it was common knowledge when I was at day school in Dublin in the mid 1950s'. Another letter-writer, who had lived near an industrial school in the 1950s and 1960s, expanding on Noel Whelan's observation, made a painful comparison. He remembered seeing boys from the school in the neighbourhood but 'never dreamed conditions were actually as appalling as the Commission describes'. His ignorance was, he reckoned, akin to that of those who had lived near Dachau concentration camp in Nazi Germany. Another letter bluntly stated: 'I cannot accept that many of those wringing their hands now knew nothing of what was happening.' On 27 May the paper announced that the letters section would be extended to two pages, the better to reflect the range of opinion being expressed in the avalanche of letters it was receiving. On the same day an editorial pondered how 'the continuing volume, passion and anger of the letters to the paper indicated that'

> We are now at a critical juncture which could herald a sea-change in our attitude to church, State and public policy.
> Religious and political leadership to match the public mood for radical renewal is badly needed. It is really a testing time for the institutional architecture of church and State constructed after independence and now found so unfit for purpose. (*Irish Times*, 27 May 2009)

In its 150-year history the *Irish Times* had been witness to many testing times, like the one the country contemporaneously faced. Indeed, two months earlier, at the end of March 2009, in the supplement it issued to celebrate the paper's 150th birthday, Geraldine Kennedy had identified the newspaper's achievement in terms that suggested its longevity could be attributed to its capacity to adapt to transitions of the kind now in train in the Republic of Ireland. She wrote with justifiable pride:

> A newspaper exists to reflect the society which it serves. The *Irish Times* is no different. It has changed and reinvented itself over and over again down

through the years, evolving, writing the first draft of history about the political, social, economic and cultural landmarks on the island of Ireland.

It has been that capacity for creative adaptation, which has, I believe, been amply demonstrated in this study, which has taken us from Victorian unionist Ireland, through revolution and the establishment of two new jurisdictions on the island, to two world wars, and in more recent years to economic transformation and the uncertainty of economic crisis, all accompanied by astonishing developments in communications technology.

Kennedy concluded her anniversary remarks by identifying the challenges the paper faced at another time of transition and modern technological change: 'And here we are, celebrating our 150th anniversary, resilient as ever but facing uncertain times with today's challenges coming from the newly-described Great Recession and the internet.' In the light of a-century-and-a-half of successful self-reinvention, it seemed apt for the editor to remind readers of the newspaper's oft-proven resilience, that resilience upon which its future will undoubtedly depend.

WORKS CITED

Adams, Bernard, *Denis Johnston: A Life*, The Lilliput Press, 2002.

Adams, Michael, *Censorship: The Irish Experience*, Dublin: Scepter Books, 1968.

Akenson, Donald Harmon, *The Church of Ireland: Ecclesiastical Reform and Revolution 1800–1885*, New Haven and London: Yale University Press, 1971.

Allen, Nicholas, *George Russell and the New Ireland, 1905–30*, Dublin: Four Courts Press, 2003.

Arnold, Matthew, 'Up to Easter', *Nineteenth Century*, Vol. 123, May 1887.

Bardon, Jonathan, *A History of Ulster*, Belfast: The Blackstaff Press, 1992.

Bartlett, Thomas, *Ireland: A History*, Cambridge: Cambridge University Press, 2010.

Bell, J. Bowyer, *The Secret Army: The IRA*, New Brunswick, NJ: Transaction Publishers, 1997.

Belton, Neil, '*Thought Fox*', London: Faber and Faber, 29 January 2013.

Best, Geoffrey, *Mid-Victorian Britain, 1851–75*, London: Weidenfeld and Nicolson, 1971.

Bew, Paul, *Ireland: The Politics of Enmity 1789–2006*, Oxford: Oxford University Press, 2007.

Blunden, Edmund (ed.) *The Poems of Wilfred Owen*, London: Chatto and Windus, 1965.

Boland, Rosita, 'The Saturday Interview: Michael Viney', *Irish Times*, 10 July 2010.

Bowen, Kurt, *Protestants in a Catholic State: Ireland's Privileged Minority*, Kingston: McGill-Queen's University Press, 1983.

Boyce, George and Alan O'Day (eds), *Ireland in Transition, 1867–1921*, London: Routledge, 2004.

Brady, Conor, *Up with the Times*, Dublin: Gill and Macmillan, 2005.

Brooke, Rupert, *The Poems: A Centenary Edition* (ed. Timothy Rogers), privately printed, 1987.

Brown, Lucy, *Victorian News and Newspapers*, Oxford: Clarendon Press, 1985.

Browne, Noel, *Against the Tide*, Dublin: Gill and Macmillan, 1986.

Byrne, Elaine A., *Political Corruption in Ireland, 1922–2010: A Crooked Harp*, Manchester and New York: Manchester University Press, 2012.

Campbell, Patrick, *My Life and Easy Times*, London: Anthony Blond, 1967.

Clissmann, Anne, *Flann O'Brien: A Critical Introduction to his Writings*, Dublin: Gill and Macmillan, 1975.

Clune, Anne, 'O'Nolan, Brian (Flann O'Brien)', *The Dictionary of Irish Biography*, Vol. 7, Dublin: Royal Irish Academy; Cambridge: Cambridge University Press, 2009.

Coleman, Marie, 'William Magennis', *Dictionary of Irish Biography*, Vol. 5, Dublin: Royal Irish Academy; Cambridge: Cambridge University Press, 2009.

Conboy, Martin, *Journalism: A Critical History*, London: Sage Publications Ltd, 2004.

Connery, Donald S., *The Irish*, London: Eyre and Spottiswoode, 1968.

Connolly, Linda, *The Irish Women's Movement: From Revolution to Devolution*, Dublin: The Lilliput Press, 2003.

Coogan, Tim Pat, *A Memoir*, London: Weidenfeld and Nicolson, 2008.

Cosgrove, Art (ed.), *Dublin Through the Ages*, Dublin: College Press, 1988.

Cronin, Anthony, *No Laughing Matter: The Life and Times of Flann O'Brien*, London: Grafton Books, 1989.

Cullen, L. M., *Eason & Son: A History*, Dublin: Eason & Son, 1989.

——*Princes and Pirates: The Dublin Chamber of Commerce, 1783–1983,* Dublin: The Chamber of Commerce, 1983.

Curtis, L. P., Jr, 'The Anglo-Irish Predicament', *20th Century Studies*, November 1970.

d'Alton, Ian, 'In a "Comity of Cultures": The Rise and Fall of the *Irish Statesman*', in Mark O'Brien and Felix M. Larkin (eds), *Periodicals and Journalism in Twentieth-Century Ireland*, Dublin: Four Courts Press, 2014.

Daly, Mary, *Dublin: The Deposed Capital: A Social and Economic History, 1860–1914*, Cork: Cork University Press, 1984.

Dawe, Gerald and Maria Johnston (eds), *High Pop: The Irish Times Columns 1970–1976*, Belfast: Lagan Press, 2008.

de Bréadún, Deaglán, 'An cupla focal: Irish', *The Irish Times: 1859–2009*, 27 March 2009.

Downey, James, *In My Own Time: Inside Irish Politics and Society*, Dublin: Gill and Macmillan, 2009.

Dudley Edwards, Ruth, 'Inglis, Brian St John', *Dictionary of Irish Biography*, Vol. 4, Dublin: Royal Irish Academy; Cambridge: Cambridge University Press, 2009.

Dunlop, Andrew, *Fifty Years of Irish Journalism,* Dublin: Hanna and Neale, 1911.

Ellis, Walter, *The Beginning of the End: The Crippling Disadvantage of a Happy Irish Childhood*, Edinburgh and London: Mainstream Publishing, 2006.

Ferriter, Diarmaid, 'Healy, John Edward', *Dictionary of Irish Biography*, Vol. 4, Dublin: Royal Irish Academy; Cambridge: Cambridge University Press, 2009.

Fleming, Lionel, *Head or Harp*, London: Barrie and Rockliff, 1965.

Foster, John Wilson, *The Titanic Complex: A Cultural Manifest,* Vancouver, BC: Belcouver Press, 1997.

Foster, Roy, *W. B. Yeats: A Life*, Vol. 1: *The Apprentice Mage*, London and New York: Oxford University Press, 1998.

Fussell, Paul, *The Great War and Modern Memory,* New York: Oxford University Press, 1975.

Gageby, Douglas, 'The Media, 1945 –70', in J. J. Lee (ed.), *Ireland 1945–70*, Dublin: Gill and Macmillan, 1979.

Gillespie, Elgy (ed.), *Changing the TIMES: Irish Women Journalists, 1969–1981*, Dublin: The Lilliput Press, 2003.

Gray, Tony, *Mr Smyllie, Sir*, Dublin: Gill and Macmillan, 1991, 1994.

Hamilton, Hugo, *The Speckled People: Memoir of a Half-Irish Childhood*, London: Harper Perennial, 2003.

Heaney, Seamus, *Death of a Naturalist*, London: Faber and Faber, 1966.

Inglis, Brian, *West Briton*, London: Faber and Faber, 1962.

James, Dermot, *From the Margins to the Centre: A History of the Irish Times*, Dublin: The Woodfield Press, 2008.

Joyce, James, *Ulysses*, London: Oxford University Press, 1993.

Kearney, Richard, 'Richard Kearney and Dermot Moran talk to Douglas Gageby', *The Crane Bag*, Vol. 8, No. 2, 1984.

Kennedy, Dennis, *Square Peg: The Life and Times of a Northern Newspaperman South of the Border*, Dublin: Nonsuch Publishing, 2009.

Keogh, Dermot, *Jews in Twentieth-Century Ireland: Refugees, Anti-Semitism and the Holocaust*, Cork: Cork University Press, 1998.

Knowlson, James, *Damned to Fame: The Life of Samuel Beckett*, London: Bloomsbury, 1996.

Lee, J. J., *The Modernisation of Irish Society, 1848–1918*, Dublin: Gill and Macmillan, 1973.

Lee, J. J. (ed.), *Ireland, 1945–70*, Dublin: Gill and Macmillan, 1979.

Lewis, Michael, *Boomerang: The Biggest Bust*, London: Penguin Books, 2011.

Long, Patrick, 'Newman, William Alexander ('Alec')', *Dictionary of Irish Biography*, Vol. 6, Dublin: Royal Irish Academy; Cambridge: Cambridge University Press, 2008.

Lyons, F. S, L., *Ireland since the Famine*, Glasgow: Collins, 1971.

MacDonagh, Donagh, *Poems from Ireland*, Dublin: The Irish Times, 1944.

MacNeice, Louis, *Autumn Journal*, London: Faber and Faber, 1939.

—— *The Poetry of W. B. Yeats*, London, New York, Toronto: Oxford University Press, 1941.

Martin, John, *The Irish Times: Past and Present: A Record of the Journal since 1859*, Belfast: Belfast Historical and Educational Society, 2008.

Martin, Seamus, *Good Times and Bad: From the Coombe to the Kremlin: A Memoir*, Cork: The Mercier Press, 2008.

Mathews, P. J., 'Stirring Up Disloyalty: The Boer War, the Irish Literary Theatre and the Emergence of a New Separatism', *Irish University Review*, Vol. 33, No. 1, Spring–Summer 2003.

Maume, Patrick, 'De Blacam', Aodh (Hugh Saunders Blackham), *Dictionary of Irish Biography*, Vol. 3, Dublin: Royal Irish Academy; Cambridge: Cambridge University Press, 2009.

Maume, Patrick, 'Patrick Campbell', *Dictionary of Irish Biography*, Vol. 2, Dublin: Royal Irish Academy; Cambridge: Cambridge University Press, 2008.

McBride, J. P., *The Dublin University Magazine: Cultural Nationality and Tory Ideology in an Irish Literary and Political Journal 1833–1852*, PhD Thesis, Trinity College, Dublin, 1987.

McGahern, John, *Amongst Women*, London and Boston: Faber and Faber, 1990.

McGarry, Fearghal, 'Irish Newspapers and the Spanish Civil War', *Irish Historical Studies*, Vol. 33, No. 129, May 2003.

Montague, John, *New Collected Poems*, Oldcastle, Co. Meath: The Gallery Press, 2012.

Morash, Christopher, *A History of the Media in Ireland*, Cambridge: Cambridge University Press, 2010.

Munter, Robert, *The History of the Irish Newspapers, 1685–1760*, Cambridge; Cambridge University Press, 1967.

O'Brien, Conor Cruise, *Memoir: My Life and Themes*, Dublin: Poolbeg Press, 1998.

O'Brien, Justin, *The Modern Prince: Charles Haughey and The Quest For Power*, Dublin: Merlin Publishing, 2002.

O'Brien, Mark, *The Irish Times: A History*, Dublin: Four Courts Press, 2008.

—— 'Pyle, Fergus, Patrick d'Esterre', *The Dictionary of Irish Biography*, Vol. 8, Dublin: Royal Irish Academy; Cambridge: Cambridge University Press, 2009.

O'Connell, Dave, 'Press Freedom Comes Carrying a Very High Price', *Connacht Tribune*, 3 December 2009.

O'Connor, T. P. 'The New Journalism', *New Review*, Vol. 1, No. 5, October 1889.

O'Day, Alan, 'Max Weber and Leadership: Butt, Parnell and Dillon', in D. George Boyce and Alan O'Day (eds), *Ireland in Transition, 1867–1921*, London and New York: Routledge, 2004.

Ó Drisceoil, Donal, *Censorship in Ireland, 1939–1945*, Cork: Cork University Press, 1996.

O'Toole, Fintan, *The Irish Times: The Book of the Century*, Dublin: Gill and Macmillan, 1999.

O'Toole, Michael, *More Kicks Than Pence*, County Dublin: Poolbeg Press, 1992.

Owen, Wilfred, *The Poems*, London: Chatto and Windus, 1965.

Parker, Michael, *Seamus Heaney: The Making of the Poet*, London: Palgrave Macmillan, 1994.

Pine, Richard, *Charles: The Life and World of Charles Acton, 1914–1999*, Dublin: Lilliput Press, 2010.

Ramazani, Jahan, 'Irish Poetry and the News', in Fran Brearton and Alan Gillis (eds), *Modern Irish Poetry*, Oxford: Oxford University Press, 2012.

—— 'The Newspaper Press' *The Edinburgh Review*, No 102, October 1855.

Sheehy, Jeanne, *The Discovery of Ireland's Past: The Celtic Revival, 1860–1914*, London: Thames and Hudson, 1980.

St Clair, William, *The Reading Nation in the Romantic Period*, Cambridge: Cambridge University Press, 2004.

Taaffe, Carol, *Ireland Through the Looking Glass; Flann O'Brien, Myles na gCopaleen and Irish Cultural Debate*, Cork: Cork University Press, 2008.

Trollope, Anthony, *He Knew He Was Right*, Oxford: Oxford University Press, 1985.

Vinem, Richard, *A History in Fragments: Europe in the Twentieth Century*, London: Abacus Books, 2002.

West, Trevor, *Horace Plunkett, Co-operation and Politics: An Irish Biography*, Gerrards Cross, Bucks: Colin Smythe Ltd., 1986.

Whittaker, Andrew (ed.), *Bright Brilliant Days: Douglas Gageby and the Irish Times*, Dublin: A. & A. Farmar, 2006.

Whyte. J. H., *Church and State in Modern Ireland, 1923–1970*, Dublin: Gill and Macmillan, 1971.

Wills, Claire, *That Neutral Island: A Cultural History of Ireland during the Second World War*, London: Faber and Faber, 2007.

Wyse Jackson, John (ed.), *Flann O'Brien at War: Myles na gCopaleen 1940–1945*, London: Duckworth, 1999.

Yeats, W. B. *The Poems*, London: Everyman's Library, 1992.

PERMISSIONS

Excerpt from 'Docker' from *Poems 1965-1975* by Seamus Heaney. Copyright © 1980 Seamus Heaney. Reprinted by permission of Faber & Faber Ltd (UK) and Farrar, Straus and Giroux, LLC (US).

Excerpt from 'Code' from *New Selected Poems* by Eavan Boland. Copyright © 2013 Eavan Boland. Reprinted by permission of Carcanet Press Limited (UK) and W.W. Norton & Company Inc. (US).

Excerpt from 'Autumn Journal' from *Collected Poems* by Louis MacNeice. Copyright © 2007 Louis MacNeice. Reprinted by permission of David Higham Associates.

Excerpt from 'The Siege of Mullingar' from *New Collected Poems* by John Montague. Copyright © 2012 John Montague. Reprinted by kind permission of the author and The Gallery Press, Loughcrew, Oldcastle, County Meath, Ireland.

INDEX